MONTCALM AND WOLFE

MONTCALM AND WOLFE

THE FRENCH AND INDIAN WAR

FRANCIS PARKMAN

WITH A NEW FOREWORD BY
C. VANN WOODWARD
AND ILLUSTRATIONS SELECTED
SPECIALLY FOR THIS EDITION

DA CAPO PRESS • NEW YORK

Library of Congress Cataloging in Publication Data

Parkman, Francis, 1823–1893.
  Montcalm and Wolfe: the French and Indian War / Francis Parkman;
with a new foreword by C. Vann Woodward and illustrations selected
specially for this edition.—1st Da Capo Press ed.
      p.   cm.
  Previously published: New York: Atheneum, 1984.
  ISBN 0-306-80621-5
  1. United States—History—French and Indian War, 1755–1763—
Campaigns. 2. Montcalm de Saint-Véran, Louis-Joseph, marquis de,
1712–1759. 3. Wolfe, James, 1727–1759. I. Title.
E199.P255   1995
973.2′6—dc20   94-48771
                                                                          CIP

First Da Capo Press edition 1995

This Da Capo Press paperback edition of *Montcalm and Wolfe*
is an unabridged republication of the centennial edition published
in New York in 1984. It is reprinted by arrangement with the
Book-of-the-Month Club, Inc.

Published by Da Capo Press, Inc.
A Subsidiary of Plenum Publishing Corporation
233 Spring Street, New York, N.Y. 10013

Manufactured in the United States of America

To

HARVARD COLLEGE,
*the Alma Mater under whose influence the
purpose of writing it was conceived,*

THIS BOOK

is affectionately inscribed.

MAPS

ACADIA
WITH
ADJACENT ISLANDS
1755

ISLE ST JEAN or
PRINCE EDWARD ISLAND

ISLE ROYAL or
CAPE BRETON ISLAND

Cape
Egmont

Port des Espagnols

Cape Breton
Louisbourg
Gabarus Bay

O C E A N

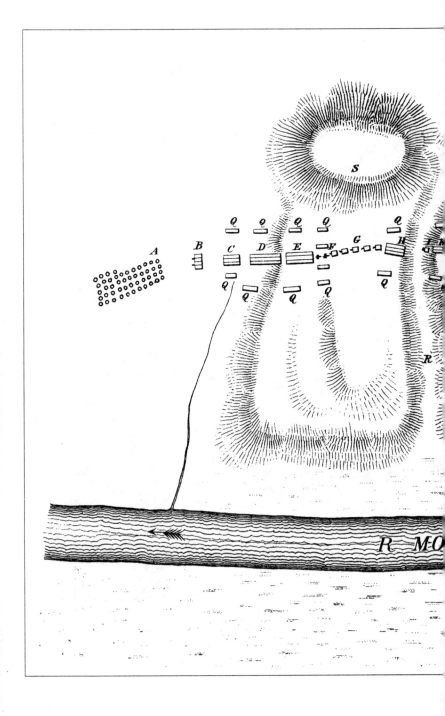

NO. 1.

A Sketch of the Field of Battle of the 9th of July, upon the Monongahela, seven miles from Fort du Quesne, shewing the Disposition of the Troops when the Action began.

EXPLANATION.

▤ British Troops; the long lines express the number of Files. ○ French and Indians. ✛ Cannon and Howitzers. ▭ Waggons, Carts, and Tumbrils. ⊢ Cattle and Packhorses.

A, French and Indians when first discovered by the Guides.

B, Guides and six light Horse.

C, Vanguard of the advanced Party.

D, Advanced Party, commanded by Lt. Col. Gage.

E, Working Party, commanded by Sir Jn. St. Clair, D.Q.M.G.

F, Two Field Pieces.

G, Waggons with Powder and Tools.

H, Rear Guard of the advanced Party.

I, Light Horse leading the Convoy. K, Sailors and Pioneers, with a Tumbril of Tools, etc. L, Three Field Pieces. M, General's Guard. N, Main Body upon the Flanks of the Convoy, with the Cattle and Packhorses between them and the Flank Guards. O, Field Piece in ye rear of ye Convoy. P, Rear Guards. Q, Flank Guards. R, A Hollow Way. S, a Hill which the Indians did most of the Execution from. T, Frazer's House.

(Signed) Pat. Mackellar, Engr.

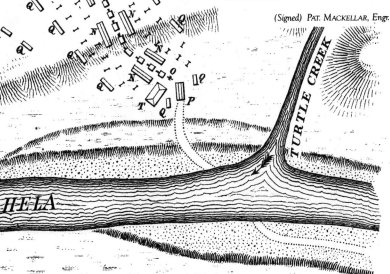

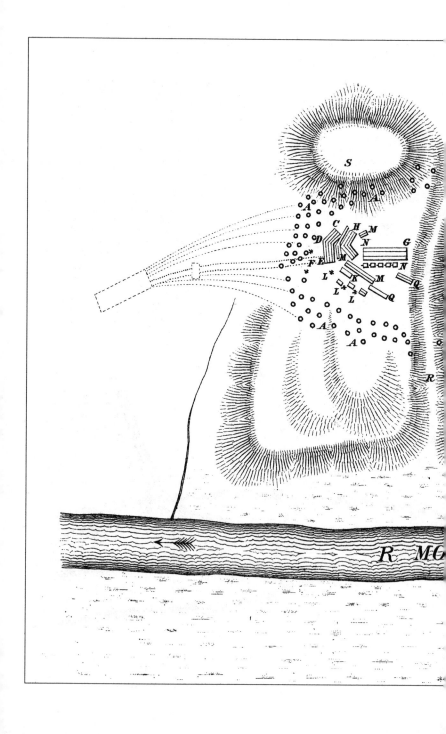

NO. 2.

A Sketch of the Field of Battle, shewing the Disposition of the Troops about 2 o'clock, when the whole of the Main Body had joined the Advanced and Working Partys, then beat back from the Ground they occupied as in Plan No. I.

EXPLANATION.

A, The French and Indian skulking behind Trees, round the British.

F, The two Field Pieces of the advanced Party abandoned.

C, D, E, H, K, M, N, Q, The whole Body of the British joined with little or no Order, but endeavouring to make Fronts towards ye Enemies Fire. L, The three Field Pieces of the main Body. P, The rear Guard divided (round the rear of the Convoy now closed up) behind Trees having been attack'd by a few Indians.

N.B. The Disposition on both Sides continued about two hours nearly as here represented, the British endeavouring to recover the Guns(F) and to gain the Hill (S) to no purpose. The British were at length beat from the Guns (L). The General was wounded soon after. They were at last beat across the Hollow Way (R) and made no further Stand. The Retreat was full of Confusion and Hurry, but after a few Miles there was a Body got to rally.

(Signed) Pat. Mackellar, Engr.

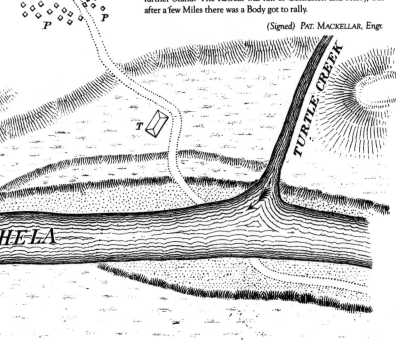

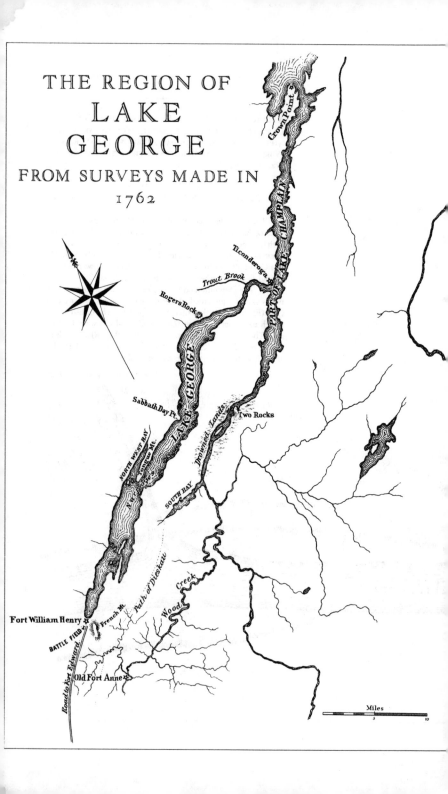

THE REGION OF
LAKE
GEORGE

FROM SURVEYS MADE IN
1762

Crown Point

PART OF LAKE CHAMPLAIN

Ticonderoga

Trout Brook

Rogers Rock

LAKE GEORGE

Sabbath Day Pt.

NORTH WEST BAY

Tongue Mt.

N.W. BAY

Drowned Lands

Two Rocks

SOUTH BAY

Path of Dieskau

Wood Creek

Fort William Henry

BATTLE FIELD

French Mt.

Road to Fort Edward

Old Fort Anne

Miles

5   10

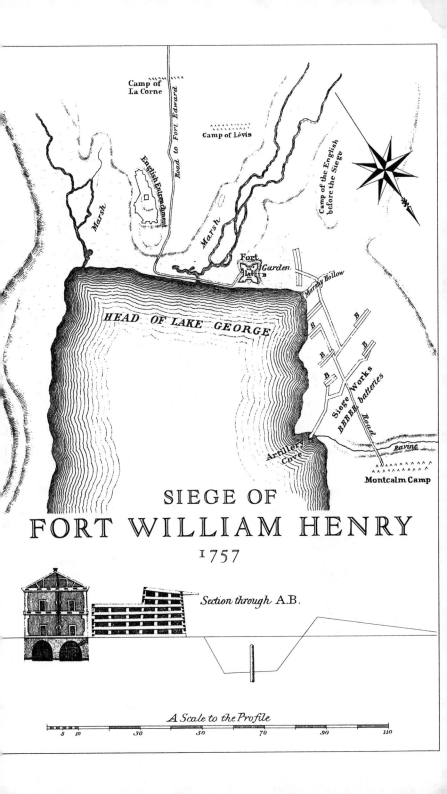

SIEGE OF
FORT WILLIAM HENRY
1757

Camp of La Corne

Camp of Lévis

Camp of the English before the Siege

English Entrenchment

Road to Fort Edward

Marsh

Marsh

Marsh

Fort
Garden
A B

HEAD OF LAKE GEORGE

Marshy Hollow

B B
B B
B B

Siege Works
BBBBB batteries

Road

Artillery Cove

Ravine

Montcalm Camp

Section through A.B.

A Scale to the Profile

5   10   30   50   70   90   110

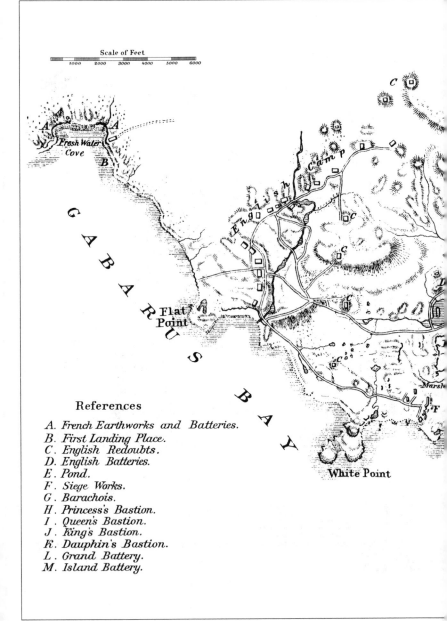

Scale of Feet

1000 2000 3000 4000 5000 6000

Fresh Water Cove

English Camp

G A B A R U S   B A Y

Flat Point

White Point

Marsh

References

A. French Earthworks and Batteries.
B. First Landing Place.
C. English Redoubts.
D. English Batteries.
E. Pond.
F. Siege Works.
G. Barachois.
H. Princess's Bastion.
I. Queen's Bastion.
J. King's Bastion.
K. Dauphin's Bastion.
L. Grand Battery.
M. Island Battery.

HARBOR

Gate

M

Goat Island

Rochford Point

Light House Point

Point

SIEGE OF LOUISBOURG

1758

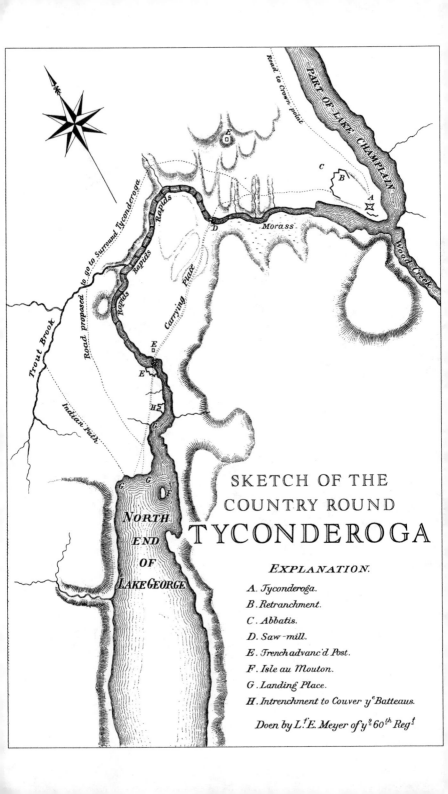

SKETCH OF THE
COUNTRY ROUND
TYCONDEROGA

EXPLANATION.

A. *Tyconderoga.*

B. *Retranchment.*

C. *Abbatis.*

D. *Saw-mill.*

E. *French advanc'd Post.*

F. *Isle au Mouton.*

G. *Landing Place.*

H. *Intrenchment to Couver y^e Batteaus.*

Doen by L.^r E. Meyer of y^e 60th Reg.^t

CONTENTS

PART TWO

16   A WINTER OF DISCONTENT   303
1757–1758

17   BIGOT   313
1753–1760

18   PITT   326
1757–1758

APPENDIXES

ILLUSTRATIONS

MAPS

Adapted, by Bernhard H. Wagner, from an 1899 edition of
Montcalm and Wolfe

PORTFOLIO

PORTFOLIO ONE

following page 176

PORTFOLIO TWO

following page 464

FOREWORD

BY

C. VANN WOODWARD

Francis Parkman thought of *Montcalm and Wolfe* as his masterpiece, and that estimate of the book has prevailed generally among most of his readers and critics since it appeared a century ago. Not long after it was published in 1884, Parkman replied to a flattering letter from his friend Henry James with the flat remark that "The subject of the book was an old hobby of mine." Hobby, indeed. That was a laconic way of describing a lifetime obsession that had seized him forty years before, during his sophomore year at Harvard, and never gave him a moment's rest thereafter. In a more unguarded letter twenty years earlier he had confessed that his great subject and the untamed forests of its setting had "possessed his waking and sleeping dreams, filling him with vague cravings impossible to satisfy."

Some years after conceiving the idea of writing the story of the "Old French War," Parkman says that he "enlarged the plan to include the whole course of the American conflict between France and England; or, in other words, the history of the American forest; for this was the light in which I regarded it. My theme fascinated me, and I was haunted with wilderness images day and night." Instead of concentrating on the Seven Years War, the enlarged plan spanned more than two centuries and depicted the waning of the Middle Ages as revealed in the decline of French absolutism, feudalism, and Roman Catholicism in the struggle for a continent.

His labors eventually resulted in seven works later entitled *France and England in North America*. Each of these works was intended to stand alone, but together they were to recount the rise and fall of French empire in the New World—the focus was always on France—in three stages. The first was the age of discovery and exploration, covered in *Pioneers of France in the New World, The Jesuits in North America in the Seventeenth Century,* and *LaSalle and the Discovery of the Great West.* The second stage was the empire at its peak, pictured in *The Old Regime in Canada* and *Count Frontenac and New France under Louis XIV.* The third was the decline and fall, contained in *A Half-Century of Conflict,* and reaching dramatic climax with the fall of Quebec in 1759 in *Montcalm and Wolfe.*

Outlined in this fashion, the roll call of majestic titles sounds like the steady march of lofty ambition to triumphant fulfillment. Actually the march was quite unsteady, plagued constantly with anguish, and the fulfillment was painfully delayed.

Francis Parkman sprang from a long line of New England clergymen going back on his mother's side to John Cotton. Born in 1823 to Boston parents of wealth and high social position in the Brahmin caste, Francis shared with the other members of his immediate family afflictions of despondency, severe headaches, and poor eyesight. In adult life, however, his ailments seemed far more numerous than those of his parents and siblings. They included heart trouble, terrible headaches, semi-blindness, water on the knee, rheumatism, and arthritis, together with prolonged insomnia and wracking "hypochondria," or depression. Judging from available evidence, several modern psychiatrists agree that his symptoms indicate an underlying neurosis in which he unconsciously created for himself "a struggle situation" that became the keynote of his life and work. Only by heroic and relentless battle against tremendous odds could he seem to maintain his self-esteem.

Parkman called his afflictions "the Enemy" and described them as "a suite of exhausting disorders, so reducing him that circulation at the extremities ceased, the light of the sun became insupportable, and a wild whirl possessed his brain, joined to a universal turmoil of the nervous system." His way of meeting "the Enemy" was by a "counter-attack" of furious work, so long as that was possible. But for years no brain work was possible at all and for long periods he could work only for brief intervals, two hours a day for five minutes at a time. Six lines of manuscript a day were about his limit during half of one year. Some years were better than others, but his health was never fully restored and his progress was always painfully handicapped.

For all that, the volumes he planned appeared with some regularity during the two decades following the Civil War. They enjoyed a remarkable popular success in their time. It was still a time of history as literature and historians as men of letters, and for that time and kind of history Parkman had no peer on his side of the Atlantic and few—a Carlyle or a Macaulay—on the other. History of that school—call it Romantic or Whig—was written to entertain and inspire as well as to inform and instruct. It was peopled by readily identifiable heroes and villains on whose actions and quirks of character hung historic decisions of mighty consequence. They might decide or disclose the destiny of nations and the conquest of continents, or tip the scale in strife between future and past, progress and reaction, good and evil, right and wrong. Such history retained the ancient form of story, could become moral drama, and required more art than science.

The art of history as Parkman practiced it called for more than research and a report of the present on the past. He sought by creative imagination to bring the past to life. He tried to imbue himself with the life and spirit of the time, events, and people he described, to become a sharer and a participant in the crises and adventures of which he wrote, and by that means to recapture the historical experience of actual participants as *they* perceived it. He explored the wilderness in desperate quests, he wrote, for "such personal experience as should, in some sense, identify him with his theme." One such quest that nearly cost him his life was the youthful adventure described in his first book, *The Oregon Trail* (1849). "It was essential to his plan," he later explained, "to gain an inside view of Indian life." Lush descriptions of wilderness scenery—forest, lake, river, mountain, and plain—were often based on his own explorations and notes. He had been there himself.

At times Parkman can write like the most romantic exponent of the Great Man theory of history, as when he sees "England spring into fresh life under the kindling influence of one great man"—William Pitt. Or when he writes of the loss of General Howe at Ticonderoga, "The death of one man was the ruin of fifteen thousand." It is true that personalities loom larger than life in his narrative. His eloquent eulogies to Wolfe and Washington, as earlier to LaSalle and Frontenac, are memorable examples. But Howard Doughty is justified in saying that in general "the individual figures for Parkman as the lengthened shadow of history," rather than vice versa. However lavishly he pictures his heroes, he takes care to fill in circumstances and impersonal forces at work in their triumphs and to acknowledge implicitly that had one man not been there, another would most likely have come along. The great man is more important for him as a symbol or an embodiment than as a determinant of history. At times, to be sure, the symbolic figures seem rather arbitrarily chosen.

In the romantic school the historian serves as judge as well as artist. He sits in judgment on the performance of cultures and nations as well as men in the crises they face. Thus in *Montcalm and Wolfe,* when speaking of the French and Indian War, Parkman writes:

> This war was the strife of a united and concentrated few against a divided and discordant many. It was the strife, too, of the past against the future; of the old against the new; of moral and intellectual torpor against moral and intellectual life, of barren absolutism against a liberty, crude, incoherent, and chaotic, yet full of prolific vitality.

While some ambiguities are admitted, there is rarely much doubt about which side embodies the past, the old, the torpor, or "barren absolutism," and which the future, the new, the vitality, and liberty—crude though it be. France of the Old Order is pitted against Anglo-America and the chaotic future. Parkman's allegiances are quite clearly with the forces of "progress," and all things are judged from that standpoint. French absolutism, feudalism, and Roman institutions, magnificent and colorful as they were, are destined to go down before the Anglo-American forces of progress.

For Parkman there were, as I have said, certain ambiguities. He could not withhold admiration from the masculine virtues he so much admired and emulated and saw embodied in the indomitable courage and fortitude of the French discoverers, explorers, warriors, rulers, and even some of the missionary Jesuits. Their Anglo-American opponents, on the other hand, were not always as admirable in their disorder, discord, and undisciplined selfishness and materialism, however loyal they were to the cause of liberty. In their New World ordeal, however, the French fell prey to the rigid despotism of their rulers on the one side or the anarchy and savagery of the forest on the other. The English stood for a compromise of liberty and self-rule between the treacherous extremes. Or so it seemed to Francis Parkman.

Montcalm and Wolfe presented the historian with his greatest challenge and the amplest opportunity for the use of his gifts for narration and portraiture. The centuries of obscure struggle in the American forest had finally precipitated a war that "set the world on fire." Parkman deftly sketches the European rivalries and power struggles and their imperial leaders—English, French, Prussian, Austrian, Russian—that were plunged into the Seven Years War. Then he turns with masterful confidence and ardor to his true subject, the war in America, which he called "the most picturesque and dramatic of American wars." It had everything romantic his imagination could desire—dramatic unity, noble settings, clear symbolism, genuine suspense, narrative climax, and a splendid curtain. Furthermore, from Parkman's point of view, it came out "right."

The two aristocratic generals who give the book its title are fully and sympathetically portrayed. The Marquis de Montcalm as a youth applied himself to books, especially Latin, Greek, and history, and aspired all his life to become a member of the French Academy. He also established a reputation for military valor, and was known for "his southern vivacity of emotion and an impetuous volubility that sometimes forgot prudence." His opposite number, James Wolfe, was frail and slender with a facial profile "by no means shaped to express resolution," and yet "his nature was a compound of tenderness and fire, which last sometimes showed itself in sharp and unpleasant flashes."

Men in the ranks receive more general attention, and martial pageantry is not neglected: French troops in "white uniform faced with blue, red, yellow, and violet," and their Indian allies "with every ornament most suited to disfigure them in European eyes, painted with vermilion, white, green, yellow, and black made of soot," each face combining "all these different colors methodically laid on with the help of a little tallow." British regulars could match their French counterparts in gaudiness of uniform, with colonial militia on both sides usually in more nondescript attire. Problems of logistics, armament, transportation, morale, and the politics of war receive close attention.

The battle pieces roll by swiftly—Louisbourg, Ticonderoga, Fort Frontenac, Fort Duquesne, Niagara—all leading to the grand climax on the Plains of Abraham before Quebec, high above the waters of the St. Lawrence. There the French, with more than sixteen thousand men, including Indians, all under Montcalm, faced the British under Wolfe with fewer than nine thousand available for land operations. While the actual fighting fell to the troops, the decisive advantage of the British lay in their superior naval power commanding the river approaches below. Measured by numbers engaged and losses sustained, the action was relatively small, but measured by results and sheer drama of action and suspense, the Battle of Quebec has few equals in military annals. What with both Montcalm and Wolfe dying of wounds in the battle, Parkman faced the challenge of a lifetime. He rose to the occasion. Of the signing of the French capitulation at the end of the battle, he could write with some degree of accuracy, "Half the continent had changed hands at the scratch of a pen."

The reader who opens the pages of *Montcalm and Wolfe* for the first time faces a rich experience. To appreciate it fully, however, the late-twentieth-century reader should be prepared for certain peculiarities and limitations of a nineteenth-century historian. Some of these limitations are not to be explained away or excused by differences of time and point of view. Too often Parkman could ignore evidence that was not in accord with his views, permit his bias to control his judgment, or sketch characterizations that are little better than hostile caricatures. Pages turn up which strongly suggest that his central theme is a conflict between the forces of light and the forces of darkness. These faults are by no means nineteenth-century peculiarities, and they have marred the pages of historians in all periods—including our own.

Other qualities of Parkman's prose and mind, however, require us to remind ourselves constantly that he was a man of *his* time and not ours. An occasional lushness of prose might prompt reflection that fashions in these matters are subject to change. So it is also with his treatment of heroes and villains and his tendency to draw a moral and point a lesson. Modern sensibilities will be nettled by his casual stereotypes of national character and by the sharp distinction he draws between "civilization" and "savagery." Even more difficult to take is his portrayal (not always consistent or invariably negative) of the Indian as a beast of the forest, "man, wolf, and devil, all in one," and as a race inevitably and rightly doomed.

In such matters as these the twentieth-century reader might learn something from the nineteenth-century historian and his often successful efforts to overcome the gaps of time between himself and the people of the eighteenth and seventeenth centuries and earlier about whom he was writing. He may have been less than fair to some of them, but he did not dismiss them because they thought and wrote like people of their time instead of his. Should we fall into the fallacy he avoided we would cut ourselves off not only from Parkman but from many other worthies of earlier times who were well worth knowing.

New Haven, 1984.

PREFACE

T he names on the titlepage stand as representative of the two nations whose final contest for the control of North America is the subject of the book.

A very large amount of unpublished material has been used in its preparation, consisting for the most part of documents copied from the archives and libraries of France and England, especially from the Archives de la Marine et des Colonies, the Archives de la Guerre, and the Archives Nationales at Paris, and the Public Record Office and the British Museum at London. The papers copied for the present work in France alone exceed six thousand folio pages of manuscript, additional and supplementary to the "Paris Documents" procured for the State of New York under the agency of Mr. Brodhead. The copies made in England form ten volumes, besides many English documents consulted in the original manuscript. Great numbers of autograph letters, diaries, and other writings of persons engaged in the war have also been examined on this side of the Atlantic.

I owe to the kindness of the present Marquis de Montcalm the permission to copy all the letters written by his ancestor, General Montcalm, when in America, to members of his family in France. General Montcalm, from his first arrival in Canada to a few days before his death, also carried on an active correspondence with one of his chief officers, Bourlamaque, with whom he was on terms of intimacy. These autograph letters are now preserved in a private collection. I have examined them, and obtained copies of the whole. They form an interesting complement to the official correspondence of the writer, and throw the most curious side-lights on the persons and events of the time.

Besides manuscripts, the printed matter in the form of books, pamphlets, contemporary newspapers, and other publications relating to the American part of the Seven Years War, is varied and abundant; and I believe I may safely say that nothing in it of much consequence has escaped me. The liberality of some of the older States of the Union, especially New York and Pennsylvania, in printing the voluminous records of their colonial history, has saved me a deal of tedious labor.

The whole of this published and unpublished mass of evidence has been read and collated with extreme care, and more than common pains have been taken to secure accuracy of statement. The study of books and papers, however, could not alone answer the purpose. The plan of the work was formed in early youth; and though various causes have long delayed its execution, it has always been kept in view. Meanwhile, I have visited and examined every spot where events of any importance in connection with the contest took place, and have observed with attention such scenes and persons as might help to illustrate those I meant to describe. In short, the subject has been studied as much from life and in the open air as at the library table. . . .

Boston, Sept. 16, 1884.

INTRODUCTION

It is the nature of great events to obscure the great events that came before them. The Seven Years War in Europe is seen but dimly through revolutionary convulsions and Napoleonic tempests; and the same contest in America is half lost to sight behind the storm-cloud of the War of Independence. Few at this day see the momentous issues involved in it, or the greatness of the danger that it averted. The strife that armed all the civilized world began here. "Such was the complication of political interests," says Voltaire, "that a cannon-shot fired in America could give the signal that set Europe in a blaze." Not quite. It was not a cannon-shot, but a volley from the hunting-pieces of a few backwoodsmen, commanded by a Virginian youth, George Washington.

To us of this day, the result of the American part of the war seems a foregone conclusion. It was far from being so; and very far from being so regarded by our forefathers. The numerical superiority of the British colonies was offset by organic weaknesses fatal to vigorous and united action. Nor at the outset did they, or the mother-country, aim at conquering Canada, but only at pushing back her boundaries. Canada—using the name in its restricted sense—was a position of great strength; and even when her dependencies were overcome, she could hold her own against forces far superior. Armies could reach her only by three routes,—the Lower St. Lawrence on the east, the Upper St. Lawrence on the west, and Lake Champlain on the south. The first access was guarded by a fortress almost impregnable by nature, and the second by a long chain of dangerous rapids; while the third offered a series of points easy to defend. During this same war, Frederic of Prussia held his ground triumphantly against greater odds, though his kingdom was open on all sides to attack.

It was the fatuity of Louis XV. and his Pompadour that made the conquest of Canada possible. Had they not broken the traditional policy of France, allied themselves to Austria, her ancient enemy, and plunged needlessly into the European war, the whole force of the kingdom would have been turned, from the first, to the humbling of England and the defence of the French colonies. The French soldiers left dead on inglorious Continental battle-fields could have saved Canada, and perhaps made good her claim to the vast territories of the West.

But there were other contingencies. The possession of Canada was a question of diplomacy as well as of war. If England conquered her, she might restore her, as she had lately restored Cape Breton. She had an interest in keeping France alive on the American continent. More than one clear eye saw, at the middle of the last century, that the subjection of Canada would lead to a revolt of the British colonies. So long as an active and enterprising enemy threatened their borders, they could not break with the mother-country, because they needed her help. And if the arms of France had prospered in the other hemisphere; if she had gained in Europe or Asia territories with which to buy back what she had lost in America, then, in all likelihood, Canada would have passed again into her hands.

The most momentous and far-reaching question ever brought to issue on this continent was: Shall France remain here, or shall she not? If, by diplomacy or war, she had preserved but the half, or less than the half, of her American possessions, then a barrier would have been set to the spread of the English-speaking races; there would have been no Revolutionary War; and for a long time, at least, no independence. It was not a question of scanty populations strung along the banks of the St. Lawrence; it was—or under a government of any worth it would have been—a question of the armies and generals of France. America owes much to the imbecility of Louis XV. and the ambitious vanity and personal dislikes of his mistress.

The Seven Years War made England what she is. It crippled the commerce of her rival, ruined France in two continents, and blighted her as a colonial power. It gave England the control of the seas and the mastery of North America and India, made her the first of commercial nations, and prepared that vast colonial system that has planted new

Englands in every quarter of the globe. And while it made England what she is, it supplied to the United States the indispensable condition of their greatness, if not of their national existence.

Before entering on the story of the great contest, we will look at the parties to it on both sides of the Atlantic.

PART ONE

Ⅱ

The Combatants

1745–1755

ENGLAND IN THE EIGHTEENTH CENTURY · HER POLITICAL AND SOCIAL
ASPECTS · HER MILITARY CONDITION · FRANCE · HER POWER AND
IMPORTANCE · SIGNS OF DECAY · THE COURT, THE NOBLES, THE CLERGY,
THE PEOPLE · THE KING AND POMPADOUR · THE PHILOSOPHERS ·
GERMANY · PRUSSIA · FREDERIC II. · RUSSIA · STATE OF EUROPE · WAR
OF THE AUSTRIAN SUCCESSION · AMERICAN COLONIES OF FRANCE AND
ENGLAND · CONTRASTED SYSTEMS AND THEIR RESULTS · CANADA · ITS
STRONG MILITARY POSITION · FRENCH CLAIMS TO THE CONTINENT ·
BRITISH COLONIES · NEW ENGLAND · VIRGINIA · PENNSYLVANIA · NEW
YORK · JEALOUSIES, DIVISIONS, INTERNAL DISPUTES, MILITARY
WEAKNESS

The latter half of the reign of George II. was one of the
most prosaic periods in English history. The civil wars
and the Restoration had had their enthusiasms, religion and liberty on
one side, and loyalty on the other; but the old fires declined when
William III. came to the throne, and died to ashes under the House of
Hanover. Loyalty lost half its inspiration when it lost the tenet of the
divine right of kings; and nobody could now hold that tenet with any
consistency except the defeated and despairing Jacobites. Nor had anybody as yet proclaimed the rival dogma of the divine right of the people. The reigning monarch held his crown neither of God nor of the
nation, but of a parliament controlled by a ruling class. The Whig

aristocracy had done a priceless service to English liberty. It was full of political capacity, and by no means void of patriotism; but it was only a part of the national life. Nor was it at present moved by political emotions in any high sense. It had done its great work when it expelled the Stuarts and placed William of Orange on the throne; its ascendency was now complete. The Stuarts had received their death-blow at Culloden; and nothing was left to the dominant party but to dispute on subordinate questions, and contend for office among themselves. The Tory squires sulked in their country-houses, hunted foxes, and grumbled against the reigning dynasty; yet hardly wished to see the nation convulsed by a counter-revolution and another return of the Stuarts.

If politics had run to commonplace, so had morals; and so too had religion. Despondent writers of the day even complained that British courage had died out. There was little sign to the common eye that under a dull and languid surface, forces were at work preparing a new life, material, moral, and intellectual. As yet, Whitefield and Wesley had not wakened the drowsy conscience of the nation, nor the voice of William Pitt roused it like a trumpet-peal.

It was the unwashed and unsavory England of Hogarth, Fielding, Smollett, and Sterne; of Tom Jones, Squire Western, Lady Bellaston, and Parson Adams; of the "Rake's Progress" and "Marriage à la Mode;" of the lords and ladies who yet live in the undying gossip of Horace Walpole, be-powdered, be-patched, and be-rouged, flirting at masked balls, playing cards till daylight, retailing scandal, and exchanging double meanings. Beau Nash reigned king over the gaming-tables of Bath; the ostrich-plumes of great ladies mingled with the peacock-feathers of courtesans in the rotunda at Ranelagh Gardens; and young lords in velvet suits and embroidered ruffles played away their patrimony at White's Chocolate-House or Arthur's Club. Vice was bolder than to-day, and manners more courtly, perhaps, but far more coarse.

The humbler clergy were thought—sometimes with reason—to be no fit company for gentlemen, and country parsons drank their ale in the squire's kitchen. The passenger-wagon spent the better part of a fortnight in creeping from London to York. Travellers carried pistols against footpads and mounted highwaymen. Dick Turpin and Jack Sheppard were popular heroes. Tyburn counted its victims by scores; and as yet no Howard had appeared to reform the inhuman abominations of the prisons.

The middle class, though fast rising in importance, was feebly and imperfectly represented in parliament. The boroughs were controlled by the nobility and gentry, or by corporations open to influence or bribery. Parliamentary corruption had been reduced to a system; and offices, sinecures, pensions, and gifts of money were freely used to keep ministers in power. The great offices of state were held by men sometimes of high ability, but of whom not a few divided their lives among politics, cards, wine, horse-racing, and women, till time and the gout sent them to the waters of Bath. The dull, pompous, and irascible old King had two ruling passions,— money, and his Continental dominions of Hanover. His elder son, the Prince of Wales, was a centre of opposition to him. His younger son, the Duke of Cumberland, a character far more pronounced and vigorous, had won the day at Culloden, and lost it at Fontenoy; but whether victor or vanquished, had shown the same vehement bull-headed courage, of late a little subdued by fast growing corpulency. The Duke of Newcastle, the head of the government, had gained power and kept it by his rank and connections, his wealth, his county influence, his control of boroughs, and the extraordinary assiduity and devotion with which he practised the arts of corruption. Henry Fox, grasping, unscrupulous, with powerful talents, a warm friend after his fashion, and a most indulgent father; Carteret, with his strong, versatile intellect and jovial intrepidity; the two Townshends, Mansfield, Halifax, and Chesterfield,—were conspicuous figures in the politics of the time. One man towered above them all. Pitt had many enemies and many critics. They called him ambitious, audacious, arrogant, theatrical, pompous, domineering; but what he has left for posterity is a loftiness of soul, undaunted courage, fiery and passionate eloquence, proud incorruptibility, domestic virtues rare in his day, unbounded faith in the cause for which he stood, and abilities which without wealth or strong connections were destined to place him on the height of power. The middle class, as yet almost voiceless, looked to him as its champion; but he was not the champion of a class. His patriotism was as comprehensive as it was haughty and unbending. He lived for England, loved her with intense devotion, knew her, believed in her, and made her greatness his own; or rather, he was himself England incarnate.

The nation was not then in fighting equipment. After the peace of Aix-la-Chapelle, the army within the three kingdoms had been reduced to about eighteen thousand men. Added to these were the garrisons of Minorca and Gibraltar, and six or seven independent companies in the American colonies. Of sailors, less than seventeen thousand were left in the Royal Navy. Such was the condition of England on the eve of one of the most formidable wars in which she was ever engaged.

Her rival across the Channel was drifting slowly and unconsciously towards the cataclysm of the Revolution; yet the old monarchy, full of

the germs of decay, was still imposing and formidable. The House of
Bourbon held the three thrones of France, Spain, and Naples; and their
threatened union in a family compact was the terror of European diplomacy. At home France was the foremost of the Continental nations;
and she boasted herself second only to Spain as a colonial power. She
disputed with England the mastery of India, owned the islands of Bourbon and Mauritius, held important possessions in the West Indies, and
claimed all North America except Mexico and a strip of sea-coast. Her
navy was powerful, her army numerous, and well appointed; but she
lacked the great commanders of the last reign. Soubise, Maillebois,
Contades, Broglie, and Clermont were but weak successors of Condé,
Turenne, Vendôme, and Villars. Marshal Richelieu was supreme in the
arts of gallantry, and more famous for conquests of love than of war.
The best generals of Louis XV. were foreigners. Lowendal sprang from
the royal house of Denmark; and Saxe, the best of all, was one of the
three hundred and fifty-four bastards of Augustus the Strong, Elector of
Saxony and King of Poland. He was now, 1750, dying at Chambord,
his iron constitution ruined by debaucheries.

The triumph of the Bourbon monarchy was complete. The government had become one great machine of centralized administration,
with a king for its head; though a king who neither could nor would
direct it. All strife was over between the Crown and the nobles; feudalism was robbed of its vitality, and left the mere image of its former
self, with nothing alive but its abuses, its caste privileges, its exactions,
its pride and vanity, its power to vex and oppress. In England, the
nobility were a living part of the nation, and if they had privileges,
they paid for them by constant service to the state; in France, they had
no political life, and were separated from the people by sharp lines of
demarcation. From warrior chiefs, they had changed to courtiers. Those
of them who could afford it, and many who could not, left their estates
to the mercy of stewards, and gathered at Versailles to revolve about
the throne as glittering satellites, paid in pomp, empty distinctions, or
rich sinecures, for the power they had lost. They ruined their vassals to
support the extravagance by which they ruined themselves. Such as
stayed at home were objects of pity and scorn. "Out of your Majesty's
presence," said one of them, "we are not only wretched, but ridiculous."

Versailles was like a vast and gorgeous theatre, where all were actors
and spectators at once; and all played their parts to perfection. Here
swarmed by thousands this silken nobility, whose ancestors rode cased
in iron. Pageant followed pageant. A picture of the time preserves for

us an evening in the great hall of the Château, where the King, with piles of louis d'or before him, sits at a large oval green table, throwing the dice, among princes and princesses, dukes and duchesses, ambassadors, marshals of France, and a vast throng of courtiers, like an animated bed of tulips; for men and women alike wear bright and varied colors. Above are the frescos of Le Brun; around are walls of sculptured and inlaid marbles, with mirrors that reflect the restless splendors of the scene and the blaze of chandeliers, sparkling with crystal pendants. Pomp, magnificence, profusion, were a business and a duty at the Court. Versailles was a gulf into which the labor of France poured its earnings; and it was never full.

Here the graces and charms were a political power. Women had prodigious influence, and the two sexes were never more alike. Men not only dressed in colors, but they wore patches and carried muffs. The robust qualities of the old nobility still lingered among the exiles of the provinces, while at Court they had melted into refinements tainted with corruption. Yet if the butterflies of Versailles had lost virility, they had not lost courage. They fought as gayly as they danced. In the halls which they haunted of yore, turned now into a historical picture-gallery, one sees them still, on the canvas of Lenfant, Lepaon, or Vernet, facing death with careless gallantry, in their small three-cornered hats, powdered perukes, embroidered coats, and lace ruffles. Their valets served them with ices in the trenches, under the cannon of besieged towns. A troop of actors formed part of the army-train of Marshal Saxe. At night there was a comedy, a ballet, or a ball, and in the morning a battle. Saxe, however, himself a sturdy German, while he recognized their fighting value, and knew well how to make the best of it, sometimes complained that they were volatile, excitable, and difficult to manage.

The weight of the Court, with its pomps, luxuries, and wars, bore on the classes least able to support it. The poorest were taxed most; the richest not at all. The nobles, in the main, were free from imposts. The clergy, who had vast possessions, were wholly free, though they consented to make voluntary gifts to the Crown; and when, in a time of emergency, the minister Machault required them, in common with all others hitherto exempt, to contribute a twentieth of their revenues to the charges of government, they passionately refused, declaring that they would obey God rather than the King. The cultivators of the soil were ground to the earth by a threefold extortion,—the seigniorial dues, the tithes of the Church, and the multiplied exactions of the Crown, enforced with merciless rigor by the farmers of the revenue, who enriched themselves by wringing the peasant on the one hand, and cheating the King on the other. A few great cities shone with all that is most brilliant in society, intellect, and concentred wealth; while the country that paid the costs lay in ignorance and penury, crushed and despairing. On the inhabitants of towns, too, the demands of the tax-gatherer were extreme; but here the immense vitality of the French people bore up the burden. While agriculture languished, and intolerable oppression turned peasants into beggars or desperadoes; while the clergy were sapped by corruption, and the nobles enervated by luxury and ruined by extravagance, the middle class was growing in thrift and strength. Arts and commerce prospered, and the seaports were alive with foreign trade. Wealth tended from all sides towards the centre. The King did not love his capital; but he and his favorites amused themselves with adorning it. Some of the chief embellishments that make Paris what it is to-day—the Place de la Concorde, the Champs Élysées, and many of the palaces of the Faubourg St. Germain—date from this reign.

One of the vicious conditions of the time was the separation in sympathies and interests of the four great classes of the nation,—clergy, nobles, burghers, and peasants; and each of these, again, divided itself into incoherent fragments. France was an aggregate of disjointed parts, held together by a meshwork of arbitrary power, itself touched with decay. A disastrous blow was struck at the national welfare when the Government of Louis XV. revived the odious persecution of the Huguenots. The attempt to scour heresy out of France cost her the most industrious and virtuous part of her population, and robbed her of those most fit to resist the mocking scepticism and turbid passions that burst out like a deluge with the Revolution.

Her manifold ills were summed up in the King. Since the Valois, she had had no monarch so worthless. He did not want understanding, still less the graces of person. In his youth the people called him the "Well-beloved;" but by the middle of the century they so detested him that he dared not pass through Paris, lest the mob should execrate him. He had not the vigor of the true tyrant; but his languor, his hatred of all effort, his profound selfishness, his listless disregard of public duty, and his effeminate libertinism, mixed with superstitious devotion, made him no less a national curse. Louis XIII. was equally unfit to govern; but he gave the reins to the Great Cardinal. Louis XV. abandoned them to a frivolous mistress, content that she should rule on condition of amusing him. It was a hard task; yet Madame de Pompadour accomplished it by methods infamous to him and to her. She gained and long kept the power that she coveted: filled the Bastille with her enemies; made and unmade ministers; appointed and removed generals. Great questions of policy were at the mercy of her caprices. Through her frivolous vanity, her personal likes and dislikes, all the great departments of government—army, navy, war, foreign affairs, justice, finance—changed from hand to hand incessantly, and this at a time of crisis when the kingdom needed the steadiest and surest guidance. Few of the officers of state, except, perhaps, D'Argenson, could venture to disregard her. She turned out Orry, the comptroller-general, put her favorite, Machault, into his place, then made him keeper of the seals, and at last minister of marine. The Marquis de Puysieux, in the ministry of foreign affairs, and the Comte de St.-Florentin, charged with the affairs of the clergy, took their cue from her. The King stinted her in nothing. First and last, she is reckoned to have cost him thirty-six million francs,—answering now to more than as many dollars.

The prestige of the monarchy was declining with the ideas that had given it life and strength. A growing disrespect for king, ministry, and clergy was beginning to prepare the catastrophe that was still some forty years in the future. While the valleys and low places of the kingdom were dark with misery and squalor, its heights were bright with a gay society,—elegant, fastidious, witty,—craving the pleasures of the mind as well as of the senses, criticising everything, analyzing everything, believing nothing. Voltaire was in the midst of it, hating, with all his vehement soul, the abuses that swarmed about him, and assailing them with the inexhaustible shafts of his restless and piercing intellect. Montesquieu was showing to a despot-ridden age the principles of political freedom. Diderot and D'Alembert were beginning their revolutionary Encyclopædia. Rousseau was sounding the first notes of his mad eloquence,—the wild revolt of a passionate and diseased genius against a world of falsities and wrongs. The *salons* of Paris, cloyed with other pleasures, alive to all that was racy and new, welcomed the pungent doctrines, and played with them as children play with fire, thinking no danger; as time went on, even embraced them in a genuine spirit of hope and good-will for humanity. The Revolution began at the top,— in the world of fashion, birth, and intellect,—and propagated itself downwards. "We walked on a carpet of flowers," Count Ségur afterwards said, "unconscious that it covered an abyss;" till the gulf yawned at last, and swallowed them.

Eastward, beyond the Rhine, lay the heterogeneous patchwork of the Holy Roman, or Germanic, Empire. The sacred bonds that throughout the Middle Ages had held together its innumerable fragments, had lost their strength. The Empire decayed as a whole; but not so the parts that composed it. In the south the House of Austria reigned over a formidable assemblage of states; and in the north the House of Brandenburg, promoted to royalty half a century before, had raised Prussia into an importance far beyond her extent and population. In her dissevered rags of territory lay the destinies of Germany. It was the late King, that honest, thrifty, dogged, headstrong despot, Frederic William, who had made his kingdom what it was, trained it to the perfection of drill, and left it to his son, Frederic II. the best engine of war in Europe. Frederic himself had passed between the upper and nether millstones of paternal discipline. Never did prince undergo such an apprenticeship. His father set him to the work of an overseer, or steward, flung plates at his head in the family circle, thrashed him with his rattan in public, bullied him for submitting to such treatment, and imprisoned him for trying to run away from it. He came at last out of purgatory; and Europe felt him to her farthest bounds. This bookish, philosophizing, verse-making cynic and profligate was soon to approve himself the first warrior of his time, and one of the first of all time.

Another power had lately risen on the European world. Peter the Great, half hero, half savage, had roused the inert barbarism of Russia into a titanic life. His daughter Elizabeth had succeeded to his throne,—heiress of his sensuality, if not of his talents.

Over all the Continent the aspect of the times was the same. Power had everywhere left the plains and the lower slopes, and gathered at the summits. Popular life was at a stand. No great idea stirred the nations to their depths. The religious convulsions of the sixteenth and seventeenth centuries were over, and the earthquake of the French Revolution had not begun. At the middle of the eighteenth century the history of Europe turned on the balance of power; the observance of treaties; inheritance and succession; rivalries of sovereign houses struggling to win power or keep it, encroach on neighbors, or prevent neighbors from encroaching; bargains, intrigue, force, diplomacy, and the musket, in the interest not of peoples but of rulers. Princes, great and small, brooded over some real or fancied wrong, nursed some dubious claim born of a marriage, a will, or an ancient covenant fished out of the abyss of time, and watched their moment to make it good. The general opportunity came when, in 1740, the Emperor Charles VI. died and bequeathed his personal dominions of the House of Austria to his daughter, Maria Theresa. The chief Powers of Europe had been pledged in advance to sustain the will; and pending the event, the veteran Prince Eugene had said that two hundred thousand soldiers would be worth all their guaranties together. The two hundred thousand were not there, and not a sovereign kept his word. They flocked to share the spoil, and parcel out the motley heritage of the young Queen. Frederic of Prussia led the way, invaded her province of Silesia, seized it, and kept it. The Elector of Bavaria and the King of Spain claimed their share, and the Elector of Saxony and the King of Sardinia prepared to follow the example. France took part with Bavaria, and intrigued to set the imperial crown on the head of the Elector, thinking to ruin her old enemy, the House of Austria, and rule Germany through an emperor too weak to dispense with her support. England, jealous of her designs, trembling for the balance of power, and anxious for the Hanoverian possessions of her king, threw herself into the strife on the side of Austria. It was now that, in the Diet at Presburg, the beautiful and distressed Queen, her infant in her arms, made her memorable appeal to the wild chivalry of her Hungarian nobles; and, clashing their swords, they shouted with one voice: "Let us die for our king, Maria Theresa;" *Moriamur pro rege nostro, Mariâ Theresiâ,*—one of the most dramatic scenes in history; not quite true, perhaps, but near the truth. Then came that confusion worse confounded called the war of the Austrian Succession, with its Mollwitz, its Dettingen, its Fontenoy, and its Scotch episode of Culloden. The peace of Aix-la-Chapelle closed the strife in 1748. Europe had time to breathe; but the germs of discord remained alive.

THE AMERICAN COMBATANTS

The French claimed all America, from the Alleghanies to the Rocky Mountains, and from Mexico and Florida to the North Pole, except only the ill-defined possessions of the English on the borders of Hudson Bay; and to these vast regions, with adjacent islands, they gave the general name of New France. They controlled the highways of the continent, for they held its two great rivers. First, they had seized the St. Lawrence, and then planted themselves at the mouth of the Mississippi. Canada at the north, and Louisiana at the south, were the keys of a boundless interior, rich with incalculable possibilities. The English colonies, ranged along the Atlantic coast, had no royal road to the great inland, and were, in a manner, shut between the mountains and the

sea. At the middle of the century they numbered in all, from Georgia
to Maine, about eleven hundred and sixty thousand white inhabitants.
By the census of 1754 Canada had but fifty-five thousand.[1] Add those
of Louisiana and Acadia, and the whole white population under the
French flag might be something more than eighty thousand. Here is an
enormous disparity; and hence it has been argued that the success of
the English colonies and the failure of the French was not due to difference of religious and political systems, but simply to numerical preponderance. But this preponderance itself grew out of a difference of
systems. We have said before, and it cannot be said too often, that in
making Canada a citadel of the state religion,—a holy of holies of
exclusive Roman Catholic orthodoxy,—the clerical monitors of the
Crown robbed their country of a trans-Atlantic empire. New France
could not grow with a priest on guard at the gate to let in none but
such as pleased him. One of the ablest of Canadian governors, La Galissonière, seeing the feebleness of the colony compared with the vast-
ness of its claims, advised the King to send ten thousand peasants to
occupy the valley of the Ohio, and hold back the British swarm that
was just then pushing its advance-guard over the Alleghanies. It needed
no effort of the King to people his waste domain, not with ten thousand peasants, but with twenty times ten thousand Frenchmen of every
station,—the most industrious, most instructed, most disciplined by
adversity and capable of self-rule, that the country could boast. While
La Galissonière was asking for colonists, the agents of the Crown, set
on by priestly fanaticism, or designing selfishness masked with fanaticism, were pouring volleys of musketry into Huguenot congregations, im-
prisoning for life those innocent of all but their faith,—the men in the
galleys, the women in the pestiferous dungeons of Aigues Mortes,—
hanging their ministers, kidnapping their children, and reviving, in
short, the dragonnades. Now, as in the past century, many of the victims escaped to the British colonies, and became a part of them. The
Huguenots would have hailed as a boon the permission to emigrate
under the fleur-de-lis, and build up a Protestant France in the valleys
of the West. It would have been a bane of absolutism, but a national
glory; would have set bounds to English colonization, and changed the
face of the continent. The opportunity was spurned. The dominant
Church clung to its policy of rule and ruin. France built its best colony

---

[1]*Censuses of Canada*, iv. 61. Rameau (*La France aux Colonies*, ii. 81) estimates the Canadian
population, in 1755, at sixty-six thousand, besides *voyageurs*, Indian traders, etc. Vaudreuil, in
1760, places it at seventy thousand.

on a principle of exclusion, and failed; England reversed the system, and succeeded.

I have shown elsewhere the aspects of Canada, where a rigid scion of the old European tree was set to grow in the wilderness. The military Governor, holding his miniature Court on the rock of Quebec; the feudal proprietors, whose domains lined the shores of the St. Lawrence; the peasant; the roving bushranger; the half-tamed savage, with crucifix and scalping-knife; priests; friars; nuns; and soldiers,—mingled to form a society the most picturesque on the continent. What distinguished it from the France that produced it was a total absence of revolt against the laws of its being,—an absolute conservatism, an unquestioning acceptance of Church and King. The Canadian, ignorant of everything but what the priest saw fit to teach him, had never heard of Voltaire; and if he had known him, would have thought him a devil. He had, it is true, a spirit of insubordination born of the freedom of the forest; but if his instincts rebelled, his mind and soul were passively submissive. The unchecked control of a hierarchy robbed him of the independence of intellect and character, without which, under the conditions of modern life, a people must resign itself to a position of inferiority. Yet Canada had a vigor of her own. It was not in spiritual deference only that she differed from the country of her birth. Whatever she had caught of its corruptions, she had caught nothing of its effeminacy. The mass of her people lived in a rude poverty,—not abject, like the peasant of old France, nor ground down by the tax-gatherer; while those of the higher ranks—all more or less engaged in pursuits of war or adventure, and inured to rough journeyings and forest exposures—were rugged as their climate. Even the French regular troops, sent out to defend the colony, caught its hardy spirit, and set an example of stubborn fighting which their comrades at home did not always emulate.

Canada lay ensconced behind rocks and forests. All along her southern boundaries, between her and her English foes, lay a broad tract of wilderness, shaggy with primeval woods. Innumerable streams gurgled beneath their shadows; innumerable lakes gleamed in the fiery sunsets; innumerable mountains bared their rocky foreheads to the wind. These wastes were ranged by her savage allies, Micmacs, Etechémins, Abenakis, Caughnawagas; and no enemy could steal upon her unawares. Through the midst of them stretched Lake Champlain, pointing straight to the heart of the British settlements,—a watery thoroughfare of mutual attack, and the only approach by which, without a long _détour_ by wilderness or sea, a hostile army could come within striking distance of the colony. The French advanced post of Fort Frederic, called Crown Point by the English, barred the narrows of the lake, which thence spread northward to the portals of Canada guarded by Fort St. Jean. Southwestward, some fourteen hundred miles as a bird flies, and twice as far by the practicable routes of travel, was Louisiana, the second of the two heads of New France; while between lay the realms of solitude where the Mississippi rolled its sullen tide, and the Ohio wound its belt of silver through the verdant woodlands.

To whom belonged this world of prairies and forests? France claimed it by right of discovery and occupation. It was her explorers who, after De Soto, first set foot on it. The question of right, it is true, mattered little; for, right or wrong, neither claimant would yield her pretensions so long as she had strength to uphold them; yet one point is worth a moment's notice. The French had established an excellent system in the distribution of their American lands. Whoever received a grant from the Crown was required to improve it, and this within reasonable time. If he did not, the land ceased to be his, and was given to another more able or industrious. An international extension of her own principle would have destroyed the pretensions of France to all the countries of the West. She had called them hers for three fourths of a century, and they were still a howling waste, yielding nothing to civilization but beaver-skins, with here and there a fort, trading-post, or mission, and three or four puny hamlets by the Mississippi and the Detroit. We have seen how she might have made for herself an indisputable title, and peopled the solitudes with a host to maintain it. She would not; others were at hand who both would and could; and the late claimant, disinherited and forlorn, would soon be left to count the cost of her bigotry.

The thirteen British colonies were alike, insomuch as they all had representative governments, and a basis of English law. But the differences among them were great. Some were purely English; others were made up of various races, though the Anglo-Saxon was always predominant. Some had one prevailing religious creed; others had many creeds. Some had charters, and some had not. In most cases the governor was appointed by the Crown; in Pennsylvania and Maryland he was appointed by a feudal proprietor, and in Connecticut and Rhode Island he was chosen by the people. The differences of disposition and character were still greater than those of form.

The four northern colonies, known collectively as New England, were an exception to the general rule of diversity. The smallest, Rhode Island, had features all its own; but the rest were substantially one in nature and origin. The principal among them, Massachusetts, may serve as the type of all. It was a mosaic of little village republics, firmly cemented together, and formed into a single body politic through representatives sent to the "General Court" at Boston. Its government, originally theocratic, now tended to democracy, ballasted as yet by strong traditions of respect for established worth and ability, as well as by the influence of certain families prominent in affairs for generations. Yet there were no distinct class-lines, and popular power, like popular education, was widely diffused. Practically Massachusetts was almost independent of the mother-country. Its people were purely English, of sound yeoman stock, with an abundant leaven drawn from the best of the Puritan gentry; but their original character had been somewhat modified by changed conditions of life. A harsh and exacting creed, with its stiff formalism and its prohibition of wholesome recreation; excess in the pursuit of gain,—the only resource left to energies robbed of their natural play; the struggle for existence on a hard and barren soil; and the isolation of a narrow village life,—joined to produce, in the meaner sort, qualities which were unpleasant, and sometimes repulsive. Puritanism was not an unmixed blessing. Its view of human nature was dark, and its attitude towards it one of repression. It strove to crush out not only what is evil, but much that is innocent and salutary. Human nature so treated will take its revenge, and for every vice that it loses find another instead. Nevertheless, while New England Puritanism bore its peculiar crop of faults, it produced also many good and sound fruits. An uncommon vigor, joined to the hardy virtues of a masculine race, marked the New England type. The sinews, it is true, were hardened at the expense of blood and flesh,—and this literally as well as figuratively; but the staple of character was a sturdy conscientiousness, an undespairing courage, patriotism, public spirit, sagacity, and a strong good sense. A great change, both for better and for worse, has since come over it, due largely to reaction against the unnatural rigors of the past. That mixture, which is now too common, of cool emotions with excitable brains, was then rarely seen. The New England colonies abounded in high examples of public and private virtue, though not always under the most prepossessing forms. They were conspicuous, moreover, for intellectual activity, and were by no means without intellectual eminence. Massachusetts had produced at least two men whose fame had crossed the sea,—Edwards, who out of the grim theology of Calvin mounted to sublime heights of mystical speculation; and Franklin, famous already by his discoveries in electricity. On the other hand, there were few genuine New Englanders who, however personally modest, could divest themselves of the notion that they belonged to a people in an especial manner the object of divine approval; and this self-righteousness, along with certain other traits, failed to commend the Puritan colonies to the favor of their fellows. Then, as now, New England was best known to her neighbors by her worst side.

In one point, however, she found general applause. She was regarded as the most military among the British colonies. This reputation was well founded, and is easily explained. More than all the rest, she lay open to attack. The long waving line of the New England border, with its lonely hamlets and scattered farms, extended from the Kennebec to beyond the Connecticut, and was everywhere vulnerable to the guns and tomahawks of the neighboring French and their savage allies. The colonies towards the south had thus far been safe from danger. New York alone was within striking distance of the Canadian war-parties. That province then consisted of a line of settlements up the Hudson and the Mohawk, and was little exposed to attack except at its northern end, which was guarded by the fortified town of Albany, with its outlying posts, and by the friendly and warlike Mohawks, whose "castles" were close at hand. Thus New England had borne the heaviest brunt of the preceding wars, not only by the forest, but also by the sea; for the French of Acadia and Cape Breton confronted her coast, and she was often at blows with them. Fighting had been a necessity with her, and she had met the emergency after a method extremely defective, but the best that circumstances would permit. Having no trained officers and no disciplined soldiers, and being too poor to maintain either, she borrowed her warriors from the workshop and the plough, and officered them with lawyers, merchants, mechanics, or farmers. To compare them with good regular troops would be folly; but they did, on the whole, better than could have been expected, and in the last war achieved the brilliant success of the capture of Louisbourg. This exploit, due partly to native hardihood and partly to good luck, greatly enhanced the military repute of New England, or rather was one of the chief sources of it.

The great colony of Virginia stood in strong contrast to New England. In both the population was English; but the one was Puritan with Roundhead traditions, and the other, so far as concerned its governing class, Anglican with Cavalier traditions. In the one, every man, woman, and child could read and write; in the other, Sir William Berkeley once thanked God that there were no free schools, and no prospect of any for a century. The hope had found fruition. The lower classes of Virginia were as untaught as the warmest friend of popular ignorance could wish. New England had a native literature more than respectable under the circumstances, while Virginia had none; numerous industries, while Virginia was all agriculture, with but a single crop; a homogeneous society and a democratic spirit, while her rival was an aristocracy. Virginian society was distinctly stratified. On the lowest level were the negro slaves, nearly as numerous as all the rest together; next, the indented servants and the poor whites, of low origin, good-humored, but boisterous, and sometimes vicious; next, the small and despised class of tradesmen and mechanics; next, the farmers and lesser planters, who were mainly of good English stock, and who merged insensibly into the ruling class of the great landowners. It was these last who represented the colony and made the laws. They may be described as English country squires transplanted to a warm climate and turned slave-masters. They sustained their position by entails, and constantly undermined it by the reckless profusion which ruined them at last. Many of them were well born, with an immense pride of descent, increased by the habit of domination. Indolent and energetic by turns; rich in natural gifts and often poor in book-learning, though some, in the lack of good teaching at home, had been bred in the English universities; high-spirited, generous to a fault; keeping open house in their capacious mansions, among vast tobacco-fields and toiling negroes, and living in a rude pomp where the fashions of St. James were somewhat oddly grafted on the roughness of the plantation,—what they wanted in schooling was supplied by an education which books alone would have been impotent to give, the education which came with the possession and exercise of political power, and the sense of a position to maintain, joined to a bold spirit of independence and a patriotic attachment to the Old Dominion. They were few in number; they raced, gambled, drank, and swore; they did everything that in Puritan eyes was most reprehensible; and in the day of need they gave the United Colonies a body of statesmen and orators which had no equal on the continent. A vigorous aristocracy favors the growth of personal eminence, even in those who are not of it, but only near it.

The essential antagonism of Virginia and New England was afterwards to become, and to remain for a century, an element of the first influence in American history. Each might have learned much from the other; but neither did so till, at last, the strife of their contending principles shook the continent. Pennsylvania differed widely from both. She was a conglomerate of creeds and races,—English, Irish, Germans, Dutch, and Swedes; Quakers, Lutherans, Presbyterians, Romanists, Moravians, and a variety of nondescript sects. The Quakers prevailed in the eastern districts; quiet, industrious, virtuous, and serenely obstinate. The Germans were strongest towards the centre of the colony, and were chiefly peasants; successful farmers, but dull, ignorant, and superstitious. Towards the west were the Irish, of whom some were Celts, always quarrelling with their German neighbors, who detested them; but the greater part were Protestants of Scotch descent, from Ulster; a vigorous border population. Virginia and New England had each a strong distinctive character. Pennsylvania, with her heterogeneous population, had none but that which she owed to the sober neutral tints of Quaker existence. A more thriving colony there was not on the continent. Life, if monotonous, was smooth and contented. Trade and the arts grew. Philadelphia, next to Boston, was the largest town in British America; and was, moreover, the intellectual centre of the middle and southern colonies. Unfortunately, for her credit in the approaching war, the Quaker influence made Pennsylvania noncombatant. Politically, too, she was an anomaly; for, though utterly unfeudal in disposition and character, she was under feudal superiors in the persons of the representatives of William Penn, the original grantee.

New York had not as yet reached the relative prominence which her geographical position and inherent strength afterwards gave her. The English, joined to the Dutch, the original settlers, were the dominant population; but a half-score of other languages were spoken in the province, the chief among them being that of the Huguenot French in the southern parts, and that of the Germans on the Mohawk. In religion, the province was divided between the Anglican Church, with government support and popular dislike, and numerous dissenting sects, chiefly Lutherans, Independents, Presbyterians, and members of the Dutch Reformed Church. The little city of New York, like its great successor, was the most cosmopolitan place on the continent, and probably the gayest. It had, in abundance, balls, concerts, theatricals, and evening clubs, with plentiful dances and other amusements for the poorer classes. Thither in the winter months came the great hereditary proprietors on the Hudson; for the old Dutch feudality still held its own, and the manors of Van Renselaer, Cortland, and Livingston, with their seigniorial privileges, and the great estates and numerous tenantry of the Schuylers and other leading families, formed the basis of an aristocracy, some of whose members had done good service to the province, and were destined to do more. Pennsylvania was feudal in form, and not in spirit; Virginia in spirit, and not in form; New England in neither; and New York largely in both. This social crystallization had, it is true, many opponents. In politics, as in religion, there were sharp antagonisms and frequent quarrels. They centred in the city; for in the well-stocked dwellings of the Dutch farmers along the Hudson there reigned a tranquil and prosperous routine; and the Dutch border town of Albany had not its like in America for unruffled conservatism and quaint picturesqueness.

Of the other colonies, the briefest mention will suffice: New Jersey, with its wholesome population of farmers; tobacco-growing Maryland, which, but for its proprietary government and numerous Roman Catholics, might pass for another Virginia, inferior in growth, and less decisive in features; Delaware, a modest appendage of Pennsylvania; wild and rude North Carolina; and, farther on, South Carolina and Georgia, too remote from the seat of war to take a noteworthy part in it. The attitude of these various colonies towards each other is hardly conceivable to an American of the present time. They had no political tie except a common allegiance to the British Crown. Communication between them was difficult and slow, by rough roads traced often through primeval forests. Between some of them there was less of sympathy than of jealousy kindled by conflicting interests or perpetual disputes concerning boundaries. The patriotism of the colonist was bounded by the lines of his government, except in the compact and kindred colonies of New England, which were socially united, though politically distinct. The country of the New Yorker was New York, and the country of the Virginian was Virginia. The New England colonies had once confederated; but, kindred as they were, they had long ago dropped apart. William Penn proposed a plan of colonial union wholly fruitless. James II. tried to unite all the northern colonies under one government; but the attempt came to naught. Each stood aloof, jealously independent. At rare intervals, under the pressure of an emergency, some of them would try to act in concert; and, except in New England, the results had been most discouraging. Nor was it this segregation only that unfitted them for war. They were all subject to popular legislatures, through whom alone money and men could be raised; and these elective bodies were sometimes factious and selfish, and not always either far-sighted or reasonable. Moreover, they were in a state of ceaseless friction with their governors, who represented the king, or, what was worse, the feudal proprietary. These disputes, though varying in intensity, were found everywhere except in the two small colonies which chose their own governors; and they were premonitions of the movement towards independence which ended in the war of Revolution. The occasion of difference mattered little. Active or latent, the quarrel was always present. In New York it turned on a question of the governor's salary; in Pennsylvania on the taxation of the proprietary estates; in Virginia on a fee exacted for the issue of land patents. It was sure to arise whenever some public crisis gave the representatives of the people an opportunity of extorting concessions from the representative of the Crown, or gave the representative of the Crown an opportunity to gain a point for prerogative. That is to say, the time when action was most needed was the time chosen for obstructing it.

In Canada there was no popular legislature to embarrass the central power. The people, like an army, obeyed the word of command,—a military advantage beyond all price.

Divided in government; divided in origin, feelings, and principles; jealous of each other, jealous of the Crown; the people at war with the executive, and, by the fermentation of internal politics, blinded to an outward danger that seemed remote and vague,—such were the conditions under which the British colonies drifted into a war that was to decide the fate of the continent.

This war was the strife of a united and concentred few against a divided and discordant many. It was the strife, too, of the past against the future; of the old against the new; of moral and intellectual torpor against moral and intellectual life; of barren absolutism against a liberty, crude, incoherent, and chaotic, yet full of prolific vitality.

2

Céloron de Bienville

1749–1752

La Galissonière · English Encroachment · Mission of Céloron ·
The Great West · Its European Claimants · Its Indian Population ·
English Fur-Traders · Céloron on the Alleghany · His Reception
· His Difficulties · Descent of the Ohio · Covert Hostility ·
Ascent of the Miami · La Demoiselle · Dark Prospects for France
· Christopher Gist · George Croghan · Their Western Mission ·
Pickawillany · English Ascendency · English Dissension and
Rivalry · The Key of the Great West

When the peace of Aix-la-Chapelle was signed, the Marquis de la Galissonière ruled over Canada. Like all the later Canadian governors, he was a naval officer; and, a few years after, he made himself famous by a victory, near Minorca, over the English admiral Byng,—an achievement now remembered chiefly by the fate of the defeated commander, judicially murdered as the scapegoat of an imbecile ministry. Galissonière was a humpback; but his deformed person was animated by a bold spirit and a strong and penetrating intellect. He was the chief representative of the American policy of France. He felt that, cost what it might, she must hold fast to Canada, and link her to Louisiana by chains of forts strong enough to hold back the British colonies, and cramp their growth by confinement within narrow limits; while French settlers, sent from the mother-country, should spread and multiply in the broad valleys of the interior.

It is true, he said, that Canada and her dependencies have always been a burden; but they are necessary as a barrier against English ambition; and to abandon them is to abandon ourselves; for if we suffer our enemies to become masters in America, their trade and naval power will grow to vast proportions, and they will draw from their colonies a wealth that will make them preponderant in Europe.[1]

The treaty had done nothing to settle the vexed question of boundaries between France and her rival. It had but staved off the inevitable conflict. Meanwhile, the English traders were crossing the mountains from Pennsylvania and Virginia, poaching on the domain which France claimed as hers, ruining the French fur-trade, seducing the Indian allies of Canada, and stirring them up against her. Worse still, English land speculators were beginning to follow. Something must be done, and that promptly, to drive back the intruders, and vindicate French rights in the valley of the Ohio. To this end the Governor sent Céloron de Bienville thither in the summer of 1749.

He was a chevalier de St. Louis and a captain in the colony troops. Under him went fourteen officers and cadets, twenty soldiers, a hundred and eighty Canadians, and a band of Indians, all in twenty-three birch-bark canoes. They left La Chine on the fifteenth of June, and pushed up the rapids of the St. Lawrence, losing a man and damaging several canoes on the way. Ten days brought them to the mouth of the Oswegatchie, where Ogdensburg now stands. Here they found a Sulpitian priest, Abbé Piquet, busy at building a fort, and lodging for the present under a shed of bark like an Indian. This enterprising father, ostensibly a missionary, was in reality a zealous political agent, bent on winning over the red allies of the English, retrieving French prestige, and restoring French trade. Thus far he had attracted but two Iroquois to his new establishment; and these he lent to Céloron.

Reaching Lake Ontario, the party stopped for a time at the French fort of Frontenac, but avoided the rival English post of Oswego, on the southern shore, where a trade in beaver skins, disastrous to French interests, was carried on, and whither many tribes, once faithful to Canada, now made resort. On the sixth of July Céloron reached Niagara. This, the most important pass of all the western wilderness, was guarded by a small fort of palisades on the point where the river joins the lake. Thence, the party carried their canoes over the portage road by the cataract, and launched them upon Lake Erie. On the fifteenth they landed on the lonely shore where the town of Portland now

---

[1]La Galissonière, *Mémoire sur les Colonies de la France dans l'Amérique septentrionale.*

stands; and for the next seven days were busied in shouldering canoes and baggage up and down the steep hills, through the dense forest of beech, oak, ash, and elm, to the waters of Chautauqua Lake, eight or nine miles distant. Here they embarked again, steering southward over the sunny waters, in the stillness and solitude of the leafy hills, till they came to the outlet, and glided down the peaceful current in the shade of the tall forests that overarched it. This prosperity was short. The stream was low, in spite of heavy rains that had drenched them on the carrying place. Father Bonnecamp, chaplain of the expedition, wrote, in his Journal: "In some places—and they were but too frequent—the water was only two or three inches deep; and we were reduced to the sad necessity of dragging our canoes over the sharp pebbles, which, with all our care and precaution, stripped off large slivers of the bark. At last, tired and worn, and almost in despair of ever seeing La Belle Rivière, we entered it at noon of the 29th." The part of the Ohio, or "La Belle Rivière," which they had thus happily reached, is now called the Alleghany. The Great West lay outspread before them, a realm of wild and waste fertility.

French America had two heads,—one among the snows of Canada, and one among the cane-brakes of Louisiana; one communicating with the world through the Gulf of St. Lawrence, and the other through the Gulf of Mexico. These vital points were feebly connected by a chain of military posts,— slender, and often interrupted,—circling through the wilderness nearly three thousand miles. Midway between Canada and Louisiana lay the valley of the Ohio. If the English should seize it, they would sever the chain of posts, and cut French America asunder. If the French held it, and entrenched themselves well along its eastern limits, they would shut their rivals between the Alleghanies and the sea, control all the tribes of the West, and turn them, in case of war, against the English borders,—a frightful and insupportable scourge.

The Indian population of the Ohio and its northern tributaries was relatively considerable. The upper or eastern half of the valley was occupied by mingled hordes of Delawares, Shawanoes, Wyandots, and Iroquois, or Indians of the Five Nations, who had migrated thither from their ancestral abodes within the present limits of the State of New York, and who were called Mingoes by the English traders. Along with them were a few wandering Abenakis, Nipissings, and Ottawas. Farther west, on the waters of the Miami, the Wabash, and other neighboring streams, was the seat of a confederacy formed of the various bands of the Miamis and their kindred or affiliated tribes. Still farther west, towards the Mississippi, were the remnants of the Illinois.

France had done but little to make good her claims to this grand domain. East of the Miami she had no military post whatever. Westward, on the Maumee, there was a small wooden fort, another on the St. Joseph, and two on the Wabash. On the meadows of the Mississippi, in the Illinois country, stood Fort Chartres,—a much stronger work, and one of the chief links of the chain that connected Quebec with New Orleans. Its four stone bastions were impregnable to musketry; and, here in the depths of the wilderness, there was no fear that cannon would be brought against it. It was the centre and citadel of a curious little forest settlement, the only vestige of civilization through all this region. At Kaskaskia, extended along the borders of the stream, were seventy or eighty French houses; thirty or forty at Cahokia, opposite the site of St. Louis; and a few more at the intervening hamlets of St. Philippe and Prairie à la Roche,—a picturesque but thriftless population, mixed with Indians, totally ignorant, busied partly with the fur-trade, and partly with the raising of corn for the market of New Orleans. They communicated with it by means of a sort of row galley, of eighteen or twenty oars, which made the voyage twice a year, and usually spent ten weeks on the return up the river.[1]

The Pope and the Bourbons had claimed this wilderness for seventy years, and had done scarcely more for it than the Indians, its natural owners. Of the western tribes, even of those living at the French posts, the Hurons or Wyandots alone were Christian.[2] The devoted zeal of the early missionaries and the politic efforts of their successors had failed alike. The savages of the Ohio and the Mississippi, instead of being tied to France by the mild bonds of the faith, were now in a state which the French called defection or revolt; that is, they received and welcomed the English traders.

These traders came in part from Virginia, but chiefly from Pennsylvania. Dinwiddie, governor of Virginia, says of them: "They appear to me to be in general a set of abandoned wretches;" and Hamilton, governor of Pennsylvania, replies: "I concur with you in opinion that they are a very licentious people."[3] Indian traders, of whatever nation, are rarely models of virtue; and these, without doubt, were rough and law-

---

[1]Gordon, *Journal, 1766*, appended to Pownall, *Topographical Description*. In the Dépôt des Cartes de la Marine at Paris, C. 4,040, are two curious maps of the Illinois colony, made a little after the middle of the century. In 1753 the Marquis Duquesne denounced the colonists as debauched and lazy.

[2]"De toutes les nations domiciliées dans les postes des pays d'en haut, il n'y a que les hurons du détroit qui aient embrassé la Réligion chretienne." *Mémoire du Roy pour servir d'instruction au S^r. Marquis de Lajonquière.*

[3]*Dinwiddie to Hamilton, 21 May, 1753. Hamilton to Dinwiddie, — May, 1753.*

less men, with abundant blackguardism and few scruples. Not all of them, however, are to be thus qualified. Some were of a better stamp; among whom were Christopher Gist, William Trent, and George Croghan. These and other chief traders hired men on the frontiers, crossed the Alleghanies with goods packed on the backs of horses, descended into the valley of the Ohio, and journeyed from stream to stream and village to village along the Indian trails, with which all this wilderness was seamed, and which the traders widened to make them practicable. More rarely, they carried their goods on horses to the upper waters of the Ohio, and embarked them in large wooden canoes, in which they descended the main river, and ascended such of its numerous tributaries as were navigable. They were bold and enterprising; and French writers, with alarm and indignation, declare that some of them had crossed the Mississippi and traded with the distant Osages. It is said that about three hundred of them came over the mountains every year.

On reaching the Alleghany, Céloron de Bienville entered upon the work assigned him, and began by taking possession of the country. The men were drawn up in order; Louis XV. was proclaimed lord of all that region, the arms of France, stamped on a sheet of tin, were nailed to a tree, a plate of lead was buried at its foot, and the notary of the expedition drew up a formal act of the whole proceeding. The leaden plate was inscribed as follows: "Year 1749, in the reign of Louis Fifteenth, King of France. We, Céloron, commanding the detachment sent by the Marquis de la Galissonière, commander-general of New France, to restore tranquillity in certain villages of these cantons, have buried this plate at the confluence of the Ohio and the Kanaouagon [*Conewango*], this 29th July, as a token of renewal of possession heretofore taken of the aforesaid River Ohio, of all streams that fall into it, and all lands on both sides to the source of the aforesaid streams, as the preceding Kings of France have enjoyed or ought to have enjoyed it, and which they have upheld by force of arms and by treaties, notably by those of Ryswick, Utrecht, and Aix-la-Chapelle."

This done, the party proceeded on its way, moving downward with the current, and passing from time to time rough openings in the forest, with clusters of Indian wigwams, the inmates of which showed a strong inclination to run off at their approach. To prevent this, Chabert de Joncaire was sent in advance, as a messenger of peace. He was himself half Indian, being the son of a French officer and a Seneca squaw, speaking fluently his maternal tongue, and, like his father, holding an important place in all dealings between the French and the tribes who spoke dialects of the Iroquois. On this occasion his success was not complete. It needed all his art to prevent the alarmed savages from taking to the woods. Sometimes, however, Céloron succeeded in gaining an audience; and at a village of Senecas called La Paille Coupée he read them a message from La Galissonière couched in terms sufficiently imperative: "My children, since I was at war with the English, I have learned that they have seduced you; and not content with corrupting your hearts, have taken advantage of my absence to invade lands which are not theirs, but mine; and therefore I have resolved to send you Monsieur de Céloron to tell you my intentions, which are that I will not endure the English on my land. Listen to me, children; mark well the word that I send you; follow my advice, and the sky will always be calm and clear over your villages. I expect from you an answer worthy of true children." And he urged them to stop all trade with the intruders, and send them back to whence they came. They promised compliance; "and," says the chaplain, Bonnecamp, "we should all have been satisfied if we had thought them sincere; but nobody doubted that fear had extorted their answer."

Four leagues below French Creek, by a rock scratched with Indian hieroglyphics, they buried another leaden plate. Three days after, they reached the Delaware village of Attiqué, at the site of Kittanning, whose twenty-two wigwams were all empty, the owners having fled. A little farther on, at an old abandoned village of Shawanoes, they found six English traders, whom they warned to begone, and return no more at their peril. Being helpless to resist, the traders pretended obedience; and Céloron charged them with a letter to the Governor of Pennsylvania, in which he declared that he was "greatly surprised" to find Englishmen trespassing on the domain of France. "I know," concluded the letter, "that our Commandant-General would be very sorry to be forced to use violence; but his orders are precise, to leave no foreign traders within the limits of his government."[1]

On the next day they reached a village of Iroquois under a female chief, called Queen Alequippa by the English, to whom she was devoted. Both Queen and subjects had fled; but among the deserted wigwams were six more Englishmen, whom Céloron warned off like the others, and who, like them, pretended to obey. At a neighboring town they found only two withered ancients, male and female, whose united ages, in the judgment of the chaplain, were full two centuries. They passed the site of the future Pittsburg; and some seventeen miles below

---

[1] Céloron, *Journal.* Compare the letter as translated in *N. Y. Col. Docs.*, VI. 532; also *Colonial Records of Pa.*, V. 425.

approached Chiningué, called Logstown by the English, one of the chief places on the river.[1] Both English and French flags were flying over the town, and the inhabitants, lining the shore, greeted their visitors with a salute of musketry,—not wholly welcome, as the guns were charged with ball. Céloron threatened to fire on them if they did not cease. The French climbed the steep bank, and encamped on the plateau above, betwixt the forest and the village, which consisted of some fifty cabins and wigwams, grouped in picturesque squalor, and tenanted by a mixed population, chiefly of Delawares, Shawanoes, and Mingoes. Here, too, were gathered many fugitives from the deserted towns above. Céloron feared a night attack. The camp was encircled by a ring of sentries; the officers walked the rounds till morning; a part of the men were kept under arms, and the rest ordered to sleep in their clothes. Joncaire discovered through some women of his acquaintance that an attack was intended. Whatever the danger may have been, the precautions of the French averted it; and instead of a battle, there was a council. Céloron delivered to the assembled chiefs a message from the Governor more conciliatory than the former, "Through the love I bear you, my children, I send you Monsieur de Céloron to open your eyes to the designs of the English against your lands. The establishments they mean to make, and of which you are certainly ignorant, tend to your complete ruin. They hide from you their plans, which are to settle here and drive you away, if I let them. As a good father who tenderly loves his children, and though far away from them bears them always in his heart, I must warn you of the danger that threatens you. The English intend to rob you of your country; and that they may succeed, they begin by corrupting your minds. As they mean to seize the Ohio, which belongs to me, I send to warn them to retire."

The reply of the chiefs, though sufficiently humble, was not all that could be wished. They begged that the intruders might stay a little longer, since the goods they brought were necessary to them. It was in fact, these goods, cheap, excellent, and abundant as they were, which formed the only true bond between the English and the Western tribes. Logstown was one of the chief resorts of the English traders; and at this moment there were ten of them in the place. Céloron warned them off. "They agreed," says the chaplain, "to all that was demanded, well resolved, no doubt, to do the contrary as soon as our backs were turned."

Having distributed gifts among the Indians, the French proceeded on

[1]There was another Chiningué, the Shenango of the English, on the Alleghany.

their way, and at or near the mouth of Wheeling Creek buried another
plate of lead. They repeated the same ceremony at the mouth of the
Muskingum. Here, half a century later, when this region belonged to
the United States, a party of boys, bathing in the river, saw the plate
protruding from the bank where the freshets had laid it bare, knocked
it down with a long stick, melted half of it into bullets, and gave what
remained to a neighbor from Marietta, who, hearing of this mysterious
relic, inscribed in an unknown tongue, came to rescue it from their
hands.[1] It is now in the cabinet of the American Antiquarian Society.[2]
On the eighteenth of August, Céloron buried yet another plate, at the
mouth of the Great Kenawha. This, too, in the course of a century,
was unearthed by the floods, and was found in 1846 by a boy at play,
by the edge of the water.[3] The inscriptions on all these plates were
much alike, with variations of date and place.

The weather was by turns rainy and hot; and the men, tired and
famished, were fast falling ill. On the twenty-second they approached
Scioto, called by the French St. Yotoc, or Sinioto, a large Shawanoe
town at the mouth of the river which bears the same name. Greatly
doubting what welcome awaited them, they filled their powder-horns
and prepared for the worst. Joncaire was sent forward to propitiate the
inhabitants; but they shot bullets through the flag that he carried, and
surrounded him, yelling and brandishing their knives. Some were for
killing him at once; others for burning him alive. The interposition of
a friendly Iroquois saved him; and at length they let him go. Céloron
was very uneasy at the reception of his messenger. "I knew," he writes,
"the weakness of my party, two thirds of which were young men who
had never left home before, and would all have run at the sight of ten
Indians. Still, there was nothing for me but to keep on; for I was short
of provisions, my canoes were badly damaged, and I had no pitch or
bark to mend them. So I embarked again, ready for whatever might
happen. I had good officers, and about fifty men who could be trusted."

As they neared the town, the Indians swarmed to the shore, and
began the usual salute of musketry. "They fired," says Céloron, "full a
thousand shots; for the English give them powder for nothing." He
prudently pitched his camp on the farther side of the river, posted
guards, and kept close watch. Each party distrusted and feared the

---

[1]O. H. Marshall, in *Magazine of American History, March, 1878.*
[2]For papers relating to it, see *Trans. Amer. Antiq. Soc.,* II.
[3]For a fac-simile of the inscription on this plate, see *Olden Time,* I. 288. Céloron calls the Kenawha, *Chinodahichetha.* The inscriptions as given in his Journal correspond with those on the plates
discovered.

other. At length, after much ado, many debates, and some threatening movements on the part of the alarmed and excited Indians, a council took place at the tent of the French commander; the chiefs apologized for the rough treatment of Joncaire, and Céloron replied with a rebuke, which would doubtless have been less mild, had he felt himself stronger. He gave them also a message from the Governor, modified, apparently, to suit the circumstances; for while warning them of the wiles of the English, it gave no hint that the King of France claimed mastery of their lands. Their answer was vague and unsatisfactory. It was plain that they were bound to the enemy by interest, if not by sympathy. A party of English traders were living in the place; and Céloron summoned them to withdraw, on pain of what might ensue. "My instructions," he says, "enjoined me to do this, and even to pillage the English; but I was not strong enough; and as these traders were established in the village and well supported by the Indians, the attempt would have failed, and put the French to shame." The assembled chiefs having been regaled with a cup of brandy each,—the only part of the proceeding which seemed to please them,—Céloron reimbarked, and continued his voyage.

On the thirtieth they reached the Great Miami, called by the French, Rivière à la Roche; and here Céloron buried the last of his leaden plates. They now bade farewell to the Ohio, or, in the words of the chaplain, to "La Belle Rivière,—that river so little known to the French, and unfortunately too well known to the English." He speaks of the multitude of Indian villages on its shores, and still more on its northern branches. "Each, great or small, has one or more English traders, and each of these has hired men to carry his furs. Behold, then, the English well advanced upon our lands, and, what is worse, under the protection of a crowd of savages whom they have drawn over to them, and whose number increases daily."

The course of the party lay up the Miami; and they toiled thirteen days against the shallow current before they reached a village of the Miami Indians, lately built at the mouth of the rivulet now called Loramie Creek. Over it ruled a chief to whom the French had given the singular name of La Demoiselle, but whom the English, whose fast friend he was, called Old Britain. The English traders who lived here had prudently withdrawn, leaving only two hired men in the place. The object of Céloron was to induce the Demoiselle and his band to leave this new abode and return to their old villages near the French fort on the Maumee, where they would be safe from English seduction. To this end, he called them to a council, gave them ample gifts, and

made them an harangue in the name of the Governor. The Demoiselle
took the gifts, thanked his French father for his good advice, and promised to follow it at a more convenient time.[1] In vain Céloron insisted
that he and his tribesmen should remove at once. Neither blandishments nor threats would prevail, and the French commander felt that
his negotiation had failed.

He was not deceived. Far from leaving his village, the Demoiselle,
who was Great Chief of the Miami Confederacy, gathered his followers
to the spot, till, less than two years after the visit of Céloron, its population had increased eightfold. Pique Town, or Pickawillany, as the
English called it, became one of the greatest Indian towns of the West,
the centre of English trade and influence, and a capital object of French
jealousy.

Céloron burned his shattered canoes, and led his party across the
long and difficult portage to the French post on the Maumee, where he
found Raymond, the commander, and all his men, shivering with fever
and ague. They supplied him with wooden canoes for his voyage down
the river; and, early in October, he reached Lake Erie, where he was
detained for a time by a drunken debauch of his Indians, who are called
by the chaplain "a species of men made to exercise the patience of
those who have the misfortune to travel with them." In a month more
he was at Fort Frontenac; and as he descended thence to Montreal, he
stopped at the Oswegatchie, in obedience to the Governor, who had
directed him to report the progress made by the Sulpitian, Abbé Piquet,
at his new mission. Piquet's new fort had been burned by Indians,
prompted, as he thought, by the English of Oswego; but the priest,
buoyant and undaunted, was still resolute for the glory of God and the
confusion of the heretics.

At length Céloron reached Montreal; and, closing his Journal, wrote
thus: "Father Bonnecamp, who is a Jesuit and a great mathematician,
reckons that we have travelled twelve hundred leagues; I and my officers think we have travelled more. All I can say is, that the nations of
these countries are very ill-disposed towards the French, and devoted
entirely to the English."[2] If his expedition had done no more, it had at

---

[1]Céloron, *Journal*. Compare *A Message from the Twightwees* (Miamis) in *Colonial Records of Pa.*,
V. 437, where they say that they refused the gifts.

[2]*Journal de la Campagne que moy Céloron, Chevalier de l'Ordre Royal et Militaire de St. Louis, Capitaine Commandant un détachement envoyé dans la Belle Rivière par les ordres de M. le Marquis de La
Galissonière*, etc.

*Relation d'un voyage dans la Belle Rivière sous les ordres de M. de Céloron, par le Père Bonnecamp,
en 1749.*

least revealed clearly the deplorable condition of French interests in the West.

While Céloron was warning English traders from the Ohio, a plan was on foot in Virginia for a new invasion of the French domain. An association was formed to settle the Ohio country; and a grant of five hundred thousand acres was procured from the King, on condition that a hundred families should be established upon it within seven years, a fort built, and a garrison maintained. The Ohio Company numbered among its members some of the chief men of Virginia, including two brothers of Washington; and it had also a London partner, one Hanbury, a person of influence, who acted as its agent in England. In the year after the expedition of Céloron, its governing committee sent the trader Christopher Gist to explore the country and select land. It must be "good level land," wrote the Committee; "we had rather go quite down to the Mississippi than take mean, broken land."[1] In November Gist reached Logstown, the Chiningué of Céloron, where he found what he calls a "parcel of reprobate Indian traders." Those whom he so stigmatizes were Pennsylvanians, chiefly Scotch-Irish, between whom and the traders from Virginia there was great jealousy. Gist was told that he "should never go home safe." He declared himself the bearer of a message from the King. This imposed respect, and he was allowed to proceed. At the Wyandot village of Muskingum he found the trader George Croghan, sent to the Indians by the Governor of Pennsylvania, to renew the chain of friendship.[2] "Croghan," he says, "is a mere idol among his countrymen, the Irish traders;" yet they met amicably, and the Pennsylvanian had with him a companion, Andrew Montour, the interpreter, who proved of great service to Gist. As Montour was a conspicuous person in his time, and a type of his class, he merits a passing notice. He was the reputed grandson of a French governor and an Indian squaw. His half-breed mother, Catharine Montour, was a native of Canada, whence she was carried off by the Iroquois, and adopted by them. She lived in a village at the head of Seneca Lake, and still held the belief, inculcated by the guides of her youth, that Christ was a Frenchman crucified by the English.[3] Her son Andrew is

---

[1] Instructions to Gist, in appendix to Pownall, *Topographical Description of North America*.

[2] *Mr. Croghan's Transactions with the Indians*, in N. Y. Col. Docs., VII. 267; *Croghan to Hamilton, 16 Dec. 1750*.

[3] This is stated by Count Zinzendorf, who visited her among the Senecas. Compare *Frontenac and New France under Louis XIV.*, p. 271. In a plan of the "Route of the Western Army," made in 1779, and of which a tracing is before me, the village where she lived is still called "French Catharine's Town."

thus described by the Moravian Zinzendorf, who knew him: "His face is like that of a European, but marked with a broad Indian ring of bear's-grease and paint drawn completely round it. He wears a coat of fine cloth of cinnamon color, a black necktie with silver spangles, a red satin waistcoat, trousers over which hangs his shirt, shoes and stockings, a hat, and brass ornaments, something like the handle of a basket, suspended from his ears."[1] He was an excellent interpreter, and held in high account by his Indian kinsmen.

After leaving Muskingum, Gist, Croghan, and Montour went together to a village on White Woman's Creek,—so called from one Mary Harris, who lived here. She was born in New England, was made prisoner when a child forty years before, and had since dwelt among her captors, finding such comfort as she might in an Indian husband and a family of young half-breeds. "She still remembers," says Gist, "that they used to be very religious in New England, and wonders how white men can be so wicked as she has seen them in these woods." He and his companions now journeyed southwestward to the Shawanoe town at the mouth of the Scioto, where they found a reception very different from that which had awaited Céloron. Thence they rode northwestward along the forest path that led to Pickawillany, the Indian town on the upper waters of the Great Miami. Gist was delighted with the country; and reported to his employers that "it is fine, rich, level land, well timbered with large walnut, ash, sugar trees and cherry trees; well watered with a great number of little streams and rivulets; full of beautiful natural meadows, with wild rye, blue-grass, and clover, and abounding with turkeys, deer, elks, and most sorts of game, particularly buffaloes, thirty or forty of which are frequently seen in one meadow." A little farther west, on the plains of the Wabash and the Illinois, he would have found them by thousands.

They crossed the Miami on a raft, their horses swimming after them; and were met on landing by a crowd of warriors, who, after smoking with them, escorted them to the neighboring town, where they were greeted by a fusillade of welcome. "We entered with English colors before us, and were kindly received by their king, who invited us into his own house and set our colors upon the top of it; then all the white men and traders that were there came and welcomed us." This "king" was Old Britain, or La Demoiselle. Great were the changes here since Céloron, a year and a half before, had vainly enticed him to change his abode, and dwell in the shadow of the fleur-de-lis. The town had

---

[1] Journal of Zinzendorf, quoted in Schweinitz, *Life of David Zeisberger*, 112, *note*.

grown to four hundred families, or about two thousand souls; and the English traders had built for themselves and their hosts a fort of pickets, strengthened with logs.

There was a series of councils in the long house, or town-hall. Croghan made the Indians a present from the Governor of Pennsylvania; and he and Gist delivered speeches of friendship and good advice, which the auditors received with the usual monosyllabic plaudits, ejected from the depths of their throats. A treaty of peace was solemnly made between the English and the confederate tribes, and all was serenity and joy; till four Ottawas, probably from Detroit, arrived with a French flag, a gift of brandy and tobacco, and a message from the French commandant inviting the Miamis to visit him. Whereupon the great war-chief rose, and, with "a fierce tone and very warlike air," said to the envoys: "Brothers the Ottawas, we let you know, by these four strings of wampum, that we will not hear anything the French say, nor do anything they bid us." Then addressing the French as if actually present: "Fathers, we have made a road to the sun-rising, and have been taken by the hand by our brothers the English, the Six Nations, the Delawares, Shawanoes, and Wyandots.[1] We assure you, in that road we will go; and as you threaten us with war in the spring, we tell you that we are ready to receive you." Then, turning again to the four envoys: "Brothers the Ottawas, you hear what I say. Tell that to your fathers the French, for we speak it from our hearts." The chiefs then took down the French flag which the Ottawas had planted in the town, and dismissed the envoys with their answer of defiance.

On the next day the town-crier came with a message from the Demoiselle, inviting his English guests to a "feather dance," which Gist thus describes: "It was performed by three dancing-masters, who were painted all over of various colors, with long sticks in their hands, upon the ends of which were fastened long feathers of swans and other birds, neatly woven in the shape of a fowl's wing; in this disguise they performed many antic tricks, waving their sticks and feathers about with great skill, to imitate the flying and fluttering of birds, keeping exact time with their music." This music was the measured thumping of an Indian drum. From time to time a warrior would leap up, and the drum and the dancers would cease as he struck a post with his tomahawk, and in a loud voice recounted his exploits. Then the music and the dance began anew, till another warrior caught the martial fire, and

---

[1]Compare *Message of Miamis and Hurons to the Governor of Pennsylvania* in N. Y. Col. Docs., VI. 594; and *Report of Croghan* in *Colonial Records of Pa.*, V. 522, 523.

bounded into the circle to brandish his tomahawk and vaunt his prowess.

On the first of March Gist took leave of Pickawillany, and returned towards the Ohio. He would have gone to the Falls, where Louisville now stands, but for a band of French Indians reported to be there, who would probably have killed him. After visiting a deposit of mammoth bones on the south shore, long the wonder of the traders, he turned eastward, crossed with toil and difficulty the mountains about the sources of the Kenawha, and after an absence of seven months reached his frontier home on the Yadkin, whence he proceeded to Roanoke with the report of his journey.[1]

All looked well for the English in the West; but under this fair outside lurked hidden danger. The Miamis were hearty in the English cause, and so perhaps were the Shawanoes; but the Delawares had not forgotten the wrongs that drove them from their old abodes east of the Alleghanies, while the Mingoes, or emigrant Iroquois, like their brethren of New York, felt the influence of Joncaire and other French agents, who spared no efforts to seduce them.[2] Still more baneful to British interests were the apathy and dissensions of the British colonies themselves. The Ohio Company had built a trading-house at Will's Creek, a branch of the Potomac, to which the Indians resorted in great numbers; whereupon the jealous traders of Pennsylvania told them that the Virginians meant to steal away their lands. This confirmed what they had been taught by the French emissaries, whose intrigues it powerfully aided. The governors of New York, Pennsylvania, and Virginia saw the importance of Indian alliances, and felt their own responsibility in regard to them; but they could do nothing without their assemblies. Those of New York and Pennsylvania were largely composed of tradesmen and farmers, absorbed in local interests, and possessed by two motives,—the saving of the people's money, and opposition to the governor, who stood for the royal prerogative. It was Hamilton, of Pennsylvania, who had sent Croghan to the Miamis to "renew the chain of friendship;" and when the envoy returned, the Assembly rejected his report. "I was condemned," he says, "for bringing expense on the Government, and the Indians were neglected."[3] In the same year Hamilton again sent him over the mountains, with a present for

---

[1] *Journal of Christopher Gist*, in appendix to Pownall, *Topographical Description*. Mr. Croghan's *Transactions with the Indians* in N. Y. Col. Docs., VII. 267.

[2] Joncaire made anti-English speeches to the Ohio Indians under the eyes of the English themselves, who did not molest him. *Journal of George Croghan, 1751,* in *Olden Time*, I. 136.

[3] *Mr. Croghan's Transactions with the Indians*, N. Y. Col. Docs., VII. 267.

the Mingoes and Delawares. Croghan succeeded in persuading them that it would be for their good if the English should build a fortified trading-house at the fork of the Ohio, where Pittsburg now stands; and they made a formal request to the Governor that it should be built accordingly. But, in the words of Croghan, the Assembly "rejected the proposal, and condemned me for making such a report." Yet this post on the Ohio was vital to English interests. Even the Penns, proprietaries of the province, never lavish of their money, offered four hundred pounds towards the cost of it, besides a hundred a year towards its maintenance; but the Assembly would not listen.[1] The Indians were so well convinced that a strong English trading-station in their country would add to their safety and comfort, that when Pennsylvania refused it, they repeated the proposal to Virginia; but here, too, it found for the present little favor.

The question of disputed boundaries had much to do with this most impolitic inaction. A large part of the valley of the Ohio, including the site of the proposed establishment, was claimed by both Pennsylvania and Virginia; and each feared that whatever money it might spend there would turn to the profit of the other. This was not the only evil that sprang from uncertain ownership. "Till the line is run between the two provinces," says Dinwiddie, governor of Virginia, "I cannot appoint magistrates to keep the traders in good order."[2] Hence they did what they pleased, and often gave umbrage to the Indians. Clinton, of New York, appealed to his Assembly for means to assist Pennsylvania in "securing the fidelity of the Indians on the Ohio," and the Assembly refused.[3] "We will take care of our Indians, and they may take care of theirs:" such was the spirit of their answer. He wrote to the various provinces, inviting them to send commissioners to meet the tribes at Albany, "in order to defeat the designs and intrigues of the French." All turned a deaf ear except Massachusetts, Connecticut, and South Carolina, who sent the commissioners, but supplied them very meagerly with the indispensable presents.[4] Clinton says further: "The Assembly of this province have not given one farthing for Indian affairs, nor for a year past have they provided for the subsistence of the garrison at

---

[1] *Colonial Records of Pa.*, V. 515, 529, 547. At a council at Logstown (1751), the Indians said to Croghan: "The French want to cheat us out of our country; but we will stop them, and, Brothers the English, you must help us. We expect that you will build a strong house on the River Ohio, that in case of war we may have a place to secure our wives and children, likewise our brothers that come to trade with us." *Report of Treaty at Logstown, Ibid.*, V. 538.

[2] *Dinwiddie to the Lords of Trade, 6 Oct. 1752.*

[3] *Journals of New York Assembly*, II. 283, 284. *Colonial Records of Pa.* V. 466.

[4] *Clinton to Hamilton, 18 Dec. 1750. Clinton to Lords of Trade, 13 June, 1751; Ibid., 17 July, 1751.*

Oswego, which is the key for the commerce between the colonies and the inland nations of Indians."[1]

In the heterogeneous structure of the British colonies, their clashing interests, their internal disputes, and the misplaced economy of penny-wise and short-sighted assembly-men, lay the hope of France. The rulers of Canada knew the vast numerical preponderance of their rivals; but with their centralized organization they felt themselves more than a match for any one English colony alone. They hoped to wage war under the guise of peace, and to deal with the enemy in detail; and they at length perceived that the fork of the Ohio, so strangely neglected by the English, formed, together with Niagara, the key of the Great West. Could France hold firmly these two controlling passes, she might almost boast herself mistress of the continent.

---

[1] *Clinton to Bedford, 30 July, 1750.*

NOTE.—The Journal of Céloron (Archives de la Marine) is very long and circumstantial, including the *procès verbaux*, and reports of councils with Indians. The Journal of the chaplain, Bonnecamp (Dépôt de la Marine), is shorter, but is the work of an intelligent and observing man. The author, a Jesuit, was skilled in mathematics, made daily observations, and constructed a map of the route, still preserved at the Dépôt de la Marine. Concurrently with these French narratives, one may consult the English letters and documents bearing on the same subjects, in the Colonial Records of Pennsylvania, the Archives of Pennsylvania, and the Colonial Documents of New York.

Three of Céloron's leaden plates have been found,—the two mentioned in the text, and another which was never buried, and which the Indians, who regarded these mysterious tablets as "bad medicine," procured by a trick from Joncaire, or, according to Governor Clinton, stole from him. A Cayuga chief brought it to Colonel Johnson, on the Mohawk, who interpreted the "Devilish writing" in such a manner as best to inspire horror of French designs.

3
Conflict for the West
1749–1753

THE FIVE NATIONS · CAUGHNAWAGA · ABBÉ PIQUET · HIS SCHEMES · HIS JOURNEY · FORT FRONTENAC · TORONTO · NIAGARA · OSWEGO · SUCCESS OF PIQUET · DETROIT · LA JONQUIÈRE · HIS INTRIGUES · HIS TRIALS · HIS DEATH · ENGLISH INTRIGUES · CRITICAL STATE OF THE WEST · PICKAWILLANY DESTROYED · DUQUESNE · HIS GRAND ENTERPRISE

The Iroquois, or Five Nations, sometimes called Six Nations after the Tuscaroras joined them, had been a power of high importance in American international politics. In a certain sense they may be said to have held the balance between their French and English neighbors; but their relative influence had of late declined. So many of them had emigrated and joined the tribes of the Ohio, that the centre of Indian population had passed to that region. Nevertheless, the Five Nations were still strong enough in their ancient abodes to make their alliance an object of the utmost consequence to both the European rivals. At the western end of their "Long House," or belt of confederated villages, Joncaire intrigued to gain them for France; while in the east he was counteracted by the young colonel of militia, William Johnson, who lived on the Mohawk, and was already well skilled in managing Indians. Johnson sometimes lost his temper; and once wrote to Governor Clinton to complain of the "confounded wicked things the French had infused into the Indians' heads; among the rest that the English were determined, the first opportunity, to de-

stroy them all. I assure your Excellency I had hard work to beat these
and several other cursed villanous things, told them by the French, out
of their heads."[1]

In former times the French had hoped to win over the Five Nations
in a body, by wholesale conversion to the Faith; but the attempt had
failed. They had, however, made within their own limits an asylum for
such converts as they could gain, whom they collected together at
Caughnawaga, near Montreal, to the number of about three hundred
warriors.[2] These could not be trusted to fight their kinsmen, but willingly made forays against the English borders. Caughnawaga, like various other Canadian missions, was divided between the Church, the
army, and the fur-trade. It had a chapel, fortifications, and storehouses;
two Jesuits, an officer, and three chief traders. Of these last, two were
maiden ladies, the Demoiselles Desauniers; and one of the Jesuits, their
friend Father Tournois, was their partner in business. They carried on
by means of the Mission Indians, and in collusion with influential persons in the colony, a trade with the Dutch at Albany, illegal, but very
profitable.[3]

Besides this Iroquois mission, which was chiefly composed of Mohawks and Oneidas, another was now begun farther westward, to win
over the Onondagas, Cayugas, and Senecas. This was the establishment
of Father Piquet, which Céloron had visited in its infancy when on his
way to the Ohio, and again on his return. Piquet was a man in the
prime of life, of an alert, vivacious countenance, by no means unpre-
possessing;[4] an enthusiastic schemer, with great executive talents; ardent, energetic, vain, self-confident, and boastful. The enterprise seems
to have been of his own devising; but it found warm approval from the
Government.[5] La Présentation, as he called the new mission, stood on
the bank of the River Oswegatchie where it enters the St. Lawrence.
Here the rapids ceased, and navigation was free to Lake Ontario. The
place commanded the main river, and could bar the way to hostile war-
parties or contraband traders. Rich meadows, forests, and abundance of
fish and game, made it attractive to Indians, and the Oswegatchie gave
access to the Iroquois towns. Piquet had chosen his site with great skill.

[1] *Johnson to Clinton, 28 April, 1749.*
[2] The estimate of a French official report, 1736, and of Sir William Johnson, 1763.
[3] *La Jonquière au Ministre, 27 Fév. 1750. Ibid., 29 Oct. 1751. Ordres du Roy et Dépêches des Ministres, 1751. Notice biographique de la Jonquière.* La Jonquière, governor of Canada, at last broke
up their contraband trade, and ordered Tournois to Quebec.
[4] I once saw a contemporary portrait of him at the mission of Two Mountains, where he had been
stationed.
[5] *Rouillé à la Jonquière, 1749.* The Intendant Bigot gave him money and provisions. *N. Y. Col.
Docs.*, X. 204.

His activity was admirable. His first stockade was burned by Indian incendiaries; but it rose quickly from its ashes, and within a year or two the mission of La Présentation had a fort of palisades flanked with blockhouses, a chapel, a storehouse, a barn, a stable, ovens, a saw-mill, broad fields of corn and beans, and three villages of Iroquois, containing, in all, forty-nine bark lodges, each holding three or four families, more or less converted to the Faith; and, as time went on, this number increased. The Governor had sent a squad of soldiers to man the fort, and five small cannon to mount upon it. The place was as safe for the new proselytes as it was convenient and agreeable. The Pennsylvanian interpreter, Conrad Weiser, was told at Onondaga, the Iroquois capital, that Piquet had made a hundred converts from that place alone; and that, "having clothed them all in very fine clothes, laced with silver and gold, he took them down and presented them to the French Governor at Montreal, who received them very kindly, and made them large presents."[1]

Such were some of the temporal attractions of La Présentation. The nature of the spiritual instruction bestowed by Piquet and his fellow-priests may be partly inferred from the words of a proselyte warrior, who declared with enthusiasm that he had learned from the Sulpitian mis-sionary that the King of France was the eldest son of the wife of Jesus Christ.[2] This he of course took in a literal sense, the mystic idea of the Church as the spouse of Christ being beyond his savage comprehension. The effect was to stimulate his devotion to the Great Onontio beyond the sea, and to the lesser Onontio who represented him as Governor of Canada.

Piquet was elated by his success; and early in 1752 he wrote to the Governor and Intendant: "It is a great miracle that, in spite of envy, contradiction, and opposition from nearly all the Indian villages, I have formed in less than three years one of the most flourishing missions in Canada. I find myself in a position to extend the empire of my good masters, Jesus Christ and the King, even to the extremities of this new world; and, with some little help from you, to do more than France and England have been able to do with millions of money and all their troops."[3]

---

[1] *Journal of Conrad Weiser, 1750.*
[2] Lalande, *Notice de l'Abbé Piquet*, in *Lettres Édifiantes.* See also Tassé in *Revue Canadienne, 1870*, p. 9.
[3] *Piquet à la Jonquière et Bigot, 8 Fév. 1752.* See Appendix A. In spite of Piquet's self-laudation, and in spite also of the detraction of the author of the *Mémoires sur le Canada, 1749–1760*, there can be no doubt of his practical capacity and his fertility of resource. Duquesne, when governor of the colony, highly praises "ses talents et son activité pour le service de Sa Majesté."

The letter from which this is taken was written to urge upon the Government a scheme in which the zealous priest could see nothing impracticable. He proposed to raise a war-party of thirty-eight hundred Indians, eighteen hundred of whom were to be drawn from the Canadian missions, the Five Nations, and the tribes of the Ohio, while the remaining two thousand were to be furnished by the Flatheads, or Choctaws, who were at the same time to be supplied with missionaries. The united force was first to drive the English from the Ohio, and next attack the Dog Tribe, or Cherokees, who lived near the borders of Virginia, with the people of which they were on friendly terms. "If," says Piquet, "the English of Virginia give any help to this last-named tribe,— which will not fail to happen,—they [*the war-party*] will do their utmost against them, through a grudge they bear them by reason of some old quarrels." In other words, the missionary hopes to set a host of savages to butchering English settlers in time of peace![1] His wild project never took effect, though the Governor, he says, at first approved it.

In the preceding year the "Apostle of the Iroquois," as he was called, made a journey to muster recruits for his mission, and kept a copious diary on the way. By accompanying him, one gets a clear view of an important part of the region in dispute between the rival nations. Six Canadians paddled him up the St. Lawrence, and five Indian converts followed in another canoe. Emerging from among the Thousand Islands, they stopped at Fort Frontenac, where Kingston now stands. Once the place was a great resort of Indians; now none were here, for the English post of Oswego, on the other side of the lake, had greater attractions. Piquet and his company found the pork and bacon very bad, and he complains that "there was not brandy enough in the fort to wash a wound." They crossed to a neighboring island, where they were soon visited by the chaplain of the fort, the storekeeper, his wife, and three young ladies, glad of an excursion to relieve the monotony of the garrison. "My hunters," says Piquet, "had supplied me with means of giving them a pretty good entertainment. We drank, with all our hearts, the health of the authorities, temporal and ecclesiastical, to the sound of our musketry, which was very well fired, and delighted the islanders." These islanders were a band of Indians who lived here. Piquet gave them a feast, then discoursed of religion, and at last persuaded them to remove to the new mission.

During eight days he and his party coasted the northern shore of

[1] Appendix A.

Lake Ontario, with various incidents, such as an encounter between his dog Cerberus and a wolf, to the disadvantage of the latter, and the meeting with "a very fine negro of twenty-two years, a fugitive from Virginia." On the twenty-sixth of June they reached the new fort of Toronto, which offered a striking contrast to their last stopping-place. "The wine here is of the best; there is nothing wanting in this fort; everything is abundant, fine, and good." There was reason for this. The Northern Indians were flocking with their beaver-skins to the English of Oswego; and in April, 1749, an officer named Portneuf had been sent with soldiers and workmen to build a stockaded trading-house at Toronto, in order to intercept them,—not by force, which would have been ruinous to French interests, but by a tempting supply of goods and brandy.[1] Thus the fort was kept well stocked, and with excellent effect. Piquet found here a band of Mississagas, who would otherwise, no doubt, have carried their furs to the English. He was strongly impelled to persuade them to migrate to La Présentation; but the Governor had told him to confine his efforts to other tribes; and lest, he says, the ardor of his zeal should betray him to disobedience, he reimbarked, and encamped six leagues from temptation.

Two days more brought him to Niagara, where he was warmly received by the commandant, the chaplain, and the storekeeper,—the triumvirate who ruled these forest outposts, and stood respectively for their three vital principles, war, religion, and trade. Here Piquet said mass; and after resting a day, set out for the trading-house at the portage of the cataract, recently built, like Toronto, to stop the Indians on their way to Oswego.[2] Here he found Joncaire, and here also was encamped a large band of Senecas; though, being all drunk, men, women, and children, they were in no condition to receive the Faith, or appreciate the temporal advantages that attended it. On the next morning, finding them partially sober, he invited them to remove to La Présentation; "but as they had still something left in their bottles, I could get no answer till the following day." "I pass in silence," pursues the missionary, "an infinity of talks on this occasion. Monsieur de Joncaire forgot nothing that could help me, and behaved like a great servant of God and the King. My recruits increased every moment. I went to say my breviary while my Indians and the Senecas, without loss of time, assembled to hold a council with Monsieur de Joncaire." The

[1]On Toronto, *La Jonquière et Bigot au Ministre, 1749. La Jonquière au Ministre, 30 Août, 1750. N. Y. Col. Docs.*, X. 201, 246.
[2]*La Jonquière au Ministre, 23 Fév. 1750. Ibid., 6 Oct. 1751.* Compare *Colonial Records of Pa.*, V. 508.

result of the council was an entreaty to the missionary not to stop at
Oswego, lest evil should befall him at the hands of the English. He
promised to do as they wished, and presently set out on his return to
Fort Niagara, attended by Joncaire and a troop of his new followers.
The journey was a triumphal progress. "Whenever we passed a camp or
a wigwam, the Indians saluted me by firing their guns, which happened
so often that I thought all the trees along the way were charged with
gunpowder; and when we reached the fort, Monsieur de Becancour received us with great ceremony and the firing of cannon, by which my
savages were infinitely flattered."

His neophytes were gathered into the chapel for the first time in their
lives, and there rewarded with a few presents. He now prepared to turn
homeward, his flock at the mission being left in his absence without a
shepherd; and on the sixth of July he embarked, followed by a swarm
of canoes. On the twelfth they stopped at the Genesee, and went to
visit the Falls, where the city of Rochester now stands. On the way,
the Indians found a populous resort of rattlesnakes, and attacked the
gregarious reptiles with great animation, to the alarm of the missionary,
who trembled for his bare-legged retainers. His fears proved needless.
Forty-two dead snakes, as he avers, requited the efforts of the sports-
men, and not one of them was bitten. When he returned to camp in
the afternoon he found there a canoe loaded with kegs of brandy. "The
English," he says, "had sent it to meet us, well knowing that this was
the best way to cause disorder among my new recruits and make them
desert me. The Indian in charge of the canoe, who had the look of a
great rascal, offered some to me first, and then to my Canadians and
Indians. I gave out that it was very probably poisoned, and immediately
embarked again."

He encamped on the fourteenth at Sodus Bay, and strongly advises
the planting of a French fort there. "Nevertheless," he adds, "it would
be still better to destroy Oswego, and on no account let the English
build it again." On the sixteenth he came in sight of this dreaded post.
Several times on the way he had met fleets of canoes going thither or
returning, in spite of the rival attractions of Toronto and Niagara. No
English establishment on the continent was of such ill omen to the
French. It not only robbed them of the fur-trade, by which they lived,
but threatened them with military and political, no less than commercial, ruin. They were in constant dread lest ships of war should be built
here, strong enough to command Lake Ontario, thus separating Canada
from Louisiana, and cutting New France asunder. To meet this danger,
they soon after built at Fort Frontenac a large three-masted vessel,

mounted with heavy cannon; thus, as usual, forestalling their rivals by promptness of action.[1] The ground on which Oswego stood was claimed by the Province of New York, which alone had control of it; but through the purblind apathy of the Assembly, and their incessant quarrels with the Governor, it was commonly left to take care of itself. For some time they would vote no money to pay the feeble little garrison; and Clinton, who saw the necessity of maintaining it, was forced to do so on his own personal credit.[2] "Why can't your Governor and your great men [the Assembly] agree?" asked a Mohawk chief of the interpreter, Conrad Weiser.[3]

Piquet kept his promise not to land at the English fort; but he approached in his canoe, and closely observed it. The shores, now covered by the city of Oswego, were then a desolation of bare hills and fields, studded with the stumps of felled trees, and hedged about with a grim border of forests. Near the strand, by the mouth of the Onondaga, were the houses of some of the traders; and on the higher ground behind them stood a huge block-house with a projecting upper story. This building was surrounded by a rough wall of stone, with flankers at the angles, forming what was called the fort.[4] Piquet reconnoitred it from his canoe with the eye of a soldier. "It is commanded," he says, "on almost every side; two batteries, of three twelve-pounders each, would be more than enough to reduce it to ashes." And he enlarges on the evils that arise from it. "It not only spoils our trade, but puts the English into communication with a vast number of our Indians, far and near. It is true that they like our brandy better than English rum; but they prefer English goods to ours, and can buy for two beaver-skins at Oswego a better silver bracelet than we sell at Niagara for ten."

The burden of these reflections was lightened when he approached Fort Frontenac. "Never was reception more solemn. The Nipissings and Algonkins, who were going on a war-party with Monsieur Belêtre, formed a line of their own accord, and saluted us with three volleys of musketry, and cries of joy without end. All our little bark vessels replied in the same way. Monsieur de Verchères and Monsieur de Valtry ordered the cannon of the fort to be fired; and my Indians, transported with joy at the honor done them, shot off their guns incessantly, with cries and acclamations that delighted everybody." A goodly band of recruits joined him, and he pursued his voyage to La Présentation,

---

[1] *Lieutenant Lindesay to Johnson, July, 1751.*
[2] *Clinton to Lords of Trade, 30 July, 1750.*
[3] *Journal of Conrad Weiser, 1750.*
[4] Compare *Doc. Hist. N. Y.*, I. 463.

while the canoes of his proselytes followed in a swarm to their new home; "that establishment"—thus in a burst of enthusiasm he closes his Journal—"that establishment which I began two years ago, in the midst of opposition; that establishment which may be regarded as a key of the colony; that establishment which officers, interpreters, and traders thought a chimæra,—that establishment, I say, forms already a mission of Iroquois savages whom I assembled at first to the number of only six, increased last year to eighty-seven, and this year to three hundred and ninety-six, without counting more than a hundred and fifty whom Monsieur Chabert de Joncaire is to bring me this autumn. And I certify that thus far I have received from His Majesty—for all favor, grace, and assistance—no more than a half pound of bacon and two pounds of bread for daily rations; and that he has not yet given a pin to the chapel, which I have maintained out of my own pocket, for the greater glory of my masters, God and the King."[1]

In his late journey he had made the entire circuit of Lake Ontario. Beyond lay four other inland oceans, to which Fort Niagara was the key. As that all-essential post controlled the passage from Ontario to Erie, so did Fort Detroit control that from Erie to Huron, and Fort Michillimackinac that from Huron to Michigan; while Fort Ste. Marie, at the outlet of Lake Superior, had lately received a garrison, and changed from a mission and trading-station to a post of war.[2] This immense extent of inland navigation was safe in the hands of France so long as she held Niagara. Niagara lost, not only the lakes, but also the Valley of the Ohio was lost with it. Next in importance was Detroit. This was not a military post alone, but also a settlement; and, except the hamlets about Fort Chartres, the only settlement that France owned in all the West. There were, it is true, but a few families; yet the hope of growth seemed good; for to such as liked a wilderness home, no spot in America had more attraction. Father Bonnecamp stopped here for a day on his way back from the expedition of Céloron. "The situation," he says, "is charming. A fine river flows at the foot of the fortifications; vast meadows, asking only to be tilled, extend beyond the sight. Nothing can be more agreeable than the climate. Winter lasts hardly two months. European grains and fruits grow here far better than in many parts of France. It is the Touraine and Beauce of Can-

---

[1] *Journal qui peut servir de Mémoire et de Relation du Voyage que j'ay fait sur le Lac Ontario pour attirer au nouvel Établissement de La Présentation les Sauvages Iroquois des Cinq Nations, 1751.* The last passage given above is condensed in the rendering, as the original is extremely involved and ungrammatical.

[2] *La Jonquière au Ministre, 24 Août, 1750.*

ada."[1] The white flag of the Bourbons floated over the compact little palisaded town, with its population of soldiers and fur-traders; and from the block-houses which served as bastions, one saw on either hand the small solid dwellings of the *habitants*, ranged at intervals along the margin of the water; while at a little distance three Indian villages—Ottawa, Pottawattamie, and Wyandot—curled their wigwam smoke into the pure summer air.[2]

When Céloron de Bienville returned from the Ohio, he went, with a royal commission, sent him a year before, to command at Detroit.[3] His late chaplain, the very intelligent Father Bonnecamp, speaks of him as fearless, energetic, and full of resource; but the Governor calls him haughty and insubordinate. Great efforts were made, at the same time, to build up Detroit as a centre of French power in the West. The methods employed were of the debilitating, paternal character long familiar to Canada. All emigrants with families were to be carried thither at the King's expense; and every settler was to receive in free gift a gun, a hoe, an axe, a ploughshare, a scythe, a sickle, two augers, large and small, a sow, six hens, a cock, six pounds of powder, and twelve pounds of lead; while to these favors were added many others. The result was that twelve families were persuaded to go, or about a twentieth part of the number wanted.[4] Detroit was expected to furnish supplies to the other posts for five hundred miles around, control the neighboring Indians, thwart English machinations, and drive off English interlopers.

La Galissonière no longer governed Canada. He had been honorably recalled, and the Marquis de la Jonquière sent in his stead.[5] La Jonquière, like his predecessor, was a naval officer of high repute; he was tall and imposing in person, and of undoubted capacity and courage; but old and, according to his enemies, very avaricious.[6] The Colonial Minister gave him special instructions regarding that thorn in the side of Canada, Oswego. To attack it openly would be indiscreet, as the two nations were at peace; but there was a way of dealing with it less haz-

[1] *Relation du Voiage de la Belle Rivière, 1749.*
[2] A plan of Detroit is before me, made about this time by the engineer Lery.
[3] *Le Ministre à la Jonquière et Bigot, 14 Mai, 1749. Le Ministre à Céloron, 23 Mai, 1749.*
[4] *Ordonnance du 2 Jan. 1750. La Jonquière et Bigot au Ministre, 1750.* Forty-six persons of all ages and both sexes had been induced by La Galissonière to go the year before. *Lettres communes de la Jonquière et Bigot, 1749.* The total fixed population of Detroit and its neighborhood in 1750 is stated at four hundred and eighty-three souls. In the following two years, a considerable number of young men came of their own accord, and Céloron wrote to Montreal to ask for girls to marry them.
[5] *Le Ministre à la Galissonière, 14 Mai, 1749.*
[6] *Mémoires sur le Canada, 1749–1760.* The charges made here and elsewhere are denied, somewhat faintly, by a descendant of La Jonquière in his elaborate *Notice biographique* of his ancestor.

ardous, if not more lawful. This was to attack it vicariously by means of the Iroquois. "If Abbé Piquet succeeds in his mission," wrote the Minister to the new Governor, "we can easily persuade these savages to destroy Oswego. This is of the utmost importance; but act with great caution."[1] In the next year the Minister wrote again: "The only means that can be used for such an operation in time of peace are those of the Iroquois. If by making these savages regard such an establishment [Oswego] as opposed to their liberty, and, so to speak, a usurpation by which the English mean to get possession of their lands, they could be induced to undertake its destruction, an operation of the sort is not to be neglected; but M. le Marquis de la Jonquière should feel with what circumspection such an affair should be conducted, and he should labor to accomplish it in a manner not to commit himself."[2] To this La Jonquière replies that it will need time; but that he will gradually bring the Iroquois to attack and destroy the English post. He received stringent orders to use every means to prevent the English from encroaching, but to act towards them at the same time "with the greatest politeness."[3] This last injunction was scarcely fulfilled in a correspondence which he had with Clinton, governor of New York, who had written to complain of the new post at the Niagara portage as an invasion of English territory, and also of the arrest of four English traders in the country of the Miamis. Niagara, like Oswego, was in the country of the Five Nations, whom the treaty of Utrecht declared "subject to the dominion of Great Britain."[4] This declaration, preposterous in itself, was binding on France, whose plenipotentiaries had signed the treaty. The treaty also provided that the subjects of the two Crowns "shall enjoy full liberty of going and coming on account of trade," and Clinton therefore demanded that La Jonquière should disavow the arrest of the four traders and punish its authors. The French Governor replied with great asperity, spurned the claim that the Five Nations were British subjects, and justified the arrest.[5] He presently went further. Rewards were offered by his officers for the scalps of Croghan and of another trader named Lowry.[6] When this reached the ears of William Johnson, on the Mo-

---

[1] *Le Ministre à La Jonquière, Mai, 1749.* The instructions given to La Jonquière before leaving France also urge the necessity of destroying Oswego.

[2] *Ordres du Roy et Dépêches des Ministres; à MM. de la Jonquière et Bigot, 15 Avril, 1750.* See Appendix A. for original.

[3] *Ordres du Roy et Dépêches des Ministres, 1750.*

[4] Chalmers, *Collection of Treaties,* I. 382.

[5] *La Jonquière à Clinton, 10 Août, 1751.*

[6] Deposition of Morris Turner and Ralph Kilgore, in *Colonial Records of Pa.,* V. 482. The deponents had been prisoners at Detroit.

hawk, he wrote to Clinton in evident anxiety for his own scalp: "If the French go on so, there is no man can be safe in his own house; for I can at any time get an Indian to kill any man for a small matter. Their going on in that manner is worse than open war."

The French on their side made counter-accusations. The captive traders were examined on oath before La Jonquière, and one of them, John Patton, is reported to have said that Croghan had instigated Indians to kill Frenchmen.[1] French officials declared that other English traders were guilty of the same practices; and there is very little doubt that the charge was true.

The dispute with the English was not the only source of trouble to the Governor. His superiors at Versailles would not adopt his views, and looked on him with distrust. He advised the building of forts near Lake Erie, and his advice was rejected. "Niagara and Detroit," he was told, "will secure forever our communications with Louisiana."[2] "His Majesty," again wrote the Colonial Minister, "thought that expenses would diminish after the peace; but, on the contrary, they have increased. There must be great abuses. You and the Intendant must look to it."[3] Great abuses there were; and of the money sent to Canada for the service of the King the larger part found its way into the pockets of peculators. The colony was eaten to the heart with official corruption; and the centre of it was François Bigot, the intendant. The Minister directed La Jonquière's attention to certain malpractices which had been reported to him; and the old man, deeply touched, replied: "I have reached the age of sixty-six years, and there is not a drop of blood in my veins that does not thrill for the service of my King. I will not conceal from you that the slightest suspicion on your part against me would cut the thread of my days."[4]

Perplexities increased; affairs in the West grew worse and worse. La Jonquière ordered Céloron to attack the English at Pickawillany; and Céloron could not or would not obey. "I cannot express," writes the Governor, "how much this business troubles me; it robs me of sleep; it makes me ill." Another letter of rebuke presently came from Versailles. "Last year you wrote that you would soon drive the English from the Ohio; but private letters say that you have done nothing. This is deplorable. If not expelled, they will seem to acquire a right against us.

---

[1] *Précis des Faits, avec leurs Pièces justificatives,* 100.
[2] *Ordres du Roy et Dépêches des Ministres, 1750.*
[3] *Ibid.,* 6 Juin, *1751.*
[4] *La Jonquière au Ministre, 19 Oct. 1751.*

Send force enough at once to drive them off, and cure them of all wish to return."[1] La Jonquière answered with bitter complaints against Céloron, and then begged to be recalled. His health, already shattered, was ruined by fatigue and vexation; and he took to his bed. Before spring he was near his end.[2] It is said that, though very rich, his habits of thrift so possessed his last hours that, seeing wax-candles burning in his chamber, he ordered others of tallow to be brought instead, as being good enough to die by. Thus frugally lighted on its way, his spirit fled; and the Baron de Longueuil took his place till a new governor should arrive.

Sinister tidings came thick from the West. Raymond, commandant at the French fort on the Maumee, close to the centre of intrigue, wrote: "My people are leaving me for Detroit. Nobody wants to stay here and have his throat cut. All the tribes who go to the English at Pickawillany come back loaded with gifts. I am too weak to meet the danger. Instead of twenty men, I need five hundred. . . . We have made peace with the English, yet they try continually to make war on us by means of the Indians; they intend to be masters of all this upper country. The tribes here are leaguing together to kill all the French, that they may have nobody on their lands but their English brothers. This I am told by Coldfoot, a great Miami chief, whom I think an honest man, if there is any such thing among Indians. . . . If the English stay in this country we are lost. We must attack, and drive them out." And he tells of war-belts sent from tribe to tribe, and rumors of plots and conspiracies far and near.

Without doubt, the English traders spared no pains to gain over the Indians by fair means or foul; sold them goods at low rates, made ample gifts, and gave gunpowder for the asking. Saint-Ange, who commanded at Vincennes, wrote that a storm would soon burst on the heads of the French. Joncaire reported that all the Ohio Indians sided with the English. Longueuil informed the Minister that the Miamis had scalped two soldiers; that the Piankishaws had killed seven Frenchmen; and that a squaw who had lived with one of the slain declared that the tribes of the Wabash and Illinois were leaguing with the Osages for a combined insurrection. Every letter brought news of murder. Small-pox had broken out at Detroit. "It is to be wished," says Longueuil, "that it would spread among our rebels; it would be fully as good as an army. . . . We

[1] *Ordres du Roy et Dépêches des Ministres,* 1751.
[2] He died on the sixth of March, 1752 (*Bigot au Ministre, 6 Mai*); not on the seventeenth of May, as stated in the *Mémoires sur le Canada, 1749–1760.*

are menaced with a general outbreak, and even Toronto is in danger. . . . Before long the English on the Miami will gain over all the surrounding tribes, get possession of Fort Chartres, and cut our communications with Louisiana."[1]

The moving spirit of disaffection was the chief called Old Britain, or the Demoiselle, and its focus was his town of Pickawillany, on the Miami. At this place it is said that English traders sometimes mustered to the number of fifty or more. "It is they," wrote Longueuil, "who are the instigators of revolt and the source of all our woes."[2] Whereupon the Colonial Minister reiterated his instructions to drive them off and plunder them, which he thought would "effectually disgust them," and bring all trouble to an end.[3]

La Jonquière's remedy had been more heroic, for he had ordered Céloron to attack the English and their red allies alike; and he charged that officer with arrogance and disobedience because he had not done so. It is not certain that obedience was easy; for though, besides the garrison of regulars, a strong body of militia was sent up to Detroit to aid the stroke,[4] the Indians of that post, whose co-operation was thought necessary, proved half-hearted, intractable, and even touched with disaffection. Thus the enterprise languished till, in June, aid came from another quarter. Charles Langlade, a young French trader married to a squaw at Green Bay, and strong in influence with the tribes of that region, came down the lakes from Michillimackinac with a fleet of canoes manned by two hundred and fifty Ottawa and Ojibwa warriors; stopped a while at Detroit; then embarked again, paddled up the Maumee to Raymond's fort at the portage, and led his greased and painted rabble through the forest to attack the Demoiselle and his English friends. They approached Pickawillany at about nine o'clock on the morning of the twenty-first. The scared squaws fled from the cornfields into the town, where the wigwams of the Indians clustered about the fortified warehouse of the traders. Of these there were at the time only eight in the place. Most of the Indians also were gone on their summer hunt, though the Demoiselle remained with a band of his tribesmen. Great was the screeching of war-whoops and clatter of guns. Three of the traders were caught outside the fort. The remaining five closed the gate, and stood on their defence. The fight was soon over. Fourteen Miamis were shot down, the Demoiselle among the rest. The five white

---

[1] *Dépêches de Longueuil; Lettres de Raymond; Benoit de Saint-Clerc à la Jonquière, Oct. 1751.*
[2] *Longueuil au Ministre, 21 Avril, 1752.*
[3] *Le Ministre à la Jonquière, 1752. Le Ministre à Duquesne, 9 Juillet, 1752.*
[4] *La Jonquière à Céloron, 1 Oct. 1751.*

men held out till the afternoon, when three of them surrendered, and
two, Thomas Burney and Andrew McBryer, made their escape. One of
the English prisoners being wounded, the victors stabbed him to death.
Seventy years of missionaries had not weaned them from cannibalism,
and they boiled and eat* the Demoiselle.[1]

The captive traders, plundered to the skin, were carried by Langlade
to Duquesne, the new governor, who highly praised the bold leader of
the enterprise, and recommended him to the Minister for such reward
as befitted one of his station. "As he is not in the King's service, and
has married a squaw, I will ask for him only a pension of two hundred
francs, which will flatter him infinitely."

The Marquis Duquesne, sprung from the race of the great naval commander of that name, had arrived towards midsummer; and he began
his rule by a general review of troops and militia. His lofty bearing
offended the Canadians; but he compelled their respect, and, according
to a writer of the time, showed from the first that he was born to
command. He presently took in hand an enterprise which his predecessor would probably have accomplished, had the Home Government encouraged him. Duquesne, profiting by the infatuated neglect of the
British provincial assemblies, prepared to occupy the upper waters of
the Ohio, and secure the passes with forts and garrisons. Thus the Virginian and Pennsylvanian traders would be debarred all access to the
West, and the tribes of that region, bereft henceforth of English guns,
knives, hatchets, and blankets, English gifts and English cajoleries,
would be thrown back to complete dependence on the French. The
moral influence, too, of such a movement would be incalculable; for
the Indian respects nothing so much as a display of vigor and daring,
backed by force. In short, the intended enterprise was a master-stroke,
and laid the axe to the very root of disaffection. It is true that, under
the treaty, commissioners had been long in session at Paris to settle the
question of American boundaries; but there was no likelihood that they
would come to agreement; and if France would make good her Western
claims, it behooved her, while there was yet time, to prevent her rival
from fastening a firm grasp on the countries in dispute.

Yet the Colonial Minister regarded the plan with distrust. "Be on
your guard," he wrote to Duquesne, "against new undertakings; private
interests are generally at the bottom of them. It is through these that

*Here Parkman uses the archaic form of the past tense, usually pronounced et.—Ed.
[1]On the attack of Pickawillany, Longueuil au Ministre, 18 Août, 1752; Duquesne au Ministre, 25
Oct. 1752; Colonial Records of Pa., V. 599; Journal of William Trent, 1752. Trent was on the spot
a few days after the affair.

new posts are established. Keep only such as are indispensable, and suppress the others. The expenses of the colony are enormous; and they have doubled since the peace." Again, a little later: "Build on the Ohio such forts as are absolutely necessary, but no more. Remember that His Majesty suspects your advisers of interested views."[1]

No doubt there was justice in the suspicion. Every military movement, and above all the establishment of every new post, was an opportunity to the official thieves with whom the colony swarmed. Some band of favored knaves grew rich; while a much greater number, excluded from sharing the illicit profits, clamored against the undertaking, and wrote charges of corruption to Versailles. Thus the Minister was kept tolerably well informed; but was scarcely the less helpless, for with the Atlantic between, the disorders of Canada defied his control. Duquesne was exasperated by the opposition that met him on all hands, and wrote to the Minister: "There are so many rascals in this country that one is forever the butt of their attacks."[2]

It seems that unlawful gain was not the only secret spring of the movement. An officer of repute says that the Intendant, Bigot, enterprising in his pleasures as in his greed, was engaged in an intrigue with the wife of Chevalier Péan; and wishing at once to console the husband and to get rid of him, sought for him a high command at a distance from the colony. Therefore while Marin, an able officer, was made first in rank, Péan was made second. The same writer hints that Duquesne himself was influenced by similar motives in his appointment of leaders.[3]

He mustered the colony troops, and ordered out the Canadians. With the former he was but half satisfied; with the latter he was delighted; and he praises highly their obedience and alacrity. "I had not the least trouble in getting them to march. They came on the minute, bringing their own guns, though many people tried to excite them to revolt; for the whole colony opposes my operations." The expedition set out early in the spring of 1753. The whole force was not much above a thousand men, increased by subsequent detachments to fifteen hundred; but to the Indians it seemed a mighty host; and one of their orators declared that the lakes and rivers were covered with boats and soldiers from Montreal to Presquisle.[4] Some Mohawk hunters by the St. Lawrence saw them as they passed, and hastened home to tell the

---

[1] *Ordres du Roy et Dépêches des Ministres, 1753.*

[2] *Duquesne au Ministre, 29 Sept. 1754.*

[3] Pouchot, *Mémoire sur la dernière Guerre de l'Amérique septentrionale* (ed. 1781), I. 8.

[4] *Duquesne au Ministre, 27 Oct. 1753.*

news to Johnson, whom they wakened at midnight, "whooping and hollowing in a frightful manner."[1] Lieutenant Holland at Oswego saw a fleet of canoes upon the lake, and was told by a roving Frenchman that they belonged to an army of six thousand men going to the Ohio, "to cause all the English to quit those parts."[2]

The main body of the expedition landed at Presquisle, on the southeastern shore of Lake Erie, where the town of Erie now stands; and here for a while we leave them.

[1] *Johnson to Clinton, 20 April, 1753*, in N. Y. Col. Docs., VI. 778.
[2] *Holland to Clinton, 15 May, 1753*, in N. Y. Col. Docs., VI. 780.

4

Conflict for Acadia

1710–1754

ACADIA CEDED TO ENGLAND · ACADIANS SWEAR FIDELITY · HALIFAX FOUNDED · FRENCH INTRIGUE · ACADIAN PRIESTS · MILDNESS OF ENGLISH RULE · COVERT HOSTILITY OF ACADIANS · THE NEW OATH · TREACHERY OF VERSAILLES · INDIANS INCITED TO WAR · CLERICAL AGENTS OF REVOLT · ABBÉ LE LOUTRE · ACADIANS IMPELLED TO EMIGRATE · MISERY OF THE EMIGRANTS · HUMANITY OF CORNWALLIS AND HOPSON · FANATICISM AND VIOLENCE OF LE LOUTRE · CAPTURE OF THE "ST. FRANÇOIS" · THE ENGLISH AT BEAUBASSIN · LE LOUTRE DRIVES OUT THE INHABITANTS · MURDER OF HOWE · BEAUSÉJOUR · INSOLENCE OF LE LOUTRE · HIS HARSHNESS TO THE ACADIANS · THE BOUNDARY COMMISSION · ITS FAILURE · APPROACHING WAR

While in the West all the signs of the sky foreboded storm, another tempest was gathering in the East, less in extent, but not less in peril. The conflict in Acadia has a melancholy interest, since it ended in a catastrophe which prose and verse have joined to commemorate, but of which the causes have not been understood.

Acadia—that is to say, the peninsula of Nova Scotia, with the addition, as the English claimed, of the present New Brunswick and some adjacent country—was conquered by General Nicholson in 1710, and formally transferred by France to the British Crown, three years later, by the treaty of Utrecht. By that treaty it was "expressly provided" that such of the French inhabitants as "are willing to remain there and to be subject to the Kingdom of Great Britain, are to enjoy the free exercise of their religion according to the usage of the Church of Rome, as far as the laws of Great Britain do allow the same;" but that any who choose may remove, with their effects, if they do so within a year. Very few availed themselves of this right; and after the end of the year those who remained were required to take an oath of allegiance to King George. There is no doubt that in a little time they would have complied, had they been let alone; but the French authorities of Canada and Cape Breton did their utmost to prevent them, and employed agents to keep them hostile to England. Of these the most efficient were the French priests, who, in spite of the treaty, persuaded their flocks that they were still subjects of King Louis. Hence rose endless perplexity to the English commanders at Annapolis, who more than suspected that the Indian attacks with which they were harassed were due mainly to French instigation.[1] It was not till seventeen years after the treaty that the Acadians could be brought to take the oath without qualifications which made it almost useless. The English authorities seem to have shown throughout an unusual patience and forbearance. At length, about 1730, nearly all the inhabitants signed by crosses, since few of them could write, an oath recognizing George II. as sovereign of Acadia, and promising fidelity and obedience to him.[2] This restored comparative quiet till the war of 1745, when some of the Acadians remained neutral, while some took arms against the English, and many others aided the enemy with information and supplies.

English power in Acadia, hitherto limited to a feeble garrison at Annapolis and a feebler one at Canseau, received at this time a great accession. The fortress of Louisbourg, taken by the English during the war, had been restored by the treaty; and the French at once prepared to make it a military and naval station more formidable than ever. Upon this the British Ministry resolved to establish another station as a counterpoise; and the harbor of Chebucto, on the south coast of Acadia, was chosen as the site of it. Thither in June, 1749, came a fleet of transports loaded with emigrants, tempted by offers of land and a home in the New World. Some were mechanics, tradesmen, farmers, and laborers; others were sailors, soldiers, and subaltern officers thrown out

[1] See the numerous papers in *Selections from the Public Documents of the Province of Nova Scotia* (Halifax, 1869), pp. 1–165; a Government publication of great value.

[2] The oath was *literatim* as follows: "Je Promets et Jure Sincerement en Foi de Chrétien que Je serai entierement Fidele, et Obeierai Vraiment Sa Majesté Le Roy George Second, qui (*sic*) Je reconnoi pour Le Souvrain Seigneur de l'Accadie ou Nouvelle Ecosse. Ainsi Dieu me Soit en Aide."

of employment by the peace. Including women and children, they counted in all about twenty-five hundred. Alone of all the British colonies on the continent, this new settlement was the offspring, not of private enterprise, but of royal authority. Yet it was free like the rest, with the same popular representation and local self-government. Edward Cornwallis, uncle of Lord Cornwallis of the Revolutionary War, was made governor and commander-in-chief. Wolfe calls him "a man of approved courage and fidelity;" and even the caustic Horace Walpole speaks of him as "a brave, sensible young man, of great temper and good nature."

Before summer was over, the streets were laid out, and the building-lot of each settler was assigned to him; before winter closed, the whole were under shelter, the village was fenced with palisades and defended by redoubts of timber, and the battalions lately in garrison at Louisbourg manned the wooden ramparts. Succeeding years brought more emigrants, till in 1752 the population was above four thousand. Thus was born into the world the city of Halifax. Along with the crumbling old fort and miserably disciplined garrison at Annapolis, besides six or seven small detached posts to watch the Indians and Acadians, it comprised the whole British force on the peninsula; for Canseau had been destroyed by the French.

The French had never reconciled themselves to the loss of Acadia, and were resolved, by diplomacy or force, to win it back again; but the building of Halifax showed that this was to be no easy task, and filled them at the same time with alarm for the safety of Louisbourg. On one point, at least, they saw their policy clear. The Acadians, though those of them who were not above thirty-five had been born under the British flag, must be kept French at heart, and taught that they were still French subjects. In 1748 they numbered eighty-eight hundred and fifty communicants, or from twelve to thirteen thousand souls; but an emigration, of which the causes will soon appear, had reduced them in 1752 to but little more than nine thousand.[1] These were divided into six principal parishes, one of the largest being that of Annapolis. Other centres of population were Grand Pré, on the basin of Mines; Beaubassin, at the head of Chignecto Bay; Pisiquid, now Windsor; and Cobequid, now Truro. Their priests, who were missionaries controlled by the diocese of Quebec, acted also as their magistrates, ruling them for this world

[1] *Description de l'Acadie, avec le Nom des Paroisses et le Nombre des Habitants, 1748. Mémoire à présenter à la Cour sur la Necessité de fixer les Limites de l'Acadie*, par l'Abbé de l'Isle-Dieu, 1753 (1754?). Compare the estimates in *Censuses of Canada* (Ottawa, 1876).

and the next. Being subject to a French superior, and being, moreover, wholly French at heart, they formed in this British province a wheel within a wheel, the inner movement always opposing the outer.

Although, by the twelfth article of the treaty of Utrecht, France had solemnly declared the Acadians to be British subjects, the Government of Louis XV. intrigued continually to turn them from subjects into enemies. Before me is a mass of English documents on Acadian affairs from the peace of Aix-la-Chapelle to the catastrophe of 1755, and above a thousand pages of French official papers from the archives of Paris, memorials, reports, and secret correspondence, relating to the same matters. With the help of these and some collateral lights, it is not difficult to make a correct diagnosis of the political disease that ravaged this miserable country. Of a multitude of proofs, only a few can be given here; but these will suffice.

It was not that the Acadians had been ill-used by the English; the reverse was the case. They had been left in free exercise of their worship, as stipulated by treaty. It is true that, from time to time, there were loud complaints from French officials that religion was in danger, because certain priests had been rebuked, arrested, brought before the Council at Halifax, suspended from their functions, or required, on pain of banishment, to swear that they would do nothing against the interests of King George. Yet such action on the part of the provincial authorities seems, without a single exception, to have been the consequence of misconduct on the part of the priest, in opposing the Government and stirring his flock to disaffection. La Jonquière, the determined adversary of the English, reported to the bishop that they did not oppose the ecclesiastics in the exercise of their functions, and an order of Louis XV. admits that the Acadians have enjoyed liberty of religion.[1] In a long document addressed in 1750 to the Colonial Minister at Versailles, Roma, an officer at Louisbourg, testifies thus to the mildness of British rule, though he ascribes it to interested motives. "The fear that the Acadians have of the Indians is the controlling motive which makes them side with the French. The English, having in view the conquest of Canada, wished to give the French of that colony, in their conduct towards the Acadians, a striking example of the mildness of their government. Without raising the fortune of any of the inhabitants, they have supplied them for more than thirty-five years with the necessaries of life, often on credit and with an excess of con-

---

[1] *La Jonquière à l'Évêque de Québec, 14 Juin, 1750. Mémoire du Roy pour servir d'Instruction au Comte de Raymond, commandant pour Sa Majesté à l'Isle Royale* [Cape Breton], *24 Avril, 1751.*

fidence, without troubling their debtors, without pressing them, without wishing to force them to pay. They have left them an appearance of liberty so excessive that they have not intervened in their disputes or even punished their crimes. They have allowed them to refuse with insolence certain moderate rents payable in grain and lawfully due. They have passed over in silence the contemptuous refusal of the Acadians to take titles from them for the new lands which they chose to occupy.[1]

"We know very well," pursues Roma, "the fruits of this conduct in the last war; and the English know it also. Judge then what will be the wrath and vengeance of this cruel nation." The fruits to which Roma alludes were the hostilities, open or secret, committed by the Acadians against the English. He now ventures the prediction that the enraged conquerors will take their revenge by drafting all the young Acadians on board their ships of war, and there destroying them by slow starvation. He proved, however, a false prophet. The English Governor merely required the inhabitants to renew their oath of allegiance, without qualification or evasion.

It was twenty years since the Acadians had taken such an oath; and meanwhile a new generation had grown up. The old oath pledged them to fidelity and obedience; but they averred that Phillips, then governor of the province, had given them, at the same time, assurance that they should not be required to bear arms against either French or Indians. In fact, such service had not been demanded of them, and they would have lived in virtual neutrality, had not many of them broken their oaths and joined the French war-parties. For this reason Cornwallis thought it necessary that, in renewing the pledge, they should bind themselves to an allegiance as complete as that required of other British subjects. This spread general consternation. Deputies from the Acadian settlements appeared at Halifax, bringing a paper signed with the marks of a thousand persons. The following passage contains the pith of it. "The inhabitants in general, sir, over the whole extent of this country are resolved not to take the oath which your Excellency requires of us; but if your Excellency will grant us our old oath, with an exemption for ourselves and our heirs from taking up arms, we will accept it."[2] The answer of Cornwallis was by no means so stern as it has been represented.[3] After the formal reception he talked in private with the

---

[1] See Appendix B.
[2] *Public Documents of Nova Scotia,* 173.
[3] See *Ibid.,* 174, where the answer is printed.

deputies; and "they went home in good humor, promising great things."[1]

The refusal of the Acadians to take the required oath was not wholly spontaneous, but was mainly due to influence from without. The French officials of Cape Breton and Isle St. Jean, now Prince Edward Island, exerted themselves to the utmost, chiefly through the agency of the priests, to excite the people to refuse any oath that should commit them fully to British allegiance. At the same time means were used to induce them to migrate to the neighboring islands under French rule, and efforts were also made to set on the Indians to attack the English. But the plans of the French will best appear in a despatch sent by La Jonquière to the Colonial Minister in the autumn of 1749.

"Monsieur Cornwallis issued an order on the tenth of the said month [*August*], to the effect that if the inhabitants will remain faithful subjects of the King of Great Britain, he will allow them priests and public exercise of their religion, with the understanding that no priest shall officiate without his permission or before taking an oath of fidelity to the King of Great Britain. Secondly, that the inhabitants shall not be exempted from defending their houses, their lands, and the Government. Thirdly, that they shall take an oath of fidelity to the King of Great Britain, on the twenty-sixth of this month, before officers sent them for that purpose."

La Jonquière proceeds to say that on hearing these conditions the Acadians were filled with perplexity and alarm, and that he, the governor, had directed Boishébert, his chief officer on the Acadian frontier, to encourage them to leave their homes and seek asylum on French soil. He thus recounts the steps he has taken to harass the English of Halifax by means of their Indian neighbors. As peace had been declared, the operation was delicate; and when three of these Indians came to him from their missionary, Le Loutre, with letters on the subject, La Jonquière was discreetly reticent. "I did not care to give them any advice upon the matter, and confined myself to a promise that I would on no account abandon them; and I have provided for supplying them with everything, whether arms, ammunition, food, or other necessaries. It is to be desired that these savages should succeed in thwarting the designs of the English, and even their settlement at Halifax. They are bent on doing so; and if they can carry out their plans, it is certain that they will give the English great trouble, and so harass them that they will be a great obstacle in their path. These savages are to act

---

[1] *Cornwallis to the Board of Trade, 11 Sept. 1749.*

alone; neither soldier nor French inhabitant is to join them; everything will be done of their own motion, and without showing that I had any knowledge of the matter. This is very essential; therefore I have written to the Sieur de Boishébert to observe great prudence in his measures, and to act very secretly, in order that the English may not perceive that we are providing for the needs of the said savages.

"It will be the missionaries who will manage all the negotiation, and direct the movements of the savages, who are in excellent hands, as the Reverend Father Germain and Monsieur l'Abbé Le Loutre are very capable of making the most of them, and using them to the greatest advantage for our interests. They will manage their intrigue in such a way as not to appear in it."

La Jonquière then recounts the good results which he expects from these measures: first, the English will be prevented from making any new settlements; secondly, we shall gradually get the Acadians out of their hands; and lastly, they will be so discouraged by constant Indian attacks that they will renounce their pretensions to the parts of the country belonging to the King of France. "I feel, Monseigneur,"—thus the Governor concludes his despatch,—"all the delicacy of this negotiation; be assured that I will conduct it with such precaution that the English will not be able to say that my orders had any part in it."[1]

He kept his word, and so did the missionaries. The Indians gave great trouble on the outskirts of Halifax, and murdered many harmless settlers; yet the English authorities did not at first suspect that they were hounded on by their priests, under the direction of the Governor of Canada, and with the privity of the Minister at Versailles. More than this; for, looking across the sea, we find royalty itself lending its august countenance to the machination. Among the letters read before the King in his cabinet in May, 1750, was one from Desherbiers, then commanding at Louisbourg, saying that he was advising the Acadians not to take the oath of allegiance to the King of England; another from Le Loutre, declaring that he and Father Germain were consulting together how to disgust the English with their enterprise of Halifax; and a third from the Intendant, Bigot, announcing that Le Loutre was using the Indians to harass the new settlement, and that he himself was sending them powder, lead, and merchandise, "to confirm them in their good designs."[2]

To this the Minister replies in a letter to Desherbiers: "His Majesty

---

[1] *La Jonquière au Ministre, 9 Oct. 1749.* See Appendix B.
[2] *Resumé des Lettres lues au Travail du Roy, Mai, 1750.*

is well satisfied with all you have done to thwart the English in their new establishment. If the dispositions of the savages are such as they seem, there is reason to hope that in the course of the winter they will succeed in so harassing the settlers that some of them will become disheartened." Desherbiers is then told that His Majesty desires him to aid English deserters in escaping from Halifax.[1] Supplies for the Indians are also promised; and he is informed that twelve medals are sent him by the frigate "La Mutine," to be given to the chiefs who shall most distinguish themselves. In another letter Desherbiers is enjoined to treat the English authorities with great politeness.[2]

When Count Raymond took command at Louisbourg, he was instructed, under the royal hand, to give particular attention to the affairs of Acadia, especially in two points,—the management of the Indians, and the encouraging of Acadian emigration to countries under French rule. "His Majesty," says the document, "has already remarked that the savages have been most favorably disposed. It is of the utmost importance that no means be neglected to keep them so. The missionaries among them are in a better position than anybody to contribute to this end, and His Majesty has reason to be satisfied with the pains they take therein. The Sieur de Raymond will excite these missionaries not to slacken their efforts; but he will warn them at the same time so to contain their zeal as not to compromise themselves with the English, and give just occasion of complaint."[3] That is, the King orders his representative to encourage the missionaries in instigating their flocks to butcher English settlers, but to see that they take care not to be found out. The injunction was hardly needed. "Monsieur Desherbiers," says a letter of earlier date, "has engaged Abbé Le Loutre to distribute the usual presents among the savages, and Monsieur Bigot has placed in his hands an additional gift of cloth, blankets, powder, and ball, to be given them in case they harass the English at Halifax. This missionary is to induce them to do so."[4] In spite of these efforts, the Indians began to relent in their hostilities; and when Longueuil became provisional governor of Canada, he complained to the Minister that it was very difficult to prevent them from making peace with the English, though Father Germain was doing his best to keep them on the warpath.[5] La

---

[1] In 1750 nine captured deserters from Phillips's regiment declared on their trial that the French had aided them and supplied them all with money. *Public Documents of Nova Scotia*, 193.

[2] *Le Ministre à Desherbiers*, 23 Mai, 1750; Ibid., 31 Mai, 1750.

[3] *Mémoire du Roy pour servir d'Instruction au Comte de Raymond*, 24 Avril, 1751.

[4] *Lettre commune de Desherbiers et Bigot au Ministre*, 15 Août, 1749.

[5] *Longueuil au Ministre*, 26 Avril, 1752.

Jonquière, too, had done his best, even to the point of departing from his original policy of allowing no soldier or Acadian to take part with them. He had sent a body of troops under La Corne, an able partisan officer, to watch the English frontier; and in the same vessel was sent a supply of "merchandise, guns, and munitions for the savages and the Acadians who may take up arms with them; and the whole is sent under pretext of trading in furs with the savages."[1] On another occasion La Jonquière wrote: "In order that the savages may do their part courageously, a few Acadians, dressed and painted in their way, could join them to strike the English. I cannot help consenting to what these savages do, because we have our hands tied [*by the peace*], and so can do nothing ourselves. Besides, I do not think that any inconvenience will come of letting the Acadians mingle among them, because if they [*the Acadians*] are captured, we shall say that they acted of their own accord."[2] In other words, he will encourage them to break the peace; and then, by means of a falsehood, have them punished as felons. Many disguised Acadians did in fact join the Indian war-parties; and their doing so was no secret to the English. "What we call here an Indian war," wrote Hopson, successor of Cornwallis, "is no other than a pretence for the French to commit hostilities on His Majesty's subjects."

At length the Indians made peace, or pretended to do so. The chief of Le Loutre's mission, who called himself Major Jean-Baptiste Cope, came to Halifax with a deputation of his tribe, and they all affixed their totems to a solemn treaty. In the next summer they returned with ninety or a hundred warriors, were well entertained, presented with gifts, and sent homeward in a schooner. On the way they seized the vessel and murdered the crew. This is told by Prévost, intendant at Louisbourg, who does not say that French instigation had any part in the treachery.[3] It is nevertheless certain that the Indians were paid for this or some contemporary murder; for Prévost, writing just four weeks later, says: "Last month the savages took eighteen English scalps, and Monsieur Le Loutre was obliged to pay them eighteen hundred livres, Acadian money, which I have reimbursed him."[4]

From the first, the services of this zealous missionary had been beyond price. Prévost testifies that, though Cornwallis does his best to

---

[1] *Bigot au Ministre, 1749.*
[2] *Dépêches de la Jonquière, 1 Mai, 1751.* See Appendix B.
[3] *Prévost au Ministre, 12 Mars, 1753; Ibid., 17 July, 1753.* Prévost was *ordonnateur*, or intendant, at Louisbourg. The treaty will be found in full in *Public Documents of Nova Scotia,* 683.
[4] *Prévost au Ministre, 16 Août, 1753.*

induce the Acadians to swear fidelity to King George, Le Loutre keeps them in allegiance to King Louis, and threatens to set his Indians upon them unless they declare against the English. "I have already," adds Prévost, "paid him 11,183 livres for his daily expenses; and I never cease advising him to be as economical as possible, and always to take care not to compromise himself with the English Government."[1] In consequence of "good service to religion and the state," Le Loutre received a pension of eight hundred livres, as did also Maillard, his brother missionary on Cape Breton. "The fear is," writes the Colonial Minister to the Governor of Louisbourg, "that their zeal may carry them too far. Excite them to keep the Indians in our interest, but do not let them compromise us. Act always so as to make the English appear as aggressors."[2]

All the Acadian clergy, in one degree or another, seem to have used their influence to prevent the inhabitants from taking the oath, and to persuade them that they were still French subjects. Some were noisy, turbulent, and defiant; others were too tranquil to please the officers of the Crown. A missionary at Annapolis is mentioned as old, and therefore inefficient; while the curé at Grand Pré, also an elderly man, was too much inclined to confine himself to his spiritual functions. It is everywhere apparent that those who chose these priests, and sent them as missionaries into a British province, expected them to act as enemies of the British Crown. The maxim is often repeated that duty to religion is inseparable from duty to the King of France. The Bishop of Quebec desired the Abbé de l'Isle-Dieu to represent to the Court the need of more missionaries to keep the Acadians Catholic and French; but, he adds, there is danger that they (the missionaries) will be required to take an oath to do nothing contrary to the interests of the King of Great Britain.[3] It is a wonder that such a pledge was not always demanded. It was exacted in a few cases, notably in that of Girard, priest at Cobequid, who, on charges of instigating his flock to disaffection, had been sent prisoner to Halifax, but released on taking an oath in the above terms. Thereupon he wrote to Longueuil at Quebec that his

[1] *Ibid.*, 22 *Juillet, 1750.*

[2] *Le Ministre au Comte de Raymond, 21 Juillet, 1752.* It is curious to compare these secret instructions, given by the Minister to the colonial officials, with a letter which the same Minister, Rouillé, wrote ostensibly to La Jonquière, but which was really meant for the eye of the British Minister at Versailles, Lord Albemarle, to whom it was shown in proof of French good faith. It was afterwards printed, along with other papers, in a small volume called *Précis des Faits, avec leurs Pièces justificatives* which was sent by the French Government to all the courts of Europe to show that the English alone were answerable for the war. The letter, it is needless to say, breathes the highest sentiments of international honor.

[3] L'Isle-Dieu, *Mémoire sur l'État actuel des Missions, 1753* (1754?).

parishioners wanted to submit to the English, and that he, having sworn to be true to the British King, could not prevent them. "Though I don't pretend to be a casuist," writes Longueuil, "I could not help answering him that he is not obliged to keep such an oath, and that he ought to labor in all zeal to preserve and increase the number of the faithful." Girard, to his credit, preferred to leave the colony, and retired to Isle St. Jean.[1]

Cornwallis soon discovered to what extent the clergy stirred their flocks to revolt; and he wrote angrily to the Bishop of Quebec: "Was it you who sent Le Loutre as a missionary to the Micmacs? and is it for their good that he excites these wretches to practise their cruelties against those who have shown them every kindness? The conduct of the priests of Acadia has been such that by command of His Majesty I have published an Order declaring that if any one of them presumes to exercise his functions without my express permission he shall be dealt with according to the laws of England."[2]

The English, bound by treaty to allow the Acadians the exercise of their religion, at length conceived the idea of replacing the French priests by others to be named by the Pope at the request of the British Government. This, becoming known to the French, greatly alarmed them, and the Intendant at Louisbourg wrote to the Minister that the matter required serious attention.[3] It threatened, in fact, to rob them of their chief agents of intrigue; but their alarm proved needless, as the plan was not carried into execution.

The French officials would have been better pleased had the conduct of Cornwallis been such as to aid their efforts to alienate the Acadians; and one writer, while confessing the "favorable treatment" of the English towards the inhabitants, denounces it as a snare.[4] If so, it was a snare intended simply to reconcile them to English rule. Nor was it without effect. "We must give up altogether the idea of an insurrection in Acadia," writes an officer of Cape Breton. "The Acadians cannot be trusted; they are controlled by fear of the Indians, which leads them to breathe French sentiments, even when their inclinations are English. They will yield to their interests; and the English will make it impossible that they should either hurt them or serve us, unless we take measures different from those we have hitherto pursued."[5]

During all this time, constant efforts were made to stimulate Acadian

[1] *Longueuil au Ministre, 27 Avril, 1752.*
[2] *Cornwallis to the Bishop of Quebec, 1 Dec. 1749.*
[3] *Daudin, prêtre, à Prévost, 23 Oct. 1753. Prévost au Ministre, 24 Nov. 1753.*
[4] *Mémoire à présenter à la Cour, 1753.*
[5] *Roma au Ministre, 11 Mars, 1750.*

emigration to French territory, and thus to strengthen the French frontier. In this work the chief agent was Le Loutre. "This priest," says a
French writer of the time, "urged the people of Les Mines, Port Royal
[*Annapolis*], and other places, to come and join the French, and promised to all, in the name of the Governor, to settle and support them
for three years, and even indemnify them for any losses they might
incur; threatening if they did not do as he advised, to abandon them,
deprive them of their priests, have their wives and children carried off,
and their property laid waste by the Indians."[1] Some passed over the
isthmus to the shores of the gulf, and others made their way to the
Strait of Canseau. Vessels were provided to convey them, in the one
case to Isle St. Jean, now Prince Edward Island, and in the other to
Isle Royale, called by the English, Cape Breton. Some were eager to
go; some went with reluctance; some would scarcely be persuaded to go
at all. "They leave their homes with great regret," reports the Governor
of Isle St. Jean, speaking of the people of Cobequid, "and they began
to move their luggage only when the savages compelled them."[2] These
savages were the flock of Abbé Le Loutre, who was on the spot to direct
the emigration. Two thousand Acadians are reported to have left the
peninsula before the end of 1751, and many more followed within the
next two years. Nothing could exceed the misery of a great part of these
emigrants, who had left perforce most of their effects behind. They
became disheartened and apathetic. The Intendant at Louisbourg says
that they will not take the trouble to clear the land, and that some of
them live, like Indians, under huts of spruce-branches.[3] The Governor
of Isle St. Jean declares that they are dying of hunger.[4] Girard, the
priest who had withdrawn to this island rather than break his oath to
the English, writes: "Many of them cannot protect themselves day or
night from the severity of the cold. Most of the children are entirely
naked; and when I go into a house they are all crouched in the ashes,
close to the fire. They run off and hide themselves, without shoes,
stockings, or shirts. They are not all reduced to this extremity but
nearly all are in want."[5] Mortality among them was great, and would
have been greater but for rations supplied by the French Government.

During these proceedings, the English Governor, Cornwallis, seems
to have justified the character of good temper given him by Horace

[1] *Mémoires sur le Canada, 1749–1760.*
[2] *Bonaventure à Desherbiers, 26 Juin, 1751.*
[3] *Prévost au Ministre, 25 Nov. 1750.*
[4] *Bonaventure, ut supra.*
[5] *Girard à (Bonaventure?), 27 Oct. 1753.*

Walpole. His attitude towards the Acadians remained on the whole patient and conciliatory. "My friends," he replied to a deputation of them asking a general permission to leave the province, "I am not ignorant of the fact that every means has been used to alienate the hearts of the French subjects of His Britannic Majesty. Great advantages have been promised you elsewhere, and you have been made to imagine that your religion was in danger. Threats even have been resorted to in order to induce you to remove to French territory. The savages are made use of to molest you; they are to cut the throats of all who remain in their native country, attached to their own interests and faithful to the Government. You know that certain officers and missionaries, who came from Canada last autumn, have been the cause of all our trouble during the winter. Their conduct has been horrible, without honor, probity, or conscience. Their aim is to embroil you with the Government. I will not believe that they are authorized to do so by the Court of France, that being contrary to good faith and the friendship established between the two Crowns."

What foundation there was for this amiable confidence in the Court of Versailles has been seen already. "When you declared your desire to submit yourselves to another Government," pursues Cornwallis, "our determination was to hinder nobody from following what he imagined to be his interest. We know that a forced service is worth nothing, and that a subject compelled to be so against his will is not far from being an enemy. We confess, however, that your determination to go gives us pain. We are aware of your industry and temperance, and that you are not addicted to any vice or debauchery. This province is your country. You and your fathers have cultivated it; naturally you ought yourselves to enjoy the fruits of your labor. Such was the design of the King, our master. You know that we have followed his orders. You know that we have done everything to secure to you not only the occupation of your lands, but the ownership of them forever. We have given you also every possible assurance of the free and public exercise of the Roman Catholic religion. But I declare to you frankly that, according to our laws, nobody can possess lands or houses in the province who shall refuse to take the oath of allegiance to his King when required to do so. You know very well that there are ill-disposed and mischievous persons among you who corrupt the others. Your inexperience, your ignorance of the affairs of government, and your habit of following the counsels of those who have not your real interests at heart, make it an easy matter to seduce you. In your petitions you ask for a general leave to quit the province. The only manner in which you can do so is to follow the regulations already established, and provide yourselves with our passport. And we declare that nothing shall prevent us from giving such passports to all who ask for them, the moment peace and tranquillity are re-established."[1] He declares as his reason for not giving them at once, that on crossing the frontier "you will have to pass the French detachments and savages assembled there, and that they compel all the inhabitants who go there to take up arms" against the English. How well this reason was founded will soon appear.

Hopson, the next governor, described by the French themselves as a "mild and peaceable officer," was no less considerate in his treatment of the Acadians; and at the end of 1752 he issued the following order to his military subordinates: "You are to look on the French inhabitants in the same light as the rest of His Majesty's subjects, as to the protection of the laws and government; for which reason nothing is to be taken from them by force, or any price set upon their goods but what they themselves agree to. And if at any time the inhabitants should obstinately refuse to comply with what His Majesty's service may require of them, you are not to redress yourself by military force or in any unlawful manner, but to lay the case before the Governor and wait his orders thereon."[2] Unfortunately, the mild rule of Cornwallis and Hopson was not always maintained under their successor, Lawrence.

Louis Joseph Le Loutre, vicar-general of Acadia and missionary to the Micmacs, was the most conspicuous person in the province, and more than any other man was answerable for the miseries that overwhelmed it. The sheep of which he was the shepherd dwelt, at a day's journey from Halifax, by the banks of the River Shubenacadie, in small cabins of logs, mixed with wigwams of birch-bark. They were not a docile flock; and to manage them needed address, energy, and money,—with all of which the missionary was provided. He fed their traditional dislike of the English, and fanned their fanaticism, born of the villanous counterfeit of Christianity which he and his predecessors had imposed on them. Thus he contrived to use them on the one hand to murder the English, and on the other to terrify the Acadians; yet not without cost to the French Government; for they had learned the value of money, and, except when their blood was up, were slow to take scalps without pay. Le Loutre was a man of boundless egotism, a violent spirit of domination, an intense hatred of the English, and a

[1] The above passages are from two addresses of Cornwallis, read to the Acadian deputies in April and May, 1750. The combined extracts here given convey the spirit of the whole. See *Public Documents of Nova Scotia*, 185–190.

[2] *Public Documents of Nova Scotia*, 197.

fanaticism that stopped at nothing. Towards the Acadians he was a despot; and this simple and superstitious people, extremely susceptible to the influence of their priests, trembled before him. He was scarcely less masterful in his dealings with the Acadian clergy; and, aided by his quality of the Bishop's vicar-general, he dragooned even the unwilling into aiding his schemes. Three successive governors of New France thought him invaluable, yet feared the impetuosity of his zeal, and vainly tried to restrain it within safe bounds. The Bishop, while approving his objects, thought his medicines too violent, and asked in a tone of reproof: "Is it right for you to refuse the Acadians the sacraments, to threaten that they shall be deprived of the services of a priest, and that the savages shall treat them as enemies?"[1] "Nobody," says a French Catholic contemporary, "was more fit than he to carry discord and desolation into a country."[2] Cornwallis called him "a good-for-nothing scoundrel," and offered a hundred pounds for his head.[3]

The authorities at Halifax, while exasperated by the perfidy practised on them, were themselves not always models of international virtue. They seized a French vessel in the Gulf of St. Lawrence, on the charge—probably true—that she was carrying arms and ammunition to the Acadians and Indians. A less defensible act was the capture of the armed brig "St. François," laden with supplies for a fort lately re-established by the French, at the mouth of the River St. John, on ground claimed by both nations. Captain Rous, a New England officer commanding a frigate in the Royal Navy, opened fire on the "St. François," took her after a short cannonade, and carried her into Halifax, where she was condemned by the court. Several captures of small craft, accused of illegal acts, were also made by the English. These proceedings, being all of an overt nature, gave the officers of Louis XV. precisely what they wanted,—an occasion for uttering loud complaints, and denouncing the English as breakers of the peace.

But the movement most alarming to the French was the English occupation of Beaubassin,—an act perfectly lawful in itself, since, without reasonable doubt, the place was within the limits of Acadia, and therefore on English ground.[4] Beaubassin was a considerable settlement on the isthmus that joins the Acadian peninsula to the mainland.

---

[1] *L'Évêque de Québec à Le Loutre*; translation in *Public Documents of Nova Scotia*, 240.

[2] *Mémoires sur le Canada, 1749–1760.*

[3] On Le Loutre, compare *Public Documents of Nova Scotia*, 178–180, *note*, with authorities there cited; *N. Y. Col. Docs.*, X. 11; *Mémoires sur le Canada, 1749–1760* (Quebec, 1838).

[4] La Jonquière himself admits that he thought so. "Cette partie là étant, à ce que je crois, dépendante de l'Acadie." *La Jonquière au Ministre*, 3 Oct. 1750.

Northwest of the settlement lay a wide marsh, through which ran a
stream called the Missaguash, some two miles beyond which rose a hill
called Beauséjour. On and near this hill were stationed the troops and
Canadians sent under Boishébert and La Corne to watch the English
frontier. This French force excited disaffection among the Acadians
through all the neighboring districts, and constantly helped them to
emigrate. Cornwallis therefore resolved to send an English force to the
spot; and accordingly, towards the end of April, 1750, Major Lawrence
landed at Beaubassin with four hundred men. News of their approach
had come before them, and Le Loutre was here with his Micmacs,
mixed with some Acadians whom he had persuaded or bullied to join
him. Resolved that the people of Beaubassin should not live under English influence, he now with his own hand set fire to the parish church,
while his white and red adherents burned the houses of the inhabitants,
and thus compelled them to cross to the French side of the river.[1] This
was the first forcible removal of the Acadians. It was as premature as it
was violent; since Lawrence, being threatened by La Corne, whose
force was several times greater than his own, presently reimbarked. In
the following September he returned with seventeen small vessels and
about seven hundred men, and again attempted to land on the strand
of Beaubassin. La Jonquière says that he could only be resisted indi-
rectly, because he was on the English side of the river. This indirect
resistance was undertaken by Le Loutre, who had thrown up a breastwork along the shore and manned it with his Indians and his painted
and be-feathered Acadians. Nevertheless the English landed, and, with
some loss, drove out the defenders. Le Loutre himself seems not to have
been among them; but they kept up for a time a helter-skelter fight,
encouraged by two other missionaries, Germain and Lalerne, who were
near being caught by the English.[2] Lawrence quickly routed them, took
possession of the cemetery, and prepared to fortify himself. The village
of Beaubassin, consisting, it is said, of a hundred and forty houses, had
been burned in the spring; but there were still in the neighborhood, on
the English side, many hamlets and farms, with barns full of grain and
hay. Le Loutre's Indians now threatened to plunder and kill the inhab-

---

[1] It has been erroneously stated that Beaubassin was burned by its own inhabitants. "Laloutre,
ayant vu que les Acadiens ne paroissoient pas fort pressés d'abandonner leurs biens, avoit lui-
même mis le feu à l'Église, et l'avoit fait mettre aux maisons des habitants par quelques-uns de
ceux qu'il avoit gagnés," etc. *Mémoires sur le Canada, 1749–1760.* "Les sauvages y mirent le feu."
Précis des Faits, 85. "Les sauvages mirent le feu aux maisons." *Prévost au Ministre, 22 Juillet, 1750.*
[2] La Vallière, *Journal de ce qui s'est passé à Chenitou* [Chignecto] *et autres parties des Frontières de
l'Acadie, 1750–1751.* La Vallière was an officer on the spot.

itants if they did not take arms against the English. Few complied, and the greater part fled to the woods.[1] On this the Indians and their Acadian allies set the houses and barns on fire, and laid waste the whole district, leaving the inhabitants no choice but to seek food and shelter with the French.[2]

The English fortified themselves on a low hill by the edge of the marsh, planted palisades, built barracks, and named the new work Fort Lawrence. Slight skirmishes between them and the French were frequent. Neither party respected the dividing line of the Missaguash, and a petty warfare of aggression and reprisal began, and became chronic. Before the end of the autumn there was an atrocious act of treachery. Among the English officers was Captain Edward Howe, an intelligent and agreeable person, who spoke French fluently, and had been long stationed in the province. Le Loutre detested him; dreading his influence over the Acadians, by many of whom he was known and liked. One morning, at about eight o'clock, the inmates of Fort Lawrence saw what seemed an officer from Beauséjour, carrying a flag, and followed by several men in uniform, wading through the sea of grass that stretched beyond the Missaguash. When the tide was out, this river was but an ugly trench of reddish mud gashed across the face of the marsh, with a thread of half-fluid slime lazily crawling along the bottom; but at high tide it was filled to the brim with an opaque torrent that would have overflowed, but for the dikes thrown up to confine it. Behind the dike on the farther bank stood the seeming officer, waving his flag in sign that he desired a parley. He was in reality no officer, but one of Le Loutre's Indians in disguise, Étienne Le Bâtard, or, as others say, the great chief, Jean-Baptiste Cope. Howe, carrying a white flag, and accompanied by a few officers and men, went towards the river to hear what he had to say. As they drew near, his looks and language excited their suspicion. But it was too late; for a number of Indians, who had hidden behind the dike during the night, fired upon Howe across the stream, and mortally wounded him. They continued their fire on his companions, but could not prevent them from carrying the dying man to the fort. The French officers, indignant at this villany, did not hesitate to charge it upon Le Loutre; "for," says one of them, "what is not a wicked priest capable of doing?" But Le Loutre's brother missionary, Maillard, declares that it was purely an effect of

[1] *Prévost au Ministre, 27 Sept. 1750.*
[2] "Les sauvages et Accadiens mirent le feu dans toutes les maisons et granges, pleines de bled et de fourrages, ce qui a causé une grande disette." La Vallière, *ut supra.*

religious zeal on the part of the Micmacs, who, according to him, bore a deadly grudge against Howe because, fourteen years before, he had spoken words disrespectful to the Holy Virgin.[1] Maillard adds that the Indians were much pleased with what they had done. Finding, however, that they could effect little against the English troops, they changed their field of action, repaired to the outskirts of Halifax, murdered about thirty settlers, and carried off eight or ten prisoners.

Strong reinforcements came from Canada. The French began a fort on the hill of Beauséjour, and the Acadians were required to work at it with no compensation but rations. They were thinly clad, some had neither shoes nor stockings, and winter was begun. They became so dejected that it was found absolutely necessary to give them wages enough to supply their most pressing needs. In the following season Fort Beauséjour was in a state to receive a garrison. It stood on the crown of the hill, and a vast panorama stretched below and around it. In front lay the Bay of Chignecto, winding along the fertile shores of Chipody and Memeramcook. Far on the right spread the great Tantemar marsh; on the left lay the marsh of the Missaguash; and on a knoll beyond it, not three miles distant, the red flag of England waved over the palisades of Fort Lawrence, while hills wrapped in dark forests bounded the horizon.

How the homeless Acadians from Beaubassin lived through the winter is not very clear. They probably found shelter at Chipody and its neighborhood, where there were thriving settlements of their countrymen. Le Loutre, fearing that they would return to their lands and submit to the English, sent some of them to Isle St. Jean. "They refused to go," says a French writer; "but he compelled them at last, by threatening to make the Indians pillage them, carry off their wives and children, and even kill them before their eyes. Nevertheless he kept about him such as were most submissive to his will."[2] In the spring after the English occupied Beaubassin, La Jonquière issued a strange proclamation. It commanded all Acadians to take forthwith an oath of fidelity to the King of France, and to enroll themselves in the French militia, on pain of being treated as rebels.[3] Three years after, Lawrence, who

---

[1] Maillard, *Les Missions Micmaques*. On the murder of Howe, *Public Documents of Nova Scotia*, 194, 195, 210; *Mémoires sur le Canada, 1749–1760*, where it is said that Le Loutre was present at the deed; La Vallière, *Journal*, who says that some Acadians took part in it; *Dépêches de la Jonquière*, who says "les sauvages de l'Abbé le Loutre l'ont tué par trahison;" and *Prévost au Ministre, 27 Oct. 1750.*

[2] *Mémoires sur le Canada, 1749–1760.*

[3] *Ordonnance du 12 Avril, 1751.*

then governed the province, proclaimed in his turn that all Acadians who had at any time sworn fidelity to the King of England, and who should be found in arms against him, would be treated as criminals.[1] Thus were these unfortunates ground between the upper and nether millstones. Le Loutre replied to this proclamation of Lawrence by a letter in which he outdid himself. He declared that any of the inhabitants who had crossed to the French side of the line, and who should presume to return to the English, would be treated as enemies by his Micmacs; and in the name of these, his Indian adherents, he demanded that the entire eastern half of the Acadian peninsula, including the ground on which Fort Lawrence stood, should be at once made over to their sole use and sovereign ownership,[2]—"which being read and considered," says the record of the Halifax Council, "the contents appeared too insolent and absurd to be answered."

The number of Acadians who had crossed the line and were collected about Beauséjour was now large. Their countrymen of Chipody began to find them a burden, and they lived chiefly on Government rations. Le Loutre had obtained fifty thousand livres from the Court in order to dike in, for their use, the fertile marshes of Memeramcook; but the relief was distant, and the misery pressing. They complained that they had been lured over the line by false assurances, and they applied secretly to the English authorities to learn if they would be allowed to return to their homes. The answer was that they might do so with full enjoyment of religion and property, if they would take a simple oath of fidelity and loyalty to the King of Great Britain, qualified by an oral intimation that they would not be required for the present to bear arms.[3] When Le Loutre heard this, he mounted the pulpit, broke into fierce invectives, threatened the terrified people with excommunication, and preached himself into a state of exhaustion.[4] The military commandant at Beauséjour used gentler means of prevention; and the Acadians, unused for generations to think or act for themselves, remained restless, but indecisive, waiting till fate should settle for them the question, under which king?

Meanwhile, for the past three years, the commissioners appointed under the treaty of Aix-la-Chapelle to settle the question of boundaries between France and England in America had been in session at Paris,

---

[1] *Écrit donné aux Habitants réfugiés à Beauséjour, 10 Août, 1754.*
[2] *Copie de la Lettre de M. l'Abbé Le Loutre, Prêtre Missionnaire des Sauvages de l'Accadie, à M. Lawrence à Halifax, 26 Août, 1754.* There is a translation in *Public Documents of Nova Scotia.*
[3] *Public Documents of Nova Scotia,* 205, 209.
[4] Compare *Mémoires, 1749–1760,* and *Public Documents of Nova Scotia,* 229, 230.

waging interminable war on paper; La Galissonière and Silhouette for France, Shirley and Mildmay for England. By the treaty of Utrecht, Acadia belonged to England; but what was Acadia? According to the English commissioners, it comprised not only the peninsula now called Nova Scotia, but all the immense tract of land between the River St. Lawrence on the north, the Gulf of the same name on the east, the Atlantic on the south, and New England on the west.[1] The French commissioners, on their part, maintained that the name Acadia belonged of right only to about a twentieth part of this territory, and that it did not even cover the whole of the Acadian peninsula, but only its southern coast, with an adjoining belt of barren wilderness. When the French owned Acadia, they gave it boundaries as comprehensive as those claimed for it by the English commissioners; now that it belonged to a rival, they cut it down to a paring of its former self. The denial that Acadia included the whole peninsula was dictated by the need of a winter communication between Quebec and Cape Breton, which was possible only with the eastern portions in French hands. So new was this denial that even La Galissonière himself, the foremost in making it, had declared without reservation two years before that Acadia was the entire peninsula.[2] "If," says a writer on the question, "we had to do with a nation more tractable, less grasping, and more conciliatory, it would be well to insist also that Halifax should be given up to us." He thinks that, on the whole, it would be well to make the demand in any case, in order to gain some other point by yielding this one.[3] It is curious that while denying that the country was Acadia, the French invariably called the inhabitants Acadians. Innumerable public documents, commissions, grants, treaties, edicts, signed by French kings and ministers, had recognized Acadia as extending over New Brunswick and a part of Maine. Four censuses of Acadia while it belonged to the French had recognized the mainland as included in it; and so do also the early French maps. Its prodigious shrinkage was simply the consequence of its possession by an alien.

Other questions of limits, more important and equally perilous, called loudly for solution. What line should separate Canada and her

[1] The commission of De Monts, in 1603, defines Acadia as extending from the fortieth to the forty-sixth degrees of latitude,—that is, from central New Brunswick to southern Pennsylvania. Neither party cared to produce the document.

[2] "L'Acadie suivant ses anciennes limites est la presquisle bornée par son isthme." *La Galissonière au Ministre, 25 Juillet, 1749.* The English commissioners were, of course, ignorant of this admission.

[3] *Mémoire de l'Abbé de l'Isle-Dieu, 1753 (1754?).*

western dependencies from the British colonies? Various principles of demarcation were suggested, of which the most prominent on the French side was a geographical one. All countries watered by streams falling into the St. Lawrence, the Great Lakes, and the Mississippi were to belong to her. This would have planted her in the heart of New York and along the crests of the Alleghanies, giving her all the interior of the continent, and leaving nothing to England but a strip of sea-coast. Yet in view of what France had achieved; of the patient gallantry of her explorers, the zeal of her missionaries, the adventurous hardi-hood of her bushrangers, revealing to civilized mankind the existence of this wilderness world, while her rivals plodded at their workshops, their farms, or their fisheries,—in view of all this, her pretensions were moderate and reasonable compared with those of England. The treaty of Utrecht had declared the Iroquois, or Five Nations, to be British subjects; therefore it was insisted that all countries conquered by them belonged to the British Crown. But what was an Iroquois conquest? The Iroquois rarely occupied the countries they overran. Their military expeditions were mere raids, great or small. Sometimes, as in the case of the Hurons, they made a solitude and called it peace; again, as in the case of the Illinois, they drove off the occupants of the soil, who returned after the invaders were gone. But the range of their war-parties was prodigious; and the English laid claim to every mountain, forest, or prairie where an Iroquois had taken a scalp. This would give them not only the country between the Alleghanies and the Mississippi, but also that between Lake Huron and the Ottawa, thus reducing Canada to the patch on the American map now represented by the province of Quebec,—or rather, by a part of it, since the extension of Acadia to the St. Lawrence would cut off the present counties of Gaspé, Ri-mouski, and Bonaventure. Indeed among the advocates of British claims there were those who denied that France had any rights what-ever on the south side of the St. Lawrence.[1] Such being the attitude of the two contestants, it was plain that there was no resort but the last argument of kings. Peace must be won with the sword.

[1] The extent of British claims is best shown on two maps of the time, Mitchell's *Map of the British and French Dominions in North America*, and Huske's *New and Accurate Map of North America*; both are in the British Museum. Dr. John Mitchell, in his *Contest in America* (London, 1757), pushes the English claim to its utmost extreme, and denies that the French were rightful owners of anything in North America except the town of Quebec and the trading-post of Tadoussac. Besides the claim founded on the subjection of the Iroquois to the British Crown, the English somewhat inconsistently advanced others founded on titles obtained by treaty from these same tribes, and others still, founded on the original grants of some of the colonies, which ran indefinitely westward across the continent.

The commissioners at Paris broke up their sessions, leaving as the monument of their toils four quarto volumes of allegations, arguments, and documentary proofs.[1] Out of the discussion rose also a swarm of fugitive publications in French, English, and Spanish; for the question of American boundaries had become European. There was one among them worth notice from its amusing absurdity. It is an elaborate disquisition, under the title of *Roman politique*, by an author faithful to the traditions of European diplomacy, and inspired at the same time by the new philosophy of the school of Rousseau. He insists that the balance of power must be preserved in America as well as in Europe, because "Nature," "the aggrandizement of the human soul," and the "felicity of man" are unanimous in demanding it. The English colonies are more populous and wealthy than the French; therefore the French should have more land, to keep the balance. Nature, the human soul, and the felicity of man require that France should own all the country beyond the Alleghanies and all Acadia but a strip of the south coast, according to the "sublime negotiations" of the French commissioners, of which the writer declares himself a "religious admirer."[2]

We know already that France had used means sharper than negotiation to vindicate her claim to the interior of the continent; had marched to the sources of the Ohio to entrench herself there, and hold the passes of the West against all comers. It remains to see how she fared in her bold enterprise.

[1] *Mémoires des Commissaires de Sa Majesté Très Chrétienne et de ceux de Sa Majesté Brittanique.* Paris, 1755. Several editions appeared.

[2] *Roman politique sur l'État présent des Affaires de l'Amérique* (Amsterdam, 1756). For extracts from French Documents, see Appendix B.

5

Washington

1753, 1754

THE FRENCH OCCUPY THE SOURCES OF THE OHIO · THEIR
SUFFERINGS · FORT LE BŒUF · LEGARDEUR DE SAINT-PIERRE · MISSION
OF WASHINGTON · ROBERT DINWIDDIE · HE OPPOSES THE FRENCH · HIS
DISPUTE WITH THE BURGESSES · HIS ENERGY · HIS APPEALS FOR HELP ·
FORT DUQUESNE · DEATH OF JUMONVILLE · WASHINGTON AT THE GREAT
MEADOWS · COULON DE VILLIERS · FORT NECESSITY

Towards the end of spring the vanguard of the expedition
sent by Duquesne to occupy the Ohio landed at Presqu'-
isle, where Erie now stands. This route to the Ohio, far better than that
which Céloron had followed, was a new discovery to the French; and
Duquesne calls the harbor "the finest in nature." Here they built a fort
of squared chestnut logs, and when it was finished they cut a road of
several leagues through the woods to Rivière aux Bœufs, now French
Creek. At the farther end of this road they began another wooden fort
and called it Fort Le Bœuf. Thence, when the water was high, they
could descend French Creek to the Alleghany, and follow that stream
to the main current of the Ohio.

It was heavy work to carry the cumbrous load of baggage across the
portages. Much of it is said to have been superfluous, consisting of vel-
vets, silks, and other useless and costly articles, sold to the King at
enormous prices as necessaries of the expedition.[1] The weight of the

[1]Pouchot, *Mémoires sur la dernière Guerre de l'Amérique Septentrionale*, I. 8.

task fell on the Canadians, who worked with cheerful hardihood, and did their part to admiration. Marin, commander of the expedition, a gruff, choleric old man of sixty-three, but full of force and capacity, spared himself so little that he was struck down with dysentery, and, refusing to be sent home to Montreal, was before long in a dying state. His place was taken by Péan, of whose private character there is little good to be said, but whose conduct as an officer was such that Duquesne calls him a prodigy of talents, resources, and zeal.[1] The subalterns deserve no such praise. They disliked the service, and made no secret of their discontent. Rumors of it filled Montreal; and Duquesne wrote to Marin: "I am surprised that you have not told me of this change. Take note of the sullen and discouraged faces about you. This sort are worse than useless. Rid yourself of them at once; send them to Montreal, that I may make an example of them."[2] Péan wrote at the end of September that Marin was in extremity; and the Governor, disturbed and alarmed, for he knew the value of the sturdy old officer, looked anxiously for a successor. He chose another veteran, Legardeur de Saint-Pierre, who had just returned from a journey of exploration towards the Rocky Mountains,[3] and whom Duquesne now ordered to the Ohio.

Meanwhile the effects of the expedition had already justified it. At first the Indians of the Ohio had shown a bold front. One of them, a chief whom the English called the Half-King, came to Fort Le Bœuf and ordered the French to leave the country; but was received by Marin with such contemptuous haughtiness that he went home shedding tears of rage and mortification. The Western tribes were daunted. The Miamis, but yesterday fast friends of the English, made humble submission to the French, and offered them two English scalps to signalize their repentance; while the Sacs, Pottawattamies, and Ojibwas were loud in professions of devotion.[4] Even the Iroquois, Delawares, and Shawanoes on the Alleghany had come to the French camp and offered their help in carrying the baggage. It needed but perseverance and success in the enterprise to win over every tribe from the mountains to the Mississippi. To accomplish this and to curb the English, Duquesne had planned a third fort, at the junction of French Creek with the Alleghany, or at some point lower down; then, leaving the three posts well

---

[1] *Duquesne au Ministre, 2 Nov. 1753*; compare *Mémoire pour Michel-Jean Hugues Péan.*

[2] *Duquesne à Marin, 27 Août, 1753.*

[3] *Mémoire ou Journal sommaire du Voyage de Jacques Legardeur de Saint-Pierre.*

[4] *Rapports de Conseils avec les Sauvages à Montreal, Juillet, 1753. Duquesne au Ministre, 31 Oct. 1753.* Letter of Dr. Shuckburgh in *N. Y. Col. Docs.*, VI. 806.

garrisoned, Péan was to descend the Ohio with the whole remaining force, impose terror on the wavering tribes, and complete their conversion. Both plans were thwarted; the fort was not built, nor did Péan descend the Ohio. Fevers, lung diseases, and scurvy made such deadly havoc among troops and Canadians, that the dying Marin saw with bitterness that his work must be left half done. Three hundred of the best men were kept to garrison Forts Presquisle and Le Bœuf; and then, as winter approached, the rest were sent back to Montreal. When they arrived, the Governor was shocked at their altered looks. "I reviewed them, and could not help being touched by the pitiable state to which fatigues and exposures had reduced them. Past all doubt, if these emaciated figures had gone down the Ohio as intended, the river would have been strewn with corpses, and the evil-disposed savages would not have failed to attack the survivors, seeing that they were but spectres."[1]

Legardeur de Saint-Pierre arrived at the end of autumn, and made his quarters at Fort Le Bœuf. The surrounding forests had dropped their leaves, and in gray and patient desolation bided the coming winter. Chill rains drizzled over the gloomy "clearing," and drenched the palisades and log-built barracks, raw from the axe. Buried in the wilderness, the military exiles resigned themselves as they might to months of monotonous solitude; when, just after sunset on the eleventh of December, a tall youth came out of the forest on horseback, attended by a companion much older and rougher than himself, and followed by several Indians and four or five white men with packhorses. Officers from the fort went out to meet the strangers; and, wading through mud and sodden snow, they entered at the gate. On the next day the young leader of the party, with the help of an interpreter, for he spoke no French, had an interview with the commandant, and gave him a letter from Governor Dinwiddie. Saint-Pierre and the officer next in rank, who knew a little English, took it to another room to study it at their ease; and in it, all unconsciously, they read a name destined to stand one of the noblest in the annals of mankind; for it introduced Major George Washington, Adjutant-General of the Virginia militia.[2]

Dinwiddie, jealously watchful of French aggression, had learned through traders and Indians that a strong detachment from Canada had entered the territories of the King of England, and built forts on Lake Erie and on a branch of the Ohio. He wrote to challenge the invasion

---

[1] *Duquesne au Ministre, 29 Nov. 1753.* On this expedition, compare the letter of Duquesne in *N. Y. Col. Docs.*, X. 255, and the deposition of Stephen Coffen, *Ibid.*, VI. 835.
[2] *Journal of Major Washington. Journal of Mr. Christopher Gist.*

and summon the invaders to withdraw; and he could find none so fit to bear his message as a young man of twenty-one. It was this rough Scotchman who launched Washington on his illustrious career.

Washington set out for the trading station of the Ohio Company on Will's Creek; and thence, at the middle of November, struck into the wilderness with Christopher Gist as a guide, Vanbraam, a Dutchman, as French interpreter, Davison, a trader, as Indian interpreter, and four woodsmen as servants. They went to the forks of the Ohio, and then down the river to Logstown, the Chiningué of Céloron de Bienville. There Washington had various parleys with the Indians; and thence, after vexatious delays, he continued his journey towards Fort Le Bœuf, accompanied by the friendly chief called the Half-King and by three of his tribesmen. For several days they followed the traders' path, pelted with unceasing rain and snow, and came at last to the old Indian town of Venango, where French Creek enters the Alleghany. Here there was an English trading-house; but the French had seized it, raised their flag over it, and turned it into a military outpost.[1] Joncaire was in command, with two subalterns; and nothing could exceed their civility. They invited the strangers to supper; and, says Washington, "the wine, as they dosed themselves pretty plentifully with it, soon banished the restraint which at first appeared in their conversation, and gave a license to their tongues to reveal their sentiments more freely. They told me that it was their absolute design to take possession of the Ohio, and, by G—, they would do it; for that although they were sensible the English could raise two men for their one, yet they knew their motions were too slow and dilatory to prevent any undertaking of theirs."[2]

With all their civility, the French officers did their best to entice away Washington's Indians; and it was with extreme difficulty that he could persuade them to go with him. Through marshes and swamps, forests choked with snow, and drenched with incessant rain, they toiled on for four days more, till the wooden walls of Fort Le Bœuf appeared at last, surrounded by fields studded thick with stumps, and half-encircled by the chill current of French Creek, along the banks of which lay more than two hundred canoes, ready to carry troops in the spring. Washington describes Legardeur de Saint-Pierre as "an elderly gentleman with much the air of a soldier." The letter sent him by Dinwiddie

[1]Marin had sent sixty men in August to seize the house, which belonged to the trader Fraser. *Dépêches de Duquesne*. They carried off two men whom they found here. Letter of Fraser in *Colonial Records of Pa.*, V. 659.

[2]*Journal of Washington*, as printed at Williamsburg, just after his return.

expressed astonishment that his troops should build forts upon lands "so notoriously known to be the property of the Crown of Great Britain." "I must desire you," continued the letter, "to acquaint me by whose authority and instructions you have lately marched from Canada with an armed force, and invaded the King of Great Britain's territories. It becomes my duty to require your peaceable departure; and that you would forbear prosecuting a purpose so interruptive of the harmony and good understanding which His Majesty is desirous to continue and cultivate with the Most Christian King. I persuade myself you will receive and entertain Major Washington with the candor and politeness natural to your nation; and it will give me the greatest satisfaction if you return him with an answer suitable to my wishes for a very long and lasting peace between us."

Saint-Pierre took three days to frame the answer. In it he said that he should send Dinwiddie's letter to the Marquis Duquesne and wait his orders; and that meanwhile he should remain at his post, according to the commands of his general. "I made it my particular care," so the letter closed, "to receive Mr. Washington with a distinction suitable to your dignity as well as his own quality and great merit."[1] No form of courtesy had, in fact, been wanting. "He appeared to be extremely complaisant," says Washington, "though he was exerting every artifice to set our Indians at variance with us. I saw that every stratagem was practised to win the Half-King to their interest." Neither gifts nor brandy were spared; and it was only by the utmost pains that Washington could prevent his red allies from staying at the fort, conquered by French blandishments.

After leaving Venango on his return, he found the horses so weak that, to arrive the sooner, he left them and their drivers in charge of Vanbraam and pushed forward on foot, accompanied by Gist alone. Each was wrapped to the throat in an Indian "matchcoat," with a gun in his hand and a pack at his back. Passing an old Indian hamlet called Murdering Town, they had an adventure which threatened to make good the name. A French Indian, whom they met in the forest, fired at them, pretending that his gun had gone off by chance. They caught him, and Gist would have killed him; but Washington interposed, and they let him go.[2] Then, to escape pursuit from his tribesmen, they walked all night and all the next day. This brought them to the banks

[1]"La Distinction qui convient à votre Dignitté à sa Qualité et à son grand Mérite." Copy of original letter sent by Dinwiddie to Governor Hamilton.
[2]Journal of Mr. Christopher Gist, in Mass. Hist. Coll., 3rd Series, V.

of the Alleghany. They hoped to have found it dead frozen; but it was all alive and turbulent, filled with ice sweeping down the current. They made a raft, shoved out into the stream, and were soon caught helplessly in the drifting ice. Washington, pushing hard with his setting-pole, was jerked into the freezing river; but caught a log of the raft, and dragged himself out. By no efforts could they reach the farther bank, or regain that which they had left; but they were driven against an island, where they landed, and left the raft to its fate. The night was excessively cold, and Gist's feet and hands were badly frost-bitten. In the morning, the ice had set, and the river was a solid floor. They crossed it, and succeeded in reaching the house of the trader Fraser, on the Monongahela. It was the middle of January when Washington arrived at Williamsburg and made his report to Dinwiddie.

Robert Dinwiddie was lieutenant-governor of Virginia, in place of the titular governor, Lord Albemarle, whose post was a sinecure. He had been clerk in a government office in the West Indies; then surveyor of customs in the "Old Dominion,"—a position in which he made himself cordially disliked; and when he rose to the governorship he carried his unpopularity with him. Yet Virginia and all the British colonies owed him much; for, though past sixty, he was the most watchful sentinel against French aggression and its most strenuous opponent. Scarcely had Marin's vanguard appeared at Presquisle, when Dinwiddie warned the Home Government of the danger, and urged, what he had before urged in vain on the Virginian Assembly, the immediate building of forts on the Ohio. There came in reply a letter, signed by the King, authorizing him to build the forts at the cost of the Colony, and to repel force by force in case he was molested or obstructed. Moreover, the King wrote, "If you shall find that any number of persons shall presume to erect any fort or forts within the limits of our province of Virginia, you are first to require of them peaceably to depart; and if, notwithstanding your admonitions, they do still endeavor to carry out any such unlawful and unjustifiable designs, we do hereby strictly charge and command you to drive them off by force of arms."[1]

The order was easily given; but to obey it needed men and money, and for these Dinwiddie was dependent on his Assembly, or House of Burgesses. He convoked them for the first of November, sending Washington at the same time with the summons to Saint-Pierre. The burgesses met. Dinwiddie exposed the danger, and asked for means to meet it.[2] They seemed more than willing to comply; but debates presently

[1] *Instructions to Our Trusty and Well-beloved Robert Dinwiddie, Esq., 28 Aug. 1753.*
[2] *Address of Lieutenant-Governor Dinwiddie to the Council and Burgesses, 1 Nov. 1753.*

arose concerning the fee of a pistole, which the Governor had demanded on each patent of land issued by him. The amount was trifling, but the principle was doubtful. The aristocratic republic of Virginia was intensely jealous of the slightest encroachment on its rights by the Crown or its representative. The Governor defended the fee. The burgesses replied that "subjects cannot be deprived of the least part of their property without their consent," declared the fee unlawful, and called on Dinwiddie to confess it to be so. He still defended it. They saw in his demand for supplies a means of bringing him to terms, and refused to grant money unless he would recede from his position. Dinwiddie rebuked them for "disregarding the designs of the French, and disputing the rights of the Crown;" and he "prorogued them in some anger."[1]

Thus he was unable to obey the instructions of the King. As a temporary resource, he ventured to order a draft of two hundred men from the militia. Washington was to have command, with the trader, William Trent, as his lieutenant. His orders were to push with all speed to the forks of the Ohio, and there build a fort; "but in case any attempts are made to obstruct the works by any persons whatsoever, to restrain all such offenders, and, in case of resistance, to make prisoners of, or kill and destroy them."[2] The Governor next sent messengers to the Catawbas, Cherokees, Chickasaws, and Iroquois of the Ohio, inviting them to take up the hatchet against the French, "who, under pretence of embracing you, mean to squeeze you to death." Then he wrote urgent letters to the governors of Pennsylvania, the Carolinas, Maryland, and New Jersey, begging for contingents of men, to be at Wills Creek in March at the latest. But nothing could be done without money; and trusting for a change of heart on the part of the burgesses, he summoned them to meet again on the fourteenth of February. "If they come in good temper," he wrote to Lord Fairfax, a nobleman settled in the colony, "I hope they will lay a fund to qualify me to send four or five hundred men more to the Ohio, which, with the assistance of our neighboring colonies, may make some figure."

The session began. Again, somewhat oddly, yet forcibly, the Governor set before the Assembly the peril of the situation, and begged them to postpone less pressing questions to the exigency of the hour.[3] This time they listened; and voted ten thousand pounds in Virginia currency to defend the frontier. The grant was frugal, and they jealously placed

---

[1] *Dinwiddie Papers.*
[2] *Ibid. Instructions to Major George Washington, January, 1754.*
[3] *Speech of Lieutenant-Governor Dinwiddie to the Council and Burgesses, 14 Feb., 1754.*

its expenditure in the hands of a committee of their own.[1] Dinwiddie, writing to the Lords of Trade, pleads necessity as his excuse for submitting to their terms. "I am sorry," he says, "to find them too much in a republican way of thinking." What vexed him still more was their sending an agent to England to complain against him on the irrepressible question of the pistole fee; and he writes to his London friend, the merchant Hanbury: "I have had a great deal of trouble from the factious disputes and violent heats of a most impudent, troublesome party here in regard to that silly fee of a pistole. Surely every thinking man will make a distinction between a fee and a tax. Poor people! I pity their ignorance and narrow, ill-natured spirits. But, my friend, consider that I could by no means give up this fee without affronting the Board of Trade and the Council here who established it." His thoughts were not all of this harassing nature, and he ends his letter with the following petition: "Now, sir, as His Majesty is pleased to make me a military officer, please send for Scott, my tailor, to make me a proper suit of regimentals, to be here by His Majesty's birthday. I do not much like gayety in dress, but I conceive this necessary. I do not much care for lace on the coat, but a neat embroidered button-hole; though you do not deal that way, I know you have a good taste, that I may show my friend's fancy in that suit of clothes; a good laced hat and two pair stockings, one silk, the other fine thread."[2]

If the Governor and his English sometimes provoke a smile, he deserves admiration for the energy with which he opposed the public enemy, under circumstances the most discouraging. He invited the Indians to meet him in council at Winchester, and, as bait to attract them, coupled the message with a promise of gifts. He sent circulars from the King to the neighboring governors, calling for supplies, and wrote letter upon letter to rouse them to effort. He wrote also to the more distant governors, Delancey of New York, and Shirley of Massachusetts, begging them to make what he called a "faint" against Canada, to prevent the French from sending so large a force to the Ohio. It was to the nearer colonies, from New Jersey to South Carolina, that he looked for direct aid; and their several governors were all more or less active to procure it; but as most of them had some standing dispute with their assemblies, they could get nothing except on terms with which they would not, and sometimes could not, comply. As the lands invaded by the French belonged to one of the two rival claimants,

[1]See the bill in Hening, *Statutes of Virginia,* VI. 417.
[2]*Dinwiddie to Hanbury, 12 March, 1754; Ibid., 10 May, 1754.*

Virginia and Pennsylvania, the other colonies had no mind to vote money to defend them. Pennsylvania herself refused to move. Hamilton, her governor, could do nothing against the placid obstinacy of the Quaker non-combatants and the stolid obstinacy of the German farmers who chiefly made up his Assembly. North Carolina alone answered the appeal, and gave money enough to raise three or four hundred men. Two independent companies maintained by the King in New York, and one in South Carolina, had received orders from England to march to the scene of action; and in these, with the scanty levies of his own and the adjacent province, lay Dinwiddie's only hope. With men abundant and willing, there were no means to put them into the field, and no commander whom they would all obey.

From the brick house at Williamsburg pompously called the Governor's Palace, Dinwiddie despatched letters, orders, couriers, to hasten the tardy reinforcements of North Carolina and New York, and push on the raw soldiers of the Old Dominion, who now numbered three hundred men. They were called the Virginia regiment; and Joshua Fry, an English gentleman, bred at Oxford, was made their colonel, with Washington as next in command. Fry was at Alexandria with half the so-called regiment, trying to get it into marching order; Washington, with the other half, had pushed forward to the Ohio Company's storehouse at Wills Creek, which was to form a base of operations. His men were poor whites, brave, but hard to discipline; without tents, ill armed, and ragged as Falstaff's recruits. Besides these, a band of backwoodsmen under Captain Trent had crossed the mountains in February to build a fort at the forks of the Ohio, where Pittsburg now stands,— a spot which Washington had examined when on his way to Fort Le Bœuf, and which he had reported as the best for the purpose. The hope was that Trent would fortify himself before the arrival of the French, and that Washington and Fry would join him in time to secure the position. Trent had begun the fort; but for some unexplained reason had gone back to Wills Creek, leaving Ensign Ward with forty men at work upon it. Their labors were suddenly interrupted. On the seventeenth of April a swarm of bateaux and canoes came down the Alleghany, bringing, according to Ward, more than a thousand Frenchmen, though in reality not much above five hundred, who landed, planted cannon against the incipient stockade, and summoned the ensign to surrender, on pain of what might ensue.[1] He complied, and was allowed to depart with his men. Retracing his steps over the mountains, he

[1] See the summons in *Précis des Faits*, 101.

reported his mishap to Washington; while the French demolished his unfinished fort, began a much larger and better one, and named it Fort Duquesne.

They had acted with their usual promptness. Their Governor, a practised soldier, knew the value of celerity, and had set his troops in motion with the first opening of spring. He had no refractory assembly to hamper him; no lack of money, for the King supplied it; and all Canada must march at his bidding. Thus, while Dinwiddie was still toiling to muster his raw recruits, Duquesne's lieutenant, Contrecœur, successor of Saint-Pierre, had landed at Presquisle with a much greater force, in part regulars, and in part Canadians.

Dinwiddie was deeply vexed when a message from Washington told him how his plans were blighted; and he spoke his mind to his friend Hanbury: "If our Assembly had voted the money in November which they did in February, it's more than probable the fort would have been built and garrisoned before the French had approached; but these things cannot be done without money. As there was none in our treasury, I have advanced my own to forward the expedition; and if the independent companies from New York come soon, I am in hopes the eyes of the other colonies will be opened; and if they grant a proper supply of men, I hope we shall be able to dislodge the French or build a fort on that river. I congratulate you on the increase of your family. My wife and two girls join in our most sincere respects to good Mrs. Hanbury."[1]

The seizure of a king's fort by planting cannon against it and threatening it with destruction was in his eyes a beginning of hostilities on the part of the French; and henceforth both he and Washington acted much as if war had been declared. From their station at Wills Creek, the distance by the traders' path to Fort Duquesne was about a hundred and forty miles. Midway was a branch of the Monongahela called Redstone Creek, at the mouth of which the Ohio Company had built another storehouse. Dinwiddie ordered all the forces to cross the mountains and assemble at this point, until they should be strong enough to advance against the French. The movement was critical in presence of an enemy as superior in discipline as he was in numbers, while the natural obstacles were great. A road for cannon and wagons must be cut through a dense forest and over two ranges of high mountains, besides countless hills and streams. Washington set all his force to the work, and they spent a fortnight in making twenty miles. To-

[1] *Dinwiddie to Hanbury, 10 May, 1754.*

wards the end of May, however, Dinwiddie learned that he had crossed the main ridge of the Alleghanies, and was encamped with a hundred and fifty men near the parallel ridge of Laurel Hill, at a place called the Great Meadows. Trent's backwoodsmen had gone off in disgust; Fry, with the rest of the regiment, was still far behind; and Washington was daily expecting an attack. Close upon this, a piece of good news, or what seemed such, came over the mountains and gladdened the heart of the Governor. He heard that a French detachment had tried to surprise Washington, and that he had killed or captured the whole. The facts were as follows.

Washington was on the Youghiogany, a branch of the Monongahela, exploring it in hopes that it might prove navigable, when a messenger came to him from his old comrade, the Half-King, who was on the way to join him. The message was to the effect that the French had marched from their fort, and meant to attack the first English they should meet. A report came soon after that they were already at the ford of the Youghiogany, eighteen miles distant. Washington at once repaired to the Great Meadows, a level tract of grass and bushes, bordered by wooded hills, and traversed in one part by a gully, which with a little labor the men turned into an entrenchment, at the same time cutting away the bushes and clearing what the young commander called "a charming field for an encounter." Parties were sent out to scour the woods, but they found no enemy. Two days passed; when, on the morning of the twenty-seventh, Christopher Gist, who had lately made a settlement on the farther side of Laurel Hill, twelve or thirteen miles distant, came to the camp with news that fifty Frenchmen had been at his house towards noon of the day before, and would have destroyed everything but for the intervention of two Indians whom he had left in charge during his absence. Washington sent seventy-five men to look for the party; but the search was vain, the French having hidden themselves so well as to escape any eye but that of an Indian. In the evening a runner came from the Half-King, who was encamped with a few warriors some miles distant. He had sent to tell Washington that he had found the tracks of two men, and traced them towards a dark glen in the forest, where in his belief all the French were lurking.

Washington seems not to have hesitated a moment. Fearing a stratagem to surprise his camp, he left his main force to guard it, and at ten o'clock set out for the Half-King's wigwams at the head of forty men. The night was rainy, and the forest, to use his own words, "as black as pitch." "The path," he continues, "was hardly wide enough for one man; we often lost it, and could not find it again for fifteen or twenty minutes, and we often tumbled over each other in the dark."[1] Seven of his men were lost in the woods and left behind. The rest groped their way all night, and reached the Indian camp at sunrise. A council was held with the Half-King, and he and his warriors agreed to join in striking the French. Two of them led the way. The tracks of the two French scouts seen the day before were again found, and, marching in single file, the party pushed through the forest into the rocky hollow where the French were supposed to be concealed. They were there in fact; and they snatched their guns the moment they saw the English. Washington gave the word to fire. A short fight ensued. Coulon de Jumonville, an ensign in command, was killed, with nine others; twenty-two were captured, and none escaped but a Canadian who had fled at the beginning of the fray. After it was over, the prisoners told Washington that the party had been sent to bring him a summons from Contrecœur, the commandant at Fort Duquesne.

Five days before, Contrecœur had sent Jumonville to scour the country as far as the dividing ridge of the Alleghanies. Under him were another officer, three cadets, a volunteer, an interpreter, and twenty-eight men. He was provided with a written summons, to be delivered to any English he might find. It required them to withdraw from the domain of the King of France, and threatened compulsion by force of arms in case of refusal. But before delivering the summons Jumonville was ordered to send two couriers back with all speed to Fort Duquesne to inform the commandant that he had found the English, and to acquaint him when he intended to communicate with them.[2] It is difficult to imagine any object for such an order except that of enabling Contrecœur to send to the spot whatever force might be needed to attack the English on their refusal to withdraw. Jumonville had sent the two couriers, and had hidden himself, apparently to wait the result. He lurked nearly two days within five miles of Washington's camp, sent out scouts to reconnoitre it, but gave no notice of his presence; played to perfection the part of a skulking enemy, and brought destruction on himself by conduct which can only be ascribed to a sinister motive on the one hand, or to extreme folly on the other. French deserters told Washington that the party came as spies, and were to show the sum-

---

[1] *Journal of Washington* in *Précis des Faits*, 109. This Journal, which is entirely distinct from that before cited, was found by the French among the baggage left on the field after the defeat of Braddock in 1755, and a translation of it was printed by them as above. The original has disappeared.
[2] The summons and the instructions to Jumonville are in *Précis des Faits*.

mons only if threatened by a superior force. This last assertion is confirmed by the French officer Pouchot, who says that Jumonville, seeing himself the weaker party, tried to show the letter he had brought.[1]

French writers say that, on first seeing the English, Jumonville's interpreter called out that he had something to say to them; but Washington, who was at the head of his men, affirms this to be absolutely false. The French say further that Jumonville was killed in the act of reading the summons. This is also denied by Washington, and rests only on the assertion of the Canadian who ran off at the outset, and on the alleged assertion of Indians who, if present at all, which is unlikely, escaped like the Canadian before the fray began. Druillon, an officer with Jumonville, wrote two letters to Dinwiddie after his capture, to claim the privileges of the bearer of a summons; but while bringing forward every other circumstance in favor of the claim, he does not pretend that the summons was read or shown either before or during the action. The French account of the conduct of Washington's Indians is no less erroneous. "This murder," says a chronicler of the time, "produced on the minds of the savages an effect very different from that which the cruel Vvasinghton had promised himself. They have a horror of crime; and they were so indignant at that which had just been perpetrated before their eyes, that they abandoned him, and offered themselves to us in order to take vengeance."[2] Instead of doing this, they boasted of their part in the fight, scalped all the dead Frenchmen, sent one scalp to the Delawares as an invitation to take up the hatchet for the English, and distributed the rest among the various Ohio tribes to the same end.

Coolness of judgment, a profound sense of public duty, and a strong self-control, were even then the characteristics of Washington; but he was scarcely twenty-two, was full of military ardor, and was vehement and fiery by nature. Yet it is far from certain that, even when age and experience had ripened him, he would have forborne to act as he did, for there was every reason for believing that the designs of the French were hostile; and though by passively waiting the event he would have thrown upon them the responsibility of striking the first blow, he would have exposed his small party to capture or destruction by giving them time to gain reinforcements from Fort Duquesne. It was inevitable that the killing of Jumonville should be greeted in France by an outcry of real or assumed horror; but the Chevalier de Lévis, second in command

[1] Pouchot, *Mémoire sur la dernière Guerre.*
[2] Poulin de Lumina, *Histoire de la Guerre contre les Anglois,* 15.

to Montcalm, probably expresses the true opinion of Frenchmen best fitted to judge when he calls it "a pretended assassination."[1] Judge it as we may, this obscure skirmish began the war that set the world on fire.[2]

Washington returned to the camp at the Great Meadows; and, expecting soon to be attacked, sent for reinforcements to Colonel Fry, who was lying dangerously ill at Wills Creek. Then he set his men to work at an entrenchment, which he named Fort Necessity, and which must have been of the slightest, as they finished it within three days.[3] The Half-King now joined him, along with the female potentate known as Queen Alequippa, and some thirty Indian families. A few days after, Gist came from Wills Creek with news that Fry was dead. Washington succeeded to the command of the regiment, the remaining three companies of which presently appeared and joined their comrades, raising the whole number to three hundred. Next arrived the independent company from South Carolina; and the Great Meadows became an animated scene, with the wigwams of the Indians, the camp-sheds of the rough Virginians, the cattle grazing on the tall grass or drinking at the lazy brook that traversed it; the surrounding heights and forests; and over all, four miles away, the lofty green ridge of Laurel Hill.

The presence of the company of regulars was a doubtful advantage. Captain Mackay, its commander, holding his commission from the King, thought himself above any officer commissioned by the Governor. There was great courtesy between him and Washington; but Mackay would take no orders, nor even the countersign, from the colonel of volunteers. Nor would his men work, except for an additional shilling a day. To give this was impossible, both from want of money, and from the discontent it would have bred in the Virginians, who worked for nothing besides their daily pay of eightpence. Washington, already a leader of men, possessed himself in a patience extremely dif-

---

[1] Lévis, *Mémoire sur la Guerre du Canada.*

[2] On this affair, Sparks, *Writings of Washington,* II. 25–48, 447. *Dinwiddie Papers.* Letter of Contrecœur in *Précis des Faits. Journal of Washington, Ibid.* Washington to Dinwiddie, 3 June, 1754. Dussieux, *Le Canada sous la Domination Française,* 118. Gaspé, *Anciens Canadiens,* appendix, 396. The assertion of Abbé de l'Isle-Dieu, that Jumonville showed a flag of truce, is unsupported. Adam Stephen, who was in the fight, says that the guns of the English were so wet that they had to trust mainly to the bayonet. The Half-King boasted that he killed Jumonville with his tomahawk. Dinwiddie highly approved Washington's conduct.

In 1755 the widow of Jumonville received a pension of one hundred and fifty francs. In 1775 his daughter, Charlotte Aimable, wishing to become a nun, was given by the King six hundred francs for her "trousseau" on entering the convent. *Dossier de Jumonville et de sa Veuve, 22 Mars, 1755. Mémoire pour Mlle. de Jumonville, 10 Juillet, 1775. Réponse du Garde des Sceaux, 25 Juillet, 1775.*

[3] *Journal of Washington* in *Précis des Faits.*

ficult to his passionate temper; but the position was untenable, and the presence of the military drones demoralized his soldiers. Therefore, leaving Mackay at the Meadows, he advanced towards Gist's settlement, cutting a wagon road as he went.

On reaching the settlement the camp was formed and an entrenchment thrown up. Deserters had brought news that strong reinforcements were expected at Fort Duquesne, and friendly Indians repeatedly warned Washington that he would soon be attacked by overwhelming numbers. Forty Indians from the Ohio came to the camp, and several days were spent in councils with them; but they proved for the most part to be spies of the French. The Half-King stood fast by the English, and sent out three of his young warriors as scouts. Reports of attack thickened. Mackay and his men were sent for, and they arrived on the twenty-eighth of June. A council of war was held at Gist's house; and as the camp was commanded by neighboring heights, it was resolved to fall back. The horses were so few that the Virginians had to carry much of the baggage on their backs, and drag nine swivels over the broken and rocky road. The regulars, though they also were raised in the provinces, refused to give the slightest help. Toiling on for two days, they reached the Great Meadows on the first of July. The position, though perhaps the best in the neighborhood, was very unfavorable, and Washington would have retreated farther, but for the condition of his men. They were spent with fatigue, and there was no choice but to stay and fight.

Strong reinforcements had been sent to Fort Duquesne in the spring, and the garrison now consisted of about fourteen hundred men. When news of the death of Jumonville reached Montreal, Coulon de Villiers, brother of the slain officer, was sent to the spot with a body of Indians from all the tribes in the colony. He made such speed that at eight o'clock on the morning of the twenty-sixth of June he reached the fort with his motley following. Here he found that five hundred Frenchmen and a few Ohio Indians were on the point of marching against the English, under Chevalier Le Mercier; but in view of his seniority in rank and his relationship to Jumonville, the command was now transferred to Villiers. Hereupon, the march was postponed; the newly-arrived warriors were called to council, and Contrecœur thus harangued them: "The English have murdered my children; my heart is sick; to-morrow I shall send my French soldiers to take revenge. And now, men of the Saut St. Louis, men of the Lake of Two Mountains, Hurons, Abenakis, Iroquois of La Présentation, Nipissings, Algonquins, and Ottawas,—I invite you all by this belt of wampum to join your French father and help him to crush the assassins. Take this hatchet, and with it two barrels of wine for a feast." Both hatchet and wine were cheerfully accepted. Then Contrecœur turned to the Delawares, who were also present: "By these four strings of wampum I invite you, if you are true children of Onontio, to follow the example of your brethren;" and with some hesitation they also took up the hatchet.

The next day was spent by the Indians in making moccasons for the march, and by the French in preparing for an expedition on a larger scale than had been at first intended. Contrecœur, Villiers, Le Mercier, and Longueuil, after deliberating together, drew up a paper to the effect that "it was fitting (*convenable*) to march against the English with the greatest possible number of French and savages, in order to avenge ourselves and chastise them for having violated the most sacred laws of civilized nations;" that, though their conduct justified the French in disregarding the existing treaty of peace, yet, after thoroughly punishing them, and compelling them to withdraw from the domain of the King, they should be told that, in pursuance of his royal orders, the French looked on them as friends. But it was further agreed that should the English have withdrawn to their own side of the mountains, "they should be followed to their settlements to destroy them and treat them as enemies, till that nation should give ample satisfaction and completely change its conduct."[1]

The party set out on the next morning, paddled their canoes up the Monongahela, encamped, heard Mass; and on the thirtieth reached the deserted storehouse of the Ohio Company at the mouth of Redstone Creek. It was a building of solid logs, well looploled for musketry. To please the Indians by asking their advice, Villiers called all the chiefs to council; which, being concluded to their satisfaction, he left a sergeant's guard at the storehouse to watch the canoes, and began his march through the forest. The path was so rough that at the first halt the chaplain declared he could go no farther, and turned back for the storehouse, though not till he had absolved the whole company in a body. Thus lightened of their sins, they journeyed on, constantly sending out scouts. On the second of July they reached the abandoned camp of Washington at Gist's settlement; and here they bivouacked, tired, and drenched all night by rain. At daybreak they marched again, and passed through the gorge of Laurel Hill. It rained without ceasing; but

---

[1] *Journal de Campagne de M. de Villiers depuis son Arrivée au Fort Duquesne jusqu' à son Retour au dit Fort.* These and other passages are omitted in the Journal as printed in *Précis des Faits.* Before me is a copy from the original in the Archives de la Marine.

Villiers pushed his way through the dripping forest to see the place, half a mile from the road, where his brother had been killed, and where several bodies still lay unburied. They had learned from a deserter the position of the enemy, and Villiers filled the woods in front with a swarm of Indian scouts. The crisis was near. He formed his men in column, and ordered every officer to his place.

Washington's men had had a full day at Fort Necessity; but they spent it less in resting from their fatigue than in strengthening their rampart with logs. The fort was a simple square enclosure, with a trench said by a French writer to be only knee deep. On the south, and partly on the west, there was an exterior embankment, which seems to have been made, like a rifle-pit, with the ditch inside. The Virginians had but little ammunition, and no bread whatever, living chiefly on fresh beef. They knew the approach of the French, who were reported to Washington as nine hundred strong, besides Indians. Towards eleven o'clock a wounded sentinel came in with news that they were close at hand; and they presently appeared at the edge of the woods, yelling, and firing from such a distance that their shot fell harmless. Washington drew up his men on the meadow before the fort, thinking, he says, that the enemy, being greatly superior in force, would attack at once; and choosing for some reason to meet them on the open plain. But Villiers had other views. "We approached the English," he writes, "as near as possible, without uselessly exposing the lives of the King's subjects;" and he and his followers made their way through the forest till they came opposite the fort, where they stationed themselves on two densely wooded hills, adjacent, though separated by a small brook. One of these was about a hundred paces from the English, and the other about sixty. Their position was such that the French and Indians, well sheltered by trees and bushes, and with the advantage of higher ground, could cross their fire upon the fort and enfilade a part of it. Washington had meanwhile drawn his followers within the entrenchment; and the firing now began on both sides. Rain fell all day. The raw earth of the embankment was turned to soft mud, and the men in the ditch of the outwork stood to the knee in water. The swivels brought back from the camp at Gist's farm were mounted on the rampart; but the gunners were so ill protected that the pieces were almost silenced by the French musketry. The fight lasted nine hours. At times the fire on both sides was nearly quenched by the showers, and the bedrenched combatants could do little but gaze at each other through a gray veil of mist and rain. Towards night, however, the fusillade revived, and became sharp again until dark. At eight o'clock the French called out to propose a parley.

Villiers thus gives his reasons for these overtures. "As we had been wet all day by the rain, as the soldiers were very tired, as the savages said that they would leave us the next morning, and as there was a report that drums and the firing of cannon had been heard in the distance, I proposed to M. Le Mercier to offer the English a conference." He says further that ammunition was falling short, and that he thought the enemy might sally in a body and attack him.[1] The English, on their side, were in a worse plight. They were half starved, their powder was nearly spent, their guns were foul, and among them all they had but two screw-rods to clean them. In spite of his desperate position, Washington declined the parley, thinking it a pretext to introduce a spy; but when the French repeated their proposal and requested that he would send an officer to them, he could hesitate no longer. There were but two men with him who knew French, Ensign Peyroney, who was disabled by a wound, and the Dutchman, Captain Vanbraam. To him the unpalatable errand was assigned. After a long absence he returned with articles of capitulation offered by Villiers; and while the officers gathered about him in the rain, he read and interpreted the paper by the glimmer of a sputtering candle kept alight with difficulty. Objection was made to some of the terms, and they were changed. Vanbraam, however, apparently anxious to get the capitulation signed and the affair ended, mistranslated several passages, and rendered the words *l'assassinat du Sieur de Jumonville* as *the death of the Sieur de Jumonville.*[2] As thus understood, the articles were signed about midnight. They provided that the English should march out with drums beating and the honors of war, carrying with them one of their swivels and all their other property; that they should be protected against insult from French or Indians; that the prisoners taken in the affair of Jumonville should be set free; and that two officers should remain as hostages for their safe return to Fort Duquesne. The hostages chosen were Vanbraam and a brave but eccentric Scotchman, Robert Stobo, an acquaintance of the novelist Smollett, said to be the original of his Lismahago.

Washington reports that twelve of the Virginians were killed on the spot, and forty-three wounded, while of the casualties in Mackay's company no returns appear. Villiers reports his own loss at only twenty in

---

[1] *Journal de Villiers*, original. Omitted in the Journal as printed by the French Government. A short and very incorrect abstract of this Journal will be found in *N. Y. Col. Docs.*, X.

[2] See Appendix C. On the fight at Great Meadows, compare Sparks, *Writings of Washington*, II. 456–468; also a letter of Colonel Innes to Governor Hamilton, written a week after the event, in *Colonial Records of Pa.*, VI. 50, and a letter of Adam Stephen in *Pennsylvania Gazette, 1754.*

all.[1] The numbers engaged are uncertain. The six companies of the Virginia regiment counted three hundred and five men and officers, and Mackay's company one hundred; but many were on the sick list, and some had deserted. About three hundred and fifty may have taken part in the fight. On the side of the French, Villiers says that the detachment as originally formed consisted of five hundred white men. These were increased after his arrival at Fort Duquesne, and one of the party reports that seven hundred marched on the expedition.[2] The number of Indians joining them is not given; but as nine tribes and communities contributed to it, and as two barrels of wine were required to give the warriors a parting feast, it must have been considerable. White men and red, it seems clear that the French force was more than twice that of the English, while they were better posted and better sheltered, keeping all day under cover, and never showing themselves on the open meadow. There were no Indians with Washington. Even the Half-King held aloof; though, being of a caustic turn, he did not spare his comments on the fight, telling Conrad Weiser, the provincial interpreter, that the French behaved like cowards, and the English like fools.[3]

In the early morning the fort was abandoned and the retreat began. The Indians had killed all the horses and cattle, and Washington's men were so burdened with the sick and wounded, whom they were obliged to carry on their backs, that most of the baggage was perforce left behind. Even then they could march but a few miles, and then encamped to wait for wagons. The Indians increased the confusion by plundering, and threatening an attack. They knocked to pieces the medicine-chest, thus causing great distress to the wounded, two of whom they murdered and scalped. For a time there was danger of panic; but order was restored, and the wretched march began along the forest road that led over the Alleghanies, fifty-two miles to the station at Wills Creek. Whatever may have been the feelings of Washington, he has left no

---

[1] Dinwiddie writes to the Lords of Trade that thirty in all were killed, and seventy wounded, on the English side; and the commissary Varin writes to Bigot that the French lost seventy-two killed and wounded.

[2] *A Journal had from Thomas Forbes, lately a Private Soldier in the King of France's Service.* (Public Record Office.) Forbes was one of Villiers' soldiers. The commissary Varin puts the number of French at six hundred, besides Indians.

[3] *Journal of Conrad Weiser,* in *Colonial Records of Pa.*, VI. 150. The Half-King also remarked that Washington "was a good-natured man, but had no experience, and would by no means take advice from the Indians, but was always driving them on to fight by his directions; that he lay at one place from one full moon to the other, and made no fortifications at all, except that little thing upon the meadow, where he thought the French would come up to him in open field."

record of them. His immense fortitude was doomed to severer trials in the future; yet perhaps this miserable morning was the darkest of his life. He was deeply moved by sights of suffering; and all around him were wounded men borne along in torture, and weary men staggering under the living load. His pride was humbled, and his young ambition seemed blasted in the bud. It was the fourth of July. He could not foresee that he was to make that day forever glorious to a new-born nation hailing him as its father.

The defeat at Fort Necessity was doubly disastrous to the English, since it was a new step and a long one towards the ruin of their interest with the Indians; and when, in the next year, the smouldering war broke into flame, nearly all the western tribes drew their scalping-knives for France.

Villiers went back exultant to Fort Duquesne, burning on his way the buildings of Gist's settlement and the storehouse at Redstone Creek. Not an English flag now waved beyond the Alleghanies.[1]

---

[1] See Appendix C.

6

The Signal of Battle

1754, 1755

TROUBLES OF DINWIDDIE · GATHERING OF THE BURGESSES · VIRGINIAN
SOCIETY · REFRACTORY LEGISLATORS · THE QUAKER ASSEMBLY · IT
REFUSES TO RESIST THE FRENCH · APATHY OF NEW YORK · SHIRLEY AND
THE GENERAL COURT OF MASSACHUSETTS · SHORT-SIGHTED POLICY ·
ATTITUDE OF ROYAL GOVERNORS · INDIAN ALLIES WAVER · CONVENTION
AT ALBANY · SCHEME OF UNION · IT FAILS · DINWIDDIE AND GLEN ·
DINWIDDIE CALLS ON ENGLAND FOR HELP · THE DUKE OF NEWCASTLE ·
WEAKNESS OF THE BRITISH CABINET · ATTITUDE OF FRANCE · MUTUAL
DISSIMULATION · BOTH POWERS SEND TROOPS TO AMERICA · COLLISION ·
CAPTURE OF THE "ALCIDE" AND THE "LIS"

The defeat of Washington was a heavy blow to the Governor, and he angrily ascribed it to the delay of the expected reinforcements. The King's companies from New York had reached Alexandria, and crawled towards the scene of action with thin ranks, bad discipline, thirty women and children, no tents, no blankets, no knapsacks, and for munitions one barrel of spoiled gunpowder.[1] The case was still worse with the regiment from North Carolina. It was commanded by Colonel Innes, a countryman and friend of Dinwiddie, who wrote to him: "Dear James, I now wish that we had none from your colony but yourself, for I foresee nothing but confusion among

---

[1] *Dinwiddie to the Lords of Trade, 24 July, 1754. Ibid. to Delancey, 20 June, 1754.*

them." The men were, in fact, utterly unmanageable. They had been promised three shillings a day, while the Virginians had only eight-pence; and when they heard on the march that their pay was to be reduced, they mutinied, disbanded, and went home.

"You may easily guess," says Dinwiddie to a London correspondent, "the great fatigue and trouble I have had, which is more than I ever went through in my life." He rested his hopes on the session of his Assembly, which was to take place in August; for he thought that the late disaster would move them to give him money for defending the colony. These meetings of the burgesses were the great social as well as political event of the Old Dominion, and gave a gathering signal to the Virginian gentry scattered far and wide on their lonely plantations. The capital of the province was Williamsburg, a village of about a thousand inhabitants, traversed by a straight and very wide street, and adorned with various public buildings, conspicuous among which was William and Mary College, a respectable structure, unjustly likened by Jefferson to a brick kiln with a roof. The capitol, at the other end of the town, had been burned some years before, and had just risen from its ashes. Not far distant was the so-called Governor's Palace, where Dinwiddie with his wife and two daughters exercised such official hospitality as his moderate salary and Scottish thrift would permit.[1]

In these seasons of festivity the dull and quiet village was transfig-ured. The broad, sandy street, scorching under a southern sun, was thronged with coaches and chariots brought over from London at heavy cost in tobacco, though soon to be bedimmed by Virginia roads and negro care; racing and hard-drinking planters; clergymen of the Estab-lishment, not much more ascetic than their boon companions of the laity; ladies, with manners a little rusted by long seclusion; black coach-men and footmen, proud of their masters and their liveries; young cav-aliers, booted and spurred, sitting their thoroughbreds with the careless grace of men whose home was the saddle. It was a proud little provin-cial society, which might seem absurd in its lofty self-appreciation, had it not soon approved itself so prolific in ability and worth.[2]

The burgesses met, and Dinwiddie made them an opening speech, inveighing against the aggressions of the French, their "contempt of treaties," and "ambitious views for universal monarchy;" and he con-

---

[1] For a contemporary account of Williamsburg, Burnaby, *Travels in North America*, 6. Smyth, *Tour in America*, I. 17, describes it some years later.

[2] The English traveller Smyth, in his *Tour*, gives a curious and vivid picture of Virginian life. For the social condition of this and other colonies before the Revolution, one cannot do better than to consult Lodge's *Short History of the English Colonies*.

cluded: "I could expatiate very largely on these affairs, but my heart burns with resentment at their insolence. I think there is no room for many arguments to induce you to raise a considerable supply to enable me to defeat the designs of these troublesome people and enemies of mankind." The burgesses in their turn expressed the "highest and most becoming resentment," and promptly voted twenty thousand pounds; but on the third reading of the bill they added to it a rider which touched the old question of the pistole fee, and which, in the view of the Governor, was both unconstitutional and offensive. He remonstrated in vain; the stubborn republicans would not yield, nor would he; and again he prorogued them. This unexpected defeat depressed him greatly. "A governor," he wrote, "is really to be pitied in the discharge of his duty to his king and country, in having to do with such obstinate, self-conceited people. . . . I cannot satisfy the burgesses unless I prostitute the rules of government. I have gone through monstrous fatigues. Such wrong-headed people, I thank God, I never had to do with before."[1] A few weeks later he was comforted; for, having again called the burgesses, they gave him the money, without trying this time to humiliate him.[2]

In straining at a gnat and swallowing a camel, aristocratic Virginia was far outdone by democratic Pennsylvania. Hamilton, her governor, had laid before the Assembly a circular letter from the Earl of Holdernesse directing him, in common with other governors, to call on his province for means to repel any invasion which might be made "within the undoubted limits of His Majesty's dominion."[3] The Assembly of Pennsylvania was curiously unlike that of Virginia, as half and often more than half of its members were Quaker tradesmen in sober raiment and broad-brimmed hats; while of the rest, the greater part were Germans who cared little whether they lived under English rule or French, provided that they were left in peace upon their farms. The House replied to the Governor's call: "It would be highly presumptuous in us to pretend to judge of the undoubted limits of His Majesty's dominions;" and they added: "the Assemblies of this province are generally composed of a majority who are constitutionally principled against war, and represent a well-meaning, peaceable people."[4] They then adjourned, telling the Governor that, "As those our limits have not been clearly ascertained to our satisfaction, we fear the precipitate call upon

[1] Dinwiddie to Hamilton, 6 Sept., 1754. Ibid. to J. Abercrombie, 1 Sept., 1754.
[2] Hening, VI. 435.
[3] The Earl of Holdernesse to the Governors in America, 28 Aug. 1753.
[4] Colonial Records of Pa., V. 748.

us as the province invaded cannot answer any good purpose at this time."

In the next month they met again, and again Hamilton asked for means to defend the country. The question was put, Should the Assembly give money for the King's use? and the vote was feebly affirmative. Should the sum be twenty thousand pounds? The vote was overwhelming in the negative. Fifteen thousand, ten thousand, and five thousand, were successively proposed, and the answer was always, No. The House would give nothing but five hundred pounds for a present to the Indians; after which they adjourned "to the sixth of the month called May."[1] At their next meeting they voted to give the Governor ten thousand pounds; but under conditions which made them for some time independent of his veto, and which, in other respects, were contrary to his instructions from the King, as well as from the proprietaries of the province, to whom he had given bonds to secure his obedience. He therefore rejected the bill, and they adjourned. In August they passed a similar vote, with the same result. At their October meeting they evaded his call for supplies. In December they voted twenty thousand pounds, hampered with conditions which were sure to be refused, since Morris, the new governor, who had lately succeeded Hamilton, was under the same restrictions as his predecessor. They told him, however, that in the present case they felt themselves bound by no Act of Parliament, and added: "We hope the Governor, notwithstanding any penal bond he may have entered into, will on reflection think himself at liberty and find it consistent with his safety and honor to give his assent to this bill." Morris, who had taken the highest legal advice on the subject in England, declined to compromise himself, saying: "Consider, gentlemen, in what light you will appear to His Majesty while, instead of contributing towards your own defence, you are entering into an ill-timed controversy concerning the validity of royal instructions which may be delayed to a more convenient time without the least injury to the rights of the people."[2] They would not yield, and told him "that they had rather the French should conquer them than give up their privileges."[3] "Truly," remarks Dinwiddie, "I think they have given their senses a long holiday."

New York was not much behind her sisters in contentious stubbornness. In answer to the Governor's appeal, the Assembly replied: "It

---

[1] *Pennsylvania Archives*, II. 235. *Colonial Records of Pa.*, VI. 22–26. *Works of Franklin*, III. 265.
[2] *Colonial Records of Pa.*, VI. 215.
[3] *Morris to Penn*, 1 Jan. 1755.

appears that the French have built a fort at a place called French Creek, at a considerable distance from the River Ohio, which may, but does not by any evidence or information appear to us to be an invasion of any of His Majesty's colonies."[1] So blind were they as yet to "manifest destiny!" Afterwards, however, on learning the defeat of Washington, they gave five thousand pounds to aid Virginia.[2] Maryland, after long delay, gave six thousand. New Jersey felt herself safe behind the other colonies, and would give nothing. New England, on the other hand, and especially Massachusetts, had suffered so much from French war-parties that they were always ready to fight. Shirley, the governor of Massachusetts, had returned from his bootless errand to settle the boundary question at Paris. His leanings were strongly monarchical; yet he believed in the New Englanders, and was more or less in sympathy with them. Both he and they were strenuous against the French, and they had mutually helped each other to reap laurels in the last war. Shirley was cautious of giving umbrage to his Assembly, and rarely quarrelled with it, except when the amount of his salary was in question. He was not averse to a war with France; for though bred a lawyer, and now past middle life, he flattered himself with hopes of a high military command. On the present occasion, making use of a rumor that the French were seizing the carrying-place between the Chaudière and the Kennebec, he drew from the Assembly a large grant of money, and induced them to call upon him to march in person to the scene of danger. He accordingly repaired to Falmouth (now Portland); and, though the rumor proved false, sent eight hundred men under Captain John Winslow to build two forts on the Kennebec as a measure of precaution.[3]

While to these northern provinces Canada was an old and pestilent enemy, those towards the south scarcely knew her by name; and the idea of French aggression on their borders was so novel and strange that they admitted it with difficulty. Mind and heart were engrossed in strife with their governors: the universal struggle for virtual self-rule. But the war was often waged with a passionate stupidity. The colonist was not then an American; he was simply a provincial, and a narrow one. The time was yet distant when these dissevered and jealous communities should weld themselves into one broad nationality, capable, at need,

---

[1] Address of the Assembly to Lieutenant-Governor Delancey, 23 April, 1754. Lords of Trade to Delancey, 5 July, 1754.
[2] Delancey to Lords of Trade, 8 Oct. 1754.
[3] Massachusetts Archives, 1754. Hutchinson, III. 26. Conduct of Major-General Shirley briefly stated. Journals of the Board of Trade, 1754.

of the mightiest efforts to purge itself of disaffection and vindicate its commanding unity.

In the interest of that practical independence which they had so much at heart, two conditions were essential to the colonists. The one was a field for expansion, and the other was mutual help. Their first necessity was to rid themselves of the French, who, by shutting them between the Alleghanies and the sea, would cramp them into perpetual littleness. With France on their backs, growing while they had no room to grow, they must remain in helpless wardship, dependent on England, whose aid they would always need; but with the West open before them, their future was their own. King and Parliament would respect perforce the will of a people spread from the ocean to the Mississippi, and united in action as in aims. But in the middle of the last century the vision of the ordinary colonist rarely reached so far. The immediate victory over a governor, however slight the point at issue, was more precious in his eyes than the remote though decisive advantage which he saw but dimly.

The governors, representing the central power, saw the situation from the national point of view. Several of them, notably Dinwiddie and Shirley, were filled with wrath at the proceedings of the French; and the former was exasperated beyond measure at the supineness of the provinces. He had spared no effort to rouse them, and had failed. His instincts were on the side of authority; but, under the circumstances, it is hardly to be imputed to him as a very deep offence against human liberty that he advised the compelling of the colonies to raise men and money for their own defence, and proposed, in view of their "intolerable obstinacy and disobedience to his Majesty's commands," that Parliament should tax them half-a-crown a head. The approaching war offered to the party of authority temptations from which the colonies might have saved it by opening their purse-strings without waiting to be told.

The Home Government, on its part, was but half-hearted in the wish that they should unite in opposition to the common enemy. It was very willing that the several provinces should give money and men, but not that they should acquire military habits and a dangerous capacity of acting together. There was one kind of union, however, so obviously necessary, and at the same time so little to be dreaded, that the British Cabinet, instructed by the governors, not only assented to it, but urged it. This was joint action in making treaties with the Indians. The practice of separate treaties, made by each province in its own interest, had bred endless disorders. The adhesion of all the tribes had been so shaken, and the efforts of the French to alienate them were so vigorous and effective, that not a moment was to be lost. Joncaire had gained over most of the Senecas, Piquet was drawing the Onondagas more and more to his mission, and the Dutch of Albany were alienating their best friends, the Mohawks, by encroaching on their lands. Their chief, Hendrick, came to New York with a deputation of the tribe to complain of their wrongs; and finding no redress, went off in anger, declaring that the covenant chain was broken.[1] The authorities in alarm called William Johnson to their aid. He succeeded in soothing the exasperated chief, and then proceeded to the confederate council at Onondaga, where he found the assembled sachems full of anxieties and doubts. "We don't know what you Christians, English and French, intend," said one of their orators. "We are so hemmed in by you both that we have hardly a hunting-place left. In a little while, if we find a bear in a tree, there will immediately appear an owner of the land to claim the property and hinder us from killing it, by which we live. We are so perplexed between you that we hardly know what to say or think."[2] No man had such power over the Five Nations as Johnson. His dealings with them were at once honest, downright, and sympathetic. They loved and trusted him as much as they detested the Indian commissioners at Albany, whom the province of New York had charged with their affairs, and who, being traders, grossly abused their office.

It was to remedy this perilous state of things that the Lords of Trade and Plantations directed the several governors to urge on their assemblies the sending of commissioners to make a joint treaty with the wavering tribes.[3] Seven of the provinces, New York, Pennsylvania, Maryland, and the four New England colonies, acceded to the plan, and sent to Albany, the appointed place of meeting, a body of men who for character and ability had never had an equal on the continent, but whose powers from their respective assemblies were so cautiously limited as to preclude decisive action. They met in the court-house of the little frontier city. A large "chain-belt" of wampum was provided, on which the King was symbolically represented, holding in his embrace the colonies, the Five Nations, and all their allied tribes. This was presented to the assembled warriors, with a speech in which the misdeeds of the French were not forgotten. The chief, Hendrick, made a much better speech in reply. "We do now solemnly renew and

[1] *N. Y. Col. Docs.*, VI. 788. *Colonial Records of Pa.*, V. 625.
[2] *N. Y. Col. Docs.*, VI. 813.
[3] *Circular Letter of Lords of Trade to Governors in America, 18 Sept. 1753. Lords of Trade to Sir Danvers Osborne*, in *N. Y. Col. Docs.*, VI. 800.

brighten the covenant chain. We shall take the chain-belt to Onondaga, where our council-fire always burns, and keep it so safe that neither thunder nor lightning shall break it." The commissioners had blamed them for allowing so many of their people to be drawn away to Piquet's mission. "It is true," said the orator, "that we live disunited. We have tried to bring back our brethren, but in vain; for the Governor of Canada is like a wicked, deluding spirit. You ask why we are so dispersed. The reason is that you have neglected us for these three years past." Here he took a stick and threw it behind him. "You have thus thrown us behind your back; whereas the French are a subtle and vigilant people, always using their utmost endeavors to seduce and bring us over to them." He then told them that it was not the French alone who invaded the country of the Indians. "The Governor of Virginia and the Governor of Canada are quarrelling about lands which belong to us, and their quarrel may end in our destruction." And he closed with a burst of sarcasm. "We would have taken Crown Point [*in the last war*], but you prevented us. Instead, you burned your own fort at Saratoga and ran away from it,—which was a shame and a scandal to you. Look about your country and see: you have no fortifications; no, not even in this city. It is but a step from Canada hither, and the French may come and turn you out of doors. You desire us to speak from the bottom of our hearts, and we shall do it. Look at the French: they are men; they are fortifying everywhere. But you are all like women, bare and open, without fortifications."[1]

Hendrick's brother Abraham now took up the word, and begged that Johnson might be restored to the management of Indian affairs, which he had formerly held; "for," said the chief, "we love him and he us, and he has always been our good and trusty friend." The commissioners had not power to grant the request, but the Indians were assured that it should not be forgotten; and they returned to their villages soothed, but far from satisfied. Nor were the commissioners empowered to take any effective steps for fortifying the frontier.

The congress now occupied itself with another matter. Its members were agreed that great danger was impending; that without wise and just treatment of the tribes, the French would gain them all, build forts along the back of the British colonies, and, by means of ships and troops from France, master them one by one, unless they would combine for mutual defence. The necessity of some form of union had at

---

[1] *Proceedings of the Congress at Albany, N. Y. Col. Docs.*, VI. 853. A few verbal changes, for the sake of brevity, are made in the above extracts.

length begun to force itself upon the colonial mind. A rough woodcut had lately appeared in the *Pennsylvania Gazette,* figuring the provinces under the not very flattering image of a snake cut to pieces, with the motto, "Join, or die." A writer of the day held up the Five Nations for emulation, observing that if ignorant savages could confederate, British colonists might do as much.[1] Franklin, the leading spirit of the congress, now laid before it his famous project of union, which has been too often described to need much notice here. Its fate is well known. The Crown rejected it because it gave too much power to the colonies; the colonies, because it gave too much power to the Crown, and because it required each of them to transfer some of its functions of self-government to a central council. Another plan was afterwards devised by the friends of prerogative, perfectly agreeable to the King, since it placed all power in the hands of a council of governors, and since it involved compulsory taxation of the colonists, who, for the same reasons, would have doggedly resisted it, had an attempt been made to carry it into effect.[2]

Even if some plan of union had been agreed upon, long delay must have followed before its machinery could be set in motion; and meantime there was need of immediate action. War-parties of Indians from Canada, set on, it was thought, by the Governor, were already burning and murdering among the border settlements of New York and New Hampshire. In the south Dinwiddie grew more and more alarmed, "for the French are like so many locusts; they are collected in bodies in a most surprising manner; their number now on the Ohio is from twelve hundred to fifteen hundred." He writes to Lord Granville that, in his opinion, they aim to conquer the continent, and that "the obstinacy of this stubborn generation" exposes the country "to the merciless rage of a rapacious enemy." What vexed him even more than the apathy of the assemblies was the conduct of his brother-governor, Glen of South Carolina, who, apparently piqued at the conspicuous part Dinwiddie was acting, wrote to him in a "very dictatorial style," found fault with his measures, jested at his activity in writing letters, and even questioned the right of England to lands on the Ohio; till he was moved at last to retort: "I cannot help observing that your letters and arguments would have been more proper from a French officer than from one of His Majesty's governors. My conduct has met with His Majesty's gra-

---

[1] Kennedy, *Importance of gaining and preserving the Friendship of the Indians.*
[2] On the Albany plan of union, *Franklin's Works,* I. 177. Shirley thought it "a great strain upon the prerogative of the Crown," and was for requiring the colonies to raise money and men "without farther consulting them upon any points whatever." *Shirley to Robinson, 24 Dec. 1754.*

cious approbation; and I am sorry it has not received yours." Thus discouraged, even in quarters where he had least reason to expect it, he turned all his hopes to the Home Government; again recommended a tax by Act of Parliament, and begged, in repeated letters, for arms, munitions, and two regiments of infantry.[1] His petition was not made in vain.

England at this time presented the phenomenon of a prime minister who could not command the respect of his own servants. A more preposterous figure than the Duke of Newcastle never stood at the head of a great nation. He had a feverish craving for place and power, joined to a total unfitness for both. He was an adept in personal politics, and was so busied with the arts of winning and keeping office that he had no leisure, even if he had had ability, for the higher work of government. He was restless, quick in movement, rapid and confused in speech, lavish of worthless promises, always in a hurry, and at once headlong, timid, and rash. "A borrowed importance and real insignificance," says Walpole, who knew him well, "gave him the perpetual air of a solicitor. . . . He had no pride, though infinite self-love. He loved business immoderately; yet was only always doing it, never did it. When left to himself, he always plunged into difficulties, and then shuddered for the consequences." Walpole gives an anecdote showing the state of his ideas on colonial matters. General Ligonier suggested to him that Annapolis ought to be defended. "To which he replied with his lisping, evasive hurry: 'Annapolis, Annapolis! Oh, yes, Annapolis must be defended; to be sure, Annapolis should be defended,—where is Annapolis?'"[2] Another contemporary, Smollett, ridicules him in his novel of *Humphrey Clinker*, and tells a similar story, which, founded in fact or not, shows in what estimation the minister was held: "Captain C. treated the Duke's character without any ceremony. 'This wiseacre,' said he, 'is still abed; and I think the best thing he can do is to sleep on till Christmas; for when he gets up he does nothing but expose his own folly. In the beginning of the war he told me in a great fright that thirty thousand French had marched from Acadia to Cape Breton. Where did they find transports? said I.—Transports! cried he, I tell you they marched by land.—By land to the island of Cape Breton!—What, is Cape Breton an island?—Certainly.—Ha! are you sure of that?—When I pointed it out on the map, he examined it earnestly

---

[1] *Dinwiddie Papers*; letters to Granville, Albemarle, Halifax, Fox, Holdernesse, Horace Walpole, and Lords of Trade.
[2] Walpole, *George II.*, I. 344.

with his spectacles; then, taking me in his arms,—My dear C., cried he, you always bring us good news. Egad! I'll go directly and tell the King that Cape Breton is an island.' "

His wealth, county influence, flagitious use of patronage, and long-practised skill in keeping majorities in the House of Commons by means that would not bear the light, made his support necessary to Pitt himself, and placed a fantastic political jobber at the helm of England in a time when she needed a patriot and a statesman. Newcastle was the growth of the decrepitude and decay of a great party, which had fulfilled its mission and done its work. But if the Whig soil had become poor for a wholesome crop, it was never so rich for toadstools.

Sir Thomas Robinson held the Southern Department, charged with the colonies; and Lord Mahon remarks of him that the Duke had achieved the feat of finding a secretary of state more incapable than himself. He had the lead of the House of Commons. "Sir Thomas Robinson lead us!" said Pitt to Henry Fox; "the Duke might as well send his jackboot to lead us." The active and aspiring Halifax was at the head of the Board of Trade and Plantations. The Duke of Cumberland commanded the army,—an indifferent soldier, though a brave one; harsh, violent, and headlong. Anson, the celebrated navigator, was First Lord of the Admiralty,—a position in which he disappointed everybody.

In France the true ruler was Madame de Pompadour, once the King's mistress, now his procuress, and a sort of feminine prime minister. Machault d'Arnouville was at the head of the Marine and Colonial Department. The diplomatic representatives of the two Crowns were more conspicuous for social than for political talents. Of Mirepoix, French ambassador at London, Marshal Saxe had once observed: "It is a good appointment; he can teach the English to dance." Walpole says concerning him: "He could not even learn to pronounce the names of our games of cards,—which, however, engaged most of the hours of his negotiation. We were to be bullied out of our colonies by an apprentice at whist!" Lord Albemarle, English ambassador at Versailles, is held up by Chesterfield as an example to encourage his son in the pursuit of the graces: "What do you think made our friend Lord Albemarle colonel of a regiment of Guards, Governor of Virginia, Groom of the Stole, and ambassador to Paris,—amounting in all to sixteen or seventeen thousand pounds a year? Was it his birth? No; a Dutch gentleman only. Was it his estate? No; he had none. Was it his learning, his parts, his political abilities and application? You can answer these questions as easily and as soon as I can ask them. What was it then? Many people wondered; but I do not, for I know, and will tell you,— it was his air, his address, his manners, and his graces."

The rival nations differed widely in military and naval strength. England had afloat more than two hundred ships of war, some of them of great force; while the navy of France counted little more than half the number. On the other hand, England had reduced her army to eighteen thousand men, and France had nearly ten times as many under arms. Both alike were weak in leadership. That rare son of the tempest, a great commander, was to be found in neither of them since the death of Saxe.

In respect to the approaching crisis, the interests of the two Powers pointed to opposite courses of action. What France needed was time. It was her policy to put off a rupture, wreathe her face in diplomatic smiles, and pose in an attitude of peace and good faith, while increasing her navy, reinforcing her garrisons in America, and strengthening her positions there. It was the policy of England to attack at once, and tear up the young encroachments while they were yet in the sap, before they could strike root and harden into stiff resistance.

When, on the fourteenth of November, the King made his opening speech to the Houses of Parliament, he congratulated them on the prevailing peace, and assured them that he should improve it to promote the trade of his subjects, "and protect those possessions which constitute one great source of their wealth." America was not mentioned; but his hearers understood him, and made a liberal grant for the service of the year.[1] Two regiments, each of five hundred men, had already been ordered to sail for Virginia, where their numbers were to be raised by enlistment to seven hundred.[2] Major-General Braddock, a man after the Duke of Cumberland's own heart, was appointed to the chief command. The two regiments—the forty-fourth and the forty-eighth—embarked at Cork in the middle of January. The soldiers detested the service, and many had deserted. More would have done so had they foreseen what awaited them.

This movement was no sooner known at Versailles than a counter expedition was prepared on a larger scale. Eighteen ships of war were fitted for sea at Brest and Rochefort, and the six battalions of La Reine, Bourgogne, Languedoc, Guienne, Artois, and Béarn, three thousand

[1] Entick, *Late War*, I. 118.
[2] *Robinson to Lords of the Admiralty*, 30 Sept. 1754. Ibid., *to Board of Ordnance*, 10 Oct. 1754. Ibid., *Circular Letter to American Governors*, 26 Oct. 1754. *Instructions to our Trusty and Well-beloved Edward Braddock*, 25 Nov. 1754.

men in all, were ordered on board for Canada. Baron Dieskau, a German veteran who had served under Saxe, was made their general; and with him went the new governor of French America, the Marquis de Vaudreuil, destined to succeed Duquesne, whose health was failing under the fatigues of his office. Admiral Dubois de la Motte commanded the fleet; and lest the English should try to intercept it, another squadron of nine ships, under Admiral Macnamara, was ordered to accompany it to a certain distance from the coast. There was long and tedious delay. Doreil, commissary of war, who had embarked with Vaudreuil and Dieskau in the same ship, wrote from the harbor of Brest on the twenty-ninth of April: "At last I think we are off. We should have been outside by four o'clock this morning, if M. de Macnamara had not been obliged to ask Count Dubois de la Motte to wait till noon to mend some important part of the rigging (I don't know the name of it) which was broken. It is precious time lost, and gives the English the advantage over us of two tides. I talk of these things as a blind man does of colors. What is certain is that Count Dubois de la Motte is very impatient to get away, and that the King's fleet destined for Canada is in very able and zealous hands. It is now half-past two. In half an hour all may be ready, and we may get out of the harbor before night." He was again disappointed; it was the third of May before the fleet put to sea.[1]

During these preparations there was active diplomatic correspondence between the two Courts. Mirepoix demanded why British troops were sent to America. Sir Thomas Robinson answered that there was no intention to disturb the peace or offend any Power whatever; yet the secret orders to Braddock were the reverse of pacific. Robinson asked on his part the purpose of the French armament at Brest and Rochefort; and the answer, like his own, was a protestation that no hostility was meant. At the same time Mirepoix in the name of the King proposed that orders should be given to the American governors on both sides to refrain from all acts of aggression. But while making this proposal the French Court secretly sent orders to Duquesne to attack and destroy Fort Halifax, one of the two forts lately built by Shirley on the Kennebec,—a river which, by the admission of the French themselves, belonged to the English. But, in making this attack, the French Governor was expressly enjoined to pretend that he acted with-

---

[1] *Lettres de Cremille, de Rostaing, et de Doreil au Ministre, Avril 18, 24, 28, 29, 1755. Liste des Vaisseaux de Guerre qui composent l'Escadre armée à Brest, 1755. Journal of M. de Vaudreuil's Voyage to Canada,* in N. Y. Col. Docs., X. 297. Pouchot, I. 25.

out orders.[1] He was also told that, if necessary, he might make use of the Indians to harass the English.[2] Thus there was good faith on neither part; but it is clear through all the correspondence that the English expected to gain by precipitating an open rupture, and the French by postponing it. Projects of convention were proposed on both sides, but there was no agreement. The English insisted as a preliminary condition that the French should evacuate all the western country as far as the Wabash. Then ensued a long discussion of their respective claims, as futile as the former discussion at Paris on Acadian boundaries.[3]

The British Court knew perfectly the naval and military preparations of the French. Lord Albemarle had died at Paris in December; but the secretary of the embassy, De Cosne, sent to London full information concerning the fleet at Brest and Rochefort.[4] On this, Admiral Boscawen, with eleven ships of the line and one frigate, was ordered to intercept it; and as his force was plainly too small, Admiral Holbourne, with seven more ships, was sent, nearly three weeks after, to join him if he could. Their orders were similar,—to capture or destroy any French vessels bound to North America.[5] Boscawen, who got to sea before La Motte, stationed himself near the southern coast of Newfoundland to cut him off; but most of the French squadron eluded him, and safely made their way, some to Louisbourg, and the others to Quebec. Thus the English expedition was, in the main, a failure. Three of the French ships, however, lost in fog and rain, had become separated from the rest, and lay rolling and tossing on an angry sea not far from Cape Race. One of them was the "Alcide," commanded by Captain Hocquart; the others were the "Lis" and the "Dauphin." The wind fell; but the fogs continued at intervals; till, on the afternoon of the seventh of June, the weather having cleared, the watchman on the maintop saw the distant ocean studded with ships. It was the fleet of Boscawen. Hocquart, who gives the account, says that in the morning they were within three leagues of him, crowding all sail in pursuit. Towards eleven o'clock one of them, the "Dunkirk," was abreast of him to windward, within short speaking distance; and the ship of the Admiral, dis-

[1] *Machault à Duquesne, 17 Fév. 1755.* The letter of Mirepoix proposing mutual abstinence from aggression, is dated on the 6th of the same month. The French dreaded Fort Halifax, because they thought it prepared the way for an advance on Quebec by way of the Chaudière.
[2] *Ibid.*
[3] This correspondence is printed among the *Pièces justificatives* of the *Précis des Faits.*
[4] Particulars in Entick, I. 121.
[5] *Secret Instructions for our Trusty and Well-beloved Edward Boscawen, Esq., Vice-Admiral of the Blue, 16 April, 1755. Most secret Instructions for Francis Holbourne, Esq., Rear-Admiral of the Blue, 9 May, 1755. Robinson to Lords of the Admiralty, 8 May, 1755.*

playing a red flag as a signal to engage, was not far off. Hocquart called out: "Are we at peace, or war?" He declares that Howe, captain of the "Dunkirk," replied in French: "La paix, la paix." Hocquart then asked the name of the British admiral; and on hearing it said: "I know him; he is a friend of mine." Being asked his own name in return, he had scarcely uttered it when the batteries of the "Dunkirk" belched flame and smoke, and volleyed a tempest of iron upon the crowded decks of the "Alcide." She returned the fire, but was forced at length to strike her colors. Rostaing, second in command of the troops, was killed; and six other officers, with about eighty men, were killed or wounded.[1] At the same time the "Lis" was attacked and overpowered. She had on board eight companies of the battalions of La Reine and Languedoc. The third French ship, the "Dauphin," escaped under cover of a rising fog.[2]

Here at last was an end to negotiation. The sword was drawn and brandished in the eyes of Europe.

[1] *Liste des Officiers tués et blessés dans le Combat de l'Alcide et du Lis.*

[2] Hocquart's account is given in full by Pichon, *Lettres et Mémoires pour servir à l'Histoire du Cap-Breton*. The short account in *Précis des Faits*, 272, seems, too, to be drawn from Hocquart. Also *Boscawen to Robinson, 22 June, 1755. Vaudreuil au Ministre, 24 Juillet, 1755.* Entick, I. 137.

Some English accounts say that Captain Howe, in answer to the question, "Are we at peace, or war?" returned, "I don't know; but you had better prepare for war." Boscawen places the action on the 10th, instead of the 8th, and puts the English loss at seven killed and twenty-seven wounded.

7
Braddock
1755

"I have the pleasure to acquaint you that General Braddock came to my house last Sunday night," writes Dinwiddie, at the end of February, to Governor Dobbs of North Carolina. Braddock had landed at Hampton from the ship "Centurion," along with young Commodore Keppel, who commanded the American squadron. "I am mighty glad," again writes Dinwiddie, "that the General is arrived, which I hope will give me some ease; for these twelve months past I have been a perfect slave." He conceived golden opinions of his guest. "He is, I think, a very fine officer, and a sensible, considerate gentleman. He and I live in great harmony."

Had he known him better, he might have praised him less. William Shirley, son of the Governor of Massachusetts, was Braddock's secretary; and after an acquaintance of some months wrote to his friend Governor Morris: "We have a general most judiciously chosen for being disqualified for the service he is employed in in almost every respect. He may be brave for aught I know, and he is honest in pecuniary matters."[1] The astute Franklin, who also had good opportunity of knowing him, says: "This general was, I think, a brave man, and might probably have made a good figure in some European war. But he had too much self-confidence; too high an opinion of the validity of regular troops; too mean a one of both Americans and Indians."[2] Horace Walpole, in his function of gathering and immortalizing the gossip of his time, has left a sharply drawn sketch of Braddock in two letters to Sir Horace Mann, written in the summer of this year: "I love to give you an idea of our characters as they rise upon the stage of history. Braddock is a very Iroquois in disposition. He had a sister who, having gamed away all her little fortune at Bath, hanged herself with a truly English deliberation, leaving only a note upon the table with those lines: 'To die is landing on some silent shore,' etc. When Braddock was told of it, he only said: 'Poor Fanny! I always thought she would play till she would be forced to *tuck herself up*.' " Under the name of Miss Sylvia S——, Goldsmith, in his life of Nash, tells the story of this unhappy woman. She was a rash but warm-hearted creature, reduced to penury and dependence, not so much by a passion for cards as by her lavish generosity to a lover ruined by his own follies, and with whom her relations are said to have been entirely innocent. Walpole continues: "But a more ridiculous story of Braddock, and which is recorded in heroics by Fielding in his *Covent Garden Tragedy*, was an amorous discussion he had formerly with a Mrs. Upton, who kept him. He had gone the greatest lengths with her pin-money, and was still craving. One day, that he was very pressing, she pulled out her purse and showed him that she had but twelve or fourteen shillings left. He twitched it from her: 'Let me see that.' Tied up at the other end he found five guineas. He took them, tossed the empty purse in her face, saying: 'Did you mean to cheat me?' and never went near her more. Now you are acquainted with General Braddock."

"He once had a duel with Colonel Gumley, Lady Bath's brother, who had been his great friend. As they were going to engage, Gumley, who had good-humor and wit (Braddock had the latter), said: 'Braddock, you are a poor dog! Here, take my purse; if you kill me, you will be forced to run away, and then you will not have a shilling to support you.' Braddock refused the purse, insisted on the duel, was disarmed,

---

[1] *Shirley the younger to Morris, 23 May, 1755.*
[2] Franklin, *Autobiography*.

and would not even ask his life. However, with all his brutality, he has
lately been governor of Gibraltar, where he made himself adored, and
where scarce any governor was endured before."[1]

Another story is told of him by an accomplished actress of the time,
George Anne Bellamy, whom Braddock had known from girlhood, and
with whom his present relations seem to have been those of an elderly
adviser and friend. "As we were walking in the Park one day, we heard
a poor fellow was to be chastised; when I requested the General to beg
off the offender. Upon his application to the general officer, whose
name was Dury, he asked Braddock how long since he had divested
himself of the brutality and insolence of his manners? To which the
other replied: 'You never knew me insolent to my inferiors. It is only
to such rude men as yourself that I behave with the spirit which I think
they deserve.' "

Braddock made a visit to the actress on the evening before he left
London for America. "Before we parted," she says, "the General told
me that he should never see me more; for he was going with a handful
of men to conquer whole nations; and to do this they must cut their
way through unknown woods. He produced a map of the country, saying at the same time: 'Dear Pop, we are sent like sacrifices to the altar,' "[2]—a strange presentiment for a man of his sturdy temper.

Whatever were his failings, he feared nothing, and his fidelity and
honor in the discharge of public trusts were never questioned. "Desperate in his fortune, brutal in his behavior, obstinate in his sentiments,"
again writes Walpole, "he was still intrepid and capable."[3] He was a
veteran in years and in service, having entered the Coldstream Guards
as ensign in 1710.

The transports bringing the two regiments from Ireland all arrived
safely at Hampton, and were ordered to proceed up the Potomac to
Alexandria, where a camp was to be formed. Thither, towards the end
of March, went Braddock himself, along with Keppel and Dinwiddie,
in the Governor's coach; while his aide-de-camp, Orme, his secretary,
Shirley, and the servants of the party followed on horseback. Braddock
had sent for the elder Shirley and other provincial governors to meet
him in council; and on the fourteenth of April they assembled in a tent
of the newly formed encampment. Here was Dinwiddie, who thought
his troubles at an end, and saw in the red-coated soldiery the near

[1] *Letters of Horace Walpole* (1866), II. 459, 461. It is doubtful if Braddock was ever governor of
Gibraltar; though, as Mr. Sargent shows, he once commanded a regiment there.
[2] *Apology for the Life of George Anne Bellamy, written by herself*, II. 204 (London, 1786).
[3] Walpole, *George II.*, I. 390.

fruition of his hopes. Here, too, was his friend and ally, Dobbs of North
Carolina; with Morris of Pennsylvania, fresh from Assembly quarrels;
Sharpe of Maryland, who, having once been a soldier, had been made
a sort of provisional commander-in-chief before the arrival of Braddock;
and the ambitious Delancey of New York, who had lately led the opposition against the Governor of that province, and now filled the office himself,—a position that needed all his manifold adroitness. But,
next to Braddock, the most noteworthy man present was Shirley, governor of Massachusetts. There was a fountain of youth in this old lawyer. A few years before, when he was boundary commissioner in Paris,
he had had the indiscretion to marry a young Catholic French girl, the
daughter of his landlord; and now, when more than sixty years old, he
thirsted for military honors, and delighted in contriving operations of
war. He was one of a very few in the colonies who at this time entertained the idea of expelling the French from the continent. He held
that Carthage must be destroyed; and, in spite of his Parisian marriage,
was the foremost advocate of the root-and-branch policy. He and Lawrence, governor of Nova Scotia, had concerted an attack on the French
fort of Beauséjour; and, jointly with others in New England, he had
planned the capture of Crown Point, the key of Lake Champlain. By
these two strokes and by fortifying the portage between the Kennebec
and the Chaudière, he thought that the northern colonies would be
saved from invasion, and placed in a position to become themselves
invaders. Then, by driving the enemy from Niagara, securing that important pass, and thus cutting off the communication between Canada
and her interior dependencies, all the French posts in the West would
die of inanition.[1] In order to commend these schemes to the Home
Government, he had painted in gloomy colors the dangers that beset
the British colonies. Our Indians, he said, will all desert us if we submit
to French encroachment. Some of the provinces are full of negro slaves,
ready to rise against their masters, and of Roman Catholics, Jacobites,
indented servants, and other dangerous persons, who would aid the
French in raising a servile insurrection. Pennsylvania is in the hands of
Quakers, who will not fight, and of Germans, who are likely enough to
join the enemy. The Dutch of Albany would do anything to save their
trade. A strong force of French regulars might occupy that place without resistance, then descend the Hudson, and, with the help of a naval
force, capture New York and cut the British colonies asunder.[2]

    The plans against Crown Point and Beauséjour had already found the

[1] *Correspondence of Shirley, 1754, 1755.*
[2] *Shirley to Robinson, 24 Jan. 1755.*

approval of the Home Government and the energetic support of all the New England colonies. Preparation for them was in full activity; and it was with great difficulty that Shirley had disengaged himself from these cares to attend the council at Alexandria. He and Dinwiddie stood in the front of opposition to French designs. As they both defended the royal prerogative and were strong advocates of taxation by Parliament, they have found scant justice from American writers. Yet the British colonies owed them a debt of gratitude, and the American States owe it still.

Braddock laid his instructions before the Council, and Shirley found them entirely to his mind; while the General, on his part, fully approved the schemes of the Governor. The plan of the campaign was settled. The French were to be attacked at four points at once. The two British regiments lately arrived were to advance on Fort Duquesne; two new regiments, known as Shirley's and Pepperell's, just raised in the provinces, and taken into the King's pay, were to reduce Niagara; a body of provincials from New England, New York, and New Jersey was to seize Crown Point; and another body of New England men to capture Beauséjour and bring Acadia to complete subjection. Braddock himself was to lead the expedition against Fort Duquesne. He asked Shirley, who, though a soldier only in theory, had held the rank of colonel since the last war, to charge himself with that against Niagara; and Shirley eagerly assented. The movement on Crown Point was intrusted to Colonel William Johnson, by reason of his influence over the Indians and his reputation for energy, capacity, and faithfulness. Lastly, the Acadian enterprise was assigned to Lieutenant-Colonel Monckton, a regular officer of merit.

To strike this-fourfold blow in time of peace was a scheme worthy of Newcastle and of Cumberland. The pretext was that the positions to be attacked were all on British soil; that in occupying them the French had been guilty of invasion; and that to expel the invaders would be an act of self-defence. Yet in regard to two of these positions, the French, if they had no other right, might at least claim one of prescription. Crown Point had been twenty-four years in their undisturbed possession, while it was three quarters of a century since they first occupied Niagara; and, though New York claimed the ground, no serious attempt had been made to dislodge them.

Other matters now engaged the Council. Braddock, in accordance with his instructions, asked the governors to urge upon their several assemblies the establishment of a general fund for the service of the campaign; but the governors were all of opinion that the assemblies would refuse,—each being resolved to keep the control of its money in its own hands; and all present, with one voice, advised that the colonies should be compelled by Act of Parliament to contribute in due proportion to the support of the war. Braddock next asked if, in the judgment of the Council, it would not be well to send Colonel Johnson with full powers to treat with the Five Nations, who had been driven to the verge of an outbreak by the misconduct of the Dutch Indian commissioners at Albany. The measure was cordially approved, as was also another suggestion of the General, that vessels should be built at Oswego to command Lake Ontario. The Council then dissolved.

Shirley hastened back to New England, burdened with the preparation for three expeditions and the command of one of them. Johnson, who had been in the camp, though not in the Council, went back to Albany, provided with a commission as sole superintendent of Indian affairs, and charged, besides, with the enterprise against Crown Point; while an express was despatched to Monckton at Halifax, with orders to set at once to his work of capturing Beauséjour.[1]

In regard to Braddock's part of the campaign, there had been a serious error. If, instead of landing in Virginia and moving on Fort Duquesne by the long and circuitous route of Wills Creek, the two regiments had disembarked at Philadelphia and marched westward, the way would have been shortened, and would have lain through one of the richest and most populous districts on the continent, filled with supplies of every kind. In Virginia, on the other hand, and in the adjoining province of Maryland, wagons, horses, and forage were scarce. The enemies of the Administration ascribed this blunder to the influence of the Quaker merchant, John Hanbury, whom the Duke of Newcastle had consulted as a person familiar with American affairs. Hanbury, who was a prominent stockholder in the Ohio Company, and who traded largely in Virginia, saw it for his interest that the troops should pass that way; and is said to have brought the Duke to this opinion.[2] A writer of the time thinks that if they had landed in Pennsylvania, forty thousand pounds would have been saved in money, and six weeks in time.[3]

---

[1] *Minutes of a Council held at the Camp at Alexandria, in Virginia, April 14, 1755. Instructions to Major-General Braddock, 25 Nov. 1754. Secret Instructions to Major-General Braddock, same date. Napier to Braddock, written by Order of the Duke of Cumberland, 25 Nov. 1754,* in *Précis des Faits, Pièces justificatives,* 168. Orme, *Journal of Braddock's Expedition. Instructions to Governor Shirley. Correspondence of Shirley. Correspondence of Braddock* (Public Record Office). *Johnson Papers. Dinwiddie Papers. Pennsylvania Archives,* II.

[2] *Shebbeare's Tracts,* Letter I. Dr. Shebbeare was a political pamphleteer, pilloried by one ministry, and rewarded by the next. He certainly speaks of Hanbury, though he does not give his name. Compare Sargent, 107, 162.

[3] *Gentleman's Magazine,* Aug. 1755.

Not only were supplies scarce, but the people showed such unwillingness to furnish them, and such apathy in aiding the expedition, that even Washington was provoked to declare that "they ought to be chastised."[1] Many of them thought that the alarm about French encroachment was a device of designing politicians; and they did not awake to a full consciousness of the peril till it was forced upon them by a deluge of calamities, produced by the purblind folly of their own representatives, who, instead of frankly promoting the expedition, displayed a perverse and exasperating narrowness which chafed Braddock to fury. He praises the New England colonies, and echoes Dinwiddie's declaration that they have shown a "fine martial spirit," and he commends Virginia as having done far better than her neighbors; but for Pennsylvania he finds no words to express his wrath.[2] He knew nothing of the intestine war between proprietaries and people, and hence could see no palliation for a conduct which threatened to ruin both the expedition and the colony. Everything depended on speed, and speed was impossible; for stores and provisions were not ready, though notice to furnish them had been given months before. The quartermaster-general, Sir John Sinclair, "stormed like a lion rampant," but with small effect.[3] Contracts broken or disavowed, want of horses, want of wagons, want of forage, want of wholesome food, or sufficient food of any kind, caused such delay that the report of it reached England, and drew from Walpole the comment that Braddock was in no hurry to be scalped. In reality he was maddened with impatience and vexation.

A powerful ally presently came to his aid in the shape of Benjamin Franklin, then postmaster-general of Pennsylvania. That sagacious personage,—the sublime of common-sense, about equal in his instincts and motives of character to the respectable average of the New England that produced him, but gifted with a versatile power of brain rarely matched on earth,—was then divided between his strong desire to repel a danger of which he saw the imminence, and his equally strong antagonism to the selfish claims of the Penns, proprietaries of Pennsylvania. This last motive had determined his attitude towards their representative, the Governor, and led him into an opposition as injurious to the military good name of the province as it was favorable to its political longings. In the present case there was no such conflict of inclinations; he could help Braddock without hurting Pennsylvania. He and his son

[1]*Writings of Washington*, II. 78. He speaks of the people of Pennsylvania.
[2]*Braddock to Robinson, 18 March, 19 April, 5 June, 1755*, etc. On the attitude of Pennsylvania, *Colonial Records of Pa.*, VI., *passim.*
[3]*Colonial Records of Pa.*, VI. 368.

had visited the camp, and found the General waiting restlessly for the report of the agents whom he had sent to collect wagons. "I stayed with him," says Franklin, "several days, and dined with him daily. When I was about to depart, the returns of wagons to be obtained were brought in, by which it appeared that they amounted only to twenty-five, and not all of these were in serviceable condition." On this the General and his officers declared that the expedition was at an end, and denounced the Ministry for sending them into a country void of the means of transportation. Franklin remarked that it was a pity they had not landed in Pennsylvania, where almost every farmer had his wagon. Braddock caught eagerly at his words, and begged that he would use his influence to enable the troops to move. Franklin went back to Pennsylvania, issued an address to the farmers appealing to their interest and their fears, and in a fortnight procured a hundred and fifty wagons, with a large number of horses.[1] Braddock, grateful to his benefactor, and enraged at everybody else, pronounced him "Almost the only instance of ability and honesty I have known in these provinces."[2] More wagons and more horses gradually arrived, and at the eleventh hour the march began.

On the tenth of May Braddock reached Wills Creek, where the whole force was now gathered, having marched thither by detachments along the banks of the Potomac. This old trading-station of the Ohio Company had been transformed into a military post and named Fort Cumberland. During the past winter the independent companies which had failed Washington in his need had been at work here to prepare a base of operations for Braddock. Their axes had been of more avail than their muskets. A broad wound had been cut in the bosom of the forest, and the murdered oaks and chestnuts turned into ramparts, barracks, and magazines. Fort Cumberland was an enclosure of logs set upright in the ground, pierced with loopholes, and armed with ten small cannon. It stood on a rising ground near the point where Wills Creek joined the Potomac, and the forest girded it like a mighty hedge, or rather like a paling of gaunt brown stems upholding a canopy of green. All around spread illimitable woods, wrapping hill, valley, and mountain. The spot was an oasis in a desert of leaves,—if the name oasis can be given to anything so rude and harsh. In this rugged area, or "clearing," all Braddock's force was now assembled, amounting, regulars, provin-

---

[1]Franklin, *Autobiography. Advertisement of B. Franklin for Wagons; Address to the Inhabitants of the Counties of York, Lancaster, and Cumberland,* in *Pennsylvania Archives,* II. 294.

[2]*Braddock to Robinson, 5 June, 1755.* The letters of Braddock here cited are the originals in the Public Record Office.

cials, and sailors, to about twenty-two hundred men. The two regiments, Halket's and Dunbar's, had been completed by enlistment in Virginia to seven hundred men each. Of Virginians there were nine companies of fifty men, who found no favor in the eyes of Braddock or his officers. To Ensign Allen of Halket's regiment was assigned the duty of "making them as much like soldiers as possible,"[1]—that is, of drilling them like regulars. The General had little hope of them, and informed Sir Thomas Robinson that "their slothful and languid disposition renders them very unfit for military service,"—a point on which he lived to change his mind. Thirty sailors, whom Commodore Keppel had lent him, were more to his liking, and were in fact of value in many ways. He had now about six hundred baggage-horses, besides those of the artillery, all weakening daily on their diet of leaves; for no grass was to be found. There was great show of discipline, and little real order. Braddock's executive capacity seems to have been moderate, and his dogged, imperious temper, rasped by disappointments, was in constant irritation. "He looks upon the country, I believe," writes Washington, "as void of honor or honesty. We have frequent disputes on this head, which are maintained with warmth on both sides, especially on his, as he is incapable of arguing without it, or giving up any point he asserts, be it ever so incompatible with reason or common sense."[2] Braddock's secretary, the younger Shirley, writing to his friend Governor Morris, spoke thus irreverently of his chief: "As the King said of a neighboring governor of yours [Sharpe], when proposed for the command of the American forces about a twelvemonth ago, and recommended as a very honest man, though not remarkably able, 'a little more ability and a little less honesty upon the present occasion might serve our turn better.' It is a joke to suppose that secondary officers can make amends for the defects of the first; the mainspring must be the mover. As to the others, I don't think we have much to boast; some are insolent and ignorant, others capable, but rather aiming at showing their own abilities than making a proper use of them. I have a very great love for my friend Orme, and think it uncommonly fortunate for our leader that he is under the influence of so honest and capable a man; but I wish for the sake of the public he had some more experience of business, particularly in America. I am greatly disgusted at seeing an expedition (as it is called), so ill-concerted originally in England, so improperly conducted since in America."[3]

[1]Orme, *Journal*.
[2]*Writings of Washington*, II. 77.
[3]*Shirley the younger to Morris, 23 May, 1755*, in *Colonial Records of Pa.*, VI. 404.

Captain Robert Orme, of whom Shirley speaks, was aide-de-camp to Braddock, and author of a copious and excellent Journal of the expedition, now in the British Museum.[1] His portrait, painted at full length by Sir Joshua Reynolds, hangs in the National Gallery at London. He stands by his horse, a gallant young figure, with a face pale, yet rather handsome, booted to the knee, his scarlet coat, ample waistcoat, and small three-cornered hat all heavy with gold lace. The General had two other aides-de-camp, Captain Roger Morris and Colonel George Washington, whom he had invited, in terms that do him honor, to become one of his military family.

It has been said that Braddock despised not only provincials, but Indians. Nevertheless he took some pains to secure their aid, and complained that Indian affairs had been so ill conducted by the provinces that it was hard to gain their confidence. This was true; the tribes had been alienated by gross neglect. Had they been protected from injustice and soothed by attentions and presents, the Five Nations, Delawares, and Shawanoes would have been retained as friends. But their complaints had been slighted, and every gift begrudged. The trader Croghan brought, however, about fifty warriors, with as many women and children, to the camp at Fort Cumberland. They were objects of great curiosity to the soldiers, who gazed with astonishment on their faces, painted red, yellow, and black, their ears slit and hung with pendants, and their heads close shaved, except the feathered scalp-lock at the crown. "In the day," says an officer, "they are in our camp, and in the night they go into their own, where they dance and make a most horrible noise." Braddock received them several times in his tent, ordered the guard to salute them, made them speeches, caused cannon to be fired and drums and fifes to play in their honor, regaled them with rum, and gave them a bullock for a feast; whereupon, being much pleased, they danced a war-dance, described by one spectator as "droll and odd, showing how they scalp and fight;" after which, says another, "they set up the most horrid song or cry that ever I heard."[2] These warriors, with a few others, promised the General to join him on the march; but he apparently grew tired of them, for a famous chief, called Scarroyaddy, afterwards complained: "He looked upon us as dogs, and would never hear anything that we said to him." Only eight of them remained with him to the end.[3]

---

[1] Printed by Sargent, in his excellent monograph of Braddock's Expedition.

[2] *Journal of a Naval Officer*, in Sargent. *The Expedition of Major-General Braddock, being Extracts of Letters from an Officer* (London, 1755).

[3] *Statement of George Croghan*, in Sargent, appendix iii.

Another ally appeared at the camp. This was a personage long known in Western fireside story as Captain Jack, the Black Hunter, or the Black Rifle. It was said of him that, having been a settler on the farthest frontier, in the Valley of the Juniata, he returned one evening to his cabin and found it burned to the ground by Indians, and the bodies of his wife and children lying among the ruins. He vowed undying vengeance, raised a band of kindred spirits, dressed and painted like Indians, and became the scourge of the red man and the champion of the white. But he and his wild crew, useful as they might have been, shocked Braddock's sense of military fitness; and he received them so coldly that they left him.[1]

It was the tenth of June before the army was well on its march. Three hundred axemen led the way, to cut and clear the road; and the long train of packhorses, wagons, and cannon toiled on behind, over the stumps, roots, and stones of the narrow track, the regulars and provincials marching in the forest close on either side. Squads of men were thrown out on the flanks, and scouts ranged the woods to guard against surprise; for, with all his scorn of Indians and Canadians, Braddock did not neglect reasonable precautions. Thus, foot by foot, they advanced into the waste of lonely mountains that divided the streams flowing to the Atlantic from those flowing to the Gulf of Mexico,—a realm of forests ancient as the world. The road was but twelve feet wide, and the line of march often extended four miles. It was like a thin, long party-colored snake, red, blue, and brown, trailing slowly through the depth of leaves, creeping round inaccessible heights, crawling over ridges, moving always in dampness and shadow, by rivulets and waterfalls, crags and chasms, gorges and shaggy steeps. In glimpses only, through jagged boughs and flickering leaves, did this wild primeval world reveal itself, with its dark green mountains, flecked with the morning mist, and its distant summits pencilled in dreamy blue. The army passed the main Alleghany, Meadow Mountain, and Great Savage Mountain, and traversed the funereal pine-forest afterwards called the Shades of Death. No attempt was made to interrupt their march, though the commandant of Fort Duquesne had sent out parties for that purpose. A few French and Indians hovered about them, now and then scalping a straggler or inscribing filthy insults on trees; while others fell upon the border settlements which the advance of the troops had left defenceless. Here they were more successful, butchering about thirty persons, chiefly women and children.

---

[1] See several traditional accounts and contemporary letters in *Hazard's Pennsylvania Register*, IV, 389, 390, 416; V. 191.

It was the eighteenth of June before the army reached a place called the Little Meadows, less than thirty miles from Fort Cumberland. Fever and dysentery among the men, and the weakness and worthlessness of many of the horses, joined to the extreme difficulty of the road, so retarded them that they could move scarcely more than three miles a day. Braddock consulted with Washington, who advised him to leave the heavy baggage to follow as it could, and push forward with a body of chosen troops. This counsel was given in view of a report that five hundred regulars were on the way to reinforce Fort Duquesne. It was adopted. Colonel Dunbar was left to command the rear division, whose powers of movement were now reduced to the lowest point. The advance corps, consisting of about twelve hundred soldiers, besides officers and drivers, began its march on the nineteenth with such artillery as was thought indispensable, thirty wagons, and a large number of packhorses. "The prospect," writes Washington to his brother, "conveyed infinite delight to my mind, though I was excessively ill at the time. But this prospect was soon clouded, and my hopes brought very low indeed when I found that, instead of pushing on with vigor without regarding a little rough road, they were halting to level every mole-hill, and to erect bridges over every brook, by which means we were four days in getting twelve miles." It was not till the seventh of July that they neared the mouth of Turtle Creek, a stream entering the Monongahela about eight miles from the French fort. The way was direct and short, but would lead them through a difficult country and a defile so perilous that Braddock resolved to ford the Monongahela to avoid this danger, and then ford it again to reach his destination.

Fort Duquesne stood on the point of land where the Alleghany and the Monongahela join to form the Ohio, and where now stands Pittsburg, with its swarming population, its restless industries, the clang of its forges, and its chimneys vomiting foul smoke into the face of heaven. At that early day a white flag fluttering over a cluster of palisades and embankments betokened the first intrusion of civilized men upon a scene which, a few months before, breathed the repose of a virgin wilderness, voiceless but for the lapping of waves upon the pebbles, or the note of some lonely bird. But now the sleep of ages was broken, and bugle and drum told the astonished forest that its doom was pronounced and its days numbered. The fort was a compact little work, solidly built and strong, compared with others on the continent. It was a square of four bastions, with the water close on two sides, and the other two protected by ravelins, ditch, glacis, and covered way. The ramparts on these sides were of squared logs, filled in with earth, and ten feet or more thick. The two water sides were enclosed by a massive stockade of upright logs, twelve feet high, mortised together and loopholed. The armament consisted of a number of small cannon mounted on the bastions. A gate and drawbridge on the east side gave access to the area within, which was surrounded by barracks for the soldiers, officers' quarters, the lodgings of the commandant, a guard-house, and a storehouse, all built partly of logs and partly of boards. There were no casemates, and the place was commanded by a high woody hill beyond the Monongahela. The forest had been cleared away to the distance of more than a musket shot from the ramparts, and the stumps were hacked level with the ground. Here, just outside the ditch, bark cabins had been built for such of the troops and Canadians as could not find room within; and the rest of the open space was covered with Indian corn and other crops.[1]

The garrison consisted of a few companies of the regular troops stationed permanently in the colony, and to these were added a considerable number of Canadians. Contrecœur still held the command.[2] Under him were three other captains, Beaujeu, Dumas, and Ligneris. Besides the troops and Canadians, eight hundred Indian warriors, mustered from far and near, had built their wigwams and camp-sheds on the open ground, or under the edge of the neighboring woods,—very little to the advantage of the young corn. Some were baptized savages settled in Canada,—Caughnawagas from Saut St. Louis, Abenakis from St. Francis, and Hurons from Lorette, whose chief bore the name of Anastase, in honor of that Father of the Church. The rest were unmitigated heathen,—Pottawattamies and Ojibwas from the northern lakes under Charles Langlade, the same bold partisan who had led them, three years before, to attack the Miamis at Pickawillany; Shawanoes and Mingoes from the Ohio; and Ottawas from Detroit, commanded, it is said, by that most redoubtable of savages, Pontiac. The law of the survival of the fittest had wrought on this heterogeneous crew through countless generations; and with the primitive Indian, the fittest was the hardiest, fiercest, most adroit, and most wily. Baptized and heathen alike, they had just enjoyed a diversion greatly to their taste. A young Pennsylvanian named James Smith, a spirited and intelligent boy of eighteen, had been waylaid by three Indians on the western borders of the province and led captive to the fort. When the

---

[1]M'Kinney's *Description of Fort Duquesne, 1756*, in *Hazard's Pennsylvania Register*, VIII. 318. *Letters of Robert Stobo, Hostage at Fort Duquesne, 1754*, in *Colonial Records of Pa.*, VI. 141, 161. Stobo's *Plan of Fort Duquesne, 1754*. *Journal of Thomas Forbes, 1755*. *Letter of Captain Haslet, 1758*, in *Olden Time*, I. 184. *Plan of Fort Duquesne* in Public Record Office.
[2]See Appendix D.

party came to the edge of the clearing, his captors, who had shot and
scalped his companion, raised the scalp-yell; whereupon a din of responsive whoops and firing of guns rose from all the Indian camps, and
their inmates swarmed out like bees, while the French in the fort shot
off muskets and cannon to honor the occasion. The unfortunate boy,
the object of this obstreperous rejoicing, presently saw a multitude of
savages, naked, hideously bedaubed with red, blue, black, and brown,
and armed with sticks or clubs, ranging themselves in two long parallel
lines, between which he was told that he must run, the faster the better, as they would beat him all the way. He ran with his best speed,
under a shower of blows, and had nearly reached the end of the course,
when he was knocked down. He tried to rise, but was blinded by a
handful of sand thrown into his face; and then they beat him till he
swooned. On coming to his senses he found himself in the fort, with
the surgeon opening a vein in his arm and a crowd of French and
Indians looking on. In a few days he was able to walk with the help of
a stick; and, coming out from his quarters one morning, he saw a memorable scene.[1]

Three days before, an Indian had brought the report that the English
were approaching; and the Chevalier de la Perade was sent out to reconnoitre.[2] He returned on the next day, the seventh, with news that
they were not far distant. On the eighth the brothers Normanville went
out, and found that they were within six leagues of the fort. The
French were in great excitement and alarm; but Contrecœur at length
took a resolution, which seems to have been inspired by Beaujeu.[3] It
was determined to meet the enemy on the march, and ambuscade them
if possible at the crossing of the Monongahela, or some other favorable
spot. Beaujeu proposed the plan to the Indians, and offered them the
war-hatchet; but they would not take it. "Do you want to die, my
father, and sacrifice us besides?" That night they held a council, and in
the morning again refused to go. Beaujeu did not despair. "I am determined," he exclaimed, "to meet the English. What! will you let your
father go alone?"[4] The greater part caught fire at his words, promised
to follow him, and put on their war-paint. Beaujeu received the com-
munion, then dressed himself like a savage, and joined the clamorous

---

[1] *Account of Remarkable Occurrences in the Life of Colonel James Smith, written by himself.* Perhaps
the best of all the numerous narratives of captives among the Indians.
[2] *Relation de Godefroy*, in Shea, *Bataille du Malangueulé* (Monongahela).
[3] Dumas, however, declares that Beaujeu adopted the plan at his suggestion. *Dumas au Ministre,
24 Juillet, 1756.*
[4] *Relation depuis le Départ des Trouppes de Québec jusqu'au 30 du Mois de Septembre, 1755.*

throng. Open barrels of gunpowder and bullets were set before the gate of the fort, and James Smith, painfully climbing the rampart with the help of his stick, looked down on the warrior rabble as, huddling together, wild with excitement, they scooped up the contents to fill their powder-horns and pouches. Then, band after band, they filed off along the forest track that led to the ford of the Monongahela. They numbered six hundred and thirty-seven; and with them went thirty-six French officers and cadets, seventy-two regular soldiers, and a hundred and forty-six Canadians, or about nine hundred in all.[1] At eight o'clock the tumult was over. The broad clearing lay lonely and still, and Contrecœur, with what was left of his garrison, waited in suspense for the issue.

It was near one o'clock when Braddock crossed the Monongahela for the second time. If the French made a stand anywhere, it would be, he thought, at the fording-place, but Lieutenant-Colonel Gage, whom he sent across with a strong advance-party, found no enemy, and quietly took possession of the farther shore. Then the main body followed. To impose on the imagination of the French scouts, who were doubtless on the watch, the movement was made with studied regularity and order. The sun was cloudless, and the men were inspirited by the prospect of near triumph. Washington afterwards spoke with admiration of the spectacle.[2] The music, the banners, the mounted officers, the troop of light cavalry, the naval detachment, the red-coated regulars, the blue-coated Virginians, the wagons and tumbrils, cannon, howitzers, and coehorns, the train of packhorses, and the droves of cattle, passed in long procession through the rippling shallows, and slowly entered the bordering forest. Here, when all were over, a short halt was ordered for rest and refreshment.

Why had not Beaujeu defended the ford? This was his intention in the morning; but he had been met by obstacles, the nature of which is not wholly clear. His Indians, it seems, had proved refractory. Three hundred of them left him, went off in another direction, and did not rejoin him till the English had crossed the river.[3] Hence perhaps it was that, having left Fort Duquesne at eight o'clock, he spent half the day in marching seven miles, and was more than a mile from the fording-

---

[1] *Liste des Officiers, Cadets, Soldats, Miliciens, et Sauvages qui composaient le Détachement qui a été au devant d'un Corps de 2,000 Anglois à 3 Lieues du Fort Duquesne, le 9 Juillet, 1755; joint à la Lettre de M. Bigot du 6 Août, 1755.*

[2] Compare the account of another eye-witness, Dr. Walker, in *Hazard's Pennsylvania Register*, VI. 104.

[3] *Relation de Godefroy*, in Shea, *Bataille du Malangueulé.*

place when the British reached the eastern shore. The delay, from whatever cause arising, cost him the opportunity of laying an ambush either at the ford or in the gullies and ravines that channelled the forest through which Braddock was now on the point of marching.

Not far from the bank of the river, and close by the British line of march, there was a clearing and a deserted house that had once belonged to the trader Fraser. Washington remembered it well. It was here that he found rest and shelter on the winter journey homeward from his mission to Fort Le Bœuf. He was in no less need of rest at this moment; for recent fever had so weakened him that he could hardly sit his horse. From Fraser's house to Fort Duquesne the distance was eight miles by a rough path, along which the troops were now beginning to move after their halt. It ran inland for a little; then curved to the left, and followed a course parallel to the river along the base of a line of steep hills that here bordered the valley. These and all the country were buried in dense and heavy forest, choked with bushes and the carcases of fallen trees. Braddock has been charged with marching blindly into an ambuscade; but it was not so. There was no ambuscade; and had there been one, he would have found it. It is true that he did not reconnoitre the woods very far in advance of the head of the column; yet, with this exception, he made elaborate dispositions to prevent surprise. Several guides, with six Virginian light horsemen, led the way. Then, a musket-shot behind, came the vanguard; then three hundred soldiers under Gage; then a large body of axemen, under Sir John Sinclair, to open the road; then two cannon with tumbrils and tool-wagons; and lastly the rear-guard, closing the line, while flanking-parties ranged the woods on both sides. This was the advance-column. The main body followed with little or no interval. The artillery and wagons moved along the road, and the troops filed through the woods close on either hand. Numerous flanking-parties were thrown out a hundred yards and more to right and left; while, in the space between them and the marching column, the pack horses and cattle, with their drivers, made their way painfully among the trees and thickets; since, had they been allowed to follow the road, the line of march would have been too long for mutual support. A body of regulars and provincials brought up the rear.

Gage, with his advance-column, had just passed a wide and bushy ravine that crossed their path, and the van of the main column was on the point of entering it, when the guides and light horsemen in the front suddenly fell back; and the engineer, Gordon, then engaged in marking out the road, saw a man, dressed like an Indian, but wearing the gorget of an officer, bounding forward along the path.[1] He stopped when he discovered the head of the column, turned, and waved his hat. The forest behind was swarming with French and savages. At the signal of the officer, who was probably Beaujeu, they yelled the war-whoop, spread themselves to right and left, and opened a sharp fire under cover of the trees. Gage's column wheeled deliberately into line, and fired several volleys with great steadiness against the now invisible assailants. Few of them were hurt; the trees caught the shot, but the noise was deafening under the dense arches of the forest. The greater part of the Canadians, to borrow the words of Dumas, "fled shamefully, crying 'Sauve qui peut!' "[2] Volley followed volley, and at the third Beaujeu dropped dead. Gage's two cannon were now brought to bear, on which the Indians, like the Canadians, gave way in confusion, but did not, like them, abandon the field. The close scarlet ranks of the English were plainly to be seen through the trees and the smoke; they were moving forward, cheering lustily, and shouting "God save the King!" Dumas, now chief in command, thought that all was lost. "I advanced," he says, "with the assurance that comes from despair, exciting by voice and gesture the few soldiers that remained. The fire of my platoon was so sharp that the enemy seemed astonished." The Indians, encouraged, began to rally. The French officers who commanded them showed admirable courage and address; and while Dumas and Ligneris, with the regulars and what was left of the Canadians, held the ground in front, the savage warriors, screeching their war-cries, swarmed through the forest along both flanks of the English, hid behind trees, bushes, and fallen trunks, or crouched in gullies and ravines, and opened a deadly fire on the helpless soldiery, who, themselves completely visible, could see no enemy, and wasted volley after volley on the impassive trees. The most destructive fire came from a hill on the English right, where the Indians lay in multitudes, firing from their lurking-places on the living target below. But the invisible death was everywhere, in front, flank, and rear. The British cheer was heard no more. The troops broke their ranks and huddled together in a bewildered mass, shrinking from the bullets that cut them down by scores.

When Braddock heard the firing in the front, he pushed forward with the main body to the support of Gage, leaving four hundred men in the rear, under Sir Peter Halket, to guard the baggage. At the moment

---

[1] *Journal of the Proceeding of the Detachment of Seamen*, in Sargent.
[2] *Dumas au Ministre, 24 Juillet, 1756. Contrecœur à Vaudreuil, 14 Juillet, 1755.* See Appendix D, where extracts are given.

of his arrival Gage's soldiers had abandoned their two cannon, and were falling back to escape the concentrated fire of the Indians. Meeting the advancing troops, they tried to find cover behind them. This threw the whole into confusion. The men of the two regiments became mixed together; and in a short time the entire force, except the Virginians and the troops left with Halket, were massed in several dense bodies within a small space of ground, facing some one way and some another, and all alike exposed without shelter to the bullets that pelted them like hail. Both men and officers were new to this blind and frightful warfare of the savage in his native woods. To charge the Indians in their hiding-places would have been useless. They would have eluded pursuit with the agility of wildcats, and swarmed back, like angry hornets, the moment that it ceased. The Virginians alone were equal to the emergency. Fighting behind trees like the Indians themselves, they might have held the enemy in check till order could be restored, had not Braddock, furious at a proceeding that shocked all his ideas of courage and discipline, ordered them, with oaths, to form into line. A body of them under Captain Waggoner made a dash for a fallen tree lying in the woods, far out towards the lurking-places of the Indians, and, crouching behind the huge trunk, opened fire; but the regulars, seeing the smoke among the bushes, mistook their best friends for the enemy, shot at them from behind, killed many, and forced the rest to return. A few of the regulars also tried in their clumsy way to fight behind trees; but Braddock beat them with his sword, and compelled them to stand with the rest, an open mark for the Indians. The panic increased; the soldiers crowded together, and the bullets spent themselves in a mass of human bodies. Commands, entreaties, and threats were lost upon them. "We would fight," some of them answered, "if we could see anybody to fight with." Nothing was visible but puffs of smoke. Officers and men who had stood all the afternoon under fire afterwards declared that they could not be sure they had seen a single Indian. Braddock ordered Lieutenant-Colonel Burton to attack the hill where the puffs of smoke were thickest, and the bullets most deadly. With infinite difficulty that brave officer induced a hundred men to follow him; but he was soon disabled by a wound, and they all faced about. The artillerymen stood for some time by their guns, which did great damage to the trees and little to the enemy. The mob of soldiers, stupefied with terror, stood panting, their foreheads beaded with sweat, loading and firing mechanically, sometimes into the air, sometimes among their own comrades, many of whom they killed. The ground, strewn with dead and wounded men, the bounding of maddened horses, the clatter and roar of musketry and cannon, mixed with the spiteful report of rifles and the yells that rose from the indefatigable throats of six hundred unseen savages, formed a chaos of anguish and terror scarcely paralleled even in Indian war. "I cannot describe the horrors of that scene," one of Braddock's officers wrote three weeks after; "no pen could do it. The yell of the Indians is fresh on my ear, and the terrific sound will haunt me till the hour of my dissolution."[1]

Braddock showed a furious intrepidity. Mounted on horseback, he dashed to and fro, storming like a madman. Four horses were shot under him, and he mounted a fifth. Washington seconded his chief with equal courage; he too no doubt using strong language, for he did not measure words when the fit was on him. He escaped as by miracle. Two horses were killed under him, and four bullets tore his clothes. The conduct of the British officers was above praise. Nothing could surpass their undaunted self-devotion; and in their vain attempts to lead on the men, the havoc among them was frightful. Sir Peter Halket was shot dead. His son, a lieutenant in his regiment, stooping to raise the body of his father, was shot dead in turn. Young Shirley, Braddock's secretary, was pierced through the brain. Orme and Morris, his aides-de-camp, Sinclair, the quartermaster-general, Gates and Gage, both afterwards conspicuous on opposite sides in the War of the Revolution, and Gladwin, who, eight years later, defended Detroit against Pontiac, were all wounded. Of eighty-six officers, sixty-three were killed or disabled;[2] while out of thirteen hundred and seventy-three non-commissioned officers and privates, only four hundred and fifty-nine came off unharmed.[3]

Braddock saw that all was lost. To save the wreck of his force from annihilation, he at last commanded a retreat; and as he and such of his officers as were left strove to withdraw the half-frenzied crew in some semblance of order, a bullet struck him down. The gallant bulldog fell from his horse, shot through the arm into the lungs. It is said, though on evidence of no weight, that the bullet came from one of his own men. Be this as it may, there he lay among the bushes, bleeding, gasping, unable even to curse. He demanded to be left where he was. Cap-

---

[1] *Leslie to a Merchant of Philadelphia, 30 July, 1755*, in *Hazard's Pennsylvania Register*, V. 191. Leslie was a lieutenant of the Forty-fourth.

[2] *A List of the Officers who were present, and of those killed and wounded, in the Action on the Banks of the Monongahela, 9 July, 1755* (Public Record Office, America and West Indies, LXXXII.).

[3] Statement of the engineer, Mackellar. By another account, out of a total, officers and men, of 1,460, the number of all ranks who escaped was 583. Braddock's force, originally 1,200, was increased, a few days before the battle, by detachments from Dunbar.

tain Stewart and another provincial bore him between them to the rear.

It was about this time that the mob of soldiers, having been three hours under fire, and having spent their ammunition, broke away in a blind frenzy, rushed back towards the ford, "and when," says Washington, "we endeavored to rally them, it was with as much success as if we had attempted to stop the wild bears of the mountains." They dashed across, helter-skelter, plunging through the water to the farther bank, leaving wounded comrades, cannon, baggage, the military chest, and the General's papers, a prey to the Indians. About fifty of these followed to the edge of the river. Dumas and Ligneris, who had now only about twenty Frenchmen with them, made no attempt to pursue, and went back to the fort, because, says Contrecœur, so many of the Canadians had "retired at the first fire." The field, abandoned to the savages, was a pandemonium of pillage and murder.[1]

James Smith, the young prisoner at Fort Duquesne, had passed a day of suspense, waiting the result. "In the afternoon I again observed a great noise and commotion in the fort, and, though at that time I could not understand French, I found it was the voice of joy and triumph, and feared that they had received what I called bad news. I had observed some of the old-country soldiers speak Dutch; as I spoke Dutch, I went to one of them and asked him what was the news. He told me that a runner had just arrived who said that Braddock would certainly be defeated; that the Indians and French had surrounded him, and were

---

[1] "Nous prîmes le parti de nous retirer en vue de rallier notre petite armée." *Dumas au Ministre, 24 Juillet, 1756.*

On the defeat of Braddock, besides authorities already cited,—*Shirley to Robinson, 5 Nov. 1755,* accompanying the plans of the battle reproduced in this volume (Public Record Office, *America and West Indies,* LXXXII.). The plans were drawn at Shirley's request by Patrick Mackellar, chief engineer of the expedition, who was with Gage in the advance column when the fight began. They were examined and fully approved by the chief surviving officers, and they closely correspond with another plan made by the aide-de-camp Orme,—which, however, shows only the beginning of the affair.

Report of the Court of Inquiry into the Behavior of the Troops at the Monongahela. Letters of Dinwiddie. Letters of Gage. Burd to Morris, 25 July, 1755. Sinclair to Robinson, 3 Sept. Rutherford to ———, 12 July. Writings of Washington, II. 68–93. *Review of Military Operations in North America.* Entick, I. 145. *Gentleman's Magazine* (1755), 378, 426. *Letter to a Friend on the Ohio Defeat* (Boston, 1755).

Contrecœur à Vaudreuil, 14 Juillet, 1755. Estat de l'Artillerie, etc., qui se sont trouvés sur le Champ de Bataille. Vaudreuil au Ministre, 5 Août, 1755. Bigot au Ministre, 27 Août. Relation du Combat du 9 Juillet. Relation depuis le Départ des Trouppes de Québec jusqu'au 30 du Mois de Septembre. Lotbinière à d'Argenson, 24 Oct. Relation officielle imprimée au Louvre. Relation de Godefroy (Shea). Extraits du Registre du Fort Duquesne (Ibid.). Relation de diverses Mouvements (Ibid.). Pouchot, I. 37.

concealed behind trees and in gullies, and kept a constant fire upon the English; and that they saw the English falling in heaps; and if they did not take the river, which was the only gap, and make their escape, there would not be one man left alive before sundown. Some time after this, I heard a number of scalp-halloos, and saw a company of Indians and French coming in. I observed they had a great number of bloody scalps, grenadiers' caps, British canteens, bayonets, etc., with them. They brought the news that Braddock was defeated. After that another company came in, which appeared to be about one hundred, and chiefly Indians; and it seemed to me that almost every one of this company was carrying scalps. After this came another company with a number of wagon-horses, and also a great many scalps. Those that were coming in and those that had arrived kept a constant firing of small arms, and also the great guns in the fort, which were accompanied with the most hideous shouts and yells from all quarters, so that it appeared to me as though the infernal regions had broke loose.

"About sundown I beheld a small party coming in with about a dozen prisoners, stripped naked, with their hands tied behind their backs and their faces and parts of their bodies blacked; these prisoners they burned to death on the bank of Alleghany River, opposite the fort. I stood on the fort wall until I beheld them begin to burn one of these men; they had him tied to a stake, and kept touching him with firebrands, red-hot irons, etc., and he screaming in a most doleful manner, the Indians in the meantime yelling like infernal spirits. As this scene appeared too shocking for me to behold, I retired to my lodging, both sore and sorry. When I came into my lodgings I saw Russel's *Seven Sermons*, which they had brought from the field of battle, which a Frenchman made a present of to me."

The loss of the French was slight, but fell chiefly on the officers, three of whom were killed, and four wounded. Of the regular soldiers, all but four escaped untouched. The Canadians suffered still less, in proportion to their numbers, only five of them being hurt. The Indians, who won the victory, bore the principal loss. Of those from Canada, twenty-seven were killed and wounded; while the casualties among the Western tribes are not reported.[1] All of these last went off the next morning with their plunder and scalps, leaving Contrecœur in great anxiety lest the remnant of Braddock's troops, reinforced by the division under Dunbar, should attack him again. His doubts would have vanished had he known the condition of his defeated enemy.

---

[1] *Liste des Officiers, Soldats, Miliciens, et Sauvages de Canada qui ont été tués et blessés le 9 Juillet, 1755.*

In the pain and languor of a mortal wound, Braddock showed un-flinching resolution. His bearers stopped with him at a favorable spot beyond the Monongahela; and here he hoped to maintain his position till the arrival of Dunbar. By the efforts of the officers about a hundred men were collected around him; but to keep them there was impossible. Within an hour they abandoned him, and fled like the rest. Gage, however, succeeded in rallying about eighty beyond the other fording-place; and Washington, on an order from Braddock, spurred his jaded horse towards the camp of Dunbar to demand wagons, provisions, and hospital stores.

Fright overcame fatigue. The fugitives toiled on all night, pursued by spectres of horror and despair; hearing still the war-whoops and the shrieks; possessed with the one thought of escape from this wilderness of death. In the morning some order was restored. Braddock was placed on a horse; then, the pain being insufferable, he was carried on a litter, Captain Orme having bribed the carriers by the promise of a guinea and a bottle of rum apiece. Early in the succeeding night, such as had not fainted on the way reached the deserted farm of Gist. Here they met wagons and provisions, with a detachment of soldiers sent by Dun-bar, whose camp was six miles farther on; and Braddock ordered them to go to the relief of the stragglers left behind.

At noon of that day a number of wagoners and packhorse-drivers had come to Dunbar's camp with wild tidings of rout and ruin. More fugi-tives followed; and soon after a wounded officer was brought in upon a sheet. The drums beat to arms. The camp was in commotion; and many soldiers and teamsters took to flight, in spite of the sentinels, who tried in vain to stop them.[1] There was a still more disgraceful scene on the next day, after Braddock, with the wreck of his force, had arrived. Orders were given to destroy such of the wagons, stores, and ammuni-tion as could not be carried back at once to Fort Cumberland. Whether Dunbar or the dying General gave these orders is not clear; but it is certain that they were executed with shameful alacrity. More than a hundred wagons were burned; cannon, coehorns, and shells were burst or buried; barrels of gunpowder were staved, and the contents thrown into a brook; provisions were scattered through the woods and swamps. Then the whole command began its retreat over the mountains to Fort Cumberland, sixty miles distant. This proceeding, for which, in view of the condition of Braddock, Dunbar must be held answerable, excited the utmost indignation among the colonists. If he could not advance,

[1] *Depositions of Matthew Laird, Michael Hoover, and Jacob Hoover, Wagoners, in Colonial Records of Pa.*, VI. 482.

they thought, he might at least have fortified himself and held his ground till the provinces could send him help; thus covering the frontier, and holding French war-parties in check.

Braddock's last moment was near. Orme, who, though himself severely wounded, was with him till his death, told Franklin that he was totally silent all the first day, and at night said only, "Who would have thought it?" that all the next day he was again silent, till at last he muttered, "We shall better know how to deal with them another time," and died a few minutes after. He had nevertheless found breath to give orders at Gist's for the succor of the men who had dropped on the road. It is said, too, that in his last hours "he could not bear the sight of a red coat," but murmured praises of "the blues," or Virginians, and said that he hoped he should live to reward them.[1] He died at about eight o'clock in the evening of Sunday, the thirteenth. Dunbar had begun his retreat that morning, and was then encamped near the Great Meadows. On Monday the dead commander was buried in the road; and men, horses, and wagons passed over his grave, effacing every sign of it, lest the Indians should find and mutilate the body.

Colonel James Innes, commanding at Fort Cumberland, where a crowd of invalids with soldiers' wives and other women had been left when the expedition marched, heard of the defeat, only two days after it happened, from a wagoner who had fled from the field on horseback. He at once sent a note of six lines to Lord Fairfax: "I have this moment received the most melancholy news of the defeat of our troops, the General killed, and numbers of our officers; our whole artillery taken. In short, the account I have received is so very bad, that as, please God, I intend to make a stand here, 't is highly necessary to raise the militia everywhere to defend the frontiers." A boy whom he sent out on horseback met more fugitives, and came back on the fourteenth with reports as vague and disheartening as the first. Innes sent them to Dinwiddie.[2] Some days after, Dunbar and his train arrived in miserable disorder, and Fort Cumberland was turned into a hospital for the shattered fragments of a routed and ruined army.

On the sixteenth a letter was brought in haste to one Buchanan at Carlisle, on the Pennsylvanian frontier:—

SIR,—I thought it proper to let you know that I was in the battle where we were defeated. And we had about eleven hundred and fifty private

---

[1] *Bolling to his Son,* 13 Aug. 1755. Bolling was a Virginian gentleman whose son was at school in England.

[2] *Innes to Dinwiddie,* 14 July, 1755.

men, besides officers and others. And we were attacked the ninth day about twelve o'clock, and held till about three in the afternoon, and then we were forced to retreat, when I suppose we might bring off about three hundred whole men, besides a vast many wounded. Most of our officers were either wounded or killed; General Braddock is wounded, but I hope not mortal; and Sir John Sinclair and many others, but I hope not mortal. All the train is cut off in a manner. Sir Peter Halket and his son, Captain Polson, Captain Gethen, Captain Rose, Captain Tatten killed, and many others. Captain Ord of the train is wounded, but I hope not mortal. We lost all our artillery entirely, and everything else.

To Mr. John Smith and Buchannon, and give it to the next post, and let him show this to Mr. George Gibson in Lancaster, and Mr. Bingham, at the sign of the Ship, and you'll oblige,

Yours to command,
JOHN CAMPBELL, *Messenger.*[1]

The evil tidings quickly reached Philadelphia, where such confidence had prevailed that certain over-zealous persons had begun to collect money for fireworks to celebrate the victory. Two of these, brother physicians named Bond, came to Franklin and asked him to subscribe; but the sage looked doubtful. "Why, the devil!" said one of them, "you surely don't suppose the fort will not be taken?" He reminded them that war is always uncertain; and the subscription was deferred.[2] The Governor laid the news of the disaster before his Council, telling them at the same time that his opponents in the Assembly would not believe it, and had insulted him in the street for giving it currency.[3]

Dinwiddie remained tranquil at Williamsburg, sure that all would go well. The brief note of Innes, forwarded by Lord Fairfax, first disturbed his dream of triumph; but on second thought he took comfort. "I am willing to think that account was from a deserter who, in a great panic, represented what his fears suggested. I wait with impatience for another express from Fort Cumberland, which I expect will greatly contradict the former." The news got abroad, and the slaves showed signs of excitement. "The villany of the negroes on any emergency is what I always feared," continues the Governor. "An example of one or two at first may prevent these creatures entering into combinations and wicked designs."[4] And he wrote to Lord Halifax: "The negro slaves have been very audacious on the news of defeat on the Ohio. These poor creatures

---

[1] *Colonial Records of Pa.*, VI. 481

[2] *Autobiography of Franklin.*

[3] *Colonial Records of Pa.*, VI. 480.

[4] *Dinwiddie to Colonel Charles Carter, 18 July, 1755.*

imagine the French will give them their freedom. We have too many here; but I hope we shall be able to keep them in proper subjection." Suspense grew intolerable. "It's monstrous they should be so tardy and dilatory in sending down any farther account." He sent Major Colin Campbell for news; when, a day or two later, a courier brought him two letters, one from Orme, and the other from Washington, both written at Fort Cumberland on the eighteenth. The letter of Orme began thus: "My dear Governor, I am so extremely ill in bed with the wound I have received that I am under the necessity of employing my friend Captain Dobson as my scribe." Then he told the wretched story of defeat and humiliation. "The officers were absolutely sacrificed by their unparalleled good behavior; advancing before their men sometimes in bodies, and sometimes separately, hoping by such an example to engage the soldiers to follow them; but to no purpose. Poor Shirley was shot through the head, Captain Morris very much wounded. Mr. Washington had two horses shot under him, and his clothes shot through in several places; behaving the whole time with the greatest courage and resolution."

Washington wrote more briefly, saying that, as Orme was giving a full account of the affair, it was needless for him to repeat it. Like many others in the fight, he greatly underrated the force of the enemy, which he placed at three hundred, or about a third of the actual number,—a natural error, as most of the assailants were invisible. "Our poor Virginians behaved like men, and died like soldiers; for I believe that out of three companies that were there that day, scarce thirty were left alive. Captain Peronney and all his officers down to a corporal were killed. Captain Polson shared almost as hard a fate, for only one of his escaped. In short, the dastardly behavior of the English soldiers exposed all those who were inclined to do their duty to almost certain death. It is imagined (I believe with great justice, too) that two thirds of both killed and wounded received their shots from our own cowardly dogs of soldiers, who gathered themselves into a body, contrary to orders, ten and twelve deep, would then level, fire, and shoot down the men before them."[1]

To Orme, Dinwiddie replied: "I read your letter with tears in my eyes; but it gave me much pleasure to see your name at the bottom, and more so when I observed by the postscript that your wound is not dangerous. But pray, dear sir, is it not possible by a second attempt to

[1] These extracts are taken from the two letters preserved in the Public Record Office, *America and West Indies*, LXXIV. LXXXII.

retrieve the great loss we have sustained? I presume the General's char-
iot is at the fort. In it you may come here, and my house is heartily at
your command. Pray take care of your valuable health; keep your spirits
up, and I doubt not of your recovery. My wife and girls join me in most
sincere respects and joy at your being so well, and I always am, with
great truth, dear friend, your affectionate humble servant."

To Washington he is less effusive, though he had known him much
longer. He begins, it is true, "Dear Washington," and congratulates
him on his escape; but soon grows formal, and asks: "Pray, sir, with the
number of them remaining, is there no possibility of doing something
on the other side of the mountains before the winter months? Surely
you must mistake. Colonel Dunbar will not march to winter-quarters in
the middle of summer, and leave the frontiers exposed to the invasions
of the enemy! No; he is a better officer, and I have a different opinion
of him. I sincerely wish you health and happiness, and am, with great
respect, sir, your obedient, humble servant."

Washington's letter had contained the astonishing announcement
that Dunbar meant to abandon the frontier and march to Philadelphia.
Dinwiddie, much disturbed, at once wrote to that officer, though without betraying any knowledge of his intention. "Sir, the melancholy
account of the defeat of our forces gave me a sensible and real concern"—on which he enlarges for a while; then suddenly changes style:
"Dear Colonel, is there no method left to retrieve the dishonor done
to the British arms? As you now command all the forces that remain,
are you not able, after a proper refreshment of your men, to make a
second attempt? You have four months now to come of the best
weather of the year for such an expedition. What a fine field for honor
will Colonel Dunbar have to confirm and establish his character as a
brave officer." Then, after suggesting plans of operation, and entering
into much detail, the fervid Governor concludes: "It gives me great
pleasure that under our great loss and misfortunes the command de-
volves on an officer of so great military judgment and established character. With my sincere respect and hearty wishes for success to all your
proceedings, I am, worthy sir, your most obedient, humble servant."

Exhortation and flattery were lost on Dunbar. Dinwiddie received
from him in reply a short, dry note, dated on the first of August, and
acquainting him that he should march for Philadelphia on the second.
This, in fact, he did, leaving the fort to be defended by invalids and a
few Virginians. "I acknowledge," says Dinwiddie, "I was not brought
up to arms; but I think common sense would have prevailed not to
leave the frontiers exposed after having opened a road over the moun-

tains to the Ohio, by which the enemy can the more easily invade us. . . . Your great colonel," he writes to Orme, "is gone to a peaceful colony, and left our frontiers open. . . . The whole conduct of Colonel Dunbar appears to me monstrous. . . . To march off all the regulars, and leave the fort and frontiers to be defended by four hundred sick and wounded, and the poor remains of our provincial forces, appears to me absurd."[1]

He found some comfort from the burgesses, who gave him forty thousand pounds, and would, he thinks, have given a hundred thousand if another attempt against Fort Duquesne had been set afoot. Shirley, too, whom the death of Braddock had made commander-in-chief, approved the Governor's plan of renewing offensive operations, and instructed Dunbar to that effect; ordering him, however, should they prove impracticable, to march for Albany in aid of the Niagara expedition.[2] The order found him safe in Philadelphia. Here he lingered for a while; then marched to join the northern army, moving at a pace which made it certain that he could not arrive in time to be of the least use.

Thus the frontier was left unguarded; and soon, as Dinwiddie had foreseen, there burst upon it a storm of blood and fire.

[1] Dinwiddie's view of Dunbar's conduct is fully justified by the letters of Shirley, Governor Morris, and Dunbar himself.

[2] *Orders for Colonel Thomas Dunbar, 12 Aug. 1755.* These supersede a previous order of August 6, by which Shirley had directed Dunbar to march northward at once.

8

Removal
of the Acadians
1755–1763

By the plan which the Duke of Cumberland had ordained and Braddock had announced in the Council at
Alexandria, four blows were to be struck at once to force back the
French boundaries, lop off the dependencies of Canada, and reduce her
from a vast territory to a petty province. The first stroke had failed,
and had shattered the hand of the striker; it remains to see what fortune
awaited the others.

It was long since a project of purging Acadia of French influence had germinated in the fertile mind of Shirley. We have seen in a former chapter the condition of that afflicted province. Several thousands of its inhabitants, wrought upon by intriguing agents of the French Government; taught by their priests that fidelity to King Louis was inseparable from fidelity to God, and that to swear allegiance to the British Crown was eternal perdition; threatened with plunder and death at the hands of the savages whom the ferocious missionary, Le Loutre, held over them in terror,—had abandoned, sometimes willingly, but oftener under constraint, the fields which they and their fathers had tilled, and crossing the boundary line of the Missaguash, had placed themselves under the French flag planted on the hill of Beauséjour.[1] Here, or in the neighborhood, many of them had remained, wretched and half starved; while others had been transported to Cape Breton, Isle St. Jean, or the coasts of the Gulf,—not so far, however, that they could not on occasion be used to aid in an invasion of British Acadia.[2] Those of their countrymen who still lived under the British flag were chiefly the inhabitants of the district of Mines and of the valley of the River Annapolis, who, with other less important settlements, numbered a little more than nine thousand souls. We have shown already, by the evidence of the French themselves, that neither they nor their emigrant countrymen had been oppressed or molested in matters temporal or spiritual, but that the English authorities, recognizing their value as an industrious population, had labored to reconcile them to a change of rulers which on the whole was to their advantage. It has been shown also how, with a heartless perfidy and a reckless disregard of their welfare and safety, the French Government and its agents labored to keep them hostile to the Crown of which it had acknowledged them to be subjects. The result was, that though they did not, like their emigrant countrymen, abandon their homes, they remained in a state of restless disaffection, refused to supply English garrisons with provisions, except at most exorbitant rates, smuggled their produce to the French across the line, gave them aid and intelligence, and sometimes, disguised as Indians, robbed and murdered English settlers. By the new-fangled construction

---

[1]See ante, Chapter 4.

[2]Rameau (La France aux Colonies, I. 63) estimates the total emigration from 1748 to 1755 at 8,600 souls,—which number seems much too large. This writer, though vehemently anti-English, gives the following passage from a letter of a high French official: "que les Acadiens émigrés et en grande misère comptaient se retirer à Québec et demander des terres, mais il conviendrait mieux qu'ils restent où ils sont, afin d'avoir le voisinage de l'Acadie bien peuplé et défriché, pour approvisionner l'Isle Royale [Cape Breton] et tomber en cas de guerre sur l'Acadie." Rameau, I. 133.

of the treaty of Utrecht which the French boundary commissioners had devised,[1] more than half the Acadian peninsula, including nearly all the cultivated land and nearly all the population of French descent, was claimed as belonging to France, though England had held possession of it more than forty years. Hence, according to the political ethics adopted at the time by both nations, it would be lawful for France to reclaim it by force. England, on her part, it will be remembered, claimed vast tracts beyond the isthmus; and, on the same pretext, held that she might rightfully seize them and capture Beauséjour, with the other French garrisons that guarded them.

On the part of France, an invasion of the Acadian peninsula seemed more than likely. Honor demanded of her that, having incited the Acadians to disaffection, and so brought on them the indignation of the English authorities, she should intervene to save them from the consequences. Moreover the loss of the Acadian peninsula had been gall and wormwood to her; and in losing it she had lost great material advantages. Its possession was necessary to connect Canada with the Island of Cape Breton and the fortress of Louisbourg. Its fertile fields and agricultural people would furnish subsistence to the troops and garrisons in the French maritime provinces, now dependent on supplies illicitly brought by New England traders, and liable to be cut off in time of war when they were needed most. The harbors of Acadia, too, would be invaluable as naval stations from which to curb and threaten the northern English colonies. Hence the intrigues so assiduously practised to keep the Acadians French at heart, and ready to throw off British rule at any favorable moment. British officers believed that should a French squadron with a sufficient force of troops on board appear in the Bay of Fundy, the whole population on the Basin of Mines and along the Annapolis would rise in arms, and that the emigrants beyond the isthmus, armed and trained by French officers, would come to their aid. This emigrant population, famishing in exile, looked back with regret to the farms they had abandoned; and, prevented as they were by Le Loutre and his colleagues from making their peace with the English, they would, if confident of success, have gladly joined an invading force to regain their homes by reconquering Acadia for Louis XV. In other parts of the continent it was the interest of France to put off hostilities; if Acadia alone had been in question, it would have been her interest to precipitate them.

Her chances of success were good. The French could at any time

[1] *Supra*, pp. 71–72.

send troops from Louisbourg or Quebec to join those maintained upon the isthmus; and they had on their side of the lines a force of militia and Indians amounting to about two thousand, while the Acadians within the peninsula had about an equal number of fighting men who, while calling themselves neutrals, might be counted on to join the invaders. The English were in no condition to withstand such an attack. Their regular troops were scattered far and wide through the province, and were nowhere more than equal to the local requirement; while of militia, except those of Halifax, they had few or none whom they dared to trust. Their fort at Annapolis was weak and dilapidated, and their other posts were mere stockades. The strongest place in Acadia was the French fort of Beauséjour, in which the English saw a continual menace.

Their apprehensions were well grounded. Duquesne, governor of Canada, wrote to Le Loutre, who virtually shared the control of Beauséjour with Vergor, its commandant: "I invite both yourself and M. Vergor to devise a plausible pretext for attacking them [*the English*] vigorously."[1] Three weeks after this letter was written, Lawrence, governor of Nova Scotia, wrote to Shirley from Halifax: "Being well informed that the French have designs of encroaching still farther upon His Majesty's rights in this province, and that they propose, the moment they have repaired the fortifications of Louisbourg, to attack our fort at Chignecto [*Fort Lawrence*], I think it high time to make some effort to drive them from the north side of the Bay of Fundy."[2] This letter was brought to Boston by Lieutenant-Colonel Monckton, who was charged by Lawrence to propose to Shirley the raising of two thousand men in New England for the attack of Beauséjour and its dependent forts. Almost at the moment when Lawrence was writing these proposals to Shirley, Shirley was writing with the same object to Lawrence, enclosing a letter from Sir Thomas Robinson, concerning which he said: "I construe the contents to be orders to us to act in concert for taking *any* advantages to drive the French of Canada out of Nova Scotia. If that is your sense of them, and your honor will be pleased to let me know whether you want any and what assistance to enable you to execute the orders, I will endeavor to send you such assistance from this province as you shall want."[3]

The letter of Sir Thomas Robinson, of which a duplicate had already been sent to Lawrence, was written in answer to one of Shirley inform-

[1] *Duquesne à Le Loutre*, 15 *Oct.* 1754; extract in *Public Documents of Nova Scotia*, 239.
[2] *Lawrence to Shirley*, 5 *Nov.* 1754. *Instructions of Lawrence to Monckton*, 7 *Nov.* 1754.
[3] *Shirley to Lawrence*, 7 *Nov.* 1754.

ing the Minister that the Indians of Nova Scotia, prompted by the French, were about to make an attack on all the English settlements east of the Kennebec; whereupon Robinson wrote: "You will without doubt have given immediate intelligence thereof to Colonel Lawrence, and will have concerted the properest measures with him for taking all possible advantage in Nova Scotia itself from the absence of those Indians, in case Mr. Lawrence shall have force enough to attack the forts erected by the French in those parts, without exposing the English settlements; and I am particularly to acquaint you that if you have not already entered into such a concert with Colonel Lawrence, it is His Majesty's pleasure that you should immediately proceed thereupon."[1]

The Indian raid did not take place; but not the less did Shirley and Lawrence find in the Minister's letter their authorization for the attack of Beauséjour. Shirley wrote to Robinson that the expulsion of the French from the forts on the isthmus was a necessary measure of self-defence; that they meant to seize the whole country as far as Mines Basin, and probably as far as Annapolis, to supply their Acadian rebels with land; that of these they had, without reckoning Indians, fourteen hundred fighting men on or near the isthmus, and two hundred and fifty more on the St. John, with whom, aided by the garrison of Beauséjour, they could easily take Fort Lawrence; that should they succeed in this, the whole Acadian population would rise in arms, and the King would lose Nova Scotia. We should anticipate them, concludes Shirley, and strike the first blow.[2]

He opened his plans to his Assembly in secret session, and found them of one mind with himself. Preparation was nearly complete, and the men raised for the expedition, before the Council at Alexandria, recognized it as a part of a plan of the summer campaign.

The French fort of Beauséjour, mounted on its hill between the marshes of Missaguash and Tantemar, was a regular work, pentagonal in form, with solid earthern ramparts, bomb-proofs, and an armament of twenty-four cannon and one mortar. The commandant, Duchambon de Vergor, a captain in the colony regulars, was a dull man of no education, of stuttering speech, unpleasing countenance, and doubtful

[1] *Robinson to Shirley, 5 July, 1754.*
[2] *Shirley to Robinson, 8 Dec. 1754. Ibid., 24 Jan. 1755.* The Record Office contains numerous other letters of Shirley on the subject. "I am obliged to your Honor for communicating to me the French Mémoire, which, with other reasons, puts it out of doubt that the French are determined to begin an offensive war on the peninsula as soon as ever they shall think themselves strengthened enough to venture upon it, and that they have thoughts of attempting it in the ensuing spring. I enclose your Honor extracts from two letters from Annapolis Royal, which show that the French inhabitants are in expectation of its being begun in the spring." *Shirley to Lawrence, 6 Jan. 1755.*

character. He owed his place to the notorious Intendant, Bigot, who, it is said, was in his debt for disreputable service in an affair of gallantry, and who had ample means of enabling his friends to enrich themselves by defrauding the King. Beauséjour was one of those plague-spots of official corruption which dotted the whole surface of New France. Bigot, sailing for Europe in the summer of 1754, wrote thus to his confederate: "Profit by your place, my dear Vergor; clip and cut—you are free to do what you please—so that you can come soon to join me in France and buy an estate near me."[1] Vergor did not neglect his opportunities. Supplies in great quantities were sent from Quebec for the garrison and the emigrant Acadians. These last got but a small part of them. Vergor and his confederates sent the rest back to Quebec, or else to Louisbourg, and sold them for their own profit to the King's agents there, who were also in collusion with him.

Vergor, however, did not reign alone. Le Loutre, by force of energy, capacity, and passionate vehemence, held him in some awe, and divided his authority. The priest could count on the support of Duquesne, who had found, says a contemporary, that "he promised more than he could perform, and that he was a knave," but who nevertheless felt compelled to rely upon him for keeping the Acadians on the side of France. There was another person in the fort worthy of notice. This was Thomas Pichon, commissary of stores, a man of education and intelligence, born in France of an English mother. He was now acting the part of a traitor, carrying on a secret correspondence with the commandant of Fort Lawrence, and acquainting him with all that passed at Beauséjour. It was partly from this source that the hostile designs of the French became known to the authorities of Halifax, and more especially the proceedings of "Moses," by which name Pichon always designated Le Loutre, because he pretended to have led the Acadians from the land of bondage.[2]

These exiles, who cannot be called self-exiled, in view of the outrageous means used to force most of them from their homes, were in a deplorable condition. They lived in constant dread of Le Loutre, backed by Vergor and his soldiers. The savage missionary, bad as he was, had in him an ingredient of honest fanaticism, both national and religious; though hatred of the English held a large share in it. He

---

[1] *Mémoires sur le Canada, 1749–1760.* This letter is also mentioned in another contemporary document, *Mémoire sur les Fraudes commises dans la Colonie.*

[2] Pichon, called also Tyrrell from the name of his mother, was author of *Genuine Letters and Memoirs relating to Cape Breton,*—a book of some value. His papers are preserved at Halifax, and some of them are printed in the *Public Documents of Nova Scotia.*

would gladly, if he could, have formed the Acadians into a permanent settlement on the French side of the line, not out of love for them, but in the interest of the cause with which he had identified his own ambition. His efforts had failed. There was not land enough for their subsistence and that of the older settlers; and the suffering emigrants pined more and more for their deserted farms. Thither he was resolved that they should not return. "If you go," he told them, "you will have neither priests nor sacraments, but will die like miserable wretches."[1] The assertion was false. Priests and sacraments had never been denied them. It is true that Daudin, priest of Pisiquid, had lately been sent to Halifax for using insolent language to the commandant, threatening him with an insurrection of the inhabitants, and exciting them to sedition; but on his promise to change conduct, he was sent back to his parishioners.[2] Vergor sustained Le Loutre, and threatened to put in irons any of the exiles who talked of going back to the English. Some of them bethought themselves of an appeal to Duquesne, and drew up a petition asking leave to return home. Le Loutre told the signers that if they did not efface their marks from the paper they should have neither sacraments in this life nor heaven in the next. He nevertheless allowed two of them to go to Quebec as deputies, writing at the same time to the Governor, that his mind might be duly prepared. Duquesne replied: "I think that the two rascals of deputies whom you sent me will not soon recover from the fright I gave them, notwithstanding the emollient I administered after my reprimand; and since I told them that they were indebted to you for not being allowed to rot in a dungeon, they have promised me to comply with your wishes."[3]

An entire heartlessness marked the dealings of the French authorities with the Acadians. They were treated as mere tools of policy, to be used, broken, and flung away. Yet, in using them, the sole condition of their efficiency was neglected. The French Government, cheated of enormous sums by its own ravenous agents, grudged the cost of sending a single regiment to the Acadian border. Thus unsupported, the Acadians remained in fear and vacillation, aiding the French but feebly, though a ceaseless annoyance and menace to the English.

This was the state of affairs at Beauséjour while Shirley and Lawrence were planning its destruction. Lawrence had empowered his agent, Monckton, to draw without limit on two Boston merchants, Apthorp

---

[1] *Pichon to Captain Scott*, 14 Oct. 1754, in *Public Documents of Nova Scotia*, 229.

[2] *Public Documents of Nova Scotia*, 223, 224, 226, 227, 238.

[3] *Public Documents of Nova Scotia*, 239.

and Hancock. Shirley, as commander-in-chief of the province of Massachusetts, commissioned John Winslow to raise two thousand volunteers. Winslow was sprung from the early governors of Plymouth colony; but, though well-born, he was ill-educated, which did not prevent him from being both popular and influential. He had strong military inclinations, had led a company of his own raising in the luckless attack on Carthagena, had commanded the force sent in the preceding summer to occupy the Kennebec, and on various other occasions had left his Marshfield farm to serve his country. The men enlisted readily at his call, and were formed into a regiment, of which Shirley made himself the nominal colonel. It had two battalions, of which Winslow, as lieutenant-colonel, commanded the first, and George Scott the second, both under the orders of Monckton. Country villages far and near, from the western borders of the Connecticut to' uttermost Cape Cod, lent soldiers to the new regiment. The muster-rolls preserve their names, vocations, birthplaces, and abode. Obadiah, Nehemiah, Jedediah, Jonathan, Ebenezer, Joshua, and the like Old Testament names abound upon the list. Some are set down as "farmers," "yeomen," or "husbandmen;" others as "shopkeepers," others as "fishermen," and many as "laborers;" while a great number were handicraftsmen of various trades, from blacksmiths to wig-makers. They mustered at Boston early in April, where clothing, haversacks, and blankets were served out to them at the charge of the King; and the crooked streets of the New England capital were filled with staring young rustics. On the next Saturday the following mandate went forth: "The men will behave very orderly on the Sabbath Day, and either stay on board their transports, or else go to church, and not stroll up and down the streets." The transports, consisting of about forty sloops and schooners, lay at Long Wharf; and here on Monday a grand review took place,—to the gratification, no doubt, of a populace whose amusements were few. All was ready except the muskets, which were expected from England, but did not come. Hence the delay of a month, threatening to ruin the enterprise. When Shirley returned from Alexandria he found, to his disgust, that the transports still lay at the wharf where he had left them on his departure.[1] The muskets arrived at length, and the fleet sailed on the twenty-second of May. Three small frigates, the "Success," the "Mermaid," and the "Siren," commanded by the ex-privateersman, Captain Rous, acted as convoy; and on the twenty-sixth the whole force safely reached Annapolis. Thence after some delay they sailed up the Bay of

[1] *Shirley to Robinson, 20 June, 1755.*

Fundy, and at sunset on the first of June anchored within five miles of the hill of Beauséjour.

At two o'clock on the next morning a party of Acadians from Chipody roused Vergor with the news. In great alarm, he sent a messenger to Louisbourg to beg for help, and ordered all the fighting men of the neighborhood to repair to the fort. They counted in all between twelve and fifteen hundred;[1] but they had no appetite for war. The force of the invaders daunted them; and the hundred and sixty regulars who formed the garrison of Beauséjour were too few to revive their confidence. Those of them who had crossed from the English side dreaded what might ensue should they be caught in arms; and, to prepare an excuse beforehand, they begged Vergor to threaten them with punishment if they disobeyed his order. He willingly complied, promised to have them killed if they did not fight, and assured them at the same time that the English could never take the fort.[2] Three hundred of them thereupon joined the garrison, and the rest, hiding their families in the woods, prepared to wage guerilla war against the invaders.

Monckton, with all his force, landed unopposed, and encamped at night on the fields around Fort Lawrence, whence he could contemplate Fort Beauséjour at his ease. The regulars of the English garrison joined the New England men; and then, on the morning of the fourth, they marched to the attack. Their course lay along the south bank of the Missaguash to where it was crossed by a bridge called Pont-à-Buot. This bridge had been destroyed; and on the farther bank there was a large blockhouse and a breastwork of timber defended by four hundred regulars, Acadians, and Indians. They lay silent and unseen till the head of the column reached the opposite bank; then raised a yell and opened fire, causing some loss. Three field-pieces were brought up, the defenders were driven out, and a bridge was laid under a spattering fusillade from behind bushes, which continued till the English had crossed the stream. Without further opposition, they marched along the road to Beauséjour, and, turning to the right, encamped among the woody hills half a league from the fort. That night there was a grand illumination, for Vergor set fire to the church and all the houses outside the ramparts.[3]

---

[1] *Mémoires sur le Canada, 1749–1760.* An English document, *State of the English and French Forts in Nova Scotia,* says 1,200 to 1,400.

[2] *Mémoires sur le Canada, 1749–1760.*

[3] Winslow, *Journal and Letter Book. Mémoires sur le Canada, 1749–1760.* Letters from officers on the spot in *Boston Evening Post* and *Boston News Letter. Journal of Surgeon John Thomas.*

The English spent some days in preparing their camp and reconnoitring the ground. Then Scott, with five hundred provincials, seized upon a ridge within easy range of the works. An officer named Vannes came out to oppose him with a hundred and eighty men, boasting that he would do great things; but on seeing the enemy, quietly returned, to become the laughing-stock of the garrison. The fort fired furiously, but with little effect. In the night of the thirteenth, Winslow, with a part of his own battalion, relieved Scott, and planted in the trenches two small mortars, brought to the camp on carts. On the next day they opened fire. One of them was disabled by the French cannon, but Captain Hazen brought up two more, of larger size, on ox-wagons; and, in spite of heavy rain, the fire was brisk on both sides.

Captain Rous, on board his ship in the harbor, watched the bombardment with great interest. Having occasion to write to Winslow, he closed his letter in a facetious strain. "I often hear of your success in plunder, particularly a coach.[1] I hope you have some fine horses for it, at least four, to draw it, that it may be said a New England colonel [*rode in*] his coach and four in Nova Scotia. If you have any good saddle-horses in your stable, I should be obliged to you for one to ride round the ship's deck on for exercise, for I am not likely to have any other."

Within the fort there was little promise of a strong defence. Le Loutre, it is true, was to be seen in his shirt-sleeves, with a pipe in his mouth, directing the Acadians in their work of strengthening the fortifications.[2] They, on their part, thought more of escape than of fighting. Some of them vainly begged to be allowed to go home; others went off without leave,— which was not difficult, as only one side of the place was attacked. Even among the officers there were some in whom interest was stronger than honor, and who would rather rob the King than die for him. The general discouragement was redoubled when, on the fourteenth, a letter came from the commandant of Louisbourg to say that he could send no help, as British ships blocked the way. On the morning of the sixteenth, a mischance befell, recorded in these words in the diary of Surgeon John Thomas: "One of our large shells fell through what they called their bomb-proof, where a number of their officers were sitting, killed six of them dead, and one Ensign Hay, which the Indians had took prisoner a few days agone and carried to

---

[1] "11 June. Capt. Adams went with a Company of Raingers, and Returned at 11 Clock with a Coach and Sum other Plunder." *Journal of John Thomas.*

[2] *Journal of Pichon*, cited by Beamish Murdoch.

the fort." The party was at breakfast when the unwelcome visitor burst in. Just opposite was a second bomb-proof, where was Vergor himself, with Le Loutre, another priest, and several officers, who felt that they might at any time share the same fate. The effect was immediate. The English, who had not yet got a single cannon into position, saw to their surprise a white flag raised on the rampart. Some officers of the garrison protested against surrender; and Le Loutre, who thought that he had everything to fear at the hands of the victors, exclaimed that it was better to be buried under the ruins of the fort than to give it up; but all was in vain, and the valiant Vannes was sent out to propose terms of capitulation. They were rejected, and others offered, to the following effect: the garrison to march out with the honors of war and to be sent to Louisbourg at the charge of the King of England, but not to bear arms in America for the space of six months. The Acadians to be pardoned the part they had just borne in the defence, "seeing that they had been compelled to take arms on pain of death." Confusion reigned all day at Beauséjour. The Acadians went home loaded with plunder. The French officers were so busy in drinking and pillaging that they could hardly be got away to sign the capitulation. At the appointed hour, seven in the evening, Scott marched in with a body of provincials, raised the British flag on the ramparts, and saluted it by a general discharge of the French cannon, while Vergor as a last act of hospitality gave a supper to the officers.[1]

Le Loutre was not to be found; he had escaped in disguise with his box of papers, and fled to Baye Verte to join his brother missionary, Manach. Thence he made his way to Quebec, where the Bishop received him with reproaches. He soon embarked for France; but the English captured him on the way, and kept him eight years in Elizabeth Castle, on the Island of Jersey. Here on one occasion a soldier on guard made a dash at the father, tried to stab him with his bayonet, and was prevented with great difficulty. He declared that, when he was with his regiment in Acadia, he had fallen into the hands of Le Loutre, and narrowly escaped being scalped alive, the missionary having doomed him to this fate, and with his own hand drawn a knife round his head as a beginning of the operation. The man swore so fiercely that he would have his revenge, that the officer in command transferred him to another post.[2]

---

[1]On the capture of Beauséjour, _Mémoires sur le Canada, 1749–1760_; Pichon, _Cape Breton_, 318; _Journal of Pichon_, cited by Murdoch; and the English accounts already mentioned.

[2]Knox, _Campaigns in North America_, I. 114, _note_. Knox, who was stationed in Nova Scotia, says that Le Loutre left behind him "a most remarkable character for inhumanity."

Throughout the siege, the Acadians outside the fort, aided by Indians, had constantly attacked the English, but were always beaten off with loss. There was an affair of this kind on the morning of the surrender, during which a noted Micmac chief was shot, and being brought into the camp, recounted the losses of his tribe; "after which, and taking a dram or two, he quickly died," writes Winslow in his Journal.

Fort Gaspereau, at Baye Verte, twelve miles distant, was summoned by letter to surrender. Villeray, its commandant, at once complied; and Winslow went with a detachment to take possession.[1] Nothing remained but to occupy the French post at the mouth of the St. John. Captain Rous, relieved at last from inactivity, was charged with the task; and on the thirtieth he appeared off the harbor, manned his boats, and rowed for shore. The French burned their fort, and withdrew beyond his reach.[2] A hundred and fifty Indians, suddenly converted from enemies to pretended friends, stood on the strand, firing their guns into the air as a salute, and declaring themselves brothers of the English. All Acadia was now in British hands. Fort Beauséjour became Fort Cumberland,—the second fort in America that bore the name of the royal Duke.

The defence had been of the feeblest. Two years later, on pressing demands from Versailles, Vergor was brought to trial, as was also Villeray. The Governor, Vaudreuil, and the Intendant, Bigot, who had returned to Canada, were in the interest of the chief defendant. The court-martial was packed; adverse evidence was shuffled out of sight; and Vergor, acquitted and restored to his rank, lived to inflict on New France another and a greater injury.[3]

Now began the first act of a deplorable drama. Monckton, with his small body of regulars, had pitched their tents under the walls of Beauséjour. Winslow and Scott, with the New England troops, lay not far off. There was little intercourse between the two camps. The British officers bore themselves towards those of the provincials with a supercilious coldness common enough on their part throughout the war. July had passed in what Winslow calls "an indolent manner," with prayers every day in the Puritan camp, when, early in August, Monckton sent for him, and made an ominous declaration. "The said Monckton was so free as to acquaint me that it was determined to remove all the French inhabitants out of the province, and that he should send for all

[1]Winslow, Journal. Villeray au Ministre, 20 Sept. 1755.
[2]Drucour au Ministre, 1 Déc. 1755.
[3]Mémoire sur les Fraudes commises dans la Colonie, 1759. Mémoires sur le Canada, 1749–1760.

the adult males from Tantemar, Chipody, Aulac, Beauséjour, and Baye Verte to read the Governor's orders; and when that was done, was determined to retain them all prisoners in the fort. And this is the first conference of a public nature I have had with the colonel since the reduction of Beauséjour; and I apprehend that no officer of either corps has been made more free with."

Monckton sent accordingly to all the neighboring settlements, commanding the male inhabitants to meet him at Beauséjour. Scarcely a third part of their number obeyed. These arrived on the tenth, and were told to stay all night under the guns of the fort. What then befell them will appear from an entry in the diary of Winslow under date of August eleventh: "This day was one extraordinary to the inhabitants of Tantemar, Oueskak, Aulac, Baye Verte, Beauséjour, and places adjacent; the male inhabitants, or the principal of them, being collected together in Fort Cumberland to hear the sentence, which determined their property, from the Governor and Council of Halifax; which was that they were declared rebels, their lands, goods, and chattels forfeited to the Crown, and their bodies to be imprisoned. Upon which the gates of the fort were shut, and they all confined, to the amount of four hundred men and upwards." Parties were sent to gather more, but caught very few, the rest escaping to the woods.

Some of the prisoners were no doubt among those who had joined the garrison at Beauséjour, and had been pardoned for doing so by the terms of the capitulation. It was held, however, that, though forgiven this special offence, they were not exempted from the doom that had gone forth against the great body of their countrymen. We must look closely at the motives and execution of this stern sentence.

At any time up to the spring of 1755 the emigrant Acadians were free to return to their homes on taking the ordinary oath of allegiance required of British subjects. The English authorities of Halifax used every means to persuade them to do so; yet the greater part refused. This was due not only to Le Loutre and his brother priests, backed by the military power, but also to the Bishop of Quebec, who enjoined the Acadians to demand of the English certain concessions, the chief of which were that the priests should exercise their functions without being required to ask leave of the Governor, and that the inhabitants should not be called upon for military service of any kind. The Bishop added that the provisions of the treaty of Utrecht were insufficient, and that others ought to be exacted.[1] The oral declaration of the English authorities, that for the present the Acadians should not be required to

---

[1] *L'Évêque de Québec à Le Loutre, Nov. 1754*, in *Public Documents of Nova Scotia*, 240.

bear arms, was not thought enough. They, or rather their prompters, demanded a written pledge.

The refusal to take the oath without reservation was not confined to the emigrants. Those who remained in the peninsula equally refused it, though most of them were born and had always lived under the British flag. Far from pledging themselves to complete allegiance, they showed continual signs of hostility. In May three pretended French deserters were detected among them inciting them to take arms against the English.[1]

On the capture of Beauséjour the British authorities found themselves in a position of great difficulty. The New England troops were enlisted for the year only, and could not be kept in Acadia. It was likely that the French would make a strong effort to recover the province, sure as they were of support from the great body of its people. The presence of this disaffected population was for the French commanders a continual inducement to invasion; and Lawrence was not strong enough to cope at once with attack from without and insurrection from within.

Shirley had held for some time that there was no safety for Acadia but in ridding it of the Acadians. He had lately proposed that the lands of the district of Chignecto, abandoned by their emigrant owners, should be given to English settlers, who would act as a check and a counterpoise to the neighboring French population. This advice had not been acted upon. Nevertheless Shirley and his brother Governor of Nova Scotia were kindred spirits, and inclined to similar measures. Colonel Charles Lawrence had not the good-nature and conciliatory temper which marked his predecessors, Cornwallis and Hopson. His energetic will was not apt to relent under the softer sentiments, and the behavior of the Acadians was fast exhausting his patience. More than a year before, the Lords of Trade had instructed him that they had no right to their lands if they persisted in refusing the oath.[2] Lawrence replied, enlarging on their obstinacy, treachery, and "ingratitude for the favor, indulgence, and protection they have at all times so undeservedly received from His Majesty's Government;" declaring at the same time that, "while they remain without taking the oaths, and have incendiary French priests among them, there are no hopes of their amendment;" and that "it would be much better, if they refuse the oaths, that they were away."[3] "We were in hopes," again wrote the

[1] *Ibid.*, 242.
[2] *Lords of Trade to Lawrence, 4 March, 1754.*
[3] *Lawrence to Lords of Trade, 1 Aug. 1754.*

Lords of Trade, "that the lenity which had been shown to those people by indulging them in the free exercise of their religion and the quiet possession of their lands, would by degrees have gained their friendship and assistance, and weaned their affections from the French; but we are sorry to find that this lenity has had so little effect, and that they still hold the same conduct, furnishing them with labor, provisions, and intelligence, and concealing their designs from us." In fact, the Acadians, while calling themselves neutrals, were an enemy encamped in the heart of the province. These are the reasons which explain and palliate a measure too harsh and indiscriminate to be wholly justified.

Abbé Raynal, who never saw the Acadians, has made an ideal picture of them,[1] since copied and improved in prose and verse, till Acadia has become Arcadia. The plain realities of their condition and fate are touching enough to need no exaggeration. They were a simple and very ignorant peasantry, industrious and frugal till evil days came to discourage them; living aloof from the world, with little of that spirit of adventure which an easy access to the vast fur-bearing interior had developed in their Canadian kindred; having few wants, and those of the rudest; fishing a little and hunting in the winter, but chiefly employed in cultivating the meadows along the River Annapolis, or rich marshes reclaimed by dikes from the tides of the Bay of Fundy. The British Government left them entirely free of taxation. They made clothing of flax and wool of their own raising, hats of similar materials, and shoes or moccasons of moose and seal skin. They bred cattle, sheep, hogs, and horses in abundance; and the valley of the Annapolis, then as now, was known for the profusion and excellence of its apples. For drink, they made cider or brewed spruce-beer. French officials describe their dwellings as wretched wooden boxes, without ornaments or conveniences, and scarcely supplied with the most necessary furniture.[2] Two or more families often occupied the same house; and their way of life, though simple and virtuous, was by no means remarkable for cleanliness. Such as it was, contentment reigned among them, undisturbed by what modern America calls progress. Marriages were early, and population grew apace. This humble society had its disturbing elements; for the Acadians, like the Canadians, were a litigious race, and neighbors often quarrelled about their boundaries. Nor were they without a bountiful share of jealousy, gossip, and backbiting, to relieve the monotony of their lives; and every village had its turbulent spirits, sometimes by fits, though rarely long, contumacious even towards the curé, the guide,

---

[1] *Histoire philosophique et politique*, VI. 242 (ed. 1772).
[2] *Beauharnois et Hocquart au Comte de Maurepas*, 12 Sept. 1745.

counsellor, and ruler of his flock. Enfeebled by hereditary mental subjection, and too long kept in leading-strings to walk alone, they needed
him, not for the next world only, but for this; and their submission,
compounded of love and fear, was commonly without bounds. He was
their true government; to him they gave a frank and full allegiance,
and dared not disobey him if they would. Of knowledge he gave them
nothing; but he taught them to be true to their wives and constant at
confession and Mass, to stand fast for the Church and King Louis, and
to resist heresy and King George; for, in one degree or another, the
Acadian priest was always the agent of a double-headed foreign
power,—the Bishop of Quebec allied with the Governor of Canada.[1]

When Monckton and the Massachusetts men laid siege to Beauséjour, Governor Lawrence thought the moment favorable for exacting
an unqualified oath of allegiance from the Acadians. The presence of a
superior and victorious force would help, he thought, to bring them to
reason; and there were some indications that this would be the result.
A number of Acadian families, who at the promptings of Le Loutre had
emigrated to Cape Breton, had lately returned to Halifax, promising to
be true subjects of King George if they could be allowed to repossess
their lands. They cheerfully took the oath; on which they were rein-
stated in their old homes, and supplied with food for the winter.[2] Their
example unfortunately found few imitators.

Early in June the principal inhabitants of Grand Pré and other settlements about the Basin of Mines brought a memorial, signed with their
crosses, to Captain Murray, the military commandant in their district,
and desired him to send it to Governor Lawrence, to whom it was
addressed. Murray reported that when they brought it to him they behaved with the greatest insolence, though just before they had been
unusually submissive. He thought that this change of demeanor was
caused by a report which had lately got among them of a French fleet
in the Bay of Fundy; for it had been observed that any rumor of an
approaching French force always had a similar effect. The deputies who
brought the memorial were sent with it to Halifax, where they laid it
before the Governor and Council. It declared that the signers had kept
the qualified oath they had taken, "in spite of the solicitations and
dreadful threats of another power," and that they would continue to

---

[1]Franquet, *Journal, 1751*, says of the Acadians: "Ils aiment l'argent, n'ont dans toute leur conduite
que leur intérêt pour objet, sont, indifféremment des deux sexes, d'une inconsidération dans leurs
discours qui dénote de la méchanceté." Another observer, Dieréville, gives a more favorable picture.

[2]*Public Documents of Nova Scotia*, 228.

prove "an unshaken fidelity to His Majesty, provided that His Majesty shall allow us the same liberty that he has [*hitherto*] granted us." Their memorial then demanded, in terms highly offensive to the Council, that the guns, pistols, and other weapons, which they had lately been required to give up, should be returned to them. They were told in reply that they had been protected for many years in the enjoyment of their lands, though they had not complied with the terms on which the lands were granted; "that they had always been treated by the Government with the greatest lenity and tenderness, had enjoyed more privileges than other English subjects, and had been indulged in the free exercise of their religion;" all which they acknowledged to be true. The Governor then told them that their conduct had been undutiful and ungrateful; "that they had discovered a constant disposition to assist His Majesty's enemies and to distress his subjects; that they had not only furnished the enemy with provisions and ammunition, but had refused to supply the [*English*] inhabitants or Government, and when they did supply them, had exacted three times the price for which they were sold at other markets." The hope was then expressed that they would no longer obstruct the settlement of the province by aiding the Indians to molest and kill English settlers; and they were rebuked for saying in their memorial that they would be faithful to the King only on certain conditions. The Governor added that they had some secret reason for demanding their weapons, and flattered themselves that French troops were at hand to support their insolence. In conclusion, they were told that now was a good opportunity to prove their sincerity by taking the oath of allegiance, in the usual form, before the Council. They replied that they had not made up their minds on that point, and could do nothing till they had consulted their constituents. Being reminded that the oath was personal to themselves, and that six years had already been given them to think about it, they asked leave to retire and confer together. This was granted, and at the end of an hour they came back with the same answer as before; whereupon they were allowed till ten o'clock on the next morning for a final decision.[1]

At the appointed time the Council again met, and the deputies were brought in. They persisted stubbornly in the same refusal. "They were then informed," says the record, "that the Council could no longer look on them as subjects to His Britannic Majesty, but as subjects to the King of France, and as such they must hereafter be treated; and they were ordered to withdraw." A discussion followed in the Council.

[1] *Minutes of Council at Halifax, 3 July, 1755,* in *Public Documents of Nova Scotia,* 247–255.

It was determined that the Acadians should be ordered to send new deputies to Halifax, who should answer for them, once for all, whether they would accept the oath or not; that such as refused it should not thereafter be permitted to take it; and "that effectual measures ought to be taken to remove all such recusants out of the province."

The deputies, being then called in and told this decision, became alarmed, and offered to swear allegiance in the terms required. The answer was that it was too late; that as they had refused the oath under persuasion, they could not be trusted when they took it under compulsion. It remained to see whether the people at large would profit by their example.

"I am determined," wrote Lawrence to the Lords of Trade, "to bring the inhabitants to a compliance, or rid the province of such perfidious subjects."[1] First, in answer to the summons of the Council, the deputies from Annapolis appeared, declaring that they had always been faithful to the British Crown, but flatly refusing the oath. They were told that, far from having been faithful subjects, they had always secretly aided the Indians, and that many of them had been in arms against the English; that the French were threatening the province; and that its affairs had reached a crisis when its inhabitants must either pledge themselves without equivocation to be true to the British Crown, or else must leave the country. They all declared that they would lose their lands rather than take the oath. The Council urged them to consider the matter seriously, warning them that, if they now persisted in refusal, no farther choice would be allowed them; and they were given till ten o'clock on the following Monday to make their final answer.

When that day came, another body of deputies had arrived from Grand Pré and the other settlements of the Basin of Mines; and being called before the Council, both they and the former deputation absolutely refused to take the oath of allegiance. These two bodies represented nine tenths of the Acadian population within the peninsula. "Nothing," pursues the record of the Council, "now remained to be considered but what measures should be taken to send the inhabitants away, and where they should be sent to." If they were sent to Canada, Cape Breton, or the neighboring islands, they would strengthen the enemy, and still threaten the province. It was therefore resolved to distribute them among the various English colonies, and to hire vessels for the purpose with all despatch.[2]

[1]*Lawrence to Lords of Trade, 18 July, 1755.*
[2]*Minutes of Council, 4 July–28 July,* in *Public Documents of Nova Scotia,* 255–267. Copies of these and other parts of the record were sent at the time to England, and are now in the Public Record Office, along with the letters of Lawrence.

The oath, the refusal of which had brought such consequences, was a simple pledge of fidelity and allegiance to King George II. and his successors. Many of the Acadians had already taken an oath of fidelity, though with the omission of the word "allegiance," and, as they insisted, with a saving clause exempting them from bearing arms. The effect of this was that they did not regard themselves as British subjects, and claimed, falsely as regards most of them, the character of neutrals. It was to put an end to this anomalous state of things that the oath without reserve had been demanded of them. Their rejection of it, reiterated in full view of the consequences, is to be ascribed partly to a fixed belief that the English would not execute their threats, partly to ties of race and kin, but mainly to superstition. They feared to take part with heretics against the King of France, whose cause, as already stated, they had been taught to regard as one with the cause of God; they were constrained by the dread of perdition. "If the Acadians are miserable, remember that the priests are the cause of it," writes the French officer Boishébert to the missionary Manach.[1]

The Council having come to a decision, Lawrence acquainted Monckton with the result, and ordered him to seize all the adult males in the neighborhood of Beauséjour; and this, as we have seen, he promptly did. It remains to observe how the rest of the sentence was carried into effect.

Instructions were sent to Winslow to secure the inhabitants on or near the Basin of Mines and place them on board transports, which, he was told, would soon arrive from Boston. His orders were stringent: "If you find that fair means will not do with them, you must proceed by the most vigorous measures possible, not only in compelling them to embark, but in depriving those who shall escape of all means of shelter or support, by burning their houses and by destroying everything that

---

[1] On the oath and its history, compare a long note by Mr. Akin in *Public Documents of Nova Scotia*, 263–267. Winslow in his Journal gives an abstract of a memorial sent him by the Acadians, in which they say that they had refused the oath, and so forfeited their lands, from motives of religion. I have shown in a former chapter that the priests had been the chief instruments in preventing them from accepting the English government. Add the following:—

"Les malheurs des Accadiens sont beaucoup moins leur ouvrage que le fruit des sollicitations et des démarches des missionnaires." *Vaudreuil au Ministre, 6 Mai, 1760.*

"Si nous avons la guerre, et si les Accadiens sont misérables, souvenez-vous que ce sont les prêtres qui en sont la cause." *Boishébert à Manach, 21 Fév. 1760.* Both these writers had encouraged the priests in their intrigues so long as these were likely to profit the French Government, and only blamed them after they failed to accomplish what was expected of them.

"Nous avons six missionnaires dont l'occupation perpetuelle est de porter les esprits au fanatisme et à la vengeance. . . . Je ne puis supporter dans nos prêtres ces odieuses déclamations qu'ils font tous les jours aux sauvages: 'Les Anglois sont les ennemis de Dieu, les compagnons du Diable.' " Pichon, *Lettres et Mémoires pour servir à l'Histoire du Cap-Breton,* 160, 161. (La Haye, 1760.)

may afford them the means of subsistence in the country." Similar orders were given to Major Handfield, the regular officer in command at Annapolis.

On the fourteenth of August Winslow set out from his camp at Fort Beauséjour, or Cumberland, on his unenviable errand. He had with him but two hundred and ninety-seven men. His mood of mind was not serene. He was chafed because the regulars had charged his men with stealing sheep; and he was doubly vexed by an untoward incident that happened on the morning of his departure. He had sent forward his detachment under Adams, the senior captain, and they were marching by the fort with drums beating and colors flying, when Monckton sent out his aide-de-camp with a curt demand that the colors should be given up, on the ground that they ought to remain with the regiment. Whatever the soundness of the reason, there was no courtesy in the manner of enforcing it. "This transaction raised my temper some," writes Winslow in his Diary; and he proceeds to record his opinion that "it is the most ungenteel, ill-natured thing that ever I saw." He sent Monckton a quaintly indignant note, in which he observed that the affair "looks odd, and will appear so in future history;" but his commander, reckless of the judgments of posterity, gave him little satisfaction.

Thus ruffled in spirit, he embarked with his men and sailed down Chignecto Channel to the Bay of Fundy. Here, while they waited the turn of the tide to enter the Basin of Mines, the shores of Cumberland lay before them dim in the hot and hazy air, and the promontory of Cape Split, like some misshapen monster of primeval chaos, stretched its portentous length along the glimmering sea, with head of yawning rock, and ridgy back bristled with forests. Borne on the rushing flood, they soon drifted through the inlet, glided under the rival promontory of Cape Blomedon, passed the red sandstone cliffs of Lyon's Cove, and descried the mouths of the rivers Canard and Des Habitants, where fertile marshes, diked against the tide, sustained a numerous and thriving population. Before them spread the boundless meadows of Grand Pré, waving with harvests or alive with grazing cattle; the green slopes behind were dotted with the simple dwellings of the Acadian farmers, and the spire of the village church rose against a background of woody hills. It was a peaceful, rural scene, soon to become one of the most wretched spots on earth. Winslow did not land for the present, but held his course to the estuary of the River Pisiquid, since called the Avon. Here, where the town of Windsor now stands, there was a stockade called Fort Edward, where a garrison of regulars under Captain Alexander Murray kept watch over the surrounding settlements. The New England men pitched their tents on shore, while the sloops that had brought them slept on the soft bed of tawny mud left by the fallen tide.

Winslow found a warm reception, for Murray and his officers had been reduced too long to their own society not to welcome the coming of strangers. The two commanders conferred together. Both had been ordered by Lawrence to "clear the whole country of such bad subjects;" and the methods of doing so had been outlined for their guidance. Having come to some understanding with his brother officer concerning the duties imposed on both, and begun an acquaintance which soon grew cordial on both sides, Winslow embarked again and retraced his course to Grand Pré, the station which the Governor had assigned him. "Am pleased," he wrote to Lawrence, "with the place proposed by your Excellency for our reception [*the village church*]. I have sent for the elders to remove all sacred things, to prevent their being defiled by heretics." The church was used as a storehouse and place of arms; the men pitched their tents between it and the graveyard; while Winslow took up his quarters in the house of the priest, where he could look from his window on a tranquil scene. Beyond the vast tract of grassland to which Grand Pré owed its name, spread the blue glistening breast of the Basin of Mines; beyond this again, the distant mountains of Cobequid basked in the summer sun; and nearer, on the left, Cape Blomedon reared its bluff head of rock and forest above the sleeping waves.

As the men of the settlement greatly outnumbered his own, Winslow set his followers to surrounding the camp with a stockade. Card-playing was forbidden, because it encouraged idleness, and pitching quoits in camp, because it spoiled the grass. Presently there came a letter from Lawrence expressing a fear that the fortifying of the camp might alarm the inhabitants. To which Winslow replied that the making of the stockade had not alarmed them in the least, since they took it as a proof that the detachment was to spend the winter with them; and he added, that as the harvest was not yet got in, he and Murray had agreed not to publish the Governor's commands till the next Friday. He concludes: "Although it is a disagreeable part of duty we are put upon, I am sensible it is a necessary one, and shall endeavor strictly to obey your Excellency's orders."

On the thirtieth, Murray, whose post was not many miles distant, made him a visit. They agreed that Winslow should summon all the male inhabitants about Grand Pré to meet him at the church and hear the King's orders, and that Murray should do the same for those around Fort Edward. Winslow then called in his three captains,—Adams,

Hobbs, and Osgood,—made them swear secrecy, and laid before them his instructions and plans; which latter they approved. Murray then returned to his post, and on the next day sent Winslow a note containing the following: "I think the sooner we strike the stroke the better, therefore will be glad to see you here as soon as conveniently you can. I shall have the orders for assembling ready written for your approbation, only the day blank, and am hopeful everything will succeed according to our wishes. The gentlemen join me in our best compliments to you and the Doctor."

On the next day, Sunday, Winslow and the Doctor, whose name was Whitworth, made the tour of the neighborhood, with an escort of fifty men, and found a great quantity of wheat still on the fields. On Tuesday Winslow "set out in a whale-boat with Dr. Whitworth and Adjutant Kennedy, to consult with Captain Murray in this critical conjuncture." They agreed that three in the afternoon of Friday should be the time of assembling; then between them they drew up a summons to the inhabitants, and got one Beauchamp, a merchant, to "put it into French." It ran as follows:—

BY John Winslow, Esquire, Lieutenant-Colonel and Commander of His Majesty's troops at Grand Pré, Mines, River Canard, and places adjacent.

To the inhabitants of the districts above named, as well ancients as young men and lads.

Whereas His Excellency the Governor has instructed us of his last resolution respecting the matters proposed lately to the inhabitants, and has ordered us to communicate the same to the inhabitants in general in person, His Excellency being desirous that each of them should be fully satisfied of His Majesty's intentions, which he has also ordered us to communicate to you, such as they have been given him.

We therefore order and strictly enjoin by these presents to all the inhabitants, as well of the above-named districts as of all the other districts, both old men and young men, as well as all the lads of ten years of age, to attend at the church in Grand Pré on Friday, the fifth instant, at three of the clock in the afternoon, that we may impart what we are ordered to communicate to them; declaring that no excuse will be admitted on any pretence whatsoever, on pain of forfeiting goods and chattels in default.

Given at Grand Pré, the second of September, in the twenty-ninth year of His Majesty's reign, A.D. 1755.

A similar summons was drawn up in the name of Murray for the inhabitants of the district of Fort Edward.

Captain Adams made a reconnoissance of the rivers Canard and Des Habitants, and reported "a fine country and full of inhabitants, a beautiful church, and abundance of the goods of the world." Another reconnoissance by Captains Hobbs and Osgood among the settlements behind Grand Pré brought reports equally favorable. On the fourth, another letter came from Murray: "All the people quiet, and very busy at their harvest; if this day keeps fair, all will be in here in their barns. I hope to-morrow will crown all our wishes." The Acadians, like the bees, were to gather a harvest for others to enjoy. The summons was sent out that afternoon. Powder and ball were served to the men, and all were ordered to keep within the lines.

On the next day the inhabitants appeared at the hour appointed, to the number of four hundred and eighteen men. Winslow ordered a table to be set in the middle of the church, and placed on it his instructions and the address he had prepared. Here he took his stand in his laced uniform, with one or two subalterns from the regulars at Fort Edward, and such of the Massachusetts officers as were not on guard duty; strong, sinewy figures, bearing, no doubt, more or less distinctly, the peculiar stamp with which toil, trade, and Puritanism had imprinted the features of New England. Their commander was not of the prevailing type. He was fifty-three years of age, with double chin, smooth forehead, arched eyebrows, close powdered wig, and round, rubicund face, from which the weight of an odious duty had probably banished the smirk of self-satisfaction that dwelt there at other times.[1] Nevertheless, he had manly and estimable qualities. The congregation of peasants, clad in rough homespun, turned their sunburned faces upon him, anxious and intent; and Winslow "delivered them by interpreters the King's orders in the following words," which, retouched in orthography and syntax, ran thus:—

GENTLEMEN,—I have received from His Excellency, Governor Lawrence, the King's instructions, which I have in my hand. By his orders you are called together to hear His Majesty's final resolution concerning the French inhabitants of this his province of Nova Scotia, who for almost half a century have had more indulgence granted them than any of his subjects in any part of his dominions. What use you have made of it you yourselves best know.

The duty I am now upon, though necessary, is very disagreeable to my natural make and temper, as I know it must be grievous to you, who are of the same species. But it is not my business to animadvert on the orders

[1] See his portrait, at the rooms of the Massachusetts Historical Society.

I have received, but to obey them; and therefore without hesitation I shall deliver to you His Majesty's instructions and commands, which are that your lands and tenements and cattle and live-stock of all kinds are forfeited to the Crown, with all your other effects, except money and household goods, and that you yourselves are to be removed from this his province.

The peremptory orders of His Majesty are that all the French inhabitants of these districts be removed; and through His Majesty's goodness I am directed to allow you the liberty of carrying with you your money and as many of your household goods as you can take without overloading the vessels you go in. I shall do everything in my power that all these goods be secured to you, and that you be not molested in carrying them away, and also that whole families shall go in the same vessel; so that this removal, which I am sensible must give you a great deal of trouble, may be made as easy as His Majesty's service will admit; and I hope that in whatever part of the world your lot may fall, you may be faithful subjects, and a peaceable and happy people.

I must also inform you that it is His Majesty's pleasure that you remain in security under the inspection and direction of the troops that I have the honor to command.

He then declared them prisoners of the King. "They were greatly struck," he says, "at this determination, though I believe they did not imagine that they were actually to be removed." After delivering the address, he returned to his quarters at the priest's house, whither he was followed by some of the elder prisoners, who begged leave to tell their families what had happened, "since they were fearful that the surprise of their detention would quite overcome them." Winslow consulted with his officers, and it was arranged that the Acadians should choose twenty of their number each day to revisit their homes, the rest being held answerable for their return.

A letter, dated some days before, now came from Major Handfield at Annapolis, saying that he had tried to secure the men of that neighborhood, but that many of them had escaped to the woods. Murray's report from Fort Edward came soon after, and was more favorable: "I have succeeded finely, and have got a hundred and eighty-three men into my possession." To which Winslow replied: "I have the favor of yours of this day, and rejoice at your success, and also for the smiles that have attended the party here." But he adds mournfully: "Things are now very heavy on my heart and hands." The prisoners were lodged in the church, and notice was sent to their families to bring them food. "Thus," says the Diary of the commander, "ended the memorable fifth of September, a day of great fatigue and trouble."

There was one quarter where fortune did not always smile. Major Jedediah Preble, of Winslow's battalion, wrote to him that Major Frye had just returned from Chipody, whither he had gone with a party of men to destroy the settlements and bring off the women and children. After burning two hundred and fifty-three buildings he had reimbarked, leaving fifty men on shore at a place called Peticodiac to give a finishing stroke to the work by burning the "Mass House," or church. While thus engaged, they were set upon by three hundred Indians and Acadians, led by the partisan officer Boishébert. More than half their number were killed, wounded, or taken. The rest ensconced themselves behind the neighboring dikes, and Frye, hastily landing with the rest of his men, engaged the assailants for three hours, but was forced at last to reimbark.[1] Captain Speakman, who took part in the affair, also sent Winslow an account of it, and added: "The people here are much concerned for fear your party should meet with the same fate (being in the heart of a numerous devilish crew), which I pray God avert."

Winslow had indeed some cause for anxiety. He had captured more Acadians since the fifth; and had now in charge nearly five hundred able-bodied men, with scarcely three hundred to guard them. As they were allowed daily exercise in the open air, they might by a sudden rush get possession of arms and make serious trouble. On the Wednesday after the scene in the church some unusual movements were observed among them, and Winslow and his officers became convinced that they could not safely be kept in one body. Five vessels, lately arrived from Boston, were lying within the mouth of the neighboring river. It was resolved to place fifty of the prisoners on board each of these, and keep them anchored in the Basin. The soldiers were all ordered under arms, and posted on an open space beside the church and behind the priest's house. The prisoners were then drawn up before them, ranked six deep,—the young unmarried men, as the most dangerous, being told off and placed on the left, to the number of a hundred and forty-one. Captain Adams, with eighty men, was then ordered to guard them to the vessels. Though the object of the movement had been explained to them, they were possessed with the idea that they were to be torn from their families and sent away at once; and they all, in great excitement, refused to go. Winslow told them that there must be no parley or delay; and as they still refused, a squad of soldiers advanced towards them with fixed bayonets; while he him-

[1] Also *Boishébert à Drucourt*, 10 Oct. *1755*, an exaggerated account. *Vaudreuil au Ministre*, 18 Oct. *1755*, sets Boishébert's force at one hundred and twenty-five men.

self, laying hold of the foremost young man, commanded him to move forward. "He obeyed; and the rest followed, though slowly, and went off praying, singing, and crying, being met by the women and children all the way (which is a mile and a half) with great lamentation, upon their knees, praying." When the escort returned, about a hundred of the married men were ordered to follow the first party; and, "the ice being broken," they readily complied. The vessels were anchored at a little distance from shore, and six soldiers were placed on board each of them as a guard. The prisoners were offered the King's rations, but preferred to be supplied by their families, who, it was arranged, should go in boats to visit them every day; "and thus," says Winslow, "ended this troublesome job." He was not given to effusions of feeling, but he wrote to Major Handfield: "This affair is more grievous to me than any service I was ever employed in."[1]

Murray sent him a note of congratulation: "I am extremely pleased that things are so clever at Grand Pré, and that the poor devils are so resigned. Here they are more patient than I could have expected for people in their circumstances; and what surprises me still more is the indifference of the women, who really are, or seem, quite unconcerned. I long much to see the poor wretches embarked and our affair a little settled; and then I will do myself the pleasure of meeting you and drinking their good voyage."

This agreeable consummation was still distant. There was a long and painful delay. The provisions for the vessels which were to carry the prisoners did not come; nor did the vessels themselves, excepting the five already at Grand Pré. In vain Winslow wrote urgent letters to George Saul, the commissary, to bring the supplies at once. Murray, at Fort Edward, though with less feeling than his brother officer, was quite as impatient of the burden of suffering humanity on his hands. "I am amazed what can keep the transports and Saul. Surely our friend at Chignecto is willing to give us as much of our neighbors' company as he well can."[2] Saul came at last with a shipload of provisions; but the lagging transports did not appear. Winslow grew heartsick at the daily sight of miseries which he himself had occasioned, and wrote to a friend at Halifax: "I know they deserve all and more than they feel; yet it hurts me to hear their weeping and wailing and gnashing of teeth. I am

---

[1]Haliburton, who knew Winslow's Journal only by imperfect extracts, erroneously states that the men put on board the vessels were sent away immediately. They remained at Grand Pré several weeks, and were then sent off at intervals with their families.

[2]*Murray to Winslow, 26 Sept. 1755.*

in hopes our affairs will soon put on another face, and we get transports, and I rid of the worst piece of service that ever I was in."

After weeks of delay, seven transports came from Annapolis; and Winslow sent three of them to Murray, who joyfully responded: "Thank God, the transports are come at last. So soon as I have shipped off my rascals, I will come down and settle matters with you, and enjoy ourselves a little."

Winslow prepared for the embarkation. The Acadian prisoners and their families were divided into groups answering to their several villages, in order that those of the same village might, as far as possible, go in the same vessel. It was also provided that the members of each family should remain together; and notice was given them to hold themselves in readiness. "But even now," he writes, "I could not persuade the people I was in earnest." Their doubts were soon ended. The first embarkation took place on the eighth of October, under which date the Diary contains this entry: "Began to embark the inhabitants, who went off very solentarily [*sic*] and unwillingly, the women in great distress, carrying off their children in their arms; others carrying their decrepit parents in their carts, with all their goods; moving in great confusion, and appeared a scene of woe and distress."[1]

Though a large number were embarked on this occasion, still more remained; and as the transports slowly arrived, the dismal scene was repeated at intervals, with more order than at first, as the Acadians had learned to accept their fate as a certainty. So far as Winslow was concerned, their treatment seems to have been as humane as was possible under the circumstances; but they complained of the men, who disliked and despised them. One soldier received thirty lashes for stealing fowls from them; and an order was issued forbidding soldiers or sailors, on pain of summary punishment, to leave their quarters without permission, "that an end may be put to distressing this distressed people." Two of the prisoners, however, while trying to escape, were shot by a reconnoitring party.

At the beginning of November Winslow reported that he had sent off fifteen hundred and ten persons, in nine vessels, and that more than six hundred still remained in his district.[2] The last of these were not embarked till late in December. Murray finished his part of the work at

---

[1] In spite of Winslow's care, some cases of separation of families occurred; but they were not numerous.

[2] *Winslow to Monckton, 3 Nov. 1755.*

the end of October, having sent from the district of Fort Edward eleven hundred persons in four frightfully crowded transports.[1] At the close of that month sixteen hundred and sixty-four had been sent from the district of Annapolis, where many others escaped to the woods.[2] A detachment which was ordered to seize the inhabitants of the district of Cobequid failed entirely, finding the settlements abandoned. In the country about Fort Cumberland, Monckton, who directed the operation in person, had very indifferent success, catching in all but little more than a thousand.[3] Le Guerne, missionary priest in this neighborhood, gives a characteristic and affecting incident of the embarkation. "Many unhappy women, carried away by excessive attachment to their husbands, whom they had been allowed to see too often, and closing their ears to the voice of religion and their missionary, threw themselves blindly and despairingly into the English vessels. And now was seen the saddest of spectacles; for some of these women, solely from a religious motive, refused to take with them their grown-up sons and daughters."[4] They would expose their own souls to perdition among heretics, but not those of their children.

When all, or nearly all, had been sent off from the various points of departure, such of the houses and barns as remained standing were burned, in obedience to the orders of Lawrence, that those who had escaped might be forced to come in and surrender themselves. The whole number removed from the province, men, women, and children, was a little above six thousand. Many remained behind; and while some of these withdrew to Canada, Isle St. Jean, and other distant retreats, the rest lurked in the woods or returned to their old haunts, whence they waged, for several years a guerilla warfare against the English. Yet their strength was broken, and they were no longer a danger to the province.

Of their exiled countrymen, one party overpowered the crew of the vessel that carried them, ran her ashore at the mouth of the St. John, and escaped.[5] The rest were distributed among the colonies from Massachusetts to Georgia, the master of each transport having been provided with a letter from Lawrence addressed to the Governor of the

[1] *Ibid.*

[2] *Captain Adams to Winslow, 29 Nov. 1755;* see also Knox, I. 85, who exactly confirms Adams's figures.

[3] *Monckton to Winslow, 7 Oct. 1755.*

[4] *Le Guerne à Prévost, 10 Mars, 1756.*

[5] *Lettre commune de Drucour et Prévost au Ministre, 6 Avril, 1756. Vaudreuil au Ministre, 1 Juin, 1756.*

province to which he was bound, and desiring him to receive the un-welcome strangers. The provincials were vexed at the burden imposed upon them; and though the Acadians were not in general ill-treated, their lot was a hard one. Still more so was that of those among them who escaped to Canada. The chronicle of the Ursulines of Quebec, speaking of these last, says that their misery was indescribable, and attributes it to the poverty of the colony. But there were other causes. The exiles found less pity from kindred and fellow Catholics than from the heretics of the English colonies. Some of them who had made their way to Canada from Boston, whither they had been transported, sent word to a gentleman of that place who had befriended them, that they wished to return.[1] Bougainville, the celebrated navigator, then aide-de-camp to Montcalm, says concerning them: "They are dying by whole-sale. Their past and present misery, joined to the rapacity of the Ca-nadians, who seek only to squeeze out of them all the money they can, and then refuse them the help so dearly bought, are the cause of this mortality." "A citizen of Quebec," he says farther on, "was in debt to one of the partners of the Great Company [*Government officials leagued for plunder*]. He had no means of paying. They gave him a great number of Acadians to board and lodge. He starved them with hunger and cold, got out of them what money they had, and paid the extortioner. *Quel pays! Quels mœurs!*"[2]

Many of the exiles eventually reached Louisiana, where their descen-dants now form a numerous and distinct population. Some, after in-credible hardship, made their way back to Acadia, where, after the peace, they remained unmolested, and, with those who had escaped seizure, became the progenitors of the present Acadians, now settled in various parts of the British maritime provinces, notably at Madawaska, on the upper St. John, and at Clare, in Nova Scotia. Others were sent from Virginia to England; and others again, after the complete conquest of the country, found refuge in France.

In one particular the authors of the deportation were disappointed in its results. They had hoped to substitute a loyal population for a disaf-fected one; but they failed for some time to find settlers for the vacated lands. The Massachusetts soldiers, to whom they were offered, would not stay in the province; and it was not till five years later that families of British stock began to occupy the waste fields of the Acadians. This

---

[1] Hutchinson, *Hist. Mass.*, III. 42, *note*.
[2] Bougainville, *Journal, 1756–1758*. His statements are sustained by *Mémoires sur le Canada, 1749–1760*.

goes far to show that a longing to become their heirs had not, as has been alleged, any considerable part in the motives for their removal.

New England humanitarianism, melting into sentimentality at a tale of woe, has been unjust to its own. Whatever judgment may be passed on the cruel measure of wholesale expatriation, it was not put in exe-cution till every resource of patience and persuasion had been tried in vain. The agents of the French Court, civil, military, and ecclesiastical, had made some act of force a necessity. We have seen by what vile practices they produced in Acadia a state of things intolerable, and impossible of continuance. They conjured up the tempest; and when it burst on the heads of the unhappy people, they gave no help. The Government of Louis XV. began with making the Acadians its tools, and ended with making them its victims.[1]

---

[1]It may not be remembered that the predecessor of Louis XV., without the slightest provocation or the pretence of any, gave orders that the whole Protestant population of the colony of New York, amounting to about eighteen thousand, should be seized, despoiled of their property, placed on board his ships, and dispersed among the other British colonies in such a way that they could not reunite. Want of power alone prevented the execution of the order. See *Frontenac and New France under Louis XIV.*, 189, 190.

9
Dieskau

1755

The next stroke of the campaign was to be the capture of
Crown Point, that dangerous neighbor which, for a
quarter of a century, had threatened the northern colonies. Shirley, in
January, had proposed an attack on it to the Ministry; and in February,
without waiting their reply, he laid the plan before his Assembly. They
accepted it, and voted money for the pay and maintenance of twelve
hundred men, provided the adjacent colonies would contribute in due
proportion.[1] Massachusetts showed a military activity worthy of the
reputation she had won. Forty-five hundred of her men, or one in eight
of her adult males, volunteered to fight the French, and enlisted for the

---

[1]*Governor Shirley's Message to his Assembly, 13 Feb. 1755. Resolutions of the Assembly of Massachusetts, 18 Feb. 1755.* Shirley's original idea was to build a fort on a rising ground near Crown Point,
in order to command it. This was soon abandoned for the more honest and more practical plan
of direct attack.

various expeditions, some in the pay of the province, and some in that of the King.[1] It remained to name a commander for the Crown Point enterprise. Nobody had power to do so, for Braddock was not yet come; but that time might not be lost, Shirley, at the request of his Assembly, took the responsibility on himself. If he had named a Massachusetts officer, it would have roused the jealousy of the other New England colonies; and he therefore appointed William Johnson of New York, thus gratifying that important province and pleasing the Five Nations, who at this time looked on Johnson with even more than usual favor. Hereupon, in reply to his request, Connecticut voted twelve hundred men, New Hampshire five hundred, and Rhode Island four hundred, all at their own charge; while New York, a little later, promised eight hundred more. When, in April, Braddock and the Council at Alexandria approved the plan and the commander, Shirley gave Johnson the commission of major-general of the levies of Massachusetts; and the governors of the other provinces contributing to the expedition gave him similar commissions for their respective contingents. Never did general take the field with authority so heterogeneous.

He had never seen service, and knew nothing of war. By birth he was Irish, of good family, being nephew of Admiral Sir Peter Warren, who, owning extensive wild lands on the Mohawk, had placed the young man in charge of them nearly twenty years before. Johnson was born to prosper. He had ambition, energy, an active mind, a tall, strong person, a rough, jovial temper, and a quick adaptation to his surroundings. He could drink flip with Dutch boors, or Madeira with royal governors. He liked the society of the great, would intrigue and flatter when he had an end to gain, and foil a rival without looking too closely at the means; but compared with the Indian traders who infested the border, he was a model of uprightness. He lived by the Mohawk in a fortified house which was a stronghold against foes and a scene of hospitality to friends, both white and red. Here—for his tastes were not fastidious—presided for many years a Dutch or German wench whom he finally married; and after her death a young Mohawk squaw took her place. Over his neighbors, the Indians of the Five Nations, and all others of their race with whom he had to deal, he acquired a remarkable influence. He liked them, adopted their ways, and treated them kindly or sternly as the case required, but always with a justice and honesty in strong contrast with the rascalities of the commission of Albany traders who had lately managed their affairs, and whom they so

---

[1]*Correspondence of Shirley,* Feb. *1755.* The number was much increased later in the season.

detested that one of their chiefs called them "not men, but devils." Hence, when Johnson was made Indian superintendent there was joy through all the Iroquois confederacy. When, in addition, he was made a general, he assembled the warriors in council to engage them to aid the expedition.

This meeting took place at his own house, known as Fort Johnson; and as more than eleven hundred Indians appeared at his call, his larder was sorely taxed to entertain them. The speeches were interminable. Johnson, a master of Indian rhetoric, knew his audience too well not to contest with them the palm of insufferable prolixity. The climax was reached on the fourth day, and he threw down the war-belt. An Oneida chief took it up; Stevens, the interpreter, began the war-dance, and the assembled warriors howled in chorus. Then a tub of punch was brought in, and they all drank the King's health.[1] They showed less alacrity, however, to fight his battles, and scarcely three hundred of them would take the war-path. Too many of their friends and relatives were enlisted for the French.

While the British colonists were preparing to attack Crown Point, the French of Canada were preparing to defend it. Duquesne, recalled from his post, had resigned the government to the Marquis de Vaudreuil, who had at his disposal the battalions of regulars that had sailed in the spring from Brest under Baron Dieskau. His first thought was to use them for the capture of Oswego; but the letters of Braddock, found on the battle-field, warned him of the design against Crown Point; while a reconnoitring party which had gone as far as the Hudson brought back news that Johnson's forces were already in the field. Therefore the plan was changed, and Dieskau was ordered to lead the main body of his troops, not to Lake Ontario, but to Lake Champlain. He passed up the Richelieu, and embarked in boats and canoes for Crown Point. The veteran knew that the foes with whom he had to deal were but a mob of countrymen. He doubted not of putting them to rout, and meant never to hold his hand till he had chased them back to Albany.[2] "Make all haste," Vaudreuil wrote to him; "for when you return we shall send you to Oswego to execute our first design."[3]

Johnson on his part was preparing to advance. In July about three thousand provincials were encamped near Albany, some on the "Flats" above the town, and some on the meadows below. Hither, too, came

[1] Report of Conference between Major-General Johnson and the Indians, June, 1755.

[2] Bigot au Ministre, 27 Août, 1755. Ibid., 5 Sept. 1755.

[3] Mémoire pour servir d'Instruction à M. le Baron de Dieskau, Maréchal des Camps et Armées du Roy, 15 Août, 1755.

a swarm of Johnson's Mohawks,—warriors, squaws, and children. They adorned the General's face with war-paint, and he danced the war-dance; then with his sword he cut the first slice from the ox that had been roasted whole for their entertainment. "I shall be glad," wrote the surgeon of a New England regiment, "if they fight as eagerly as they ate their ox and drank their wine."

Above all things the expedition needed promptness; yet everything moved slowly. Five popular legislatures controlled the troops and the supplies. Connecticut had refused to send her men till Shirley promised that her commanding officer should rank next to Johnson. The whole movement was for some time at a deadlock because the five governments could not agree about their contributions of artillery and stores.[1] The New Hampshire regiment had taken a short cut for Crown Point across the wilderness of Vermont; but had been recalled in time to save them from probable destruction. They were now with the rest in the camp at Albany, in such distress for provisions that a private subscription was proposed for their relief.[2]

Johnson's army, crude as it was, had in it good material. Here was Phineas Lyman, of Connecticut, second in command, once a tutor at Yale College, and more recently a lawyer,—a raw soldier, but a vigorous and brave one; Colonel Moses Titcomb, of Massachusetts, who had fought with credit at Louisbourg; and Ephraim Williams, also colonel of a Massachusetts regiment, a tall and portly man, who had been a captain in the last war, member of the General Court, and deputy-sheriff. He made his will in the camp at Albany, and left a legacy to found the school which has since become Williams College. His relative, Stephen Williams, was chaplain of his regiment, and his brother Thomas was its surgeon. Seth Pomeroy, gunsmith at Northampton, who, like Titcomb, had seen service at Louisbourg, was its lieutenant-colonel. He had left a wife at home, an excellent matron, to whom he was continually writing affectionate letters, mingling household cares with news of the camp, and charging her to see that their eldest boy, Seth, then in college at New Haven, did not run off to the army. Pomeroy had with him his brother Daniel; and this he thought was enough. Here, too, was a man whose name is still a household word in New England,—the sturdy Israel Putnam, private in a Connecticut regiment; and another as bold as he, John Stark, lieutenant in the New Hampshire levies, and the future victor of Bennington.

---

[1] *The Conduct of Major-General Shirley briefly stated* (London, 1758).
[2] *Blanchard to Wentworth, 28 Aug. 1755,* in *Provincial Papers of New Hampshire,* VI, 429.

The soldiers were no soldiers, but farmers and farmers' sons who had volunteered for the summer campaign. One of the corps had a blue uniform faced with red. The rest wore their daily clothing. Blankets had been served out to them by the several provinces, but the greater part brought their own guns; some under the penalty of a fine if they came without them, and some under the inducement of a reward.[1] They had no bayonets, but carried hatchets in their belts as a sort of substitute.[2] At their sides were slung powder-horns, on which, in the leisure of the camp, they carved quaint devices with the points of their jack-knives. They came chiefly from plain New England homesteads,— rustic abodes, unpainted and dingy, with long well-sweeps, capacious barns, rough fields of pumpkins and corn, and vast kitchen chimneys, above which in winter hung squashes to keep them from frost, and guns to keep them from rust.

As to the manners and morals of the army there is conflict of evidence. In some respects nothing could be more exemplary. "Not a chicken has been stolen," says William Smith, of New York; while, on the other hand, Colonel Ephraim Williams writes to Colonel Israel Williams, then commanding on the Massachusetts frontier: "We are a wicked, profane army, especially the New York and Rhode Island troops. Nothing to be heard among a great part of them but the language of Hell. If Crown Point is taken, it will not be for our sakes, but for those good people left behind."[3] There was edifying regularity in respect to form. Sermons twice a week, daily prayers, and frequent psalm-singing alternated with the much-needed military drill.[4] "Prayers among us night and morning," writes Private Jonathan Caswell, of Massachusetts, to his father. "Here we lie, knowing not when we shall march for Crown Point; but I hope not long to tarry. Desiring your prayers to God for me as I am agoing to war, I am Your Ever Dutiful Son."[5]

To Pomeroy and some of his brothers in arms it seemed that they were engaged in a kind of crusade against the myrmidons of Rome. "As you have at heart the Protestant cause," he wrote to his friend Israel Williams, "so I ask an interest in your prayers that the Lord of Hosts would go forth with us and give us victory over our unreasonable, encroaching, barbarous, murdering enemies."

[1] *Proclamation of Governor Shirley, 1755.*
[2] *Second Letter to a Friend on the Battle of Lake George.*
[3] *Papers of Colonel Israel Williams.*
[4] *Massachusetts Archives.*
[5] *Jonathan Caswell to John Caswell, 6 July, 1755.*

Both Williams the surgeon and Williams the colonel chafed at the incessant delays. "The expedition goes on very much as a snail runs," writes the former to his wife; "it seems we may possibly see Crown Point this time twelve months." The Colonel was vexed because everything was out of joint in the department of transportation: wagoners mutinous for want of pay; ordnance stores, camp-kettles, and provisions left behind. "As to rum," he complains, "it won't hold out nine weeks. Things appear most melancholy to me." Even as he was writing, a report came of the defeat of Braddock; and, shocked at the blow, his pen traced the words: "The Lord have mercy on poor New England!"

Johnson had sent four Mohawk scouts to Canada. They returned on the twenty-first of August with the report that the French were all astir with preparation, and that eight thousand men were coming to defend Crown Point. On this a council of war was called; and it was resolved to send to the several colonies for reinforcements.[1] Meanwhile the main body had moved up the river to the spot called the Great Carrying Place, where Lyman had begun a fortified storehouse, which his men called Fort Lyman, but which was afterwards named Fort Edward. Two Indian trails led from this point to the waters of Lake Champlain, one by way of Lake George, and the other by way of Wood Creek. There was doubt which course the army should take. A road was begun to Wood Creek; then it was countermanded, and a party was sent to explore the path to Lake George. "With submission to the general officers," Surgeon Williams again writes, "I think it a very grand mistake that the business of reconnoitring was not done months agone." It was resolved at last to march for Lake George; gangs of axemen were sent to hew out the way; and on the twenty-sixth two thousand men were ordered to the lake, while Colonel Blanchard, of New Hampshire, remained with five hundred to finish and defend Fort Lyman.

The train of Dutch wagons, guarded by the homely soldiery, jolted slowly over the stumps and roots of the newly made road, and the regiments followed at their leisure. The hardships of the way were not without their consolations. The jovial Irishman who held the chief command made himself very agreeable to the New England officers. "We went on about four or five miles," says Pomeroy in his Journal, "then stopped, ate pieces of broken bread and cheese, and drank some fresh lemon-punch and the best of wine with General Johnson and some of the field-officers." It was the same on the next day. "Stopped

[1] *Minutes of Council of War, 22 Aug. 1755. Ephraim Williams to Benjamin Dwight, 22 Aug. 1755.*

about noon and dined with General Johnson by a small brook under a tree; ate a good dinner of cold boiled and roast venison; drank good fresh lemon-punch and wine."

That afternoon they reached their destination, fourteen miles from Fort Lyman. The most beautiful lake in America lay before them; then more beautiful than now, in the wild charm of untrodden mountains and virgin forests. "I have given it the name of Lake George," wrote Johnson to the Lords of Trade, "not only in honor of His Majesty, but to ascertain his undoubted dominion here." His men made their camp on a piece of rough ground by the edge of the water, pitching their tents among the stumps of the newly felled trees. In their front was a forest of pitch-pine; on their right, a marsh, choked with alders and swamp-maples; on their left, the low hill where Fort George was afterwards built; and at their rear, the lake. Little was done to clear the forest in front, though it would give excellent cover to an enemy. Nor did Johnson take much pains to learn the movements of the French in the direction of Crown Point, though he sent scouts towards South Bay and Wood Creek. Every day stores and bateaux, or flat boats, came on wagons from Fort Lyman; and preparation moved on with the leisure that had marked it from the first. About three hundred Mohawks came to the camp, and were regarded by the New England men as nuisances. On Sunday the gray-haired Stephen Williams preached to these savage allies a long Calvinistic sermon, which must have sorely perplexed the interpreter whose business it was to turn it into Mohawk; and in the afternoon young Chaplain Newell, of Rhode Island, expounded to the New England men the somewhat untimely text, "Love your enemies." On the next Sunday, September seventh, Williams preached again, this time to the whites from a text in Isaiah. It was a peaceful day, fair and warm, with a few light showers; yet not wholly a day of rest, for two hundred wagons came up from Fort Lyman, loaded with bateaux. After the sermon there was an alarm. An Indian scout came in about sunset, and reported that he had found the trail of a body of men moving from South Bay towards Fort Lyman. Johnson called for a volunteer to carry a letter of warning to Colonel Blanchard, the commander. A wagoner named Adams offered himself for the perilous service, mounted, and galloped along the road with the letter. Sentries were posted, and the camp fell asleep.

While Johnson lay at Lake George, Dieskau prepared a surprise for him. The German Baron had reached Crown Point at the head of three thousand five hundred and seventy-three men, regulars, Canadians, and

Indians.[1] He had no thought of waiting there to be attacked. The troops were told to hold themselves ready to move at a moment's notice. Officers—so ran the order—will take nothing with them but one spare shirt, one spare pair of shoes, a blanket, a bearskin, and provisions for twelve days; Indians are not to amuse themselves by taking scalps till the enemy is entirely defeated, since they can kill ten men in the time required to scalp one.[2] Then Dieskau moved on, with nearly all his force, to Carillon, or Ticonderoga, a promontory commanding both the routes by which alone Johnson could advance, that of Wood Creek and that of Lake George.

The Indian allies were commanded by Legardeur de Saint-Pierre, the officer who had received Washington on his embassy to Fort Le Bœuf. These unmanageable warriors were a constant annoyance to Dieskau, being a species of humanity quite new to him. "They drive us crazy," he says, "from morning till night. There is no end to their demands. They have already eaten five oxen and as many hogs, without counting the kegs of brandy they have drunk. In short, one needs the patience of an angel to get on with these devils; and yet one must always force himself to seem pleased with them."[3]

They would scarcely even go out as scouts. At last, however, on the fourth of September, a reconnoitring party came in with a scalp and an English prisoner caught near Fort Lyman. He was questioned under the threat of being given to the Indians for torture if he did not tell the truth; but, nothing daunted, he invented a patriotic falsehood; and thinking to lure his captors into a trap, told them that the English army had fallen back to Albany, leaving five hundred men at Fort Lyman, which he represented as indefensible. Dieskau resolved on a rapid movement to seize the place. At noon of the same day, leaving a part of his force at Ticonderoga, he embarked the rest in canoes and advanced along the narrow prolongation of Lake Champlain that stretched southward through the wilderness to where the town of Whitehall now stands. He soon came to a point where the lake dwindled to a mere canal, while two mighty rocks, capped with stunted forests, faced each other from the opposing banks. Here he left an officer named Roquemaure with a detachment of troops, and again advanced along a belt of quiet water traced through the midst of a deep marsh, green at that season with sedge and water-weeds, and known to the

[1]*Vaudreuil au Ministre, 25 Sept. 1755.*
[2]*Livre d'Ordres, Août, Sept. 1755.*
[3]*Dieskau à Vaudreuil, 1 Sept. 1755.*

English as the Drowned Lands. Beyond, on either hand, crags feathered with birch and fir, or hills mantled with woods, looked down on the long procession of canoes.[1] As they neared the site of Whitehall, a passage opened on the right, the entrance to a sheet of lonely water slumbering in the shadow of woody mountains, and forming the lake then, as now, called South Bay. They advanced to its head, landed where a small stream enters it, left the canoes under a guard, and began their march through the forest. They counted in all two hundred and sixteen regulars of the battalions of Languedoc and La Reine, six hundred and eighty-four Canadians, and about six hundred Indians.[2] Every officer and man carried provisions for eight days in his knapsack. They encamped at night by a brook, and in the morning, after hearing Mass, marched again. The evening of the next day brought them near the road that led to Lake George. Fort Lyman was but three miles distant. A man on horseback galloped by; it was Adams, Johnson's unfortunate messenger. The Indians shot him, and found the letter in his pocket. Soon after, ten or twelve wagons appeared in charge of mutinous drivers, who had left the English camp without orders. Several of them were shot, two were taken, and the rest ran off. The two captives declared that, contrary to the assertion of the prisoner at Ticonderoga, a large force lay encamped at the lake. The Indians now held a council, and presently gave out that they would not attack the fort, which they thought well supplied with cannon, but that they were willing to attack the camp at Lake George. Remonstrance was lost upon them. Dieskau was not young, but he was daring to rashness, and inflamed to emulation by the victory over Braddock. The enemy were reported greatly to outnumber him; but his Canadian advisers had assured him that the English colony militia were the worst troops on the face of the earth. "The more there are," he said to the Canadians and Indians, "the more we shall kill;" and in the morning the order was given to march for the lake.

They moved rapidly on through the waste of pines, and soon entered the rugged valley that led to Johnson's camp. On their right was a gorge where, shadowed in bushes, gurgled a gloomy brook; and beyond rose the cliffs that buttressed the rocky heights of French Mountain, seen by glimpses between the boughs. On their left rose gradually the lower slopes of West Mountain. All was rock, thicket, and forest; there was

---

[1] I passed this way three weeks ago. There are some points where the scene is not much changed since Dieskau saw it.

[2] *Mémoire sur l'Affaire du 8 Septembre.*

no open space but the road along which the regulars marched, while the Canadians and Indians pushed their way through the woods in such order as the broken ground would permit.

They were three miles from the lake, when their scouts brought in a prisoner who told them that a column of English troops was approaching. Dieskau's preparations were quickly made. While the regulars halted on the road, the Canadians and Indians moved to the front, where most of them hid in the forest along the slopes of West Mountain, and the rest lay close among the thickets on the other side. Thus, when the English advanced to attack the regulars in front, they would find themselves caught in a double ambush. No sight or sound betrayed the snare; but behind every bush crouched a Canadian or a savage, with gun cocked and ears intent, listening for the tramp of the approaching column.

The wagoners who escaped the evening before had reached the camp about midnight, and reported that there was a war-party on the road near Fort Lyman. Johnson had at this time twenty-two hundred effective men, besides his three hundred Indians.[1] He called a council of war in the morning, and a resolution was taken which can only be explained by a complete misconception as to the force of the French. It was determined to send out two detachments of five hundred men each, one towards Fort Lyman, and the other towards South Bay, the object being, according to Johnson, "to catch the enemy in their retreat."[2] Hendrick, chief of the Mohawks, a brave and sagacious warrior, expressed his dissent after a fashion of his own. He picked up a stick and broke it; then he picked up several sticks, and showed that together they could not be broken. The hint was taken, and the two detachments were joined in one. Still the old savage shook his head. "If they are to be killed," he said, "they are too many; if they are to fight, they are too few." Nevertheless, he resolved to share their fortunes; and mounting on a gun-carriage, he harangued his warriors with a voice so animated and gestures so expressive, that the New England officers listened in admiration, though they understood not a word. One difficulty remained. He was too old and fat to go afoot; but Johnson lent him a horse, which he bestrode, and trotted to the head of the column, followed by two hundred of his warriors as fast as they could grease, paint, and befeather themselves.

---

[1] *Wraxall to Lieutenant-Governor Delancey, 10 Sept. 1755.* Wraxall was Johnson's aide-de-camp and secretary. The *Second Letter to a Friend* says twenty-one hundred whites and two hundred or three hundred Indians. Blodget, who was also on the spot, sets the whites at two thousand.

[2] *Letter to the Governors of the several Colonies, 9 Sept. 1755.*

THE COMBATANTS

In the middle of the eighteenth century the French controlled vast areas of the eastern American continent. But the English king, "dull, pompous" old George II (plate 1), whose colonies ranged only along the Atlantic Coast, had a vastly greater number of colonists than did the "worthless" French king, Louis XIV (3). Their fight for supremacy over the North American continent came to a climax in 1759, when French Quebec, defended by the Marquis de Montcalm, fell to the British general James Wolfe.

5

7

Céloron de Bienville (5), a captain of the French troops, was sent to the valley of the Ohio in 1749 to drive back English intruders. As he advanced he planted lead plates setting forth the French title to these lands. This fragment (6) from the mouth of the Muskingum River is one of three that has survived. On his way he stopped at La Preséntation, an Indian mission established by Father Piquet (7), who, like all clerical monitors of the French Crown, was attempting to convert the Indians. The conference (8), on the banks of the same Muskingum River, shows the English colonel Henry Bouquet also attempting to win over the Indians.

6

8

One of the bravest and most sagacious Indians supporting the British was Hendrick, Chief of the Mohawks (9). When the English commissioners blamed him for allowing so many of his people to be drawn away to Piquet's mission, Hendrick reminded them that "The French are a subtle and vigilant people, always using their utmost endeavors to seduce and bring us over to them." Both English and French alike had good reason to woo the Indians. The record of their cruelties in the dark frontier forests, their "taking the hair" of their victims (10), made them formidable enemies and essential allies.

9

10

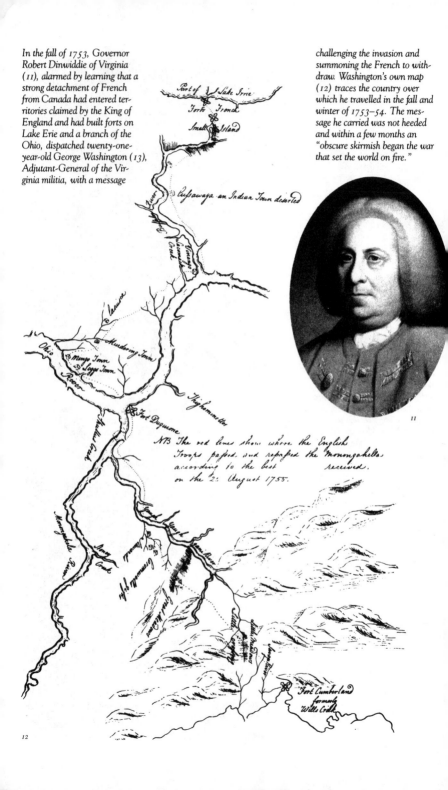

In the fall of 1753, Governor Robert Dinwiddie of Virginia (11), alarmed by learning that a strong detachment of French from Canada had entered territories claimed by the King of England and had built forts on Lake Erie and a branch of the Ohio, dispatched twenty-one-year-old George Washington (13), Adjutant-General of the Virginia militia, with a message challenging the invasion and summoning the French to withdraw. Washington's own map (12) traces the country over which he travelled in the fall and winter of 1753–54. The message he carried was not heeded and within a few months an "obscure skirmish began the war that set the world on fire."

14

15

17

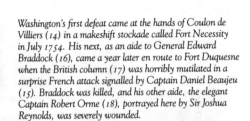

Washington's first defeat came at the hands of Coulon de Villiers (*14*) in a makeshift stockade called Fort Necessity in July *1754*. His next, as an aide to General Edward Braddock (*16*), came a year later en route to Fort Duquesne when the British column (*17*) was horribly mutilated in a surprise French attack signalled by Captain Daniel Beaujeu (*15*). Braddock was killed, and his other aide, the elegant Captain Robert Orme (*18*), portrayed here by Sir Joshua Reynolds, was severely wounded.

16

18

19

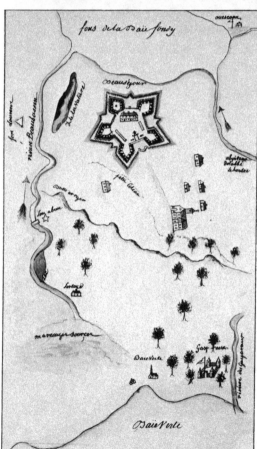

20

21

The conflict over Acadia was a long
and unhappy one. In 1710 it was
conquered and transferred by Franc
the British Crown. But the rebellion
continued for years—fanned by Fre
officials and priests and in particula
Louis Joseph Le Loutre, the fanatic

Vicar-General. In the plan (20) of Fort Beauséjour (19), which the French built across the river from the English Fort Lawrence, Abbé Le Loutre's church and hunting blind are delineated. Charles de Boishébert (21), chief French officer on the Acadian frontier, also encouraged the Acadians to migrate to the neighboring islands under French rule and prodded the Indians to harass the English at Halifax (22). In 1755 the incredible but inevitable took place, and six thousand Acadian men, women, and children were exiled to the English colonies (23).

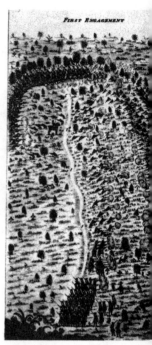

FIRST ENGAGEMENT

Niagara River.

LAKE ONTARIO

A VIEW of NIAGARA FORT,
taken by Sir William Johnson,
on the 25th of July 1759.
Drawn on the Spot in 1758.

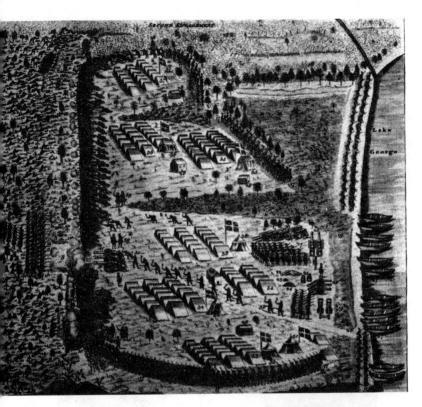

William Johnson (24) had "ambition, energy, an active mind, a tall, strong person," and, more important, a remarkable influence over his neighbors, the Indians of the Five Nations. In 1755 he was sent to Lake George to rout the French, and plate 25 shows the two engagements as drawn by an eyewitness. At left, his men are ambushed by the waiting French; at right, in the main battle, his soldiers with their three cannon defend their camp and inflict heavy losses on the advancing French troops. That same year Major-General William Shirley (27), the "lawyer-soldier," planned an attack on Fort Niagara—"the key to the interior" (26). Although that mission was abandoned owing to lack of provisions and the unexpected strength of the opposition awaiting him, that important post was finally captured in 1759 by Johnson, leaving "Detroit, Michillimackinac, the Illinois, and all the other French interior posts...severed from Canada."

27

28

29

30

31

32

33

Among the important Frenchmen in America during the conflict were
Canada's governors, the Marquis de la Galissonière (28), the Marquis
de la Jonquière (29), and the Marquis de Vaudreuil (30), and its military
men, Montcalm (33) and his aides, Colonel Louis Antoine de
Bougainville (31), and Duc François de Lévis (32).

In 1756 the Earl of Loudon (34) came to take command of the English forces in America, replacing Shirley just before the French descended in force upon Oswego (35) on Lake Ontario and took it with all its garrison. Loudon, "a rough Scotch lord, hot and irascible" blamed Shirley for the loss of this strategic fort. France's triumph here was the "greatest that the French arms had yet achieved in America."

To the east a different sort of war was being waged up and down Lake George and Lake Champlain by a bo of New England rangers under their captain, Robert Rogers of New Hampshire (37). On skates and snow shoes they made excursions to intercept provisions on their way to the French fort at Crown Point (36), making a plan of its works, capturing prisoners, burning houses and barns, and killing cattle.

34

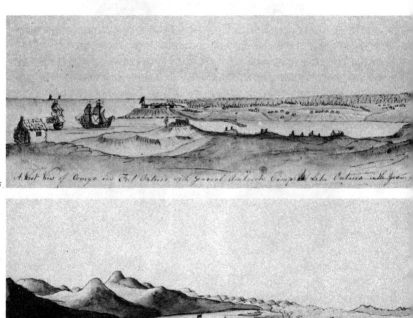

A West View of Oswego and Fort Ontario, with General Abercromby Camp at Lake Ontario with year

35

36

37

38

Two little ships operating on Lake Ontario: Lejeorge of the English fleet (38) and Lamarquisse de Vaudreuil of the French fleet (39), taken from an old French map.

39

Saint-Luc de la Corne (40) was called "general of the Indians." In 1757, under Montcalm's leadership, he led a body of Indians in an attack on Fort William Henry at the head of Lake George. After a long and bloody siege, the English surrendered and Montcalm called the Indian chiefs to council and asked them to promise to restrain their young warriors from any disorder. The woodcut on the title page of a contemporary pamphlet (41) shows the savage slaughter that occurred at Fort William Henry. La Corne stood by. A witness reported: "None, either officer or soldier, protected the said wounded men."

40

The CRUEL

MASSACRE

Of the PROTESTANTS, in

North America;

Shewing how the French and Indians join together to scalp the English, and the manner of their Scalping, &c. &c.

Printed and Sold in Aldermary Church-Yard, Bow Lane, LONDON.

41

Captain Elisha Hawley was in his tent, finishing a letter which he had just written to his brother Joseph; and these were the last words: "I am this minute agoing out in company with five hundred men to see if we can intercept 'em in their retreat, or find their canoes in the Drowned Lands; and therefore must conclude this letter." He closed and directed it; and in an hour received his death-wound.

It was soon after eight o'clock when Ephraim Williams left the camp with his regiment, marched a little distance, and then waited for the rest of the detachment under Lieutenant-Colonel Whiting. Thus Dieskau had full time to lay his ambush. When Whiting came up, the whole moved on together, so little conscious of danger that no scouts were thrown out in front or flank; and, in full security, they entered the fatal snare. Before they were completely involved in it, the sharp eye of old Hendrick detected some sign of an enemy. At that instant, whether by accident or design, a gun was fired from the bushes. It is said that Dieskau's Iroquois, seeing Mohawks, their relatives, in the van, wished to warn them of danger. If so, the warning came too late. The thickets on the left blazed out a deadly fire, and the men fell by scores. In the words of Dieskau, the head of the column "was doubled up like a pack of cards." Hendrick's horse was shot down, and the chief was killed with a bayonet as he tried to rise. Williams, seeing a rising ground on his right, made for it, calling on his men to follow; but as he climbed the slope, guns flashed from the bushes, and a shot through the brain laid him dead. The men in the rear pressed forward to support their comrades, when a hot fire was suddenly opened on them from the forest along their right flank. Then there was a panic; some fled outright, and the whole column recoiled. The van now became the rear, and all the force of the enemy rushed upon it, shouting and screeching. There was a moment of total confusion; but a part of Williams's regiment rallied under command of Whiting, and covered the retreat, fighting behind trees like Indians, and firing and falling back by turns, bravely aided by some of the Mohawks and by a detachment which Johnson sent to their aid. "And a very handsome retreat they made," writes Pomeroy; "and so continued till they came within about three quarters of a mile of our camp. This was the last fire our men gave our enemies, which killed great numbers of them; they were seen to drop as pigeons." So ended the fray long known in New England fireside story as the "bloody morning scout." Dieskau now ordered a halt, and sounded his trumpets to collect his scattered men. His Indians, however, were sullen and unmanageable, and the Canadians also showed signs of wavering. The veteran who commanded them all, Legardeur

de Saint-Pierre, had been killed. At length they were persuaded to
move again, the regulars leading the way.

About an hour after Williams and his men had begun their march, a
distant rattle of musketry was heard at the camp; and as it grew nearer
and louder, the listeners knew that their comrades were on the retreat.
Then, at the eleventh hour, preparations were begun for defence. A
sort of barricade was made along the front of the camp, partly of wagons, and partly of inverted bateaux, but chiefly of the trunks of trees
hastily hewn down in the neighboring forest and laid end to end in a
single row. The line extended from the southern slopes of the hill on
the left across a tract of rough ground to the marshes on the right. The
forest, choked with bushes and clumps of rank ferns, was within a few
yards of the barricade, and there was scarcely time to hack away the
intervening thickets. Three cannon were planted to sweep the road
that descended through the pines, and another was dragged up to the
ridge of the hill. The defeated party began to come in; first, scared
fugitives both white and red; then, gangs of men bringing the wounded;
and at last, an hour and a half after the first fire was heard, the main
detachment was seen marching in compact bodies down the road.

Five hundred men were detailed to guard the flanks of the camp.
The rest stood behind the wagons or lay flat behind the logs and inverted bateaux, the Massachusetts men on the right, and the Connecticut men on the left. Besides Indians, this actual fighting force was
between sixteen and seventeen hundred rustics, very few of whom had
been under fire before that morning. They were hardly at their posts
when they saw ranks of white-coated soldiers moving down the road,
and bayonets that to them seemed innumerable glittering between the
boughs. At the same time a terrific burst of war-whoops rose along the
front; and, in the words of Pomeroy, "the Canadians and Indians, helter-skelter, the woods full of them, came running with undaunted courage right down the hill upon us, expecting to make us flee."[1] Some of
the men grew uneasy; while the chief officers, sword in hand, threatened instant death to any who should stir from their posts.[2] If Dieskau
had made an assault at that instant, there could be little doubt of the
result.

This he well knew; but he was powerless. He had his small force of
regulars well in hand; but the rest, red and white, were beyond control,
scattering through the woods and swamps, shouting, yelling, and firing

[1] *Seth Pomeroy to his Wife,* 10 *Sept.* 1755.
[2] *Dr. Perez Marsh to William Williams,* 25 *Sept.* 1755.

from behind trees. The regulars advanced with intrepidity towards the camp where the trees were thin, deployed, and fired by platoons, till Captain Eyre, who commanded the artillery, opened on them with grape, broke their ranks, and compelled them to take to cover. The fusillade was now general on both sides, and soon grew furious. "Perhaps," Seth Pomeroy wrote to his wife, two days after, "the hailstones from heaven were never much thicker than their bullets came; but, blessed be God! that did not in the least daunt or disturb us." Johnson received a flesh-wound in the thigh, and spent the rest of the day in his tent. Lyman took command; and it is a marvel that he escaped alive, for he was four hours in the heat of the fire, directing and animating the men. "It was the most awful day my eyes ever beheld," wrote Surgeon Williams to his wife; "there seemed to be nothing but thunder and lightning and perpetual pillars of smoke." To him, his colleague Doctor Pynchon, one assistant, and a young student called "Billy," fell the charge of the wounded of his regiment. "The bullets flew about our ears all the time of dressing them; so we thought best to leave our tent and retire a few rods behind the shelter of a log-house." On the adjacent hill stood one Blodget, who seems to have been a sutler, watching, as well as bushes, trees, and smoke would let him, the progress of the fight, of which he soon after made and published a curious bird's-eye view. As the wounded men were carried to the rear, the wagoners about the camp took their guns and powder-horns, and joined in the fray. A Mohawk, seeing one of these men still unarmed, leaped over the barricade, tomahawked the nearest Canadian, snatched his gun, and darted back unhurt. The brave savage found no imitators among his tribesmen, most of whom did nothing but utter a few war-whoops, saying that they had come to see their English brothers fight. Some of the French Indians opened a distant flank fire from the high ground beyond the swamp on the right, but were driven off by a few shells dropped among them.

Dieskau had directed his first attack against the left and centre of Johnson's position. Making no impression here, he tried to force the right, where lay the regiments of Titcomb, Ruggles, and Williams. The fire was hot for about an hour. Titcomb was shot dead, a rod in front of the barricade, firing from behind a tree like a common soldier. At length Dieskau, exposing himself within short range of the English line, was hit in the leg. His adjutant, Montreuil, himself wounded, came to his aid, and was washing the injured limb with brandy, when the unfortunate commander was again hit in the knee and thigh. He seated himself behind a tree, while the Adjutant called two Canadians to carry him to the rear. One of them was instantly shot down. Montreuil took his place; but Dieskau refused to be moved, bitterly denounced the Canadians and Indians, and ordered the Adjutant to leave him and lead the regulars in a last effort against the camp.

It was too late. Johnson's men, singly or in small squads, were already crossing their row of logs; and in a few moments the whole dashed forward with a shout, falling upon the enemy with hatchets and the butts of their guns. The French and their allies fled. The wounded General still sat helpless by the tree, when he saw a soldier aiming at him. He signed to the man not to fire; but he pulled trigger, shot him across the hips, leaped upon him, and ordered him in French to surrender. "I said," writes Dieskau, " 'You rascal, why did you fire? You see a man lying in his blood on the ground, and you shoot him!' He answered: 'How did I know that you had not got a pistol? I had rather kill the devil than have the devil kill me.' 'You are a Frenchman?' I asked. 'Yes,' he replied; 'it is more than ten years since I left Canada;' whereupon several others fell on me and stripped me. I told them to carry me to their general, which they did. On learning who I was, he sent for surgeons, and, though wounded himself, refused all assistance till my wounds were dressed."[1]

It was near five o'clock when the final rout took place. Some time before, several hundred of the Canadians and Indians had left the field and returned to the scene of the morning fight, to plunder and scalp the dead. They were resting themselves near a pool in the forest, close beside the road, when their repose was interrupted by a volley of bullets. It was fired by a scouting party from Fort Lyman, chiefly backwoodsmen, under Captains Folsom and McGinnis. The assailants were greatly outnumbered; but after a hard fight the Canadians and Indians broke and fled. McGinnis was mortally wounded. He continued to give orders till the firing was over; then fainted, and was carried, dying, to the camp. The bodies of the slain, according to tradition, were thrown into the pool, which bears to this day the name of Bloody Pond.

The various bands of fugitives rejoined each other towards night, and encamped in the forest; then made their way round the southern shoulder of French Mountain, till, in the next evening, they reached their canoes. Their plight was deplorable; for they had left their knapsacks behind, and were spent with fatigue and famine.

Meanwhile their captive general was not yet out of danger. The Mo-

---

[1] *Dialogue entre le Maréchal de Saxe et le Baron de Dieskau aux Champs Élysées.* This paper is in the Archives de la Guerre, and was evidently written or inspired by Dieskau himself. In spite of its fanciful form, it is a sober statement of the events of the campaign. There is a translation of it in *N. Y. Col. Docs.*, X. 340.

hawks were furious at their losses in the ambush of the morning, and above all at the death of Hendrick. Scarcely were Dieskau's wounds dressed, when several of them came into the tent. There was a long and angry dispute in their own language between them and Johnson, after which they went out very sullenly. Dieskau asked what they wanted. "What do they want?" returned Johnson. "To burn you, by God, eat you, and smoke you in their pipes, in revenge for three or four of their chiefs that were killed. But never fear; you shall be safe with me, or else they shall kill us both."[1] The Mohawks soon came back, and another talk ensued, excited at first, and then more calm; till at length the visitors, seemingly appeased, smiled, gave Dieskau their hands in sign of friendship, and quietly went out again. Johnson warned him that he was not yet safe; and when the prisoner, fearing that his presence might incommode his host, asked to be removed to another tent, a captain and fifty men were ordered to guard him. In the morning an Indian, alone and apparently unarmed, loitered about the entrance, and the stupid sentinel let him pass in. He immediately drew a sword from under a sort of cloak which he wore, and tried to stab Dieskau; but was prevented by the Colonel to whom the tent belonged, who seized upon him, took away his sword, and pushed him out. As soon as his wounds would permit, Dieskau was carried on a litter, strongly escorted, to Fort Lyman, whence he was sent to Albany, and afterwards to New York. He is profuse in expressions of gratitude for the kindness shown him by the colonial officers, and especially by Johnson. Of the provincial soldiers he remarked soon after the battle that in the morning they fought like good boys, about noon like men, and in the afternoon like devils.[2] In the spring of 1757 he sailed for England, and was for a time at Falmouth; whence Colonel Matthew Sewell, fearing that he might see and learn too much, wrote to the Earl of Holdernesse: "The Baron has great penetration and quickness of apprehension. His long service under Marshal Saxe renders him a man of real consequence, to be cautiously observed. His circumstances deserve compassion, for indeed they are very melancholy, and I much doubt of his being ever perfectly cured." He was afterwards a long time at Bath, for the benefit of the waters. In 1760 the famous Diderot met him at Paris, cheerful and full of anecdote, though wretchedly shattered by his wounds. He died a few years later.

On the night after the battle the yeomen warriors felt the truth of

---

[1] See the story as told by Dieskau to the celebrated Diderot, at Paris, in 1760. *Mémoires de Diderot*, I. 402 (1830). Compare *N. Y. Col. Docs.*, X. 343.

[2] *Dr. Perez Marsh to William Williams, 25 Sept. 1755.*

the saying that, next to defeat, the saddest thing is victory. Comrades and friends by scores lay scattered through the forest. As soon as he could snatch a moment's leisure, the overworked surgeon sent the dismal tidings to his wife: "My dear brother Ephraim was killed by a ball through his head; poor brother Josiah's wound I fear will prove mortal; poor Captain Hawley is yet alive, though I did not think he would live two hours after bringing him in." Daniel Pomeroy was shot dead; and his brother Seth wrote the news to his wife Rachel, who was just delivered of a child: "Dear Sister, this brings heavy tidings; but let not your heart sink at the news, though it be your loss of a dear husband. Monday the eighth instant was a memorable day; and truly you may say, had not the Lord been on our side, we must all have been swallowed up. My brother, being one that went out in the first engagement, received a fatal shot through the middle of the head." Seth Pomeroy found a moment to write also to his own wife, whom he tells that another attack is expected; adding, in quaintly pious phrase: "But as God hath begun to show mercy, I hope he will go on to be gracious." Pomeroy was employed during the next few days with four hundred men in what he calls "the melancholy piece of business" of burying the dead. A letter-writer of the time does not approve what was done on this occasion. "Our people," he says, "not only buried the French dead, but buried as many of them as might be without the knowledge of our Indians, to prevent their being scalped. This I call an excess of civility;" his reason being that Braddock's dead soldiers had been left to the wolves.

The English loss in killed, wounded, and missing was two hundred and sixty-two;[1] and that of the French by their own account, two hundred and twenty-eight,[2]—a somewhat modest result of five hours' fighting. The English loss was chiefly in the ambush of the morning, where the killed greatly outnumbered the wounded, because those who fell and could not be carried away were tomahawked by Dieskau's Indians. In the fight at the camp, both Indians and Canadians kept themselves so well under cover that it was very difficult for the New England men to pick them off, while they on their part lay close behind their row of logs. On the French side, the regular officers and troops bore the brunt of the battle and suffered the chief loss, nearly all of the former and nearly half of the latter being killed or wounded.

Johnson did not follow up his success. He says that his men were

---

[1] *Return of Killed, Wounded, and Missing at the Battle of Lake George.*

[2] *Doreil au Ministre, 20 Oct. 1755.* Surgeon Williams gives the English loss as two hundred and sixteen killed, and ninety-six wounded. Pomeroy thinks that the French lost four or five hundred. Johnson places their loss at four hundred.

tired. Yet five hundred of them had stood still all day, and boats enough for their transportation were lying on the beach. Ten miles down the lake, a path led over a gorge of the mountains to South Bay, where Dieskau had left his canoes and provisions. It needed but a few hours to reach and destroy them; but no such attempt was made. Nor, till a week after, did Johnson send out scouts to learn the strength of the enemy at Ticonderoga. Lyman strongly urged him to make an effort to seize that important pass; but Johnson thought only of holding his own position. "I think," he wrote, "we may expect very shortly a more formidable attack." He made a solid breastwork to defend his camp; and as reinforcements arrived, set them at building a fort on a rising ground by the lake. It is true that just after the battle he was deficient in stores, and had not bateaux enough to move his whole force. It is true, also, that he was wounded, and that he was too jealous of Lyman to delegate the command to him; and so the days passed till, within a fortnight, his nimble enemy were entrenched at Ticonderoga in force enough to defy him.

The Crown Point expedition was a failure disguised under an incidental success. The northern provinces, especially Massachusetts and Connecticut, did what they could to forward it, and after the battle sent a herd of raw recruits to the scene of action. Shirley wrote to Johnson from Oswego; declared that his reasons for not advancing were insufficient, and urged him to push for Ticonderoga at once. Johnson replied that he had not wagons enough, and that his troops were ill-clothed, ill-fed, discontented, insubordinate, and sickly. He complained that discipline was out of the question, because the officers were chosen by popular election; that many of them were no better than the men, unfit for command, and like so many "heads of a mob."[1] The reinforcements began to come in, till, in October, there were thirty-six hundred men in the camp; and as most of them wore summer clothing and had but one thin domestic blanket, they were half frozen in the chill autumn nights.

Johnson called a council of war; and as he was suffering from inflamed eyes, and was still kept in his tent by his wound, he asked Lyman to preside,—not unwilling, perhaps, to shift the responsibility upon him. After several sessions and much debate, the assembled officers decided that it was inexpedient to proceed.[2] Yet the army lay more than a month longer at the lake, while the disgust of the men increased

[1] *Shirley to Johnson, 19 Sept. 1755. Ibid., 24 Sept. 1755. Johnson to Shirley, 22 Sept. 1755. Johnson to Phipps, 10 Oct. 1755* (Massachusetts Archives).
[2] *Reports of Council of War, 11–21 Oct. 1755.*

daily under the rains, frosts, and snows of a dreary November. On the twenty-second, Chandler, chaplain of one of the Massachusetts regiments, wrote in the interleaved almanac that served him as a diary: "The men just ready to mutiny. Some clubbed their firelocks and marched, but returned back. Very rainy night. Miry water standing in the tents. Very distressing time among the sick." The men grew more and more unruly, and went off in squads without asking leave. A difficult question arose: Who should stay for the winter to garrison the new forts, and who should command them? It was settled at last that a certain number of soldiers from each province should be assigned to this ungrateful service, and that Massachusetts should have the first officer, Connecticut the second, and New York the third. Then the camp broke up. "Thursday the 27th," wrote the chaplain in his almanac, "we set out about ten of the clock, marched in a body, about three thousand, the wagons and baggage in the centre, our colonel much insulted by the way." The soldiers dispersed to their villages and farms, where in blustering winter nights, by the blazing logs of New England hearthstones, they told their friends and neighbors the story of the campaign.

The profit of it fell to Johnson. If he did not gather the fruits of victory, at least he reaped its laurels. He was a courtier in his rough way. He had changed the name of Lac St. Sacrement to Lake George, in compliment to the King. He now changed that of Fort Lyman to Fort Edward, in compliment to one of the King's grandsons; and, in compliment to another, called his new fort at the lake, William Henry. Of General Lyman he made no mention in his report of the battle, and his partisans wrote letters traducing that brave officer; though Johnson is said to have confessed in private that he owed him the victory. He himself found no lack of eulogists; and, to quote the words of an able but somewhat caustic and prejudiced opponent, "to the panegyrical pen of his secretary, Mr. Wraxall, and the *sic volo sic jubeo* of Lieutenant-Governor Delancey, is to be ascribed that mighty renown which echoed through the colonies, reverberated to Europe, and elevated a raw, inexperienced youth into a kind of second Marlborough."[1] Parliament gave him five thousand pounds, and the King made him a baronet.

---

[1] *Review of Military Operations in North America, in a Letter to a Nobleman* (ascribed to William Livingston).

On the Battle of Lake George a mass of papers will be found in the *N. Y. Col. Docs.*, Vols. VI. and X. Those in Vol. VI., taken chiefly from the archives of New York, consist of official and private letters, reports, etc., on the English side. Those in Vol. X. are drawn chiefly from the archives of the French War Department, and include the correspondence of Dieskau and his adjutant Montreuil. I have examined most of them in the original. Besides these I have obtained from the Archives de la Marine and other sources a number of important additional papers, which have never been printed, including Vaudreuil's reports to the Minister of War, and his strictures on Dieskau, whom he accuses of disobeying orders by dividing his force; also the translation of an English journal of the campaign found in the pocket of a captured officer, and a long account of the battle sent by Bigot to the Minister of Marine, 4 Oct. 1755.

I owe to the kindness of Theodore Pomeroy, Esq., a copy of the Journal of Lieutenant-Colonel Seth Pomeroy, whose letters also are full of interest; as are those of Surgeon Williams, from the collection of William L. Stone, Esq. The papers of Colonel Israel Williams, in the Library of the Massachusetts Historical Society, contain many other curious letters relating to the campaign, extracts from some of which are given in the text. One of the most curious records of the battle is *A Prospective-Plan of the Battle near Lake George, with an Explanation thereof, containing a full, though short, History of that important Affair, by Samuel Blodget, occasionally at the Camp when the Battle was fought.* It is an engraving, printed at Boston soon after the fight, of which it gives a clear idea. Four years after, Blodget opened a shop in Boston, where, as appears by his advertisements in the newspapers, he sold "English Goods, also English Hatts, etc." The engraving is reproduced in the *Documentary History of New York*, IV., and elsewhere. The *Explanation thereof* is only to be found complete in the original. This, as well as the anonymous *Second Letter to a Friend*, also printed at Boston in 1755, is excellent for the information it gives as to the condition of the ground where the conflict took place, and the position of the combatants. The unpublished Archives of Massachusetts; the correspondence of Sir William Johnson; the *Review of Military Operations in North America*; Dwight, *Travels in New England and New York*, III.; and Hoyt, *Antiquarian Researches on Indian Wars*,—should also be mentioned. Dwight and Hoyt drew their information from aged survivors of the battle. I have repeatedly examined the localities.

In the odd effusion of the colonial muse called *Tilden's Poems, chiefly to Animate and Rouse the Soldiers*, printed 1756, is a piece styled *The Christian Hero, or New England's Triumph*, beginning with the invocation,—

> "O Heaven, indulge my feeble Muse,
> Teach her what numbers for to choose!"

and containing the following stanza:—

> "Their Dieskau we from them detain,
> While Canada aloud complains
> And counts the numbers of their slain
> And makes a dire complaint;
> The Indians to their demon gods;
> And with the French there's little odds,
> While images receive their nods,
> Invoking rotten saints."

10

Shirley–Border War

1755, 1756

The capture of Niagara was to finish the work of the summer. This alone would have gained for England the control of the valley of the Ohio, and made Braddock's expedition superfluous. One marvels at the short-sightedness, the dissensions, the apathy which had left this key of the interior so long in the hands of France without an effort to wrest it from her. To master Niagara would be to cut the communications of Canada with the whole system of French forts and settlements in the West, and leave them to perish like limbs of a girdled tree.

Major-General Shirley, in the flush of his new martial honors, was to try his prentice hand at the work. The lawyer-soldier could plan a campaign boldly and well. It remained to see how he would do his part towards executing it. In July he arrived at Albany, the starting-point of his own expedition as well as that of Johnson. This little Dutch city was an outpost of civilization. The Hudson, descending from the northern wilderness, connected it with the lakes and streams that formed the thoroughfare to Canada; while the Mohawk, flowing from the west, was a liquid pathway to the forest homes of the Five Nations. Before the war was over, a little girl, Anne MacVicar, daughter of a Highland officer, was left at Albany by her father, and spent several years there in the house of Mrs. Schuyler, aunt of General Schuyler of the Revolution. Long after, married and middle-aged, she wrote down her recollections of the place,—the fort on the hill behind; the great street, grassy and broad, that descended thence to the river, with market, guard-house, town hall, and two churches in the middle, and rows of quaint Dutch-built houses on both sides, each detached from its neighbors, each with its well, garden, and green, and its great overshadowing tree. Before every house was a capacious porch, with seats where the people gathered in the summer twilight; old men at one door, matrons at another, young men and girls mingling at a third; while the cows with their tinkling bells came from the common at the end of the town, each stopping to be milked at the door of its owner; and children, porringer in hand, sat on the steps, watching the process and waiting their evening meal.

Such was the quiet picture painted on the memory of Anne Mac-Vicar, and reproduced by the pen of Mrs. Anne Grant.[1] The patriarchal, semi-rural town had other aspects, not so pleasing. The men were mainly engaged in the fur-trade, sometimes legally with the Five Nations, and sometimes illegally with the Indians of Canada,—an occupation which by no means tends to soften the character. The Albany Dutch traders were a rude, hard race, loving money, and not always scrupulous as to the means of getting it. Coming events, too, were soon to have their effect on this secluded community. Regiments, red and blue, trumpets, drums, banners, artillery trains, and all the din of war transformed its peaceful streets, and brought some attaint to domestic morals hitherto commendable; for during the next five years Albany was to be the principal base of military operations on the continent.

Shirley had left the place, and was now on his way up the Mohawk. His force, much smaller than at first intended, consisted of the New Jersey regiment, which mustered five hundred men, known as the Jersey Blues, and of the fiftieth and fifty-first regiments, called respectively

---

[1]*Memoirs of an American Lady* (Mrs. Schuyler), Chap. VI. A genuine picture of colonial life, and a charming book, though far from being historically trustworthy. Compare the account of Albany in Kalm, II. 102.

Shirley's and Pepperell's. These, though paid by the King and counted as regulars, were in fact raw provincials, just raised in the colonies, and wearing their gay uniforms with an awkward, unaccustomed air. How they gloried in them may be gathered from a letter of Sergeant James Gray, of Pepperell's, to his brother John: "I have two Holland shirts, found me by the King, and two pair of shoes and two pair of worsted stockings; a good silver-laced hat (the lace I could sell for four dollars); and my clothes is as fine scarlet broadcloth as ever you did see. A sergeant here in the King's regiment is counted as good as an ensign with you; and one day in every week we must have our hair or wigs powdered."[1] Most of these gorgeous warriors were already on their way to Oswego, their first destination.

Shirley followed, embarking at the Dutch village of Schenectady, and ascending the Mohawk with about two hundred of the so-called regulars in bateaux. They passed Fort Johnson, the two villages of the Mohawks, and the Palatine settlement of German Flats; left behind the last trace of civilized man, rowed sixty miles through a wilderness, and reached the Great Carrying Place, which divided the waters that flow to the Hudson from those that flow to Lake Ontario. Here now stands the city which the classic zeal of its founders has adorned with the name of Rome. Then all was swamp and forest, traversed by a track that led to Wood Creek,—which is not to be confounded with the Wood Creek of Lake Champlain. Thither the bateaux were dragged on sledges and launched on the dark and tortuous stream, which, fed by a decoction of forest leaves that oozed from the marshy shores, crept in shadow through depths of foliage, with only a belt of illumined sky gleaming between the jagged tree-tops. Tall and lean with straining towards the light, their rough, gaunt stems trickling with perpetual damps, stood on either hand the silent hosts of the forest. The skeletons of their dead, barkless, blanched, and shattered, strewed the mud-banks and shallows; others lay submerged, like bones of drowned mammoths, thrusting lank, white limbs above the sullen water; and great trees, entire as yet, were flung by age or storms athwart the current,—a bristling barricade of matted boughs. There was work for the axe as well as for the oar; till at length Lake Oneida opened before them, and they rowed all day over its sunny breast, reached the outlet, and drifted down the shallow eddies of the Onondaga, between walls of verdure, silent as death, yet haunted everywhere with ambushed danger. It was twenty days after leaving Schenectady when they neared the mouth of the river; and Lake Ontario greeted them, stretched like a sea

[1] *James Gray to John Gray, 11 July, 1755.*

to the pale brink of the northern sky, while on the bare hill at their left stood the miserable little fort of Oswego.

Shirley's whole force soon arrived; but not the needful provisions and stores. The machinery of transportation and the commissariat was in the bewildered state inevitable among a peaceful people at the beginning of a war; while the news of Braddock's defeat produced such an effect on the boatmen and the draymen at the carrying-places, that the greater part deserted. Along with these disheartening tidings, Shirley learned the death of his eldest son, killed at the side of Braddock. He had with him a second son, Captain John Shirley, a vivacious young man, whom his father and his father's friends in their familiar correspondence always called "Jack." John Shirley's letters give a lively view of the situation.

"I have sat down to write to you,"—thus he addresses Governor Morris, of Pennsylvania, who seems to have had a great liking for him,—"because there is an opportunity of sending you a few lines; and if you will promise to excuse blots, interlineations, and grease (for this is written in the open air, upon the head of a pork-barrel, and twenty people about me), I will begin another half-sheet. We are not more than about fifteen hundred men fit for duty; but that, I am pretty sure, if we can go in time in our sloop, schooner, row-galleys, and whale-boats, will be sufficient to take Frontenac; after which we may venture to go upon the attack of Niagara, but not before. I have not the least doubt with myself of knocking down both these places yet this fall, if we can get away in a week. If we take or destroy their two vessels at Frontenac, and ruin their harbor there, and destroy the two forts of that and Niagara, I shall think we have done great things. Nobody holds it out better than my father and myself. We shall all of us relish a good house over our heads, being all encamped, except the General and some few field-officers, who have what are called at Oswego houses; but they would in other countries be called only sheds, except the fort, where my father is. Adieu, dear sir; I hope my next will be directed from Frontenac. Yours most affectionately, John Shirley."[1]

---

[1] The young author of this letter was, like his brother, a victim of the war.

"Permit me, good sir, to offer you my hearty condolence upon the death of my friend Jack, whose worth I admired, and feel for him more than I can express. . . . Few men of his age had so many friends." *Governor Morris to Shirley, 27 Nov. 1755.*

"My heart bleeds for Mr. Shirley. He must be overwhelmed with Grief when he hears of Capt. John Shirley's Death, of which I have an Account by the last Post from New York, where he died of a Flux and Fever that he had contracted at Oswego. The loss of Two Sons in one Campaign scarcely admits of Consolation. I feel the Anguish of the unhappy Father, and mix my Tears very heartily with his. I have had an intimate Acquaintance with Both of Them for many Years, and know well their inestimable Value." *Morris to Dinwiddie, 29 Nov. 1755.*

Fort Frontenac lay to the northward, fifty miles or more across the lake. Niagara lay to the westward, at the distance of four or five days by boat or canoe along the south shore. At Frontenac there was a French force of fourteen hundred regulars and Canadians.[1] They had vessels and canoes to cross the lake and fall upon Oswego as soon as Shirley should leave it to attack Niagara; for Braddock's captured papers had revealed to them the English plan. If they should take it, Shirley would be cut off from his supplies and placed in desperate jeopardy, with the enemy in his rear. Hence it is that John Shirley insists on taking Frontenac before attempting Niagara. But the task was not easy; for the French force at the former place was about equal in effective strength to that of the English at Oswego. At Niagara, too, the French had, at the end of August, nearly twelve hundred Canadians and Indians from Fort Duquesne and the upper lakes.[2] Shirley was but imperfectly informed by his scouts of the unexpected strength of the opposition that awaited him; but he knew enough to see that his position was a difficult one. His movement on Niagara was stopped, first by want of provisions, and secondly because he was check-mated by the troops at Frontenac. He did not despair. Want of courage was not among his failings, and he was but too ready to take risks. He called a council of officers, told them that the total number of men fit for duty was thirteen hundred and seventy-six, and that as soon as provisions enough should arrive he would embark for Niagara with six hundred soldiers and as many Indians as possible, leaving the rest to defend Oswego against the expected attack from Fort Frontenac.[3]

"All I am uneasy about is our provisions," writes John Shirley to his friend Morris; "our men have been upon half allowance of bread these three weeks past, and no rum given to 'em. My father yesterday called all the Indians together and made 'em a speech on the subject of General Johnson's engagement, which he calculated to inspire them with a spirit of revenge." After the speech he gave them a bullock for a feast, which they roasted and ate, pretending that they were eating the Governor of Canada! Some provisions arriving, orders were given to embark on the next day; but the officers murmured their dissent. The weather was persistently bad, their vessels would not hold half the party, and the bateaux, made only for river navigation, would infallibly founder on the treacherous and stormy lake. "All the field-officers," says John

---

[1] *Bigot au Ministre, 27 Août, 1755.*
[2] *Ibid., 5 Sept. 1755.*
[3] *Minutes of a Council of War at Oswego, 18 Sept. 1755.*

Shirley, "think it too rash an attempt; and I have heard so much of it that I think it my duty to let my father know what I hear." Another council was called; and the General, reluctantly convinced of the danger, put the question whether to go or not. The situation admitted but one reply. The council was of opinion that for the present the enterprise was impracticable; that Oswego should be strengthened, more vessels built, and preparation made to renew the attempt as soon as spring opened.[1] All thoughts of active operations were now suspended, and during what was left of the season the troops exchanged the musket for the spade, saw, and axe. At the end of October, leaving seven hundred men at Oswego, Shirley returned to Albany, and narrowly escaped drowning on the way, while passing a rapid in a whale-boat, to try the fitness of that species of craft for river navigation.[2]

Unfortunately for him, he had fallen out with Johnson, whom he had made what he was, but who now turned against him,—a seeming ingratitude not wholly unprovoked. Shirley had diverted the New Jersey regiment, destined originally for Crown Point, to his own expedition against Niagara. Naturally inclined to keep all the reins in his own hands, he had encroached on Johnson's new office of Indian superintendent, held conferences with the Five Nations, and employed agents of his own to deal with them. These agents were persons obnoxious to Johnson, being allied with the clique of Dutch traders at Albany, who hated him because he had supplanted them in the direction of Indian affairs; and in a violent letter to the Lords of Trade, he inveighs against their "licentious and abandoned proceedings," "villanous conduct," "scurrilous falsehoods," and "base and insolent behavior."[3] "I am considerable enough," he says, "to have enemies and to be envied;"[4] and he declares he has proof that Shirley told the Mohawks that he, Johnson, was an upstart of his creating, whom he had set up and could pull down. Again, he charges Shirley's agents with trying to "debauch the Indians from joining him;" while Shirley, on his side, retorts the same complaint against his accuser.[5] When, by the death of Braddock, Shirley became commander-in-chief, Johnson grew so restive at being sub-

[1] *Ibid.*, *27 Sept. 1755.*

[2] On the Niagara expedition, *Braddock's Instructions to Major-General Shirley. Correspondence of Shirley, 1755. Conduct of Major-General Shirley* (London, 1758). Letters of John Shirley in *Pennsylvania Archives*, II. Bradstreet to Shirley, *17 Aug. 1755.* MSS. in Massachusetts Archives. *Review of Military Operations in North America. Gentleman's Magazine, 1757,* p. 73. *London Magazine, 1759,* p. 594. Trumbull, *Hist. Connecticut,* II. 370.

[3] *Johnson to the Lords of Trade, 3 Sept. 1755.*

[4] *Ibid., 17 Jan. 1756.*

[5] *John Shirley to Governor Morris, 12 Aug. 1755.*

ject to his instructions that he declined to hold the management of Indian affairs unless it was made independent of his rival. The dispute became mingled with the teapot-tempest of New York provincial politics. The Lieutenant-Governor, Delancey, a politician of restless ambition and consummate dexterity, had taken umbrage at Shirley, of whose rising honors, not borne with remarkable humility, he appears to have been jealous. Delancey had hitherto favored the Dutch faction in the Assembly, hostile to Johnson; but he now changed attitude, and joined hands with him against the object of their common dislike. The one was strong in the prestige of a loudly-trumpeted victory, and the other had means of influence over the Ministry. Their coalition boded ill to Shirley, and he soon felt its effects.[1]

The campaign was now closed,—a sufficiently active one, seeing that the two nations were nominally at peace. A disastrous rout on the Monongahela, failure at Niagara, a barren victory at Lake George, and three forts captured in Acadia, were the disappointing results on the part of England. Nor had her enemies cause to boast. The Indians, it is true, had won a battle for them: but they had suffered mortifying defeat from a raw militia; their general was a prisoner; and they had lost Acadia past hope.

The campaign was over; but not its effects. It remains to see what befell from the rout of Braddock and the unpardonable retreat of Dunbar from the frontier which it was his duty to defend. Dumas had replaced Contrecœur in the command of Fort Duquesne; and his first care was to set on the Western tribes to attack the border settlements. His success was triumphant. The Delawares and Shawanoes, old friends of the English, but for years past tending to alienation through neglect and ill-usage, now took the lead against them. Many of the Mingoes, or Five Nation Indians on the Ohio, also took up the hatchet, as did various remoter tribes. The West rose like a nest of hornets, and swarmed in fury against the English frontier. Such was the consequence of the defeat of Braddock aided by the skilful devices of the French commander. "It is by means such as I have mentioned," says Dumas, "varied in every form to suit the occasion, that I have succeeded in ruining the three adjacent provinces, Pennsylvania, Maryland, and Virginia, driving off the inhabitants, and totally destroying the settlements over a tract of country thirty leagues wide, reckoning from the line of Fort Cumberland. M. de Contrecœur had not been gone a week before

---

[1]On this affair, see various papers in *N. Y. Col. Docs.*, VI., VII. Smith, *Hist. New York*, Part II., Chaps. IV. V. *Review of Military Operations in North America.* Both Smith and Livingston, the author of the *Review*, were personally cognizant of the course of the dispute.

I had six or seven different war-parties in the field at once, always accompanied by Frenchmen. Thus far, we have lost only two officers and a few soldiers; but the Indian villages are full of prisoners of every age and sex. The enemy has lost far more since the battle than on the day of his defeat."[1]

Dumas, required by the orders of his superiors to wage a detestable warfare against helpless settlers and their families, did what he could to temper its horrors, and enjoined the officers who went with the Indians to spare no effort to prevent them from torturing prisoners.[2] The attempt should be set down to his honor; but it did not avail much. In the record of cruelties committed this year on the borders, we find repeated instances of children scalped alive. "They kill all they meet," writes a French priest; "and after having abused the women and maidens, they slaughter or burn them."[3]

Washington was now in command of the Virginia regiment, consisting of a thousand men, raised afterwards to fifteen hundred. With these he was to protect a frontier of three hundred and fifty miles against more numerous enemies, who could choose their time and place of attack. His headquarters were at Winchester. His men were an ungovernable crew, enlisted chiefly on the turbulent border, and resenting every kind of discipline as levelling them with negroes; while the sympathizing House of Burgesses hesitated for months to pass any law for enforcing obedience, lest it should trench on the liberties of free white men. The service was to the last degree unpopular. "If we talk of obliging men to serve their country," wrote Landon Carter, "we are sure to hear a fellow mumble over the words 'liberty' and 'property' a thousand times."[4] The people, too, were in mortal fear of a slave insurrection, and therefore dared not go far from home.[5] Meanwhile a panic reigned along the border. Captain Waggoner, passing a gap in the Blue Ridge, could hardly make his way for the crowd of fugitives. "Every day," writes Washington, "we have accounts of such cruelties and barbarities as are shocking to human nature. It is not possible to conceive the situation and danger of this miserable country. Such numbers of French and Indians are all around that no road is safe."

These frontiers had always been at peace. No forts of refuge had thus

---

[1] *Dumas au Ministre, 24 Juillet, 1756.*

[2] *Mémoires de Famille de l'Abbé Casgrain,* cited in *Le Foyer Canadien,* III. 26, where an extract is given from an order of Dumas to Baby, a Canadian officer. Orders of Contrecœur and Ligneris to the same effect are also given. A similar order, signed by Dumas, was found in the pocket of Douville, an officer killed by the English on the frontier. *Writings of Washington,* II. 137, *note.*

[3] *Rev. Claude Godefroy Cocquard, S. J., à son Frère, Mars (?), 1757.*

[4] Extract in *Writings of Washington,* II. 145, *note.*

[5] *Letters of Dinwiddie, 1755.*

far been built, and the scattered settlers had no choice but flight. Their
first impulse was to put wife and children beyond reach of the tomahawk. As autumn advanced, the invading bands grew more and more
audacious. Braddock had opened a road for them by which they could
cross the mountains at their ease; and scouts from Fort Cumberland
reported that this road was beaten by as many feet as when the English
army passed last summer. Washington was beset with difficulties. Men
and officers alike were unruly and mutinous. He was at once blamed
for their disorders and refused the means of repressing them. Envious
detractors published slanders against him. A petty Maryland captain,
who had once had a commission from the King, refused to obey his
orders, and stirred up factions among his officers. Dinwiddie gave him
cold support. The temper of the old Scotchman, crabbed at the best,
had been soured by disappointment, vexation, weariness, and ill-
health. He had, besides, a friend and countryman, Colonel Innes,
whom, had he dared, he would gladly have put in Washington's place.
He was full of zeal in the common cause, and wanted to direct the
defence of the borders from his house at Williamsburg, two hundred
miles distant. Washington never hesitated to obey; but he accompanied
his obedience by a statement of his own convictions and his reasons for
them, which, though couched in terms the most respectful, galled his
irascible chief. The Governor acknowledged his merit; but bore him no
love, and sometimes wrote to him in terms which must have tried his
high temper to the utmost. Sometimes, though rarely, he gave words
to his emotion.

"Your Honor," he wrote in April, "may see to what unhappy straits
the distressed inhabitants and myself are reduced. I see inevitable destruction in so clear a light, that unless vigorous measures are taken by
the Assembly, and speedy assistance sent from below, the poor inhabitants that are now in forts must unavoidably fall, while the remainder
are flying before the barbarous foe. In fine, the melancholy situation of
the people; the little prospect of assistance; the gross and scandalous
abuse cast upon the officers in general, which is reflecting upon me in
particular for suffering misconduct of such extraordinary kinds; and the
distant prospect, if any, of gaining honor and reputation in the service,—cause me to lament the hour that gave me a commission, and
would induce me at any other time than this of imminent danger to
resign, without one hesitating moment, a command from which I never
expect to reap either honor or benefit, but, on the contrary, have almost an absolute certainty of incurring displeasure below, while the
murder of helpless families may be laid to my account here.

"The supplicating tears of the women and moving petitions of the men melt me into such deadly sorrow, that I solemnly declare, if I know my own mind, I could offer myself a willing sacrifice to the butchering enemy, provided that would contribute to the people's ease."[1]

In the turmoil around him, patriotism and public duty seemed all to be centred in the breast of one heroic youth. He was respected and generally beloved, but he did not kindle enthusiasm. His were the qualities of an unflagging courage, an all-enduring fortitude, and a deep trust. He showed an astonishing maturity of character, and the kind of mastery over others which begins with mastery over self. At twenty-four he was the foremost man, and acknowledged as such, along the whole long line of the western border.

To feel the situation, the nature of these frontiers must be kept in mind. Along the skirts of the southern and middle colonies ran for six or seven hundred miles a loose, thin, dishevelled fringe of population, the half-barbarous pioneers of advancing civilization. Their rude dwellings were often miles apart. Buried in woods, the settler lived in an appalling loneliness. A low-browed cabin of logs, with moss stuffed in the chinks to keep out the wind, roof covered with sheets of bark, chimney of sticks and clay, and square holes closed by a shutter in place of windows; an unkempt matron, lean with hard work, and a brood of children with bare heads and tattered garments eked out by deerskin,— such was the home of the pioneer in the remoter and wilder districts. The scene around bore witness to his labors. It was the repulsive transition from savagery to civilization, from the forest to the farm. The victims of his axe lay strewn about the dismal "clearing" in a chaos of prostrate trunks, tangled boughs, and withered leaves, waiting for the fire that was to be the next agent in the process of improvement; while around, voiceless and grim, stood the living forest, gazing on the desolation, and biding its own day of doom. The owner of the cabin was miles away, hunting in the woods for the wild turkey and venison which were the chief food of himself and his family till the soil could be tamed into the bearing of crops.

Towards night he returned; and as he issued from the forest shadows he saw a column of blue smoke rising quietly in the still evening air. He ran to the spot; and there, among the smouldering logs of his dwelling, lay, scalped and mangled, the dead bodies of wife and children. A war-party had passed that way. Breathless, palpitating, his brain on fire, he rushed through the thickening night to carry the alarm to his nearest neighbor, three miles distant.

[1] *Writings of Washington*, II. 143.

Such was the character and the fate of many incipient settlements of the utmost border. Farther east, they had a different aspect. Here, small farms with well-built log-houses, cattle, crops of wheat and Indian corn, were strung at intervals along some woody valley of the lower Alleghanies: yesterday a scene of hardy toil; to-day swept with destruction from end to end. There was no warning; no time for concert, perhaps none for flight. Sudden as the leaping panther, a pack of human wolves burst out of the forest, did their work, and vanished.

If the country had been an open one, like the plains beyond the Mississippi, the situation would have been less frightful; but the forest was everywhere, rolled over hill and valley in billows of interminable green,—a leafy maze, a mystery of shade, a universal hiding-place, where murder might lurk unseen at its victim's side, and Nature seemed formed to nurse the mind with wild and dark imaginings. The detail of blood is set down in the untutored words of those who saw and felt it. But there was a suffering that had no record,—the mortal fear of women and children in the solitude of their wilderness homes, haunted, waking and sleeping, with nightmares of horror that were but the forecast of an imminent reality. The country had in past years been so peaceful, and the Indians so friendly, that many of the settlers, especially on the Pennsylvanian border, had no arms, and were doubly in need of help from the Government. In Virginia they had it, such as it was. In Pennsylvania they had for months none whatever; and the Assembly turned a deaf ear to their cries.

Far to the east, sheltered from danger, lay staid and prosperous Philadelphia, the home of order and thrift. It took its stamp from the Quakers, its original and dominant population, set apart from the other colonists not only in character and creed, but in the outward symbols of a peculiar dress and a daily sacrifice of grammar on the altar of religion. The even tenor of their lives counteracted the effects of climate, and they are said to have been perceptibly more rotund in feature and person than their neighbors. Yet, broad and humanizing as was their faith, they were capable of extreme bitterness towards opponents, clung tenaciously to power, and were jealous for the ascendency of their sect, which had begun to show signs of wavering. On other sects they looked askance; and regarded the Presbyterians in particular with a dislike which in moments of crisis rose to detestation.[1] They held it sin to fight, and above all to fight against Indians.

[1] See a crowd of party pamphlets, Quaker against Presbyterian, which appeared at Philadelphia in 1764, abusively acrimonious on both sides.

Here was one cause of military paralysis. It was reinforced by another. The old standing quarrel between governor and assembly had grown more violent than ever; and this as a direct consequence of the public distress, which above all things demanded harmony. The dispute turned this time on a single issue,—that of the taxation of the proprietary estates. The estates in question consisted of vast tracts of wild land, yielding no income, and at present to a great extent worthless, being overrun by the enemy.[1] The Quaker Assembly had refused to protect them; and on one occasion had rejected an offer of the proprietaries to join them in paying the cost of their defence.[2] But though they would not defend the land, they insisted on taxing it; and farther insisted that the taxes upon it should be laid by the provincial assessors. By a law of the province, these assessors were chosen by popular vote; and in consenting to this law, the proprietaries had expressly provided that their estates should be exempted from all taxes to be laid by officials in whose appointment they had no voice.[3] Thomas and Richard Penn, the present proprietaries, had debarred their deputy, the Governor, both by the terms of his commission and by special instruction, from consenting to such taxation, and had laid him under heavy bonds to secure his obedience. Thus there was another side to the question than that of the Assembly; though our American writers have been slow to acknowledge it.

Benjamin Franklin was leader in the Assembly and shared its views. The feudal proprietorship of the Penn family was odious to his democratic nature. It was, in truth, a pestilent anomaly, repugnant to the genius of the people; and the disposition and character of the present proprietaries did not tend to render it less vexatious. Yet there were considerations which might have tempered the impatient hatred with which the colonists regarded it. The first proprietary, William Penn, had used his feudal rights in the interest of a broad liberalism; and through them had established the popular institutions and universal tolerance which made Pennsylvania the most democratic province in America, and nursed the spirit of liberty which now revolted against his heirs. The one absorbing passion of Pennsylvania was resistance to their deputy, the Governor. The badge of feudalism, though light, was

---

[1] The productive estates of the proprietaries were taxed through the tenants.

[2] The proprietaries offered to contribute to the cost of building and maintaining a fort on the spot where the French soon after built Fort Duquesne. This plan, vigorously executed, would have saved the province from a deluge of miseries. One of the reasons assigned by the Assembly for rejecting it was that it would irritate the enemy. See *supra*, pp. 34–35.

[3] *A Brief View of the Conduct of Pennsylvania for the year 1755.*

insufferably irritating; and the sons of William Penn were moreover detested by the Quakers as renegades from the faith of their father. Thus the immediate political conflict engrossed mind and heart; and in the rancor of their quarrel with the proprietaries, the Assembly forgot the French and Indians.

In Philadelphia and the eastern districts the Quakers could ply their trades, tend their shops, till their farms, and discourse at their ease on the wickedness of war. The midland counties, too, were for the most part tolerably safe. They were occupied mainly by crude German peasants, who nearly equalled in number all the rest of the population, and who, gathered at the centre of the province, formed a mass politically indigestible. Translated from servitude to the most ample liberty, they hated the thought of military service, which reminded them of former oppression, cared little whether they lived under France or England, and, thinking themselves out of danger, had no mind to be taxed for the defence of others. But while the great body of the Germans were sheltered from harm, those of them who lived farther westward were not so fortunate. Here, mixed with Scotch Irish Presbyterians and Celtic Irish Catholics, they formed a rough border population, the discordant elements of which could rarely unite for common action; yet, though confused and disjointed, they were a living rampart to the rest of the colony. Against them raged the furies of Indian war; and, maddened with distress and terror, they cried aloud for help.

Petition after petition came from the borders for arms and ammunition, and for a militia law to enable the people to organize and defend themselves. The Quakers resisted. "They have taken uncommon pains," writes Governor Morris to Shirley, "to prevent the people from taking up arms."[1] Braddock's defeat, they declared, was a just judgment on him and his soldiers for molesting the French in their settlements on the Ohio.[2] A bill was passed by the Assembly for raising fifty thousand pounds for the King's use by a tax which included the proprietary lands. The Governor, constrained by his instructions and his bonds, rejected it. "I can only say," he told them, "that I will readily pass a bill for striking any sum in paper money the present exigency may require, provided funds are established for sinking the same in five years." Messages long and acrimonious were exchanged between the parties. The Assembly, had they chosen, could easily have raised money enough by methods not involving the point in dispute; but they

[1] *Morris to Shirley, 16 Aug. 1755.*
[2] *Morris to Sir Thomas Robinson, 28 Aug. 1755.*

thought they saw in the crisis a means of forcing the Governor to yield. The Quakers had an alternative motive: if the Governor gave way, it was a political victory; if he stood fast, their non-resistance principles would triumph, and in this triumph their ascendency as a sect would be confirmed. The debate grew every day more bitter and unmannerly. The Governor could not yield; the Assembly would not. There was a complete deadlock. The Assembly requested the Governor "not to make himself the hateful instrument of reducing a free people to the abject state of vassalage."[1] As the raising of money and the control of its expenditure was in their hands; as he could not prorogue or dissolve them, and as they could adjourn on their own motion to such time as pleased them; as they paid his support, and could withhold it if he offended them,—which they did in the present case,—it seemed no easy task for him to reduce them to vassalage. "What must we do," pursued the Assembly, "to please this kind governor, who takes so much pains to render us obnoxious to our sovereign and odious to our fellow-subjects? If we only tell him that the difficulties he meets with are not owing to the causes he names,—which indeed have no existence,—but to his own want of skill and abilities for his station, he takes it extremely amiss, and says 'we forget all decency to those in authority.' We are apt to think there is likewise some decency due to the Assembly as a part of the government; and though we have not, like the Governor, had a courtly education, but are plain men, and must be very imperfect in our politeness, yet we think we have no chance of improving by his example."[2] Again, in another Message, the Assembly, with a thrust at Morris himself, tell him that colonial governors have often been "transient persons, of broken fortunes, greedy of money, destitute of all concern for those they govern, often their enemies, and endeavoring not only to oppress, but to defame them."[3] In such unseemly fashion was the battle waged. Morris, who was himself a provincial, showed more temper and dignity; though there was not too much on either side. "The Assembly," he wrote to Shirley, "seem determined to take advantage of the country's distress to get the whole power of government into their own hands." And the Assembly proclaimed on their part that the Governor was taking advantage of the country's distress to reduce the province to "Egyptian bondage."

[1] *Colonial Records of Pa.*, VI. 584.
[2] *Message of the Assembly to the Governor, 29 Sept. 1755* (written by Franklin), in *Colonial Records of Pa.*, VI. 631, 632.
[3] *Writings of Franklin*, III. 447. The Assembly at first suppressed this paper, but afterwards printed it.

Petitions poured in from the miserable frontiersmen. "How long will those in power, by their quarrels, suffer us to be massacred?" demanded William Trent, the Indian trader. "Two and forty bodies have been buried on Patterson's Creek; and since they have killed more, and keep on killing."[1] Early in October news came that a hundred persons had been murdered near Fort Cumberland. Repeated tidings followed of murders on the Susquehanna; then it was announced that the war-parties had crossed that stream, and were at their work on the eastern side. Letter after letter came from the sufferers, bringing such complaints as this: "We are in as bad circumstances as ever any poor Christians were ever in; for the cries of widowers, widows, fatherless and motherless children, are enough to pierce the most hardest of hearts. Likewise it's a very sorrowful spectacle to see those that escaped with their lives with not a mouthful to eat, or bed to lie on, or clothes to cover their nakedness, or keep them warm, but all they had consumed into ashes. These deplorable circumstances cry aloud for your Honor's most wise consideration; for it is really very shocking for the husband to see the wife of his bosom her head cut off, and the children's blood drunk like water, by these bloody and cruel savages."[2]

Morris was greatly troubled. "The conduct of the Assembly," he wrote to Shirley, "is to me shocking beyond parallel." "The inhabitants are abandoning their plantations, and we are in a dreadful situation," wrote John Harris from the east bank of the Susquehanna. On the next day he wrote again: "The Indians are cutting us off every day, and I had a certain account of about fifteen hundred Indians, besides French, being on their march against us and Virginia, and now close on our borders, their scouts scalping our families on our frontiers daily." The report was soon confirmed; and accounts came that the settlements in the valley called the Great Cove had been completely destroyed. All this was laid before the Assembly. They declared the accounts exaggerated, but confessed that outrages had been committed; hinted that the fault was with the proprietaries; and asked the Governor to explain why the Delawares and Shawanoes had become unfriendly. "If they have suffered wrongs," said the Quakers, "we are resolved to do all in our power to redress them, rather than entail upon ourselves and our posterity the calamities of a cruel Indian war." The Indian records were searched, and several days spent in unsuccessful efforts to prove fraud in a late land-purchase.

---

[1] *Trent to James Burd, 4 Oct. 1755.*
[2] *Adam Hoops to Governor Morris, 3 Nov. 1755.*

Post after post still brought news of slaughter. The upper part of Cumberland County was laid waste. Edward Biddle wrote from Reading: "The drum is beating and bells ringing, and all the people under arms. This night we expect an attack. The people exclaim against the Quakers." "We seem to be given up into the hands of a merciless enemy," wrote John Elder from Paxton. And he declares that more than forty persons have been killed in that neighborhood, besides numbers carried off. Meanwhile the Governor and Assembly went on fencing with words and exchanging legal subtleties; while, with every cry of distress that rose from the west, each hoped that the other would yield.

On the eighth of November the Assembly laid before Morris for his concurrence a bill for emitting bills of credit to the amount of sixty thousand pounds, to be sunk in four years by a tax including the proprietary estates.[1] "I shall not," he replied, "enter into a dispute whether the proprietaries ought to be taxed or not. It is sufficient for me that they have given me no power in that case; and I cannot think it consistent either with my duty or safety to exceed the powers of my commission, much less to do what that commission expressly prohibits."[2] He stretched his authority, however, so far as to propose a sort of compromise by which the question should be referred to the King; but they refused it; and the quarrel and the murders went on as before. "We have taken," said the Assembly, "every step in our power, consistent with the just rights of the freemen of Pennsylvania, for the relief of the poor distressed inhabitants; and we have reason to believe that they themselves would not wish us to go farther. Those who would give up essential liberty to purchase a little temporary safety deserve neither liberty nor safety."[3] Then the borderers deserved neither; for, rather than be butchered, they would have let the proprietary lands lie untaxed for another year. "You have in all," said the Governor, "proposed to me five money bills, three of them rejected because contrary to royal instructions; the other two on account of the unjust method proposed for taxing the proprietary estate. If you are disposed to relieve your country, you have many other ways of granting money to which I shall have no objection. I shall put one proof more both of your sincerity and mine in our professions of regard for the public, by offering to agree to any bill in the present exigency which it is consistent with my duty to pass; lest, before our present disputes can be brought to an issue, we

[1] *Colonial Records of Pa.*, VI. 682.
[2] *Message of the Governor to the Assembly, 8 Nov. 1755,* in *Colonial Records of Pa.*, VI. 684.
[3] *Message of the Assembly to the Governor, 11 Nov. Ibid.*, VI. 692. The words are Franklin's.

should neither have a privilege to dispute about, nor a country to dispute in."[1] They stood fast; and with an obstinacy for which the Quakers were chiefly answerable, insisted that they would give nothing, except by a bill taxing real estate, and including that of the proprietaries.

But now the Assembly began to feel the ground shaking under their feet. A paper, called a "Representation," signed by some of the chief citizens, was sent to the House, calling for measures of defence. "You will forgive us, gentlemen," such was its language, "if we assume characters somewhat higher than that of humble suitors praying for the defence of our lives and properties as a matter of grace or favor on your side. You will permit us to make a positive and immediate demand of it."[2] This drove the Quakers mad. Preachers, male and female, harangued in the streets, denouncing the iniquity of war. Three of the sect from England, two women and a man, invited their brethren of the Assembly to a private house, and fervently exhorted them to stand firm. Some of the principal Quakers joined in an address to the House, in which they declared that any action on its part "inconsistent with the peaceable testimony we profess and have borne to the world appears to us in its consequences tò be destructive of our religious liberties."[3] And they protested that they would rather "suffer" than pay taxes for such ends. Consistency, even in folly, has in it something respectable; but the Quakers were not consistent. A few years after, when heated with party-passion and excited by reports of an irruption of incensed Presbyterian borderers, some of the pacific sectaries armed for battle; and the streets of Philadelphia beheld the curious conjunction of musket and broad-brimmed hat.[4]

The mayor, aldermen, and common council next addressed the Assembly, adjuring them, "in the most solemn manner, before God and in the name of all our fellow-citizens," to provide for defending the lives and property of the people.[5] A deputation from a band of Indians on the Susquehanna, still friendly to the province, came to ask whether the English meant to fight or not; for, said their speaker, "if they will not stand by us, we will join the French." News came that the settlement of Tulpehocken, only sixty miles distant, had been destroyed; and then that the Moravian settlement of Gnadenhütten was burned, and

[1] *Message of the Governor to the Assembly, 22 Nov. 1755, in Colonial Records of Pa.*, VI. 714.
[2] *Pennsylvania Archives*, II. 485.
[3] *Ibid.*, II. 487.
[4] See *Conspiracy of Pontiac*, II. 143, 152.
[5] *A Remonstrance*, etc., in *Colonial Records of Pa.*, VI. 734.

nearly all its inmates massacred. Colonel William Moore wrote to the Governor that two thousand men were coming from Chester County to compel him and the Assembly to defend the province; and Conrad Weiser wrote that more were coming from Berks on the same errand. Old friends of the Assembly began to cry out against them. Even the Germans, hitherto their fast allies, were roused from their attitude of passivity, and four hundred of them came in procession to demand measures of war. A band of frontiersmen presently arrived, bringing in a wagon the bodies of friends and relatives lately murdered, displaying them at the doors of the Assembly, cursing the Quakers, and threatening vengeance.[1]

Finding some concession necessary, the House at length passed a militia law,—probably the most futile ever enacted. It specially exempted the Quakers, and constrained nobody; but declared it lawful, for such as chose, to form themselves into companies and elect officers by ballot. The company officers thus elected might, if they saw fit, elect, also by ballot, colonels, lieutenant-colonels, and majors. These last might then, in conjunction with the Governor, frame articles of war; to which, however, no officer or man was to be subjected unless, after three days' consideration, he subscribed them in presence of a justice of the peace, and declared his willingness to be bound by them.[2]

This mockery could not appease the people; the Assembly must raise money for men, arms, forts, and all the detested appliances of war. Defeat absolute and ignominious seemed hanging over the House, when an incident occurred which gave them a decent pretext for retreat. The Governor informed them that he had just received a letter from the proprietaries, giving to the province five thousand pounds sterling to aid in its defence, on condition that the money should be accepted as a free gift, and not as their proportion of any tax that was or might be laid by the Assembly. They had not learned the deplorable state of the country, and had sent the money in view of the defeat of Braddock and its probable consequences. The Assembly hereupon yielded, struck out from the bill before them the clause taxing the proprietary estates, and, thus amended, presented it to the Governor, who by his signature made it a law.[3]

The House had failed to carry its point. The result disappointed

---

[1] Mante, 47; Entick, I. 377.

[2] This remarkable bill, drawn by Franklin, was meant for political rather than military effect. It was thought that Morris would refuse to pass it, and could therefore be accused of preventing the province from defending itself; but he avoided the snare by signing it.

[3] *Minutes of Council, 27 Nov. 1755.*

Franklin, and doubly disappointed the Quakers. His maxim was: Beat
the Governor first, and then beat the enemy; theirs: Beat the Governor, and let the enemy alone. The measures that followed, directed in
part by Franklin himself, held the Indians in check, and mitigated the
distress of the western counties; yet there was no safety for them
throughout the two or three years when France was cheering on her
hell-hounds against this tormented frontier.

As in Pennsylvania, so in most of the other colonies there was conflict between assemblies and governors, to the unspeakable detriment of
the public service. In New York, though here no obnoxious proprietary
stood between the people and the Crown, the strife was long and severe. The point at issue was an important one,—whether the Assembly
should continue their practice of granting yearly supplies to the Governor, or should establish a permanent fund for the ordinary expenses
of government,—thus placing him beyond their control. The result was
a victory for the Assembly.

Month after month the great continent lay wrapped in snow. Far
along the edge of the western wilderness men kept watch and ward in
lonely blockhouses, or scoured the forest on the track of prowling war-
parties. The provincials in garrison at forts Edward, William Henry,
and Oswego dragged out the dreary winter; while bands of New England
rangers, muffled against the piercing cold, caps of fur on their heads,
hatchets in their belts, and guns in their mittened hands, glided on
skates along the gleaming ice-floor of Lake George, to spy out the secrets of Ticonderoga, or seize some careless sentry to tell them tidings
of the foe. Thus the petty war went on; but the big war was frozen into
torpor, ready, like a hibernating bear, to wake again with the birds, the
bees, and the flowers.[1]

[1]On Pennsylvanian disputes,—*A Brief State of the Province of Pennsylvania* (London, 1755). *A
Brief View of the Conduct of Pennsylvania* (London, 1756). These are pamphlets on the Governor's
side, by William Smith, D.D., Provost of the College of Pennsylvania. *An Answer to an invidious
Pamphlet, intituled a Brief State*, etc. (London, 1755). Anonymous. *A True and Impartial State of
the Province of Pennsylvania* (Philadelphia, 1759). Anonymous. The last two works attack the first
two with great vehemence. The *True and Impartial State* is an able presentation of the case of the
Assembly, omitting, however, essential facts. But the most elaborate work on the subject is the
Historical Review of the Constitution and Government of Pennsylvania, inspired and partly written by
Franklin. It is hotly partisan, and sometimes sophistical and unfair. Articles on the quarrel will
also be found in the provincial newspapers, especially the *New York Mercury*, and in the *Gentleman's Magazine* for 1755 and 1756. But it is impossible to get any clear and just view of it without
wading through the interminable documents concerning it in the *Colonial Records of Pennsylvania*
and the *Pennsylvania Archives*.

II

Montcalm

1712–1756

WAR DECLARED · STATE OF EUROPE · POMPADOUR AND MARIA
THERESA · INFATUATION OF THE FRENCH COURT · THE EUROPEAN WAR ·
MONTCALM TO COMMAND IN AMERICA · HIS EARLY LIFE · AN
INTRACTABLE PUPIL · HIS MARRIAGE · HIS FAMILY · HIS CAMPAIGNS ·
PREPARATION FOR AMERICA · HIS ASSOCIATES · LÉVIS, BOURLAMAQUE,
BOUGAINVILLE · EMBARKATION · THE VOYAGE · ARRIVAL · VAUDREUIL ·
FORCES OF CANADA · TROOPS OF THE LINE, COLONY TROOPS, MILITIA,
INDIANS · THE MILITARY SITUATION · CAPTURE OF FORT BULL ·
MONTCALM AT TICONDEROGA

On the eighteenth of May, 1756, England, after a year
of open hostility, at length declared war. She had attacked France by land and sea, turned loose her ships to prey on French
commerce, and brought some three hundred prizes into her ports. It
was the act of a weak Government, supplying by spasms of violence
what it lacked in considerate resolution. France, no match for her am-
phibious enemy in the game of marine depredation, cried out in horror;
and to emphasize her complaints and signalize a pretended good faith
which her acts had belied, ostentatiously released a British frigate captured by her cruisers. She in her turn declared war on the ninth of
June: and now began the most terrible conflict of the eighteenth century; one that convulsed Europe and shook America, India, the coasts
of Africa, and the islands of the sea.

In Europe the ground was trembling already with the coming earthquake. Such smothered discords, such animosities, ambitions, jealousies, possessed the rival governments; such entanglements of treaties and alliances, offensive or defensive, open or secret,—that a blow at one point shook the whole fabric. Hanover, like the heel of Achilles, was the vulnerable part for which England was always trembling. Therefore she made a defensive treaty with Prussia, by which each party bound itself to aid the other, should its territory be invaded. England thus sought a guaranty against France, and Prussia against Russia. She had need. Her King, Frederic the Great, had drawn upon himself an avalanche. Three women—two empresses and a concubine—controlled the forces of the three great nations, Austria, Russia, and France; and they all hated him: Elizabeth of Russia, by reason of a distrust fomented by secret intrigue and turned into gall by the biting tongue of Frederic himself, who had jibed at her amours, compared her to Messalina, and called her "*infâme catin du Nord;*" Maria Theresa of Austria, because she saw in him a rebellious vassal of the Holy Roman Empire, and, above all, because he had robbed her of Silesia; Madame de Pompadour, because when she sent him a message of compliment, he answered, "*Je ne la connais pas,*" forbade his ambassador to visit her, and in his mocking wit spared neither her nor her royal lover. Feminine pique, revenge, or vanity had then at their service the mightiest armaments of Europe.

The recovery of Silesia and the punishment of Frederic for his audacity in seizing it, possessed the mind of Maria Theresa with the force of a ruling passion. To these ends she had joined herself in secret league with Russia; and now at the prompting of her minister Kaunitz she courted the alliance of France. It was a reversal of the hereditary policy of Austria; joining hands with an old and deadly foe, and spurning England, of late her most trusty ally. But France could give powerful aid against Frederic; and hence Maria Theresa, virtuous as she was high-born and proud, stooped to make advances to the all-powerful mistress of Louis XV., wrote her flattering letters, and addressed her, it is said, as "*Ma chère cousine.*" Pompadour was delighted, and could hardly do enough for her imperial friend. She ruled the King, and could make and unmake ministers at will. They hastened to do her pleasure, disguising their subserviency by dressing it out in specious reasons of state. A conference at her summer-house, called Babiole, "Bawble," prepared the way for a treaty which involved the nation in the anti-Prussian war, and made it the instrument of Austria in the attempt to humble Frederic,— an attempt which if successful would give the hereditary enemy of France a predominance over Germany. France engaged to aid the cause with twenty-four thousand men; but in the zeal of her rulers began with a hundred thousand. Thus the three great Powers stood leagued against Prussia. Sweden and Saxony joined them; and the Empire itself, of which Prussia was a part, took arms against its obnoxious member.

Never in Europe had power been more centralized, and never in France had the reins been held by persons so pitiful, impelled by motives so contemptible. The levity, vanity, and spite of a concubine became a mighty engine to influence the destinies of nations. Louis XV., enervated by pleasures and devoured by *ennui*, still had his emotions; he shared Pompadour's detestation of Frederic, and he was tormented at times by a lively fear of damnation. But how damn a king who had entered the lists as champion of the Church? England was Protestant, and so was Prussia; Austria was supremely Catholic. Was it not a merit in the eyes of God to join her in holy war against the powers of heresy? The King of the Parc-aux-Cerfs* would propitiate Heaven by a new crusade.

Henceforth France was to turn her strength against her European foes; and the American war, the occasion of the universal outbreak, was to hold in her eyes a second place. The reasons were several: the vanity of Pompadour, infatuated by the advances of the Empress-Queen, and eager to secure her good graces; the superstition of the King; the anger of both against Frederic; the desire of D'Argenson, minister of war, that the army, and not the navy, should play the foremost part; and the passion of courtiers and nobles, ignorant of the naval service, to win laurels in a continental war,—all conspired to one end. It was the interest of France to turn her strength against her only dangerous rival; to continue as she had begun, in building up a naval power that could face England on the seas and sustain her own rising colonies in America, India, and the West Indies: for she too might have multiplied herself, planted her language and her race over all the globe, and grown with the growth of her children, had she not been at the mercy of an effeminate profligate, a mistress turned procuress, and the favorites to whom they delegated power.

Still, something must be done for the American war; at least there must be a new general to replace Dieskau. None of the Court favorites

---

*Here Parkman alludes to the notorious retreat, built at Versailles on the site of a "hunting box," where Louis XV "received and gave hospitality to young women of easy virtue." In Parkman's day, lurid tales of "an immense park . . . and a whole troop of innocent does pursued by a libidinous monarch" had not yet been discredited. See Pierre Gaxotte, *Louis XV and His Times* (Philadelphia, 1934), pp. 129–130.—Ed.

wanted a command in the backwoods, and the minister of war was free to choose whom he would. His choice fell on Louis Joseph, Marquis de Montcalm-Gozon de Saint-Véran.

Montcalm was born in the south of France, at the Château of Candiac, near Nîmes, on the twenty-ninth of February, 1712. At the age of six he was placed in the charge of one Dumas, a natural son of his grandfather. This man, a conscientious pedant, with many theories of education, ruled his pupil stiffly; and, before the age of fifteen, gave him a good knowledge of Latin, Greek, and history. Young Montcalm had a taste for books, continued his reading in such intervals of leisure as camps and garrisons afforded, and cherished to the end of his life the ambition of becoming a member of the Academy. Yet, with all his liking for study, he sometimes revolted against the sway of the pedagogue who wrote letters of complaint to his father protesting against the "judgments of the vulgar, who, contrary to the experience of ages, say that if children are well reproved they will correct their faults." Dumas, however, was not without sense, as is shown by another letter to the elder Montcalm, in which he says that the boy had better be ignorant of Latin and Greek "than know them as he does without knowing how to read, write, and speak French well." The main difficulty was to make him write a good hand,—a point in which he signally failed to the day of his death. So refractory was he at times, that his master despaired. "M. de Montcalm," Dumas informs the father, "has great need of docility, industry, and willingness to take advice. What will become of him?" The pupil, aware of these aspersions, met them by writing to his father his own ideas of what his aims should be. "First, to be an honorable man, of good morals, brave, and a Christian. Secondly, to read in moderation; to know as much Greek and Latin as most men of the world; also the four rules of arithmetic, and something of history, geography, and French and Latin *belles-lettres*, as well as to have a taste for the arts and sciences. Thirdly, and above all, to be obedient, docile, and very submissive to your orders and those of my dear mother; and also to defer to the advice of M. Dumas. Fourthly, to fence and ride as well as my small abilities will permit."[1]

If Louis de Montcalm failed to satisfy his preceptor, he had a brother who made ample amends. Of this infant prodigy it is related that at six years he knew Latin, Greek, and Hebrew, and had some acquaintance with arithmetic, French history, geography, and heraldry. He was destined for the Church, but died at the age of seven; his precocious brain having been urged to fatal activity by the exertions of Dumas.

---

[1] This passage is given by Somervogel from the original letter.

Other destinies and a more wholesome growth were the lot of young Louis. At fifteen he joined the army as ensign in the regiment of Hainaut. Two years after, his father bought him a captaincy, and he was first under fire at the siege of Philipsbourg. His father died in 1735, and left him heir to a considerable landed estate, much embarrassed by debt. The Marquis de la Fare, a friend of the family, soon after sought for him an advantageous marriage to strengthen his position and increase his prospects of promotion; and he accordingly espoused Mademoiselle Angélique Louise Talon du Boulay,— a union which brought him influential alliances and some property. Madame de Montcalm bore him ten children, of whom only two sons and four daughters were living in 1752. "May God preserve them all," he writes in his autobiography, "and make them prosper for this world and the next! Perhaps it will be thought that the number is large for so moderate a fortune, especially as four of them are girls; but does God ever abandon his children in their need?

> " 'Aux petits des oiseaux il donne la pâture,
>   Et sa bonté s'étend sur toute la nature.' "

He was pious in his soldierly way, and ardently loyal to Church and King.

His family seat was Candiac; where, in the intervals of campaigning, he found repose with his wife, his children, and his mother, who was a woman of remarkable force of character and who held great influence over her son. He had a strong attachment to this home of his childhood; and in after years, out of the midst of the American wilderness, his thoughts turned longingly towards it. *"Quand reverrai-je mon cher Candiac!"*

In 1741 Montcalm took part in the Bohemian campaign. He was made colonel of the regiment of Auxerrois two years later, and passed unharmed through the severe campaign of 1744. In the next year he fought in Italy under Maréchal de Maillebois. In 1746, at the disastrous action under the walls of Piacenza, where he twice rallied his regiment, he received five sabre-cuts,—two of which were in the head,—and was made prisoner. Returning to France on parole, he was promoted in the year following to the rank of brigadier; and being soon after exchanged, rejoined the army, and was again wounded by a musket-shot. The peace of Aix-la-Chapelle now gave him a period of rest.[1] At length, being on

---

[1] The account of Montcalm up to this time is chiefly from his unpublished autobiography, preserved by his descendants, and entitled *Mémoires pour servir à l'Histoire de ma Vie.* Somervogel, *Comme on servait autrefois;* Bonnechose, *Montcalm et le Canada;* Martin, *Le Marquis de Montcalm; Éloge de Montcalm; Autre Éloge de Montcalm; Mémoires sur le Canada, 1749–1760,* and other writings in print and manuscript have also been consulted.

a visit to Paris late in the autumn of 1755, the minister, D'Argenson, hinted to him that he might be appointed to command the troops in America. He heard no more of the matter till, after his return home, he received from D'Argenson a letter dated at Versailles the twenty-fifth of January, at midnight. "Perhaps, Monsieur," it began, "you did not expect to hear from me again on the subject of the conversation I had with you the day you came to bid me farewell at Paris. Nevertheless I have not forgotten for a moment the suggestion I then made you; and it is with the greatest pleasure that I announce to you that my views have prevailed. The King has chosen you to command his troops in North America, and will honor you on your departure with the rank of major-general."

The Chevalier de Lévis, afterwards Marshal of France, was named as his second in command, with the rank of brigadier, and the Chevalier de Bourlamaque as his third, with the rank of colonel; but what especially pleased him was the appointment of his eldest son to command a regiment in France. He set out from Candiac for the Court, and occupied himself on the way with reading Charlevoix. "I take great pleasure in it," he writes from Lyons to his mother; "he gives a pleasant account of Quebec. But be comforted; I shall always be glad to come home." At Paris he writes again: "Don't expect any long letter from me before the first of March; all my business will be done by that time, and I shall begin to breathe again. I have not yet seen the Chevalier de Montcalm [*his son*]. Last night I came from Versailles, and am going back to-morrow. The King gives me twenty-five thousand francs a year, as he did to M. Dieskau, besides twelve thousand for my equipment, which will cost me above a thousand crowns more; but I cannot stop for that. I embrace my dearest and all the family." A few days later his son joined him. "He is as thin and delicate as ever, but grows prodigiously tall."

On the second of March he informs his mother, "My affairs begin to get on. A good part of the baggage went off the day before yesterday in the King's wagons; an assistant-cook and two liverymen yesterday. I have got a good cook. Estève, my secretary, will go on the eighth; Joseph and Déjean will follow me. To-morrow evening I go to Versailles till Sunday, and will write from there to Madame de Montcalm [*his wife*]. I have three aides-de-camp; one of them, Bougainville, a man of parts, pleasant company. Madame Mazade was happily delivered on Wednesday; in extremity on Friday with a malignant fever; Saturday and yesterday, reports favorable. I go there twice a day, and am just going now. She has a girl. I embrace you all." Again, on the fifteenth: "In a few hours I set out for Brest. Yesterday I presented my son, with whom I am well pleased, to all the royal family. I shall have a secretary at Brest, and will write more at length." On the eighteenth he writes from Rennes to his wife: "I arrived, dearest, this morning, and stay here all day. I shall be at Brest on the twenty-first. Everything will be on board on the twenty-sixth. My son has been here since yesterday for me to coach him and get him a uniform made, in which he will give thanks for his regiment at the same time that I take leave in my embroidered coat. Perhaps I shall leave debts behind. I wait impatiently for the bills. You have my will; I wish you would get it copied, and send it to me before I sail."

Reaching Brest, the place of embarkation, he writes to his mother: "I have business on hand still. My health is good, and the passage will be a time of rest. I embrace you, and my dearest, and my daughters. Love to all the family. I shall write up to the last moment."

No translation can give an idea of the rapid, abrupt, elliptical style of this familiar correspondence, where the meaning is sometimes suggested by a single word, unintelligible to any but those for whom it is written.

At the end of March Montcalm, with all his following, was ready to embark; and three ships of the line, the "Léopard," the "Héros," and the "Illustre," fitted out as transports, were ready to receive the troops; while the General, with Lévis and Bourlamaque, were to take passage in the frigates "Licorne," "Sauvage," and "Sirène." "I like the Chevalier de Lévis," says Montcalm, "and I think he likes me." His first aide-de-camp, Bougainville, pleased him, if possible, still more. This young man, son of a notary, had begun life as an advocate in the Parliament of Paris, where his abilities and learning had already made him conspicuous, when he resigned the gown for the sword, and became a captain of dragoons. He was destined in later life to win laurels in another career, and to become one of the most illustrious of French navigators. Montcalm, himself a scholar, prized his varied talents and accomplishments, and soon learned to feel for him a strong personal regard.

The troops destined for Canada were only two battalions, one belonging to the regiment of La Sarre, and the other to that of Royal Roussillon. Louis XV. and Pompadour sent a hundred thousand men to fight the battles of Austria, and could spare but twelve hundred to reinforce New France. These troops marched into Brest at early morning, breakfasted in the town, and went at once on board the transports, "with an incredible gayety," says Bougainville. "What a nation is ours! Happy he who commands it, and commands it worthily!"[1] Montcalm

---

[1] *Journal de Bougainville.* This is a fragment; his Journal proper begins a few weeks later.

and he embarked in the "Licorne," and sailed on the third of April, leaving Lévis and Bourlamaque to follow a few days after.[1]

The voyage was a rough one. "I have been fortunate," writes Montcalm to his wife, "in not being ill nor at all incommoded by the heavy gale we had in Holy Week. It was not so with those who were with me, especially M. Estève, my secretary, and Joseph, who suffered cruelly,—seventeen days without being able to take anything but water. The season was very early for such a hard voyage, and it was fortunate that the winter has been so mild. We had very favorable weather till Monday the twelfth; but since then till Saturday evening we had rough weather, with a gale that lasted ninety hours, and put us in real danger. The forecastle was always under water, and the waves broke twice over the quarter-deck. From the twenty-seventh of April to the evening of the fourth of May we had fogs, great cold, and an amazing quantity of icebergs. On the thirtieth, when luckily the fog lifted for a time, we counted sixteen of them. The day before, one drifted under the bowsprit, grazed it, and might have crushed us if the deck-officer had not called out quickly, *Luff.* After speaking of our troubles and sufferings, I must tell you of our pleasures, which were fishing for cod and eating it. The taste is exquisite. The head, tongue, and liver are morsels worthy of an epicure. Still, I would not advise anybody to make the voyage for their sake. My health is as good as it has been for a long time. I found it a good plan to eat little and take no supper; a little tea now and then, and plenty of lemonade. Nevertheless I have taken very little liking for the sea, and think that when I shall be so happy as to rejoin you I shall end my voyages there. I don't know when this letter will go. I shall send it by the first ship that returns to France, and keep on writing till then. It is pleasant, I know, to hear particulars about the people one loves, and I thought that my mother and you, my dearest and most beloved, would be glad to read all these dull details. We heard Mass on Easter Day. All the week before, it was impossible, because the ship rolled so that I could hardly keep my legs. If I had dared, I think I should have had myself lashed fast. I shall not soon forget that Holy Week."

This letter was written on the eleventh of May, in the St. Lawrence, where the ship lay at anchor, ten leagues below Quebec, stopped by ice from proceeding farther. Montcalm made his way to the town by land, and soon after learned with great satisfaction that the other ships were safe in the river below. "I see," he writes again, "that I shall have

[1]*Lévis à ——, 5 Avril, 1756.*

plenty of work. Our campaign will soon begin. Everything is in motion. Don't expect details about our operations; generals never speak of movements till they are over. I can only tell you that the winter has been quiet enough, though the savages have made great havoc in Pennsylvania and Virginia, and carried off, according to their custom, men, women, and children. I beg you will have High Mass said at Montpellier or Vauvert to thank God for our safe arrival and ask for good success in future."[1]

Vaudreuil, the governor-general, was at Montreal, and Montcalm sent a courier to inform him of his arrival. He soon went thither in person, and the two men met for the first time. The new general was not welcome to Vaudreuil, who had hoped to command the troops himself, and had represented to the Court that it was needless and inexpedient to send out a general officer from France.[2] The Court had not accepted his views;[3] and hence it was with more curiosity than satisfaction that he greeted the colleague who had been assigned him. He saw before him a man of small stature, with a lively countenance, a keen eye, and, in moments of animation, rapid, vehement utterance, and nervous gesticulation. Montcalm, we may suppose, regarded the Governor with no less attention. Pierre François Rigaud, Marquis de Vaudreuil, was son of Philippe de Vaudreuil, who had governed Canada early in the century; and he himself had been governor of Louisiana. He had not the force of character which his position demanded, lacked decision in times of crisis; and though tenacious of authority, was more jealous in asserting than self-reliant in exercising it. One of his traits was a sensitive egotism, which made him forward to proclaim his own part in every success, and to throw on others the burden of every failure. He was facile by nature, and capable of being led by such as had skill and temper for the task. But the impetuous Montcalm was not of their number; and the fact that he was born in France would in itself have thrown obstacles in his way to the good graces of the Governor. Vaudreuil, Canadian by birth, loved the colony and its people, and distrusted Old France and all that came out of it. He had been bred, moreover, to the naval service; and, like other Canadian governors, his official correspondence was with the minister of marine, while that of Montcalm was with the minister of war. Even had Nature made him less suspicious, his relations with the General would have been critical.

[1] These extracts are translated from copies of the original letters, in possession of the present Marquis de Montcalm.
[2] *Vaudreuil au Ministre, 30 Oct. 1755.*
[3] *Ordres du Roy et Dépêches des Ministres, Fév. 1756.*

Montcalm commanded the regulars from France, whose very presence
was in the eyes of Vaudreuil an evil, though a necessary one. Their
chief was, it is true, subordinate to him in virtue of his office of governor;[1] yet it was clear that for the conduct of the war the trust of the
Government was mainly in Montcalm; and the Minister of War had
even suggested that he should have the immediate command, not only
of the troops from France, but of the colony regulars and the militia.
An order of the King to this effect was sent to Vaudreuil, with instructions to communicate it to Montcalm or withhold it, as he should think
best.[2] He lost no time in replying that the General "ought to concern
himself with nothing but the command of the troops from France;" and
he returned the order to the minister who sent it.[3] The Governor and
the General represented the two parties which were soon to divide
Canada,—those of New France and of Old.

A like antagonism was seen in the forces commanded by the two
chiefs. These were of three kinds,—the *troupes de terre*, troops of the
line, or regulars from France; the *troupes de la marine*, or colony regulars; and lastly the militia. The first consisted of the four battalions that
had come over with Dieskau and the two that had come with Montcalm, comprising in all a little less than three thousand men.[4] Besides
these, the battalions of Artois and Bourgogne, to the number of eleven
hundred men, were in garrison at Louisbourg. All these troops wore a
white uniform, faced with blue, red, yellow, or violet,[5] a black three-
cornered hat, and gaiters, generally black, from the foot to the knee.
The subaltern officers in the French service were very numerous, and
were drawn chiefly from the class of lesser nobles. A well-informed
French writer calls them "a generation of *petits-maîtres*, dissolute, frivolous, heedless, light-witted; but brave always, and ready to die with

---

[1]*Le Ministre à Vaudreuil, 15 Mars, 1756. Commission du Marquis de Montcalm. Mémoire du Roy
pour servir d'Instruction au Marquis de Montcalm.*
[2]*Ordres du Roy et Dépêches des Ministres, 1756. Le Ministre à Vaudreuil, 15 Mars, 1756.*
[3]*Vaudreuil au Ministre, 16 Juin, 1756.* "Qu'il ne se mêle que du commandement des troupes de
terre."
[4]Of about twelve hundred who came with Montcalm, nearly three hundred were now in hospital.
The four battalions that came with Dieskau are reported at the end of May to have sixteen
hundred and fifty-three effective men. *État de la Situation actuelle des Bataillons*, appended to Montcalm's despatch of 12 June. Another document, *Détail de ce qui s'est passé en Canada, Juin, 1755,
jusqu'à Juin, 1756*, sets the united effective strength of the battalions in Canada at twenty-six
hundred and seventy-seven, which was increased by recruits which arrived from France about
midsummer.
[5]Except, perhaps, the battalion of Béarn, which formerly wore, and possibly wore still, a uniform
of light blue.

their soldiers, though not to suffer with them."[1] In fact the course of the war was to show plainly that in Europe the regiments of France were no longer what they had once been. It was not so with those who fought in America. Here, for enduring gallantry, officers and men alike deserve nothing but praise.

The *troupes de la marine* had for a long time formed the permanent military establishment of Canada. Though attached to the naval department, they served on land, and were employed as a police within the limits of the colony, or as garrisons of the outlying forts, where their officers busied themselves more with fur-trading than with their military duties. Thus they had become ill-disciplined and inefficient, till the hard hand of Duquesne restored them to order. They originally consisted of twenty-eight independent companies, increased in 1750 to thirty companies, at first of fifty, and afterwards of sixty-five men each, forming a total of nineteen hundred and fifty rank and file. In March, 1757, ten more companies were added. Their uniform was not unlike that of the troops attached to the War Department, being white, with black facings. They were enlisted for the most part in France; but when their term of service expired, and even before, in time of peace, they were encouraged to become settlers in the colony as was also the case with their officers, of whom a great part were of European birth. Thus the relations of the *troupes de la marine* with the colony were close; and they formed a sort of connecting link between the troops of the line and the native militia.[2] Besides these colony regulars, there was a company of colonial artillery, consisting this year of seventy men, and replaced in 1757 by two companies of fifty men each.

All the effective male population of Canada, from fifteen years to sixty, was enrolled in the militia, and called into service at the will of the Governor. They received arms, clothing, equipment, and rations from the King, but no pay; and instead of tents they made themselves huts of bark or branches. The best of them were drawn from the upper parts of the colony, where habits of bushranging were still in full activity. Their fighting qualities were much like those of the Indians, whom

---

[1] Susane, *Ancienne Infanterie Française.* In the atlas of this work are colored plates of the uniforms of all the regiments of foot.

[2] On the *troupes de la marine,*—*Mémoire pour servir d'Instruction à MM. Jonquière et Bigot, 30 Avril, 1749. Ordres du Roy et Dépêches des Ministres, 1750. Ibid., 1755. Ibid., 1757. Instruction pour Vaudreuil, 22 Mars, 1755. Ordonnance pour l'Augmentation de Soldats dans les Compagnies de Canada, 14 Mars, 1755. Duquesne au Ministre, 26 Oct. 1753. Ibid., 30 Oct. 1753. Ibid., 29 Fév. 1754. Duquesne à Marin, 27 Août, 1753. Atlas de Susane.*

they rivalled in endurance and in the arts of forest war. As bush-fighters they had few equals; they fought well behind earthworks, and were good at a surprise or sudden dash; but for regular battle on the open field they were of small account, being disorderly, and apt to break and take to cover at the moment of crisis. They had no idea of the great operations of war. At first they despised the regulars for their ignorance of woodcraft, and thought themselves able to defend the colony alone; while the regulars regarded them in turn with a contempt no less unjust. They were excessively given to gasconade, and every true Canadian boasted himself a match for three Englishmen at least. In 1750 the militia of all ranks counted about thirteen thousand; and eight years later the number had increased to about fifteen thousand.[1] Until the last two years of the war, those employed in actual warfare were but few. Even in the critical year 1758 only about eleven hundred were called to arms, except for two or three weeks in summer;[2] though about four thousand were employed in transporting troops and supplies, for which service they received pay.

To the white fighting force of the colony are to be added the red men. The most trusty of them were the Mission Indians, living within or near the settled limits of Canada, chiefly the Hurons of Lorette, the Abenakis of St. Francis and Batiscan, the Iroquois of Caughnawaga and La Présentation, and the Iroquois and Algonkins at the Two Mountains on the Ottawa. Besides these, all the warriors of the west and north, from Lake Superior to the Ohio, and from the Alleghanies to the Mississippi, were now at the beck of France. As to the Iroquois or Five Nations who still remained in their ancient seats within the present limits of New York, their power and pride had greatly fallen; and crowded as they were between the French and the English, they were in a state of vacillation, some leaning to one side, some to the other, and some to each in turn. As a whole, the best that France could expect from them was neutrality.

Montcalm at Montreal had more visits than he liked from his red allies. "They are *vilains messieurs*," he informs his mother, "even when fresh from their toilet, at which they pass their lives. You would not believe it, but the men always carry to war, along with their tomahawk and gun, a mirror to daub their faces with various colors, and arrange feathers on their heads and rings in their ears and noses. They think it

---

[1] *Récapitulation des Milices du Gouvernement de Canada, 1750. Dénombrement des Milices, 1758, 1759.* On the militia, see also Bougainville in Margry, *Relations et Mémoires inédits*, 60, and *N. Y. Col. Docs.*, X. 680.

[2] *Montcalm au Ministre, 1 Sept. 1758.*

a great beauty to cut the rim of the ear and stretch it till it reaches the shoulder. Often they wear a laced coat, with no shirt at all. You would take them for so many masqueraders or devils. One needs the patience of an angel to get on with them. Ever since I have been here, I have had nothing but visits, harangues, and deputations of these gentry. The Iroquois ladies, who always take part in their government, came also, and did me the honor to bring me belts of wampum, which will oblige me to go to their village and sing the war-song. They are only a little way off. Yesterday we had eighty-three warriors here, who have gone out to fight. They make war with astounding cruelty, sparing neither men, women, nor children, and take off your scalp very neatly,—an operation which generally kills you.

"Everything is horribly dear in this country; and I shall find it hard to make the two ends of the year meet, with the twenty-five thousand francs the King gives me. The Chevalier de Lévis did not join me till yesterday. His health is excellent. In a few days I shall send him to one camp, and M. de Bourlamaque to another; for we have three of them: one at Carillon, eighty leagues from here, towards the place where M. de Dieskau had his affair last year; another at Frontenac, sixty leagues; and the third at Niagara, a hundred and forty leagues. I don't know when or whither I shall go myself; that depends on the movements of the enemy. It seems to me that things move slowly in this new world; and I shall have to moderate my activity accordingly. Nothing but the King's service and the wish to make a career for my son could prevent me from thinking too much of my expatriation, my distance from you, and the dull existence here, which would be duller still if I did not manage to keep some little of my natural gayety."

The military situation was somewhat perplexing. Iroquois spies had brought reports of great preparations on the part of the English. As neither party dared offend these wavering tribes, their warriors could pass with impunity from one to the other, and were paid by each for bringing information, not always trustworthy. They declared that the English were gathering in force to renew the attempt made by Johnson the year before against Crown Point and Ticonderoga, as well as that made by Shirley against forts Frontenac and Niagara. Vaudreuil had spared no effort to meet the double danger. Lotbinière, a Canadian engineer, had been busied during the winter in fortifying Ticonderoga, while Pouchot, a captain in the battalion of Béarn, had rebuilt Niagara, and two French engineers were at work in strengthening the defences of Frontenac. The Governor even hoped to take the offensive, antici-pate the movements of the English, capture Oswego, and obtain the

complete command of Lake Ontario. Early in the spring a blow had
been struck which materially aided these schemes.

The English had built two small forts to guard the Great Carrying
Place on the route to Oswego. One of these, Fort Williams, was on the
Mohawk; the other, Fort Bull, a mere collection of storehouses surrounded by a palisade, was four miles distant, on the bank of Wood
Creek. Here a great quantity of stores and ammunition had imprudently
been collected against the opening campaign. In February Vaudreuil
sent Léry, a colony officer, with three hundred and sixty-two picked
men, soldiers, Canadians, and Indians, to seize these two posts. Towards the end of March, after extreme hardship, they reached the road
that connected them, and at half-past five in the morning captured
twelve men going with wagons to Fort Bull. Learning from them the
weakness of that place, they dashed forward to surprise it. The thirty
provincials of Shirley's regiment who formed the garrison had barely
time to shut the gate, while the assailants fired on them through the
loopholes, of which they got possession in the tumult. Léry called on
the defenders to yield; but they refused, and pelted the French for an
hour with bullets and hand-grenades. The gate was at last beat down
with axes, and they were summoned again; but again refused, and fired
hotly through the opening. The French rushed in, shouting *Vive le roi*,
and a frightful struggle followed. All the garrison were killed, except
two or three who hid themselves till the slaughter was over; the fort
was set on fire and blown to atoms by the explosion of the magazines;
and Léry then withdrew, not venturing to attack Fort Williams. Johnson, warned by Indians of the approach of the French, had pushed up
the Mohawk with reinforcements; but came too late.[1]

Vaudreuil, who always exaggerates any success in which he has had
part, says that besides bombs, bullets, cannon-balls, and other munitions, forty-five thousand pounds of gunpowder were destroyed on this
occasion. It is certain that damage enough was done to retard English
operations in the direction of Oswego sufficiently to give the French
time for securing all their posts on Lake Ontario. Before the end of
June this was in good measure done. The battalion of Béarn lay encamped before the now strong fort of Niagara, and the battalions of
Guienne and La Sarre, with a body of Canadians, guarded Frontenac

---

[1] *Bigot au Ministre, 12 Avril, 1756. Vaudreuil au Ministre, 1 Juin, 1756. Ibid., 8 Juin, 1756. Journal
de ce qui s'est passé en Canada depuis le Mois d'Octobre, 1755, jusqu'au Mois de Juin, 1756. Shirley
to Fox, 7 May, 1756. Conduct of Major General-Shirley briefly stated. Information of Captain John
Vicars, of the Fiftieth (Shirley's) Regiment.* Eastburn, *Faithful Narrative.* Entick, I. 471. The French
accounts place the number of English at sixty or eighty.

against attack. Those of La Reine and Languedoc had been sent to Ticonderoga, while the Governor, with Montcalm and Lévis, still remained at Montreal watching the turn of events.[1] Hither, too, came the intendant François Bigot, the most accomplished knave in Canada, yet indispensable for his vigor and executive skill; Bougainville, who had disarmed the jealousy of Vaudreuil, and now stood high in his good graces; and the Adjutant-General, Montreuil, clearly a vain and pragmatic personage, who, having come to Canada with Dieskau the year before, thought it behooved him to give the General the advantage of his experience. "I like M. de Montcalm very much," he writes to the minister, "and will do the impossible to deserve his confidence. I have spoken to him in the same terms as to M. Dieskau; thus: 'Trust only the French regulars for an expedition, but use the Canadians and Indians to harass the enemy. Don't expose yourself; send me to carry your orders to points of danger.' The colony officers do not like those from France. The Canadians are independent, spiteful, lying, boastful; very good for skirmishing, very brave behind a tree, and very timid when not under cover. I think both sides will stand on the defensive. It does not seem to me that M. de Montcalm means to attack the enemy; and I think he is right. In this country a thousand men could stop three thousand."[2]

"M. de Vaudreuil overwhelms me with civilities," Montcalm writes to the Minister of War. "I think that he is pleased with my conduct towards him, and that it persuades him there are general officers in France who can act under his orders without prejudice or ill-humor."[3] "I am on good terms with him," he says again; "but not in his confidence, which he never gives to anybody from France. His intentions are good, but he is slow and irresolute."[4]

Indians presently brought word that ten thousand English were coming to attack Ticonderoga. A reinforcement of colony regulars was at once despatched to join the two battalions already there; a third battalion, Royal Roussillon, was sent after them. The militia were called out and ordered to follow with all speed, while both Montcalm and Lévis hastened to the supposed scene of danger.[5] They embarked in canoes on the Richelieu, coasted the shore of Lake Champlain, passed

[1]*Correspondance de Montcalm, Vaudreuil, et Lévis.*

[2]*Montreuil au Ministre,* 12 *Juin, 1756.* The original is in cipher.

[3]*Montcalm au Ministre,* 12 *Juin, 1756.*

[4]*Ibid.,* 19 *Juin, 1756.* "Je suis bien avec luy, sans sa confiance, qu'il ne donne jamais à personne de la France." Erroneously rendered in *N. Y. Col. Docs.*, X. 421.

[5]*Montcalm au Ministre,* 26 *Juin, 1756. Détail de ce qui s'est passé, Oct. 1755– Juin, 1756.*

Fort Frederic or Crown Point, where all was activity and bustle, and reached Ticonderoga at the end of June. They found the fort, on which Lotbinière had been at work all winter, advanced towards completion. It stood on the crown of the promontory, and was a square with four bastions, a ditch, blown in some parts out of the solid rock, bomb-proofs, barracks of stone, and a system of exterior defences as yet only begun. The rampart consisted of two parallel walls ten feet apart, built of the trunks of trees, and held together by transverse logs dovetailed at both ends, the space between being filled with earth and gravel well packed.[1] Such was the first Fort Ticonderoga, or Carillon,—a structure quite distinct from the later fort of which the ruins still stand on the same spot. The forest had been hewn away for some distance around, and the tents of the regulars and huts of the Canadians had taken its place; innumerable bark canoes lay along the strand, and gangs of men toiled at the unfinished works.

Ticonderoga was now the most advanced position of the French, and Crown Point, which had before held that perilous honor, was in the second line. Lévis, to whom had been assigned the permanent command of this post of danger, set out on foot to explore the neighboring woods and mountains, and slept out several nights before he reappeared at the camp. "I do not think," says Montcalm, "that many high officers in Europe would have occasion to take such tramps as this. I cannot speak too well of him. Without being a man of brilliant parts, he has good experience, good sense, and a quick eye; and, though I had served with him before, I never should have thought that he had such promptness and efficiency. He has turned his campaigns to good account."[2] Lévis writes of his chief with equal warmth. "I do not know if the Marquis de Montcalm is pleased with me, but I am sure that I am very much so with him, and shall always be charmed to serve under his orders. It is not for me, Monseigneur, to speak to you of his merit and his talents. You know him better than anybody else; but I may have the honor of assuring you that he has pleased everybody in this colony, and manages affairs with the Indians extremely well."[3]

The danger from the English proved to be still remote, and there was ample leisure in the camp. Duchat, a young captain in the battalion of Languedoc, used it in writing to his father a long account of what he saw about him,—the forests full of game; the ducks, geese, and par-

---

[1] *Lotbinière au Ministre, 31 Oct. 1756. Montcalm au Ministre, 20 Juillet, 1756.*
[2] *Montcalm au Ministre, 20 Juillet, 1756.*
[3] *Lévis au Ministre, 17 Juillet, 1756.*

tridges; the prodigious flocks of wild pigeons that darkened the air; the bears, the beavers; and above all the Indians, their canoes, dress, ball-play, and dances. "We are making here," says the military prophet, "a place that history will not forget. The English colonies have ten times more people than ours; but these wretches have not the least knowledge of war, and if they go out to fight, they must abandon wives, children, and all that they possess. Not a week passes but the French send them a band of *hairdressers*, whom they would be very glad to dispense with. It is incredible what a quantity of scalps they bring us. In Virginia they have committed unheard-of cruelties, carried off families, burned a great many houses, and killed an infinity of people. These miserable English are in the extremity of distress, and repent too late the unjust war they began against us. It is a pleasure to make war in Canada. One is troubled neither with horses nor baggage; the King provides every-thing. But it must be confessed that if it costs no money, one pays for it in another way, by seeing nothing but pease and bacon on the mess-table. Luckily the lakes are full of fish, and both officers and soldiers have to turn fishermen."[1]

Meanwhile, at the head of Lake George, the raw bands of ever-active New England were mustering for the fray.

[1]*Relation de M. Duchat, Capitaine au Régiment de Languedoc, écrite au Camp de Carillon,* 15 Juillet, 1756.

12

Oswego

1756

THE NEW CAMPAIGN · UNTIMELY CHANGE OF COMMANDERS · ECLIPSE OF
SHIRLEY · EARL OF LOUDON · MUSTER OF PROVINCIALS · NEW ENGLAND
LEVIES · WINSLOW AT LAKE GEORGE · JOHNSON AND THE FIVE NATIONS ·
BRADSTREET AND HIS BOATMEN · FIGHT ON THE ONONDAGA · PESTILENCE
AT OSWEGO · LOUDON AND THE PROVINCIALS · NEW ENGLAND CAMPS ·
ARMY CHAPLAINS · A SUDDEN BLOW · MONTCALM ATTACKS OSWEGO · ITS
FALL

W hen, at the end of the last year, Shirley returned
from his bootless Oswego campaign, he called a
council of war at New York and laid before it his scheme for the next
summer's operations. It was a comprehensive one: to master Lake Ontario by an overpowering naval force and seize the French forts upon
it, Niagara, Frontenac, and Toronto; attack Ticonderoga and Crown
Point on the one hand, and Fort Duquesne on the other, and at the
same time perplex and divide the enemy by an inroad down the Chaudière upon the settlements about Quebec.[1] The council approved the
scheme; but to execute it the provinces must raise at least sixteen thousand men. This they refused to do. Pennsylvania and Virginia would

[1]Minutes of Council of War held at New York, 12 and 13 Dec. 1755. Shirley to Robinson, 19 Dec.
1755. The Conduct of Major-General Shirley briefly stated. Review of Military Operations in North
America.

take no active part, and were content with defending themselves. The attack on Fort Duquesne was therefore abandoned, as was also the diversion towards Quebec. The New England colonies were discouraged by Johnson's failure to take Crown Point, doubtful of the military abilities of Shirley, and embarrassed by the debts of the last campaign; but when they learned that Parliament would grant a sum of money in partial compensation for their former sacrifices,[1] they plunged into new debts without hesitation, and raised more men than the General had asked; though, with their usual jealousy, they provided that their soldiers should be employed for no other purpose than the attack on Ticonderoga and Crown Point. Shirley chose John Winslow to command them, and gave him a commission to that effect; while he, to clinch his authority, asked and obtained supplementary commissions from every government that gave men to the expedition.[2] For the movement against the forts of Lake Ontario, which Shirley meant to command in person, he had the remains of his own and Pepperell's regiments, the two shattered battalions brought over by Braddock, the "Jersey Blues," four provincial companies from North Carolina, and the four King's companies of New York. His first care was to recruit their ranks and raise them to their full complement; which, when effected, would bring them up to the insufficient strength of about forty-four hundred men.

While he was struggling with contradictions and cross purposes, a withering blow fell upon him; he learned that he was superseded in the command. The cabal formed against him, with Delancey at its head, had won over Sir Charles Hardy, the new governor of New York, and had painted Shirley's conduct in such colors that the Ministry removed him. It was essential for the campaign that a successor should be sent at once, to form plans on the spot and make preparations accordingly. The Ministry were in no such haste. It was presently announced that Colonel Daniel Webb would be sent to America, followed by General James Abercromby; who was to be followed in turn by the Earl of Loudon, the destined commander-in-chief. Shirley was to resign his command to Webb, Webb to Abercromby, and Abercromby to Loudon.[3] It chanced that the two former arrived in June at about the same time,

---

[1] *Lords of Trade to Lords of the Treasury, 12 Feb. 1756. Fox to American Governors, 13 March, 1756. Shirley to Phipps, 15 June, 1756.* The sum was £115,000, divided in proportion to the expense incurred by the several colonies; Massachusetts having £54,000, Connecticut £26,000, and New York £15,000, the rest being given to New Hampshire, Rhode Island, and New Jersey.

[2] *Letter and Order Books of General Winslow, 1756.*

[3] *Fox to Shirley, 13 March, 1756. Ibid., 31 March, 1756. Order to Colonel Webb, 31 March, 1756. Order to Major-General Abercromby, 1 April, 1756. Halifax to Shirley, 1 April, 1756. Shirley to Fox, 13 June, 1756.*

while the Earl came in July; and meanwhile it devolved on Shirley to make ready for them. Unable to divine what their plans would be, he prepared the campaign in accordance with his own.

His star, so bright a twelvemonth before, was now miserably dimmed. In both his public and private life he was the butt of adversity. He had lost two promising sons; he had made a mortifying failure as a soldier; and triumphant enemies were rejoicing in his fall. It is to the credit of his firmness and his zeal in the cause that he set himself to his task with as much vigor as if he, and not others, were to gather the fruits. His chief care was for his favorite enterprise in the direction of Lake Ontario. Making Albany his headquarters, he rebuilt the fort at the Great Carrying Place destroyed in March by the French, sent troops to guard the perilous route to Oswego, and gathered provisions and stores at the posts along the way.

Meanwhile the New England men, strengthened by the levies of New York, were mustering at Albany for the attack of Crown Point. At the end of May they moved a short distance up the Hudson, and encamped at a place called Half-Moon, where the navigation was stopped by rapids. Here and at the posts above were gathered something more than five thousand men, as raw and untrained as those led by Johnson in the summer before.[1] The four New England colonies were much alike in their way of raising and equipping men, and the example of Massachusetts may serve for them all. The Assembly or "General Court" voted the required number, and chose a committee of war authorized to impress provisions, munitions, stores, clothing, tools, and other necessaries, for which fair prices were to be paid within six months. The Governor issued a proclamation calling for volunteers. If the full number did not appear within the time named, the colonels of militia were ordered to muster their regiments, and immediately draft out of them men enough to meet the need. A bounty of six dollars was offered this year to stimulate enlistment, and the pay of a private soldier was fixed at one pound six shillings a month, Massachusetts currency. If he brought a gun, he had an additional bounty of two dollars. A powder-horn, bullet-pouch, blanket, knapsack, and "wooden bottle," or canteen, were supplied by the province; and if he brought no gun of his own, a musket was given him, for which, as for the other articles, he was to account at the end of the campaign. In the next year it was announced that the soldier should receive, besides his pay, "a coat and soldier's hat." The coat was of coarse blue cloth, to which

[1] *Letter and Order Books of Winslow, 1756.*

breeches of red or blue were afterwards added. Along with his rations, he was promised a gill of rum each day, a privilege of which he was extremely jealous, deeply resenting every abridgment of it. He was en-listed for the campaign, and could not be required to serve above a year at farthest.

The complement of a regiment was five hundred, divided into com-panies of fifty; and as the men and officers of each were drawn from the same neighborhood, they generally knew each other. The officers, though nominally appointed by the Assembly, were for the most part the virtual choice of the soldiers themselves, from whom they were often indistinguishable in character and social standing. Hence disci-pline was weak. The pay—or, as it was called, the wages—of a colonel was twelve pounds sixteen shillings, Massachusetts currency, a month; that of a captain, five pounds eight shillings,—an advance on the pay of the last year; and that of a chaplain, six pounds eight shillings.[1] Penalties were enacted against "irreligion, immorality, drunkenness, de-bauchery, and profaneness." The ordinary punishments were the wooden horse, irons, or, in bad cases, flogging.

Much difficulty arose from the different rules adopted by the var-ious colonies for the regulation of their soldiers. Nor was this the only source of trouble. Besides its war committee, the Assembly of each of the four New England colonies chose another committee "for clothing, arming, paying, victualling, and transporting" its troops. They were to go to the scene of operations, hire wagons, oxen, and horses, build boats and vessels, and charge themselves with the con-veyance of all supplies belonging to their respective governments. They were to keep in correspondence with the committee of war at home, to whom they were responsible; and the officer commanding the contingent of their colony was required to furnish them with guards and escorts. Thus four independent committees were engaged in the work of transportation at the same time, over the same roads, for the same object. Each colony chose to keep the control of its property in its own hands. The inconveniences were obvious. "I wish to God," wrote Lord Loudon to Winslow, "you could persuade your people to go all one way." The committees themselves did not always find their task agreeable. One of their number, John Ashley, of Mas-sachusetts, writes in dudgeon to Governor Phipps: "Sir, I am apt to think that things have been misrepresented to your Honor, or else I am certain I should not suffer in my character, and be styled a

[1] *Vote of General Court, 26 Feb. 1756.*

damned rascal, and ought to be put in irons, etc., when I am certain I have exerted myself to the utmost of my ability to expedite the business assigned me by the General Court." At length, late in the autumn, Loudon persuaded the colonies to forego this troublesome sort of independence, and turn over their stores to the commissary-general, receipts being duly given.[1]

From Winslow's headquarters at Half-Moon a road led along the banks of the Hudson to Stillwater, whence there was water carriage to Saratoga. Here stores were again placed in wagons and carried several miles to Upper Falls; thence by boat to Fort Edward; and thence, four-teen miles across country, to Fort William Henry at Lake George, where the army was to embark for Ticonderoga. Each of the points of transit below Fort Edward was guarded by a stockade and two or more companies of provincials. They were much pestered by Indians, who now and then scalped a straggler, and escaped with their usual nimble-ness. From time to time strong bands of Canadians and Indians ap-proached by way of South Bay or Wood Creek, and threatened more serious mischief. It is surprising that some of the trains were not cut off, for the escorts were often reckless and disorderly to the last degree. Sometimes the invaders showed great audacity. Early in June Colonel Fitch at Albany scrawls a hasty note to Winslow: "Friday, 11 o'clock: Sir, about half an hour since, a party of near fifty French and Indians had the impudence to come down to the river opposite to this city and captivate two men;" and Winslow replies with equal quaintness: "We daily discover the Indians about us; but not yet have been so happy as to obtain any of them."[2]

Colonel Jonathan Bagley commanded at Fort William Henry, where gangs of men were busied under his eye in building three sloops and making several hundred whaleboats to carry the army to Ticonderoga. The season was advancing fast, and Winslow urged him to hasten on the work; to which the humorous Bagley answered: "Shall leave no stone unturned; every wheel shall go that rum and human flesh can move."[3] A fortnight after he reports: "I must really confess I have al-

---

[1] The above particulars are gathered from the voluminous papers in the State House at Boston, *Archives, Military*, Vols. LXXV., LXXVI. These contain the military acts of the General Court, proclamations, reports of committees, and other papers relating to military affairs in 1755 and 1756. The *Letter and Order Books of Winslow*, in the Library of the Massachusetts Historical Society, have supplied much concurrent matter. See also *Colonial Records of R. I.*, V., and *Provincial Papers of N. H.*, VI.

[2] Vaudreuil, in his despatch of 12 August, gives particulars of these raids, with an account of the scalps taken on each occasion. He thought the results disappointing.

[3] *Bagley to Winslow, 2 July, 1756.*

most wore the men out, poor dogs. Pray where are the committee, or what are they about?" He sent scouts to watch the enemy, with results not quite satisfactory. "There is a vast deal of news here; every party brings abundance, but all different." Again, a little later: "I constantly keep out small scouting parties to the eastward and westward of the lake, and make no discovery but the tracks of small parties who are plaguing us constantly; but what vexes me most, we can't catch one of the sons of ————. I have sent out skulking parties some distance from the sentries in the night, to lie still in the bushes to intercept them; but the flies are so plenty, our people can't bear them."[1] Colonel David Wooster, at Fort Edward, was no more fortunate in his attempts to take satisfaction on his midnight visitors; and reports that he has not thus far been able "to give those villains a dressing."[2] The English, however, were fast learning the art of forest war, and the partisan chief, Captain Robert Rogers, began already to be famous. On the seventeenth of June he and his band lay hidden in the bushes within the outposts of Ticonderoga, and made a close survey of the fort and surrounding camps.[3] His report was not cheering. Winslow's so-called army had now grown to nearly seven thousand men; and these, it was plain, were not too many to drive the French from their stronghold.

While Winslow pursued his preparations, tried to settle disputes of rank among the colonels of the several colonies, and strove to bring order out of the little chaos of his command, Sir William Johnson was engaged in a work for which he was admirably fitted. This was the attaching of the Five Nations to the English interest. Along with his patent of baronetcy, which reached him about this time, he received, direct from the Crown, the commission of "Colonel, Agent, and Sole Superintendent of the Six Nations and other Northern Tribes."[4] Henceforth he was independent of governors and generals, and responsible to the Court alone. His task was a difficult one. The Five Nations would fain have remained neutral, and let the European rivals fight it out; but, on account of their local position, they could not. The exactions and lies of the Albany traders, the frauds of land-speculators, the contradictory action of the different provincial governments, joined to English weakness and mismanagement in the last war, all conspired to alienate them and to aid the efforts of the French agents, who cajoled and threatened them by turns. But for Johnson these intrigues would

[1] *Ibid.*, 15 July, 1756.
[2] *Wooster to Winslow*, 2 June, 1756.
[3] *Report of Rogers*, 19 June, 1756. Much abridged in his published *Journals*.
[4] *Fox to Johnson*, 13 March, 1756. *Papers of Sir William Johnson*.

have prevailed. He had held a series of councils with them at Fort Johnson during the winter, and not only drew from them a promise to stand by the English, but persuaded all the confederated tribes, except the Cayugas, to consent that the English should build forts near their chief towns, under the pretext of protecting them from the French.[1]

In June he went to Onondaga, well escorted, for the way was dangerous. This capital of the Confederacy was under a cloud. It had just lost one Red Head, its chief sachem; and first of all it behooved the baronet to condole their affliction. The ceremony was long, with compliments, lugubrious speeches, wampum-belts, the scalp of an enemy to replace the departed, and a final glass of rum for each of the assembled mourners. The conferences lasted a fortnight; and when Johnson took his leave, the tribes stood pledged to lift the hatchet for the English.[2]

When he returned to Fort Johnson a fever seized him, and he lay helpless for a time; then rose from his sick bed to meet another congregation of Indians. These were deputies of the Five Nations, with Mohegans from the Hudson, and Delawares and Shawanoes from the Susquehanna, whom he had persuaded to visit him in hope that he might induce them to cease from murdering the border settlers. All their tribesmen were in arms against the English; but he prevailed at last, and they accepted the war-belt at his hands. The Delawares complained that their old conquerors, the Five Nations, had forced them "to wear the petticoat," that is, to be counted not as warriors but as women. Johnson, in presence of all the Assembly, now took off the figurative garment, and pronounced them henceforth men. A grand war-dance followed. A hundred and fifty Mohawks, Oneidas, Onondagas, Delawares, Shawanoes, and Mohegans stamped, whooped, and yelled all night.[3] In spite of Piquet, the two Joncaires, and the rest of the French agents, Johnson had achieved a success. But would the Indians keep their word? It was more than doubtful. While some of them treated with him on the Mohawk, others treated with Vaudreuil at Montreal.[4] A display of military vigor on the English side, crowned by some signal victory, would alone make their alliance sure.

It was not the French only who thwarted the efforts of Johnson; for while he strove to make friends of the Delawares and Shawanoes, Gov-

[1]*Conferences between Sir William Johnson and the Indians, Dec. 1755, to Feb. 1756,* in *N. Y. Col. Docs.,* VII. 44–74. *Account of Conferences held and Treaties made between Sir William Johnson, Bart., and the Indian Nations of North America* (London, 1756).

[2]*Minutes of Councils at Onondaga, 19 June to 3 July, 1756,* in *N. Y. Col. Docs.,* VII. 134–150

[3]*Minutes of Councils at Fort Johnson, 9 July to 12 July,* in *N. Y. Col. Docs.,* VII. 152–160.

[4]*Conferences between M. de Vaudreuil and the Five Nations, 28 July to 20 Aug.,* in *N. Y. Col. Docs.,* X. 445–453.

ernor Morris of Pennsylvania declared war against them, and Governor
Belcher of New Jersey followed his example; though persuaded at last
to hold his hand till the baronet had tried the virtue of pacific measures.[1]

What Shirley longed for was the collecting of a body of Five Nation
warriors at Oswego to aid him in his cherished enterprise against Niagara and Frontenac. The warriors had promised him to come; but
there was small hope that they would do so. Meanwhile he was at
Albany pursuing his preparations, posting his scanty force in the forts
newly built on the Mohawk and the Great Carrying Place, and sending
forward stores and provisions. Having no troops to spare for escorts, he
invented a plan which, like everything he did, was bitterly criticised.
He took into pay two thousand boatmen, gathered from all parts of the
country, including many whalemen from the eastern coasts of New
England, divided them into companies of fifty, armed each with a gun
and a hatchet, and placed them under the command of Lieutenant-
Colonel John Bradstreet.[2] Thus organized, they would, he hoped, require no escort. Bradstreet was a New England officer who had been a
captain in the last war, somewhat dogged and self-opinioned, but
brave, energetic, and well fitted for this kind of service.

In May Vaudreuil sent Coulon de Villiers with eleven hundred soldiers, Canadians, and Indians, to harass Oswego and cut its communications with Albany.[3] Nevertheless Bradstreet safely conducted a
convoy of provisions and military stores to the garrison; and on the
third of July set out on his return with the empty boats. The party were
pushing their way up the river in three divisions. The first of these,
consisting of a hundred boats and three hundred men, with Bradstreet
at their head, were about nine miles from Oswego, when, at three in
the afternoon, they received a heavy volley from the forest on the east
bank. It was fired by a part of Villiers' command, consisting, by English
accounts, of about seven hundred men. A considerable number of the
boatmen were killed or disabled, and the others made for the shelter of
the western shore. Some prisoners were taken in the confusion; and if
the French had been content to stop here, they might fairly have
claimed a kind of victory: but, eager to push their advantage, they tried
to cross under cover of an island just above. Bradstreet saw the movement, and landed on the island with six or eight followers, among

[1] *Johnson to Lords of Trade, 28 May, 1756. Ibid., 17 July, 1756. Johnson to Shirley, 24 April, 1756.*
Colonial Records of Pa., VII. 75, 88, 194.
[2] *Shirley to Fox, 7 May, 1756. Shirley to Abercromby, 27 June, 1756. Loudon to Fox, 19 Aug. 1756.*
[3] *Détail de ce qui s'est passé en Canada, Oct. 1755–Juin, 1756.*

whom was young Captain Schuyler, afterwards General Schuyler of the Revolution. Their fire kept the enemy in check till others joined them, to the number of about twenty. These a second and a third time beat back the French, who now gave over the attempt, and made for another ford at some distance above. Bradstreet saw their intention; and collecting two hundred and fifty men, was about to advance up the west bank to oppose them, when Dr. Kirkland, a surgeon, came to tell him that the second division of boats had come up, and that the men had landed. Bradstreet ordered them to stay where they were, and defend the lower crossing: then hastened forward; but when he reached the upper ford, the French had passed the river, and were ensconced in a pine-swamp near the shore. Here he attacked them; and both parties fired at each other from behind trees for an hour, with little effect. Bradstreet at length encouraged his men to make a rush at the enemy, who were put to flight and driven into the river, where many were shot or drowned as they tried to cross. Another party of the French had meanwhile passed by a ford still higher up to support their comrades; but the fight was over before they reached the spot, and they in their turn were set upon and driven back across the stream. Half an hour after, Captain Patten arrived from Onondaga with the grenadiers of Shirley's regiment; and late in the evening two hundred men came from Oswego to reinforce the victors. In the morning Bradstreet prepared to follow the French to their camp, twelve miles distant; but was prevented by a heavy rain which lasted all day. On the Monday following, he and his men reached Albany, bringing two prisoners, eighty French muskets, and many knapsacks picked up in the woods. He had lost between sixty and seventy killed, wounded, and taken.[1]

This affair was trumpeted through Canada as a victory of the French. Their notices of it are discordant, though very brief. One of them says that Villiers had four hundred men. Another gives him five hundred, and a third eight hundred, against fifteen hundred English, of whom they killed eight hundred, or an Englishman apiece. A fourth writer boasts that six hundred Frenchmen killed nine hundred English. A fifth contents himself with four hundred; but thinks that forty more would have been slain if the Indians had not fired too soon. He says further that there were three hundred boats; and presently forgetting himself,

---

[1] *Letter of J. Choate, Albany, 12 July, 1756*, in Massachusetts Archives, LV. *Three Letters from Albany, July, Aug. 1756*, in Doc. Hist. of N. Y., I. 482. *Review of Military Operations. Shirley to Fox, 26 July, 1756. Abercromby to Sir Charles Hardy, 11 July, 1756*. Niles, in *Mass. Hist. Coll., Fourth Series*, V. 417. Lossing, *Life of Schuyler*, I. 131 (1860). Mante, 60. Bradstreet's conduct on this occasion afterwards gained for him the warm praises of Wolfe.

adds that five hundred were taken or destroyed. A sixth announces a great capture of stores and provisions, though all the boats were empty. A seventh reports that the Canadians killed about three hundred, and would have killed more but for the bad quality of their tomahawks. An eighth, with rare modesty, puts the English loss at fifty or sixty. That of Villiers is given in every proportion of killed or wounded, from one up to ten. Thus was Canada roused to martial ardor, and taught to look for future triumphs cheaply bought.[1]

The success of Bradstreet silenced for a time the enemies of Shirley. His cares, however, redoubled. He was anxious for Oswego, as the two prisoners declared that the French meant to attack it, instead of waiting to be attacked from it. Nor was the news from that quarter reassuring. The engineer, Mackellar, wrote that the works were incapable of defence; and Colonel Mercer, the commandant, reported general discontent in the garrison.[2] Captain John Vicars, an invalid officer of Shirley's regiment, arrived at Albany with yet more deplorable accounts. He had passed the winter at Oswego, where he declared the dearth of food to have been such that several councils of war had been held on the question of abandoning the place from sheer starvation. More than half his regiment died of hunger or disease; and, in his own words, "had the poor fellows lived they must have eaten one another." Some of the men were lodged in barracks, though without beds, while many lay all winter in huts on the bare ground. Scurvy and dysentery made frightful havoc. "In January," says Vicars, "we were informed by the Indians that we were to be attacked. The garrison was then so weak that the strongest guard we proposed to mount was a subaltern and twenty men; but we were seldom able to mount more than sixteen or eighteen, and half of those were obliged to have sticks in their hands to support them. The men were so weak that the sentries often fell down on their posts, and lay there till the relief came and lifted them up." His own company of fifty was reduced to ten. The other regiment of the garrison, Pepperell's, or the fifty-first, was quartered at Fort Ontario, on the other side of the river; and being better sheltered, suffered less.

The account given by Vicars of the state of the defences was scarcely more flattering. He reported that the principal fort had no cannon on

[1]Nouvelles du Camp établi au Portage de Chouaguen, première Relation. Ibid., Séconde Relation, 10 Juillet, 1756. Bougainville, Journal, who gives the report as he heard it. Lettre du R. P. Cocquard, S. J., 1756. Vaudreuil au Ministre, 10 Juillet, 1756. Ursulines de Québec, II. 292. N. Y. Col. Docs., X. 434, 467, 477, 483. Some prisoners taken in the first attack were brought to Montreal, where their presence gave countenance to these fabrications.
[2]Mackellar to Shirley, June, 1756. Mercer to Shirley, 2 July, 1756.

the side most exposed to attack. Two pieces had been mounted on the trading-house in the centre; but as the concussion shook down stones from the wall whenever they were fired, they had since been removed. The second work, called Fort Ontario, he had not seen since it was finished, having been too ill to cross the river. Of the third, called New Oswego, or "Fort Rascal," he testifies thus: "It never was finished, and there were no loopholes in the stockades; so that they could not fire out of the fort but by opening the gate and firing out of that."[1]

Through the spring and early summer Shirley was gathering recruits, often of the meanest quality, and sending them to Oswego to fill out the two emaciated regiments. The place must be defended at any cost. Its fall would ruin not only the enterprise against Niagara and Fron-tenac, but also that against Ticonderoga and Crown Point; since, hav-ing nothing more to fear on Lake Ontario, the French could unite their whole force on Lake Champlain, whether for defence or attack.

Towards the end of June Abercromby and Webb arrived at Albany, bringing a reinforcement of nine hundred regulars, consisting of Ot-way's regiment, or a part of it, and a body of Highlanders. Shirley resigned his command, and Abercromby requested him to go to New York, wait there till Lord Loudon arrived, and lay before him the state of affairs.[2] Shirley waited till the twenty-third of July, when the Earl at length appeared. He was a rough Scotch lord, hot and irascible; and the communications of his predecessor, made, no doubt, in a manner somewhat pompous and self-satisfied, did not please him. "I got from Major-General Shirley," he says, "a few papers of very little use; only he insinuated to me that I would find everything prepared, and have nothing to do but to pull laurels; which I understand was his constant conversation before my arrival."[3]

Loudon sailed up the Hudson in no placid mood. On reaching Al-bany he abandoned the attempt against Niagara and Frontenac; and had resolved to turn his whole force against Ticonderoga, when he was met by an obstacle that both perplexed and angered him. By a royal order lately issued, all general and field officers with provincial com-missions were to take rank only as eldest captains when serving in con-junction with regular troops.[4] Hence the whole provincial army, as

[1] *Information of Captain John Vicars, of the Fiftieth (Shirley's) Regiment*, enclosed with a despatch of Lord Loudon. Vicars was a veteran British officer who left Oswego with Bradstreet on the third of July. *Shirley to Loudon, 5 Sept. 1756.*
[2] *Shirley to Fox, 4 July, 1756.*
[3] *Loudon (to Fox?), 19 Aug. 1756.*
[4] *Order concerning the Rank of Provincial General and Field Officers in North America. Given at our Court at Kensington, 12 May, 1756.*

Winslow observes, might be put under the command of any British major.[1] The announcement of this regulation naturally caused great discontent. The New England officers held a meeting, and voted with one voice that in their belief its enforcement would break up the provincial army and prevent the raising of another. Loudon, hearing of this, desired Winslow to meet him at Albany for a conference on the subject. Thither Winslow went with some of his chief officers. The Earl asked them to dinner, and there was much talk, with no satisfactory result; whereupon, somewhat chafed, he required Winslow to answer in writing, yes or no, whether the provincial officers would obey the commander-in-chief and act in conjunction with the regulars. Thus forced to choose between acquiescence and flat mutiny, they declared their submission to his orders, at the same time asking as a favor that they might be allowed to act independently; to which Loudon gave for the present an unwilling assent. Shirley, who, in spite of his removal from command, had the good of the service deeply at heart, was much troubled at this affair, and wrote strong letters to Winslow in the interest of harmony.[2]

Loudon next proceeded to examine the state of the provincial forces, and sent Lieutenant-Colonel Burton, of the regulars, to observe and report upon it. Winslow by this time had made a forward movement, and was now at Lake George with nearly half his command, while the rest were at Fort Edward under Lyman, or in detachments at Saratoga and the other small posts below. Burton found Winslow's men encamped with their right on what are now the grounds of Fort William Henry Hotel, and their left extending southward between the mountain in their front and the marsh in their rear. "There are here," he reports, "about twenty-five hundred men, five hundred of them sick, the greatest part of them what they call poorly; they bury from five to eight daily, and officers in proportion; extremely indolent, and dirty to a degree." Then, in vernacular English, he describes the infectious condition of the fort, which was full of the sick. "Their camp," he proceeds, "is nastier than anything I could conceive; their ——, kitchens, graves, and places for slaughtering cattle all mixed through their encampment; a great waste of provisions, the men having just what they please; no great command kept up. Colonel Gridley governs the general; not in the least alert; only one advanced guard of a subaltern and twenty-four men. The cannon and stores in great confusion." Of the

---

[1] *Winslow to Shirley, 21 Aug. 1756.*
[2] *Correspondence of Loudon, Abercromby, and Shirley, July, Aug. 1756. Record of Meeting of Provincial Officers, July, 1756. Letter and Order Books of Winslow.*

camp at Fort Edward he gives a better account. "It is much cleaner than at Fort William Henry, but not sufficiently so to keep the men healthy; a much better command kept up here. General Lyman very ready to order out to work and to assist the engineers with any number of men they require, and keeps a succession of scouting-parties out towards Wood Creek and South Bay."[1]

The prejudice of the regular officer may have colored the picture, but it is certain that the sanitary condition of the provincial camps was extremely bad. "A grievous sickness among the troops," writes a Massachusetts surgeon at Fort Edward; "we bury five or six a day. Not more than two thirds of our army fit for duty. Long encampments are the bane of New England men."[2] Like all raw recruits, they did not know how to take care of themselves; and their officers had not the experience, knowledge, or habit of command to enforce sanitary rules. The same evils were found among the Canadians when kept long in one place. Those in the camp of Villiers are reported at this time as nearly all sick.[3]

Another penman, very different from the military critic, was also on the spot, noting down every day what he saw and felt. This was John Graham, minister of Suffield, in Connecticut, and now chaplain of Lyman's regiment. His spirit, by nature far from buoyant, was depressed by bodily ailments, and still more by the extremely secular character of his present surroundings. It appears by his Diary that he left home "under great exercise of mind," and was detained at Albany for a time, being, as he says, taken with an ague-fit and a quinsy; but at length he reached the camp at Fort Edward, where deep despondency fell upon him. "Labor under great discouragements," says the Diary, under date of July twenty-eighth; "for find my business but mean in the esteem of many, and think there's not much for a chaplain to do." Again, Tuesday, August seventeenth: "Breakfasted this morning with the General. But a graceless meal; never a blessing asked, nor thanks given. At the evening sacrifice a more open scene of wickedness. The General and head officers, with some of the regular officers, in General Lyman's tent, within four rods of the place of public prayers. None came to prayers; but they fixed a table without the door of the tent, where a head colonel was posted to make punch in the sight of all, they within drinking, talking, and laughing during the whole of the service, to the

---

[1] *Burton to Loudon, 27 Aug. 1756.*
[2] *Dr. Thomas Williams to Colonel Israel Williams, 28 Aug. 1756.*
[3] Bougainville, *Journal.*

disturbance and disaffection of most present. This was not only a bare neglect, but an open contempt, of the worship of God by the heads of this army. 'Twas but last Sabbath that General Lyman spent the time of divine service in the afternoon in his tent, drinking in company with Mr. Gordon, a regular officer. I have oft heard cursing and swearing in his presence by some provincial field-officers, but never heard a reproof nor so much as a check to them come from his mouth, though he never uses such language himself. Lord, what is man! Truly, the May-game of Fortune! Lord, make me know my duty, and what I ought to do!"

That night his sleep was broken and his soul troubled by angry voices under his window, where one Colonel Glasier was berating, in unhallowed language, the captain of the guard; and here the chaplain's Journal abruptly ends.[1]

A brother minister, bearing no likeness to the worthy Graham, appeared on the same spot some time after. This was Chaplain William Crawford, of Worcester, who, having neglected to bring money to the war, suffered much annoyance, aggravated by what he thought a want of due consideration for his person and office. His indignation finds vent in a letter to his townsman, Timothy Paine, member of the General Court: "No man can reasonably expect that I can with any propriety discharge the duty of a chaplain when I have nothing either to eat or drink, nor any conveniency to write a line other than to sit down upon a stump and put a piece of paper upon my knee. As for Mr. Weld [*another chaplain*], he is easy and silent whatever treatment he meets with, and I suppose they thought to find me the same easy and ductile person; but may the wide yawning earth devour me first! The state of the camp is just such as one at home would guess it to be,—nothing but a hurry and confusion of vice and wickedness, with a stygian atmosphere to breathe in."[2] The vice and wickedness of which he complains appear to have consisted in a frequent infraction of the standing order against "Curseing and Swareing," as well as of that which required attendance on daily prayers, and enjoined "the people to appear in a decent manner, clean and shaved," at the two Sunday sermons.[3]

At the beginning of August Winslow wrote to the committees of the

---

[1] I owe to my friend George S. Hale, Esq., the opportunity of examining the autograph Journal; it has since been printed in the *Magazine of American History* for March, 1882.

[2] The autograph letter is in Massachusetts Archives, LVI. no. 142. The same volume contains a letter from Colonel Frye, of Massachusetts, in which he speaks of the forlorn condition in which Chaplain Weld reached the camp. Of Chaplain Crawford, he says that he came decently clothed, but without bed or blanket, till he, Frye, lent them to him, and got Captain Learned to take him into his tent. Chaplains usually had a separate tent, or shared that of the colonel.

[3] *Letter and Order Books of Winslow.*

several provinces: "It looks as if it won't be long before we are fit for a remove,"—that is, for an advance on Ticonderoga. On the twelfth Loudon sent Webb with the forty-fourth regiment and some of Bradstreet's boatmen to reinforce Oswego.[1] They had been ready for a month; but confusion and misunderstanding arising from the change of command had prevented their departure.[2] Yet the utmost anxiety had prevailed for the safety of that important post, and on the twenty-eighth Surgeon Thomas Williams wrote: "Whether Oswego is yet ours is uncertain. Would hope it is, as the reverse would be such a terrible shock as the country never felt, and may be a sad omen of what is coming upon poor sinful New England. Indeed we can't expect anything but to be severely chastened till we are humbled for our pride and haughtiness."[3]

His foreboding proved true. Webb had scarcely reached the Great Carrying Place, when tidings of disaster fell upon him like a thunderbolt. The French had descended in force upon Oswego, taken it with all its garrison; and, as report ran, were advancing into the province, six thousand strong. Wood Creek had just been cleared, with great labor, of the trees that choked it. Webb ordered others to be felled and thrown into the stream to stop the progress of the enemy; then, with shameful precipitation, he burned the forts of the Carrying Place, and retreated down the Mohawk to German Flats. Loudon ordered Winslow to think no more of Ticonderoga, but to stay where he was and hold the French in check. All was astonishment and dismay at the sudden blow. "Oswego has changed masters, and I think we may justly fear that the whole of our country will soon follow, unless a merciful God prevent, and awake a sinful people to repentance and reformation." Thus wrote Dr. Thomas Williams to his wife from the camp at Fort Edward. "Such a shocking affair has never found a place in English annals," wrote the surgeon's young relative, Colonel William Williams. "The loss is beyond account; but the dishonor done His Majesty's arms is infinitely greater."[4] It remains to see how the catastrophe befell.

Since Vaudreuil became chief of the colony he had nursed the plan of seizing Oswego, yet hesitated to attempt it. Montcalm declares that he confirmed the Governor's wavering purpose; but Montcalm himself had hesitated. In July, however, there came exaggerated reports that

---

[1] *Loudon (to Fox?), 19 Aug. 1756.*
[2] *Conduct of Major-General Shirley briefly stated. Shirley to Loudon, 4 Sept. 1756. Shirley to Fox, 16 Sept. 1756.*
[3] *Thomas Williams to Colonel Israel Williams, 28 Aug. 1756.*
[4] *Colonel William Williams to Colonel Israel Williams, 30 Aug. 1756.*

the English were moving upon Ticonderoga in greatly increased numbers; and both Vaudreuil and the General conceived that a feint against
Oswego would draw off the strength of the assailants, and, if promptly
and secretly executed, might even be turned successfully into a real
attack. Vaudreuil thereupon recalled Montcalm from Ticonderoga.[1]
Leaving that post in the keeping of Lévis and three thousand men, he
embarked on Lake Champlain, rowed day and night, and reached
Montreal on the nineteenth. Troops were arriving from Quebec, and
Indians from the far west. A band of Menomonies from beyond Lake
Michigan, naked, painted, plumed, greased, stamping, uttering sharp
yelps, shaking feathered lances, brandishing tomahawks, danced the
war-dance before the Governor, to the thumping of the Indian drum.
Bougainville looked on astonished, and thought of the Pyrrhic dance
of the Greeks.

Montcalm and he left Montreal on the twenty-first, and reached Fort
Frontenac in eight days. Rigaud, brother of the Governor, had gone
thither some time before, and crossed with seven hundred Canadians
to the south side of the lake, where Villiers was encamped at Niaouré
Bay, now Sackett's Harbor, with such of his detachment as war and
disease had spared. Rigaud relieved him, and took command of the
united bands. With their aid the engineer, Descombles, reconnoitred
the English forts, and came back with the report that success was certain.[2] It was but a confirmation of what had already been learned from
deserters and prisoners, who declared that the main fort was but a loopholed wall held by six or seven hundred men, ill fed, discontented, and
mutinous.[3] Others said that they had been driven to desert by the want
of good food, and that within a year twelve hundred men had died of
disease at Oswego.[4]

The battalions of La Sarre, Guienne, and Béarn, with the colony
regulars, a body of Canadians, and about two hundred and fifty Indians,
were destined for the enterprise. The whole force was a little above
three thousand, abundantly supplied with artillery. La Sarre and
Guienne were already at Fort Frontenac. Béarn was at Niagara, whence
it arrived in a few days, much buffeted by the storms of Lake Ontario.
On the fourth of August all was ready. Montcalm embarked at night
with the first division, crossed in darkness to Wolf Island, lay there
hidden all day, and embarking again in the evening, joined Rigaud at

[1]Vaudreuil au Ministre, 12 Août, 1756. Montcalm à sa Femme, 20 Juillet, 1756.
[2]Vaudreuil au Ministre, 4 Août, 1756. Vaudreuil à Bourlamaque, — Juin, 1756.
[3]Bougainville, Journal.
[4]Vaudreuil au Ministre, 10 Juillet, 1756. Résumé des Nouvelles du Canada, Sept. 1756.

Niaouré Bay at seven o'clock in the morning of the sixth. The second division followed, with provisions, hospital train, and eighty artillery boats; and on the eighth all were united at the bay. On the ninth Rigaud, covered by the universal forest, marched in advance to protect the landing of the troops. Montcalm followed with the first division; and, coasting the shore in bateaux, landed at midnight of the tenth within half a league of the first English fort. Four cannon were planted in battery upon the strand, and the men bivouacked by their boats. So skilful were the assailants and so careless the assailed that the English knew nothing of their danger, till in the morning, a reconnoitring canoe discovered the invaders. Two armed vessels soon came to cannonade them; but their light guns were no match for the heavy artillery of the French, and they were forced to keep the offing.

Descombles, the engineer, went before dawn to reconnoitre the fort, with several other officers and a party of Indians. While he was thus employed, one of these savages, hungry for scalps, took him in the gloom for an Englishman, and shot him dead. Captain Pouchot, of the battalion of Béarn, replaced him; and the attack was pushed vigorously. The Canadians and Indians, swarming through the forest, fired all day on the fort under cover of the trees. The second division came up with twenty-two more cannon; and at night the first parallel was marked out at a hundred and eighty yards from the rampart. Stumps were grubbed up, fallen trunks shoved aside, and a trench dug, sheltered by fascines, gabions, and a strong abattis.

Fort Ontario, counted as the best of the three forts at Oswego, stood on a high plateau at the east or right side of the river where it entered the lake. It was in the shape of a star, and was formed of trunks of trees set upright in the ground, hewn flat on two sides, and closely fitted together,—an excellent defence against musketry or swivels, but worth-less against cannon. The garrison, three hundred and seventy in all, were the remnant of Pepperell's regiment, joined to raw recruits lately sent up to fill the places of the sick and dead. They had eight small cannon and a mortar, with which on the next day, Friday, the thir-teenth, they kept up a brisk fire till towards night; when, after growing more rapid for a time, it ceased, and the fort showed no sign of life. Not a cannon had yet opened on them from the trenches; but it was certain that with the French artillery once in action, their wooden ram-part would be shivered to splinters. Hence it was that Colonel Mercer, commandant at Oswego, thinking it better to lose the fort than to lose both fort and garrison, signalled to them from across the river to aban-don their position and join him on the other side. Boats were sent to bring them off; and they passed over unmolested, after spiking their cannon and firing off their ammunition or throwing it into the well.

The fate of Oswego was now sealed. The principal work, called Old Oswego, or Fort Pepperell, stood at the mouth of the river on the west side, nearly opposite Fort Ontario, and less than five hundred yards distant from it. The trading-house, which formed the centre of the place, was built of rough stone laid in clay, and the wall which enclosed it was of the same materials; both would crumble in an instant at the touch of a twelve-pound shot. Towards the west and south they had been protected by an outer line of earthworks, mounted with cannon, and forming an entrenched camp; while the side towards Fort Ontario was left wholly exposed, in the rash confidence that this work, standing on the opposite heights, would guard against attack from that quarter. On a hill, a fourth of a mile beyond Old Oswego, stood the unfinished stockade called New Oswego, Fort George, or, by reason of its worthlessness, Fort Rascal. It had served as a cattle pen before the French appeared, but was now occupied by a hundred and fifty Jersey provincials. Old Oswego with its outwork was held by Shirley's regiment, chiefly invalids and raw recruits, to whom were now joined the garrison of Fort Ontario and a number of sailors, boatmen, and laborers.

Montcalm lost no time. As soon as darkness set in he began a battery at the brink of the height on which stood the captured fort. His whole force toiled all night, digging, setting gabions, and dragging up cannon, some of which had been taken from Braddock. Before daybreak twenty heavy pieces had been brought to the spot, and nine were already in position. The work had been so rapid that the English imagined their enemies to number six thousand at least. The battery soon opened fire. Grape and round shot swept the intrenchment and crashed through the rotten masonry. The English, says a French officer, "were exposed to their shoe-buckles." Their artillery was pointed the wrong way, in expectation of an attack, not from the east, but from the west. They now made a shelter of pork-barrels, three high and three deep, planted cannon behind them, and returned the French fire with some effect.

Early in the morning Montcalm had ordered Rigaud to cross the river with the Canadians and Indians. There was a ford three quarters of a league above the forts;[1] and here they passed over unopposed, the English not having discovered the movement.[2] The only danger was from the river. Some of the men were forced to swim, others waded to the

[1] Bougainville, *Journal.*
[2] Pouchot, I. 76.

waist, and others to the neck; but they all crossed safely, and presently showed themselves at the edge of the woods, yelling and firing their guns, too far for much execution, but not too far to discourage the garrison.

The garrison were already disheartened. Colonel Mercer, the soul of the defence, had just been cut in two by a cannon-shot while directing the gunners. Up to this time the defenders had behaved with spirit; but despair now seized them, increased by the screams and entreaties of the women, of whom there were more than a hundred in the place. There was a council of officers, and then the white flag was raised. Bougainville went to propose terms of capitulation. "The cries, threats, and hideous howlings of our Canadians and Indians," says Vaudreuil, "made them quickly decide." "This," observes the Reverend Father Claude Godefroy Cocquard, "reminds me of the fall of Jericho before the shouts of the Israelites." The English surrendered prisoners of war, to the number, according to the Governor, of sixteen hundred,[1] which included the sailors, laborers, and women. The Canadians and Indians broke through all restraint, and fell to plundering. There was an opening of rum-barrels and a scene of drunkenness, in which some of the prisoners had their share; while others tried to escape in the confusion, and were tomahawked by the excited savages. Many more would have been butchered, but for the efforts of Montcalm, who by unstinted promises succeeded in appeasing his ferocious allies, whom he dared not offend. "It will cost the King," he says, "eight or ten thousand livres in presents."[2]

The loss on both sides is variously given. By the most trustworthy accounts, that of the English did not reach fifty killed, and that of the French was still less. In the forts and vessels were found above a hundred pieces of artillery, most of them swivels and other light guns, with a large quantity of powder, shot, and shell. The victors burned the forts and the vessels on the stocks, destroyed such provisions and stores as they could not carry away, and made the place a desert. The priest Piquet, who had joined the expedition, planted amid the ruin a

[1] *Vaudreuil au Ministre, 20 Août, 1756.* He elsewhere makes the number somewhat greater. That the garrison, exclusive of civilians, did not exceed at the utmost fourteen hundred, is shown by *Shirley to Loudon, 5 Sept. 1756.* Loudon had charged Shirley with leaving Oswego weakly garrisoned; and Shirley replies by alleging that the troops there were in number as above. It was of course his interest to make them appear as numerous as possible. In the printed *Conduct of Major-General Shirley briefly stated*, they are put at only ten hundred and fifty.

[2] Several English writers say, however, that fifteen or twenty young men were given up to the Indians to be adopted in place of warriors lately killed.

tall cross, graven with the words, *In hoc signo vincunt*; and near it was set a pole bearing the arms of France, with the inscription, *Manibus date lilia plenis*. Then the army decamped, loaded with prisoners and spoil, descended to Montreal, hung the captured flags in the churches, and sang Te Deum in honor of their triumph.

It was the greatest that the French arms had yet achieved in America. The defeat of Braddock was an Indian victory; this last exploit was the result of bold enterprise and skilful tactics. With its laurels came its fruits. Hated Oswego had been laid in ashes, and the would-be assailants forced to a vain and hopeless defence. France had conquered the undisputed command of Lake Ontario, and her communications with the West were safe. A small garrison at Niagara and another at Frontenac would now hold those posts against any effort that the English could make this year; and the whole French force could concentrate at Ticonderoga, repel the threatened attack, and perhaps retort it by seizing Albany. If the English, on the other side, had lost a great material advantage, they had lost no less in honor. The news of the surrender was received with indignation in England and in the colonies. Yet the behavior of the garrison was not so discreditable as it seemed. The position was indefensible, and they could have held out at best but a few days more. They yielded too soon; but unless Webb had come to their aid, which was not to be expected, they must have yielded at last.

The French had scarcely gone, when two English scouts, Thomas Harris and James Conner, came with a party of Indians to the scene of desolation. The ground was strewn with broken casks and bread sodden with rain. The remains of burnt bateaux and whaleboats were scattered along the shore. The great stone trading-house in the old fort was a smoking ruin; Fort Rascal was still burning on the neighboring hill; Fort Ontario was a mass of ashes and charred logs, and by it stood two poles on which were written words which the visitors did not understand. They went back to Fort Johnson with their story; and Oswego reverted for a time to the bears, foxes, and wolves.[1]

---

[1] On the capture of Oswego, the authorities examined here have been very numerous, and only the best need be named. *Livre d'Ordres, Campagne de 1756*, contains all orders from headquarters. *Mémoire pour servir d'Instruction à M. le Marquis de Montcalm, 21 Juillet, 1756, signé Vaudreuil*. Bougainville, *Journal*. *Vaudreuil au Ministre, 15 Juin, 1756* (designs against Oswego). *Ibid.*, *13 Août, 1755*. *Ibid.*, *30 Août*. Pouchot, I. 67–81. *Relation de la Prise des Forts de Chouaguen*. *Bigot au Ministre, 3 Sept. 1756*. *Journal du Siége de Chouaguen*. *Précis des Événements, 1756*. *Montcalm au Ministre, 20 Juillet, 1756*. *Ibid.*, *28 Août, 1756*. *Desandrouins à ——, même date*. *Montcalm à sa Femme, 30 Août*. Translations of several of the above papers, along with others less important, will be found in *N. Y. Col. Docs.*, X., and *Doc. Hist. N. Y.*, I.

State of Facts relating to the Loss of Oswego, in London Magazine for 1757, p. 14. Correspondence of Shirley. Correspondence of Loudon. Littlehales to Loudon, 30 Aug. 1756. Hardy to Lords of Trade, 5 Sept. 1756. Conduct of Major-General Shirley briefly stated. Declaration of some Soldiers of Shirley's Regiment, in N. Y. Col. Docs., VII. 126. Letter from an officer present, in Boston Evening Post of 16 May, 1757. The published plans and drawings of Oswego at this time are very inexact.

13

Partisan War

1756, 1757

FAILURE OF SHIRLEY'S PLAN · CAUSES · LOUDON AND SHIRLEY · CLOSE
OF THE CAMPAIGN · THE WESTERN BORDER · ARMSTRONG DESTROYS
KITTANNING · THE SCOUTS OF LAKE GEORGE · WAR PARTIES FROM
TICONDEROGA · ROBERT ROGERS · THE RANGERS · THEIR HARDIHOOD
AND DARING · DISPUTES AS TO QUARTERS OF TROOPS · EXPEDITION OF
ROGERS · A DESPERATE BUSH-FIGHT · ENTERPRISE OF VAUDREUIL ·
RIGAUD ATTACKS FORT WILLIAM HENRY

Shirley's grand scheme for cutting New France in twain
had come to wreck. There was an element of boyishness
in him. He made bold plans without weighing too closely his means of
executing them. The year's campaign would in all likelihood have succeeded if he could have acted promptly; if he had had ready to his hand
a well-trained and well-officered force, furnished with material of war
and means of transportation, and prepared to move as soon as the
streams and lakes of New York were open, while those of Canada were
still sealed with ice. But timely action was out of his power. The army
that should have moved in April was not ready to move till August. Of
the nine discordant semi-republics whom he asked to join in the work,
three or four refused, some of the others were lukewarm, and all were
slow. Even Massachusetts, usually the foremost, failed to get all her
men into the field till the season was nearly ended. Having no military
establishment, the colonies were forced to improvise a new army for

243

every campaign. Each of them watched its neighbors, or, jealous lest it should do more than its just share, waited for them to begin. Each popular assembly acted under the eye of a frugal constituency, who, having little money, were as chary of it as their descendants are lavish; and most of them were shaken by internal conflicts, more absorbing than the great question on which hung the fate of the continent. Only the four New England colonies were fully earnest for the war, and one, even of these, was ready to use the crisis as a means of extorting concessions from its Governor in return for grants of money and men. When the lagging contingents came together at last, under a commander whom none of them trusted, they were met by strategical difficulties which would have perplexed older soldiers and an abler general; for they were forced to act on the circumference of a vast semicircle, in a labyrinth of forests, without roads, and choked with every kind of obstruction.

Opposed to them was a trained army, well organized and commanded, focused at Montreal, and moving for attack or defence on two radiating lines,—one towards Lake Ontario, and the other towards Lake Champlain,—supported by a martial peasantry, supplied from France with money and material, dependent on no popular vote, having no will but that of its chief, and ready on the instant to strike to right or left as the need required. It was a compact military absolutism confronting a heterogeneous group of industrial democracies, where the force of numbers was neutralized by diffusion and incoherence. A long and dismal apprenticeship waited them before they could hope for success; nor could they ever put forth their full strength without a radical change of political conditions and an awakened consciousness of common interests and a common cause. It was the sense of powerlessness arising from the want of union that, after the fall of Oswego, spread alarm through the northern and middle colonies, and drew these desponding words from William Livingston, of New Jersey: "The colonies are nearly exhausted, and their funds already anticipated by expensive unexecuted projects. Jealous are they of each other; some ill-constituted, others shaken with intestine divisions, and, if I may be allowed the expression, parsimonious even to prodigality. Our assemblies are diffident of their governors, governors despise their assemblies; and both mutually misrepresent each other to the Court of Great Britain." Military measures, he proceeds, demand secrecy and despatch; but when so many divided provinces must agree to join in them, secrecy and despatch are impossible. In conclusion he exclaims: "Canada must be demolished,—*Delenda est Carthago*,—or we are undone."[1] But Loudon was not Scipio, and cis-Atlantic Carthage was to stand for some time longer.

The Earl, in search of a scapegoat for the loss of Oswego, naturally chose Shirley, attacked him savagely, told him that he was of no use in America, and ordered him to go home to England without delay.[2] Shirley, who was then in Boston, answered this indecency with dignity and effect.[3] The chief fault was with Loudon himself, whose late arrival in America had caused a change of command and of plans in the crisis of the campaign. Shirley well knew the weakness of Oswego; and in early spring had sent two engineers to make it defensible, with particular instructions to strengthen Fort Ontario.[4] But they, thinking that the chief danger lay on the west and south, turned all their attention thither, and neglected Ontario till it was too late. Shirley was about to reinforce Oswego with a strong body of troops when the arrival of Abercromby took the control out of his hands and caused ruinous delay. He cannot, however, be acquitted of mismanagement in failing to supply the place with wholesome provisions in the preceding autumn, before the streams were stopped with ice. Hence came the ravages of disease and famine which, before spring, reduced the garrison to a hundred and forty effective men. Yet there can be no doubt that the change of command was a blunder. This is the view of Franklin, who knew Shirley well, and thus speaks of him: "He would in my opinion, if continued in place, have made a much better campaign than that of Loudon, which was frivolous, expensive, and disgraceful to our nation beyond conception. For though Shirley was not bred a soldier, he was sensible and sagacious in himself, and attentive to good advice from others, capable of forming judicious plans, and quick and active in carrying them into execution."[5] He sailed for England in the autumn, disappointed and poor; the bull-headed Duke of Cumberland had been deeply prejudiced against him, and it was only after long waiting that this strenuous champion of British interests was rewarded in his old age with the petty government of the Bahamas.

Loudon had now about ten thousand men at his command, though

[1] *Review of Military Operations*, 187, 189 (Dublin, 1757).

[2] *Loudon to Shirley*, 6 *Sept. 1756*.

[3] The correspondence on both sides is before me, copied from the originals in the Public Record Office.

[4] "The principal thing for which I sent Mr. Mackellar to Oswego was to strengthen Fort Ontario as much as he possibly could." *Shirley to Loudon*, 4 *Sept. 1756*.

[5] *Works of Franklin*, I. 220.

not all fit for duty. They were posted from Albany to Lake George. The Earl himself was at Fort Edward, while about three thousand of the provincials still lay, under Winslow, at the lake. Montcalm faced them at Ticonderoga, with five thousand three hundred regulars and Canadians, in a position where they could defy three times their number.[1] "The sons of Belial are too strong for me," jocosely wrote Winslow;[2] and he set himself to intrenching his camp; then had the forest cut down for the space of a mile from the lake to the mountains, so that the trees, lying in what he calls a "promiscuous manner," formed an almost impenetrable abattis. An escaped prisoner told him that the French were coming to visit him with fourteen thousand men;[3] but Montcalm thought no more of stirring than Loudon himself; and each stood watching the other, with the lake between them, till the season closed.

Meanwhile the western borders were still ravaged by the tomahawk. New York, New Jersey, Pennsylvania, Maryland, and Virginia all writhed under the infliction. Each had made a chain of blockhouses and wooden forts to cover its frontier, and manned them with disorderly bands, lawless, and almost beyond control.[4] The case was at the worst in Pennsylvania, where the tedious quarrelling of Governor and Assembly, joined to the doggedly pacific attitude of the Quakers, made vigorous defence impossible. Rewards were offered for prisoners and scalps, so bountiful that the hunting of men would have been a profitable vocation, but for the extreme wariness and agility of the game.[5] Some of the forts were well built stockades; others were almost worthless; but the enemy rarely molested even the feeblest of them, preferring to ravage the lonely and unprotected farms. There were two or three exceptions. A Virginian fort was attacked by a war-party under an officer named Douville, who was killed, and his followers were put to flight.[6] The assailants were more fortunate at a small stockade called Fort Granville, on the Juniata. A large body of French and Indians attacked it in August while most of the garrison were absent protecting the farmers at their harvest; they set it on fire, and, in spite of a most

[1]"Nous sommes tant à Carillon qu'aux postes avancés 5,300 hommes." Bougainville, Journal.
[2]Winslow to Loudon, 29 Sept. 1756.
[3]Examination of Sergeant James Archibald.
[4]In the Public Record Office, America and West Indies, LXXXII., is a manuscript map showing the positions of such of these posts as were north of Virginia. They are thirty-five in number, from the head of James River to a point west of Esopus, on the Hudson.
[5]Colonial Records of Pa., VII. 76.
[6]Washington to Morris,—April, 1756.

gallant resistance by the young lieutenant left in command, took it, and killed all but one of the defenders.[1]

What sort of resistance the Pennsylvanian borderers would have made under political circumstances less adverse may be inferred from an exploit of Colonel John Armstrong, a settler of Cumberland. After the loss of Fort Granville the Governor of the province sent him with three hundred men to attack the Delaware town of Kittanning, a populous nest of savages on the Alleghany, between the two French posts of Duquesne and Venango. Here most of the war-parties were fitted out, and the place was full of stores and munitions furnished by the French. Here, too, lived the redoubted chief called Captain Jacobs, the terror of the English border. Armstrong set out from Fort Shirley, the farthest outpost, on the last of August, and, a week after, was within six miles of the Indian town. By rapid marching and rare good luck, his party had escaped discovery. It was ten o'clock at night, with a bright moon. The guides were perplexed, and knew neither the exact position of the place nor the paths that led to it. The adventurers threaded the forest in single file, over hills and through hollows, bewildered and anxious, stopping to watch and listen. At length they heard in the distance the beating of an Indian drum and the whooping of warriors in the war-dance. Guided by the sounds, they cautiously moved forward, till those in the front, scrambling down a rocky hill, found themselves on the banks of the Alleghany, about a hundred rods below Kittanning. The moon was near setting; but they could dimly see the town beyond a great intervening field of corn. "At that moment," says Armstrong, "an Indian whistled in a very singular manner, about thirty perches from our front, in the foot of the cornfield." He thought they were discovered; but one Baker, a soldier well versed in Indian ways, told him that it was only some village gallant calling to a young squaw. The party then crouched in the bushes, and kept silent. The moon sank behind the woods, and fires soon glimmered through the field, kindled to drive off mosquitoes by some of the Indians who, as the night was warm, had come out to sleep in the open air. The eastern sky began to redden with the approach of day. Many of the party, spent with a rough march of thirty miles, had fallen asleep. They were now cautiously roused; and Armstrong ordered nearly half of them to make their way along the ridge of a bushy hill that overlooked the town, till they came opposite to it, in order to place it between two fires. Twenty minutes were al-

[1]*Colonial Records of Pa.*, VII. 232, 242; *Pennsylvania Archives*, II. 744.

lowed them for the movement; but they lost their way in the dusk, and reached their station too late. When the time had expired, Armstrong gave the signal to those left with him, who dashed into the cornfield, shooting down the astonished savages or driving them into the village, where they turned and made desperate fight.

It was a cluster of thirty log-cabins, the principal being that of the chief, Jacobs, which was loopholed for musketry, and became the centre of resistance. The fight was hot and stubborn. Armstrong ordered the town to be set on fire, which was done, though not without loss; for the Delawares at this time were commonly armed with rifles, and used them well. Armstrong himself was hit in the shoulder. As the flames rose and the smoke grew thick, a warrior in one of the houses sang his death-song, and a squaw in the same house was heard to cry and scream. Rough voices silenced her, and then the inmates burst out, but were instantly killed. The fire caught the house of Jacobs, who, trying to escape through an opening in the roof, was shot dead. Bands of Indians were gathering beyond the river, firing from the other bank, and even crossing to help their comrades; but the assailants held to their work till the whole place was destroyed. "During the burning of the houses," says Armstrong, "we were agreeably entertained by the quick succession of charged guns, gradually firing off as reached by the fire; but much more so with the vast explosion of sundry bags and large kegs of gunpowder, wherewith almost every house abounded; the prisoners afterwards informing us that the Indians had frequently said they had a sufficient stock of ammunition for ten years' war with the English."

These prisoners were eleven men, women, and children, captured in the border settlements, and now delivered by their countrymen. The day was far spent when the party withdrew, carrying their wounded on Indian horses, and moving perforce with extreme slowness, though expecting an attack every moment. None took place; and they reached the settlements at last, having bought their success with the loss of seventeen killed and thirteen wounded.[1] A medal was given to each officer, not by the Quaker-ridden Assembly, but by the city council of Philadelphia.

The report of this affair made by Dumas, commandant at Fort Duquesne, is worth noting. He says that Attiqué, the French name of

---

[1] *Report of Armstrong to Governor Denny, 14 Sept. 1756*, in *Colonial Records of Pa.*, VII. 257,—a modest yet very minute account. *A List of the Names of the Persons killed, wounded, and missing in the late Expedition against the Kittanning*. Hazard, *Pennsylvania Register*, I. 366.

Kittanning, was attacked by "le Général Wachinton," with three or four hundred men on horseback; that the Indians gave way; but that five or six Frenchmen who were in the town held the English in check till the fugitives rallied; that Washington and his men then took to flight, and would have been pursued but for the loss of some barrels of gunpowder which chanced to explode during the action. Dumas adds that several large parties are now on the track of the enemy, and he hopes will cut them to pieces. He then asks for a supply of provisions and merchandise to replace those which the Indians of Attiqué had lost by a fire.[1] Like other officers of the day, he would admit nothing but successes in the department under his command.

Vaudreuil wrote singular despatches at this time to the minister at Versailles. He takes credit to himself for the number of war-parties that his officers kept always at work, and fills page after page with details of the *coups* they had struck; how one brought in two English scalps, another three, another one, and another seven. He owns that they committed frightful cruelties, mutilating and sometimes burning their prisoners; but he expresses no regret, and probably felt none, since he declares that the object of this murderous warfare was to punish the English till they longed for peace.[2]

The waters and mountains of Lake George, and not the western borders, were the chief centre of partisan war. Ticonderoga was a hornet's nest, pouring out swarms of savages to infest the highways and byways of the wilderness. The English at Fort William Henry, having few Indians, could not retort in kind; but they kept their scouts and rangers in active movement. What they most coveted was prisoners, as sources of information. One Kennedy, a lieutenant of provincials, with five followers, white and red, made a march of rare audacity, passed all the French posts, took a scalp and two prisoners on the Richelieu, and burned a magazine of provisions between Montreal and St. John. The party were near famishing on the way back; and Kennedy was brought into Fort William Henry in a state of temporary insanity from starvation.[3] Other provincial officers, Peabody, Hazen, Waterbury, and Miller, won a certain distinction in this adventurous service, though few were so conspicuous as the blunt and sturdy Israel Putnam. Winslow writes in October that he has just returned from the best "scout" yet made, and that, being a man of strict truth, he may be entirely

[1] *Dumas à Vaudreuil, 9 Sept. 1756,* cited in *Bigot au Ministre, 6 Oct. 1756,* and in *Bougainville, Journal.*

[2] *Dépêches de Vaudreuil, 1756.*

[3] *Minute of Lieutenant Kennedy's Scout. Winslow to Loudon, 20 Sept. 1756.*

trusted.[1] Putnam had gone with six followers down Lake George in a whaleboat to a point on the east side, opposite the present village of Hague, hid the boat, crossed northeasterly to Lake Champlain, three miles from the French fort, climbed the mountain that overlooks it, and made a complete reconnoissance; then approached it, chased three Frenchmen, who escaped within the lines, climbed the mountain again, and moving westward along the ridge, made a minute survey of every outpost between the fort and Lake George.[2] These adventures were not always fortunate. On the nineteenth of September Captain Hodges and fifty men were ambushed a few miles from Fort William Henry by thrice their number of Canadians and Indians, and only six escaped. Thus the record stands in the *Letter Book* of Winslow.[3] By visiting the encampments of Ticonderoga, one may learn how the blow was struck.

After much persuasion, much feasting, and much consumption of tobacco and brandy, four hundred Indians, Christians from the Missions and heathen from the far west, were persuaded to go on a grand war-party with the Canadians. Of these last there were a hundred,—a wild crew, bedecked and bedaubed like their Indian companions. Perière, an officer of colony regulars, had nominal command of the whole; and among the leaders of the Canadians was the famous bush-fighter, Marin. Bougainville was also of the party. In the evening of the sixteenth they all embarked in canoes at the French advance-post commanded by Contrecœur, near the present steamboat-landing, passed in the gloom under the bare steeps of Rogers Rock, paddled a few hours, landed on the west shore, and sent scouts to reconnoitre. These came back with their reports on the next day, and an Indian crier called the chiefs to council. Bougainville describes them as they stalked gravely to the place of meeting, wrapped in colored blankets, with lances in their hands. The accomplished young aide-de-camp studied his strange companions with an interest not unmixed with disgust. "Of all caprice," he says, "Indian caprice is the most capricious." They were insolent to the French, made rules for them which they did not observe themselves, and compelled the whole party to move when and whither they pleased. Hiding the canoes, and lying close in the forest by day, they all held their nocturnal course southward, by the lofty heights of Black Mountain, and among the islets of the Narrows, till the eigh-

[1] *Winslow to Loudon,* 16 Oct. 1756.
[2] *Report of a Scout to Ticonderoga, Oct. 1756,* signed Israel Putnam.
[3] Compare Massachusetts Archives, LXXVI. 81.

teenth. That night the Indian scouts reported that they had seen the fires of an encampment on the west shore; on which the whole party advanced to the attack, an hour before dawn, filing silently under the dark arches of the forest, the Indians nearly naked, and streaked with their war-paint of vermilion and soot. When they reached the spot, they found only the smouldering fires of a deserted bivouac. Then there was a consultation; ending, after much dispute, with the choice by the Indians of a hundred and ten of their most active warriors to attempt some stroke in the neighborhood of the English fort. Marin joined them with thirty Canadians, and they set out on their errand; while the rest encamped to await the result. At night the adventurers returned, raising the death-cry and firing their guns; somewhat depressed by losses they had suffered, but boasting that they had surprised fifty-three English, and killed or taken all but one. It was a modest and perhaps an involuntary exaggeration. "The very recital of the cruelties they committed on the battle-field is horrible," writes Bougainville. "The ferocity and insolence of these black-souled barbarians makes one shudder. It is an abominable kind of war. The air one breathes is contagious of insensibility and hardness."[1] This was but one of many such parties sent out from Ticonderoga this year.

Early in September a band of New England rangers came to Winslow's camp, with three prisoners taken within the lines of Ticonderoga. Their captain was Robert Rogers, of New Hampshire,—a strong, well-knit figure, in dress and appearance more woodsman than soldier, with a clear, bold eye, and features that would have been good but for the ungainly proportions of the nose.[2] He had passed his boyhood in the rough surroundings of a frontier village. Growing to manhood, he engaged in some occupation which, he says, led him to frequent journeyings in the wilderness between the French and English settlements, and gave him a good knowledge of both.[3] It taught him also to speak a little French. He does not disclose the nature of this mysterious employment; but there can be little doubt that it was a smuggling trade with Canada. His character leaves much to be desired. He had been charged with forgery, or complicity in it, seems to have had no scruple in matters of business, and after the war was accused of treasonable dealings with the French and Spaniards in the west.[4] He was ambitious

[1] Bougainville, *Journal*.
[2] A large engraved portrait of him, nearly at full length, is before me, printed at London in 1776.
[3] Rogers, *Journals, Introduction* (1765).
[4] *Provincial Papers of New Hampshire*, VI. 364. *Correspondence of Gage, 1766. N. Y. Col. Docs.*, VII. 990. Caleb Stark, *Memoir and Correspondence of John Stark*, 386.

and violent, yet able in more ways than one, by no means uneducated, and so skilled in woodcraft, so energetic and resolute, that his services were invaluable. In recounting his own adventures, his style is direct, simple, without boasting, and to all appearance without exaggeration. During the past summer he had raised a band of men, chiefly New Hampshire borderers, and made a series of daring excursions which gave him a prominent place in this hardy byplay of war. In the spring of the present year he raised another company, and was commissioned as its captain, with his brother Richard as his first lieutenant, and the intrepid John Stark as his second. In July still another company was formed, and Richard Rogers was promoted to command it. Before the following spring there were seven such; and more were afterwards added, forming a battalion dispersed on various service, but all under the orders of Robert Rogers, with the rank of major.[1] These rangers wore a sort of woodland uniform, which varied in the different companies, and were armed with smooth-bore guns, loaded with buckshot, bullets, or sometimes both.

The best of them were commonly employed on Lake George; and nothing can surpass the adventurous hardihood of their lives. Summer and winter, day and night, were alike to them. Embarked in whaleboats or birch-canoes, they glided under the silent moon or in the languid glare of a breathless August day, when islands floated in dreamy haze, and the hot air was thick with odors of the pine; or in the bright October, when the jay screamed from the woods, squirrels gathered their winter hoard, and congregated blackbirds chattered farewell to their summer haunts; when gay mountains basked in light, maples dropped leaves of rustling gold, sumachs glowed like rubies under the dark green of the unchanging spruce, and mossed rocks with all their painted plumage lay double in the watery mirror: that festal evening of the year, when jocund Nature disrobes herself, to wake again refreshed in the joy of her undying spring. Or, in the tomb-like silence of the winter forest, with breath frozen on his beard, the ranger strode on snow-shoes over the spotless drifts; and, like Dürer's knight, a ghastly death stalked ever at his side. There were those among them for whom this stern life had a fascination that made all other existence tame.

Rogers and his men had been in active movement since midwinter. In January they skated down Lake George, passed Ticonderoga, hid themselves by the forest-road between that post and Crown Point, intercepted two sledges loaded with provisions, and carried the drivers to

[1]Rogers, Journals. Report of the Adjutant-General of New Hampshire (1866), II. 158, 159.

Fort William Henry. In February they climbed a hill near Crown Point and made a plan of the works; then lay in ambush by the road from the fort to the neighboring village, captured a prisoner, burned houses and barns, killed fifty cattle, and returned without loss. At the end of the month they went again to Crown Point, burned more houses and barns, and reconnoitred Ticonderoga on the way back. Such excursions were repeated throughout the spring and summer. The reconnoissance of Ticonderoga and the catching of prisoners there for the sake of information were always capital objects. The valley, four miles in extent, that lay between the foot of Lake George and the French fort, was at this time guarded by four distinct outposts or fortified camps. Watched as it was at all points, and ranged incessantly by Indians in the employ of France, Rogers and his men knew every yard of the ground. On a morning in May he lay in ambush with eleven followers on a path between the fort and the nearest camp. A large body of soldiers passed; the rangers counted a hundred and eighteen, and lay close in their hiding-place. Soon after came a party of twenty-two. They fired on them, killed six, captured one, and escaped with him to Fort William Henry. In October Rogers was passing with twenty men in two whaleboats through the seeming solitude of the Narrows when a voice called to them out of the woods. It was that of Captain Shepherd, of the New Hampshire regiment, who had been captured two months before, and had lately made his escape. He told them that the French had the fullest information of the numbers and movements of the English; that letters often reached them from within the English lines; and that Lydius, a Dutch trader at Albany, was their principal correspondent.[1] Arriving at Ticonderoga, Rogers cautiously approached the fort, till, about noon, he saw a sentinel on the road leading thence to the woods. Followed by five of his men, he walked directly towards him. The man challenged, and Rogers answered in French. Perplexed for a moment, the soldier suffered him to approach; till, seeing his mistake, he called out in amazement, "*Qui êtes vous?*" "Rogers," was the answer; and the sentinel was seized, led in hot haste to the boats, and carried to the English fort, where he gave important information.

An exploit of Rogers towards midsummer greatly perplexed the French. He embarked at the end of June with fifty men in five whaleboats, made light and strong, expressly for this service, rowed about ten

---

[1] *Letter and Order Books of Winslow.* "One Lydiass . . . whom we suspect for a French spy; he lives better than anybody, without any visible means, and his daughters have had often presents from Mr. Vaudreuil." *Loudon (to Fox?), 19 Aug. 1756.*

miles down Lake George, landed on the east side, carried the boats six miles over a gorge of the mountains, launched them again in South Bay, and rowed down the narrow prolongation of Lake Champlain under cover of darkness. At dawn they were within six miles of Ticonderoga. They landed, hid their boats, and lay close all day. Embarking again in the evening, they rowed with muffled oars under the shadow of the eastern shore, and passed so close to the French fort that they heard the voices of the sentinels calling the watchword. In the morning they had left it five miles behind. Again they hid in the woods; and from their lurking-place saw bateaux passing, some northward, and some southward, along the narrow lake. Crown Point was ten or twelve miles farther on. They tried to pass it after nightfall, but the sky was too clear and the stars too bright; and as they lay hidden the next day, nearly a hundred boats passed before them on the way to Ticonderoga. Some other boats which appeared about noon landed near them, and they watched the soldiers at dinner, within a musket-shot of their lurking-place. The next night was more favorable. They embarked at nine in the evening, passed Crown Point unseen, and hid themselves as before, ten miles below. It was the seventh of July. Thirty boats and a schooner passed them, returning towards Canada. On the next night they rowed fifteen miles farther, and then sent men to reconnoitre, who reported a schooner at anchor about a mile off. They were preparing to board her, when two sloops appeared, coming up the lake at but a short distance from the land. They gave them a volley, and called on them to surrender; but the crews put off in boats and made for the opposite shore. They followed and seized them. Out of twelve men their fire had killed three and wounded two, one of whom, says Rogers in his report, "could not march, therefore we put an end to him, to prevent discovery."[1] They sank the vessels, which were laden with wine, brandy, and flour, hid their boats on the west shore, and returned on foot with their prisoners.[2]

Some weeks after, Rogers returned to the place where he had left the boats, embarked in them, reconnoitred the lake nearly to St. John, hid them again eight miles north of Crown Point, took three prisoners near that post, and carried them to Fort William Henry. In the next month the French found several English boats in a small cove north of Crown

[1] *Report of Rogers to Sir William Johnson, July, 1756.* This incident is suppressed in the printed *Journals*, which merely say that the man "soon died."

[2] Rogers, *Journals*, 20. *Shirley to Fox, 26 July, 1756.* "This afternoon Capt. Rogers came down with 4 scalps and 8 prisoners which he took on Lake Champlain, between 20 and 30 miles beyond Crown Point." *Surgeon Williams to his Wife, 16 July, 1756.*

Point. Bougainville propounds five different hypotheses to account for their being there; and exploring parties were sent out in the vain attempt to find some water passage by which they could have reached the spot without passing under the guns of two French forts.[1]

The French, on their side, still kept their war-parties in motion, and Vaudreuil faithfully chronicled in his despatches every English scalp they brought in. He believed in Indians, and sent them to Ticonderoga in numbers that were sometimes embarrassing. Even Pottawattamies from Lake Michigan were prowling about Winslow's camp and silently killing his sentinels with arrows, while their "medicine men" remained at Ticonderoga practising sorcery and divination to aid the warriors or learn how it fared with them. Bougainville writes in his Journal on the fifteenth of October: "Yesterday the old Pottawattamies who have stayed here 'made medicine' to get news of their brethren. The lodge trembled, the sorcerer sweated drops of blood, and the devil came at last and told him that the warriors would come back with scalps and prisoners. A sorcerer in the medicine lodge is exactly like the Pythoness on the tripod or the witch Canidia invoking the shades." The diviner was not wholly at fault. Three days after, the warriors came back with a prisoner.[2]

Till November, the hostile forces continued to watch each other from the opposite ends of Lake George. Loudon repeated his orders to Winslow to keep the defensive, and wrote sarcastically to the Colonial Minister: "I think I shall be able to prevent the provincials doing anything very rash, without their having it in their power to talk in the language of this country that they could have taken all Canada if they had not been prevented by the King's servants." Winslow tried to console himself for the failure of the campaign, and wrote in his odd English to Shirley: "Am sorry that this year's performance has not succeeded as was intended; have only to say I pushed things to the utmost of my power to have been sooner in motion, which was the only thing that should have carried us to Crown Point; and though I am sensible that we are doing our duty in acting on the defensive, yet it makes no *eclate* [sic], and answers to little purpose in the eyes of my constituents."

On the first of the month the French began to move off towards Canada, and before many days Ticonderoga was left in the keeping of

---

[1] Bougainville, *Journal*.

[2] This kind of divination was practised by Algonkin tribes from the earliest times. See *Pioneers of France in the New World*, 254.

five or six companies.[1] Winslow's men followed their example. Major Eyre, with four hundred regulars, took possession of Fort William Henry, and the provincials marched for home, their ranks thinned by camp diseases and small-pox.[2] In Canada the regulars were quartered on the inhabitants, who took the infliction as a matter of course. In the English provinces the question was not so simple. Most of the British troops were assigned to Philadelphia, New York, and Boston; and Loudon demanded free quarters for them, according to usage then prevailing in England during war. Nor was the demand in itself unreasonable, seeing that the troops were sent over to fight the battles of the colonies. In Philadelphia lodgings were given them in the public-houses, which, however, could not hold them all. A long dispute followed between the Governor, who seconded Loudon's demand, and the Assembly, during which about half the soldiers lay on straw in out-houses and sheds till near midwinter, many sickening, and some dying from exposure. Loudon grew furious, and threatened, if shelter were not provided, to send Webb with another regiment and billet the whole on the inhabitants; on which the Assembly yielded, and quarters were found.[3]

In New York the privates were quartered in barracks, but the officers were left to find lodging for themselves. Loudon demanded that provision should be made for them also. The city council hesitated, afraid of incensing the people if they complied. Cruger, the mayor, came to remonstrate. "God damn my blood!" replied the Earl; "if you do not billet my officers upon free quarters this day, I'll order here all the troops in North America, and billet them myself upon this city." Being no respecter of persons, at least in the provinces, he began with Oliver Delancey, brother of the late acting Governor, and sent six soldiers to lodge under his roof. Delancey swore at the unwelcome guests, on which Loudon sent him six more. A subscription was then raised among the citizens, and the required quarters were provided.[4] In Boston there was for the present less trouble. The troops were lodged in the barracks of Castle William, and furnished with blankets, cooking utensils, and other necessaries.[5]

[1] Bougainville, *Journal*. Malartic, *Journal*.

[2] *Letter and Order Books of Winslow*. Winslow to Halifax, 30 Dec. 1756.

[3] *Loudon to Denny, 28 Oct. 1756. Colonial Records of Pa.*, VII. 358–380. *Loudon to Pitt, 10 March, 1757. Notice of Colonel Bouquet, in Pennsylvania Magazine, III. 124. The Conduct of a Noble Commander in America impartially reviewed* (1758).

[4] Smith, *Hist. of N. Y.*, Part II. 242. *William Corry to Johnson, 15 Jan., 1757*, in Stone, *Life of Sir William Johnson*, II. 24, note. *Loudon to Hardy, 21 Nov. 1756*.

[5] Massachusetts Archives, LXXVI. 153.

Major Eyre and his soldiers, in their wilderness exile by the borders
of Lake George, whiled the winter away with few other excitements
than the evening howl of wolves from the frozen mountains, or some
nocturnal savage shooting at a sentinel from behind a stump on the
moonlit fields of snow. A livelier incident at last broke the monotony
of their lives. In the middle of January Rogers came with his rangers
from Fort Edward, bound on a scouting party towards Crown Point.
They spent two days at Fort William Henry in making snow-shoes and
other preparation, and set out on the seventeenth. Captain Spikeman
was second in command, with Lieutenants Stark and Kennedy, several
other subalterns, and two gentlemen volunteers enamoured of adventure. They marched down the frozen lake and encamped at the Narrows. Some of them, unaccustomed to snow-shoes, had become unfit
for travel, and were sent back, thus reducing the number to seventy-
four. In the morning they marched again, by icicled rocks and icebound
waterfalls, mountains gray with naked woods and fir-trees bowed down
with snow. On the nineteenth they reached the west shore, about four
miles south of Rogers Rock, marched west of north eight miles, and
bivouacked among the mountains. On the next morning they changed
their course, marched east of north all day, passed Ticonderoga undis-
covered, and stopped at night some five miles beyond it. The weather
was changing, and rain was coming on. They scraped away the snow
with their snow-shoes, piled it in a bank around them, made beds of
spruce-boughs, built fires, and lay down to sleep, while the sentinels
kept watch in the outer gloom. In the morning there was a drizzling
rain, and the softened snow stuck to their snow-shoes. They marched
eastward three miles through the dripping forest, till they reached the
banks of Lake Champlain, near what is now called Five Mile Point,
and presently saw a sledge, drawn by horses, moving on the ice from
Ticonderoga towards Crown Point. Rogers sent Stark along the shore
to the left to head it off, while he with another party, covered by the
woods, moved in the opposite direction to stop its retreat. He soon saw
eight or ten more sledges following the first, and sent a messenger to
prevent Stark from showing himself too soon; but Stark was already on
the ice. All the sledges turned back in hot haste. The rangers ran in
pursuit and captured three of them, with seven men and six horses,
while the rest escaped to Ticonderoga. The prisoners, being separately
examined, told an ominous tale. There were three hundred and fifty
regulars at Ticonderoga; two hundred Canadians and forty-five Indians
had lately arrived there, and more Indians were expected that evening,—all destined to waylay the communications between the English

forts, and all prepared to march at a moment's notice. The rangers were now in great peril. The fugitives would give warning of their presence, and the French and Indians, in overwhelming force, would no doubt cut off their retreat.

Rogers at once ordered his men to return to their last night's encampment, rekindle the fires, and dry their guns, which were wet by the rain of the morning. Then they marched southward in single file through the snow-encumbered forest, Rogers and Kennedy in the front, Spikeman in the centre, and Stark in the rear. In this order they moved on over broken and difficult ground till two in the afternoon, when they came upon a valley, or hollow, scarcely a musket-shot wide, which ran across their line of march, and, like all the rest of the country, was buried in thick woods. The front of the line had descended the first hill, and was mounting that on the farther side, when the foremost men heard a low clicking sound, like the cocking of a great number of guns; and in an instant a furious volley blazed out of the bushes on the ridge above them. Kennedy was killed outright, as also was Gardner, one of the volunteers. Rogers was grazed in the head by a bullet, and others were disabled or hurt. The rest returned the fire, while a swarm of French and Indians rushed upon them from the ridge and the slopes on either hand, killing several more, Spikeman among the rest, and capturing others. The rangers fell back across the hollow and regained the hill they had just descended. Stark with the rear, who were at the top when the fray began, now kept the assailants in check by a brisk fire till their comrades joined them. Then the whole party, spreading themselves among the trees that covered the declivity, stubbornly held their ground and beat back the French in repeated attempts to dislodge them. As the assailants were more than two to one, what Rogers had most to dread was a movement to outflank him and get into his rear. This they tried twice, and were twice repulsed by a party held in reserve for the purpose. The fight lasted several hours, during which there was much talk between the combatants. The French called out that it was a pity so many brave men should be lost, that large reinforcements were expected every moment, and that the rangers would then be cut to pieces without mercy; whereas if they surrendered at once they should be treated with the utmost kindness. They called to Rogers by name, and expressed great esteem for him. Neither threats nor promises had any effect, and the firing went on till darkness stopped it. Towards evening Rogers was shot through the wrist; and one of the men, John Shute, used to tell in his old age how he saw another ranger trying to bind the captain's wound with the ribbon of his own queue.

As Ticonderoga was but three miles off, it was destruction to stay where they were; and they withdrew under cover of night, reduced to forty-eight effective and six wounded men. Fourteen had been killed, and six captured. Those that were left reached Lake George in the morning, and Stark, with two followers, pushed on in advance to bring a sledge for the wounded. The rest made their way to the Narrows, where they encamped, and presently descried a small dark object on the ice far behind them. It proved to be one of their own number, Sergeant Joshua Martin, who had received a severe wound in the fight, and was left for dead; but by desperate efforts had followed on their tracks, and was now brought to camp in a state of exhaustion. He recovered, and lived to an advanced age. The sledge sent by Stark came in the morning, and the whole party soon reached the fort. Abercromby, on hearing of the affair, sent them a letter of thanks for gallant conduct.

Rogers reckons the number of his assailants at about two hundred and fifty in all. Vaudreuil says that they consisted of eighty-nine regulars and ninety Canadians and Indians. With his usual boastful exaggeration, he declares that forty English were left dead on the field, and that only three reached Fort William Henry alive. He says that the fight was extremely hot and obstinate, and admits that the French lost thirty-seven killed and wounded. Rogers makes the number much greater. That it was considerable is certain, as Lusignan, commandant at Ticonderoga, wrote immediately for reinforcements.[1]

The effects of his wound and an attack of small-pox kept Rogers quiet for a time. Meanwhile the winter dragged slowly away, and the ice of Lake George, cracking with change of temperature, uttered its strange cry of agony, heralding that dismal season when winter begins to relax its gripe, but spring still holds aloof; when the sap stirs in the sugar-maples, but the buds refuse to swell, and even the catkins of the

---

[1] Rogers, *Journals*, 38–44. Caleb Stark, *Memoir and Correspondence of John Stark*, 18, 412. *Return of Killed, Wounded, and Missing in the Action near Ticonderoga, Jan. 1757*; all the names are here given. James Abercromby, aide-de-camp to his uncle, General Abercromby, wrote to Rogers from Albany: "You cannot imagine how all ranks of people here are pleased with your conduct and your men's behavior."

The accounts of the French writers differ from each other, but agree in placing the English force at from seventy to eighty, and their own much higher. The principal report is that of *Vaudreuil au Ministre, 19 Avril, 1757* (his second letter of this date). Bougainville, Montcalm, Malartic, and Montreuil all speak of the affair, placing the English loss much higher than is shown by the returns. The story, repeated in most of the French narratives, that only three of the rangers reached Fort William Henry, seems to have arisen from the fact that Stark with two men went thither in advance of the rest. As regards the antecedents of the combat, the French and English accounts agree.

willows will not burst their brown integuments; when the forest is patched with snow, though on its sunny slopes one hears in the stillness the whisper of trickling waters that ooze from the half-thawed soil and saturated beds of fallen leaves; when clouds hang low on the darkened mountains, and cold mists entangle themselves in the tops of the pines; now a dull rain, now a sharp morning frost, and now a storm of snow powdering the waste, and wrapping it again in the pall of winter.

In this cheerless season, on St. Patrick's Day, the seventeenth of March, the Irish soldiers who formed a part of the garrison of Fort William Henry were paying homage to their patron saint in libations of heretic rum, the product of New England stills; and it is said that John Stark's rangers forgot theological differences in their zeal to share the festivity. The story adds that they were restrained by their commander, and that their enforced sobriety proved the saving of the fort. This may be doubted; for without counting the English soldiers of the garrison who had no special call to be drunk that day, the fort was in no danger till twenty-four hours after, when the revellers had had time to rally from their pious carouse. Whether rangers or British soldiers, it is certain that watchmen were on the alert during the night between the eighteenth and nineteenth, and that towards one in the morning they heard a sound of axes far down the lake, followed by the faint glow of a distant fire. The inference was plain, that an enemy was there, and that the necessity of warming himself had overcome his caution. Then all was still for some two hours, when, listening in the pitchy darkness, the watchers heard the footsteps of a great body of men approaching on the ice, which at the time was bare of snow. The garrison were at their posts, and all the cannon on the side towards the lake vomited grape and round-shot in the direction of the sound, which thereafter was heard no more.

Those who made it were a detachment, called by Vaudreuil an army, sent by him to seize the English fort. Shirley had planned a similar stroke against Ticonderoga a year before; but the provincial levies had come in so slowly, and the ice had broken up so soon, that the scheme was abandoned. Vaudreuil was more fortunate. The whole force, regulars, Canadians, and Indians, was ready to his hand. No pains were spared in equipping them. Overcoats, blankets, bearskins to sleep on, tarpaulins to sleep under, spare moccasons, spare mittens, kettles, axes, needles, awls, flint and steel, and many miscellaneous articles were provided, to be dragged by the men on light Indian sledges, along with provisions for twelve days. The cost of the expedition is set at a million francs, answering to more than as many dollars of the present time. To the disgust of the officers from France, the Governor named his brother

Rigaud for the chief command; and before the end of February the whole party was on its march along the ice of Lake Champlain. They rested nearly a week at Ticonderoga, where no less than three hundred short scaling-ladders, so constructed that two or more could be joined in one, had been made for them; and here, too, they received a reinforcement, which raised their number to sixteen hundred. Then, marching three days along Lake George, they neared the fort on the evening of the eighteenth, and prepared for a general assault before daybreak.

The garrison, including rangers, consisted of three hundred and forty-six effective men.[1] The fort was not strong, and a resolute assault by numbers so superior must, it seems, have overpowered the defenders; but the Canadians and Indians who composed most of the attacking force were not suited for such work; and, disappointed in his hope of a surprise, Rigaud withdrew them at daybreak, after trying in vain to burn the buildings outside. A few hours after, the whole body reappeared, filing off to surround the fort, on which they kept up a brisk but harmless fire of musketry. In the night they were heard again on the ice, approaching as if for an assault; and the cannon, firing towards the sound, again drove them back. There was silence for a while, till tongues of flame lighted up the gloom, and two sloops, ice-bound in the lake, and a large number of bateaux on the shore were seen to be on fire. A party sallied to save them; but it was too late. In the morning they were all consumed, and the enemy had vanished.

It was Sunday, the twentieth. Everything was quiet till noon, when the French filed out of the woods and marched across the ice in procession, ostentatiously carrying their scaling-ladders, and showing themselves to the best effect. They stopped at a safe distance, fronting towards the fort, and several of them advanced, waving a red flag. An officer with a few men went to meet them, and returned bringing Le Mercier, chief of the Canadian artillery, who, being led blindfold into the fort, announced himself as bearer of a message from Rigaud. He was conducted to the room of Major Eyre, where all the British officers were assembled; and, after mutual compliments, he invited them to give up the place peaceably, promising the most favorable terms, and threatening a general assault and massacre in case of refusal. Eyre said that he should defend himself to the last; and the envoy, again blindfolded, was led back to whence he came.

The whole French force now advanced as if to storm the works, and

[1] *Strength of the Garrison of Fort William Henry when the Enemy came before it*, enclosed in the letter of *Major Eyre to Loudon, 26 March, 1757*. There were also one hundred and twenty-eight invalids.

the garrison prepared to receive them. Nothing came of it but a fusillade, to which the British made no reply. At night the French were
heard advancing again, and each man nerved himself for the crisis. The
real attack, however, was not against the fort, but against the buildings
outside, which consisted of several storehouses, a hospital, a saw-mill,
and the huts of the rangers, besides a sloop on the stocks and piles of
planks and cord-wood. Covered by the night, the assailants crept up
with fagots of resinous sticks, placed them against the farther side of
the buildings, kindled them, and escaped before the flame rose; while
the garrison, straining their ears in the thick darkness, fired wherever
they heard a sound. Before morning all around them was in a blaze,
and they had much ado to save the fort barracks from the shower of
burning cinders. At ten o'clock the fires had subsided, and a thick fall
of snow began, filling the air with a restless chaos of large moist flakes.
This lasted all day and all the next night, till the ground and the ice
were covered to a depth of three feet and more. The French lay close
in their camps till a little before dawn on Tuesday morning, when
twenty volunteers from the regulars made a bold attempt to burn the
sloop on the stocks, with several storehouses and other structures, and
several hundred scows and whaleboats which had thus far escaped.
They were only in part successful; but they fired the sloop and some
buildings near it, and stood far out on the ice watching the flaming
vessel, a superb bonfire amid the wilderness of snow. The spectacle cost
the volunteers a fourth of their number killed and wounded.

On Wednesday morning the sun rose bright on a scene of wintry
splendor, and the frozen lake was dotted with Rigaud's retreating followers toiling towards Canada on snow-shoes. Before they reached it
many of them were blinded for a while by the insufferable glare, and
their comrades led them homewards by the hand.[1]

[1]*Eyre to Loudon,* 24 March, 1757. *Ibid.,* 25 March, enclosed in Loudon's despatch of 25 April,
1757. *Message of Rigaud to Major Eyre,* 20 March, 1757. *Letter from Fort William Henry,* 26 March,
1757, in *Boston Gazette,* No. 106, and *Boston Evening Post,* No. 1,128. *Abstract of Letters from
Albany,* in *Boston News Letter,* No. 2,860. Caleb Stark, *Memoir and Correspondence of John Stark,*
22, a curious mixture of truth and error. *Relation de la Campagne sur le Lac St. Sacrement pendant
l'Hiver,* 1757. Bougainville, *Journal.* Malartic, *Journal. Montcalm au Ministre,* 24 Avril, 1757. *Montreuil au Ministre,* 23 Avril, 1757. *Montcalm à sa Mère,* 1 Avril, 1757. *Mémoires sur le Canada,
1749–1760.*

  The French loss in killed and wounded is set by Montcalm at eleven. That of the English was
seven, slightly wounded, chiefly in sorties. They took three prisoners. Stark was touched by a
bullet, for the only time in his adventurous life.

14

Montcalm and Vaudreuil

1757

Spring came at last, and the Dutch burghers of Albany heard, faint from the far height, the clamor of the wild-fowl, streaming in long files northward to their summer home. As the aërial travellers winged their way, the seat of war lay spread beneath them like a map. First the blue Hudson, slumbering among its forests, with the forts along its banks, Half-Moon, Stillwater, Saratoga, and the geometric lines and earthen mounds of Fort Edward. Then a broad belt of dingy evergreen; and beyond, released from wintry fetters, the glistening breast of Lake George, with Fort William Henry at its side, amid charred ruins and a desolation of prostrate forests. Hence the lake stretched northward, like some broad river, trenched between mountain ranges still leafless and gray. Then they looked down on Ticonderoga, with the flag of the Bourbons, like a flickering white speck, waving on its ramparts; and next on Crown Point with its tower of stone. Lake Champlain now spread before them, widening as they flew: on the left, the mountain wilderness of the Adirondacks, like a stormy sea congealed; on the right, the long procession of the Green Mountains; and, far beyond, on the dim verge of the eastern sky, the White Mountains throned in savage solitude. They passed over the bastioned square of Fort St. John, Fort Chambly guarding the rapids of the Richelieu, and the broad belt of the St. Lawrence, with Montreal seated on its bank. Here we leave them, to build their nests and hatch their brood among the fens of the lonely North.

Montreal, the military heart of Canada, was in the past winter its social centre also, where were gathered conspicuous representatives both of Old France and of New; not men only, but women. It was a sparkling fragment of the reign of Louis XV. dropped into the American wilderness. Montcalm was here with his staff and his chief officers, now pondering schemes of war, and now turning in thought to his beloved Château of Candiac, his mother, children, and wife, to whom he sent letters with every opportunity. To his wife he writes: "Think of me affectionately; give love to my girls. I hope next year I may be with you all. I love you tenderly, dearest." He says that he has sent her a packet of marten-skins for a muff; "and another time I shall send some to our daughter; but I should like better to bring them myself." Of this eldest daughter he writes in reply to a letter of domestic news from Madame de Montcalm: "The new gown with blonde trimmings must be becoming, for she is pretty." Again, "There is not an hour in the day when I do not think of you, my mother and my children." He had the tastes of a country gentleman, and was eager to know all that was passing on his estate. Before leaving home he had set up a mill to grind olives for oil, and was well pleased to hear of its prosperity. "It seems to be a good thing, which pleases me very much. Bougainville and I talk a great deal about the oil-mill." Some time after, when the King sent him the coveted decoration of the *cordon rouge*, he informed Madame de Montcalm of the honor done him, and added: "But I think I am better pleased with what you tell me of the success of my oil-mill."

To his mother he writes of his absorbing occupations, and says: "You can tell my dearest that I have no time to occupy myself with the ladies, even if I wished to." Nevertheless he now and then found leisure for some little solace in his banishment; for he writes to Bourlamaque, whom he had left at Quebec, after a visit which he had himself made there early in the winter: "I am glad you sometimes speak of me to the three ladies in the Rue du Parloir; and I am flattered by their remembrance, especially by that of one of them, in whom I find at certain moments too much wit and too many charms for my tranquillity." These ladies of the Rue du Parloir are several times mentioned in his familiar correspondence with Bourlamaque.

His station obliged him to maintain a high standard of living, to his great financial detriment, for Canadian prices were inordinate. "I must live creditably, and so I do; sixteen persons at table every day. Once a fortnight I dine with the Governor-General and with the Chevalier de Lévis, who lives well too. He has given three grand balls. As for me, up to Lent I gave, besides dinners, great suppers, with ladies, three times a week. They lasted till two in the morning; and then there was dancing, to which company came uninvited, but sure of a welcome from those who had been at supper. It is very expensive, not very amusing, and often tedious. At Quebec, where we spent a month, I gave receptions or parties, often at the Intendant's house. I like my gallant Chevalier de Lévis very much. Bourlamaque was a good choice; he is steady and cool, with good parts. Bougainville has talent, a warm head, and warm heart; he will ripen in time. Write to Madame Cornier that I like her husband; he is perfectly well, and as impatient for peace as I am. Love to my daughters, and all affection and respect to my mother. I live only in the hope of joining you all again. Nevertheless, Montreal is as good a place as Alais even in time of peace, and better now, because the Government is here; for the Marquis de Vaudreuil, like me, spent only a month at Quebec. As for Quebec, it is as good as the best cities of France, except ten or so. Clear sky, bright sun; neither spring nor autumn, only summer and winter. July, August, and September, hot as in Languedoc: winter insupportable; one must keep always indoors. The ladies *spirituelles*, *galantes*, *dévotes*. Gambling at Quebec, dancing and conversation at Montreal. My friends the Indians, who are often unbearable, and whom I treat with perfect tranquillity and patience, are fond of me. If I were not a sort of general, though very subordinate to the Governor, I could gossip about the plans of the campaign, which it is likely will begin on the tenth or fifteenth of May. I worked at the plan of the last affair [*Rigaud's expedition to Fort William Henry*], which might have turned out better, though good as it was. I wanted only eight hundred men. If I had had my way, Monsieur de Lévis or Monsieur de Bougainville would have had charge of it. However, the thing was all right, and in good hands. The Governor, who is extremely civil to me, gave it to his brother; he thought him more used to winter marches. Adieu, my heart; I adore and love you!"

To meet his manifold social needs, he sends to his wife orders for prunes, olives, anchovies, muscat wine, capers, sausages, confectionery, cloth for liveries, and many other such items; also for scent-bags of two kinds, and perfumed pomatum for presents; closing in postscript with an injunction not to forget a dozen pint-bottles of English lavender. Some months after, he writes to Madame de Saint-Véran: "I have got everything that was sent me from Montpellier except the sausages. I have lost a third of what was sent from Bordeaux. The English captured it on board the ship called 'La Superbe;' and I have reason to fear that everything sent from Paris is lost on board 'La Liberté.' I am running into debt here. Pshaw! I must live. I do not worry myself. Best love to you, my mother."

When Rigaud was about to march with his detachment against Fort William Henry, Montcalm went over to La Prairie to see them. "I reviewed them," he writes to Bourlamaque, "and gave the officers a dinner, which, if anybody else had given it, I should have said was a grand affair. There were two tables, for thirty-six persons in all. On Wednesday there was an Assembly at Madame Varin's; on Friday the Chevalier de Lévis gave a ball. He invited sixty-five ladies, and got only thirty, with a great crowd of men. Rooms well lighted, excellent order, excellent service, plenty of refreshments of every sort all through the night; and the company stayed till seven in the morning. As for me, I went to bed early. I had had that day eight ladies at a supper given to Madame Varin. To-morrow I shall have half-a-dozen at another supper, given to I don't know whom, but incline to think it will be La Roche Beaucour. The gallant Chevalier is to give us still another ball."

Lent put a check on these festivities. "To-morrow," he tells Bourlamaque, "I shall throw myself into devotion with might and main (à corps perdu). It will be easier for me to detach myself from the world and turn heavenward here at Montreal than it would be at Quebec." And, some time after, "Bougainville spent Monday delightfully at Isle Ste. Hélène, and Tuesday devoutly with the Sulpitian Fathers at the Mountain. I was there myself at four o'clock, and did them the civility to sup in their refectory at a quarter before six."

In May there was a complete revival of social pleasures, and Montcalm wrote to Bourlamaque: "Madame de Beaubassin's supper was very gay. There were toasts to the Rue du Parloir and to the General. To-day I must give a dinner to Madame de Saint-Ours, which will be a little more serious. Péan is gone to establish himself at La Chine, and will come back with La Barolon, who goes thither with a husband of hers, bound to the Ohio with Villejoin and Louvigny. The Chevalier de Lévis amuses himself very much here. He and his friends spend all their time with Madame de Lenisse."

Under these gayeties and gallantries there were bitter heart-burnings. Montcalm hints at some of them in a letter to Bourlamaque, written at the time of the expedition to Fort William Henry, which, in the words of Montcalm, who would have preferred another commander, the Governor had ordered to march "under the banners of brother Rigaud." "After he got my letter on Sunday evening," says the disappointed General, "Monsieur de Vaudreuil sent me his secretary with the instructions he had given his brother," which he had hitherto withheld. "This gave rise after dinner to a long conversation with him; and I hope for the good of the service that his future conduct will prove the truth of his words. I spoke to him with frankness and firmness of the necessity I was under of communicating to him my reflections; but I did not name any of the persons who, to gain his good graces, busy themselves with destroying his confidence in me. I told him that he would always find me disposed to aid in measures tending to our success, even should his views, which always ought to prevail, be different from mine; but that I dared flatter myself that he would henceforward communicate his plans to me sooner; for, though his knowledge of the country gave greater weight to his opinions, he might rest satisfied that I should second him in methods and details. This explanation passed off becomingly enough, and ended with a proposal to dine on a moose's nose [*an estimed morsel*] the day after to-morrow. I burn your letters, Monsieur, and I beg you to do the same with mine, after making a note of anything you may want to keep." But Bourlamaque kept all the letters, and bound them in a volume, which still exists.[1]

Montcalm was not at this time fully aware of the feeling of Vaudreuil towards him. The touchy egotism of the Governor and his jealous attachment to the colony led him to claim for himself and the Canadians the merit of every achievement and to deny it to the French troops and their general. Before the capture of Oswego was known, he wrote to the naval minister that Montcalm would never have dared attack that place if he had not encouraged him and answered his timid objections.[2] "I am confident that I shall reduce it," he adds; "my expedition is sure to succeed if Monsieur de Montcalm follows the directions I have given him." When the good news came he immediately wrote again, declar-

---

[1]The preceding extracts are from *Lettres de Montcalm à Madame de Saint-Véran, sa Mère, et à Madame de Montcalm, sa Femme, 1756, 1757* (*Papiers de Famille*); and *Lettres de Montcalm à Bourlamaque, 1757*. See Appendix E.

[2]*Vaudreuil au Ministre de la Marine, 13 Août, 1756.*

ing that the victory was due to his brother Rigaud and the Canadians, who, he says, had been ill-used by the General, and not allowed either to enter the fort or share the plunder, any more than the Indians, who were so angry at the treatment they had met that he had great difficulty in appeasing them. He hints that the success was generally ascribed to him. "There has been a great deal of talk here; but I will not do myself the honor of repeating it to you, especially as it relates to myself. I know how to do violence to my self-love. The measures I took assured our victory, in spite of opposition. If I had been less vigilant and firm, Oswego would still be in the hands of the English. I cannot sufficiently congratulate myself on the zeal which my brother and the Canadians and Indians showed on this occasion; for without them my orders would have been given in vain. The hopes of His Britannic Majesty have vanished, and will hardly revive again; for I shall take care to crush them in the bud."[1]

The pronouns "I" and "my" recur with monotonous frequency in his correspondence. "I have laid waste all the British provinces." "By promptly uniting my forces at Carillon, I have kept General Loudon in check, though he had at his disposal an army of about twenty thousand men;"[2] and so without end, in all varieties of repetition. It is no less characteristic that he here assigns to his enemies double their actual force.

He has the faintest of praise for the troops from France. "They are generally good, but thus far they have not absolutely distinguished themselves. I do justice to the firmness they showed at Oswego; but it was only the colony troops, Canadians, and Indians who attacked the forts. Our artillery was directed by the Chevalier Le Mercier and M. Frémont [*colony officers*], and was served by our colony troops and our militia. The officers from France are more inclined to defence than attack. Far from spending the least thing here, they lay by their pay. They saved the money allowed them for refreshments, and had it in pocket at the end of the campaign. They get a profit, too, out of their provisions, by having certificates made under borrowed names, so that they can draw cash for them on their return. It is the same with the soldiers, who also sell their provisions to the King and get paid for them. In conjunction with M. Bigot, I labor to remedy all these abuses; and the rules we have established have saved the King a considerable expense. M. de Montcalm has complained very much of these rules."

---

[1]*Vaudreuil au Ministre de la Marine*, 1 Sept. 1756.
[2]*Ibid.*, 6 Nov. 1756.

The Intendant Bigot, who here appears as a reformer, was the centre of a monstrous system of public fraud and robbery; while the charges against the French officers are unsupported. Vaudreuil, who never loses an opportunity of disparaging them, proceeds thus:—

"The troops from France are not on very good terms with our Canadians. What can the soldiers think of them when they see their officers threaten them with sticks or swords? The Canadians are obliged to carry these gentry on their shoulders, through the cold water, over rocks that cut their feet; and if they make a false step they are abused. Can anything be harder? Finally, Monsieur de Montcalm is so quick-tempered that he goes to the length of striking the Canadians. How can he restrain his officers when he cannot restrain himself? Could any example be more contagious? This is the way our Canadians are treated. They deserve something better." He then enlarges on their zeal, hardihood, and bravery, and adds that nothing but their blind submission to his commands prevents many of them from showing resentment at the usage they had to endure. The Indians, he goes on to say, are not so gentle and yielding; and but for his brother Rigaud and himself, might have gone off in a rage. "After the campaign of Oswego they did not hesitate to tell me that they would go wherever I sent them, provided I did not put them under the orders of M. de Montcalm. They told me positively that they could not bear his quick temper. I shall always maintain the most perfect union and understanding with M. le Marquis de Montcalm, but I shall be forced to take measures which will assure to our Canadians and Indians treatment such as their zeal and services merit."[1]

To the subject of his complaints Vaudreuil used a different language; for Montcalm says, after mentioning that he had had occasion to punish some of the Canadians at Oswego: "I must do Monsieur de Vaudreuil the justice to say that he approved my proceedings." He treated the General with the blandest politeness. "He is a good-natured man," continues Montcalm, "mild, with no character of his own, surrounded by people who try to destroy all his confidence in the general of the troops from France. I am praised excessively, in order to make him jealous, excite his Canadian prejudices, and prevent him from dealing with me frankly, or adopting my views when he can help it."[2] He elsewhere complains that Vaudreuil gave to both him and Lévis orders

---

[1] *Vaudreuil au Ministre de la Marine*, 23 Oct. 1756. The above extracts are somewhat condensed in the translation. See the letter in Dussieux, 279.

[2] *Montcalm au Ministre de la Guerre*, 11 Juillet, 1757.

couched in such equivocal terms that he could throw the blame on them in case of reverse.[1] Montcalm liked the militia no better than the Governor liked the regulars. "I have used them with good effect, though not in places exposed to the enemy's fire. They know neither discipline nor subordination, and think themselves in all respects the first nation on earth." He is sure, however, that they like him: "I have gained the utmost confidence of the Canadians and Indians; and in the eyes of the former, when I travel or visit their camps, I have the air of a tribune of the people."[2] "The affection of the Indians for me is so strong that there are moments when it astonishes the Governor."[3] "The Indians are delighted with me," he says in another letter; "the Canadians are pleased with me; their officers esteem and fear me, and would be glad if the French troops and their general could be dispensed with; and so should I."[4] And he writes to his mother: "The part I have to play is unique: I am a general-in-chief subordinated; sometimes with everything to do, and sometimes nothing; I am esteemed, respected, beloved, envied, hated; I pass for proud, supple, stiff, yielding, polite, devout, gallant, etc.; and I long for peace."[5]

The letters of the Governor and those of the General, it will be seen, contradict each other flatly at several points. Montcalm is sustained by his friend Bougainville, who says that the Indians had a great liking for him, and that he "knew how to manage them as well as if he had been born in their wigwams."[6] And while Vaudreuil complains that the Canadians are ill-used by Montcalm, Bougainville declares that the regulars are ill-used by Vaudreuil. "One must be blind not to see that we are treated as the Spartans treated the Helots." Then he comments on the jealous reticence of the Governor. "The Marquis de Montcalm has not the honor of being consulted; and it is generally through public rumor that he first hears of Monsieur de Vaudreuil's military plans." He calls the Governor "a timid man, who can neither make a resolution nor keep one;" and he gives another trait of him, illustrating it, after his usual way, by a parallel from the classics: "When V. produces an idea he falls in love with it, as Pygmalion did with his statue. I can forgive Pygmalion, for what he produced was a masterpiece."[7]

[1]*Ibid.*, 1 Nov. 1756.
[2]*Ibid.*, 18 Sept. 1757.
[3]*Ibid.*, 4 Nov. 1757.
[4]*Ibid.*, 28 Août, 1756.
[5]*Montcalm à Madame de Saint-Véran, 23 Sept. 1757.*
[6]*Bougainville à Saint-Laurens, 19 Août, 1757.*
[7]Bougainville, *Journal.*

The exceeding touchiness of the Governor was sorely tried by certain indiscretions on the part of the General, who in his rapid and vehement utterances sometimes forgot the rules of prudence. His anger, though not deep, was extremely impetuous; and it is said that his irritation against Vaudreuil sometimes found escape in the presence of servants and soldiers.[1] There was no lack of reporters, and the Governor was told everything. The breach widened apace, and Canada divided itself into two camps: that of Vaudreuil with the colony officers, civil and military, and that of Montcalm with the officers from France. The principal exception was the Chevalier de Lévis. This brave and able commander had an easy and adaptable nature, which made him a sort of connecting link between the two parties. "One should be on good terms with everybody," was a maxim which he sometimes expressed, and on which he shaped his conduct with notable success. The Intendant Bigot also, an adroit and accomplished person, had the skill to avoid breaking with either side.

But now the season of action was near, and domestic strife must give place to efforts against the common foe. "God or devil!" Montcalm wrote to Bourlamaque, "we must do something and risk a fight. If we succeed, we can, all three of us [*you, Lévis, and I*], ask for promotion. Burn this letter." The prospects, on the whole, were hopeful. The victory at Oswego had wrought marvels among the Indians, inspired the faithful, confirmed the wavering, and daunted the ill-disposed. The whole West was astir, ready to pour itself again in blood and fire against the English border; and even the Cherokees and Choctaws, old friends of the British colonies, seemed on the point of turning against them.[2] The Five Nations were half won for France. In November a large deputation of them came to renew the chain of friendship at Montreal. "I have laid Oswego in ashes," said Vaudreuil; "the English quail before me. Why do you nourish serpents in your bosom? They mean only to enslave you." The deputies trampled under foot the medals the English had given them, and promised the "Devourer of Villages," for so they styled the Governor, that they would never more lift the hatchet against his children. The chief difficulty was to get rid of them; for, being clothed and fed at the expense of the King, they were in no haste to take leave; and learning that New Year's Day was a time of visits, gifts, and health-drinking, they declared that they would stay to share its pleasures; which they did, to their own satisfaction and the annoy-

---

[1] *Événements de la Guerre en Canada, 1759, 1760.*
[2] *Vaudreuil au Ministre de la Marine, 19 Avril, 1757.*

ance of those who were forced to entertain them and their squaws.[1] An active siding with France was to be expected only from the western bands of the Confederacy. Neutrality alone could be hoped for from the others, who were too near the English safely to declare against them; while from one of the tribes, the Mohawks, even neutrality was doubtful.

Vaudreuil, while disliking the French regulars, felt that he could not dispense with them, and had asked for a reinforcement. His request was granted; and the Colonial Minister informed him that twenty-four hundred men had been ordered to Canada to strengthen the colony regulars and the battalions of Montcalm.[2] This, according to the estimate of the Minister, would raise the regular force in Canada to sixty-six hundred rank and file.[3] The announcement was followed by another, less agreeable. It was to the effect that a formidable squadron was fitting out in British ports. Was Quebec to be attacked, or Louisbourg? Louisbourg was beyond reach of succor from Canada; it must rely on its own strength and on help from France. But so long as Quebec was threatened, all the troops in the colony must be held ready to defend it, and the hope of attacking England in her own domains must be abandoned. Till these doubts were solved, nothing could be done; and hence great activity in catching prisoners for the sake of news. A few were brought in, but they knew no more of the matter than the French themselves; and Vaudreuil and Montcalm rested for a while in suspense.

The truth, had they known it, would have gladdened their hearts. The English preparations were aimed at Louisbourg. In the autumn before, Loudon, prejudiced against all plans of his predecessor, Shirley, proposed to the Ministry a scheme of his own, involving a possible attack on Quebec, but with the reduction of Louisbourg as its immediate object,—an important object, no doubt, but one that had no direct bearing on the main question of controlling the interior of the continent. Pitt, then for a brief space at the head of the Government, accepted the suggestion, and set himself to executing it; but he was hampered by opposition, and early in April was forced to resign. Then followed a contest of rival claimants to office; and the war against

[1]*Montcalm au Ministre de la Guerre, 24 Avril, 1757; Relation de l'Ambassade des Cinq Nations à Montréal, jointe à la lettre précédente. Procès-verbal de différentes Entrevues entre M. de Vaudreuil et les Députés des Nations sauvages du 13 au 30 Déc. 1756. Malartic, Journal. Montcalm à Madame de Saint-Véran, 1 Avril, 1757.*

[2]*Ordres du Roy et Dépêches des Ministres, Mars, 1757.*

[3]*Ministerial Minute on the Military Force in Canada, 1757,* in N. Y. Col. Docs., X. 523.

France was made subordinate to disputes of personal politics. Meanwhile one Florence Hensey, a spy at London, had informed the French Court that a great armament was fitting out for America, though he could not tell its precise destination. Without loss of time three French squadrons were sent across the Atlantic, with orders to rendezvous at Louisbourg, the conjectured point of attack.

The English were as tardy as their enemies were prompt. Everything depended on speed; yet their fleet, under Admiral Holbourne, consisting of fifteen ships of the line and three frigates, with about five thousand troops on board, did not get to sea till the fifth of May, when it made sail for Halifax, where Loudon was to meet it with additional forces.

Loudon had drawn off the best part of the troops from the northern frontier, and they were now at New York waiting for embarkation. That the design might be kept secret, he laid an embargo on colonial shipping,—a measure which exasperated the colonists without answering its purpose. Now ensued a long delay, during which the troops, the provincial levies, the transports destined to carry them, and the ships of war which were to serve as escort, all lay idle. In the interval Loudon showed great activity in writing despatches and other avocations more or less proper to a commander, being always busy, without, according to Franklin, accomplishing anything. One Innis, who had come with a message from the Governor of Pennsylvania, and had waited above a fortnight for the General's reply, remarked of him that he was like St. George on a tavern sign, always on horseback, and never riding on.[1] Yet nobody longed more than he to reach the rendezvous at Halifax. He was waiting for news of Holbourne, and he waited in vain. He knew only that a French fleet had been seen off the coast strong enough to overpower his escort and sink all his transports.[2] But the season was growing late; he must act quickly if he was to act at all. He and Sir Charles Hardy agreed between them that the risk must be run; and on the twentieth of June the whole force put to sea. They met no enemy, and entered Halifax harbor on the thirtieth. Holbourne and his fleet had not yet appeared; but his ships soon came straggling in, and before the tenth of July all were at anchor before the town. Then there was more delay. The troops, nearly twelve thousand in all, were landed, and weeks were spent in drilling them and planting vegetables for their

[1] *Works of Franklin*, I. 219. Franklin intimates that while Loudon was constantly writing, he rarely sent off despatches. This is a mistake; there is abundance of them, often tediously long, in the Public Record Office.
[2] *Loudon to Pitt, 30 May, 1757.* He had not learned Pitt's resignation.

refreshment. Sir Charles Hay was put under arrest for saying that the nation's money was spent in sham battles and raising cabbages. Some attempts were made to learn the state of Louisbourg; and Captain Gorham, of the rangers, who reconnoitred it from a fishing vessel, brought back an imperfect report, upon which, after some hesitation, it was resolved to proceed to the attack. The troops were embarked again, and all was ready, when, on the fourth of August, a sloop came from Newfoundland, bringing letters found on board a French vessel lately captured. From these it appeared that all three of the French squadrons were united in the harbor of Louisbourg, to the number of twenty-two ships of the line, besides several frigates, and that the garrison had been increased to a total force of seven thousand men, ensconced in the strongest fortress of the continent. So far as concerned the naval force, the account was true. La Motte, the French admiral, had with him a fleet carrying an aggregate of thirteen hundred and sixty cannon, anchored in a sheltered harbor under the guns of the town. Success was now hopeless, and the costly enterprise was at once abandoned. Loudon with his troops sailed back for New York, and Admiral Holbourne, who had been joined by four additional ships, steered for Louisbourg, in hopes that the French fleet would come out and fight him. He cruised off the port; but La Motte did not accept the challenge.

The elements declared for France. A September gale, of fury rare even on that tempestuous coast, burst upon the British fleet. "It blew a perfect hurricane," says the unfortunate Admiral, "and drove us right on shore." One ship was dashed on the rocks, two leagues from Louisbourg. A shifting of the wind in the nick of time saved the rest from total wreck. Nine were dismasted; others threw their cannon into the sea. Not one was left fit for immediate action; and had La Motte sailed out of Louisbourg, he would have had them all at his mercy.

Delay, the source of most of the disasters that befell England and her colonies at this dismal epoch, was the ruin of the Louisbourg expedition. The greater part of La Motte's fleet reached its destination a full month before that of Holbourne. Had the reverse taken place, the fortress must have fallen. As it was, the ill-starred attempt, drawing off the British forces from the frontier, where they were needed most, did for France more than she could have done for herself, and gave Montcalm and Vaudreuil the opportunity to execute a scheme which they had nursed since the fall of Oswego.[1]

---

[1] *Despatches of Loudon, Feb. to Aug. 1757.* Knox, *Campaigns in North America,* I. 6–28. Knox was in the expedition. *Review of Mr. Pitt's Administration* (London, 1763). *The Conduct of a Noble*

Commander in America impartially reviewed (London, 1758). Beatson, *Naval and Military Memoirs*, II. 49–59. *Answer to the Letter to two Great Men* (London, 1760). Entick, II. 168, 169. *Holbourne to Loudon, 4 Aug. 1757. Holbourne to Pitt, 29 Sept. 1757. Ibid., 30 Sept. 1757. Holbourne to Pownall, 2 Nov. 1757.* Mante, 86, 97. *Relation du Désastre arrivé à la Flotte Anglaise commandée par l'Amiral Holbourne.* Chevalier Johnstone, *Campaign of Louisbourg. London Magazine*, 1757, 514. *Gentleman's Magazine*, 1757, 463, 476. *Ibid.*, 1758, 168–173.

It has been said that Loudon was scared from his task by false reports of the strength of the French at Louisbourg. This was not the case. The *Gazette de France*, 621, says that La Motte had twenty-four ships of war. Bougainville says that as early as the ninth of June there were twenty-one ships of war, including five frigates, at Louisbourg. To this the list given by Knox closely answers.

15

Fort William Henry

1757

ANOTHER BLOW · THE WAR-SONG · THE ARMY AT TICONDEROGA · INDIAN
ALLIES · THE WAR-FEAST · TREATMENT OF PRISONERS · CANNIBALISM ·
SURPRISE AND SLAUGHTER · THE WAR COUNCIL · MARCH OF LÉVIS · THE
ARMY EMBARKS · FORT WILLIAM HENRY · NOCTURNAL SCENE · INDIAN
FUNERAL · ADVANCE UPON THE FORT · GENERAL WEBB · HIS
DIFFICULTIES · HIS WEAKNESS · THE SIEGE BEGUN · CONDUCT OF THE
INDIANS · THE INTERCEPTED LETTER · DESPERATE POSITION OF THE
BESIEGED · CAPITULATION · FEROCITY OF THE INDIANS · MISSION OF
BOUGAINVILLE · MURDER OF WOUNDED MEN · A SCENE OF TERROR · THE
MASSACRE · EFFORTS OF MONTCALM · THE FORT BURNED

"I am going on the ninth to sing the war-song at the Lake of Two Mountains, and on the next day at Saut St. Louis,—a long, tiresome ceremony. On the twelfth I am off; and I count on having news to tell you by the end of this month or the beginning of next." Thus Montcalm wrote to his wife from Montreal early in July. All doubts had been solved. Prisoners taken on the Hudson and despatches from Versailles had made it certain that Loudon was bound to Louisbourg, carrying with him the best of the troops that had guarded the New York frontier. The time was come, not only to strike the English on Lake George, but perhaps to seize Fort Edward and carry terror to Albany itself. Only one difficulty remained, the want of provisions. Agents were sent to collect corn and bacon among the inhabitants; the curés and militia captains were ordered to aid in the work; and enough was presently found to feed twelve thousand men for a month.[1]

The emissaries of the Governor had been busy all winter among the tribes of the West and North; and more than a thousand savages, lured by the prospect of gifts, scalps, and plunder, were now encamped at Montreal. Many of them had never visited a French settlement before. All were eager to see Montcalm, whose exploit in taking Oswego had inflamed their imagination; and one day, on a visit of ceremony, an orator from Michillimackinac addressed the General thus: "We wanted to see this famous man who tramples the English under his feet. We thought we should find him so tall that his head would be lost in the clouds. But you are a little man, my Father. It is when we look into your eyes that we see the greatness of the pine-tree and the fire of the eagle."[2]

It remained to muster the Mission Indians settled in or near the limits of the colony; and it was to this end that Montcalm went to sing the war-song with the converts of the Two Mountains. Rigaud, Bougainville, young Longueuil, and others were of the party; and when they landed, the Indians came down to the shore, their priests at their head, and greeted the General with a volley of musketry; then received him after dark in their grand council-lodge, where the circle of wild and savage visages, half seen in the dim light of a few candles, suggested to Bougainville a midnight conclave of wizards. He acted vicariously the chief part in the ceremony. "I sang the war-song in the name of M. de Montcalm, and was much applauded. It was nothing but these words: 'Let us trample the English under our feet,' chanted over and over again, in cadence with the movements of the savages." Then came the war-feast, against which occasion Montcalm had caused three oxen to be roasted.[3] On the next day the party went to Caughnawaga, or Saut St. Louis, where the ceremony was repeated; and Bougainville, who again sang the war-song in the name of his commander, was requited by adoption into the clan of the Turtle. Three more oxen were solemnly devoured, and with one voice the warriors took up the hatchet.

---

[1] Vaudreuil, *Lettres circulaires aux Curés et aux Capitaines de Milice des Paroisses du Gouvernement de Montreal, 16 Juin, 1757.*
[2] Bougainville, *Journal.*
[3] Bougainville describes a ceremony in the Mission Church of the Two Mountains in which warriors and squaws sang in the choir. Ninety-nine years after, in 1856, I was present at a similar ceremony on the same spot, and heard the descendants of the same warriors and squaws sing like their ancestors. Great changes have since taken place at this old mission.

Meanwhile troops, Canadians and Indians, were moving by detachments up Lake Champlain. Fleets of bateaux and canoes followed each
other day by day along the capricious lake, in calm or storm, sunshine
or rain, till, towards the end of July, the whole force was gathered at
Ticonderoga, the base of the intended movement. Bourlamaque had
been there since May with the battalions of Béarn and Royal Roussillon, finishing the fort, sending out war-parties, and trying to discover
the force and designs of the English at Fort William Henry.

Ticonderoga is a high rocky promontory between Lake Champlain
on the north and the mouth of the outlet of Lake George on the south.
Near its extremity and close to the fort were still encamped the two
battalions under Bourlamaque, while bateaux and canoes were passing
incessantly up the river of the outlet. There were scarcely two miles of
navigable water, at the end of which the stream fell foaming over a
high ledge of rock that barred the way. Here the French were building
a saw-mill; and a wide space had been cleared to form an encampment
defended on all sides by an abattis, within which stood the tents of the
battalions of La Reine, La Sarre, Languedoc, and Guienne, all commanded by Lévis. Above the cascade the stream circled through the
forest in a series of beautiful rapids, and from the camp of Lévis a road
a mile and a half long had been cut to the navigable water above. At
the end of this road there was another fortified camp, formed of colony
regulars, Canadians, and Indians, under Rigaud. It was scarcely a mile
farther to Lake George, where on the western side there was an outpost, chiefly of Canadians and Indians; while advanced parties were
stationed at Bald Mountain, now called Rogers Rock, and elsewhere on
the lake, to watch the movements of the English. The various encampments just mentioned were ranged along a valley extending four miles
from Lake Champlain to Lake George, and bordered by mountains
wooded to the top.

Here was gathered a martial population of eight thousand men, including the brightest civilization and the darkest barbarism: from the
scholar-soldier Montcalm and his no less accomplished aide-de-camp;
from Lévis, conspicuous for graces of person; from a throng of courtly
young officers, who would have seemed out of place in that wilderness
had they not done their work so well in it; from these to the foulest
man-eating savage of the uttermost northwest.

Of Indian allies there were nearly two thousand. One of their tribes,
the Iowas, spoke a language which no interpreter understood; and they
all bivouacked where they saw fit: for no man could control them. "I
see no difference," says Bougainville, "in the dress, ornaments, dances,

and songs of the various western nations. They go naked, excepting a strip of cloth passed through a belt, and paint themselves black, red, blue, and other colors. Their heads are shaved and adorned with bunches of feathers, and they wear rings of brass wire in their ears. They wear beaver-skin blankets, and carry lances, bows and arrows, and quivers made of the skins of beasts. For the rest they are straight, well made, and generally very tall. Their religion is brute paganism. I will say it once for all, one must be the slave of these savages, listen to them day and night, in council and in private, whenever the fancy takes them, or whenever a dream, a fit of the vapors, or their perpetual craving for brandy, gets possession of them; besides which they are always wanting something for their equipment, arms, or toilet, and the general of the army must give written orders for the smallest trifle,—an eternal, wearisome detail, of which one has no idea in Europe."

It was not easy to keep them fed. Rations would be served to them for a week; they would consume them in three days, and come for more. On one occasion they took the matter into their own hands, and butchered and devoured eighteen head of cattle intended for the troops; nor did any officer dare oppose this "St. Bartholomew of the oxen," as Bougainville calls it. "Their paradise is to be drunk," says the young officer. Their paradise was rather a hell; for sometimes, when mad with brandy, they grappled and tore each other with their teeth like wolves. They were continually "making medicine," that is, consulting the Manitou, to whom they hung up offerings, sometimes a dead dog, and sometimes the belt-cloth which formed their only garment.

The Mission Indians were better allies than these heathen of the west; and their priests, who followed them to the war, had great influence over them. They were armed with guns, which they well knew how to use. Their dress, though savage, was generally decent, and they were not cannibals; though in other respects they retained all their traditional ferocity and most of their traditional habits. They held frequent war-feasts, one of which is described by Roubaud, Jesuit missionary of the Abenakis of St. Francis, whose flock formed a part of the company present.

"Imagine," says the father, "a great assembly of savages adorned with every ornament most suited to disfigure them in European eyes, painted with vermilion, white, green, yellow, and black made of soot and the scrapings of pots. A single savage face combines all these different colors, methodically laid on with the help of a little tallow, which serves for pomatum. The head is shaved except at the top, where there is a small tuft, to which are fastened feathers, a few beads of wampum, or some such trinket. Every part of the head has its ornament. Pendants hang from the nose and also from the ears, which are split in infancy and drawn down by weights till they flap at last against the shoulders. The rest of the equipment answers to this fantastic decoration: a shirt bedaubed with vermilion, wampum collars, silver bracelets, a large knife hanging on the breast, moose-skin moccasons, and a belt of various colors always absurdly combined. The sachems and war-chiefs are distinguished from the rest: the latter by a gorget, and the former by a medal, with the King's portrait on one side, and on the other Mars and Bellona joining hands, with the device, *Virtus et Honor.*"

Thus attired, the company sat in two lines facing each other, with kettles in the middle filled with meat chopped for distribution. To a dignified silence succeeded songs, sung by several chiefs in succession, and compared by the narrator to the howling of wolves. Then followed a speech from the chief orator, highly commended by Roubaud, who could not help admiring this effort of savage eloquence. "After the harangue," he continues, "they proceeded to nominate the chiefs who were to take command. As soon as one was named he rose and took the head of some animal that had been butchered for the feast. He raised it aloft so that all the company could see it, and cried: 'Behold the head of the enemy!' Applause and cries of joy rose from all parts of the assembly. The chief, with the head in his hand, passed down between the lines, singing his war-song, bragging of his exploits, taunting and defying the enemy, and glorifying himself beyond all measure. To hear his self-laudation in these moments of martial transport one would think him a conquering hero ready to sweep everything before him. As he passed in front of the other savages, they would respond by dull broken cries jerked up from the depths of their stomachs, and accompanied by movements of their bodies so odd that one must be well used to them to keep countenance. In the course of his song the chief would utter from time to time some grotesque witticism; then he would stop, as if pleased with himself, or rather to listen to the thousand confused cries of applause that greeted his ears. He kept up his martial promenade as long as he liked the sport; and when he had had enough, ended by flinging down the head of the animal with an air of contempt, to show that his warlike appetite craved meat of another sort."[1] Others followed with similar songs and pantomime, and the festival was closed at last by ladling out the meat from the kettles, and devouring it.

[1] *Lettre du Père . . .* (Roubaud), *Missionnaire chez les Abnakis, 21 Oct. 1757,* in *Lettres Edifiantes et Curieuses,* VI. 189 (1810).

Roubaud was one day near the fort, when he saw the shore lined
with a thousand Indians, watching four or five English prisoners, who,
with the war-party that had captured them, were approaching in a boat
from the farther side of the water. Suddenly the whole savage crew
broke away together and ran into the neighboring woods, whence they
soon emerged, yelling diabolically, each armed with a club. The
wretched prisoners were to be forced to "run the gauntlet," which
would probably have killed them. They were saved by the chief who
commanded the war-party, and who, on the persuasion of a French
officer, claimed them as his own and forbade the game; upon which,
according to rule in such cases, the rest abandoned it. On this same
day the missionary met troops of Indians conducting several bands of
English prisoners along the road that led through the forest from the
camp of Lévis. Each of the captives was held by a cord made fast about
the neck; and the sweat was starting from their brows in the extremity
of their horror and distress. Roubaud's tent was at this time in the camp
of the Ottawas. He presently saw a large number of them squatted
about a fire, before which meat was roasting on sticks stuck in the
ground; and, approaching, he saw that it was the flesh of an Englishman, other parts of which were boiling in a kettle, while near by sat
eight or ten of the prisoners, forced to see their comrade devoured.
The horror-stricken priest began to remonstrate; on which a young savage fiercely replied in broken French: "You have French taste; I have
Indian. This is good meat for me;" and the feasters pressed him to
share it.

Bougainville says that this abomination could not be prevented;
which only means that if force had been used to stop it, the Ottawas
would have gone home in a rage. They were therefore left to finish
their meal undisturbed. Having eaten one of their prisoners, they began
to treat the rest with the utmost kindness, bringing them white bread,
and attending to all their wants,—a seeming change of heart due to
the fact that they were a valuable commodity, for which the owners
hoped to get a good price at Montreal. Montcalm wished to send them
thither at once, to which after long debate the Indians consented, demanding, however, a receipt in full, and bargaining that the captives
should be supplied with shoes and blankets.[1]

These unfortunates belonged to a detachment of three hundred provincials, chiefly New Jersey men, sent from Fort William Henry under

---

[1] *Journal de l'Expédition contre le Fort George* [William Henry] *du 12 Juillet au 16 Août, 1757.*
Bougainville, *Journal. Lettre du P. Roubaud.*

command of Colonel Parker to reconnoitre the French outposts. Montcalm's scouts discovered them; on which a band of Indians, considerably more numerous, went to meet them under a French partisan named Corbière, and ambushed themselves not far from Sabbath Day Point. Parker had rashly divided his force; and at daybreak of the twenty-sixth of July three of his boats fell into the snare, and were captured without a shot. Three others followed, in ignorance of what had happened, and shared the fate of the first. When the rest drew near, they were greeted by a deadly volley from the thickets, and a swarm of canoes darted out upon them. The men were seized with such a panic that some of them jumped into the water to escape, while the Indians leaped after them and speared them with their lances like fish. "Terrified," says Bougainville, "by the sight of these monsters, their agility, their firing, and their yells, they surrendered almost without resistance." About a hundred, however, made their escape. The rest were killed or captured, and three of the bodies were eaten on the spot. The journalist adds that the victory so elated the Indians that they became insupportable; "but here in the forests of America we can no more do without them than without cavalry on the plain."[1]

Another success at about the same time did not tend to improve their manners. A hundred and fifty of them, along with a few Canadians under Marin, made a dash at Fort Edward, killed or drove in the pickets, and returned with thirty-two scalps and a prisoner. It was found, however, that the scalps were far from representing an equal number of heads, the Indians having learned the art of making two or three out of one by judicious division.[2]

Preparations were urged on with the utmost energy. Provisions, camp equipage, ammunition, cannon, and bateaux were dragged by gangs of men up the road from the camp of Lévis to the head of the rapids. The work went on through heat and rain, by day and night, till, at the end of July, all was done. Now, on the eve of departure, Montcalm, anxious for harmony among his red allies, called them to a grand council near the camp of Rigaud. Forty-one tribes and sub-tribes, Christian and heathen, from the east and from the west, were represented in it. Here were the mission savages,—Iroquois of Caughnawaga, Two Mountains, and La Présentation; Hurons of Lorette and Detroit; Nipissings of Lake

---

[1]Bougainville, *Journal*. Malartic, *Journal*. *Montcalm à Vaudreuil, 27 Juillet, 1757. Webb to Loudon, 1 Aug. 1757. Webb to Delancey, 30 July, 1757. Journal de l'Expédition contre le Fort George. London Magazine*, 1757, 457. Niles, *French and Indian Wars*. *Boston Gazette*, 15 Aug. 1757.

[2]This affair was much exaggerated at the time. I follow Bougainville, who had the facts from Marin. According to him, the thirty-two scalps represented eleven killed; which exactly answers to the English loss as stated by Colonel Frye in a letter from Fort Edward.

Nipissing; Abenakis of St. Francis, Becancour, Missisqui, and the Penobscot; Algonkins of Three Rivers and Two Mountains; Micmacs and Malecites from Acadia: in all eight hundred chiefs and warriors. With these came the heathen of the west,—Ottawas of seven distinct bands; Ojibwas from Lake Superior, and Mississagas from the region of Lakes Erie and Huron; Pottawattamies and Menomonies from Lake Michigan; Sacs, Foxes, and Winnebagoes from Wisconsin; Miamis from the prairies of Illinois, and Iowas from the banks of the Des Moines: nine hundred and seventy-nine chiefs and warriors, men of the forests and men of the plains, hunters of the moose and hunters of the buffalo, bearers of steel hatchets and stone war-clubs, of French guns and of flint-headed arrows. All sat in silence, decked with ceremonial paint, scalp-locks, eagle plumes, or horns of buffalo; and the dark and wild assemblage was edged with white uniforms of officers from France, who came in numbers to the spectacle. Other officers were also here, all belonging to the colony. They had been appointed to the command of the Indian allies, over whom, however, they had little or no real authority. First among them was the bold and hardy Saint-Luc de la Corne, who was called general of the Indians; and under him were others, each assigned to some tribe or group of tribes,—the intrepid Marin; Charles Langlade, who had left his squaw wife at Michillimackinac to join the war; Niverville, Langis, La Plante, Hertel, Longueuil, Herbin, Lorimier, Sabrevois, and Fleurimont; men familiar from childhood with forests and savages. Each tribe had its interpreter, often as lawless as those with whom he had spent his life; and for the converted tribes there were three missionaries,—Piquet for the Iroquois, Mathevet for the Nipissings, who were half heathen, and Roubaud for the Abenakis.[1]

There was some complaint among the Indians because they were crowded upon by the officers who came as spectators. This difficulty being removed, the council opened, Montcalm having already explained his plans to the chiefs and told them the part he expected them to play.

Pennahouel, chief of the Ottawas, and senior of all the Assembly, rose and said: "My father, I, who have counted more moons than any here, thank you for the good words you have spoken. I approve them. Nobody ever spoke better. It is the Manitou of War who inspires you."

Kikensick, chief of the Nipissings, rose in behalf of the Christian

---

[1] The above is chiefly from *Tableau des Sauvages qui se trouvent à l'Armée du Marquis de Montcalm, le 28 Juillet, 1757*. Forty-one tribes and sub-tribes are here named, some, however, represented by only three or four warriors. Besides those set down under the head of Christians, it is stated that a few of the Ottawas of Detroit and Michillimackinac still retained the faith.

Indians, and addressed the heathen of the west. "Brothers, we thank you for coming to help us defend our lands against the English. Our cause is good. The Master of Life is on our side. Can you doubt it, brothers, after the great blow you have just struck? It covers you with glory. The lake, red with the blood of Corlaer [*the English*] bears witness forever to your achievement. We too share your glory, and are proud of what you have done." Then, turning to Montcalm: "We are even more glad than you, my father, who have crossed the great water, not for your own sake, but to obey the great King and defend his children. He has bound us all together by the most solemn of ties. Let us take care that nothing shall separate us."

The various interpreters, each in turn, having explained this speech to the Assembly, it was received with ejaculations of applause; and when they had ceased, Montcalm spoke as follows: "Children, I am delighted to see you all joined in this good work. So long as you remain one, the English cannot resist you. The great King has sent me to protect and defend you; but above all he has charged me to make you happy and unconquerable, by establishing among you the union which ought to prevail among brothers, children of one father, the great Onontio." Then he held out a prodigious wampum belt of six thousand beads: "Take this sacred pledge of his word. The union of the beads of which it is made is the sign of your united strength. By it I bind you all together, so that none of you can separate from the rest till the English are defeated and their fort destroyed."

Pennahouel took up the belt and said: "Behold, brothers, a circle drawn around us by the great Onontio. Let none of us go out from it; for so long as we keep in it, the Master of Life will help all our undertakings." Other chiefs spoke to the same effect, and the council closed in perfect harmony.[1] Its various members bivouacked together at the camp by the lake, and by their carelessness soon set it on fire; whence the place became known as the Burned Camp. Those from the missions confessed their sins all day; while their heathen brothers hung an old coat and a pair of leggings on a pole as tribute to the Manitou. This greatly embarrassed the three priests, who were about to say Mass, but doubted whether they ought to say it in presence of a sacrifice to the devil. Hereupon they took counsel of Montcalm. "Better say it so than not at all," replied the military casuist. Brandy being prudently denied them, the allies grew restless; and the greater part paddled up the lake to a spot near the place where Parker had been defeated. Here they

[1]Bougainville, *Journal*.

encamped to wait the arrival of the army, and amused themselves meantime with killing rattlesnakes, there being a populous "den" of those reptiles among the neighboring rocks.

Montcalm sent a circular letter to the regular officers, urging them to dispense for a while with luxuries, and even comforts. "We have but few bateaux, and these are so filled with stores that a large division of the army must go by land;" and he directed that everything not absolutely necessary should be left behind, and that a canvas shelter to every two officers should serve them for a tent, and a bearskin for a bed. "Yet I do not forbid a mattress," he adds. "Age and infirmities may make it necessary to some; but I shall not have one myself, and make no doubt that all who can will willingly imitate me."[1]

The bateaux lay ready by the shore, but could not carry the whole force; and Lévis received orders to march by the side of the lake with twenty-five hundred men, Canadians, regulars, and Iroquois. He set out at daybreak of the thirtieth of July, his men carrying nothing but their knapsacks, blankets, and weapons. Guided by the unerring Indians, they climbed the steep gorge at the side of Rogers Rock, gained the valley beyond, and marched southward along a Mohawk trail which threaded the forest in a course parallel to the lake. The way was of the roughest; many straggled from the line, and two officers completely broke down. The first destination of the party was the mouth of Ganouskie Bay, now called Northwest Bay, where they were to wait for Montcalm, and kindle three fires as a signal that they had reached the rendezvous.[2]

Montcalm left a detachment to hold Ticonderoga; and then, on the first of August, at two in the afternoon, he embarked at the Burned Camp with all his remaining force. Including those with Lévis, the expedition counted about seven thousand six hundred men, of whom more than sixteen hundred were Indians.[3] At five in the afternoon they reached the place where the Indians, having finished their rattlesnake hunt, were smoking their pipes and waiting for the army. The red warriors embarked, and joined the French flotilla; and now, as evening drew near, was seen one of those wild pageantries of war which Lake

[1] *Circulaire du Marquis de Montcalm, 25 Juillet, 1757.*

[2] *Guerre du Canada, par le Chevalier de Lévis.* This manuscript of Lévis is largely in the nature of a journal.

[3] *État de l'Armée Française devant le Fort George, autrement Guillaume-Henri, le 3 Août, 1757. Tableau des Sauvages qui se trouvent à l'Armée du Marquis de Montcalm, le 28 Juillet, 1757.* This gives a total of 1,799 Indians, of whom some afterwards left the army. *État de l'Armée du Roi en Canada, sur le Lac St. Sacrement et dans les Camps de Carillon, le 29 Juillet, 1757.* This gives a total of 8,019 men, of whom about four hundred were left in garrison at Ticonderoga.

George has often witnessed. A restless multitude of birch canoes, filled with painted savages, glided by shores and islands, like troops of swimming waterfowl. Two hundred and fifty bateaux came next, moved by sail and oar, some bearing the Canadian militia, and some the battalions of Old France in trim and gay attire: first, La Reine and Languedoc; then the colony regulars; then La Sarre and Guienne; then the Canadian brigade of Courtemanche; then the cannon and mortars, each on a platform sustained by two bateaux lashed side by side, and rowed by the militia of Saint-Ours; then the battalions of Béarn and Royal Roussillon; then the Canadians of Gaspé, with the provision-bateaux and the field-hospital; and, lastly, a rear guard of regulars closed the line. So, under the flush of sunset, they held their course along the romantic lake, to play their part in the historic drama that lends a stern enchantment to its fascinating scenery. They passed the Narrows in mist and darkness; and when, a little before dawn, they rounded the high promontory of Tongue Mountain, they saw, far on the right, three fiery sparks shining through the gloom. These were the signal-fires of Lévis, to tell them that he had reached the appointed spot.[1]

Lévis had arrived the evening before, after his hard march through the sultry midsummer forest. His men had now rested for a night, and at ten in the morning he marched again. Montcalm followed at noon, and coasted the western shore, till, towards evening, he found Lévis waiting for him by the margin of a small bay not far from the English fort, though hidden from it by a projecting point of land. Canoes and bateaux were drawn up on the beach, and the united forces made their bivouac together.

The earthen mounds of Fort William Henry still stand by the brink of Lake George; and seated at the sunset of an August day under the pines that cover them, one gazes on a scene of soft and soothing beauty, where dreamy waters reflect the glories of the mountains and the sky. As it is to-day, so it was then; all breathed repose and peace. The splash of some leaping trout, or the dipping wing of a passing swallow, alone disturbed the summer calm of that unruffled mirror.

About ten o'clock at night two boats set out from the fort to reconnoitre. They were passing a point of land on their left, two miles or more down the lake, when the men on board descried through the gloom a strange object against the bank; and they rowed towards it to learn what it might be. It was an awning over the bateaux that carried

[1] The site of the present village of Bolton.

Roubaud and his brother missionaries. As the rash oarsmen drew near, the bleating of a sheep in one of the French provision-boats warned them of danger; and turning, they pulled for their lives towards the eastern shore. Instantly more than a thousand Indians threw themselves into their canoes and dashed in hot pursuit, making the lake and the mountains ring with the din of their war-whoops. The fugitives had nearly reached land when their pursuers opened fire. They replied; shot one Indian dead, and wounded another; then snatched their oars again, and gained the beach. But the whole savage crew was upon them. Several were killed, three were taken, and the rest escaped in the dark woods.[1] The prisoners were brought before Montcalm, and gave him valuable information of the strength and position of the English.[2]

The Indian who was killed was a noted chief of the Nipissings; and his tribesmen howled in grief for their bereavement. They painted his face with vermilion, tied feathers in his hair, hung pendants in his ears and nose, clad him in a resplendent war-dress, put silver bracelets on his arms, hung a gorget on his breast with a flame colored ribbon, and seated him in state on the top of a hillock, with his lance in his hand, his gun in the hollow of his arm, his tomahawk in his belt, and his kettle by his side. Then they all crouched about him in lugubrious silence. A funeral harangue followed; and next a song and solemn dance to the booming of the Indian drum. In the gray of the morning they buried him as he sat, and placed food in the grave for his journey to the land of souls.[3]

As the sun rose above the eastern mountains the French camp was all astir. The column of Lévis, with Indians to lead the way, moved through the forest towards the fort, and Montcalm followed with the main body; then the artillery boats rounded the point that had hid them from the sight of the English, saluting them as they did so with musketry and cannon; while a host of savages put out upon the lake, ranged their canoes abreast in a line from shore to shore, and advanced slowly, with measured paddle-strokes and yells of defiance.

The position of the enemy was full in sight before them. At the head of the lake, towards the right, stood the fort, close to the edge of the

---

[1] *Lettre du Père Roubaud,* 21 Oct. 1757. Roubaud, who saw the whole, says that twelve hundred Indians joined the chase, and that their yells were terrific.

[2] The remains of Fort William Henry are now—1882—crowded between a hotel and the wharf and station of a railway. While I write, a scheme is on foot to level the whole for other railway structures. When I first knew the place the ground was in much the same state as in the time of Montcalm.

[3] *Lettre du Père Roubaud.*

water. On its left was a marsh; then the rough piece of ground where Johnson had encamped two years before; then a low, flat, rocky hill, crowned with an entrenched camp; and, lastly, on the extreme left, another marsh. Far around the fort and up the slopes of the western mountain the forest had been cut down and burned, and the ground was cumbered with blackened stumps and charred carcasses and limbs of fallen trees, strewn in savage disorder one upon another.[1] This was the work of Winslow in the autumn before. Distant shouts and war-cries, the clatter of musketry, white puffs of smoke in the dismal clearing and along the scorched edge of the bordering forest, told that Lévis' Indians were skirmishing with parties of the English, who had gone out to save the cattle roaming in the neighborhood, and burn some outbuildings that would have favored the besiegers. Others were taking down the tents that stood on a plateau near the foot of the mountain on the right, and moving them to the entrenchment on the hill. The garrison sallied from the fort to support their comrades, and for a time the firing was hot.

Fort William Henry was an irregular bastioned square, formed by embankments of gravel surmounted by a rampart of heavy logs, laid in tiers crossed one upon another, the interstices filled with earth. The lake protected it on the north, the marsh on the east, and ditches with *chevaux-de-frise* on the south and west. Seventeen cannon, great and small, besides several mortars and swivels, were mounted upon it;[2] and a brave Scotch veteran, Lieutenant-Colonel Monro, of the thirty-fifth regiment, was in command.

General Webb lay fourteen miles distant at Fort Edward, with twenty-six hundred men, chiefly provincials. On the twenty-fifth of July he had made a visit to Fort William Henry, examined the place, given some orders, and returned on the twenty-ninth. He then wrote to the Governor of New York, telling him that the French were certainly coming, begging him to send up the militia, and saying: "I am determined to march to Fort William Henry with the whole army under my command as soon as I shall hear of the farther approach of the enemy." Instead of doing so he waited three days, and then sent up a detachment of two hundred regulars under Lieutenant-Colonel Young, and eight hundred Massachusetts men under Colonel Frye. This raised the force at the lake to two thousand and two hundred, including sail-

---

[1] *Précis des Événements de la Campagne de 1757 en la Nouvelle France.*

[2] *État des Effets et Munitions de Guerre qui se sont trouvés au Fort Guillaume-Henri.* There were six more guns in the entrenched camp.

ors and mechanics, and reduced that of Webb to sixteen hundred, besides half as many more distributed at Albany and the intervening
forts.[1] If, according to his spirited intention, he should go to the rescue
of Monro, he must leave some of his troops behind him to protect the
lower posts from a possible French inroad by way of South Bay. Thus
his power of aiding Monro was slight, so rashly had Loudon, intent on
Louisbourg, left this frontier open to attack. The defect, however, was
as much in Webb himself as in his resources. His conduct in the past
year had raised doubts of his personal courage; and this was the moment
for answering them. Great as was the disparity of numbers, the emergency would have justified an attempt to save Monro at any risk. That
officer sent him a hasty note, written at nine o'clock on the morning
of the third, telling him that the French were in sight on the lake; and,
in the next night, three rangers came to Fort Edward, bringing another
short note, dated at six in the evening, announcing that the firing had
begun, and closing with the words: "I believe you will think it proper
to send a reinforcement as soon as possible." Now, if ever, was the time
to move, before the fort was invested and access cut off. But Webb lay
quiet, sending expresses to New England for help which could not possibly arrive in time. On the next night another note came from Monro
to say that the French were upon him in great numbers, well supplied
with artillery, but that the garrison were all in good spirits. "I make no
doubt," wrote the hard-pressed officer, "that you will soon send us a
reinforcement;" and again on the same day: "We are very certain that
a part of the enemy have got between you and us upon the high road,
and would therefore be glad (if it meets with your approbation) the
whole army was marched."[2] But Webb gave no sign.[3]

When the skirmishing around the fort was over, La Corne, with a
body of Indians, occupied the road that led to Fort Edward, and Lévis
encamped hard by to support him, while Montcalm proceeded to examine the ground and settle his plan of attack. He made his way to the
rear of the entrenched camp and reconnoitred it, hoping to carry it by
assault; but it had a breastwork of stones and logs, and he thought the
attempt too hazardous. The ground where he stood was that where

[1]Frye, *Journal of the Attack of Fort William Henry. Webb to Loudon*, 1 Aug. 1757. *Ibid.*, 5 Aug.
1757.
[2]*Copy of four Letters from Lieutenant-Colonel Monro to Major-General Webb, enclosed in the General's
Letter of the fifth of August to the Earl of Loudon.*
[3]"The number of troops remaining under my Command at this place [*Fort Edward*], excluding the
Posts on Hudson's River, amounts to but sixteen hundred men fit for duty, with which Army, so
much inferior to that of the enemy, I did not think it prudent to pursue my first intentions of
Marching to their Assistance." *Webb to Loudon*, 5 Aug. 1757.

Dieskau had been defeated; and as the fate of his predecessor was not of flattering augury, he resolved to besiege the fort in form.

He chose for the site of his operations the ground now covered by the village of Caldwell. A little to the north of it was a ravine, beyond which he formed his main camp, while Lévis occupied a tract of dry ground beside the marsh, whence he could easily move to intercept succors from Fort Edward on the one hand, or repel a sortie from Fort William Henry on the other. A brook ran down the ravine and entered the lake at a small cove protected from the fire of the fort by a point of land; and at this place, still called Artillery Cove, Montcalm prepared to debark his cannon and mortars.

Having made his preparations, he sent Fontbrune, one of his aides-de-camp, with a letter to Monro. "I owe it to humanity," he wrote, "to summon you to surrender. At present I can restrain the savages, and make them observe the terms of a capitulation, as I might not have power to do under other circumstances; and an obstinate defence on your part could only retard the capture of the place a few days, and endanger an unfortunate garrison which cannot be relieved, in consequence of the dispositions I have made. I demand a decisive answer within an hour." Monro replied that he and his soldiers would defend themselves to the last. While the flags of truce were flying, the Indians swarmed over the fields before the fort; and when they learned the result, an Abenaki chief shouted in broken French: "You won't surrender, eh! Fire away then, and fight your best; for if I catch you, you shall get no quarter." Monro emphasized his refusal by a general discharge of his cannon.

The trenches were opened on the night of the fourth,—a task of extreme difficulty, as the ground was covered by a profusion of half-burned stumps, roots, branches, and fallen trunks. Eight hundred men toiled till daylight with pick, spade, and axe, while the cannon from the fort flashed through the darkness, and grape and round-shot whistled and screamed over their heads. Some of the English balls reached the camp beyond the ravine, and disturbed the slumbers of the officers off duty, as they lay wrapped in their blankets and bear-skins. Before daybreak the first parallel was made; a battery was nearly finished on the left, and another was begun on the right. The men now worked under cover, safe in their burrows; one gang relieved another, and the work went on all day.

The Indians were far from doing what was expected of them. Instead of scouting in the direction of Fort Edward to learn the movements of the enemy and prevent surprise, they loitered about the camp and in the trenches, or amused themselves by firing at the fort from behind stumps and logs. Some, in imitation of the French, dug little trenches for themselves, in which they wormed their way towards the rampart, and now and then picked off an artillery-man, not without loss on their own side. On the afternoon of the fifth, Montcalm invited them to a council, gave them belts of wampum, and mildly remonstrated with them. "Why expose yourselves without necessity? I grieve bitterly over the losses that you have met, for the least among you is precious to me. No doubt it is a good thing to annoy the English; but that is not the main point. You ought to inform me of everything the enemy is doing, and always keep parties on the road between the two forts." And he gently hinted that their place was not in his camp, but in that of Lévis, where missionaries were provided for such of them as were Christians, and food and ammunition for them all. They promised, with excellent docility, to do everything he wished, but added that there was something on their hearts. Being encouraged to relieve themselves of the burden, they complained that they had not been consulted as to the management of the siege, but were expected to obey orders like slaves. "We know more about fighting in the woods than you," said their orator; "ask our advice, and you will be the better for it."[1]

Montcalm assured them that if they had been neglected, it was only through the hurry and confusion of the time; expressed high appreciation of their talents for bush-fighting, promised them ample satisfaction, and ended by telling them that in the morning they should hear the big guns. This greatly pleased them, for they were extremely impatient for the artillery to begin. About sunrise the battery of the left opened with eight heavy cannon and a mortar, joined, on the next morning, by the battery of the right, with eleven pieces more. The fort replied with spirit. The cannon thundered all day, and from a hundred peaks and crags the astonished wilderness roared back the sound. The Indians were delighted. They wanted to point the guns; and to humor them, they were now and then allowed to do so. Others lay behind logs and fallen trees, and yelled their satisfaction when they saw the splinters fly from the wooden rampart.

Day after day the weary roar of the distant cannonade fell on the ears of Webb in his camp at Fort Edward. "I have not yet received the least reinforcement," he writes to Loudon; "this is the disagreeable situation we are at present in. The fort, by the heavy firing we hear from the lake, is still in our possession; but I fear it cannot long hold out against

---

[1] Bougainville, *Journal*.

so warm a cannonading if I am not reinforced by a sufficient number of militia to march to their relief." The militia were coming; but it was impossible that many could reach him in less than a week. Those from New York alone were within call, and two thousand of them arrived soon after he sent Loudon the above letter. Then, by stripping all the forts below, he could bring together forty-five hundred men; while several French deserters assured him that Montcalm had nearly twelve thousand. To advance to the relief of Monro with a force so inferior, through a defile of rocks, forests, and mountains, made by nature for ambuscades,—and this too with troops who had neither the steadiness of regulars nor the bush-fighting skill of Indians,—was an enterprise for firmer nerve than his.

He had already warned Monro to expect no help from him. At midnight of the fourth, Captain Bartman, his aide-de-camp, wrote: "The General has ordered me to acquaint you he does not think it prudent to attempt a junction or to assist you till reinforced by the militia of the colonies, for the immediate march of which repeated expresses have been sent." The letter then declared that the French were in complete possession of the road between the two forts, that a prisoner just brought in reported their force in men and cannon to be very great, and that, unless the militia came soon, Monro had better make what terms he could with the enemy.[1]

The chance was small that this letter would reach its destination; and in fact the bearer was killed by La Corne's Indians, who, in stripping the body, found the hidden paper, and carried it to the General. Montcalm kept it several days, till the English rampart was half battered down; and then, after saluting his enemy with a volley from all his cannon, he sent it with a graceful compliment to Monro. It was Bougainville who carried it, preceded by a drummer and a flag. He was met at the foot of the glacis, blindfolded, and led through the fort and along the edge of the lake to the entrenched camp, where Monro was at the time. "He returned many thanks," writes the emissary in his Diary, "for the courtesy of our nation, and protested his joy at having to do with so generous an enemy. This was his answer to the Marquis de Montcalm. Then they led me back, always with eyes blinded; and our batteries began to fire again as soon as we thought that the English grenadiers who escorted me had had time to re-enter the fort. I hope

---

[1]Frye, in his *Journal*, gives the letter in full. A spurious translation of it is appended to a piece called *Jugement impartial sur les Opérations militaires en Canada.*

General Webb's letter may induce the English to surrender the sooner."[1]

By this time the sappers had worked their way to the angle of the lake, where they were stopped by a marshy hollow, beyond which was a tract of high ground, reaching to the fort and serving as the garden of the garrison.[2] Logs and fascines in large quantities were thrown into the hollow, and hurdles were laid over them to form a causeway for the cannon. Then the sap was continued up the acclivity beyond, a trench was opened in the garden, and a battery begun, not two hundred and fifty yards from the fort. The Indians, in great number, crawled forward among the beans, maize, and cabbages, and lay there ensconced. On the night of the seventh, two men came out of the fort, apparently to reconnoitre, with a view to a sortie, when they were greeted by a general volley and a burst of yells which echoed among the mountains; followed by responsive whoops pealing through the darkness from the various camps and lurking-places of the savage warriors far and near.

The position of the besieged was now deplorable. More than three hundred of them had been killed and wounded; small-pox was raging in the fort; the place was a focus of infection, and the casemates were crowded with the sick. A sortie from the entrenched camp and another from the fort had been repulsed with loss. All their large cannon and mortars had been burst, or disabled by shot; only seven small pieces were left fit for service;[3] and the whole of Montcalm's thirty-one cannon and fifteen mortars and howitzers would soon open fire, while the walls were already breached, and an assault was imminent. Through the night of the eighth they fired briskly from all their remaining pieces. In the morning the officers held a council, and all agreed to surrender if honorable terms could be had. A white flag was raised, a drum was beat, and Lieutenant-Colonel Young, mounted on horseback, for a shot in the foot had disabled him from walking, went, followed by a few soldiers, to the tent of Montcalm.

It was agreed that the English troops should march out with the honors of war, and be escorted to Fort Edward by a detachment of French troops; that they should not serve for eighteen months; and that all French prisoners captured in America since the war began should be given up within three months. The stores, munitions, and artillery were

---

[1]Bougainville, *Journal. Bougainville au Ministre, 19 Août, 1757.*
[2]Now (1882) the site of Fort William Henry Hotel, with its grounds. The hollow is partly filled by the main road of Caldwell.
[3]Frye, *Journal.*

to be the prize of the victors, except one field-piece, which the garrison were to retain in recognition of their brave defence.

Before signing the capitulation Montcalm called the Indian chiefs to council, and asked them to consent to the conditions, and promise to restrain their young warriors from any disorder. They approved everything and promised everything. The garrison then evacuated the fort, and marched to join their comrades in the entrenched camp, which was included in the surrender. No sooner were they gone than a crowd of Indians clambered through the embrasures in search of rum and plunder. All the sick men unable to leave their beds were instantly butchered.[1] "I was witness of this spectacle," says the missionary Roubaud; "I saw one of these barbarians come out of the casemates with a human head in his hand, from which the blood ran in streams, and which he paraded as if he had got the finest prize in the world." There was little left to plunder; and the Indians, joined by the more lawless of the Canadians, turned their attention to the entrenched camp, where all the English were now collected.

The French guard stationed there could not or would not keep out the rabble. By the advice of Montcalm the English stove their rum-barrels; but the Indians were drunk already with homicidal rage, and the glitter of their vicious eyes told of the devil within. They roamed among the tents, intrusive, insolent, their visages besmirched with war-paint; grinning like fiends as they handled, in anticipation of the knife, the long hair of cowering women, of whom, as well as of children, there were many in the camp, all crazed with fright. Since the last war the New England border population had regarded Indians with a mixture of detestation and horror. Their mysterious warfare of ambush and surprise, their midnight onslaughts, their butcheries, their burnings, and all their nameless atrocities, had been for years the theme of fireside story; and the dread they excited was deepened by the distrust and dejection of the time. The confusion in the camp lasted through the afternoon. "The Indians," says Bougainville, "wanted to plunder the chests of the English; the latter resisted; and there was fear that serious disorder would ensue. The Marquis de Montcalm ran thither immediately, and used every means to restore tranquillity: prayers, threats, caresses, interposition of the officers and interpreters who have some influence over these savages."[2] "We shall be but too happy if we can prevent a massacre. Detestable position! of which nobody who has not

---

[1] *Attestation of William Arbuthnot, Captain in Frye's Regiment.*
[2] *Bougainville au Ministre, 19 Août, 1757.*

been in it can have any idea, and which makes victory itself a sorrow to the victors. The Marquis spared no efforts to prevent the rapacity of the savages and, I must say it, of certain persons associated with them, from resulting in something worse than plunder. At last, at nine o'clock in the evening, order seemed restored. The Marquis even induced the Indians to promise that, besides the escort agreed upon in the capitulation, two chiefs for each tribe should accompany the English on their way to Fort Edward."[1] He also ordered La Corne and the other Canadian officers attached to the Indians to see that no violence took place. He might well have done more. In view of the disorders of the afternoon, it would not have been too much if he had ordered the whole body of regular troops, whom alone he could trust for the purpose, to hold themselves ready to move to the spot in case of outbreak, and shelter their defeated foes behind a hedge of bayonets.

Bougainville was not to see what ensued; for Montcalm now sent him to Montreal, as a special messenger to carry news of the victory. He embarked at ten o'clock. Returning daylight found him far down the lake; and as he looked on its still bosom flecked with mists, and its quiet mountains sleeping under the flush of dawn, there was nothing in the wild tranquillity of the scene to suggest the tragedy which even then was beginning on the shore he had left behind.

The English in their camp had passed a troubled night, agitated by strange rumors. In the morning something like a panic seized them; for they distrusted not the Indians only, but the Canadians. In their haste to be gone they got together at daybreak, before the escort of three hundred regulars had arrived. They had their muskets, but no ammunition; and few or none of the provincials had bayonets. Early as it was, the Indians were on the alert; and, indeed, since midnight great numbers of them had been prowling about the skirts of the camp, showing, says Colonel Frye, "more than usual malice in their looks." Seventeen wounded men of his regiment lay in huts, unable to join the march. In the preceding afternoon Miles Whitworth, the regimental surgeon, had passed them over to the care of a French surgeon, according to an agreement made at the time of the surrender; but, the Frenchman being absent, the other remained with them attending to their wants. The French surgeon had caused special sentinels to be posted for their protection. These were now removed, at the moment when they were needed most; upon which, about five o'clock in the morning, the Indians entered the huts, dragged out the inmates, and toma-

---

[1]Bougainville, *Journal.*

hawked and scalped them all, before the eyes of Whitworth, and in presence of La Corne and other Canadian officers, as well as of a French guard stationed within forty feet of the spot; and, declares the surgeon under oath, "none, either officer or soldier, protected the said wounded men."[1] The opportune butchery relieved them of a troublesome burden.

A scene of plundering now began. The escort had by this time arrived, and Monro complained to the officers that the capitulation was broken; but got no other answer than advice to give up the baggage to the Indians in order to appease them. To this the English at length agreed; but it only increased the excitement of the mob. They demanded rum; and some of the soldiers, afraid to refuse, gave it to them from their canteens, thus adding fuel to the flame. When, after much difficulty, the column at last got out of the camp and began to move along the road that crossed the rough plain between the entrenchment and the forest, the Indians crowded upon them, impeded their march, snatched caps, coats, and weapons from men and officers, tomahawked those that resisted, and, seizing upon shrieking women and children, dragged them off or murdered them on the spot. It is said that some of the interpreters secretly fomented the disorder.[2] Suddenly there rose the screech of the war-whoop. At this signal of butchery, which was given by Abenaki Christians from the mission of the Penobscot,[3] a mob of savages rushed upon the New Hampshire men at the rear of the column, and killed or dragged away eighty of them.[4] A frightful tumult ensued, when Montcalm, Lévis, Bourlamaque, and many other French officers, who had hastened from their camp on the first news of disturbance, threw themselves among the Indians, and by promises and threats tried to allay their frenzy. "Kill me, but spare the English who are under my protection," exclaimed Montcalm. He took from one of them a young officer whom the savage had seized; upon which several other Indians immediately tomahawked their prisoners, lest they too should be taken from them. One writer says that a French grenadier was killed and two wounded in attempting to restore order; but the statement is doubtful. The English seemed paralyzed, and fortunately did not attempt a resistance, which, without ammunition as they were,

---

[1] *Affidavit of Miles Whitworth.* See Appendix F.

[2] This is stated by Pouchot and Bougainville; the latter of whom confirms the testimony of the English witnesses, that Canadian officers present did nothing to check the Indians.

[3] See note, end of chapter.

[4] Belknap, *History of New Hampshire*, says that eighty were killed. Governor Wentworth, writing immediately after the event, says "killed or captivated."

would have ended in a general massacre. Their broken column straggled forward in wild disorder, amid the din of whoops and shrieks, till they reached the French advance-guard, which consisted of Canadians; and here they demanded protection from the officers, who refused to give it, telling them that they must take to the woods and shift for themselves. Frye was seized by a number of Indians, who, brandishing spears and tomahawks, threatened him with death and tore off his clothing, leaving nothing but breeches, shoes, and shirt. Repelled by the officers of the guard, he made for the woods. A Connecticut soldier who was present says of him that he leaped upon an Indian who stood in his way, disarmed and killed him, and then escaped; but Frye himself does not mention the incident. Captain Burke, also of the Massachusetts regiment, was stripped, after a violent struggle, of all his clothes; then broke loose, gained the woods, spent the night shivering in the thick grass of a marsh, and on the next day reached Fort Edward. Jonathan Carver, a provincial volunteer, declares that, when the tumult was at its height, he saw officers of the French army walking about at a little distance and talking with seeming unconcern. Three or four Indians seized him, brandished their tomahawks over his head, and tore off most of his clothes, while he vainly claimed protection from a sentinel, who called him an English dog, and violently pushed him back among his tormentors. Two of them were dragging him towards the neighboring swamp, when an English officer, stripped of everything but his scarlet breeches, ran by. One of Carver's captors sprang upon him, but was thrown to the ground; whereupon the other went to the aid of his comrade and drove his tomahawk into the back of the Englishman. As Carver turned to run, an English boy, about twelve years old, clung to him and begged for help. They ran on together for a moment, when the boy was seized, dragged from his protector, and, as Carver judged by his shrieks, was murdered. He himself escaped to the forest, and after three days of famine reached Fort Edward.

The bonds of discipline seem for the time to have been completely broken; for while Montcalm and his chief officers used every effort to restore order, even at the risk of their lives, many other officers, chiefly of the militia, failed atrociously to do their duty. How many English were killed it is impossible to tell with exactness. Roubaud says that he saw forty or fifty corpses scattered about the field. Lévis says fifty; which does not include the sick and wounded before murdered in the camp and fort. It is certain that six or seven hundred persons were carried off, stripped, and otherwise maltreated. Montcalm succeeded in recovering more than four hundred of them in the course of the day; and many of the French officers did what they could to relieve their wants by buying back from their captors the clothing that had been torn from them. Many of the fugitives had taken refuge in the fort, whither Monro himself had gone to demand protection for his followers; and here Roubaud presently found a crowd of half-frenzied women, crying in anguish for husbands and children. All the refugees and redeemed prisoners were afterwards conducted to the entrenched camp, where food and shelter were provided for them and a strong guard set for their protection until the fifteenth, when they were sent under an escort to Fort Edward. Here cannon had been fired at intervals to guide those who had fled to the woods, whence they came dropping in from day to day, half dead with famine.

On the morning after the massacre the Indians decamped in a body and set out for Montreal, carrying with them their plunder and some two hundred prisoners, who, it is said, could not be got out of their hands. The soldiers were set to the work of demolishing the English fort; and the task occupied several days. The barracks were torn down, and the huge pine-logs of the rampart thrown into a heap. The dead bodies that filled the casemates were added to the mass, and fire was set to the whole. The mighty funeral pyre blazed all night. Then, on the sixteenth, the army reimbarked. The din of ten thousand combatants, the rage, the terror, the agony, were gone; and no living thing was left but the wolves that gathered from the mountains to feast upon the dead.[1]

---

[1] The foregoing chapter rests largely on evidence never before brought to light, including the minute *Journal* of Bougainville,—a document which can hardly be commended too much,—the correspondence of Webb, a letter of Colonel Frye, written just after the massacre, and a journal of the siege, sent by him to Governor Pownall as his official report. Extracts from these, as well as from the affidavit of Dr. Whitworth, which is also new evidence, are given in Appendix F.

The Diary of Malartic and the correspondence of Montcalm, Lévis, Vaudreuil, and Bigot, also throw light on the campaign, as well as numerous reports of the siege, official and semi-official. The long letter of the Jesuit Roubaud, printed anonymously in the *Lettres Édifiantes et Curieuses*, gives a remarkably vivid account of what he saw. He was an intelligent person, who may be trusted where he has no motive for lying. Curious particulars about him will be found in a paper called, *The deplorable Case of Mr. Roubaud*, printed in the *Historical Magazine, Second Series*, VIII. 282. Compare Verreau, *Report on Canadian Archives, 1874*.

Impressions of the massacre at Fort William Henry have hitherto been derived chiefly from the narrative of Captain Jonathan Carver, in his *Travels*. He has discredited himself by his exaggeration of the number killed; but his account of what he himself saw tallies with that of the other witnesses. He is outdone in exaggeration by an anonymous French writer of the time, who seems rather pleased at the occurrence, and affirms that all the English were killed except seven hundred, these last being captured, so that none escaped (*Nouvelles du Canada envoyées de Montréal, Août, 1757*). Carver puts killed and captured together at fifteen hundred. Vaudreuil, who always makes light of Indian barbarities, goes to the other extreme, and avers that no more than five or six were killed. Lévis and Roubaud, who saw everything, and were certain not to exaggerate the number, give the most trustworthy evidence on this point. The capitulation, having been broken by the allies of France, was declared void by the British Government.

The Signal of Butchery. Montcalm, Bougainville, and several others say that the massacre was begun by the Abenakis of Panaouski. Father Martin, in quoting the letter in which Montcalm makes this statement, inserts the word *idolâtres*, which is not in the original. Dussieux and O'Callaghan give the passage correctly. This Abenaki band, ancestors of the present Penobscots, were no idolaters, but had been converted more than half a century. In the official list of the Indian allies they are set down among the Christians. Roubaud, who had charge of them during the expedition, speaks of these and other converts with singular candor: "Vous avez dû vous apercevoir . . . que nos sauvages, pour être Chrétiens, n'en sont pas plus irrépréhensibles dans leur conduite."

PART TWO

16

A Winter of
Discontent

1757, 1758

BOASTS OF LOUDON · A MUTINOUS MILITIA · PANIC · ACCUSATIONS OF
VAUDREUIL · HIS WEAKNESS · INDIAN BARBARITIES · DESTRUCTION OF
GERMAN FLATS · DISCONTENT OF MONTCALM · FESTIVITIES AT MONTREAL
· MONTCALM'S RELATIONS WITH THE GOVERNOR · FAMINE · RIOTS ·
MUTINY · WINTER AT TICONDEROGA · A DESPERATE BUSH-FIGHT ·
DEFEAT OF THE RANGERS · ADVENTURES OF ROCHE AND PRINGLE

Loudon, on his way back from Halifax, was at sea off the
coast of Nova Scotia when a despatch-boat from Governor Pownall of Massachusetts startled him with news that Fort William Henry was attacked; and a few days after he learned by another
boat that the fort was taken and the capitulation "inhumanly and vil-
lanously broken." On this he sent Webb orders to hold the enemy in
check without risking a battle till he should himself arrive. "I am on
the way," these were his words, "with a force sufficient to turn the
scale, with God's assistance; and then I hope we shall teach the French
to comply with the laws of nature and humanity. For although I abhor
barbarity, the knowledge I have of Mr. Vaudreuil's behavior when in
Louisiana, from his own letters in my possession, and the murders committed at Oswego and now at Fort William Henry, will oblige me to
make those gentlemen sick of such inhuman villany whenever it is in
my power." He reached New York on the last day of August, and heard
that the French had withdrawn. He nevertheless sent his troops up the

Hudson, thinking, he says, that he might still attack Ticonderoga; a wild scheme, which he soon abandoned, if he ever seriously entertained it.[1]

Webb had remained at Fort Edward in mortal dread of attack. Johnson had joined him with a band of Mohawks; and on the day when Fort William Henry surrendered there had been some talk of attempting to throw succors into it by night. Then came the news of its capture; and now, when it was too late, tumultuous mobs of militia came pouring in from the neighboring provinces. In a few days thousands of them were bivouacked on the fields about Fort Edward, doing nothing, disgusted and mutinous, declaring that they were ready to fight, but not to lie still without tents, blankets, or kettles. Webb writes on the fourteenth that most of those from New York had deserted, threatening to kill their officers if they tried to stop them. Delancey ordered them to be fired upon. A sergeant was shot, others were put in arrest, and all was disorder till the seventeenth; when Webb, learning that the French were gone, sent them back to their homes.[2]

Close on the fall of Fort William Henry came crazy rumors of disaster, running like wildfire through the colonies. The number and ferocity of the enemy were grossly exaggerated; there was a cry that they would seize Albany and New York itself;[3] while it was reported that Webb, as much frightened as the rest, was for retreating to the Highlands of the Hudson.[4] This was the day after the capitulation, when a part only of the militia had yet appeared. If Montcalm had seized the moment, and marched that afternoon to Fort Edward, it is not impossible that in the confusion he might have carried it by a *coup-de-main*.

Here was an opportunity for Vaudreuil, and he did not fail to use it. Jealous of his rival's exploit, he spared no pains to tarnish it; complaining that Montcalm had stopped half way on the road to success, and, instead of following his instructions, had contented himself with one victory when he should have gained two. But the Governor had enjoined upon him as a matter of the last necessity that the Canadians should be at their homes before September to gather the crops, and he would have been the first to complain had the injunction been disre-

---

[1]*Loudon to Webb, 20 Aug. 1757. Loudon to Holdernesse, Oct. 1757. Loudon to Pownall, 16 [18?] Aug. 1757.* A passage in this last letter, in which Loudon says that he shall, if prevented by headwinds from getting into New York, disembark the troops on Long Island, is perverted by that ardent partisan, William Smith, the historian of New York, into the absurd declaration "that he should encamp on Long Island for the defence of the continent."

[2]*Delancey to [Holdernesse?], 24 Aug. 1757.*

[3]*Captain Christie to Governor Wentworth, 11 Aug. 1757. Ibid., to Governor Pownall, same date.*

[4]Smith, *Hist. N. Y.*, Part II. 254.

garded. To besiege Fort Edward was impossible, as Montcalm had no means of transporting cannon thither; and to attack Webb without them was a risk which he had not the rashness to incur.

It was Bougainville who first brought Vaudreuil the news of the success on Lake George. A day or two after his arrival, the Indians, who had left the army after the massacre, appeared at Montreal, bringing about two hundred English prisoners. The Governor rebuked them for breaking the capitulation, on which the heathen savages of the West declared that it was not their fault, but that of the converted Indians, who, in fact, had first raised the war-whoop. Some of the prisoners were presently bought from them at the price of two kegs of brandy each; and the inevitable consequences followed.

"I thought," writes Bougainville, "that the Governor would have told them they should have neither provisions nor presents till all the English were given up; that he himself would have gone to their huts and taken the prisoners from them; and that the inhabitants would be forbidden, under the severest penalties, from selling or giving them brandy. I saw the contrary; and my soul shuddered at the sights my eyes beheld. On the fifteenth, at two o'clock, in the presence of the whole town, they killed one of the prisoners, put him into the kettle, and forced his wretched countrymen to eat of him." The Intendant Bigot, the friend of the Governor, confirms this story; and another French writer says that they "compelled mothers to eat the flesh of their children."[1] Bigot declares that guns, canoes, and other presents were given to the Western tribes before they left Montreal; and he adds, "they must be sent home satisfied at any cost." Such were the pains taken to preserve allies who were useful chiefly through the terror inspired by their diabolical cruelties. This time their ferocity cost them dear. They had dug up and scalped the corpses in the graveyard of Fort William Henry, many of which were remains of victims of the small-pox; and the savages caught the disease, which is said to have made great havoc among them.[2]

Vaudreuil, in reporting what he calls "my capture of Fort William Henry," takes great credit to himself for his "generous procedures" to-

---

[1]"En chemin faisant et même en entrant à Montréal ils les ont mangés et fait manger aux autres prisonniers." *Bigot au Ministre, 24 Août, 1757.*

"Des sauvages ont fait manger aux mères la chair de leurs enfants." *Jugement impartial sur les Opérations militaires en Canada.* A French diary kept in Canada at this time, and captured at sea, is cited by Hutchinson as containing similar statements.

[2]One of these corpses was that of Richard Rogers, brother of the noted partisan Robert Rogers. He had died of small-pox some time before. *Rogers, Journals, 55, note.*

wards the English prisoners; alluding, it seems, to his having bought some of them from the Indians with the brandy which was sure to cause the murder of others.[1] His obsequiousness to his red allies did not cease with permitting them to kill and devour before his eyes those whom he was bound in honor and duty to protect. "He let them do what they pleased," says a French contemporary; "they were seen roaming about Montreal, knife in hand, threatening everybody, and often insulting those they met. When complaint was made, he said nothing. Far from it; instead of reproaching them, he loaded them with gifts, in the belief that their cruelty would then relent."[2]

Nevertheless, in about a fortnight all, or nearly all, the surviving prisoners were bought out of their clutches; and then, after a final distribution of presents and a grand debauch at La Chine, the whole savage rout paddled for their villages.

The campaign closed in November with a partisan exploit on the Mohawk. Here, at a place called German Flats, on the farthest frontier, there was a thriving settlement of German peasants from the Palatinate, who were so ill-disposed towards the English that Vaudreuil had had good hope of stirring them to revolt, while at the same time persuading their neighbors, the Oneida Indians, to take part with France.[3] As his measures to this end failed, he resolved to attack them. Therefore, at three o'clock in the morning of the twelfth of November, three hundred colony troops, Canadians and Indians, under an officer named Belêtre, wakened the unhappy peasants by a burst of yells, and attacked the small picket forts which they had built as places of refuge. These were taken one by one and set on fire. The sixty dwellings of the settlement, with their barns and outhouses, were all burned, forty or fifty of the inhabitants were killed, and about three times that number, chiefly women and children, were made prisoners, including Johan Jost Petrie, the magistrate of the place. Fort Herkimer was not far off, with a garrison of two hundred men under Captain Townshend, who at the first alarm sent out a detachment too weak to arrest the havoc; while Belêtre, unable to carry off his booty, set on his followers to the work of destruction, killed a great number of hogs, sheep, cattle, and horses, and then made a hasty retreat. Lord Howe, pushing up the river from Schenectady with troops and militia, found nothing but an abandoned slaughter-field. Vaudreuil reported the affair to the Court, and summed

[1]*Vaudreuil au Ministre, 15 Sept. 1757.*
[2]*Mémoires sur le Canada, 1749–1760.*
[3]*Dépêches de Vaudreuil, 1757.*

up the results with pompous egotism: "I have ruined the plans of the English; I have disposed the Five Nations to attack them; I have carried consternation and terror into all those parts."[1]

Montcalm, his summer work over, went to Montreal; and thence in September to Quebec, a place more to his liking. "Come as soon as you can," he wrote to Bourlamaque, "and I will tell a certain fair lady how eager you are." Even Quebec was no paradise for him; and he writes again to the same friend: "My heart and my stomach are both ill at ease, the latter being the worse." To his wife he says: "The price of everything is rising. I am ruining myself; I owe the treasurer twelve thousand francs. I long for peace and for you. In spite of the public distress, we have balls and furious gambling." In February he returned to Montreal in a sleigh on the ice of the St. Lawrence,—a mode of travelling which he describes as cold but delicious. Montreal pleased him less than ever, especially as he was not in favor at what he calls the Court, meaning the circle of the Governor-General. "I find this place so amusing," he writes ironically to Bourlamaque, "that I wish Holy Week could be lengthened, to give me a pretext for neither making nor receiving visits, staying at home, and dining there almost alone. Burn all my letters, as I do yours." And in the next week: "Lent and devotion have upset my stomach and given me a cold; which does not prevent me from having the Governor-General at dinner to-day to end his lenten fast, according to custom here." Two days after he announces: "To-day a grand dinner at Martel's; twenty-three persons, all big-wigs (*les grosses perruques*); no ladies. We still have got to undergo those of Péan, Deschambault, and the Chevalier de Lévis. I spend almost every evening in my chamber, the place I like best, and where I am least bored."

With the opening spring there were changes in the modes of amusement. Picnics began, Vaudreuil and his wife being often of the party, as too was Lévis. The Governor also made visits of compliment at the houses of the seigniorial proprietors along the river; "very much," says Montcalm, as "Henri IV. did to the bourgeois notables of Paris. I live as usual, fencing in the morning, dining, and passing the evening at

---

[1] *Loudon to Pitt, 14 Feb. 1758. Vaudreuil au Ministre, 12 Fév. 1758. Ibid., 28 Nov. 1758.* Bougainville, *Journal. Summary of M. de Belêtre's Campaign,* in *N. Y. Col. Docs.,* X. 672. Extravagant reports of the havoc made were sent to France. It was pretended that three thousand cattle, three thousand sheep (Vaudreuil says four thousand), and from five hundred to fifteen hundred horses were destroyed, with other personal property to the amount of 1,500,000 livres. These official falsehoods are contradicted in a letter from Quebec, *Daine au Maréchal de Belleisle, 19 Mai, 1758.* Lévis says that the whole population of the settlement, men, women, and children, was not above three hundred.

home or at the Governor's. Péan has gone up to La Chine to spend six days with the reigning sultana [*Péan's wife, mistress of Bigot*]. As for me, my *ennui* increases. I don't know what to do, or say, or read, or where to go; and I think that at the end of the next campaign I shall ask bluntly, blindly, for my recall, only because I am bored."[1]

His relations with Vaudreuil were a constant annoyance to him, notwithstanding the mask of mutual civility. "I never," he tells his mother, "ask for a place in the colony troops for anybody. You need not be an Œdipus to guess this riddle. Here are four lines from Corneille:—

> " 'Mon crime véritable est d'avoir aujourd'hui
> Plus de nom que . . . [*Vaudreuil*], plus de vertus que lui,
> Et c'est de là que part cette secrète haine
> Que le temps ne rendra que plus forte et plus pleine.'

Nevertheless I live here on good terms with everybody, and do my best to serve the King. If they could but do without me; if they could but spring some trap on me, or if I should happen to meet with some check!"

Vaudreuil meanwhile had written to the Court in high praise of Lévis, hinting that he, and not Montcalm, ought to have the chief command.[2]

Under the hollow gayeties of the ruling class lay a great public distress, which broke at last into riot. Towards midwinter no flour was to be had in Montreal; and both soldiers and people were required to accept a reduced ration, partly of horse-flesh. A mob gathered before the Governor's house, and a deputation of women beset him, crying out that the horse was the friend of man, and that religion forbade him to be eaten. In reply he threatened them with imprisonment and hanging; but with little effect, and the crowd dispersed, only to stir up the soldiers quartered in the houses of the town. The colony regulars, ill-disciplined at the best, broke into mutiny, and excited the battalion of Béarn to join them. Vaudreuil was helpless; Montcalm was in Quebec; and the task of dealing with the mutineers fell upon Lévis, who proved equal to the crisis, took a high tone, threatened death to the first soldier who should refuse horse-flesh, assured them at the same time that he ate it every day himself, and by a characteristic mingling of authority and tact, quelled the storm.[3]

The prospects of the next campaign began to open. Captain Pouchot

[1] *Montcalm à Bourlamaque, 22 Mai, 1758.*
[2] *Vaudreuil au Ministre de la Marine, 16 Sept. 1757. Ibid., au Ministre de la Guerre, même date.*
[3] Bougainville, *Journal. Montcalm à Mirepoix, 20 Avril, 1758.* Lévis, *Journal de la Guerre du Canada.*

had written from Niagara that three thousand savages were waiting to be let loose against the English borders. "What a scourge!" exclaims Bougainville. "Humanity groans at being forced to use such monsters. What can be done against an invisible enemy, who strikes and vanishes, swift as the lightning? It is the destroying angel." Captain Hebecourt kept watch and ward at Ticonderoga, begirt with snow and ice, and much plagued by English rangers, who sometimes got into the ditch itself.[1] This was to reconnoitre the place in preparation for a winter attack which Loudon had planned, but which, like the rest of his schemes, fell to the ground.[2] Towards midwinter a band of these intruders captured two soldiers and butchered some fifteen cattle close to the fort, leaving tied to the horns of one of them a note addressed to the commandant in these terms: "I am obliged to you, sir, for the rest you have allowed me to take and the fresh meat you have sent me. I shall take good care of my prisoners. My compliments to the Marquis of Montcalm." Signed, Rogers.[3]

A few weeks later Hebecourt had his revenge. About the middle of March a report came to Montreal that a large party of rangers had been cut to pieces a few miles from Ticonderoga, and that Rogers himself was among the slain. This last announcement proved false; but the rangers had suffered a crushing defeat. Colonel Haviland, commanding at Fort Edward, sent a hundred and eighty of them, men and officers, on a scouting party towards Ticonderoga; and Captain Pringle and Lieutenant Roche, of the twenty-seventh regiment, joined them as volunteers, no doubt through a love of hardy adventure, which was destined to be fully satisfied. Rogers commanded the whole. They passed down Lake George on the ice under cover of night, and then, as they neared the French outposts, pursued their way by land behind Rogers Rock and the other mountains of the western shore. On the preceding day, the twelfth of March, Hebecourt had received a reinforcement of two hundred Mission Indians and a body of Canadians. The Indians had no sooner arrived than, though nominally Christians, they consulted the spirits, by whom they were told that the English were coming. On this they sent out scouts, who came back breathless, declaring that they had found a great number of snow-shoe tracks. The superhuman warning being thus confirmed, the whole body of Indians, joined by a band of Canadians and a number of volunteers from the

[1] *Montcalm à Bourlamaque, 28 Mars, 1758.*
[2] *Loudon to Pitt, 14 Feb. 1758.*
[3] *Journal de ce qui s'est passé en Canada, 1757, 1758.* Compare Rogers, *Journals,* 72–75.

regulars, set out to meet the approaching enemy, and took their way up the valley of Trout Brook, a mountain gorge that opens from the west upon the valley of Ticonderoga.

Towards three o'clock on the afternoon of that day Rogers had reached a point nearly west of the mountain that bears his name. The rough and rocky ground was buried four feet in snow, and all around stood the gray trunks of the forest, bearing aloft their skeleton arms and tangled intricacy of leafless twigs. Close on the right was a steep hill, and at a little distance on the left was the brook, lost under ice and snow. A scout from the front told Rogers that a party of Indians was approaching along the bed of the frozen stream, on which he ordered his men to halt, face to that side, and advance cautiously. The Indians soon appeared, and received a fire that killed some of them and drove back the rest in confusion.

Not suspecting that they were but an advance-guard, about half the rangers dashed in pursuit, and were soon met by the whole body of the enemy. The woods rang with yells and musketry. In a few minutes some fifty of the pursuers were shot down, and the rest driven back in disorder upon their comrades. Rogers formed them all on the slope of the hill; and here they fought till sunset with stubborn desperation, twice repulsing the overwhelming numbers of the assailants, and thwarting all their efforts to gain the heights in the rear. The combatants were often not twenty yards apart, and sometimes they were mixed together. At length a large body of Indians succeeded in turning the right flank of the rangers. Lieutenant Phillips and a few men were sent by Rogers to oppose the movement; but they quickly found themselves surrounded, and after a brave defence surrendered on a pledge of good treatment. Rogers now advised the volunteers, Pringle and Roche, to escape while there was time, and offered them a sergeant as guide; but they gallantly resolved to stand by him. Eight officers and more than a hundred rangers lay dead and wounded in the snow. Evening was near and the forest was darkening fast, when the few survivors broke and fled. Rogers with about twenty followers escaped up the mountain; and gathering others about him, made a running fight against the Indian pursuers, reached Lake George, not without fresh losses, and after two days of misery regained Fort Edward with the remnant of his band. The enemy on their part suffered heavily, the chief loss falling on the Indians; who, to revenge themselves, murdered all the wounded and nearly all the prisoners, and tying Lieutenant Phillips and his men to trees, hacked them to pieces.

Captain Pringle and Lieutenant Roche had become separated from the other fugitives; and, ignorant of woodcraft, they wandered by moonlight amid the desolation of rocks and snow, till early in the night they met a man whom they knew as a servant of Rogers, and who said that he could guide them to Fort Edward. One of them had lost his snow-shoes in the fight; and, crouching over a miserable fire of broken sticks, they worked till morning to make a kind of substitute with forked branches, twigs, and a few leather strings. They had no hatchet to cut firewood, no blankets, no overcoats, and no food except part of a Bologna sausage and a little ginger which Pringle had brought with him. There was no game; not even a squirrel was astir; and their chief sustenance was juniper-berries and the inner bark of trees. But their worst calamity was the helplessness of their guide. His brain wandered; and while always insisting that he knew the country well, he led them during four days hither and thither among a labyrinth of nameless mountains, clambering over rocks, wading through snowdrifts, struggling among fallen trees, till on the fifth day they saw with despair that they had circled back to their own starting-point. On the next morning, when they were on the ice of Lake George, not far from Rogers Rock, a blinding storm of sleet and snow drove in their faces. Spent as they were, it was death to stop; and bending their heads against the blast, they fought their way forward, now on the ice, and now in the adjacent forest, till in the afternoon the storm ceased, and they found themselves on the bank of an unknown stream. It was the outlet of the lake; for they had wandered into the valley of Ticonderoga, and were not three miles from the French fort. In crossing the torrent Pringle lost his gun, and was near losing his life. All three of the party were drenched to the skin; and, becoming now for the first time aware of where they were, they resolved on yielding themselves prisoners to save their lives. Night, however, again found them in the forest. Their guide became delirious, saw visions of Indians all around, and, murmuring incoherently, straggled off a little way, seated himself in the snow, and was soon dead. The two officers, themselves but half alive, walked all night round a tree to keep the blood in motion. In the morning, again toiling on, they presently saw the fort across the intervening snowfields, and approached it, waving a white handkerchief. Several French officers dashed towards them at full speed, and reached them in time to save them from the clutches of the Indians, whose camps were near at hand. They were kindly treated, recovered from the effects of their frightful ordeal, and were afterwards exchanged. Pringle lived to old age, and died in 1800, senior major-general of the British army.[1]

---

[1]Rogers, two days after reaching Fort Edward, made a detailed report of the fight, which was printed in the *New Hampshire Gazette* and other provincial papers. It is substantially incorporated

in his published *Journals*, which also contain a long letter from Pringle to Colonel Haviland, dated at Carillon (Ticonderoga), 28 March, and giving an excellent account of his and Roche's adventures. It was sent by a flag of truce, which soon after arrived from Fort Edward with a letter for Vaudreuil. The French accounts of the fight are *Hebecourt à [Vaudreuil?], 15 Mars, 1758. Montcalm au Ministre de la Guerre, 10 Avril, 1758. Doreil à Belleisle, 30 Avril, 1758.* Bougainville, *Journal. Relation de l'Affaire de Roger, 19 Mars, 1758. Autre Relation, même date.* Lévis, *Journal.* According to Lévis, the French force consisted of 250 Indians and Canadians, and a number of officers, cadets, and soldiers. Rogers puts it at 700. Most of the French writers put the force of the rangers, correctly, at about 180. Rogers reports his loss at 125. None of the wounded seem to have escaped, being either murdered after the fight, or killed by exposure in the woods. The Indians brought in 144 scalps, having no doubt divided some of them, after their ingenious custom. Rogers threw off his overcoat during the fight, and it was found on the field, with his commission in the pocket; whence the report of his death. There is an unsupported tradition that he escaped by sliding on his snow-shoes down a precipice of Rogers Rock.

17

Bigot

1753–1760

His Life and Character · Canadian Society · Official Festivities ·
A Party of Pleasure · Hospitalities of Bigot · Desperate
Gambling · Château Bigot · Canadian Ladies · Cadet ·
La Friponne · Official Rascality · Methods of Peculation · Cruel
Frauds on the Acadians · Military Corruption · Péan · Love
and Knavery · Varin and his Partners · Vaudreuil and the
Peculators · He defends Bigot; praises Cadet and Péan ·
Canadian Finances · Peril of Bigot · Threats of the Minister ·
Evidence of Montcalm · Impending Ruin of the Confederates

At this stormy epoch of Canadian history the sinister
figure of the Intendant Bigot moves conspicuous on
the scene. Not that he was answerable for all the manifold corruption
that infected the colony, for much of it was rife before his time, and
had a vitality of its own; but his office and character made him the
centre of it, and, more than any other man, he marshalled and organized the forces of knavery.

In the dual government of Canada the Governor represented the
King and commanded the troops; while the Intendant was charged with
trade, finance, justice, and all other departments of civil administration.[1] In former times the two functionaries usually quarrelled; but between Vaudreuil and Bigot there was perfect harmony.

[1] See *Old Régime in Canada.*

François Bigot, in the words of his biographer, was "born in the bosom of the magistracy," both his father and his grandfather having held honorable positions in the parliament of Bordeaux.[1] In appearance he was not prepossessing, though his ugly, pimpled face was joined with easy and agreeable manners. In spite of indifferent health, he was untiring both in pleasure and in work, a skilful man of business, of great official experience, energetic, good-natured, free-handed, ready to oblige his friends and aid them in their needs at the expense of the King, his master; fond of social enjoyments, lavish in hospitality.

A year or two before the war began, the engineer Franquet was sent from France to strengthen Louisbourg and inspect the defences of Canada. He kept a copious journal, full of curious observation, and affording bright glimpses not only of the social life of the Intendant, but of Canadian society in the upper or official class. Thus, among various matters of the kind, he gives us the following. Bigot, who was in Quebec, had occasion to go to Montreal to meet the Governor; and this official journey was turned into a pleasure excursion, of which the King paid all the costs. Those favored with invitations, a privilege highly prized, were Franquet, with seven or eight military officers and a corresponding number of ladies, including the wife of Major Péan, of whom Bigot was enamoured. A chief steward, cooks, servants, and other attendants, followed the party. The guests had been requested to send their portmanteaus to the Intendant's Palace six days before, that they might be sent forward on sledges along with bedding, table service, cooking utensils, and numberless articles of comfort and luxury. Orders were given to the inhabitants along the way, on pain of imprisonment, to level the snowdrifts and beat the road smooth with ox-teams, as also to provide relays of horses. It is true that they were well paid for this last service; so well that the hire of a horse to Montreal and back again would cost the King the entire value of the animal. On the eighth of February the party met at the palace; and after a grand dinner set out upon their journey in twenty or more sleighs, some with two guests and a driver, and the rest with servants and attendants. The procession passed at full trot along St. Vallier street amid the shouts of an admiring crowd, stopped towards night at Pointe-aux-Trembles, where each looked for lodging; and then they all met and supped with the Intendant. The militia captain of the place was ordered to have fresh horses ready at seven in the morning, when Bigot regaled his friends with tea,

---

[1] *Procès de Bigot, Cadet, et autres, Mémoire pour Messire François Bigot, accusé, contre Monsieur le Procureur-Général du Roi, accusateur.*

coffee, and chocolate, after which they set out again, drove to Cap-Santé, and stopped two hours at the house of the militia captain to breakfast and warm themselves. In the afternoon they reached Ste. Anne-de-la-Pérade, when Bigot gave them a supper at the house in which he lodged, and they spent the evening at cards.

The next morning brought them to Three Rivers, where Madame Marin, Franquet's travelling companion, wanted to stop to see her sister, the wife of Rigaud, who was then governor of the place. Madame de Rigaud, being ill, received her visitors in bed, and ordered an ample dinner to be provided for them; after which they returned to her chamber for coffee and conversation. Then they all set out again, saluted by the cannon of the fort.

Their next stopping-place was Isle-au-Castor, where, being seated at cards before supper, they were agreeably surprised by the appearance of the Governor, who had come down from Montreal to meet them with four officers, Duchesnaye, Marin, Le Mercier, and Péan. Many were the embraces and compliments; and in the morning they all journeyed on together, stopping towards night at the largest house they could find, where their servants took away the partitions to make room, and they sat down to a supper, followed by the inevitable game of cards. On the next night they reached Montreal and were lodged at the intendency, the official residence of the hospitable Bigot. The succeeding day was spent in visiting persons of eminence and consideration, among whom are to be noted the names, soon to become notorious, of Varin, naval commissary, Martel, King's storekeeper, Antoine Penisseault, and François Maurin. A succession of festivities followed, including the benediction of three flags for a band of militia on their way to the Ohio. All persons of quality in Montreal were invited on this occasion, and the Governor gave them a dinner and a supper. Bigot, however, outdid him in the plenitude of his hospitality, since, in the week before Lent, forty guests supped every evening at his table, and dances, masquerades, and cards consumed the night.[1]

His chief abode was at Quebec, in the capacious but somewhat ugly building known as the Intendant's Palace. Here it was his custom during the war to entertain twenty persons at dinner every day; and there was also a hall for dancing, with a gallery to which the citizens were admitted as spectators.[2] The bounteous Intendant provided a separate dancing-hall for the populace; and, though at the same time he plun-

---

[1] Franquet, *Journal.*
[2] De Gaspé, *Mémoires,* 119.

dered and ruined them, his gracious demeanor long kept him a place in their hearts. Gambling was the chief feature of his entertainments, and the stakes grew deeper as the war went on. He played desperately himself, and early in 1758 lost two hundred and four thousand francs,—a loss which he well knew how to repair. Besides his official residence on the banks of the St. Charles, he had a country house about five miles distant, a massive old stone building in the woods at the foot of the mountain of Charlesbourg; its ruins are now known as Château Bigot. In its day it was called the Hermitage; though the uses to which it was applied savored nothing of asceticism. Tradition connects it and its owner with a romantic, but more than doubtful, story of love, jealousy, and murder.

The chief Canadian families were so social in their habits and so connected by intermarriage that, along with the French civil and military officers of the colonial establishment, they formed a society whose members all knew each other, like the corresponding class in Virginia. There was among them a social facility and ease rare in democratic communities; and in the ladies of Quebec and Montreal were often seen graces which visitors from France were astonished to find at the edge of a wilderness. Yet this small though lively society had anomalies which grew more obtrusive towards the close of the war. Knavery makes strange companions; and at the tables of high civil officials and colony officers of rank sat guests as boorish in manners as they were worthless in character.

Foremost among these was Joseph Cadet, son of a butcher at Quebec, who at thirteen went to sea as a pilot's boy, then kept the cows of an inhabitant of Charlesbourg, and at last took up his father's trade and prospered in it.[1] In 1756 Bigot got him appointed commissary-general, and made a contract with him which flung wide open the doors of peculation. In the next two years Cadet and his associates, Péan, Maurin, Corpron, and Penisseault, sold to the King, for about twenty-three million francs, provisions which cost them eleven millions, leaving a net profit of about twelve millions. It was not legally proved that the Intendant shared Cadet's gains; but there is no reasonable doubt that he did so. Bigot's chief profits rose, however, from other sources. It was his business to see that the King's storehouses for the supply of troops, militia, and Indians were kept well stocked. To this end he and Bréard, naval comptroller at Quebec, made a partnership with the commercial house of Gradis and Son at Bordeaux. He next told the Colo-

---

[1] *Procès de Bigot, Cadet, et autres, Mémoire pour Messire François Bigot.* Compare *Mémoires sur le Canada,* 1749–1760.

nial Minister that there were stores enough already in Canada to last
three years, and that it would be more to the advantage of the King to
buy them in the colony than to take the risk of sending them from
France.[1] Gradis and Son then shipped them to Canada in large quantities, while Bréard or his agent declared at the custom-house that they
belonged to the King, and so escaped the payment of duties. They were
then, as occasion rose, sold to the King at a huge profit, always under
fictitious names. Often they were sold to some favored merchant or
speculator, who sold them in turn to Bigot's confederate, the King's
storekeeper; and sometimes they passed through several successive
hands, till the price rose to double or triple the first cost, the Intendant
and his partners sharing the gains with friends and allies. They would
let nobody else sell to the King; and thus a grinding monopoly was
established, to the great profit of those who held it.[2]

Under the name of a trader named Claverie, Bigot, some time before
the war, set up a warehouse on land belonging to the King and not far
from his own palace. Here the goods shipped from Bordeaux were collected, to be sold in retail to the citizens, and in wholesale to favored
merchants and the King. This establishment was popularly known as
La Friponne, or The Cheat. There was another Friponne at Montreal,
which was leagued with that of Quebec, and received goods from it.

Bigot and his accomplices invented many other profitable frauds.
Thus he was charged with the disposal of the large quantity of furs
belonging to his master, which it was his duty to sell at public auction,
after due notice, to the highest bidder. Instead of this, he sold them
privately at a low price to his own confederates. It was also his duty to
provide transportation for troops, artillery, provisions, and stores, in
which he made good profit by letting to the King, at high prices, boats
or vessels which he had himself bought or hired for the purpose.[3]

Yet these and other illicit gains still left him but the second place as
public plunderer. Cadet, the commissary-general, reaped an ampler harvest, and became the richest man in the colony. One of the operations
of this scoundrel, accomplished with the help of Bigot, consisted in
buying for six hundred thousand francs a quantity of stores belonging
to the King, and then selling them back to him for one million four
hundred thousand.[4] It was further shown on his trial that in 1759 he
received 1,614,354 francs for stores furnished at the post of Miramichi,

[1] *Bigot au Ministre*, 8 Oct. 1749.
[2] *Procès de Bigot, Cadet, et autres. Mémoire sur les Fraudes commises dans la Colonie.* Compare Mémoires sur le Canada, 1749–1760.
[3] *Jugement rendu souverainement dans l'Affaire du Canada.*
[4] *Procès de Bigot, Cadet, et autres, Requête du Procureur-Général,* 19 Déc. 1761.

while the value of those actually furnished was but 889,544 francs; thus giving him a fraudulent profit of more than seven hundred and twenty-four thousand.[1] Cadet's chief resource was the falsification of accounts. The service of the King in Canada was fenced about by rigid formalities. When supplies were wanted at any of the military posts, the commandant made a requisition specifying their nature and quantity, while, before pay could be drawn for them, the King's storekeeper, the local commissary, and the inspector must set their names as vouchers to the list, and finally Bigot must sign it.[2] But precautions were useless where all were leagued to rob the King. It appeared on Cadet's trial that by gifts of wine, brandy, or money he had bribed the officers, both civil and military, at all the principal forts to attest the truth of accounts in which the supplies furnished by him were set at more than twice their true amount. Of the many frauds charged against him there was one peculiarly odious. Large numbers of refugee Acadians were to be supplied with rations to keep them alive. Instead of wholesome food, mouldered and unsalable salt cod was sent them, and paid for by the King at inordinate prices.[3] It was but one of many heartless outrages practised by Canadian officials on this unhappy people.

Cadet told the Intendant that the inhabitants were hoarding their grain, and got an order from him requiring them to sell it at a low fixed price, on pain of having it seized. Thus nearly the whole fell into his hands. Famine ensued; and he then sold it at a great profit, partly to the King, and partly to its first owners. Another of his devices was to sell provisions to the King which, being sent to the outlying forts, were falsely reported as consumed; on which he sold them to the King a second time. Not without reason does a writer of the time exclaim: "This is the land of abuses, ignorance, prejudice, and all that is monstrous in government. Peculation, monopoly, and plunder have become a bottomless abyss."[4]

The command of a fort brought such opportunities of making money that, according to Bougainville, the mere prospect of appointment to it for the usual term of three years was thought enough for a young man to marry upon. It was a favor in the gift of the Governor, who was accused of sharing the profits. These came partly from the fur-trade, and still more from frauds of various kinds. For example, a requisition was made for supplies as gifts to the Indians in order to keep them

[1] Procès de Bigot, Cadet, et autres, Mémoire pour Messire François Bigot.
[2] Mémoire sur le Canada (Archives Nationales).
[3] Mémoires sur le Canada, 1749–1760.
[4] Considérations sur l'État présent du Canada.

friendly or send them on the war-path; and their number was put many times above the truth in order to get more goods, which the commandant and his confederates then bartered for furs on their own account, instead of giving them as presents. "And," says a contemporary, addressing the Colonial Minister, "those who treat the savages so basely are officers of the King, depositaries of his authority, ministers of that Great Onontio whom they call their father."[1] At the post of Green Bay, the partisan officer Marin, and Rigaud, the Governor's brother, made in a short time a profit of three hundred and twelve thousand francs.[2] "Why is it," asks Bougainville, "that of all which the King sends to the Indians two thirds are stolen, and the rest sold to them instead of being given?"[3]

The transportation of military stores gave another opportunity of plunder. The contractor would procure from the Governor or the local commandant an order requiring the inhabitants to serve him as boatmen, drivers, or porters, under a promise of exemption that year from duty as soldiers. This saved him his chief item of expense, and the profits of his contract rose in proportion.

A contagion of knavery ran through the official life of the colony; and to resist it demanded no common share of moral robustness. The officers of the troops of the line were not much within its influence; but those of the militia and colony regulars, whether of French or Canadian birth, shared the corruption of the civil service. Seventeen of them, including six chevaliers of St. Louis and eight commandants of forts, were afterwards arraigned for fraud and malversation, though some of the number were acquitted. Bougainville gives the names of four other Canadian officers as honorable exceptions to the general demoralization,—Benoît, Repentigny, Lainé, and Le Borgne; "not enough," he observes, "to save Sodom."

Conspicuous among these military thieves was Major Péan, whose qualities as a soldier have been questioned, but who nevertheless had shown almost as much vigor in serving the King during the Ohio campaign of 1753 as he afterwards displayed effrontery in cheating him. "Le petit Péan" had married a young wife, Mademoiselle Desméloizes, Canadian like himself, well born, and famed for beauty, vivacity, and wit. Bigot, who was near sixty, became her accepted lover; and the fortune of Péan was made. His first success seems to have taken him by

[1] *Ibid.*
[2] *Mémoire sur les Fraudes commises dans la Colonie.* Bougainville, *Mémoire sur l'État de la Nouvelle France.*
[3] Bougainville, *Journal.*

surprise. He had bought as a speculation a large quantity of grain, with money of the King lent him by the Intendant. Bigot, officially omnipotent, then issued an order raising the commodity to a price far above that paid by Péan, who thus made a profit of fifty thousand crowns.[1] A few years later his wealth was estimated at from two to four million francs. Madame Péan became a power in Canada, the dispenser of favors and offices; and all who sought opportunity to rob the King hastened to pay her their court. Péan, jilted by his own wife, made prosperous love to the wife of his partner, Penisseault; who, though the daughter of a Montreal tradesman, had the air of a woman of rank, and presided with dignity and grace at a hospitable board where were gathered the clerks of Cadet and other lesser lights of the administrative hierarchy. It was often honored by the presence of the Chevalier de Lévis, who, captivated by the charms of the hostess, condescended to a society which his friends condemned as unworthy of his station. He succeeded Péan in the graces of Madame Penisseault, and after the war took her with him to France; while the aggrieved husband found consolation in the wives of the small functionaries under his orders.[2]

Another prominent name on the roll of knavery was that of Varin, commissary of marine, and Bigot's deputy at Montreal, a Frenchman of low degree, small in stature, sharp witted, indefatigable, conceited, arrogant, headstrong, capricious, and dissolute. Worthless as he was, he found a place in the Court circle of the Governor, and aspired to supplant Bigot in the intendancy. To this end, as well as to save himself from justice, he had the fatuity to turn informer and lay bare the sins of his confederates, though forced at the same time to betray his own. Among his comrades and allies may be mentioned Deschenaux, son of a shoemaker at Quebec, and secretary to the Intendant; Martel, King's storekeeper at Montreal; the humpback Maurin, who is not to be confounded with the partisan officer Marin; and Corpron, a clerk whom several tradesmen had dismissed for rascality, but who was now in the confidence of Cadet, to whom he made himself useful, and in whose service he grew rich.

Canada was the prey of official jackals,—true lion's providers, since they helped to prepare a way for the imperial beast, who, roused at last from his lethargy, was gathering his strength to seize her for his own. Honesty could not be expected from a body of men clothed with arbitrary and ill-defined powers, ruling with absolute sway an unfortunate

---

[1]*Mémoires sur le Canada, 1749-1760. Mémoire sur les Fraudes*, etc. Compare Pouchot, I. 8.
[2]*Mémoires sur le Canada, 1749-1760.*

people who had no voice in their own destinies, and answerable only to an apathetic master three thousand miles away. Nor did the Canadian Church, though supreme, check the corruptions that sprang up and flourished under its eye. The Governor himself was charged with sharing the plunder; and though he was acquitted on his trial, it is certain that Bigot had him well in hand, that he was intimate with the chief robbers, and that they found help in his weak compliances and wilful blindness. He put his stepson, Le Verrier, in command at Michillimackinac, where, by fraud and the connivance of his stepfather, the young man made a fortune.[1] When the Colonial Minister berated the Intendant for maladministration, Vaudreuil became his advocate, and wrote thus in his defence: "I cannot conceal from you, Monseigneur, how deeply M. Bigot feels the suspicions expressed in your letters to him. He does not deserve them, I am sure. He is full of zeal for the service of the King; but as he is rich, or passes as such, and as he has merit, the ill-disposed are jealous, and insinuate that he has prospered at the expense of His Majesty. I am certain that it is not true, and that nobody is a better citizen than he, or has the King's interest more at heart."[2] For Cadet, the butcher's son, the Governor asked a patent of nobility as a reward for his services.[3] When Péan went to France in 1758, Vaudreuil wrote to the Colonial Minister: "I have great confidence in him. He knows the colony and its needs. You can trust all he says. He will explain everything in the best manner. I shall be extremely sensible to any kindness you may show him, and hope that when you know him you will like him as much as I do."[4]

Administrative corruption was not the only bane of Canada. Her financial condition was desperate. The ordinary circulating medium consisted of what was known as card money, and amounted to only a million of francs. This being insufficient, Bigot, like his predecessor Hocquart, issued promissory notes on his own authority, and made them legal tender. They were for sums from one franc to a hundred, and were called *ordonnances*. Their issue was blamed at Versailles as an encroachment on the royal prerogative, though they were recognized by the Ministry in view of the necessity of the case. Every autumn those who held them to any considerable amount might bring them to the colonial treasurer, who gave in return bills of exchange on the royal treasury in France. At first these bills were promptly paid; then delays

---

[1] *Mémoires sur le Canada, 1749–1760.*
[2] *Vaudreuil au Ministre, 15 Oct. 1759.*
[3] *Ibid., 7 Nov. 1759.*
[4] *Ibid., 6 Août, 1758.*

took place, and the notes depreciated; till in 1759 the Ministry, aghast at the amount, refused payment, and the utmost dismay and confusion followed.[1]

The vast jarring, discordant mechanism of corruption grew incontrollable; it seized upon Bigot, and dragged him, despite himself, into perils which his prudence would have shunned. He was becoming a victim to the rapacity of his own confederates, whom he dared not offend by refusing his connivance and his signature to frauds which became more and more recklessly audacious. He asked leave to retire from office, in the hope that his successor would bear the brunt of the ministerial displeasure. Péan had withdrawn already, and with the fruits of his plunder bought land in France, where he thought himself safe. But though the Intendant had long been an object of distrust, and had often been warned to mend his ways,[2] yet such was his energy, his executive power, and his fertility of resource, that in the crisis of the war it was hard to dispense with him. Neither his abilities, however, nor his strong connections in France, nor an ally whom he had secured in the bureau of the Colonial Minister himself, could avail him much longer; and the letters from Versailles became appalling in rebuke and menace.

"The ship 'Britannia,'" wrote the Minister, Berryer, "laden with goods such as are wanted in the colony, was captured by a privateer from St.-Malo, and brought into Quebec. You sold the whole cargo for eight hundred thousand francs. The purchasers made a profit of two millions. You bought back a part for the King at one million, or two hundred thousand more than the price for which you sold the whole. With conduct like this it is no wonder that the expenses of the colony become insupportable. The amount of your drafts on the treasury is frightful. The fortunes of your subordinates throw suspicion on your administration." And in another letter on the same day: "How could it happen that the small-pox among the Indians cost the King a million francs? What does this expense mean? Who is answerable for it? Is it the officers who command the posts, or is it the storekeepers? You give me no particulars. What has become of the immense quantity of provisions sent to Canada last year? I am forced to conclude that the King's stores are set down as consumed from the moment they arrive, and then sold to His Majesty at exorbitant prices. Thus the King buys

---

[1] *Réflexions sommaires sur le Commerce qui s'est fait en Canada. État présent du Canada.* Compare Stevenson, *Card Money of Canada,* in *Transactions of the Historical Society of Quebec, 1873–1875.*
[2] *Ordres du Roy et Dépêches des Ministres, 1751–1758.*

stores in France, and then buys them again in Canada. I no longer wonder at the immense fortunes made in the colony."[1] Some months later the Minister writes: "You pay bills without examination, and then find an error in your accounts of three million six hundred thousand francs. In the letters from Canada I see nothing but incessant speculation in provisions and goods, which are sold to the King for ten times more than they cost in France. For the last time, I exhort you to give these things your serious attention, for they will not escape from mine."[2]

"I write, Monsieur, to answer your last two letters, in which you tell me that instead of sixteen millions, your drafts on the treasury for 1758 will reach twenty-four millions, and that this year they will rise to from thirty-one to thirty-three millions. It seems, then, that there are no bounds to the expenses of Canada. They double almost every year, while you seem to give yourself no concern except to get them paid. Do you suppose that I can advise the King to approve such an administration? or do you think that you can take the immense sum of thirty-three millions out of the royal treasury by merely assuring me that you have signed drafts for it? This, too, for expenses incurred irregularly, often needlessly, always wastefully; which make the fortune of everybody who has the least hand in them, and about which you know so little that after reporting them at sixteen millions, you find two months after that they will reach twenty-four. You are accused of having given the furnishing of provisions to one man, who, under the name of commissary-general, has set what prices he pleased; of buying for the King at second or third hand what you might have got from the producer at half the price; of having in this and other ways made the fortunes of persons connected with you; and of living in splendor in the midst of a public misery, which all the letters from the colony agree in ascribing to bad administration, and in charging M. de Vaudreuil with weakness in not preventing."[3]

These drastic utterances seem to have been partly due to a letter written by Montcalm in cipher to the Maréchal de Belleisle, then minister of war. It painted the deplorable condition of Canada, and exposed without reserve the peculations and robberies of those intrusted with its interests. "It seems," said the General, "as if they were all hastening to make their fortunes before the loss of the colony; which

[1] *Le Ministre à Bigot, 19 Jan. 1759.*
[2] *Ibid., 29 Août, 1759.*
[3] *Le Ministre à Bigot, 29 Août, 1759* (second letter of this date).

many of them perhaps desire as a veil to their conduct." He gives
among other cases that of Le Mercier, chief of Canadian artillery, who
had come to Canada as a private soldier twenty years before, and had
so prospered on fraudulent contracts that he would soon be worth
nearly a million. "I have often," continues Montcalm, "spoken of these
expenditures to M. de Vaudreuil and M. Bigot; and each throws the
blame on the other."[1] And yet at the same time Vaudreuil was assuring
the Minister that Bigot was without blame.

Some two months before Montcalm wrote this letter, the Minister,
Berryer, sent a despatch to the Governor and Intendant which filled
them with ire and mortification. It ordered them to do nothing without
consulting the general of the French regulars, not only in matters of
war, but in all matters of administration touching the defence and preservation of the colony. A plainer proof of confidence on one hand and
distrust on the other could not have been given.[2]

One Querdisien-Tremais was sent from Bordeaux as an agent of Government to make investigation. He played the part of detective,
wormed himself into the secrets of the confederates, and after six
months of patient inquisition traced out four distinct combinations for
public plunder. Explicit orders were now given to Bigot, who, seeing
no other escape, broke with Cadet, and made him disgorge two millions
of stolen money. The Commissary-General and his partners became so
terrified that they afterwards gave up nearly seven millions more.[3]
Stormy events followed, and the culprits found shelter for a time amid
the tumults of war. Peculation did not cease, but a day of reckoning
was at hand.

---

[1] *Montcalm au Ministre de la Guerre, Lettre confidentielle, 12 Avril, 1759.*
[2] *Le Ministre à Vaudreuil et Bigot, 20 Fév. 1759.*
[3] *Procès de Bigot, Cadet, et autres, Mémoire pour François Bigot, 3me partie.*

NOTE.—The printed documents of the trial of Bigot and the other peculators include the defence
of Bigot, of which the first part occupies 303 quarto pages, and the second part 764. Among the
other papers are the arguments for Péan, Varin, Saint-Blin, Boishébert, Martel, Joncaire-Chabert,
and several more, along with the elaborate *Jugement rendu,* the *Requêtes du Procureur-Général,* the
Réponse aux Mémoires de M. Bigot et du Sieur Péan, etc., forming together five quarto volumes, all
of which I have carefully examined. These are in the Library of Harvard University. There is
another set, also of five volumes, in the Library of the Historical Society of Quebec, containing
most of the papers just mentioned, and, bound with them, various others in manuscript, among
which are documents in defence of Vaudreuil (printed in part), Estève, Corpron, Penisseault,
Maurin, and Bréard. I have examined this collection also. The manuscript *Ordres du Roy et Dépêches des Ministres, 1751–1760,* as well as the letters of Vaudreuil, Bougainville, Daine, Doreil,
and Montcalm throw much light on the maladministration of the time; as do many contemporary
documents, notably those entitled *Mémoire sur les Fraudes commises dans la Colonie, État présent du
Canada,* and *Mémoire sur le Canada* (Archives Nationales). The remarkable anonymous work

printed by the Historical Society of Quebec under the title *Mémoires sur le Canada depuis 1749 jusqu'à 1760*, is full of curious matter concerning Bigot and his associates which squares well with other evidence. This is the source from which Smith, in his *History of Canada* (Quebec, 1815), drew most of his information on the subject. A manuscript which seems to be the original draft of this valuable document was preserved at the Bastile, and, with other papers, was thrown into the street when that castle was destroyed. They were gathered up, and afterwards bought by a Russian named Dubrowski, who carried them to St. Petersburg. Lord Dufferin, when minister there, procured a copy of the manuscript in question, which is now in the keeping of Abbé H. Verreau at Montreal, to whose kindness I owe the opportunity of examining it. In substance it differs little from the printed work, though the language and the arrangement often vary from it. The author, whoever he may have been, was deeply versed in Canadian affairs of the time, and though often caustic, is generally trustworthy.

18

Pitt

1757–1758

FREDERIC OF PRUSSIA · THE COALITION AGAINST HIM · HIS DESPERATE
POSITION · ROSSBACH · LEUTHEN · REVERSES OF ENGLAND · WEAKNESS
OF THE MINISTRY · A CHANGE · PITT AND NEWCASTLE · CHARACTER OF
PITT · SOURCES OF HIS POWER · HIS AIMS · LOUIS XV. · POMPADOUR ·
SHE CONTROLS THE COURT AND DIRECTS THE WAR · GLOOMY PROSPECTS
OF ENGLAND · DISASTERS · THE NEW MINISTRY · INSPIRING INFLUENCE OF
PITT · THE TIDE TURNS · BRITISH VICTORIES · PITT'S PLANS FOR AMERICA
· LOUISBOURG, TICONDEROGA, DUQUESNE · NEW COMMANDERS · NAVAL
BATTLES

The war kindled in the American forest was now raging
in full conflagration among the kingdoms of Europe; and
in the midst stood Frederic of Prussia, a veritable fire-king. He had
learned through secret agents that he was to be attacked, and that the
wrath of Maria Theresa with her two allies, Pompadour and the Empress of Russia, was soon to wreak itself upon him. With his usual
prompt audacity he anticipated his enemies, marched into Saxony, and
began the Continental war. His position seemed desperate. England,
sundered from Austria, her old ally, had made common cause with him;
but he had no other friend worth the counting. France, Russia, Austria,
Sweden, Saxony, the collective Germanic Empire, and most of the
smaller German States had joined hands for his ruin, eager to crush
him and divide the spoil, parcelling out his dominions among them-

selves in advance by solemn mutual compact. Against the five millions of Prussia were arrayed populations of more than a hundred millions. The little kingdom was open on all sides to attack, and her enemies were spurred on by the bitterest animosity. It was thought that one campaign would end the war. The war lasted seven years, and Prussia came out of it triumphant. Such a warrior as her indomitable king Europe has rarely seen. If the Seven Years War made the maritime and colonial greatness of England, it also raised Prussia to the rank of a first-class Power.

Frederic began with a victory, routing the Austrians in one of the fiercest of recorded conflicts, the battle of Prague. Then in his turn he was beaten at Kolin. All seemed lost. The hosts of the coalition were rolling in upon him like a deluge. Surrounded by enemies, in the jaws of destruction, hoping for little but to die in battle, this strange hero solaced himself with an exhaustless effusion of bad verses, sometimes mournful, sometimes cynical, sometimes indignant, and sometimes breathing a dauntless resolution; till, when his hour came, he threw down his pen to achieve those feats of arms which stamp him one of the foremost soldiers of the world.

The French and Imperialists, in overwhelming force, thought to crush him at Rossbach. He put them to shameful rout; and then, instead of bonfires and Te Deums, mocked at them in doggerel rhymes of amazing indecency. While he was beating the French, the Austrians took Silesia from him. He marched to recover it, found them strongly posted at Leuthen, eighty thousand men against thirty thousand, and without hesitation resolved to attack them. Never was he more heroic than on the eve of this, his crowning triumph. "The hour is at hand," he said to his generals. "I mean, in spite of the rules of military art, to attack Prince Karl's army, which is nearly thrice our own. This risk I must run, or all is lost. We must beat him or die, all of us, before his batteries." He burst unawares upon the Austrian right, and rolled their whole host together, corps upon corps, in a tumult of irretrievable ruin.

While her great ally was reaping a full harvest of laurels, England, dragged into the Continental war because that apple of discord, Hanover, belonged to her King, found little but humiliation. Minorca was wrested from her, and the Ministry had an innocent man shot to avert from themselves the popular indignation; while the same Ministry, scared by a phantom of invasion, brought over German troops to defend British soil. But now an event took place pregnant with glorious consequence. The reins of power fell into the hands of William Pitt. He had already held them for a brief space, forced into office at the

end of 1756 by popular clamor, in spite of the Whig leaders and against
the wishes of the King. But the place was untenable. Newcastle's Parliament would not support him; the Duke of Cumberland opposed him;
the King hated him; and in April, 1757, he was dismissed. Then ensued eleven weeks of bickering and dispute, during which, in the midst
of a great war, England was left without a government. It became clear
that none was possible without Pitt; and none with him could be permanent and strong unless joined with those influences which had thus
far controlled the majorities of Parliament. Therefore an extraordinary
union was brought about; Lord Chesterfield acting as go-between to
reconcile the ill-assorted pair. One of them brought to the alliance the
confidence and support of the people; the other, Court management,
borough interest, and parliamentary connections. Newcastle was made
First Lord of the Treasury, and Pitt, the old enemy who had repeatedly
browbeat and ridiculed him, became Secretary of State, with the lead
of the House of Commons and full control of the war and foreign affairs. It was a partnership of magpie and eagle. The dirty work of government, intrigue, bribery, and all the patronage that did not affect the
war, fell to the share of the old politician. If Pitt could appoint generals, admirals, and ambassadors, Newcastle was welcome to the rest. "I
will borrow the Duke's majorities to carry on the government," said the
new secretary; and with the audacious self-confidence that was one of
his traits, he told the Duke of Devonshire, "I am sure that I can save
this country, and that nobody else can." England hailed with one ac-
claim the undaunted leader who asked for no reward but the honor of
serving her. The hour had found the man. For the next four years this
imposing figure towers supreme in British history.

He had glaring faults, some of them of a sort not to have been expected in him. Vanity, the common weakness of small minds, was the
most disfiguring foible of this great one. He had not the simplicity
which becomes greatness so well. He could give himself theatrical airs,
strike attitudes, and dart stage lightnings from his eyes; yet he was formidable even in his affectations. Behind his great intellectual powers
lay a burning enthusiasm, a force of passion and fierce intensity of will,
that gave redoubled impetus to the fiery shafts of his eloquence; and
the haughty and masterful nature of the man had its share in the ascendency which he long held over Parliament. He would blast the labored
argument of an adversary by a look of scorn or a contemptuous wave of
the hand.

The Great Commoner was not a man of the people in the popular
sense of that hackneyed phrase. Though himself poor, being a younger

son, he came of a rich and influential family; he was patrician at heart; both his faults and his virtues, his proud incorruptibility and passionate, domineering patriotism, bore the patrician stamp. Yet he loved liberty and he loved the people, because they were the English people. The effusive humanitarianism of to-day had no part in him, and the democracy of to-day would detest him. Yet to the middle-class England of his own time, that unenfranchised England which had little representation in Parliament, he was a voice, an inspiration, and a tower of strength. He would not flatter the people; but, turning with contempt from the tricks and devices of official politics, he threw himself with a confidence that never wavered on their patriotism and public spirit. They answered him with a boundless trust, asked but to follow his lead, gave him without stint their money and their blood, loved him for his domestic virtues and his disinterestedness, believed him even in his self-contradiction, and idolized him even in his bursts of arrogant passion. It was he who waked England from her lethargy, shook off the spell that Newcastle and his fellow-enchanters had cast over her, and taught her to know herself again. A heart that beat in unison with all that was British found responsive throbs in every corner of the vast empire that through him was to become more vast. With the instinct of his fervid patriotism he would join all its far-extended members into one, not by vain assertions of parliamentary supremacy, but by bonds of sympathy and ties of a common freedom and a common cause.

The passion for power and glory subdued in him all the sordid parts of humanity, and he made the power and glory of England one with his own. He could change front through resentment or through policy; but in whatever path he moved, his objects were the same: not to curb the power of France in America, but to annihilate it; crush her navy, cripple her foreign trade, ruin her in India, in Africa, and wherever else, east or west, she had found foothold; gain for England the mastery of the seas, open to her the great highways of the globe, make her supreme in commerce and colonization; and while limiting the activities of her rival to the European continent, give to her the whole world for a sphere.

To this British Roman was opposed the pampered Sardanapalus of Versailles, with the silken favorite who by calculated adultery had bought the power to ruin France. The Marquise de Pompadour, who began life as Jeanne Poisson,—Jane Fish,—daughter of the head clerk of a banking house, who then became wife of a rich financier, and then, as mistress of the King, rose to a pinnacle of gilded ignominy, chose this time to turn out of office the two ministers who had shown most ability and force,—Argenson, head of the department of war, and Machault, head of the marine and colonies; the one because he was not subservient to her will, and the other because he had unwittingly touched the self-love of her royal paramour. She aspired to a share in the conduct of the war, and not only made and unmade ministers and generals, but discussed campaigns and battles with them, while they listened to her prating with a show of obsequious respect, since to lose her favor was to risk losing all. A few months later, when blows fell heavy and fast, she turned a deaf ear to representations of financial straits and military disasters, played the heroine, affected a greatness of soul superior to misfortune, and in her perfumed boudoir varied her tiresome graces by posing as a Roman matron. In fact she never wavered in her spite against Frederic, and her fortitude was perfect in bearing the sufferings of others and defying dangers that could not touch her.

When Pitt took office it was not over France, but over England that the clouds hung dense and black. Her prospects were of the gloomiest. "Whoever is in or whoever is out," wrote Chesterfield, "I am sure we are undone both at home and abroad: at home by our increasing debt and expenses; abroad by our ill-luck and incapacity. We are no longer a nation." And his despondency was shared by many at the beginning of the most triumphant Administration in British history. The shuffling weakness of his predecessors had left Pitt a heritage of tribulation. From America came news of Loudon's manifold failures; from Germany that of the miscarriage of the Duke of Cumberland, who, at the head of an army of Germans in British pay, had been forced to sign the convention of Kloster-Zeven, by which he promised to disband them. To these disasters was added a third, of which the new Government alone had to bear the burden. At the end of summer Pitt sent a great expedition to attack Rochefort; the military and naval commanders disagreed, and the consequence was failure. There was no light except from far-off India, where Clive won the great victory of Plassey, avenged the Black Hole of Calcutta, and prepared the ruin of the French power and the undisputed ascendency of England.

If the English had small cause as yet to rejoice in their own successes, they found comfort in those of their Prussian allies. The rout of the French at Rossbach and of the Austrians at Leuthen spread joy through their island. More than this, they felt that they had found at last a leader after their own heart; and the consciousness regenerated them. For the paltering imbecility of the old Ministry they had the unconquerable courage, the iron purpose, the unwavering faith, the inextinguishable hope, of the new one. "England has long been in labor," said Frederic of Prussia, "and at last she has brought forth a man." It was not only that instead of weak commanders Pitt gave her strong ones; the same men who had served her feebly under the blight of the New-castle Administration served her manfully and well under his robust impulsion. "Nobody ever entered his closet," said Colonel Barré, "who did not come out of it a braver man." That inspiration was felt wher-ever the British flag waved. Zeal awakened with the assurance that con-spicuous merit was sure of its reward, and that no officer who did his duty would now be made a sacrifice, like Admiral Byng, to appease public indignation at ministerial failures. As Nature, languishing in chill vapors and dull smothering fogs, revives at the touch of the sun, so did England spring into fresh life under the kindling influence of one great man.

With the opening of the year 1758 her course of Continental victo-ries began. The Duke of Cumberland, the King's son, was recalled in disgrace, and a general of another stamp, Prince Ferdinand of Bruns-wick, was placed in command of the Germans in British pay, with the contingent of English troops now added to them. The French, too, changed commanders. The Duke of Richelieu, a dissolute old beau, returned to Paris to spend in heartless gallantries the wealth he had gained by plunder; and a young soldier-churchman, the Comte de Cler-mont, took his place. Prince Ferdinand pushed him hard with an infe-rior force, drove him out of Hanover, and captured eleven thousand of his soldiers. Clermont was recalled, and was succeeded by Contades, another incapable. One of his subordinates won for him the battle of Lutterberg; but the generalship of Ferdinand made it a barren victory, and the campaign remained a success for the English. They made de-scents on the French coasts, captured St.-Servan, a suburb of St.-Malo, and burned three ships of the line, twenty-four privateers, and sixty merchantmen; then entered Cherbourg, destroyed the forts, carried off or spiked the cannon, and burned twenty-seven vessels,—a success par-tially offset by a failure on the coast of Brittany, where they were re-pulsed with some loss. In Africa they drove the French from the Guinea coast, and seized their establishment at Senegal.

It was towards America that Pitt turned his heartiest efforts. His first aim was to take Louisbourg, as a step towards taking Quebec; then Ticonderoga, that thorn in the side of the northern colonies; and lastly Fort Duquesne, the Key of the Great West. He recalled Loudon, for whom he had a fierce contempt; but there were influences which he could not disregard, and Major-General Abercromby, who was next in order of rank, an indifferent soldier, though a veteran in years, was allowed to succeed him, and lead in person the attack on Ticonderoga.[1] Pitt hoped that Brigadier Lord Howe, an admirable officer, who was joined with Abercromby, would be the real commander, and make amends for all shortcomings of his chief. To command the Louisbourg expedition, Colonel Jeffrey Amherst was recalled from the German war, and made at one leap a major-general.[2] He was energetic and resolute, somewhat cautious and slow, but with a bulldog tenacity of grip. Under him were three brigadiers, Whitmore, Lawrence, and Wolfe, of whom the youngest is the most noteworthy. In the luckless Rochefort expedition, Colonel James Wolfe was conspicuous by a dashing gallantry that did not escape the eye of Pitt, always on the watch for men to do his work. The young officer was ardent, headlong, void of fear, often rash, almost fanatical in his devotion to military duty, and reckless of life when the glory of England or his own was at stake. The third expedition, that against Fort Duquesne, was given to Brigadier John Forbes, whose qualities well fitted him for the task.

During his first short term of office, Pitt had given a new species of troops to the British army. These were the Scotch Highlanders, who had risen against the House of Hanover in 1745, and would rise against it again should France accomplish her favorite scheme of throwing a force into Scotland to excite another insurrection for the Stuarts. But they would be useful to fight the French abroad, though dangerous as their possible allies at home; and two regiments of them were now ordered to America.

Delay had been the ruin of the last year's attempt against Louisbourg. This time preparation was urged on apace; and before the end of winter two fleets had put to sea: one, under Admiral Boscawen, was destined for Louisbourg; while the other, under Admiral Osborn, sailed for the Mediterranean to intercept the French fleet of Admiral La Clue, who was about to sail from Toulon for America. Osborn, cruising between the coasts of Spain and Africa, barred the way to the Straits of Gibraltar, and kept his enemy imprisoned. La Clue made no attempt to force a passage; but several combats of detached ships took place, one of which is too remarkable to pass unnoticed. Captain Gardiner of the "Monmouth," a ship of four hundred and seventy men and sixty-four guns, engaged the French ship "Foudroyant," carrying a thousand men

[1] Order, War Office, 19 Dec. 1757.
[2] Pitt to Abercromby, 27 Jan. 1758. Instructions for our Trusty and Well-beloved Jeffrey Amherst, Esq., Major-General of our Forces in North America, 3 March, 1758.

and eighty-four guns of heavier metal than those of the Englishman. Gardiner had lately been reproved by Anson, First Lord of the Admiralty, for some alleged misconduct or shortcoming, and he thought of nothing but retrieving his honor. "We must take her," he said to his crew as the "Foudroyant" hove in sight. "She looks more than a match for us, but I will not quit her while this ship can swim or I have a soul left alive;" and the sailors answered with cheers. The fight was long and furious. Gardiner was killed by a musket shot, begging his first lieutenant with his dying breath not to haul down his flag. The lieutenant nailed it to the mast. At length the "Foudroyant" ceased from thundering, struck her colors, and was carried a prize to England.[1]

The typical British naval officer of that time was a rugged sea-dog, a tough and stubborn fighter, though no more so than the politer generations that followed, at home on the quarter-deck, but no ornament to the drawing-room, by reason of what his contemporary, Entick, the strenuous chronicler of the war, calls, not unapprovingly, "the ferocity of his manners." While Osborn held La Clue imprisoned at Toulon, Sir Edward Hawke, worthy leader of such men, sailed with seven ships of the line and three frigates to intercept a French squadron from Rochefort convoying a fleet of transports with troops for America. The French ships cut their cables and ran for the shore, where most of them stranded in the mud, and some threw cannon and munitions overboard to float themselves. The expedition was broken up. Of the many ships fitted out this year for the succor of Canada and Louisbourg, comparatively few reached their destination, and these for the most part singly or by twos and threes.

Meanwhile Admiral Boscawen with his fleet bore away for Halifax, the place of rendezvous, and Amherst, in the ship "Dublin," followed in his wake.

[1] Entick, III. 56–60.

19

Louisbourg

1758

The stormy coast of Cape Breton is indented by a small land-locked bay, between which and the ocean lies a tongue of land dotted with a few grazing sheep, and intersected by rows of stone that mark more or less distinctly the lines of what once were streets. Green mounds and embankments of earth enclose the whole space, and beneath the highest of them yawn arches and caverns of ancient masonry. This grassy solitude was once the "Dunkirk of America;" the vaulted caverns where the sheep find shelter from the rain were casemates where terrified women sought refuge from storms of shot and shell, and the shapeless green mounds were citadel, bastion, rampart, and glacis. Here stood Louisbourg; and not all the efforts of its conquerors, nor all the havoc of succeeding times, have availed to efface it. Men in hundreds toiled for months with lever, spade, and gunpowder in the work of destruction, and for more than a century it has served as a stone quarry; but the remains of its vast defences still tell their tale of human valor and human woe.

Stand on the mounds that were once the King's Bastion. The glistening sea spreads eastward three thousand miles, and its waves meet their first rebuff against this iron coast. Lighthouse Point is white with foam; jets of spray spout from the rocks of Goat Island; mist curls in clouds from the seething surf that lashes the crags of Black Point, and the sea boils like a caldron among the reefs by the harbor's mouth; but on the calm water within, the small fishing vessels rest tranquil at their moorings. Beyond lies a hamlet of fishermen by the edge of the water, and a few scattered dwellings dot the rough hills, bristled with stunted firs, that gird the quiet basin; while close at hand, within the precinct of the vanished fortress, stand two small farmhouses. All else is a solitude of ocean, rock, marsh, and forest.[1]

At the beginning of June, 1758, the place wore another aspect. Since the peace of Aix-la-Chapelle vast sums had been spent in repairing and strengthening it; and Louisbourg was the strongest fortress in French or British America. Nevertheless it had its weaknesses. The original plan of the works had not been fully carried out; and owing, it is said, to the bad quality of the mortar, the masonry of the ramparts was in so poor a condition that it had been replaced in some parts with fascines. The circuit of the fortifications was more than a mile and a half, and the town contained about four thousand inhabitants. The best buildings in it were the convent, the hospital, the King's storehouses, and the chapel and governor's quarters, which were under the same roof. Of the private houses, only seven or eight were of stone, the rest being humble wooden structures, suited to a population of fishermen. The garrison consisted of the battalions of Artois, Bourgogne, Cambis, and Volontaires Étrangers, with two companies of artillery and twenty-four of colony troops from Canada,—in all three thousand and eighty regular troops, besides officers;[2] and to these were added a body of armed inhabitants and a band of Indians. In the harbor were five ships of the line and seven frigates, carrying in all five hundred and forty-four guns and about three thousand men.[3] Two hundred and nineteen cannon and seventeen mortars were mounted on the walls and

---

[1]Louisbourg is described as I saw it ten days before writing the above, after an easterly gale.

[2]*Journal du Siége de Louisbourg.* Twenty-nine hundred regulars were able to bear arms when the siege began. *Houllière, Commandant des Troupes, au Ministre, 6 Août, 1758.*

[3]Le Prudent, 74 guns; Entreprenant, 74; Capricieux, 64; Célèbre, 64; Bienfaisant, 64; Apollon, 50; Chèvre, 22; Biche, 18; Fidèle, 22; Écho, 26; Aréthuse, 36; Comète, 30. The Bizarre, 64, sailed for France on the eighth of June, and was followed by the Comète.

outworks.[1] Of these last the most important were the Grand Battery on the shore of the harbor opposite its mouth, and the Island Battery on the rocky islet at its entrance.

The strongest front of the works was on the land side, along the base of the penensular triangle on which the town stood. This front, about twelve hundred yards in extent, reached from the sea on the left to the harbor on the right, and consisted of four bastions with their connecting curtains, the Princess's, the Queen's, the King's, and the Dauphin's. The King's Bastion formed part of the citadel. The glacis before it sloped down to an extensive marsh, which, with an adjacent pond, completely protected this part of the line. On the right, however, towards the harbor, the ground was high enough to offer advantages to an enemy, as was also the case, to a less degree, on the left, towards the sea. The best defence of Louisbourg was the craggy shore, that, for leagues on either hand, was accessible only at a few points, and even there with difficulty. All these points were vigilantly watched.

There had been signs of the enemy from the first opening of spring. In the intervals of fog, rain, and snow-squalls, sails were seen hovering on the distant sea; and during the latter part of May a squadron of nine ships cruised off the mouth of the harbor, appearing and disappearing, sometimes driven away by gales, sometimes lost in fogs, and sometimes approaching to within cannon-shot of the batteries. Their object was to blockade the port,—in which they failed; for French ships had come in at intervals, till, as we have seen, twelve of them lay safe anchored in the harbor, with more than a year's supply of provisions for the garrison.

At length, on the first of June, the southeastern horizon was white with a cloud of canvas. The long-expected crisis was come. Drucour, the governor, sent two thousand regulars, with about a thousand militia and Indians, to guard the various landing-places; and the rest, aided by the sailors, remained to hold the town.[2]

At the end of May Admiral Boscawen was at Halifax with twenty-three ships of the line, eighteen frigates and fire-ships, and a fleet of transports, on board of which were eleven thousand and six hundred soldiers, all regulars, except five hundred provincial rangers.[3] Amherst

---

[1] *État d'Artillerie*, appended to the Journal of Drucour. There were also forty-four cannon in reserve.
[2] *Rapport de Drucour. Journal du Siége.*
[3] Of this force, according to Mante, only 9,900 were fit for duty. The table printed by Knox (I. 127) shows a total of 11,112, besides officers, artillery, and rangers. The *Authentic Account of the Reduction of Louisbourg, by a Spectator*, puts the force at 11,326 men, besides officers. Entick makes the whole 11,936.

had not yet arrived, and on the twenty-eighth, Boscawen, in pursuance of his orders and to prevent loss of time, put to sea without him; but scarcely had the fleet sailed out of Halifax, when they met the ship that bore the expected general. Amherst took command of the troops; and the expedition held its way till the second of June, when they saw the rocky shore-line of Cape Breton, and descried the masts of the French squadron in the harbor of Louisbourg.

Boscawen sailed into Gabarus Bay. The sea was rough; but in the afternoon Amherst, Lawrence, and Wolfe, with a number of naval officers, reconnoitred the shore in boats, coasting it for miles, and approaching it as near as the French batteries would permit. The rocks were white with surf, and every accessible point was strongly guarded. Boscawen saw little chance of success. He sent for his captains, and consulted them separately. They thought, like him, that it would be rash to attempt a landing, and proposed a council of war. One of them alone, an old sea officer named Ferguson, advised his commander to take the responsibility himself, hold no council, and make the attempt at every risk. Boscawen took his advice, and declared that he would not leave Gabarus Bay till he had fulfilled his instructions and set the troops on shore.[1]

West of Louisbourg there were three accessible places, Freshwater Cove, four miles from the town, and Flat Point, and White Point, which were nearer, the last being within a mile of the fortifications. East of the town there was an inlet called Lorambec, also available for landing. In order to distract the attention of the enemy, it was resolved to threaten all these places, and to form the troops into three divisions, two of which, under Lawrence and Whitmore, were to advance towards Flat Point and White Point, while a detached regiment was to make a feint at Lorambec. Wolfe, with the third division, was to make the real attack and try to force a landing at Freshwater Cove, which, as it proved, was the most strongly defended of all. When on shore Wolfe was an habitual invalid, and when at sea every heave of the ship made him wretched; but his ardor was unquenchable. Before leaving England he wrote to a friend: "Being of the profession of arms, I would seek all occasions to serve; and therefore have thrown myself in the way of the American war, though I know that the very passage threatens my life, and that my constitution must be utterly ruined and undone."

On the next day, the third, the surf was so high that nothing could be attempted. On the fourth there was a thick fog and a gale. The

[1]Entick, III. 224.

frigate "Trent" struck on a rock, and some of the transports were near being stranded. On the fifth there was another fog and a raging surf. On the sixth there was fog, with rain in the morning and better weather towards noon, whereupon the signal was made and the troops entered the boats; but the sea rose again, and they were ordered back to the ships. On the seventh more fog and more surf till night, when the sea grew calmer, and orders were given for another attempt. At two in the morning of the eighth the troops were in the boats again. At daybreak the frigates of the squadron, anchoring before each point of real or pretended attack, opened a fierce cannonade on the French en-trenchments; and, a quarter of an hour after, the three divisions rowed towards the shore. That of the left, under Wolfe, consisted of four com-panies of grenadiers, with the light infantry and New England rangers, followed and supported by Fraser's Highlanders and eight more compa-nies of grenadiers. They pulled for Freshwater Cove. Here there was a crescent-shaped beach, a quarter of a mile long, with rocks at each end. On the shore above, about a thousand Frenchmen, under Lieutenant-Colonel de Saint-Julien, lay behind entrenchments covered in front by spruce and fir trees, felled and laid on the ground with the tops out-ward.[1] Eight cannon and swivels were planted to sweep every part of the beach and its approaches, and these pieces were masked by young evergreens stuck in the ground before them.

The English were allowed to come within close range unmolested. Then the batteries opened, and a deadly storm of grape and musketry was poured upon the boats. It was clear in an instant that to advance farther would be destruction; and Wolfe waved his hand as a signal to sheer off. At some distance on the right, and little exposed to the fire, were three boats of light infantry under Lieutenants Hopkins and Brown and Ensign Grant; who, mistaking the signal or wilfully misin-terpreting it, made directly for the shore before them. It was a few rods east of the beach; a craggy coast and a strand strewn with rocks and lashed with breakers, but sheltered from the cannon by a small project-ing point. The three officers leaped ashore, followed by their men. Wolfe saw the movement, and hastened to support it. The boat of Major Scott, who commanded the light infantry and rangers, next came up, and was stove in an instant; but Scott gained the shore, climbed the crags, and found himself with ten men in front of some seventy French and Indians. Half his followers were killed and wounded, and three bullets were shot through his clothes; but with

---

[1]Drucour reports 985 soldiers as stationed here under Saint-Julien; there were also some Indians. Freshwater Cove, otherwise Kennington Cove, was called La Cormorandière by the French.

admirable gallantry he held his ground till others came to his aid.[1] The remaining boats now reached the landing. Many were stove among the rocks, and others were overset; some of the men were dragged back by the surf and drowned; some lost their muskets, and were drenched to the skin: but the greater part got safe ashore. Among the foremost was seen the tall, attenuated form of Brigadier Wolfe, armed with nothing but a cane, as he leaped into the surf and climbed the crags with his soldiers. As they reached the top they formed in compact order, and attacked and carried with the bayonet the nearest French battery, a few rods distant. The division of Lawrence soon came up; and as the attention of the enemy was now distracted, they made their landing with little opposition at the farther end of the beach, whither they were followed by Amherst himself. The French, attacked on right and left, and fearing, with good reason, that they would be cut off from the town, abandoned all their cannon and fled into the woods. About seventy of them were captured and fifty killed. The rest, circling among the hills and around the marshes, made their way to Louisbourg, and those at the intermediate posts joined their flight. The English followed through a matted growth of firs till they reached the cleared ground; when the cannon, opening on them from the ramparts, stopped the pursuit. The first move of the great game was played and won.[2]

Amherst made his camp just beyond range of the French cannon, and Flat Point Cove was chosen as the landing-place of guns and stores. Clearing the ground, making roads, and pitching tents filled the rest of the day. At night there was a glare of flames from the direction of the town. The French had abandoned the Grand Battery after setting fire to the buildings in it and to the houses and fish-stages along the shore of the harbor. During the following days stores were landed as fast as the surf would permit: but the task was so difficult that from first to last more than a hundred boats were stove in accomplishing it; and such was the violence of the waves that none of the siege-guns could be got ashore till the eighteenth. The camp extended two miles along a stream that flowed down to the Cove among the low, woody hills that curved around the town and harbor. Redoubts were made to protect its front, and blockhouses to guard its left and rear from the bands of Acadians known to be hovering in the woods.

Wolfe, with twelve hundred men, made his way six or seven miles

---

[1]Pichon, *Mémoires du Cap-Breton*, 284.

[2]*Journal of Amherst*, in Mante, 117. *Amherst to Pitt, 11 June, 1758. Authentic Account of the Reduction of Louisbourg, by a Spectator,* 11. *General Orders of Amherst, 3–7 June, 1759. Letter from an Officer,* in Knox, I. 191; Entick, III. 225. The French accounts generally agree in essentials with the English. The English lost one hundred and nine, killed, wounded, and drowned.

round the harbor, took possession of the battery at Lighthouse Point which the French had abandoned, planted guns and mortars, and opened fire on the Island Battery that guarded the entrance. Other guns were placed at different points along the shore, and soon opened on the French ships. The ships and batteries replied. The artillery fight raged night and day; till on the twenty-fifth the island guns were dismounted and silenced. Wolfe then strengthened his posts, secured his communications, and returned to the main army in front of the town.

Amherst had reconnoitred the ground and chosen a hillock at the edge of the marsh, less than half a mile from the ramparts, as the point for opening his trenches. A road with an epaulement to protect it must first be made to the spot; and as the way was over a tract of deep mud covered with water-weeds and moss, the labor was prodigious. A thousand men worked at it day and night under the fire of the town and ships.

When the French looked landward from their ramparts they could see scarcely a sign of the impending storm. Behind them Wolfe's cannon were playing busily from Lighthouse Point and the heights around the harbor; but, before them, the broad flat marsh and the low hills seemed almost a solitude. Two miles distant, they could descry some of the English tents; but the greater part were hidden by the inequalities of the ground. On the right, a prolongation of the harbor reached nearly half a mile beyond the town, ending in a small lagoon formed by a projecting sandbar, and known as the Barachois. Near this bar lay moored the little frigate "Aréthuse," under a gallant officer named Vauquelin. Her position was a perilous one; but so long as she could maintain it she could sweep with her fire the ground before the works, and seriously impede the operations of the enemy. The other naval captains were less venturous; and when the English landed, they wanted to leave the harbor and save their ships. Drucour insisted that they should stay to aid the defence, and they complied; but soon left their moorings and anchored as close as possible under the guns of the town, in order to escape the fire of Wolfe's batteries. Hence there was great murmuring among the military officers, who would have had them engage the hostile guns at short range. The frigate "Écho," under cover of a fog, had been sent to Quebec for aid; but she was chased and captured; and, a day or two after, the French saw her pass the mouth of the harbor with an English flag at her mast-head.

When Wolfe had silenced the Island Battery, a new and imminent danger threatened Louisbourg. Boscawen might enter the harbor, overpower the French naval force, and cannonade the town on its weakest side. Therefore Drucour resolved to sink four large ships at the entrance; and on a dark and foggy night this was successfully accomplished. Two more vessels were afterwards sunk, and the harbor was then thought safe.

The English had at last finished their preparations, and were urging on the siege with determined vigor. The landward view was a solitude no longer. They could be seen in multitudes piling earth and fascines beyond the hillock at the edge of the marsh. On the twenty-fifth they occupied the hillock itself, and fortified themselves there under a shower of bombs. Then they threw up earth on the right, and pushed their approaches towards the Barachois, in spite of a hot fire from the frigate "Aréthuse." Next they appeared on the left towards the sea about a third of a mile from the Princess's Bastion. It was Wolfe, with a strong detachment, throwing up a redoubt and opening an entrenchment. Late on the night of the ninth of July six hundred French troops sallied to interrupt the work. The English grenadiers in the trenches fought stubbornly with bayonet and sword, but were forced back to the second line, where a desperate conflict in the dark took place; and after severe loss on both sides the French were driven back. Some days before, there had been another sortie on the opposite side, near the Barachois, resulting in a repulse of the French and the seizure by Wolfe of a more advanced position.

Various courtesies were exchanged between the two commanders. Drucour, on occasion of a flag of truce, wrote to Amherst that there was a surgeon of uncommon skill in Louisbourg, whose services were at the command of any English officer who might need them. Amherst on his part sent to his enemy letters and messages from wounded Frenchmen in his hands, adding his compliments to Madame Drucour, with an expression of regret for the disquiet to which she was exposed, begging her at the same time to accept a gift of pineapples from the West Indies. She returned his courtesy by sending him a basket of wine; after which amenities the cannon roared again. Madame Drucour was a woman of heroic spirit. Every day she was on the ramparts, where her presence roused the soldiers to enthusiasm; and every day with her own hand she fired three cannon to encourage them.

The English lines grew closer and closer, and their fire more and more destructive. Desgouttes, the naval commander, withdrew the "Aréthuse" from her exposed position, where her fire had greatly annoyed the besiegers. The shot-holes in her sides were plugged up, and in the dark night of the fourteenth of July she was towed through the obstructions in the mouth of the harbor, and sent to France to report the situation of Louisbourg. More fortunate than her predecessor, she escaped the English in a fog. Only five vessels now remained afloat in the harbor, and these were feebly manned, as the greater part of their officers and crews had come ashore, to the number of two thousand, lodging under tents in the town, amid the scarcely suppressed murmurs of the army officers.

On the eighth of July news came that the partisan Boishébert was approaching with four hundred Acadians, Canadians, and Micmacs to attack the English outposts and detachments. He did little or nothing, however, besides capturing a few stragglers. On the sixteenth, early in the evening, a party of English, led by Wolfe, dashed forward, drove off a band of French volunteers, seized a rising ground called Hauteur-de-la-Potence, or Gallows Hill, and began to entrench themselves scarcely three hundred yards from the Dauphin's Bastion. The town opened on them furiously with grape-shot; but in the intervals of the firing the sound of their picks and spades could plainly be heard. In the morning they were seen throwing up earth like moles as they burrowed their way forward; and on the twenty-first they opened another parallel, within two hundred yards of the rampart. Still their sappers pushed on. Every day they had more guns in position, and on right and left their fire grew hotter. Their pickets made a lodgment along the foot of the glacis, and fired up the slope at the French in the covered way.

The twenty-first was a memorable day. In the afternoon a bomb fell on the ship "Célèbre" and set her on fire. An explosion followed. The few men on board could not save her, and she drifted from her moorings. The wind blew the flames into the rigging of the "Entreprenant," and then into that of the "Capricieux." At night all three were in full blaze; for when the fire broke out the English batteries turned on them a tempest of shot and shell to prevent it from being extinguished. The glare of the triple conflagration lighted up the town, the trenches, the harbor, and the surrounding hills, while the burning ships shot off their guns at random as they slowly drifted westward, and grounded at last near the Barachois. In the morning they were consumed to the water's edge; and of all the squadron the "Prudent" and the "Bienfaisant" alone were left.

In the citadel, of which the King's Bastion formed the front, there was a large oblong stone building containing the chapel, lodgings for men and officers, and at the southern end the quarters of the Governor. On the morning after the burning of the ships a shell fell through the roof among a party of soldiers in the chamber below, burst, and set the place on fire. In half an hour the chapel and all the northern part of the building were in flames; and no sooner did the smoke rise above the bastion than the English threw into it a steady shower of missiles. Yet soldiers, sailors, and inhabitants hastened to the spot, and labored desperately to check the fire. They saved the end occupied by Drucour and his wife, but all the rest was destroyed. Under the adjacent rampart were the casemates, one of which was crowded with wounded officers, and the rest with women and children seeking shelter in these subterranean dens. Before the entrances there was a long barrier of timber to protect them from exploding shells; and as the wind blew the flames towards it, there was danger that it would take fire and suffocate those within. They rushed out, crazed with fright, and ran hither and thither with outcries and shrieks amid the storm of iron.

In the neighboring Queen's Bastion was a large range of barracks built of wood by the New England troops after their capture of the fortress in 1745. So flimsy and combustible was it that the French writers call it a "house of cards" and "a paper of matches." Here were lodged the greater part of the garrison: but such was the danger of fire, that they were now ordered to leave it; and they accordingly lay in the streets or along the foot of the ramparts, under shelters of timber which gave some little protection against bombs. The order was well timed; for on the night after the fire in the King's Bastion, a shell filled with combustibles set this building also in flames. A fearful scene ensued. All the English batteries opened upon it. The roar of mortars and cannon, the rushing and screaming of round-shot and grape, the hissing of fuses and the explosion of grenades and bombs mingled with a storm of musketry from the covered way and trenches; while, by the glare of the conflagration, the English regiments were seen drawn up in battle array, before the ramparts, as if preparing for an assault.

Two days after, at one o'clock in the morning, a burst of loud cheers was heard in the distance, followed by confused cries and the noise of musketry, which lasted but a moment. Six hundred English sailors had silently rowed into the harbor and seized the two remaining ships, the "Prudent" and the "Bienfaisant." After the first hubbub all was silent for half an hour. Then a light glowed through the thick fog that covered the water. The "Prudent" was burning. Being aground with the low tide, her captors had set her on fire, allowing the men on board to escape to the town in her boats. The flames soon wrapped her from stem to stern; and as the broad glare pierced the illumined mists, the English sailors, reckless of shot and shell, towed her companion-ship, with all on board, to a safe anchorage under Wolfe's batteries.

The position of the besieged was deplorable. Nearly a fourth of their number were in the hospitals; while the rest, exhausted with incessant toil, could find no place to snatch an hour of sleep; "and yet," says an officer, "they still show ardor." "To-day," he again says, on the twenty-fourth, "the fire of the place is so weak that it is more like funeral guns than a defence." On the front of the town only four cannon could fire at all. The rest were either dismounted or silenced by the musketry from the trenches. The masonry of the ramparts had been shaken by the concussion of their own guns; and now, in the Dauphin's and King's bastions, the English shot brought it down in masses. The trenches had been pushed so close on the rising grounds at the right that a great part of the covered way was enfiladed, while a battery on a hill across the harbor swept the whole front with a flank fire. Amherst had ordered the gunners to spare the houses of the town; but, according to French accounts, the order had little effect, for shot and shell fell everywhere. "There is not a house in the place," says the Diary just quoted, "that has not felt the effects of this formidable artillery. From yesterday morning till seven o'clock this evening we reckon that a thousand or twelve hundred bombs, great and small, have been thrown into the town, accompanied all the time by the fire of forty pieces of cannon, served with an activity not often seen. The hospital and the houses around it, which also serve as hospitals, are attacked with cannon and mortar. The surgeon trembles as he amputates a limb amid cries of *Gare la bombe!* and leaves his patient in the midst of the operation, lest he should share his fate. The sick and wounded, stretched on mattresses, utter cries of pain, which do not cease till a shot or the bursting of a shell ends them."[1] On the twenty-sixth the last cannon was silenced in front of the town, and the English batteries had made a breach which seemed practicable for assault.

On the day before, Drucour, with his chief officers and the engineer, Franquet, had made the tour of the covered way, and examined the state of the defences. All but Franquet were for offering to capitulate. Early on the next morning a council of war was held, at which were present Drucour, Franquet, Desgouttes, naval commander, Houllière, commander of the regulars, and the several chiefs of battalions. Franquet presented a memorial setting forth the state of the fortifications. As it was he who had reconstructed and repaired them, he was anxious

---

[1] Early in the siege Drucour wrote to Amherst asking that the hospitals should be exempt from fire. Amherst answered that shot and shell might fall on any part of so small a town, but promised to insure the sick and wounded from molestation if Drucour would send them either to the island at the mouth of the harbor, or to any of the ships, if anchored apart from the rest. The offer was declined, for reasons not stated. Drucour gives the correspondence in his Diary.

to show the quality of his work in the best light possible; and therefore, in the view of his auditors, he understated the effects of the English fire. Hence an altercation arose, ending in a unanimous decision to ask for terms. Accordingly, at ten o'clock, a white flag was displayed over the breach in the Dauphin's Bastion, and an officer named Loppinot was sent out with offers to capitulate. The answer was prompt and stern: the garrison must surrender as prisoners of war; a definite reply must be given within an hour; in case of refusal the place will be attacked by land and sea.[1]

Great was the emotion in the council; and one of its members, D'Anthonay, lieutenant-colonel of the battalion of Volontaires Étrangers, was sent to propose less rigorous terms. Amherst would not speak with him; and jointly with Boscawen despatched this note to the Governor:—

SIR,—We have just received the reply which it has pleased your Excellency to make as to the conditions of the capitulation offered you. We shall not change in the least our views regarding them. It depends on your Excellency to accept them or not; and you will have the goodness to give your answer, yes or no, within half an hour.
We have the honor to be, etc.,
E. BOSCAWEN,
J. AMHERST.[2]

Drucour answered as follows:—

GENTLEMEN,—To reply to your Excellencies in as few words as possible, I have the honor to repeat that my position also remains the same, and that I persist in my first resolution.
I have the honor to be, etc.,
THE CHEVALIER DE DRUCOUR.

In other words, he refused the English terms, and declared his purpose to abide the assault. Loppinot was sent back to the English camp with this note of defiance. He was no sooner gone than Prévost, the intendant, an officer of functions purely civil, brought the Governor a memorial which, with or without the knowledge of the military authorities, he had drawn up in anticipation of the emergency. "The violent resolution which the council continues to hold," said this document,

[1] Mante and other English writers give the text of this reply.
[2] Translated from the Journal of Drucour.

"obliges me, for the good of the state, the preservation of the King's subjects, and the averting of horrors shocking to humanity, to lay before your eyes the consequences that may ensue. What will become of the four thousand souls who compose the families of this town, of the thousand or twelve hundred sick in the hospitals, and the officers and crews of our unfortunate ships? They will be delivered over to carnage and the rage of an unbridled soldiery, eager for plunder, and impelled to deeds of horror by pretended resentment at what has formerly happened in Canada. Thus they will all be destroyed, and the memory of their fate will live forever in our colonies. . . . It remains, Monsieur," continues the paper, "to remind you that the councils you have held thus far have been composed of none but military officers. I am not surprised at their views. The glory of the King's arms and the honor of their several corps have inspired them. You and I alone are charged with the administration of the colony and the care of the King's subjects who compose it. These gentlemen, therefore, have had no regard for them. They think only of themselves and their soldiers, whose business it is to encounter the utmost extremity of peril. It is at the prayer of an intimidated people that I lay before you the considerations specified in this memorial."

"In view of these considerations," writes Drucour, "joined to the impossibility of resisting an assault, M. le Chevalier de Courserac undertook in my behalf to run after the bearer of my answer to the English commander and bring it back." It is evident that the bearer of the note had been in no hurry to deliver it, for he had scarcely got beyond the fortifications when Courserac overtook and stopped him. D'Anthonay, with Duvivier, major of the battalion of Artois, and Loppinot, the first messenger, was then sent to the English camp, empowered to accept the terms imposed. An English spectator thus describes their arrival: "A lieutenant-colonel came running out of the garrison, making signs at a distance, and bawling out as loud as he could, 'We accept! We accept!' He was followed by two others; and they were all conducted to General Amherst's headquarters."[1] At eleven o'clock at night they returned with the articles of capitulation and the following letter:—

SIR,—We have the honor to send your Excellency the articles of capitulation signed.

Lieutenant-Colonel D'Anthonay has not failed to speak in behalf of the inhabitants of the town; and it is nowise our intention to distress them, but to give them all the aid in our power.

---

[1] *Authentic Account of the Siege of Louisbourg, by a Spectator.*

Your Excellency will have the goodness to sign a duplicate of the articles and send it to us.

It only remains to assure your Excellency that we shall with great pleasure seize every opportunity to convince your Excellency that we are with the most perfect consideration,

> Sir, your Excellency's most obedient servants,

> E. Boscawen,
> J. Amherst.

The articles stipulated that the garrison should be sent to England, prisoners of war, in British ships; that all artillery, arms, munitions, and stores, both in Louisbourg and elsewhere on the Island of Cape Breton, as well as on Isle St.-Jean, now Prince Edward's Island, should be given up intact; that the gate of the Dauphin's Bastion should be delivered to the British troops at eight o'clock in the morning; and that the garrison should lay down their arms at noon. The victors, on their part, promised to give the French sick and wounded the same care as their own, and to protect private property from pillage.

Drucour signed the paper at midnight, and in the morning a body of grenadiers took possession of the Dauphin's Gate. The rude soldiery poured in, swarthy with wind and sun, and begrimed with smoke and dust; the garrison, drawn up on the esplanade, flung down their muskets and marched from the ground with tears of rage; the cross of St. George floated over the shattered rampart; and Louisbourg, with the two great islands that depended on it, passed to the British Crown. Guards were posted, a stern discipline was enforced, and perfect order maintained. The conquerors and the conquered exchanged greetings, and the English general was lavish of courtesies to the brave lady who had aided the defence so well. "Every favor she asked was granted," says a Frenchman present.

Drucour and his garrison had made a gallant defence. It had been his aim to prolong the siege till it should be too late for Amherst to cooperate with Abercromby in an attack on Canada; and in this, at least, he succeeded.

Five thousand six hundred and thirty-seven officers, soldiers, and sailors were prisoners in the hands of the victors. Eighteen mortars and two hundred and twenty-one cannon were found in the town, along with a great quantity of arms, munitions, and stores.[1] At the middle of August such of the prisoners as were not disabled by wounds or sickness were em-

---

[1] *Account of the Guns, Mortars, Shot, Shell, etc., found in the Town of Louisbourg upon its Surrender this day,* signed *Jeffrey Amherst, 27 July, 1758.*

barked for England, and the merchants and inhabitants were sent to France. Brigadier Whitmore, as governor of Louisbourg, remained with four regiments to hold guard over the desolation they had made.

The fall of the French stronghold was hailed in England with noisy rapture. Addresses of congratulation to the King poured in from all the cities of the kingdom, and the captured flags were hung in St. Paul's amid the roar of cannon and the shouts of the populace. The provinces shared these rejoicings. Sermons of thanksgiving resounded from countless New England pulpits. At Newport there were fireworks and illuminations; and, adds the pious reporter, "We have reason to believe that Christians will make wise and religious improvement of so signal a favor of Divine Providence." At Philadelphia a like display was seen, with music and universal ringing of bells. At Boston "a stately bonfire like a pyramid was kindled on the top of Fort Hill, which made a lofty and prodigious blaze;" though here certain jealous patriots protested against celebrating a victory won by British regulars, and not by New England men. At New York there was a grand official dinner at the Province Arms in Broadway, where every loyal toast was echoed by the cannon of Fort George; and illuminations and fireworks closed the day.[1] In the camp of Abercromby at Lake George, Chaplain Cleaveland, of Bagley's Massachusetts regiment, wrote: "The General put out orders that the breastwork should be lined with troops, and to fire three rounds for joy, and give thanks to God in a religious way."[2] But nowhere did the tidings find a warmer welcome than in the small detached forts scattered through the solitudes of Nova Scotia, where the military exiles, restless from inaction, listened with greedy ears for every word from the great world whence they were banished. So slow were their communications with it that the fall of Louisbourg was known in England before it had reached them all. Captain John Knox, then in garrison at Annapolis, tells how it was greeted there more than five weeks after the event. It was the sixth of September. A sloop from Boston was seen coming up the bay. Soldiers and officers ran down to the wharf to ask for news. "Every soul," says Knox, "was impatient, yet shy of asking; at length, the vessel being come near enough to be spoken to, I called out, 'What news from Louisbourg?' To which the master simply replied, and with some gravity, 'Nothing strange.' This answer, which was so coldly delivered, threw us all into great consternation, and we looked at each other without being able to speak; some

---

[1]These particulars are from the provincial newspapers.
[2]Cleaveland, *Journal.*

of us even turned away with an intent to return to the fort. At length one of our soldiers, not yet satisfied, called out with some warmth: 'Damn you, Pumpkin, is n't Louisbourg taken yet?' The poor New England man then answered: 'Taken, yes, above a month ago, and I have been there since; but if you have never heard it before, I have got a good parcel of letters for you now.' If our apprehensions were great at first, words are insufficient to express our transports at this speech, the latter part of which we hardly waited for; but instantly all hats flew off, and we made the neighboring woods resound with our cheers and huzzas for almost half an hour. The master of the sloop was amazed beyond expression, and declared he thought we had heard of the success of our arms eastward before, and had sought to banter him."[1] At night there was a grand bonfire and universal festivity in the fort and village.

Amherst proceeded to complete his conquest by the subjection of all the adjacent possessions of France. Major Dalling was sent to occupy Port Espagnol, now Sydney. Colonel Monckton was despatched to the Bay of Fundy and the River St. John with an order "to destroy the vermin who are settled there."[2] Lord Rollo, with the thirty-fifth regiment and two battalions of the sixtieth, received the submission of Isle St.-Jean, and tried to remove the inhabitants,—with small success; for out of more than four thousand he could catch but seven hundred.[3]

The ardent and indomitable Wolfe had been the life of the siege. Wherever there was need of a quick eye, a prompt decision, and a bold dash, there his lank figure was always in the front. Yet he was only half pleased with what had been done. The capture of Louisbourg, he thought, should be but the prelude of greater conquests; and he had hoped that the fleet and army would sail up the St. Lawrence and attack Quebec. Impetuous and impatient by nature, and irritable with disease, he chafed at the delay that followed the capitulation, and wrote to his father a few days after it: "We are gathering strawberries and other wild fruits of the country, with a seeming indifference about what is doing in other parts of the world. Our army, however, on the continent wants our help." Growing more anxious, he sent Amherst a note to ask his intentions; and the General replied, "What I most wish to do is to go to Quebec. I have proposed it to the Admiral, and yesterday he seemed to think it impracticable." On which Wolfe wrote again: "If the Admiral will not carry us to Quebec, reinforcements

[1]Knox, *Historical Journal*, I. 158.
[2]*Orders of Amherst to Wolfe*, 15 Aug. 1758; *Ibid. to Monckton*, 24 Aug. 1758; *Report of Monckton*, 12 Nov. 1758.
[3]*Villejouin, commandant à l'Isle St.-Jean, au Ministre*, 8 Sept. 1758.

should certainly be sent to the continent without losing a moment. This damned French garrison take up our time and attention, which might be better bestowed. The transports are ready, and a small convoy would carry a brigade to Boston or New York. With the rest of the troops we might make an offensive and destructive war in the Bay of Fundy and the Gulf of St. Lawrence. I beg pardon for this freedom, but I cannot look coolly upon the bloody inroads of those hell-hounds, the Canadians; and if nothing further is to be done, I must desire leave to quit the army."

Amherst answered that though he had meant at first to go to Quebec with the whole army, late events on the continent made it impossible; and that he now thought it best to go with five or six regiments to the aid of Abercromby. He asked Wolfe to continue to communicate his views to him, and would not hear for a moment of his leaving the army; adding, "I know nothing that can tend more to His Majesty's service than your assisting in it." Wolfe again wrote to his commander, with whom he was on terms of friendship: "An offensive, daring kind of war will awe the Indians and ruin the French. Blockhouses and a trembling defensive encourage the meanest scoundrels to attack us. If you will attempt to cut up New France by the roots, I will come with pleasure to assist."

Amherst, with such speed as his deliberate nature would permit, sailed with six regiments for Boston to reinforce Abercromby at Lake George, while Wolfe set out on an errand but little to his liking. He had orders to proceed to Gaspé, Miramichi, and other settlements on the Gulf of St. Lawrence, destroy them, and disperse their inhabitants; a measure of needless and unpardonable rigor, which, while detesting it, he executed with characteristic thoroughness. "Sir Charles Hardy and I," he wrote to his father, "are preparing to rob the fishermen of their nets and burn their huts. When that great exploit is at an end, I return to Louisbourg, and thence to England." Having finished the work, he wrote to Amherst: "Your orders were carried into execution. We have done a great deal of mischief, and spread the terror of His Majesty's arms through the Gulf, but have added nothing to the reputation of them." The destruction of property was great; yet, as Knox writes, "he would not suffer the least barbarity to be committed upon the persons of the wretched inhabitants."[1]

He returned to Louisbourg, and sailed for England to recruit his shattered health for greater conflicts.

---

[1] "Les Anglais ont très-bien traités les prisonniers qu'ils ont faits dans cette partie" [Gaspé, etc]. *Vaudreuil au Ministre, 4 Nov. 1758.*

NOTE.—Four long and minute French diaries of the siege of Louisbourg are before me. The first, that of Drucour, covers a hundred and six folio pages, and contains his correspondence with Amherst, Boscawen, and Desgouttes. The second is that of the naval captain Tourville, commander of the ship "Capricieux," and covers fifty pages. The third is by an officer of the garrison whose name does not appear. The fourth, of about a hundred pages, is by another officer of the garrison, and is also anonymous. It is an excellent record of what passed each day, and of the changing conditions, moral and physical, of the besieged. These four Journals, though clearly independent of each other, agree in nearly all essential particulars. I have also numerous letters from the principal officers, military, naval, and civil, engaged in the defence,—Drucour, Desgouttes, Houllière, Beaussier, Marolles, Tourville, Courserac, Franquet, Villejouin, Prévost, and Querdisien. These, with various other documents relating to the siege, were copied from the originals in the Archives de la Marine. Among printed authorities on the French side may be mentioned Pichon, *Lettres et Mémoires pour servir à l'Histoire du Cap-Breton*, and the *Campaign of Louisbourg*, by the Chevalier Johnstone, a Scotch Jacobite serving under Drucour.

The chief authorities on the English side are the official Journal of Amherst, printed in the *London Magazine* and in other contemporary periodicals, and also in Mante, *History of the Late War*; five letters from Amherst to Pitt, written during the siege (Public Record Office); an excellent private Journal called *An Authentic Account of the Reduction of Louisbourg, by a Spectator*, parts of which have been copied verbatim by Entick without acknowledgment; the admirable Journal of Captain John Knox, which contains numerous letters and orders relating to the siege; and the correspondence of Wolfe contained in his Life by Wright. Before me is the Diary of a captain or subaltern in the army of Amherst at Louisbourg, found in the garret of an old house at Windsor, Nova Scotia, on an estate belonging in 1760 to Chief Justice Deschamps. I owe the use of it to the kindness of George Wiggins, Esq., of Windsor, N. S. Mante gives an excellent plan of the siege operations, and another will be found in Jefferys, *Natural and Civil History of French Dominions in North America*.

20

Ticonderoga

1758

ACTIVITY OF THE PROVINCES · SACRIFICES OF MASSACHUSETTS · THE
ARMY AT LAKE GEORGE · PROPOSED INCURSION OF LÉVIS · PERPLEXITIES
OF MONTCALM · HIS PLAN OF DEFENCE · CAMP OF ABERCROMBY · HIS
CHARACTER · LORD HOWE · HIS POPULARITY · EMBARKATION OF
ABERCROMBY · ADVANCE DOWN LAKE GEORGE · LANDING · FOREST
SKIRMISH · DEATH OF HOWE · ITS EFFECTS · POSITION OF THE FRENCH ·
THE LINES OF TICONDEROGA · BLUNDERS OF ABERCROMBY · THE
ASSAULT · A FRIGHTFUL SCENE · INCIDENTS OF THE BATTLE · BRITISH
REPULSE · PANIC · RETREAT · TRIUMPH OF MONTCALM

In the last year Loudon called on the colonists for four
thousand men. This year Pitt asked them for twenty thousand, and promised that the King would supply arms, ammunition,
tents, and provisions, leaving to the provinces only the raising, clothing, and pay of their soldiers; and he added the assurance that Parliament would be asked to make some compensation even for these.[1] Thus
encouraged, cheered by the removal of Loudon, and animated by the
unwonted vigor of British military preparation, the several provincial
assemblies voted men in abundance, though the usual vexatious delays
took place in raising, equipping, and sending them to the field.

[1] *Pitt to the Colonial Governors, 30 Dec. 1757.*

In this connection, an able English writer has brought against the colonies, and especially against Massachusetts, charges which deserve attention. Viscount Bury says: "Of all the colonies, Massachusetts was the first which discovered the designs of the French and remonstrated against their aggressions; of all the colonies she most zealously promoted measures of union for the common defence, and made the greatest exertions in furtherance of her views." But he adds that there is a reverse to the picture, and that "this colony, so high-spirited, so warlike, and apparently so loyal, would never move hand or foot in her own defence till certain of repayment by the mother country."[1] The groundlessness of this charge is shown by abundant proofs, one of which will be enough. The Englishman Pownall, who had succeeded Shirley as royal governor of the province, made this year a report of its condition to Pitt. Massachusetts, he says, "has been the frontier and advanced guard of all the colonies against the enemy in Canada," and has always taken the lead in military affairs. In the three past years she has spent on the expeditions of Johnson, Winslow, and Loudon £242,356, besides about £45,000 a year to support the provincial government, at the same time maintaining a number of forts and garrisons, keeping up scouting-parties, and building, equipping, and manning a ship of twenty guns for the service of the King. In the first two months of the present year, 1758, she made a further military outlay of £172,239. Of all these sums she has received from Parliament a reimbursement of only £70,117, and hence she is deep in debt; yet, in addition, she has this year raised, paid, maintained, and clothed seven thousand soldiers placed under the command of General Abercromby, besides above twenty-five hundred more serving the King by land or sea; amounting in all to about one in four of her able-bodied men.

Massachusetts was extremely poor by the standards of the present day, living by fishing, farming, and a trade sorely hampered by the British navigation laws. Her contributions of money and men were not ordained by an absolute king, but made by the voluntary act of a free people. Pownall goes on to say that her present war-debt, due within three years, is 366,698 pounds sterling, and that to meet it she has imposed on herself taxes amounting, in the town of Boston, to thirteen shillings and twopence to every pound of income from real and personal estate; that her people are in distress, that she is anxious to continue her efforts in the public cause, but that without some further reimburse-

[1] Bury, *Exodus of the Western Nations*, II. 250, 251.

ment she is exhausted and helpless.[1] Yet in the next year she incurred a new and heavy debt. In 1760 Parliament repaid her £59,575.[2] Far from being fully reimbursed, the end of the war found her on the brink of bankruptcy. Connecticut made equal sacrifices in the common cause,—highly to her honor, for she was little exposed to danger, being covered by the neighboring provinces; while impoverished New Hampshire put one in three of her able-bodied men into the field.[3]

In June the combined British and provincial force which Abercromby was to lead against Ticonderoga was gathered at the head of Lake George; while Montcalm lay at its outlet around the walls of the French stronghold, with an army not one fourth so numerous. Vaudreuil had devised a plan for saving Ticonderoga by a diversion into the valley of the Mohawk under Lévis, Rigaud, and Longueuil, with sixteen hundred men, who were to be joined by as many Indians. The English forts of that region were to be attacked, Schenectady threatened, and the Five Nations compelled to declare for France.[4] Thus, as the Governor gave out, the English would be forced to cease from aggression, leave Montcalm in peace, and think only of defending themselves.[5] "This," writes Bougainville on the fifteenth of June, "is what M. de Vaudreuil thinks will happen, because he never doubts anything. Ticonderoga, which is the point really threatened, is abandoned without support to the troops of the line and their general. It would even be wished that they might meet a reverse, if the consequences to the colony would not be too disastrous."

The proposed movement promised, no doubt, great advantages; but it was not destined to take effect. Some rangers taken on Lake George by a partisan officer named Langy declared with pardonable exaggeration that twenty-five or thirty thousand men would attack Ticonderoga in less than a fortnight. Vaudreuil saw himself forced to abandon his Mohawk expedition, and to order Lévis and his followers, who had not yet left Montreal, to reinforce Montcalm.[6] Why they did not go at once is not clear. The Governor declares that there were not boats

---

[1] Pownall to Pitt, 30 Sept. 1758 (Public Record Office, America and West Indies, LXXI.). "The province of Massachusetts Bay has exerted itself with great zeal and at vast expense for the public service." Registers of Privy Council, 26 July, 1757.

[2] Bollan, Agent of Massachusetts, to Speaker of Assembly, 20 March, 1760. It was her share of £200,000 granted to all the colonies in the proportion of their respective efforts.

[3] Address to His Majesty from the Governor, Council, and Assembly of New Hampshire, Jan. 1759.

[4] Lévis au Ministre, 17 Juin, 1758. Doreil au Ministre, 16 Juin, 1758. Montcalm à sa Femme, 18 Avril, 1758.

[5] Correspondance de Vaudreuil, 1758. Livre d'Ordres, Juin, 1758.

[6] Bigot au Ministre, 21 Juillet, 1758.

enough. From whatever cause, there was a long delay, and Montcalm
was left to defend himself as he could.

He hesitated whether he should not fall back to Crown Point. The
engineer, Lotbinière, opposed the plan, as did also Le Mercier.[1] It was
but a choice of difficulties, and he stayed at Ticonderoga. His troops
were disposed as they had been in the summer before; one battalion,
that of Berry, being left near the fort, while the main body, under
Montcalm himself, was encamped by the saw-mill at the Falls, and the
rest, under Bourlamaque, occupied the head of the portage, with a
small advanced force at the landing-place on Lake George. It remained
to determine at which of these points he should concentrate them and
make his stand against the English. Ruin threatened him in any case;
each position had its fatal weakness or its peculiar danger, and his best
hope was in the ignorance or blundering of his enemy. He seems to
have been several days in a state of indecision.

In the afternoon of the fifth of July the partisan Langy, who had
again gone out to reconnoitre towards the head of Lake George, came
back in haste with the report that the English were embarked in great
force. Montcalm sent a canoe down Lake Champlain to hasten Lévis
to his aid, and ordered the battalion of Berry to begin a breastwork and
abattis on the high ground in front of the fort. That they were not
begun before shows that he was in doubt as to his plan of defence; and
that his whole army was not now set to work at them shows that his
doubt was still unsolved.

It was nearly a month since Abercromby had begun his camp at the
head of Lake George. Here, on the ground where Johnson had beaten
Dieskau, where Montcalm had planted his batteries, and Monro vainly
defended the wooden ramparts of Fort William Henry, were now assembled more than fifteen thousand men; and the shores, the foot of the
mountains, and the broken plains between them were studded thick
with tents. Of regulars there were six thousand three hundred and sixty-
seven, officers and soldiers, and of provincials nine thousand and
thirty-four.[2] To the New England levies, or at least to their chaplains,
the expedition seemed a crusade against the abomination of Babylon;
and they discoursed in their sermons of Moses sending forth Joshua
against Amalek. Abercromby, raised to his place by political influence,
was little but the nominal commander. "A heavy man," said Wolfe in

---

[1] *N. Y. Col. Docs.*, X. 893. Lotbinière's relative, Vaudreuil, confirms the statement. Montcalm
had not, as has been said, begun already to fall back.
[2] *Abercromby to Pitt, 12 July, 1758.*

a letter to his father; "an aged gentleman, infirm in body and mind," wrote William Parkman, a boy of seventeen, who carried a musket in a Massachusetts regiment, and kept in his knapsack a dingy little notebook, in which he jotted down what passed each day.[1] The age of the aged gentleman was fifty-two.

Pitt meant that the actual command of the army should be in the hands of Brigadier Lord Howe,[2] and he was in fact its real chief; "the noblest Englishman that has appeared in my time, and the best soldier in the British army," says Wolfe.[3] And he elsewhere speaks of him as "that great man." Abercromby testifies to the universal respect and love with which officers and men regarded him, and Pitt calls him "a character of ancient times; a complete model of military virtue."[4] High as this praise is, it seems to have been deserved. The young nobleman, who was then in his thirty-fourth year, had the qualities of a leader of men. The army felt him, from general to drummer-boy. He was its soul; and while breathing into it his own energy and ardor, and bracing it by stringent discipline, he broke through the traditions of the service and gave it new shapes to suit the time and place. During the past year he had studied the art of forest warfare, and joined Rogers and his rangers in their scouting-parties, sharing all their hardships and making himself one of them. Perhaps the reforms that he introduced were fruits of this rough self-imposed schooling. He made officers and men throw off all useless incumbrances, cut their hair close, wear leggings to protect them from briers, brown the barrels of their muskets, and carry in their knapsacks thirty pounds of meal, which they cooked for themselves; so that, according to an admiring Frenchman, they could live a month without their supply-trains.[5] "You would laugh to see the droll figure we all make," writes an officer. "Regulars as well as provincials have cut their coats so as scarcely to reach their waists. No officer or private is allowed to carry more than one blanket and a bearskin. A small portmanteau is allowed each officer. No women follow the camp to wash our linen. Lord Howe has already shown an example by going to the brook and washing his own."[6]

Here, as in all things, he shared the lot of the soldier, and required

[1] Great-uncle of the writer, and son of the Rev. Ebenezer Parkman, a graduate of Harvard, and minister of Westborough, Mass.

[2] Chesterfield, *Letters*, IV. 260 (ed. Mahon).

[3] *Wolfe to his Father, 7 Aug. 1758*, in Wright, 450.

[4] *Pitt to Grenville, 22 Aug. 1758*, in Grenville Papers, I. 262.

[5] Pouchot, *Dernière Guerre de l'Amérique*, I. 140.

[6] *Letter from Camp, 12 June, 1758*, in *Boston Evening Post*. Another, in *Boston News Letter*, contains similar statements.

his officers to share it. A story is told of him that before the army embarked he invited some of them to dinner in his tent, where they found no seats but logs, and no carpet but bearskins. A servant presently placed on the ground a large dish of pork and peas, on which his lordship took from his pocket a sheath containing a knife and fork and began to cut the meat. The guests looked on in some embarrassment; upon which he said: "Is it possible, gentlemen, that you have come on this campaign without providing yourselves with what is necessary?" And he gave each of them a sheath, with a knife and fork, like his own.

Yet this Lycurgus of the camp, as a contemporary calls him, is described as a man of social accomplishments rare even in his rank. He made himself greatly beloved by the provincial officers, with many of whom he was on terms of intimacy, and he did what he could to break down the barriers between the colonial soldiers and the British regulars. When he was at Albany, sharing with other high officers the kindly hospitalities of Mrs. Schuyler, he so won the heart of that excellent matron that she loved him like a son; and, though not given to such effusion, embraced him with tears on the morning when he left her to lead his division to the lake.[1] In Westminster Abbey may be seen the tablet on which Massachusetts pays grateful tribute to his virtues, and commemorates "the affection her officers and soldiers bore to his command."

On the evening of the fourth of July, baggage, stores, and ammunition were all on board the boats, and the whole army embarked on the morning of the fifth. The arrangements were perfect. Each corps marched without confusion to its appointed station on the beach, and the sun was scarcely above the ridge of French Mountain when all were afloat. A spectator watching them from the shore says that when the fleet was three miles on its way, the surface of the lake at that distance was completely hidden from sight.[2] There were nine hundred bateaux, a hundred and thirty-five whaleboats, and a large number of heavy flatboats carrying the artillery. The whole advanced in three divisions, the regulars in the centre, and the provincials on the flanks. Each corps had its flags and its music. The day was fair and men and officers were in the highest spirits.

Before ten o'clock they began to enter the Narrows; and the boats of the three divisions extended themselves into long files as the mountains

---

[1] Mrs. Grant, *Memoirs of an American Lady*, 226 (ed. 1876).
[2] *Letter from Lake George*, in *Boston News Letter*.

closed on either hand upon the contracted lake. From front to rear the line was six miles long. The spectacle was superb: the brightness of the summer day; the romantic beauty of the scenery; the sheen and sparkle of those crystal waters; the countless islets, tufted with pine, birch, and fir; the bordering mountains, with their green summits and sunny crags; the flash of oars and glitter of weapons; the banners, the varied uniforms, and the notes of bugle, trumpet, bagpipe, and drum, answered and prolonged by a hundred woodland echoes. "I never beheld so delightful a prospect," wrote a wounded officer at Albany a fortnight after.

Rogers with the rangers, and Gage with the light infantry, led the way in whaleboats, followed by Bradstreet with his corps of boatmen, armed and drilled as soldiers. Then came the main body. The central column of regulars was commanded by Lord Howe, his own regiment, the fifty-fifth, in the van, followed by the Royal Americans, the twenty-seventh, forty-fourth, forty-sixth, and eightieth infantry, and the Highlanders of the forty-second, with their major, Duncan Campbell of Inverawe, silent and gloomy amid the general cheer, for his soul was dark with foreshadowings of death.[1] With this central column came what are described as two floating castles, which were no doubt batteries to cover the landing of the troops. On the right hand and the left were the provincials, uniformed in blue, regiment after regiment, from Massachusetts, Connecticut, New York, New Jersey, and Rhode Island. Behind them all came the bateaux, loaded with stores and baggage, and the heavy flatboats that carried the artillery, while a rear-guard of provincials and regulars closed the long procession.[2]

At five in the afternoon they reached Sabbath-Day Point, twenty-five miles down the lake, where they stopped till late in the evening, waiting for the baggage and artillery, which had lagged behind; and here Lord Howe, lying on a bearskin by the side of the ranger, John Stark, questioned him as to the position of Ticonderoga and its best points of approach. At about eleven o'clock they set out again, and at daybreak entered what was then called the Second Narrows; that is to say, the contraction of the lake where it approaches its outlet. Close on their left, ruddy in the warm sunrise, rose the vast bare face of Rogers Rock, whence a French advanced party, under Langy and an officer named Trepezec, was watching their movements. Lord Howe,

---

[1] See Appendix G.
[2] *Letter from Lake George*, in *Boston News Letter*. Even Rogers, the ranger, speaks of the beauty of the scene.

with Rogers and Bradstreet, went in whaleboats to reconnoitre the landing. At the place which the French called the Burnt Camp, where Montcalm had embarked the summer before, they saw a detachment of the enemy too weak to oppose them. Their men landed and drove them off. At noon the whole army was on shore. Rogers, with a party of rangers, was ordered forward to reconnoitre, and the troops were formed for the march.

From this part of the shore[1] a plain covered with forest stretched northwestward half a mile or more to the mountains behind which lay the valley of Trout Brook. On this plain the army began its march in four columns, with the intention of passing round the western bank of the river of the outlet, since the bridge over it had been destroyed. Rogers, with the provincial regiments of Fitch and Lyman, led the way, at some distance before the rest. The forest was extremely dense and heavy, and so obstructed with undergrowth that it was impossible to see more than a few yards in any direction, while the ground was encumbered with fallen trees in every stage of decay. The ranks were broken, and the men struggled on as they could in dampness and shade, under a canopy of boughs that the sun could scarcely pierce. The difficulty increased when, after advancing about a mile, they came upon undulating and broken ground. They were now not far from the upper rapids of the outlet. The guides became bewildered in the maze of trunks and boughs; the marching columns were confused, and fell in one upon the other. They were in the strange situation of an army lost in the woods.

The advanced party of French under Langy and Trepezec, about three hundred and fifty in all, regulars and Canadians, had tried to retreat; but before they could do so, the whole English army had passed them, landed, and placed itself between them and their countrymen. They had no resource but to take to the woods. They seem to have climbed the steep gorge at the side of Rogers Rock and followed the Indian path that led to the valley of Trout Brook, thinking to descend it, and, by circling along the outskirts of the valley of Ticonderoga, reach Montcalm's camp at the saw-mill. Langy was used to bushranging; but he too became perplexed in the blind intricacies of the forest. Towards the close of the day he and his men had come out from the valley of Trout Brook, and were near the junction of that stream with the river of the outlet, in a state of some anxiety, for they could see nothing but brown trunks and green boughs. Could any of them have

---

[1]Between the old and new steamboat-landings, and parts adjacent.

climbed one of the great pines that here and there reared their shaggy spires high above the surrounding forest, they would have discovered where they were, but would have gained not the faintest knowledge of the enemy. Out of the woods on the right they would have seen a smoke rising from the burning huts of the French camp at the head of the portage, which Bourlamaque had set on fire and abandoned. At a mile or more in front, the saw-mill at the Falls might perhaps have been descried, and, by glimpses between the trees, the tents of the neighboring camp where Montcalm still lay with his main force. All the rest seemed lonely as the grave; mountain and valley lay wrapped in primeval woods, and none could have dreamed that, not far distant, an army was groping its way, buried in foliage; no rumbling of wagons and artillery trains, for none were there; all silent but the cawing of some crow flapping his black wings over the sea of tree-tops.

Lord Howe, with Major Israel Putnam and two hundred rangers, was at the head of the principal column, which was a little in advance of the three others. Suddenly the challenge, *Qui vive!* rang sharply from the thickets in front. *Français!* was the reply. Langy's men were not deceived; they fired out of the bushes. The shots were returned; a hot skirmish followed; and Lord Howe dropped dead, shot through the breast. All was confusion. The dull, vicious reports of musketry in thick woods, at first few and scattering, then in fierce and rapid volleys, reached the troops behind. They could hear, but see nothing. Already harassed and perplexed, they became perturbed. For all they knew, Montcalm's whole army was upon them. Nothing prevented a panic but the steadiness of the rangers, who maintained the fight alone till the rest came back to their senses. Rogers, with his reconnoitring party, and the regiments of Fitch and Lyman, were at no great distance in front. They all turned on hearing the musketry, and thus the French were caught between two fires. They fought with desperation. About fifty of them at length escaped; a hundred and forty-eight were captured, and the rest killed or drowned in trying to cross the rapids. The loss of the English was small in numbers, but immeasurable in the death of Howe. "The fall of this noble and brave officer," says Rogers, "seemed to produce an almost general languor and consternation through the whole army." "In Lord Howe," writes another contemporary, Major Thomas Mante, "the soul of General Abercromby's army seemed to expire. From the unhappy moment the General was deprived of his advice, neither order nor discipline was observed, and a strange kind of infatuation usurped the place of resolution." The death of one man was the ruin of fifteen thousand.

The evil news was despatched to Albany, and in two or three days the messenger who bore it passed the house of Mrs. Schuyler on the meadows above the town. "In the afternoon," says her biographer, "a man was seen coming from the north galloping violently without his hat. Pedrom, as he was familiarly called, Colonel Schulyer's only surviving brother, was with her, and ran instantly to inquire, well knowing that he rode express. The man galloped on, crying out that Lord Howe was killed. The mind of our good aunt had been so engrossed by her anxiety and fears for the event impending, and so impressed with the merit and magnanimity of her favorite hero, that her wonted firmness sank under the stroke, and she broke out into bitter lamentations. This had such an effect on her friends and domestics that shrieks and sobs of anguish echoed through every part of the house."

The effect of the loss was seen at once. The army was needlessly kept under arms all night in the forest, and in the morning was ordered back to the landing whence it came.[1] Towards noon, however, Bradstreet was sent with a detachment of regulars and provincials to take possession of the saw-mill at the Falls, which Montcalm had abandoned the evening before. Bradstreet rebuilt the bridges destroyed by the retiring enemy, and sent word to his commander that the way was open; on which Abercromby again put his army in motion, reached the Falls late in the afternoon, and occupied the deserted encampment of the French.

Montcalm with his main force had held this position at the Falls through most of the preceding day, doubtful, it seems, to the last whether he should not make his final stand there. Bourlamaque was for doing so; but two old officers, Bernès and Montguy, pointed out the danger that the English would occupy the neighboring heights;[2] whereupon Montcalm at length resolved to fall back. The camp was broken up at five o'clock. Some of the troops embarked in bateaux, while others marched a mile and a half along the forest road, passed the place where the battalion of Berry was still at work on the breastwork begun in the morning, and made their bivouac a little farther on, upon the cleared ground that surrounded the fort.

The peninsula of Ticonderoga consists of a rocky plateau, with low grounds on each side, bordering Lake Champlain on the one hand, and the outlet of Lake George on the other. The fort stood near the end of the peninsula, which points towards the southeast. Thence, as one goes

[1] *Abercromby to Pitt, 12 July, 1758.*
[2] Pouchot, I. 145.

westward, the ground declines a little, and then slowly rises, till, about half a mile from the fort, it reaches its greatest elevation, and begins still more gradually to decline again. Thus a ridge is formed across the plateau between the steep declivities that sink to the low grounds on right and left. Some weeks before, a French officer named Hugues had suggested the defence of this ridge by means of an abattis.[1] Montcalm approved his plan; and now, at the eleventh hour, he resolved to make his stand here. The two engineers, Pontleroy and Desandrouin, had already traced the outline of the works, and the soldiers of the battalion of Berry had made some progress in constructing them. At dawn of the seventh, while Abercromby, fortunately for his enemy, was drawing his troops back to the landing-place, the whole French army fell to their task. The regimental colors were planted along the line, and the officers, stripped to the shirt, took axe in hand and labored with their men. The trees that covered the ground were hewn down by thousands, the tops lopped off, and the trunks piled one upon another to form a massive breastwork. The line followed the top of the ridge, along which it zigzagged in such a manner that the whole front could be swept by flank-fires of musketry and grape. Abercromby describes the wall of logs as between eight and nine feet high;[2] in which case there must have been a rude *banquette*, or platform to fire from, on the inner side. It was certainly so high that nothing could be seen over it but the crowns of the soldiers' hats. The upper tier was formed of single logs, in which notches were cut to serve as loopholes; and in some places sods and bags of sand were piled along the top, with narrow spaces to fire through.[3] From the central part of the line the ground sloped away like a natural glacis; while at the sides, and especially on the left, it was undulating and broken. Over this whole space, to the distance of a musketshot from the works, the forest was cut down, and the trees left lying where they fell among the stumps, with tops turned outwards, forming one vast abattis, which, as a Massachusetts officer says, looked like a forest laid flat by a hurricane.[4] But the most formidable obstruction was immediately along the front of the breastwork, where the ground was covered with heavy boughs, overlapping and interlaced, with sharpened points bristling into the face of the assailant like the quills of a porcupine. As these works were all of wood, no vestige of

[1] *N. Y. Col. Docs.*, X. 708.

[2] *Abercromby to Barrington, 12 July, 1758.* "At least eight feet high." Rogers, *Journals*, 116.

[3] A Swiss officer of the Royal Americans, writing on the 14th, says that there were two, and in some parts three, rows of loopholes. See the letter in *Pennsylvania Archives*, III. 472.

[4] *Colonel Oliver Partridge to his Wife, 12 July, 1758.*

them remains. The earthworks now shown to tourists as the lines of Montcalm are of later construction; and though on the same ground, are not on the same plan.[1]

Here, then, was a position which, if attacked in front with musketry alone, might be called impregnable. But would Abercromby so attack it? He had several alternatives. He might attempt the flank and rear of his enemy by way of the low grounds on the right and left of the plateau, a movement which the precautions of Montcalm had made difficult, but not impossible. Or, instead of leaving his artillery idle on the strand of Lake George, he might bring it to the front and batter the breastwork, which, though impervious to musketry, was worthless against heavy cannon. Or he might do what Burgoyne did with success a score of years later, and plant a battery on the heights of Rattlesnake Hill, now called Mount Defiance, which commanded the position of the French, and whence the inside of their breastwork could be scoured with round-shot from end to end. Or, while threatening the French front with a part of his army, he could march the rest a short distance through the woods on his left to the road which led from Ticonderoga to Crown Point, and which would soon have brought him to the place called Five-Mile Point, where Lake Champlain narrows to the width of an easy rifle-shot, and where a battery of field-pieces would have cut off all Montcalm's supplies and closed his only way of retreat. As the French were provisioned for but eight days, their position would thus have been desperate. They plainly saw the danger; and Doreil declares that had the movement been made, their whole army must have surrendered.[2] Montcalm had done what he could; but the danger of his position was inevitable and extreme. His hope lay in Abercromby; and it was a hope well founded. The action of the English general answered the utmost wishes of his enemy.

Abercromby had been told by his prisoners that Montcalm had six thousand men, and that three thousand more were expected every hour. Therefore he was in haste to attack before these succors could arrive. As was the general, so was the army. "I believe," writes an officer, "we were one and all infatuated by a notion of carrying every obstacle by a mere *coup de mousqueterie*."[3] Leadership perished with Lord Howe, and nothing was left but blind, headlong valor.

---

[1]A new line of works was begun four days after the battle, to replace the log breastwork. Malartic, *Journal*. *Travaux faits à Carillon, 1758*.
[2]*Doreil au Ministre, 28 Juillet, 1758*. The Chevalier Johnstone thought that Montcalm was saved by Abercromby's ignorance of the ground. *A Dialogue in Hades* (Quebec Historical Society).
[3]See the letter in Knox, I. 148.

Clerk, chief engineer, was sent to reconnoitre the French works from Mount Defiance; and came back with the report that, to judge from what he could see, they might be carried by assault. Then, without waiting to bring up his cannon, Abercromby prepared to storm the lines.

The French finished their breastwork and abattis on the evening of the seventh, encamped behind them, slung their kettles, and rested after their heavy toil. Lévis had not yet appeared; but at twilight one of his officers, Captain Pouchot, arrived with three hundred regulars, and announced that his commander would come before morning with a hundred more. The reinforcement, though small, was welcome, and Lévis was a host in himself. Pouchot was told that the army was half a mile off. Thither he repaired, made his report to Montcalm, and looked with amazement at the prodigious amount of work accomplished in one day.[1] Lévis himself arrived in the course of the night, and approved the arrangement of the troops. They lay behind their lines till daybreak; then the drums beat, and they formed in order of battle.[2] The battalions of La Sarre and Languedoc were posted on the left, under Bourlamaque, the first battalion of Berry with that of Royal Roussillon in the centre, under Montcalm, and those of La Reine, Béarn, and Guienne on the right, under Lévis. A detachment of volunteers occupied the low grounds between the breastwork and the outlet of Lake George; while, at the foot of the declivity on the side towards Lake Champlain, were stationed four hundred and fifty colony regulars and Canadians, behind an abattis which they had made for themselves; and as they were covered by the cannon of the fort, there was some hope that they would check any flank movement which the English might attempt on that side. Their posts being thus assigned, the men fell to work again to strengthen their defences. Including those who came with Lévis, the total force of effective soldiers was now thirty-six hundred.[3]

Soon after nine o'clock a distant and harmless fire of small-arms began on the slopes of Mount Defiance. It came from a party of Indians who had just arrived with Sir William Johnson, and who, after amusing themselves in this manner for a time, remained for the rest of the day safe spectators of the fight. The soldiers worked undisturbed till noon, when volleys of musketry were heard from the forest in front. It was

[1] Pouchot, I. 137.
[2] *Livre d'Ordres, Disposition de Défense des Retranchements, 8 Juillet, 1758.*
[3] Montcalm, *Relation de la Victoire remportée à Carillon, 8 Juillet, 1758.* Vaudreuil puts the number at 4,760, besides officers, which includes the garrison and laborers at the fort. *Vaudreuil au Ministre, 28 Juillet, 1758.*

the English light troops driving in the French pickets. A cannon was fired as a signal to drop tools and form for battle. The white uniforms lined the breastwork in a triple row, with the grenadiers behind them as a reserve, and the second battalion of Berry watching the flanks and rear.

Meanwhile the English army had moved forward from its camp by the saw-mill. First came the rangers, the light infantry, and Bradstreet's armed boatmen, who, emerging into the open space, began a spattering fire. Some of the provincial troops followed, extending from left to right, and opening fire in turn; then the regulars, who had formed in columns of attack under cover of the forest, advanced their solid red masses into the sunlight, and passing through the intervals between the provincial regiments, pushed forward to the assault. Across the rough ground, with its maze of fallen trees whose leaves hung withering in the July sun, they could see the top of the breastwork, but not the men behind it; when, in an instant, all the line was obscured by a gush of smoke, a crash of exploding firearms tore the air, and grapeshot and musket-balls swept the whole space like a tempest; "a damnable fire," says an officer who heard them screaming about his ears. The English had been ordered to carry the works with the bayonet; but their ranks were broken by the obstructions through which they struggled in vain to force their way, and they soon began to fire in turn. The storm raged in full fury for an hour. The assailants pushed close to the breastwork; but there they were stopped by the bristling mass of sharpened branches, which they could not pass under the murderous cross-fires that swept them from front and flank. At length they fell back, exclaiming that the works were impregnable. Abercromby, who was at the saw-mill, a mile and a half in the rear, sent orders to attack again, and again they came on as before.

The scene was frightful: masses of infuriated men who could not go forward and would not go back; straining for an enemy they could not reach, and firing on an enemy they could not see; caught in the entanglement of fallen trees; tripped by briers, stumbling over logs, tearing through boughs; shouting, yelling, cursing, and pelted all the while with bullets that killed them by scores, stretched them on the ground, or hung them on jagged branches in strange attitudes of death. The provincials supported the regulars with spirit, and some of them forced their way to the foot of the wooden wall.

The French fought with the intrepid gayety of their nation, and shouts of *Vive le Roi!* and *Vive notre Général!* mingled with the din of musketry. Montcalm, with his coat off, for the day was hot, directed the defence of the centre, and repaired to any part of the line where the danger for the time seemed greatest. He is warm in praise of his enemy, and declares that between one and seven o'clock they attacked him six successive times. Early in the action Abercromby tried to turn the French left by sending twenty bateaux, filled with troops, down the outlet of Lake George. They were met by the fire of the volunteers stationed to defend the low grounds on that side, and, still advancing, came within range of the cannon of the fort, which sank two of them and drove back the rest.

A curious incident happened during one of the attacks. De Bassignac, a captain in the battalion of Royal Roussillon, tied his handkerchief to the end of a musket and waved it over the breastwork in defiance. The English mistook it for a sign of surrender, and came forward with all possible speed, holding their muskets crossed over their heads in both hands, and crying *Quarter*. The French made the same mistake; and thinking that their enemies were giving themselves up as prisoners, ceased firing, and mounted on the top of the breastwork to receive them. Captain Pouchot, astonished, as he says, to see them perched there, looked out to learn the cause, and saw that the enemy meant anything but surrender. Whereupon he shouted with all his might: *"Tirez! Tirez! Ne voyez-vous pas que ces gens-là vont vous enlever?"* The soldiers, still standing on the breastwork, instantly gave the English a volley, which killed some of them, and sent back the rest discomfited.[1]

This was set to the account of Gallic treachery. "Another deceit the enemy put upon us," says a military letter-writer: "they raised their hats above the breastwork, which our people fired at; they, having loopholes to fire through, and being covered by the sods, we did them little damage, except shooting their hats to pieces."[2] In one of the last assaults a soldier of the Rhode Island regiment, William Smith, managed to get through all obstructions and ensconce himself close under the breastwork, where in the confusion he remained for a time unnoticed, improving his advantages meanwhile by shooting several Frenchmen. Being at length observed, a soldier fired vertically down upon him and wounded him severely, but not enough to prevent his springing up, striking at one of his enemies over the top of the wall, and braining him with his hatchet. A British officer who saw the feat, and was struck

[1] Pouchot, I. 153. Both Niles and Entick mention the incident.
[2] *Letter from Saratoga, 12 July, 1758*, in *New Hampshire Gazette*. Compare *Pennsylvania Archives*, III. 474.

by the reckless daring of the man, ordered two regulars to bring him off; which, covered by a brisk fire of musketry, they succeeded in doing. A letter from the camp two or three weeks later reports him as in a fair way to recover, being, says the writer, much braced and invigorated by his anger against the French, on whom he was swearing to have his revenge.[1]

Toward five o'clock two English columns joined in a most determined assault on the extreme right of the French, defended by the battalions of Guienne and Béarn. The danger for a time was imminent. Montcalm hastened to the spot with the reserves. The assailants hewed their way to the foot of the breastwork; and though again and again repulsed, they again and again renewed the attack. The Highlanders fought with stubborn and unconquerable fury. "Even those who were mortally wounded," writes one of their lieutenants, "cried to their companions not to lose a thought upon them, but to follow their officers and mind the honor of their country. Their ardor was such that it was difficult to bring them off."[2] Their major, Campbell of Inverawe, found his foreboding true. He received a mortal shot, and his clansmen bore him from the field. Twenty-five of their officers were killed or wounded, and half the men fell under the deadly fire that poured from the loopholes. Captain John Campbell and a few followers tore their way through the abattis, climbed the breastwork, leaped down among the French, and were bayoneted there.[3]

As the colony troops and Canadians on the low ground were left undisturbed, Lévis sent them an order to make a sortie and attack the left flank of the charging columns. They accordingly posted themselves among the trees along the declivity, and fired upwards at the enemy, who presently shifted their position to the right, out of the line of shot. The assault still continued, but in vain; and at six there was another effort, equally fruitless. From this time till half-past seven a lingering fight was kept up by the rangers and other provincials, firing from the edge of the woods and from behind the stumps, bushes, and fallen trees in front of the lines. Its only objects were to cover their comrades, who were collecting and bringing off the wounded, and to protect the retreat of the regulars, who fell back in disorder to the Falls. As twilight came on, the last combatant withdrew, and none were left but the dead. Abercromby had lost in killed, wounded, and missing, nineteen

---

[1] *Letter from Lake George, 26 July, 1758*, in *Boston Gazette*. The story is given, without much variation, in several other letters.
[2] *Letter of Lieutenant William Grant*, in *Maclachlan's Highlands*, II. 340 (ed. 1875).
[3] *Ibid.*, II. 339.

hundred and forty-four officers and men.[1] The loss of the French, not counting that of Langy's detachment, was three hundred and seventy-seven. Bourlamaque was dangerously wounded; Bougainville slightly; and the hat of Lévis was twice shot through.[2]

Montcalm, with a mighty load lifted from his soul, passed along the lines, and gave the tired soldiers the thanks they nobly deserved. Beer, wine, and food were served out to them, and they bivouacked for the night on the level ground between the breastwork and the fort. The enemy had met a terrible rebuff; yet the danger was not over. Abercromby still had more than thirteen thousand men, and he might renew the attack with cannon. But, on the morning of the ninth, a band of volunteers who had gone out to watch him brought back the report that he was in full retreat. The saw-mill at the Falls was on fire, and the last English soldier was gone. On the morning of the tenth, Lévis, with a strong detachment, followed the road to the landing-place, and found signs that a panic had overtaken the defeated troops. They had left behind several hundred barrels of provisions and a large quantity of baggage; while in a marshy place that they had crossed was found a considerable number of their shoes, which had stuck in the mud, and which they had not stopped to recover. They had embarked on the morning after the battle, and retreated to the head of the lake in a disorder and dejection wofully contrasted with the pomp of their advance. A gallant army was sacrificed by the blunders of its chief.

Montcalm announced his victory to his wife in a strain of exaggeration that marks the exaltation of his mind. "Without Indians, almost without Canadians or colony troops,—I had only four hundred,—alone with Lévis and Bourlamaque and the troops of the line, thirty-one hundred fighting men, I have beaten an army of twenty-five thousand. They repassed the lake precipitately, with a loss of at least five thousand. This glorious day does infinite honor to the valor of our battalions. I have no time to write more. I am well, my dearest, and I embrace you." And he wrote to his friend Doreil: "The army, the too-small army of the King, has beaten the enemy. What a day for France! If I had had two hundred Indians to send out at the head of a thousand picked men under the Chevalier de Lévis, not many would have escaped. Ah, my dear Doreil, what soldiers are ours! I never saw the like. Why were they not at Louisbourg?"

On the morrow of his victory he caused a great cross to be planted

---

[1] See Appendix G.
[2] *Lévis au Ministre, 13 Juillet, 1758.*

on the battle-field, inscribed with these lines, composed by the soldier-scholar himself,—

"Quid dux? quid miles? quid strata ingentia ligna?
En Signum! en victor! Deus hîc, Deus ipse triumphat."

"Soldier and chief and rampart's strength are nought;
Behold the conquering Cross! 'T is God the triumph wrought."[1]

[1] Along with the above paraphrase I may give that of Montcalm himself, which was also inscribed on the cross:—

"Chrétien! ce ne fut point Montcalm et la prudence,
Ces arbres renversés, ces héros, leurs exploits,
Qui des Anglais confus ont brisé l'espérance;
C'est le bras de ton Dieu, vainqueur sur cette croix."

In the same letter in which Montcalm sent these lines to his mother he says: "Je vous envoie, pour vous amuser, deux chansons sur le combat du 8 Juillet, dont l'une est en style des poissardes de Paris." One of these songs, which were written by soldiers after the battle, begins,—

"Je chante des François
La valeur et la gloire,
Qui toujours sur l'Anglois
Remportent la victoire.
Ce sont des héros,
Tous nos généraux,
Et Montcalm et Lévis,
Et Bourlamaque aussi.

"Mars, qui les engendra
Pour l'honneur de la France,
D'abord les anima
De sa haute vaillance,
Et les transporta
Dans le Canada,
Où l'on voit les François
Culbuter les Anglois."

The other effusion of the military muse is in a different strain, "en style des poissardes de Paris." The following is a specimen, given *literatim*:—

"L'aumônier fit l'exhortation,
Puis il donnit l'absolution;
Aisément cela se peut croire.
Enfants, dit-il, animez-vous!
L'bon Dieu, sa mère, tout est pour vous.
S—é! j'sommes catholiques. Les Anglois sont des hérétiques.

"Ce sont des chiens; à coups d'pieds, à coups d'poings faut leur casser la gueule et la mâchoire.

"Soldats, officiers, généraux,
Chacun en ce jour fut héros.
Aisément cela se peut croire.

Montcalm, comme défunt Annibal,
S'montroit soldat et général.
S—é! sil y avoit quelqu'un qui ne l'aimît point!

"Je veux être un chien; à coups d'pieds, à coups d'poings, j'lui cass'rai la gueule et la mâchoire."
This is an allusion to Vaudreuil. On the battle of Ticonderoga, see Appendix G.

2I

Fort Frontenac

1758

The rashness of Abercromby before the fight was matched by his poltroonery after it. Such was his terror that on the evening of his defeat he sent an order to Colonel Cummings, commanding at Fort William Henry, to send all the sick and wounded and all the heavy artillery to New York without delay.[1] He himself followed so closely upon this disgraceful missive that Cummings had no time to obey it.

The defeated and humbled troops proceeded to reoccupy the ground they had left a few days before in the flush of confidence and pride; and young Colonel Williams, of Massachusetts, lost no time in sending the miserable story to his uncle Israel. His letter, which is dated "Lake George (sorrowful situation), July ye 11th," ends thus: "I have told facts; you may put the epithets upon them. In one word, what with fatigue, want of sleep, exercise of mind, and leaving the place we went to cap-

[1] *Cunningham, aide-de-camp of Abercromby, to Cummings, 8 July, 1758.*

ture, the best part of the army is unhinged. I have told enough to make you sick, if the relation acts on you as the facts have on me."

In the routed army was the sturdy John Cleaveland, minister of Ipswich, and now chaplain of Bagley's Massachusetts regiment, who regarded the retreat with a disgust that was shared by many others. "This day," he writes in his Diary, at the head of Lake George, two days after the battle, "wherever I went I found people, officers and soldiers, astonished that we left the French ground, and commenting on the strange conduct in coming off." From this time forth the provincials called their commander Mrs. Nabbycromby.[1] He thought of nothing but fortifying himself. "Towards evening," continues the chaplain, "the General, with his Rehoboam counsellors, came over to line out a fort on the rocky hill where our breastwork was last year. Now we begin to think strongly that the grand expedition against Canada is laid aside, and a foundation made totally to impoverish our country." The whole army was soon intrenched. The chaplain of Bagley's, with his brother Ebenezer, chaplain of another regiment, one day walked round the camp and carefully inspected it. The tour proved satisfactory to the militant divines, and John Cleaveland reported to his wife: "We have built an extraordinary good breastwork, sufficient to defend ourselves against twenty thousand of the enemy, though at present we have not above a third part of that number fit for duty." Many of the troops had been sent to the Mohawk, and others to the Hudson.

In the regiment of which Cleaveland was chaplain there was a young surgeon from Danvers, Dr. Caleb Rea, who also kept a copious diary, and, being of a serious turn, listened with edification to the prayers and exhortations to which the yeoman soldiery were daily summoned. In his zeal, he made an inquest among them for singers, and chose the most melodious to form a regimental choir, "the better to carry on the daily service of singing psalms;" insomuch that the New England camp was vocal with rustic harmony, sincere, if somewhat nasal. These seemly observances were not inconsistent with a certain amount of disorder among the more turbulent spirits, who, removed from the repressive influence of tight-laced village communities, sometimes indulged in conduct which grieved the conscientious surgeon. The rural New England of that time, with its narrowness, its prejudices, its oddities, its combative energy, and rugged, unconquerable strength, is among the things of the past, or lingers in remote corners where the whistle

[1]Trumbull, *Hist. Connecticut*, II. 392. "Nabby" (Abigail) was then a common female name in New England.

of the locomotive is never heard. It has spread itself in swarming millions over half a continent, changing with changing conditions; and even the part of it that clings to the ancestral hive has transformed and continues to transform itself.

The provincials were happy in their chaplains, among whom there reigned a marvellous harmony, Episcopalians, Presbyterians, and Congregationalists meeting twice a week to hold prayer-meetings together. "A rare instance indeed," says Dr. Rea, "and perhaps scarce ever was an army blessed with such a set of chaplains before." On one occasion, just before the fatal expedition, nine of them, after prayers and breakfast, went together to call upon the General. "He treated us very kindly," says the chaplain of Bagley's, "and told us that he hoped we would teach the people to do their duty and be courageous; and told us a story of a chaplain in Germany, where he was, who just before the action told the soldiers he had not time to say much, and therefore should only say: 'Be courageous; for no cowards go to heaven.' The General treated us to a bowl of punch and a bottle of wine, and then we took our leave of him."[1]

When Cleaveland and the more gifted among his brethren preached of a Sunday, officers and men of the regulars, no less than the provincials, came to listen; yet that pious Sabbatarian, Dr. Rea, saw much to afflict his conscience. "Sad, sad it is to see how the Sabbath is profaned in the camp," above all by "the horrid custom of swearing, more especially among the regulars; and I can't but charge our defeat on this sin."

It would have been well had the harmony that prevailed among the chaplains found its counterpart among the men of the sword; but between the British regular officers and those of the provinces there was anything but an equal brotherhood. It is true that Pitt, in the spirit of conciliation which he always showed towards the colonies, had procured a change in the regulations concerning the relative rank of British and provincial officers, thus putting them in a position much nearer equality; but this, while appeasing the provincials, seems to have annoyed the others. Till the campaign was nearly over, not a single provincial colonel had been asked to join in a council of war; and, complains Cleaveland, "they know no more of what is to be done than a sergeant, till the orders come out." Of the British officers, the greater part had seen but little active service. Most of them were men of family, exceedingly prejudiced and insular, whose knowledge of the world

---

[1] For the use of the Diary of Chaplain Cleaveland, as well as of his letters to his wife, I am indebted to the kindness of Miss Abby E. Cleaveland, his descendant.

was limited to certain classes of their own countrymen, and who looked down on all others, whether domestic or foreign. Towards the provincials their attitude was one of tranquil superiority, though its tranquillity was occasionally disturbed by what they regarded as absurd pretension on the part of the colony officers. One of them gave vent to his feelings in an article in the *London Chronicle*, in which he advanced the very reasonable proposition that "a farmer is not to be taken from the plough and made an officer in a day;" and he was answered wrathfully, at great length, in the *Boston Evening Post*, by a writer signing himself "A New England Man." The provincial officers, on the other hand, and especially those of New England, being no less narrow and prejudiced, filled with a sensitive pride and a jealous local patriotism, and bred up in a lofty appreciation of the merits and importance of their country, regarded British superciliousness with a resentment which their strong love for England could not overcome. This feeling was far from being confined to the officers. A provincial regiment stationed at Half-Moon, on the Hudson, thought itself affronted by Captain Cruikshank, a regular officer; and the men were so incensed that nearly half of them went off in a body. The deportment of British officers in the Seven Years War no doubt had some part in hastening on the Revolution.

What with levelling Montcalm's siege works, planting palisades, and grubbing up stumps in their bungling and laborious way, the regulars found abundant occupation. Discipline was stiff and peremptory. The wooden horse and the whipping-post were conspicuous objects in the camp, and often in use. Caleb Rea, being tender-hearted, never went to see the lash laid on; for, as he quaintly observes, "the cries were satisfactory to me, without the sight of the strokes." He and the rest of the doctors found active exercise for such skill as they had, since fever and dysentery were making scarcely less havoc than the bullets at Ticonderoga. This came from the bad state of the camps and unwholesome food. The provincial surgeons seem to have been very little impressed with the importance of sanitary regulations, and to have thought it their business not to prevent disease, but only to cure it. The one grand essential in their eyes was a well-stocked medicine-chest, rich in exhaustless stores of rhubarb, ipecacuanha, and calomel. Even this sometimes failed. Colonel Williams reports "the sick destitute of everything proper for them; medicine-chest empty; nothing but their dirty blankets for beds; Dr. Ashley dead, Dr. Wright gone home, low enough; Bille worn off his legs,—such is our case. I have near a hundred sick. Lost a sergeant and a private last night."[1] Chaplain Cleaveland himself, though strong of frame, did not escape; but he found solace in his trouble from the congenial society of a brother chaplain, Mr. Emerson, of New Hampshire, "a right-down hearty Christian minister, of savory conversation," who came to see him in his tent, breakfasted with him, and joined him in prayer. Being somewhat better, he one day thought to recreate himself with the apostolic occupation of fishing. The sport was poor; the fish bit slowly; and as he lay in his boat, still languid with his malady, he had leisure to reflect on the contrasted works of Providence and man,—the bright lake basking amid its mountains, a dream of wilderness beauty, and the swarms of harsh humanity on the shore beside him, with their passions, discords, and miseries. But it was with the strong meat of Calvinistic theology, and not with reveries like these, that he was accustomed to nourish his military flock.

While at one end of the lake the force of Abercromby was diminished by detachments and disease, that of Montcalm at the other was so increased by reinforcements that a forward movement on his part seemed possible. He contented himself, however, with strengthening the fort, reconstructing the lines that he had defended so well, and sending out frequent war-parties by way of Wood Creek and South Bay, to harass Abercromby's communications with Fort Edward. These parties, some of which consisted of several hundred men, were generally more or less successful; and one of them, under La Corne, surprised and destroyed a large wagon train escorted by forty soldiers. When Abercromby heard of it, he ordered Rogers, with a strong detachment of provincials, light infantry, and rangers, to go down the lake in boats, cross the mountains to the narrow waters of Lake Champlain, and cut off the enemy. But though Rogers set out at two in the morning, the French retreated so fast that he arrived too late. As he was on his way back, he was met by a messenger from the General with orders to intercept other French parties reported to be hovering about Fort Edward. On this he retraced his steps, marched through the forest to where Whitehall now stands, and thence made his way up Wood Creek to old Fort Anne, a relic of former wars, abandoned and falling to decay. Here, on the neglected "clearing" that surrounded the ruin, his followers encamped. They counted seven hundred in all, and consisted of about eighty rangers, a body of Connecticut men under Major Putnam,

[1] *Colonel William Williams to Colonel Israel Williams, 4 Sept. 1758.*

and a small regular force, chiefly light infantry, under Captain Dalzell, the brave officer who was afterwards killed by Pontiac's warriors at Detroit.

Up to this time Rogers had observed his usual caution, commanding silence on the march, and forbidding fires at night; but, seeing no signs of an enemy, he forgot himself; and on the following morning, the eighth of August, he and Lieutenant Irwin, of the light infantry, amused themselves by firing at a mark on a wager. The shots reached the ears of four hundred and fifty French and Indians under the famous partisan Marin, who at once took steps to reconnoitre and ambuscade his rash enemy. For nearly a mile from the old fort the forest had formerly been cut down and burned; and Nature had now begun to reassert herself, covering the open tract with a dense growth of bushes and saplings almost impervious to anything but a wild-cat, had it not been traversed by a narrow Indian path. Along this path the men were forced to march in single file. At about seven o'clock, when the two marksmen had decided their bet, and before the heavy dew of the night was dried upon the bushes, the party slung their packs and set out. Putnam was in the front with his Connecticut men; Dalzell followed with the regulars; and Rogers, with his rangers, brought up the rear of the long and slender line. Putnam himself led the way, shouldering through the bushes, gun in hand; and just as the bluff yeoman emerged from them to enter the forest-growth beyond, the air was rent with yells, the thickets before him were filled with Indians, and one of them, a Caughnawaga chief, sprang upon him, hatchet in hand. He had time to cock his gun and snap it at the breast of his assailant; but it missed fire, and he was instantly seized and dragged back into the forest, as were also a lieutenant named Tracy and three private men. Then the firing began. The French and Indians, lying across the path in a semicircle, had the advantage of position and surprise. The Connecticut men fell back among the bushes in disorder; but soon rallied, and held the enemy in check while Dalzell and Rogers—the latter of whom was nearly a mile behind—were struggling through briers and thickets to their aid. So close was the brushwood that it was full half an hour before they could get their followers ranged in some kind of order in front of the enemy; and even then each man was forced to fight for himself as best he could. Humphreys, the biographer of Putnam, blames Rogers severely for not coming at once to the aid of the Connecticut men; but two of their captains declare that he came with all possible speed; while a regular officer present highly praised him to Abercromby for cool and officer-like conduct.[1] As a man his deserts were small; as a bushfighter he was beyond reproach.

Another officer recounts from hearsay the remarkable conduct of an Indian, who sprang into the midst of the English and killed two of them with his hatchet; then mounted on a log and defied them all. One of the regulars tried to knock him down with the butt of his musket; but though the blow made him bleed, he did not fall, and would have killed his assailant if Rogers had not shot him dead.[2] The firing lasted about two hours. At length some of the Canadians gave way, and the rest of the French and Indians followed.[3] They broke into small parties to elude pursuit, and reuniting towards evening, made their bivouac on a spot surrounded by impervious swamps.

Rogers remained on the field and buried all his own dead, forty-nine in number. Then he resumed his march to Fort Edward, carrying the wounded on litters of branches till the next day, when he met a detachment coming with wagons to his relief. A party sent out soon after for the purpose reported that they had found and buried more than a hundred French and Indians. From this time forward the war-parties from Ticonderoga greatly relented in their activity.

The adventures of the captured Putnam were sufficiently remarkable. The Indians, after dragging him to the rear, lashed him fast to a tree so that he could not move a limb, and a young savage amused himself by throwing a hatchet at his head, striking it into the wood as close as possible to the mark without hitting it. A French petty officer then thrust the muzzle of his gun violently against the prisoner's body, pretended to fire it at him, and at last struck him in the face with the butt; after which dastardly proceeding he left him. The French and Indians being forced after a time to fall back, Putnam found himself between the combatants and exposed to bullets from both sides; but the enemy, partially recovering the ground they had lost, unbound him, and led him to a safe distance from the fight. When the retreat began, the Indians hurried him along with them, stripped of coat, waistcoat, shoes, and stockings, his back burdened with as many packs of the wounded as could be piled upon it, and his wrists bound so tightly together that the pain became intense. In his torment he begged them to kill him; on which a French officer who was near persuaded them to

[1] *Letter from the Camp at Lake George, 5 Sept. 1758*, signed by Captains Maynard and Giddings, and printed in the *Boston Weekly Advertiser.* "Rogers deserves much to be commended." *Abercromby to Pitt, 19 Aug. 1758.*
[2] *Thomas Barnsley to Bouquet, 7 Sept. 1758.*
[3] *Doreil au Ministre, 31 Août, 1757.*

untie his hands and take off some of the packs, and the chief who had captured him gave him a pair of moccasons to protect his lacerated feet. When they encamped at night, they prepared to burn him alive, stripped him naked, tied him to a tree, and gathered dry wood to pile about him. A sudden shower of rain interrupted their pastime; but when it was over they began again, and surrounded him with a circle of brushwood which they set on fire. As they were yelling and dancing their delight at the contortions with which he tried to avoid the rising flames, Marin, hearing what was going forward, broke through the crowd, and with a courageous humanity not too common among Canadian officers, dashed aside the burning brush, untied the prisoner, and angrily upbraided his tormentors. He then restored him to the chief who had captured him, and whose right of property in his prize the others had failed to respect. The Caughnawaga treated him at first with kindness; but, with the help of his tribesmen, took effectual means to prevent his escape, by laying him on his back, stretching his arms and legs in the form of a St. Andrew's cross, and binding the wrists and ankles fast to the stems of young trees. This was a mode of securing prisoners in vogue among Indians from immemorial time; but, not satisfied with it, they placed brushwood upon his body, and then laid across it the long slender stems of saplings, on the ends of which several warriors lay down to sleep, so that the slightest movement on his part would rouse them. Thus he passed a night of misery, which did not prevent him from thinking of the ludicrous figure he made in the hands of the tawny Philistines.

On the next night, after a painful march, he reached Ticonderoga, where he was questioned by Montcalm, and afterwards sent to Montreal in charge of a French officer, who showed him the utmost kindness. On arriving, wofully tattered, bruised, scorched, and torn, he found a friend in Colonel Schuyler, himself a prisoner on parole, who helped him in his need, and through whose good offices the future major-general of the Continental Army was included in the next exchange of prisoners.[1]

[1] On Putnam's adventures, Humphreys, 57 (1818). He had the story from Putnam himself, and seems to give it with substantial correctness, though his account of the battle is at several points erroneous. The "Molang" of his account is Marin. On the battle, besides authorities already cited, *Recollections of Thomson Maxwell*, a soldier present (*Essex Institute*, VII. 97). Rogers, *Journals*, 117. Letter from camp in *Boston Gazette*, no. 117. Another in *New Hampshire Gazette*, no. 104. *Gentleman's Magazine*, 1758, p. 498. Malartic, *Journal du Régiment de Béarn*. Lévis, *Journal de la Guerre en Canada*. The French notices of the affair are few and brief. They admit a defeat, but exaggerate the force and the losses of the English, and underrate their own. Malartic, however, says that Marin set out with four hundred men, and was soon after joined by an additional number of Indians; which nearly answers to the best English accounts.

The petty victory over Marin was followed by a more substantial success. Early in September Abercromby's melancholy camp was cheered with the tidings that the important French post of Fort Frontenac, which controlled Lake Ontario, which had baffled Shirley in his attempt against Niagara, and given Montcalm the means of conquering Oswego, had fallen into British hands. "This is a glorious piece of news, and may God have all the glory of the same!" writes Chaplain Cleaveland in his Diary. Lieutenant-Colonel Bradstreet had planned the stroke long before, and proposed it first to Loudon, and then to Abercromby. Loudon accepted it; but his successor received it coldly, though Lord Howe was warm in its favor. At length, under the pressure of a council of war, Abercromby consented that the attempt should be made, and gave Bradstreet three thousand men, nearly all provincials. With these he made his way, up the Mohawk and down the Onondaga, to the lonely and dismal spot where Oswego had once stood. By dint of much persuasion a few Oneidas joined him; though, like most of the Five Nations, they had been nearly lost to the English through the effects of the defeat at Ticonderoga. On the twenty-second of August his fleet of whaleboats and bateaux pushed out on Lake Ontario; and, three days after, landed near the French fort. On the night of the twenty-sixth Bradstreet made a lodgment within less than two hundred yards of it; and early in the morning De Noyan, the commandant, surrendered himself and his followers, numbering a hundred and ten soldiers and laborers, prisoners of war. With them were taken nine armed vessels, carrying from eight to eighteen guns, and forming the whole French naval force on Lake Ontario. The crews escaped. An enormous quantity of provisions, naval stores, munitions, and Indian goods intended for the supply of the western posts fell into the hands of the English, who kept what they could carry off, and burned the rest. In the fort were found sixty cannon and sixteen mortars, which the victors used to batter down the walls; and then, reserving a few of the best, knocked off the trunnions of the others. The Oneidas were bent on scalping some of the prisoners. Bradstreet forbade it. They begged that he would do as the French did,—turn his back and shut his eyes; but he forced them to abstain from all violence, and consoled them by a lion's share of the plunder. In accordance with the orders of Abercromby, the fort was dismantled, and all the buildings in or around it burned, as were also the vessels, except the two largest, which were reserved to carry off some of the captured goods. Then, with boats deeply laden, the detachment returned to Oswego; where, after unloading and burning the two vessels, they proceeded towards Albany, leaving a thousand of their number at the new fort which Brigadier Stanwix was building at the Great Carrying Place of the Mohawk.

Next to Louisbourg, this was the heaviest blow that the French had yet received. Their command of Lake Ontario was gone. New France was cut in two; and unless the severed parts could speedily reunite, all the posts of the interior would be in imminent jeopardy. If Bradstreet had been followed by another body of men to reoccupy and rebuild Oswego, thus recovering a harbor on Lake Ontario, all the captured French vessels could have been brought thither, and the command of this inland sea assured at once. Even as it was, the advantages were immense. A host of savage warriors, thus far inclined to France or wavering between the two belligerents, stood henceforth neutral, or gave themselves to England; while Fort Duquesne, deprived of the supplies on which it depended, could make but faint resistance to its advancing enemy.

Amherst, with five regiments from Louisbourg, came, early in October, to join Abercromby at Lake George, and the two commanders discussed the question of again attacking Ticonderoga. Both thought the season too late. A fortnight after, a deserter brought news that Montcalm was breaking up his camp. Abercromby followed his example. The opposing armies filed off each to its winter quarters, and only a few scouting parties kept alive the embers of war on the waters and mountains of Lake George.

Meanwhile Brigadier Forbes was climbing the Alleghanies, hewing his way through the forests of western Pennsylvania, and toiling inch by inch towards his goal of Fort Duquesne.[1]

---

[1] On the capture of Fort Frontenac, *Bradstreet to Abercromby, 31 Aug. 1758. Impartial Account of Lieutenant-Colonel Bradstreet's Expedition, by a Volunteer in the Expedition* (London, 1759). Letter from a New York officer to his colonel, in *Boston Gazette*, no. 182. Several letters from persons in the expedition, in *Boston Evening Post*, no. 1,203, *New Hampshire Gazette*, no. 104, and *Boston News Letter*, no. 2,932. *Abercromby to Pitt, 25 Nov. 1758. Lieutenant Macauley to Horatio Gates, 30 Aug. 1758. Vaudreuil au Ministre, 30 Oct. 1758.* Pouchot, I. 162. *Mémoires sur le Canada, 1749–1760.*

22

Fort Duquesne

1758

DINWIDDIE AND WASHINGTON · BRIGADIER FORBES · HIS ARMY ·
CONFLICTING VIEWS · DIFFICULTIES · ILLNESS OF FORBES · HIS
SUFFERINGS · HIS FORTITUDE · HIS DIFFERENCE WITH WASHINGTON · SIR
JOHN SINCLAIR · TROUBLESOME ALLIES · SCOUTING PARTIES · BOASTS OF
VAUDREUIL · FORBES AND THE INDIANS · MISSION OF CHRISTIAN
FREDERIC POST · COUNCIL OF PEACE · SECOND MISSION OF POST ·
DEFEAT OF GRANT · DISTRESS OF FORBES · DARK PROSPECTS · ADVANCE
OF THE ARMY · CAPTURE OF THE FRENCH FORT · THE SLAIN OF
BRADDOCK'S FIELD · DEATH OF FORBES

During the last year Loudon, filled with vain schemes against Louisbourg, had left the French scalping-parties to their work of havoc on the western borders. In Virginia Washington still toiled at his hopeless task of defending with a single regiment a forest frontier of more than three hundred miles; and in Pennsylvania the Assembly thought more of quarrelling with their governor than of protecting the tormented settlers. Fort Duquesne, the source of all the evil, was left undisturbed. In vain Washington urged the futility of defensive war, and the necessity of attacking the enemy in his stronghold. His position, trying at the best, was made more so by the behavior of Dinwiddie. That crusty Scotchman had conceived a dislike to him, and sometimes treated him in a manner that must have been unspeakably galling to the proud and passionate young man, who nevertheless, unconquerable in his sense of public duty, curbed himself to patience, or the semblance of it.

Dinwiddie was now gone, and a new governor had taken his place. The conduct of the war, too, had changed, and in the plans of Pitt the capture of Fort Duquesne held an important place. Brigadier John Forbes was charged with it. He was a Scotch veteran, forty-eight years of age, who had begun life as a student of medicine, and who ended it as an able and faithful soldier. Though a well-bred man of the world, his tastes were simple; he detested ceremony, and dealt frankly and plainly with the colonists, who both respected and liked him. In April he was in Philadelphia waiting for his army, which as yet had no existence; for the provincials were not enlisted, and an expected battalion of Highlanders had not arrived. It was the end of June before they were all on the march; and meanwhile the General was attacked with a painful and dangerous malady, which would have totally disabled a less resolute man.

His force consisted of provincials from Pennsylvania, Virginia, Maryland, and North Carolina, with twelve hundred Highlanders of Montgomery's regiment and a detachment of Royal Americans, amounting in all, with wagoners and camp followers, to between six and seven thousand men. The Royal American regiment was a new corps raised, in the colonies, largely from among the Germans of Pennsylvania. Its officers were from Europe; and conspicuous among them was Lieutenant-Colonel Henry Bouquet, a brave and accomplished Swiss, who commanded one of the four battalions of which the regiment was composed. Early in July he was encamped with the advance-guard at the hamlet of Raystown, now the town of Bedford, among the eastern heights of the Alleghanies. Here his tents were pitched in an opening of the forest by the banks of a small stream; and Virginians in huntingshirts, Highlanders in kilt and plaid, and Royal Americans in regulation scarlet, labored at throwing up intrenchments and palisades, while around stood the silent mountains in their mantles of green.

Now rose the question whether the army should proceed in a direct course to Fort Duquesne, hewing a new road through the forest, or march thirty-four miles to Fort Cumberland, and thence follow the road made by Braddock. It was the interest of Pennsylvania that Forbes should choose the former route, and of Virginia that he should choose the latter. The Old Dominion did not wish to see a highway cut for her rival to those rich lands of the Ohio which she called her own. Washington, who was then at Fort Cumberland with a part of his regiment, was earnest for the old road; and in an interview with Bouquet midway between that place and Raystown, he spared no effort to bring him to the same opinion. But the quartermaster-general, Sir John Sinclair, who was supposed to know the country, had advised the Pennsylvania route; and both Bouquet and Forbes were resolved to take it. It was shorter, and when once made would furnish readier and more abundant supplies of food and forage; but to make it would consume a vast amount of time and labor. Washington foretold the ruin of the expedition unless it took Braddock's road. Ardent Virginian as he was, there is no cause to believe that his decision was based on any but military reasons; but Forbes thought otherwise, and found great fault with him. Bouquet did him more justice. "Colonel Washington," he writes to the General, "is filled with a sincere zeal to aid the expedition, and is ready to march with equal activity by whatever way you choose."

The fate of Braddock had impressed itself on all the army, and inspired a caution that was but too much needed; since, except Washington's men and a few others among the provincials, the whole, from general to drummer-boy, were total strangers to that insidious warfare of the forest in which their enemies, red and white, had no rival. Instead of marching, like Braddock, at one stretch for Fort Duquesne, burdened with a long and cumbrous baggage-train, it was the plan of Forbes to push on by slow stages, establishing fortified magazines as he went, and at last, when within easy distance of the fort, to advance upon it with all his force, as little impeded as possible with wagons and pack-horses. He bore no likeness to his predecessor, except in determined resolution, and he did not hesitate to embrace military heresies which would have driven Braddock to fury. To Bouquet, in whom he placed a well-merited trust, he wrote, "I have been long in your opinion of equipping numbers of our men like the savages, and I fancy Colonel Burd, of Virginia, has most of his best people equipped in that manner. In this country we must learn the art of war from enemy Indians, or anybody else who has seen it carried on here."

His provincials displeased him, not without reason; for the greater part were but the crudest material for an army, unruly, and recalcitrant to discipline. Some of them came to the rendezvous at Carlisle with old province muskets, the locks tied on with a string; others brought fowling-pieces of their own, and others carried nothing but walking-sticks; while many had never fired a gun in their lives.[1] Forbes reported to Pitt that their officers, except a few in the higher ranks, were "an extremely bad collection of broken innkeepers, horse-jockeys, and In-

[1] *Correspondence of Forbes and Bouquet, July, August, 1758.*

dian traders;" nor is he more flattering towards the men, though as to some of them he afterwards changed his mind.[1]

While Bouquet was with the advance at Raystown, Forbes was still in Philadelphia, trying to bring the army into shape, and collecting provisions, horses, and wagons; much vexed meantime by the Assembly, whose tedious disputes about taxing the proprietaries greatly obstructed the service. "No sergeant or quartermaster of a regiment," he says, "is obliged to look into more details than I am; and if I did not see to everything myself, we should never get out of this town." July had begun before he could reach the frontier village of Carlisle, where he found everything in confusion. After restoring some order, he wrote to Bouquet: "I have been and still am but poorly, with a cursed flux, but shall move day after to-morrow." He was doomed to disappointment; and it was not till the ninth of August that he sent another letter from the same place to the same military friend. "I am now able to write after three weeks of a most violent and tormenting distemper, which, thank God, seems now much abated as to pain, but has left me as weak as a new-born infant. However, I hope to have strength enough to set out from this place on Friday next." The disease was an inflammation of the stomach and other vital organs; and when he should have been in bed, with complete repose of body and mind, he was racked continually with the toils and worries of a most arduous campaign.

He left Carlisle on the eleventh, carried on a kind of litter made of a hurdle slung between two horses; and two days later he wrote from Shippensburg: "My journey here from Carlisle raised my disorder and pains to so intolerable a degree that I was obliged to stop, and may not get away for a day or two." Again, on the eighteenth: "I am better, and partly free from the excruciating pain I suffered; but still so weak that I can scarce bear motion." He lay helpless at Shippensburg till September was well advanced. On the second he says: "I really cannot describe how I have suffered both in body and mind of late, and the relapses have been worse as the disappointment was greater;" and on the fourth, still writing to Bouquet, who in the camp at Raystown was struggling with many tribulations: "I am sorry you have met with so many cross accidents to vex you, and have such a parcel of scoundrels as the provincials to work with; *mais le vin est tiré*, and you must drop a little of the gentleman and treat them as they deserve. Seal and send off the enclosed despatch to Sir John by some sure hand. He is a very

---

[1] *Forbes to Pitt, 6 Sept. 1758.*

odd man, and I am sorry it has been my fate to have any concern with him. I am afraid our army will not admit of division, lest one half meet with a check; therefore I would consult Colonel Washington, though perhaps not follow his advice, as his behavior about the roads was no-ways like a soldier. I thank my good cousin for his letter, and have only to say that I have all my life been subject to err; but I now reform, as I go to bed at eight at night, if able to sit up so late."

Nobody can read the letters of Washington at this time without feeling that the imputations of Forbes were unjust, and that here, as elsewhere, his ruling motive was the public good.[1] Forbes himself, seeing the rugged and difficult nature of the country, began to doubt whether after all he had not better have chosen the old road of Braddock. He soon had an interview with its chief advocates, the two Virginia colonels, Washington and Burd, and reported the result to Bouquet, adding: "I told them that, whatever they thought, I had acted on the best information to be had, and could safely say for myself, and believed I might answer for you, that the good of the service was all we had at heart, not valuing provincial interests, jealousies, or suspicions one single twopence." It must be owned that, considering the slow and sure mode of advance which he had wisely adopted, the old soldier was probably right in his choice; since before the army could reach Fort Duquesne, the autumnal floods would have made the Youghiogany and the Monongahela impassable.

The Sir John mentioned by Forbes was the quartermaster-general, Sir John Sinclair, who had gone forward with Virginians and other troops from the camp of Bouquet to make the road over the main range of the Alleghanies, whence he sent back the following memorandum of his requirements: "Pickaxes, crows, and shovels; likewise more whiskey. Send me the newspapers, and tell my black to send me a candlestick and half a loaf of sugar." He was extremely inefficient; and Forbes, out of all patience with him, wrote confidentially to Bouquet that his only talent was for throwing everything into confusion. Yet he found fault with everybody else, and would discharge volleys of oaths at all who met his disapproval. From this cause or some other, Lieutenant-Colonel Stephen, of the Virginians, told him that he would break his sword rather than be longer under his orders. "As I had not sufficient strength," says Sinclair, "to take him by the neck from among his own

---

[1]Besides the printed letters, there is an autograph collection of his correspondence with Bouquet in 1758 (forming vol. 21,641, *Additional Manuscripts*, British Museum). Copies of the whole are before me.

men, I was obliged to let him have his own way, that I might not be the occasion of bloodshed." He succeeded at last in arresting him, and Major Lewis, of the same regiment, took his place.

The aid of Indians as scouts and skirmishers was of the last importance to an army so weak in the arts of woodcraft, and efforts were made to engage the services of the friendly Cherokees and Catawbas, many of whom came to the camp, where their caprice, insolence, and rapacity tried to the utmost the patience of the commanders. That of Sir John Sinclair had already been overcome by his dealings with the provincial authorities; and he wrote in good French, at the tail of a letter to the Swiss colonel: "Adieu, my dear Bouquet. The greatest curse that our Lord can pronounce against the worst of sinners is to give them business to do with provincial commissioners and friendly Indians." A band of sixty warriors told Colonel Burd that they would join the army on condition that it went by Braddock's road. "This," wrote Forbes, on hearing of the proposal, "is a new system of military discipline truly, and shows that my good friend Burd is either made a cat's-foot of himself, or little knows me if he imagines that sixty scoundrels are to direct me in my measures."[1] Bouquet, with a pliant tact rarely seen in the born Briton, took great pains to please these troublesome allies, and went so far as to adopt one of them as his son.[2] A considerable number joined the army; but they nearly all went off when the stock of presents provided for them was exhausted.

Forbes was in total ignorance of the strength and movements of the enemy. The Indians reported their numbers to be at least equal to his own; but nothing could be learned from them with certainty, by reason of their inveterate habit of lying. Several scouting-parties of whites were therefore sent forward, of which the most successful was that of a young Virginian officer, accompanied by a sergeant and five Indians. At a little distance from the French fort, the Indians stopped to paint themselves and practise incantations. The chief warrior of the party then took certain charms from an otter-skin bag and tied them about the necks of the other Indians. On that of the officer he hung the otter-skin itself; while to the sergeant he gave a small packet of paint from the same mystic receptacle. "He told us," reports the officer, "that none of us could be shot, for those things would turn the balls from us; and then shook hands with us, and told us to go and fight like men." Thus armed against fate, they mounted the high ground afterwards called Grant's Hill, where, covered by trees and bushes, they had a good view

[1] The above extracts are from the *Bouquet and Haldimand Papers*, British Museum.
[2] *Bouquet to Forbes*, 3 June, 1758.

of the fort, and saw plainly that the reports of the French force were greatly exaggerated.[1]

Meanwhile Bouquet's men pushed on the heavy work of road-making up the main range of the Alleghanies, and, what proved far worse, the parallel mountain ridge of Laurel Hill, hewing, digging, blasting, laying fascines and gabions to support the track along the sides of steep declivities, or worming their way like moles through the jungle of swamp and forest. Forbes described the country to Pitt as an "immense uninhabited wilderness, overgrown everywhere with trees and brushwood, so that nowhere can one see twenty yards." In truth, as far as eye or mind could reach, a prodigious forest vegetation spread its impervious canopy over hill, valley, and plain, and wrapped the stern and awful waste in the shadows of the tomb.

Having secured his magazines at Raystown, and built a fort there named Fort Bedford, Bouquet made a forward movement of some forty miles, crossed the main Alleghany and Laurel Hill, and, taking post on a stream called Loyalhannon Creek, began another depot of supplies as a base for the final advance on Fort Duquesne, which was scarcely fifty miles distant.

Vaudreuil had learned from prisoners the march of Forbes, and, with his usual egotism, announced to the Colonial Minister what he had done in consequence. "I have provided for the safety of Fort Duquesne." "I have sent reinforcements to M. de Ligneris, who commands there." "I have done the impossible to supply him with provisions, and I am now sending them in abundance, in order that the troops I may perhaps have occasion to send to drive off the English may not be delayed." "A stronger fort is needed on the Ohio; but I cannot build one till after the peace; then I will take care to build such a one as will thenceforth keep the English out of that country." Some weeks later he was less confident, and very anxious for news from Ligneris. He says that he has sent him all the succors he could, and ordered troops to go to his aid from Niagara, Detroit, and Illinois, as well as the militia of Detroit, with the Indians there and elsewhere in the West,—Hurons, Ottawas, Pottawattamies, Miamis, and other tribes. What he fears is that the English will not attack the fort till all these Indians have grown tired of waiting, and have gone home again.[2] This was precisely the intention of Forbes, and the chief object of his long delays.

He had another good reason for making no haste. There was hope

---

[1] *Journal of a Reconnoitring Party, Aug. 1758.* The writer seems to have been Ensign Chew, of Washington's regiment.
[2] *Vaudreuil au Ministre, Juillet, Août, Octobre 1758.*

that the Delawares and Shawanoes, who lived within easy reach of Fort
Duquesne, and who for the past three years had spread havoc throughout the English border, might now be won over from the French alliance. Forbes wrote to Bouquet from Shippensburg: "After many
intrigues with Quakers, the Provincial Commissioners, the Governor,
etc., and by the downright bullying of Sir William Johnson, I hope I
have now brought about a general convention of the Indians."[1] The
convention was to include the Five Nations, the Delawares, the Shawanoes, and other tribes, who had accepted wampum belts of invitation, and promised to meet the Governor and Commissioners of the
various provinces at the town of Easton, before the middle of September. This seeming miracle was wrought by several causes. The Indians
in the French interest, always greedy for presents, had not of late got
enough to satisfy them. Many of those destined for them had been
taken on the way from France by British cruisers, and the rest had
passed through the hands of official knaves, who sold the greater part
for their own profit. Again, the goods supplied by French fur-traders
were few and dear; and the Indians remembered with regret the abundance and comparative cheapness of those they had from the English
before the war. At the same time it was reported among them that a
British army was marching to the Ohio strong enough to drive out the
French from all that country; and the Delawares and Shawanoes of the
West began to waver in their attachment to the falling cause. The
eastern Delawares, living at Wyoming and elsewhere on the upper Susquehanna, had made their peace with the English in the summer before; and their great chief, Teedyuscung, thinking it for his interest that
the tribes of the Ohio should follow his example, sent them wampum
belts, inviting them to lay down the hatchet. The Five Nations, with
Johnson at one end of the Confederacy and Joncaire at the other,—
the one cajoling them in behalf of England, and the other in behalf of
France,—were still divided in counsel; but even among the Senecas,
the tribe most under Joncaire's influence, there was a party so far inclined to England that, like the Delaware chief, they sent wampum to
the Ohio, inviting peace. But the influence most potent in reclaiming
the warriors of the West was of a different kind. Christian Frederic
Post, a member of the Moravian brotherhood, had been sent at the
instance of Forbes as an envoy to the hostile tribes from the Governor
and Council of Pennsylvania. He spoke the Delaware language, knew
the Indians well, had lived among them, had married a converted

[1] *Forbes to Bouquet,* 18 Aug. 1758.

squaw, and, by his simplicity of character, directness, and perfect honesty, gained their full confidence. He now accepted his terrible mission,
and calmly prepared to place himself in the clutches of the tiger. He
was a plain German, upheld by a sense of duty and a single-hearted
trust in God; alone, with no great disciplined organization to impel and
support him, and no visions and illusions such as kindled and sustained
the splendid heroism of the early Jesuit martyrs. Yet his errand was no
whit less perilous. And here we may notice the contrast between the
mission settlements of the Moravians in Pennsylvania and those which
the later Jesuits and the Sulpitians had established at Caughnawaga, St.
Francis, La Présentation, and other places. The Moravians were apos-
tles of peace, and they succeeded to a surprising degree in weaning their
converts from their ferocious instincts and warlike habits; while the
Mission Indians of Canada retained all their native fierceness, and were
systematically impelled to use their tomahawks against the enemies of
the Church. Their wigwams were hung with scalps, male and female,
adult and infant; and these so-called missions were but nests of baptized
savages, who wore the crucifix instead of the medicine-bag, and were
encouraged by the Government for purposes of war.[1]

The Moravian envoy made his way to the Delaware town of Kush-
kushkee, on Beaver Creek, northwest of Fort Duquesne, where the
three chiefs known as King Beaver, Shingas, and Delaware George received him kindly, and conducted him to another town on the same
stream. Here his reception was different. A crowd of warriors, their
faces distorted with rage, surrounded him, brandishing knives and
threatening to kill him; but others took his part, and, order being at
last restored, he read them his message from the Governor, which
seemed to please them. They insisted, however, that he should go with
them to Fort Duquesne, in order that the Indians assembled there
might hear it also. Against this dangerous proposal he protested in
vain. On arriving near the fort, the French demanded that he should
be given up to them, and, being refused, offered a great reward for his
scalp; on which his friends advised him to keep close by the camp-fire,
as parties were out with intent to kill him. "Accordingly," says Post, "I
stuck to the fire as if I had been chained there. On the next day the
Indians, with a great many French officers, came out to hear what I
had to say. The officers brought with them a table, pens, ink, and

---

[1] Of the Hurons of the mission of Lorette, Bougainville says: "Ils sont toujours sauvages autant que
ceux qui sont les moins apprivoisés." And yet they had been converts under Jesuit control for
more than four generations. The case was no better at the other missions; and at St. Francis it
seems to have been worse.

paper. I spoke in the midst of them with a free conscience, and perceived by their looks that they were not pleased with what I said." The substance of his message was an invitation to the Indians to renew the old chain of friendship, joined with a warning that an English army was on its way to drive off the French, and that they would do well to stand neutral.

He addressed an audience filled with an inordinate sense of their own power and importance, believing themselves greater and braver than either of the European nations, and yet deeply jealous of both. "We have heard," they said, "that the French and English mean to kill all the Indians and divide the land among themselves." And on this string they harped continually. If they had known their true interest, they would have made no peace with the English, but would have united as one man to form a barrier of fire against their farther progress; for the West in English hands meant farms, villages, cities, the ruin of the forest, the extermination of the game, and the expulsion of those who lived on it; while the West in French hands meant but scattered posts of war and trade, with the native tribes cherished as indispensable allies.

After waiting some days, the three tribes of the Delawares met in council, and made their answer to the message brought by Post. It was worthy of a proud and warlike race, and was to the effect that since their brothers of Pennsylvania wished to renew the old peace-chain, they on their part were willing to do so, provided that the wampum belt should be sent them in the name, not of Pennsylvania alone, but of the rest of the provinces also.

Having now accomplished his errand, Post wished to return home; but the Indians were seized with an access of distrust, and would not let him go. This jealousy redoubled when they saw him writing in his notebook. "It is a troublesome cross and heavy yoke to draw this people," he says; "they can punish and squeeze a body's heart to the utmost. There came some together and examined me about what I had wrote yesterday. I told them I writ what was my duty. 'Brothers, I tell you I am not afraid of you. I have a good conscience before God and man. I tell you, brothers, there is a bad spirit in your hearts, which breeds jealousy, and will keep you ever in fear.' " At last they let him go; and, eluding a party that lay in wait for his scalp, he journeyed twelve days through the forest, and reached Fort Augusta with the report of his mission.[1]

[1] *Journal of Christian Frederic Post, July, August, September, 1758.*

As the result of it, a great convention of white men and red was held at Easton in October. The neighboring provinces had been asked to send their delegates, and some of them did so; while belts of invitation were sent to the Indians far and near. Sir William Johnson, for reasons best known to himself, at first opposed the plan; but was afterwards led to favor it and to induce tribes under his influence to join in the grand pacification. The Five Nations, with the smaller tribes lately admitted into their confederacy, the Delawares of the Susquehanna, the Mohegans, and several kindred bands, all had their representatives at the meeting. The conferences lasted nineteen days, with the inevitable formalities of such occasions, and the weary repetition of conventional metaphors and long-winded speeches. At length, every difficulty being settled, the Governor of Pennsylvania, in behalf of all the English, rose with a wampum belt in his hand, and addressed the tawny congregation thus: "By this belt we heal your wounds; we remove your grief; we take the hatchet out of your heads; we make a hole in the earth, and bury it so deep that nobody can dig it up again." Then, laying the first belt before them, he took another, very large, made of white wampum beads, in token of peace: "By this belt we renew all our treaties; we brighten the chain of friendship; we put fresh earth to the roots of the tree of peace, that it may bear up against every storm, and live and flourish while the sun shines and the rivers run." And he gave them the belt with the request that they would send it to their friends and allies, and invite them to take hold also of the chain of friendship. Accordingly all present agreed on a joint message of peace to the tribes of the Ohio.[1]

Frederic Post, with several white and Indian companions, was chosen to bear it. A small escort of soldiers that attended him as far as the Alleghany was cut to pieces on its return by a band of the very warriors to whom he was carrying his offers of friendship; and other tenants of the grim and frowning wilderness met the invaders of their domain with inhospitable greetings. "The wolves made a terrible music this night," he writes at his first bivouac after leaving Loyalhannon. When he reached the Delaware towns his reception was ominous. The young warriors said: "Anybody can see with half an eye that the English only mean to cheat us. Let us knock the messengers in the head." Some of them had attacked an English outpost, and had been repulsed; hence, in the words of Post, "They were possessed with a murdering spirit, and with bloody vengeance were thirsty and drunk. I said: 'As God has

[1] *Minutes of Conferences at Easton, October, 1758.*

stopped the mouths of the lions that they could not devour Daniel, so he will preserve us from their fury.' " The chiefs and elders were of a different mind from their fierce and capricious young men. They met during the evening in the log-house where Post and his party lodged; and here a French officer presently arrived with a string of wampum from the commandant, inviting them to help him drive back the army of Forbes. The string was scornfully rejected. "They kicked it from one to another as if it were a snake. Captain Peter took a stick, and with it flung the string from one end of the room to the other, and said: 'Give it to the French captain; he boasted of his fighting, now let us see him fight. We have often ventured our lives for him, and got hardly a loaf of bread in return; and now.he thinks we shall jump to serve him.' Then we saw the French captain mortified to the uttermost. He looked as pale as death. The Indians discoursed and joked till midnight, and the French captain sent messengers at midnight to Fort Duquesne."

There was a grand council, at which the French officer was present; and Post delivered the peace message from the council at Easton, along with another with which Forbes had charged him. "The messages pleased all the hearers except the French captain. He shook his head in bitter grief, and often changed countenance. Isaac Still [*an Indian*] ran him down with great boldness, and pointed at him, saying, 'There he sits!' They all said: 'The French always deceived us!' pointing at the French captain; who, bowing down his head, turned quite pale, and could look no one in the face. All the Indians began to mock and laugh at him. He could hold it no longer, and went out."[1]

The overtures of peace were accepted, and the Delawares, Shawanoes, and Mingoes were no longer enemies of the English. The loss was the more disheartening to the French, since, some weeks before, they had gained a success which they hoped would confirm the adhesion of all their wavering allies. Major Grant, of the Highlanders, had urged Bouquet to send him to reconnoitre Fort Duquesne, capture prisoners, and strike a blow that would animate the assailants and discourage the assailed. Bouquet, forgetting his usual prudence, consented; and Grant set out from the camp at Loyalhannon with about eight hundred men, Highlanders, Royal Americans, and provincials. On the fourteenth of September, at two in the morning, he reached the top of the rising ground thenceforth called Grant's Hill, half a mile or more from the French fort. The forest and the darkness of the night hid him completely from the enemy. He ordered Major Lewis, of the Virginians, to

---

[1] *Journal of Christian Frederic Post, October, November, 1758.*

take with him half the detachment, descend to the open plain before
the fort, and attack the Indians known to be encamped there; after
which he was to make a feigned retreat to the hill, where the rest of
the troops were to lie in ambush and receive the pursuers. Lewis set out
on his errand, while Grant waited anxiously for the result. Dawn was
near, and all was silent; till at length Lewis returned, and incensed his
commander by declaring that his men had lost their way in the dark
woods, and fallen into such confusion that the attempt was impracticable. The morning twilight now began, but the country was wrapped
in thick fog. Grant abandoned his first plan, and sent a few Highlanders
into the cleared ground to burn a warehouse that had been seen there.
He was convinced that the French and their Indians were too few to
attack him, though their numbers in fact were far greater than his
own.[1] Infatuated with this idea, and bent on taking prisoners, he had
the incredible rashness to divide his force in such a way that the several
parts could not support each other. Lewis, with two hundred men, was
sent to guard the baggage two miles in the rear, where a company of
Virginians, under Captain Bullitt, was already stationed. A hundred
Pennsylvanians were posted far off on the right, towards the Alleghany,
while Captain Mackenzie, with a detachment of Highlanders, was sent
to the left, towards the Monongahela. Then, the fog having cleared a
little, Captain Macdonald, with another company of Highlanders, was
ordered into the open plain to reconnoitre the fort and make a plan of
it, Grant himself remaining on the hill with a hundred of his own
regiment and a company of Maryland men. "In order to put on a good
countenance," he says, "and convince our men they had no reason to
be afraid, I gave directions to our drums to beat the reveille. The troops
were in an advantageous post, and I must own I thought we had nothing to fear." Macdonald was at this time on the plain, midway between
the woods and the fort, and in full sight of it. The roll of the drums
from the hill was answered by a burst of war-whoops, and the French
came swarming out like hornets, many of them in their shirts, having
just leaped from their beds. They all rushed upon Macdonald and his
men, who met them with a volley that checked their advance; on
which they surrounded him at a distance, and tried to cut off his retreat. The Highlanders broke through, and gained the woods, with the
loss of their commander, who was shot dead. A crowd of French fol-

[1] Grant to Forbes, no date. "Les rapports sur le nombre des Français varient de 3,000 à 1,200."
Bouquet à Forbes, 17 Sept. 1758. Bigot says that 3,500 daily rations were delivered at Fort Duquesne throughout the summer. Bigot au Ministre, 22 Nov. 1758. In October the number had
fallen to 1,180, which included Indians. Ligneris à Vaudreuil, 18 Oct. 1758.

lowed close, and soon put them to rout, driving them and Mackenzie's party back to the hill where Grant was posted. Here there was a hot fight in the forest, lasting about three quarters of an hour. At length the force of numbers, the novelty of the situation, and the appalling yells of the Canadians and Indians, completely overcame the Highlanders, so intrepid in the ordinary situations of war. They broke away in a wild and disorderly retreat. "Fear," says Grant, "got the better of every other passion; and I trust I shall never again see such a panic among troops."

His only hope was in the detachment he had sent to the rear under Lewis to guard the baggage. But Lewis and his men, when they heard the firing in front, had left their post and pushed forward to help their comrades, taking a straight course through the forest; while Grant was retreating along the path by which he had advanced the night before. Thus they missed each other; and when Grant reached the spot where he expected to find Lewis, he saw to his dismay that nobody was there but Captain Bullitt and his company. He cried in despair that he was a ruined man; not without reason, for the whole body of French and Indians was upon him. Such of his men as held together were forced towards the Alleghany, and, writes Bouquet, "would probably have been cut to pieces but for Captain Bullitt and his Virginians, who kept up the fight against the whole French force till two thirds of them were killed." They were offered quarter, but refused it; and the survivors were driven at last into the Alleghany, where some were drowned, and others swam over and escaped. Grant was surrounded and captured, and Lewis, who presently came up, was also made prisoner, along with some of his men, after a stiff resistance. Thus ended this mismanaged affair, which cost the English two hundred and seventy three killed, wounded, and taken. The rest got back safe to Loyalhannon.[1]

The invalid General was deeply touched by this reverse, yet expressed himself with a moderation that does him honor. He wrote to Bouquet from Raystown: "Your letter of the seventeenth I read with no less surprise than concern, as I could not believe that such an attempt would have been made without my knowledge and concurrence. The

---

[1] On Grant's defeat, *Grant to Forbes, no date,* a long and minute report, written while a prisoner. *Bouquet à Forbes, 17 Sept. 1758. Forbes to Pitt, 20 Oct. 1758. Vaudreuil au Ministre, 1 Nov. 1758.* Letters from camp in *Boston Evening Post, Boston Weekly Advertiser, Boston News Letter,* and other provincial newspapers of the time. *List of Killed, Wounded, and Missing in the Action of Sept. 14. Gentleman's Magazine, XXIX. 173. Hazard's Pennsylvania Register, VIII. 141. Olden Time, I. 179.* Vaudreuil, with characteristic exaggeration, represents all Grant's party as killed or taken, except a few who died of starvation. The returns show that 540 came back safe, out of 813.

breaking in upon our fair and flattering hopes of success touches me most sensibly. There are two wounded Highland officers just now arrived, who give so lame an account of the matter that one can draw nothing from them, only that my friend Grant most certainly lost his wits, and by his thirst of fame brought on his own perdition, and ran great risk of ours."[1]

The French pushed their advantage with spirit. Early in October a large body of them hovered in the woods about the camp at Loyalhannon, drove back a detachment sent against them, approached under cover of the trees, and, though beaten off, withdrew deliberately, after burying their dead and killing great numbers of horses and cattle.[2] But, with all their courageous energy, their position was desperate. The militia of Louisiana and the Illinois left the fort in November and went home; the Indians of Detroit and the Wabash would stay no longer; and, worse yet, the supplies destined for Fort Duquesne had been destroyed by Bradstreet at Fort Frontenac. Hence Ligneris was compelled by prospective starvation to dismiss the greater part of his force, and await the approach of his enemy with those that remained.

His enemy was in a plight hardly better than his own. Autumnal rains, uncommonly heavy and persistent, had ruined the newly-cut road. On the mountains the torrents tore it up, and in the valleys the wheels of the wagons and cannon churned it into soft mud. The horses, overworked and underfed, were fast breaking down. The forest had little food for them, and they were forced to drag their own oats and corn, as well as supplies for the army, through two hundred miles of wilderness. In the wretched condition of the road this was no longer possible. The magazines of provisions formed at Raystown and Loyalhannon to support the army on its forward march were emptied faster than they could be filled. Early in October the elements relented; the clouds broke, the sky was bright again, and the sun shone out in splendor on mountains radiant in the livery of autumn. A gleam of hope revisited the heart of Forbes. It was but a flattering illusion. The sullen clouds returned, and a chill, impenetrable veil of mist and rain hid the mountains and the trees. Dejected Nature wept and would not be comforted. Above, below, around, all was trickling, oozing, pattering, gushing. In the miserable encampments the starved horses stood steaming in the rain, and the men crouched, disgusted, under their dripping

[1] *Forbes to Bouquet, 23 Sept. 1758.*

[2] *Burd to Bouquet, 12 Oct. 1758. Bouquet à Forbes, 13 Oct. 1758. Forbes to Pitt, 20 Oct. 1758. Letter from Loyalhannon, 14 Oct.,* in *Olden Time,* I. 180. *Letters from camp,* in *Boston News Letter. Ligneris à Vaudreuil, 18 Oct. 1758. Vaudreuil au Ministre, 20 Nov. 1758.*

tents, while the drenched picket-guard in the neighboring forest paced dolefully through black mire and spongy mosses. The rain turned to snow; the descending flakes clung to the many-colored foliage, or melted from sight in the trench of half-liquid clay that was called a road. The wheels of the wagons sank in it to the hub, and to advance or retreat was alike impossible.

Forbes from his sick bed at Raystown wrote to Bouquet: "Your description of the road pierces me to the very soul." And a few days later to Pitt: "I am in the greatest distress, occasioned by rains unusual at this season, which have rendered the clay roads absolutely impracticable. If the weather does not favor, I shall be absolutely locked up in the mountains. I cannot form any judgment how I am to extricate myself, as everything depends on the weather, which snows and rains frightfully." There was no improvement. In the next week he writes to Bouquet: "These four days of constant rain have completely ruined the road. The wagons would cut it up more in an hour than we could repair in a week. I have written to General Abercromby, but have not had one scrape of a pen from him since the beginning of September; so it looks as if we were either forgot or left to our fate."[1] Wasted and tortured by disease, the perplexed commander was forced to burden himself with a multitude of details which would else have been neglected, and to do the work of commissary and quartermaster as well as general. "My time," he writes, "is disagreeably spent between business and medicine."

In the beginning of November he was carried to Loyalhannon, where the whole army was then gathered. There was a council of officers, and they resolved to attempt nothing more that season; but, a few days later, three prisoners were brought in who reported the defenceless condition of the French, on which Forbes gave orders to advance again. The wagons and all the artillery, except a few light pieces, were left behind; and on the eighteenth of November twenty-five hundred picked men marched for Fort Duquesne, without tents or baggage, and burdened only with knapsacks and blankets. Washington and Colonel Armstrong, of the Pennsylvanians, had opened a way for them by cutting a road to within a day's march of the French fort. On the evening of the twenty-fourth, the detachment encamped among the hills of Turkey Creek; and the men on guard heard at midnight a dull and heavy sound booming over the western woods. Was it a magazine exploded by accident, or were the French blowing up their works? In the morning

[1] *Forbes to Bouquet, 15 Oct. 1758. Ibid., 25 Oct. 1758. Forbes to Pitt, 20 Oct. 1758.*

the march was resumed, a strong advance-guard leading the way. Forbes came next, carried in his litter; and the troops followed in three parallel columns, the Highlanders in the centre under Montgomery, their colonel, and the Royal Americans and provincials on the right and left, under Bouquet and Washington.[1] Thus, guided by the tap of the drum at the head of each column, they moved slowly through the forest, over damp, fallen leaves, crisp with frost, beneath an endless entanglement of bare gray twigs that sighed and moaned in the bleak November wind. It was dusk when they emerged upon the open plain and saw Fort Duquesne before them, with its background of wintry hills beyond the Monongahela and the Alleghany. During the last three miles they had passed the scattered bodies of those slain two months before at the defeat of Grant; and it is said that, as they neared the fort, the Highlanders were goaded to fury at seeing the heads of their slaughtered comrades stuck on poles, round which the kilts were hung derisively, in imitation of petticoats. Their rage was vain; the enemy was gone. Only a few Indians lingered about the place, who reported that the garrison, to the number of four or five hundred, had retreated, some down the Ohio, some overland towards Presquisle, and the rest, with their commander, up the Alleghany to Venango, called by the French, Fort Machault. They had burned the barracks and storehouses, and blown up the fortifications.

The first care of the victors was to provide defence and shelter for those of their number on whom the dangerous task was to fall of keeping what they had won. A stockade was planted around a cluster of traders' cabins and soldiers' huts, which Forbes named Pittsburg, in honor of the great minister. It was not till the next autumn that General Stanwix built, hard by, the regular fortified work called Fort Pitt.[2] Captain West, brother of Benjamin West, the painter, led a detachment of Pennsylvanians, with Indian guides, through the forests of the Monongahela, to search for the bones of those who had fallen under Braddock. In the heart of the savage wood they found them in abundance, gnawed by wolves and foxes, and covered with the dead leaves of four successive autumns. Major Halket, of Forbes' staff, had joined the party; and, with the help of an Indian who was in the fight, he presently found two skeletons lying under a tree. In one of them he recognized, by a peculiarity of the teeth, the remains of his father, Sir Peter Halket, and in the other he believed that he saw the bones of a

---

[1] *Letter from a British Officer in the Expedition,* 25 Feb. *1759, Gentleman's Magazine,* XXIX. 171.
[2] *Stanwix to Pitt,* 20 Nov. *1759.*

brother who had fallen at his father's side. The young officer fainted at the sight. The two skeletons were buried together, covered with a Highland plaid, and the Pennsylvanian woodsmen fired a volley over the grave. The rest of the bones were undistinguishable; and, being carefully gathered up, they were all interred in a deep trench dug in the freezing ground.[1]

The work of the new fort was pushed on apace, and the task of holding it for the winter was assigned to Lieutenant-Colonel Mercer, of the Virginians, with two hundred provincials. The number was far too small. It was certain that, unless vigorously prevented by a counter attack, the French would gather in early spring from all their nearer western posts, Niagara, Detroit, Presquisle, Le Bœuf, and Venango, to retake the place; but there was no food for a larger garrison, and the risk must be run.

The rest of the troops, with steps quickened by hunger, began their homeward march early in December. "We would soon make M. de Ligneris shift his quarters at Venango," writes Bouquet just after the fort was taken, "if we only had provisions; but we are scarcely able to maintain ourselves a few days here. After God, the success of this expedition is entirely due to the General, who, by bringing about the treaty with the Indians at Easton, struck the French a stunning blow, wisely delayed our advance to wait the effects of that treaty, secured all our posts and left nothing to chance, and resisted the urgent solicitation to take Braddock's road, which would have been our destruction. In all his measures he has shown the greatest prudence, firmness, and ability."[2] No sooner was his work done, than Forbes fell into a state of entire prostration, so that for a time he could neither write a letter nor dictate one. He managed, however, two days after reaching Fort Duquesne, to send Amherst a brief notice of his success, adding: "I shall leave this place as soon as I am able to stand; but God knows when I shall reach Philadelphia, if I ever do."[3] On the way back, a hut with a chimney was built for him at each stopping-place, and on the twenty-eighth of December Major Halket writes from "Tomahawk Camp:" "How great was our disappointment, on coming to this ground last night, to find that the chimney was unlaid, no fire made, nor any wood cut that would burn. This distressed the General to the greatest degree, by obliging him after his long journey to sit above two hours without any

[1]Galt, *Life of Benjamin West*, I. 64 (ed. 1820).
[2]*Bouquet to Chief Justice Allen, 25 Nov. 1758.*
[3]*Forbes to Amherst, 26 Nov. 1758.*

fire, exposed to a snowstorm, which had very near destroyed him entirely; but with great difficulty, by the assistance of some cordials, he was brought to."[1] At length, carried all the way in his litter, he reached Philadelphia, where, after lingering through the winter, he died in March, and was buried with military honors in the chancel of Christ Church.

If his achievement was not brilliant, its solid value was above price. It opened the Great West to English enterprise, took from France half her savage allies, and relieved the western borders from the scourge of Indian war. From southern New York to North Carolina, the frontier populations had cause to bless the memory of the steadfast and all-enduring soldier.

So ended the campaign of 1758. The centre of the French had held its own triumphantly at Ticonderoga; but their left had been forced back by the capture of Louisbourg, and their right by that of Fort Duquesne, while their entire right wing had been well nigh cut off by the destruction of Fort Frontenac. The outlook was dark. Their own Indians were turning against them. "They have struck us," wrote Doreil to the Minister of War; "they have seized three canoes loaded with furs on Lake Ontario, and murdered the men in them: sad forerunner of what we have to fear! Peace, Monseigneur, give us peace! Pardon me, but I cannot repeat that word too often."

---

[1] *Halket to Bouquet, 28 Dec. 1758.*

NOTE.—The *Bouquet and Haldimand Papers* in the British Museum contain a mass of curious correspondence of the principal persons engaged in the expedition under Forbes; copies of it all are before me. The Public Record Office, *America and West Indies*, has also furnished much material, including the official letters of Forbes. The *Writings of Washington*, the *Archives* and *Colonial Records* of Pennsylvania, and the magazines and newspapers of the time may be mentioned among the sources of information, along with a variety of miscellaneous contemporary letters. The Journals of Christian Frederic Post are printed in full in the *Olden Time* and elsewhere.

23

The Brink of Ruin

1758, 1759

JEALOUSY OF VAUDREUIL · HE ASKS FOR MONTCALM'S RECALL · HIS
DISCOMFITURE · SCENE AT THE GOVERNOR'S HOUSE · DISGUST OF
MONTCALM · THE CANADIANS DESPONDENT · DEVICES TO ENCOURAGE
THEM · GASCONADE OF THE GOVERNOR · DEPLORABLE STATE OF THE
COLONY · MISSION OF BOUGAINVILLE · DUPLICITY OF VAUDREUIL ·
BOUGAINVILLE AT VERSAILLES · SUBSTANTIAL AID REFUSED TO CANADA ·
A MATRIMONIAL TREATY · RETURN OF BOUGAINVILLE · MONTCALM
ABANDONED BY THE COURT · HIS PLANS OF DEFENCE · SAD NEWS FROM
CANDIAC · BOASTS OF VAUDREUIL

"Never was general in a more critical position than
I was: God has delivered me; his be the praise!
He gives me health, though I am worn out with labor, fatigue, and
miserable dissensions that have determined me to ask for my recall.
Heaven grant that I may get it!"

Thus wrote Montcalm to his mother after his triumph at Ticonderoga. That great exploit had entailed a train of vexations, for it stirred
the envy of Vaudreuil, more especially as it was due to the troops of
the line, with no help from Indians, and very little from Canadians.
The Governor assured the Colonial Minister that the victory would
have bad results, though he gives no hint what these might be; that
Montcalm had mismanaged the whole affair; that he would have been
beaten but for the manifest interposition of Heaven;[1] and, finally, that

[1] *Vaudreuil au Ministre, 8 Août, 1758.*

he had failed to follow his (Vaudreuil's) directions, and had therefore enabled the English to escape. The real directions of the Governor, dictated, perhaps, by dread lest his rival should reap laurels, were to avoid a general engagement; and it was only by setting them at nought that Abercromby had been routed. After the battle a sharp correspondence passed between the two chiefs. The Governor, who had left Montcalm to his own resources before the crisis, sent him Canadians and Indians in abundance after it was over; and while he cautiously refrained from committing himself by positive orders, repeated again and again that if these reinforcements were used to harass Abercromby's communications, the whole English army would fall back to the Hudson, and leave baggage and artillery a prey to the French. These preposterous assertions and tardy succors were thought by Montcalm to be a device for giving color to the charge that he had not only failed to deserve victory, but had failed also to make use of it.[1] He did what was possible, and sent strong detachments to act in the English rear; which, though they did not, and could not, compel the enemy to fall back, caused no slight annoyance, till Rogers checked them by the defeat of Marin. Nevertheless Vaudreuil pretended on one hand that Montcalm had done nothing with the Canadians and Indians sent him, and on the other that these same Canadians and Indians had triumphed over the enemy by their mere presence at Ticonderoga. "It was my activity in sending these succors to Carillon [Ticonderoga] that forced the English to retreat. The Marquis de Montcalm might have made their retreat difficult; but it was in vain that I wrote to him, in vain that the colony troops, Canadians and Indians, begged him to pursue the enemy."[2] The succors he speaks of were sent in July and August, while the English did not fall back till the first of November. Neither army left its position till the season was over, and Abercromby did so only when he learned that the French were setting the example. Vaudreuil grew more and more bitter. "As the King has intrusted this colony to me, I cannot help warning you of the unhappy consequences that would follow if the Marquis de Montcalm should remain here. I shall keep him by me till I receive your orders. It is essential that they reach me early." "I pass over in silence all the infamous conduct and indecent talk he has held or countenanced; but I should be wanting in my duty to the King if I did not beg you to ask for his recall."[3]

He does not say what is meant by infamous conduct and indecent

---

[1] Much of the voluminous correspondence on these matters will be found in N. Y. Col. Docs., X.
[2] Vaudreuil au Ministre, 8 Avril, 1759.
[3] Ibid.

talk; but the allusion is probably to irreverent utterances touching the
Governor in which the officers from France were apt to indulge, not
always without the knowledge of their chief. Vaudreuil complained of
this to Montcalm, adding, "I am greatly above it, and I despise it."[1] To
which the General replied: "You are right to despise gossip, supposing
that there has been any. For my part, though I hear that I have been
torn to pieces without mercy in your presence, I do not believe it."[2] In
these infelicities Bigot figures as peacemaker, though with no perceptible success. Vaudreuil's cup of bitterness was full when letters came
from Versailles ordering him to defer to Montcalm on all questions of
war, or of civil administration bearing upon war.[3] He had begged hard
for his rival's recall, and in reply his rival was set over his head.

The two yokefellows were excellently fitted to exasperate each other:
Montcalm, with his southern vivacity of emotion and an impetuous,
impatient volubility that sometimes forgot prudence; and Vaudreuil, always affable towards adherents, but full of suspicious egotism and restless jealousy that bristled within him at the very thought of his
colleague. Some of the byplay of the quarrel may be seen in Montcalm's
familiar correspondence with Bourlamaque. One day the Governor, in
his own house, brought up the old complaint that Montcalm, after
taking Fort William Henry, did not take Fort Edward also. The General, for the twentieth time, gave good reasons for not making the attempt. "I ended," he tells Bourlamaque, "by saying quietly that when I
went to war I did the best I could; and that when one is not pleased
with one's lieutenants, one had better take the field in person. He was
very much moved, and muttered between his teeth that perhaps he
would; at which I said that I should be delighted to serve under him.
Madame de Vaudreuil wanted to put in her word. I said: 'Madame,
saving due respect, permit me to have the honor to say that ladies
ought not to talk war.' She kept on. I said: 'Madame, saving due respect, permit me to have the honor to say that if Madame de Montcalm
were here, and heard me talking war with Monsieur le Marquis de Vaudreuil, she would remain silent.' This scene was in presence of eight
officers, three of them belonging to the colony troops; and a pretty
story they will make of it."

These letters to Bourlamaque, in their detestable handwriting, small,
cramped, confused, without stops, and sometimes almost indeciphera-

---

[1] *Vaudreuil à Montcalm, 1 Août, 1758.*
[2] *Montcalm à Vaudreuil, 6 Août, 1758.*
[3] *Ordres du Roy et Dépêches des Ministres, 1758, 1759.*

ble, betray the writer's state of mind. "I should like as well as anybody to be Marshal of France; but to buy the honor with the life I am leading here would be too much." He recounts the last news from Fort Duquesne, just before its fall. "Mutiny among the Canadians, who want to come home; the officers busy with making money, and stealing like mandarins. Their commander sets the example, and will come back with three or four hundred thousand francs; the pettiest ensign, who does not gamble, will have ten, twelve, or fifteen thousand. The Indians don't like Ligneris, who is drunk every day. Forgive the confusion of this letter; I have not slept all night with thinking of the robberies and mismanagement and folly. *Pauvre Roi, pauvre France, cara patria!*" "Oh, when shall we get out of this country! I think I would give half that I have to go home. Pardon this digression to a melancholy man. It is not that I have not still some remnants of gayety; but what would seem such in anybody else is melancholy for a Languedocian. Burn my letter, and never doubt my attachment." "I shall always say, Happy he who is free from the proud yoke to which I am bound. When shall I see my château of Candiac, my plantations, my chestnut grove, my oil-mill, my mulberry-trees? *O bon Dieu! Bon soir; brûlez ma lettre.*"[1]

Never was dispute more untimely than that between these ill-matched colleagues. The position of the colony was desperate. Thus far the Canadians had never lost heart, but had obeyed with admirable alacrity the Governor's call to arms, borne with patience the burdens and privations of the war, and submitted without revolt to the exactions and oppressions of Cadet and his crew; loyal to their native soil, loyal to their Church, loyal to the wretched government that crushed and belittled them. When the able-bodied were ordered to the war, where four fifths of them were employed in the hard and tedious work of transportation, the women, boys, and old men tilled the fields and raised a scanty harvest, which always might be, and sometimes was, taken from them in the name of the King. Yet the least destitute among them were forced every winter to lodge soldiers in their houses, for each of whom they were paid fifteen francs a month, in return for substance devoured and wives and daughters debauched.[2]

No pains had been spared to keep up the courage of the people and feed them with flattering illusions. When the partisan officer Boishébert was tried for peculation, his counsel met the charge by extolling the

[1] The above extracts are from letters of 5 and 27 Nov. and 9 Dec. 1758, and 18 and 23 March, 1759.

[2] *Mémoire sur le moyen d'entretenir 10,000 Hommes de Troupes dans les Colonies, 1759.*

manner in which he had fulfilled the arduous duty of encouraging the Acadians, "putting on an air of triumph even in defeat; using threats, caresses, stratagems; painting our victories in vivid colors; hiding the strength and successes of the enemy; promising succors that did not and could not come; inventing plausible reasons why they did not come, and making new promises to set off the failure of the old; persuading a starved people to forget their misery; taking from some to give to others; and doing all this continually in the face of a superior enemy, that this country might be snatched from England and saved to France."[1] What Boishébert was doing in Acadia, Vaudreuil was doing on a larger scale in Canada. By indefatigable lying, by exaggerating every success and covering over every reverse, he deceived the people and in some measure himself. He had in abundance the Canadian gift of gasconade, and boasted to the Colonial Minister that one of his countrymen was a match for from three to ten Englishmen. It is possible that he almost believed it; for the midnight surprise of defenceless families and the spreading of panics among scattered border settlements were inseparable from his idea of war. Hence the high value he set on Indians, who in such work outdid the Canadians themselves. Sustained by the intoxication of flattering falsehoods, and not doubting that the blunders and weakness of the first years of the war gave the measure of English efficiency, the colonists had never suspected that they could be subdued.

But now there was a change. The reverses of the last campaign, hunger, weariness, and possibly some incipient sense of atrocious misgovernment, began to produce their effect; and some, especially in the towns, were heard to murmur that further resistance was useless. The Canadians, though brave and patient, needed, like Frenchmen, the stimulus of success. "The people are alarmed," said the modest Governor, "and would lose courage if my firmness did not rekindle their zeal to serve the King."[2]

"Rapacity, folly, intrigue, falsehood, will soon ruin this colony which has cost the King so dear," wrote Doreil to the Minister of War. "We must not flatter ourselves with vain hope; Canada is lost if we do not have peace this winter." "It has been saved by miracle in these past three years; nothing but peace can save it now, in spite of all the efforts and the talents of M. de Montcalm."[3] Vaudreuil himself became thoroughly alarmed, and told the Court in the autumn of 1758 that food,

---

[1] *Procès de Bigot, Cadet, et autres, Mémoire pour le Sieur de Boishébert.*
[2] *Vaudreuil au Ministre, 10 Avril, 1759.*
[3] *Doreil au Ministre, 31 Juillet, 1758. Ibid. 12 Août, 1758. Ibid. 31 Août, 1758. Ibid. 1 Sept. 1758.*

arms, munitions, and everything else were fast failing, and that without immediate peace or heavy reinforcements all was lost.

The condition of Canada was indeed deplorable. The St. Lawrence was watched by British ships; the harvest was meagre; a barrel of flour cost two hundred francs; most of the cattle and many of the horses had been killed for food. The people lived chiefly on a pittance of salt cod or on rations furnished by the King; all prices were inordinate; the officers from France were starving on their pay; while a legion of indigenous and imported scoundrels fattened on the general distress. "What a country!" exclaims Montcalm. "Here all the knaves grow rich, and the honest men are ruined." Yet he was resolved to stand by it to the last, and wrote to the Minister of War that he would bury himself under its ruins. "I asked for my recall after the glorious affair of the eighth of July; but since the state of the colony is so bad, I must do what I can to help it and retard its fall." The only hope was in a strong appeal to the Court; and he thought himself fortunate in persuading Vaudreuil to consent that Bougainville should be commissioned to make it, seconded by Doreil. They were to sail in different ships, in order that at least one of them might arrive safe.

Vaudreuil gave Bougainville a letter introducing him to the Colonial Minister in high terms of praise: "He is in all respects better fitted than anybody else to inform you of the state of the colony. I have given him my instructions, and you can trust entirely in what he tells you."[1] Concerning Doreil he wrote to the Minister of War: "I have full confidence in him, and he may be entirely trusted. Everybody here likes him."[2] While thus extolling the friends of his rival, the Governor took care to provide against the effects of his politic commendations, and wrote thus to his patron, the Colonial Minister: "In order to condescend to the wishes of M. de Montcalm, and leave no means untried to keep in harmony with him, I have given letters to MM. Doreil and Bougainville; but I have the honor to inform you, Monseigneur, that they do not understand the colony, and to warn you that they are creatures of M. de Montcalm."[3]

The two envoys had sailed for France. Winter was close at hand, and the harbor of Quebec was nearly empty. One ship still lingered, the last of the season, and by her Montcalm sent a letter to his mother: "You will be glad to have me write to you up to the last moment to tell

[1] *Vaudreuil au Ministre de la Marine, 4 Nov. 1758.*

[2] *Vaudreuil au Ministre de la Guerre, 11 Oct. 1758.*

[3] *Vaudreuil au Ministre de la Marine, 3 Nov. 1758.*

you for the hundredth time that, occupied as I am with the fate of New
France, the preservation of the troops, the interest of the state, and my
own glory, I think continually of you all. We did our best in 1756,
1757, and 1758; and so, God helping, we will do in 1759, unless you
make peace in Europe." Then, shut from the outer world for half a year
by barriers of ice, he waited what returning spring might bring forth.

Both Bougainville and Doreil escaped the British cruisers and safely
reached Versailles, where, in the slippery precincts of the Court, as new
to him as they were treacherous, the young aide-de-camp justified all
the confidence of his chief. He had interviews with the ministers, the
King, and, more important than all, with Madame de Pompadour,
whom he succeeded in propitiating, though not, it seems, without difficulty and delay. France, unfortunate by land and sea, with finances
ruined and navy crippled, had gained one brilliant victory, and she
owed it to Montcalm. She could pay for it in honors, if in nothing else.
Montcalm was made lieutenant-general, Lévis major-general, Bourlamaque brigadier, and Bougainville colonel and chevalier of St. Louis;
while Vaudreuil was solaced with the grand cross of that order.[1] But
when the two envoys asked substantial aid for the imperilled colony,
the response was chilling. The Colonial Minister, Berryer, prepossessed
against Bougainville by the secret warning of Vaudreuil, received him
coldly, and replied to his appeal for help: "Eh, Monsieur, when the
house is on fire one cannot occupy one's self with the stable." "At least,
Monsieur, nobody will say that you talk like a horse," was the irreverent answer.

Bougainville laid four memorials before the Court, in which he
showed the desperate state of the colony and its dire need of help. Thus
far, he said, Canada has been saved by the dissensions of the English
colonies; but now, for the first time, they are united against her, and
prepared to put forth their strength. And he begged for troops, arms,
munitions, food, and a squadron to defend the mouth of the St. Lawrence.[2] The reply, couched in a letter to Montcalm, was to the effect
that it was necessary to concentrate all the strength of the kingdom for
a decisive operation in Europe; that, therefore, the aid required could
not be sent; and that the King trusted everything to his zeal and generalship, joined with the valor of the victors of Ticonderoga.[3] All that
could be obtained was between three and four hundred recruits for the

[1] *Ordres du Roy et Dépêches des Ministres, Janvier, Février, 1759.*
[2] *Mémoire remis au Ministre par M. de Bougainville, Décembre, 1758.*
[3] *Le Ministre à Montcalm, 3 Fév. 1759.*

regulars, sixty engineers, sappers, and artillerymen, and gunpowder, arms, and provisions sufficient, along with the supplies brought over by the contractor, Cadet, to carry the colony through the next campaign.[1]

Montcalm had intrusted Bougainville with another mission, widely different. This was no less than the negotiating of suitable marriages for the eldest son and daughter of his commander, with whom, in the confidence of friendship, he had had many conversations on the matter. "He and I," Montcalm wrote to his mother, Madame de Saint-Véran, "have two ideas touching these marriages,—the first, romantic and chimerical; the second, good, practicable."[2] Bougainville, invoking the aid of a lady of rank, a friend of the family, acquitted himself well of his delicate task. Before he embarked for Canada, in early spring, a treaty was on foot for the marriage of the young Comte de Montcalm to an heiress of sixteen; while Mademoiselle de Montcalm had already become Madame d'Espineuse. "Her father will be delighted," says the successful negotiator.[3]

Again he crossed the Atlantic and sailed up the St. Lawrence as the portentous spring of 1759 was lowering over the dissolving snows of Canada. With him came a squadron bearing the supplies and the petty reinforcement which the Court had vouchsafed. "A little is precious to those who have nothing," said Montcalm on receiving them. Despatches from the ministers gave warning of a great armament fitted out in English ports for the attack of Quebec, while a letter to the General from the Maréchal de Belleisle, minister of war, told what was expected of him, and why he and the colony were abandoned to their fate. "If we sent a large reinforcement of troops," said Belleisle, "there would be great fear that the English would intercept them on the way; and as the King could never send you forces equal to those which the English are prepared to oppose to you, the attempt would have no other effect than to excite the Cabinet of London to increased efforts for preserving its superiority on the American continent.

"As we must expect the English to turn all their force against Canada, and attack you on several sides at once, it is necessary that you limit your plans of defence to the most essential points and those most closely connected, so that, being concentrated within a smaller space, each part may be within reach of support and succor from the rest. How small soever may be the space you are able to hold, it is indispensable

---

[1] *Ordres du Roy et Dépêches des Ministres, Février, 1759.*
[2] *Montcalm à Madame de Saint-Véran, 24 Sept. 1758.*
[3] *Lettres de Bougainville à Madame de Saint-Véran, 1758, 1759.*

to keep a footing in North America; for if we once lose the country entirely, its recovery will be almost impossible. The King counts on your zeal, courage, and persistency to accomplish this object, and relies on you to spare no pains and no exertions. Impart this resolution to your chief officers, and join with them to inspire your soldiers with it. I have answered for you to the King; I am confident that you will not disappoint me, and that for the glory of the nation, the good of the state, and your own preservation, you will go to the utmost extremity rather than submit to conditions as shameful as those imposed at Louisbourg, the memory of which you will wipe out."[1] "We will save this unhappy colony, or perish," was the answer of Montcalm.

It was believed that Canada would be attacked with at least fifty thousand men. Vaudreuil had caused a census to be made of the governments of Montreal, Three Rivers, and Quebec. It showed a little more than thirteen thousand effective men.[2] To these were to be added thirty-five hundred troops of the line, including the late reinforcement, fifteen hundred colony troops, a body of irregulars in Acadia, and the militia and *coureurs-de-bois* of Detroit and the other upper posts, along with from one to two thousand Indians who could still be counted on. Great as was the disparity of numbers, there was good hope that the centre of the colony could be defended; for the only avenues by which an enemy could approach were barred by the rock of Quebec, the rapids of the St. Lawrence, and the strong position of Isle-aux-Noix, at the outlet of Lake Champlain. Montcalm had long inclined to the plan of concentration enjoined on him by the Minister of War. Vaudreuil was of another mind; he insisted on still occupying Acadia and the forts of the upper country: matters on which he and the General exchanged a correspondence that widened the breach between them.

Should every effort of resistance fail, and the invaders force their way into the heart of Canada, Montcalm proposed the desperate resort of abandoning the valley of the St. Lawrence, descending the Mississippi with his troops and as many as possible of the inhabitants, and making a last stand for France among the swamps of Louisiana.[3]

In April, before Bougainville's return, he wrote to his wife: "Can we hope for another miracle to save us? I trust in God; he fought for us on the eighth of July. Come what may, his will be done! I wait the news from France with impatience and dread. We have had none for eight

---

[1] *Belleisle à Montcalm, 19 Fév. 1759.*
[2] *Vaudreuil au Ministre, 8 Avril, 1759.* The *Mémoires sur le Canada, 1749–1760,* says 15,229 effective men.
[3] *Mémoire sur le Canada remis au Ministre, 27 Déc. 1758.*

months; and who knows if much can reach us at all this year? How dearly I have to pay for the dismal privilege of figuring two or three times in the gazettes!" A month later, after Bougainville had come: "Our daughter is well married. I think I would renounce every honor to join you again; but the King must be obeyed. The moment when I see you once more will be the brightest of my life. Adieu, my heart! I believe that I love you more than ever."

Bougainville had brought sad news. He had heard before sailing from France that one of Montcalm's daughters was dead, but could not learn which of them. "I think," says the father, "that it must be poor Mirète, who was like me, and whom I loved very much." He was never to know if this conjecture was true.

To Vaudreuil came a repetition of the detested order that he should defer to Montcalm on all questions of war; and moreover that he should not take command in person except when the whole body of the militia was called out; nor, even then, without consulting his rival.[1] His ire and vexation produced an access of jealous self-assertion, and drove him into something like revolt against the ministerial command. "If the English attack Quebec, I shall always hold myself free to go thither myself with most of the troops and all the militia and Indians I can assemble. On arriving I shall give battle to the enemy; and I shall do so again and again, till I have forced him to retire, or till he has entirely crushed me by excessive superiority of numbers. My obstinacy in opposing his landing will be the more *à propos*, as I have not the means of sustaining a siege. If I succeed as I wish, I shall next march to Carillon to arrest him there. You see, Monseigneur, that the slightest change in my arrangements would have the most unfortunate consequences."[2]

Whether he made good this valorous declaration will presently be seen.

[1] *Ordres du Roy et Dépêches des Ministres, Lettre à Vaudreuil, 3 Fév. 1759.*
[2] *Vaudreuil au Ministre, 8 Avril, 1759.*
NOTE.—The Archives de la Guerre and the Archives de la Marine contain a mass of letters and documents on the subjects treated in the above chapter; these I have carefully read and collated. The other principal authorities are the correspondence of Montcalm with Bourlamaque and with his own family; the letters of Vaudreuil preserved in the Archives Nationales; and the letters of Bougainville and Doreil to Montcalm and Madame de Saint-Véran while on their mission to France. For copies of these last I am indebted to the present Marquis de Montcalm.

24

Wolfe

1758, 1759

Captain John Knox, of the forty-third regiment, had spent the winter in garrison at Fort Cumberland, on the hill of Beauséjour. For nearly two years he and his comrades had been exiles amid the wilds of Nova Scotia, and the monotonous inaction was becoming insupportable. The great marsh of Tantemar on the one side, and that of Missaguash on the other, two vast flat tracts of glaring snow, bounded by dark hills of spruce and fir, were hateful to their sight. Shooting, fishing, or skating were a dangerous relief; for the neighborhood was infested by "vermin," as they called the Acadians and their Micmac allies. In January four soldiers and a ranger were waylaid not far from the fort, disabled by bullets, and then scalped alive. They were found the next morning on the snow, contorted in the agonies of death, and frozen like marble statues. St. Patrick's Day brought more cheerful excitements. The Irish officers of the garrison gave their comrades a feast, having laid in during the autumn a stock of frozen provisions, that the festival of their saint might be duly honored. All was hilarity at Fort Cumberland, where it is recorded that punch to the value of twelve pounds sterling, with a corresponding supply of wine and beer, was consumed on this joyous occasion.[1]

About the middle of April a schooner came up the bay, bringing letters that filled men and officers with delight. The regiment was ordered to hold itself ready to embark for Louisbourg and join an expedition to the St. Lawrence, under command of Major-General Wolfe. All that afternoon the soldiers were shouting and cheering in their barracks; and when they mustered for the evening roll-call, there was another burst of huzzas. They waited in expectancy nearly three weeks, and then the transports which were to carry them arrived, bringing the provincials who had been hastily raised in New England to take their place. These Knox describes as a mean-looking set of fellows, of all ages and sizes, and without any kind of discipline; adding that their officers are sober, modest men, who, though of confined ideas, talk very clearly and sensibly, and make a decent appearance in blue, faced with scarlet, though the privates have no uniform at all.

At last the forty-third set sail, the cannon of the fort saluting them, and the soldiers cheering lustily, overjoyed to escape from their long imprisonment. A gale soon began; the transports became separated; Knox's vessel sheltered herself for a time in Passamaquoddy Bay; then passed the Grand Menan, and steered southward and eastward along the coast of Nova Scotia. A calm followed the gale; and they moved so slowly that Knox beguiled the time by fishing over the stern, and caught a halibut so large that he was forced to call for help to pull it in. Then they steered northeastward, now lost in fogs, and now tossed mercilessly on those boisterous waves; till, on the twenty-fourth of May, they saw a rocky and surf-lashed shore, with a forest of masts rising to all appearance out of it. It was the British fleet in the land-locked harbor of Louisbourg.

On the left, as they sailed through the narrow passage, lay the town, scarred with shot and shell, the red cross floating over its battered ramparts; and around in a wide semicircle rose the bristling backs of rugged hills, set thick with dismal evergreens. They passed the great ships of the fleet, and anchored among the other transports towards the head of the harbor. It was not yet free from ice; and the floating masses lay so thick in some parts that the reckless sailors, returning from leave on shore, jumped from one to another to regain their ships. There was a review of troops, and Knox went to see it; but it was over before he reached the place, where he was presently told of a characteristic reply

[1]Knox, *Historical Journal,* I. 228.

just made by Wolfe to some officers who had apologized for not having taught their men the new exercise. "Poh, poh!—new exercise—new fiddlestick. If they are otherwise well disciplined, and will fight, that 's all I shall require of them."

Knox does not record his impressions of his new commander, which must have been disappointing. He called him afterwards a British Achilles; but in person at least Wolfe bore no likeness to the son of Peleus, for never was the soul of a hero cased in a frame so incongruous. His face, when seen in profile, was singular as that of the Great Condé. The forehead and chin receded; the nose, slightly upturned, formed with the other features the point of an obtuse triangle; the mouth was by no means shaped to express resolution; and nothing but the clear, bright, and piercing eye bespoke the spirit within. On his head he wore a black three-cornered hat; his red hair was tied in a queue behind; his narrow shoulders, slender body, and long, thin limbs were cased in a scarlet frock, with broad cuffs and ample skirts that reached the knee; while on his left arm he wore a band of crape in mourning for his father, of whose death he had heard a few days before.

James Wolfe was in his thirty-third year. His father was an officer of distinction, Major-General Edward Wolfe, and he himself, a delicate and sensitive child, but an impetuous and somewhat headstrong youth, had served the King since the age of fifteen. From childhood he had dreamed of the army and the wars. At sixteen he was in Flanders, adjutant of his regiment, discharging the duties of the post in a way that gained him early promotion and, along with a painstaking assiduity, showing a precocious faculty for commanding men. He passed with credit through several campaigns, took part in the victory of Dettingen, and then went to Scotland to fight at Culloden. Next we find him at Stirling, Perth, and Glasgow, always ardent and always diligent, constant in military duty, and giving his spare hours to mathematics and Latin. He presently fell in love; and being disappointed, plunged into a variety of dissipations, contrary to his usual habits, which were far above the standard of that profligate time.

At twenty-three he was a lieutenant-colonel, commanding his regiment in the then dirty and barbarous town of Inverness, amid a disaffected and turbulent population whom it was his duty to keep in order: a difficult task, which he accomplished so well as to gain the special commendation of the King, and even the goodwill of the Highlanders themselves. He was five years among these northern hills, battling with ill-health, and restless under the intellectual barrenness of his surroundings. He felt his position to be in no way salutary, and wrote to his mother: "The fear of becoming a mere ruffian and of imbibing the tyrannical principles of an absolute commander, or giving way insensibly to the temptations of power till I became proud, insolent, and intolerable,—these considerations will make me wish to leave the regiment before next winter; that by frequenting men above myself I may know my true condition, and by discoursing with the other sex may learn some civility and mildness of carriage." He got leave of absence, and spent six months in Paris, where he was presented at Court and saw much of the best society. This did not prevent him from working hard to perfect himself in French, as well as in horsemanship, fencing, dancing, and other accomplishments, and from earnestly seeking an opportunity to study the various armies of Europe. In this he was thwarted by the stupidity and prejudice of the commander-in-chief; and he made what amends he could by extensive reading in all that bore on military matters.

His martial instincts were balanced by strong domestic inclinations. He was fond of children; and after his disappointment in love used to say that they were the only true inducement to marriage. He was a most dutiful son, and wrote continually to both his parents. Sometimes he would philosophize on the good and ill of life; sometimes he held questionings with his conscience; and once he wrote to his mother in a strain of self-accusation not to be expected from a bold and determined soldier. His nature was a compound of tenderness and fire, which last sometimes showed itself in sharp and unpleasant flashes. His excitable temper was capable almost of fierceness, and he could now and then be needlessly stern; but towards his father, mother, and friends he was a model of steady affection. He made friends readily, and kept them, and was usually a pleasant companion, though subject to sallies of imperious irritability which occasionally broke through his strong sense of good breeding. For this his susceptible constitution was largely answerable, for he was a living barometer, and his spirits rose and fell with every change of weather. In spite of his impatient outbursts, the officers whom he had commanded remained attached to him for life; and, in spite of his rigorous discipline, he was beloved by his soldiers, to whose comfort he was always attentive. Frankness, directness, essential good feeling, and a high integrity atoned for all his faults.

In his own view, as expressed to his mother, he was a person of very moderate abilities, aided by more than usual diligence; but this modest judgment of himself by no means deprived him of self-confidence, nor, in time of need, of self-assertion. He delighted in every kind of hardihood; and, in his contempt for effeminacy, once said to his mother:

"Better be a savage of some use than a gentle, amorous puppy, obnoxious to all the world." He was far from despising fame; but the controlling principles of his life were duty to his country and his profession, loyalty to the King, and fidelity to his own ideal of the perfect soldier. To the parent who was the confidant of his most intimate thoughts he said: "All that I wish for myself is that I may at all times be ready and firm to meet that fate we cannot shun, and to die gracefully and properly when the hour comes." Never was wish more signally fulfilled. Again he tells her: "My utmost desire and ambition is to look steadily upon danger;" and his desire was accomplished. His intrepidity was complete. No form of death had power to daunt him. Once and again, when bound on some deadly enterprise of war, he calmly counts the chances whether or not he can compel his feeble body to bear him on till the work is done. A frame so delicately strung could not have been insensible to danger; but forgetfulness of self, and the absorption of every faculty in the object before him, shut out the sense of fear. He seems always to have been at his best in the thick of battle; most complete in his mastery over himself and over others.

But it is in the intimacies of domestic life that one sees him most closely, and especially in his letters to his mother, from whom he inherited his frail constitution, without the beauty that distinguished her. "The greatest happiness that I wish for here is to see you happy." "If you stay much at home I will come and shut myself up with you for three weeks or a month, and play at piquet from morning till night; and you shall laugh at my short red hair as much as you please." The playing at piquet was a sacrifice to filial attachment; for the mother loved cards, and the son did not. "Don't trouble yourself about my room or my bedclothes; too much care and delicacy at this time would enervate me and complete the destruction of a tottering constitution. Such as it is, it must serve me now, and I'll make the best of it while it holds." At the beginning of the war his father tried to dissuade him from offering his services on board the fleet; and he replies in a letter to Mrs. Wolfe: "It is no time to think of what is convenient or agreeable; that service is certainly the best in which we are the most useful. For my part, I am determined never to give myself a moment's concern about the nature of the duty which His Majesty is pleased to order us upon. It will be a sufficient comfort to you two, as far as my person is concerned,—at least it will be a reasonable consolation,—to reflect that the Power which has hitherto preserved me may, if it be his pleasure, continue to do so; if not, that it is but a few days or a few years more or less, and that those who perish in their duty and in the service of their country die honorably." Then he proceeds to give particular directions about his numerous dogs, for the welfare of which in his absence he provides with anxious solicitude, especially for "my friend Cæsar, who has great merit and much good-humor."

After the unfortunate expedition against Rochefort, when the board of general officers appointed to inquire into the affair were passing the highest encomiums upon his conduct, his parents were at Bath, and he took possession of their house at Blackheath, whence he wrote to his mother: "I lie in your chamber, dress in the General's little parlor, and dine where you did. The most perceptible difference and change of affairs (exclusive of the bad table I keep) is the number of dogs in the yard; but by coaxing Ball [his father's dog] and rubbing his back with my stick, I have reconciled him with the new ones, and put them in some measure under his protection."

When about to sail on the expedition against Louisbourg, he was anxious for his parents, and wrote to his uncle, Major Wolfe, at Dublin: "I trust you will give the best advice to my mother, and such assistance, if it should be wanted, as the distance between you will permit. I mention this because the General seems to decline apace, and narrowly escaped being carried off in the spring. She, poor woman, is in a bad state of health, and needs the care of some friendly hand. She has long and painful fits of illness, which by succession and inheritance are likely to devolve on me, since I feel the early symptoms of them." Of his friends Guy Carleton, afterwards Lord Dorchester, and George Warde, the companion of his boyhood, he also asks help for his mother in his absence.

His part in the taking of Louisbourg greatly increased his reputation. After his return he went to Bath to recruit his health; and it seems to have been here that he wooed and won Miss Katherine Lowther, daughter of an ex-Governor of Barbadoes, and sister of the future Lord Lonsdale. A betrothal took place, and Wolfe wore her portrait till the night before his death. It was a little before this engagement that he wrote to his friend Lieutenant-Colonel Rickson: "I have this day signi-fied to Mr. Pitt that he may dispose of my slight carcass as he pleases, and that I am ready for any undertaking within the compass of my skill and cunning. I am in a very bad condition both with the gravel and rheumatism; but I had much rather die than decline any kind of service that offers. If I followed my own taste it would lead me into Germany. However, it is not our part to choose, but to obey. My opinion is that I shall join the army in America."

Pitt chose him to command the expedition then fitting out against

Quebec; made him a major-general, though, to avoid giving offence to older officers, he was to hold that rank in America alone; and permitted him to choose his own staff. Appointments made for merit, and not through routine and patronage, shocked the Duke of Newcastle, to whom a man like Wolfe was a hopeless enigma; and he told George II. that Pitt's new general was mad. "Mad is he?" returned the old King; "then I hope he will bite some others of my generals."

At the end of January the fleet was almost ready, and Wolfe wrote to his uncle Walter: "I am to act a greater part in this business than I wished. The backwardness of some of the older officers has in some measure forced the Government to come down so low. I shall do my best, and leave the rest to fortune, as perforce we must when there are not the most commanding abilities. We expect to sail in about three weeks. A London life and little exercise disagrees entirely with me, but the sea still more. If I have health and constitution enough for the campaign, I shall think myself a lucky man; what happens afterwards is of no great consequence." He sent to his mother an affectionate letter of farewell, went to Spithead, embarked with Admiral Saunders in the ship "Neptune," and set sail on the seventeenth of February. In a few hours the whole squadron was at sea, the transports, the frigates, and the great line-of-battle ships, with their ponderous armament and their freight of rude humanity armed and trained for destruction; while on the heaving deck of the "Neptune," wretched with seasickness and racked with pain, stood the gallant invalid who was master of it all.

The fleet consisted of twenty-two ships of the line, with frigates, sloops-of-war, and a great number of transports. When Admiral Saunders arrived with his squadron off Louisbourg, he found the entrance blocked by ice, and was forced to seek harborage at Halifax. The squadron of Admiral Holmes, which had sailed a few days earlier, proceeded to New York to take on board troops destined for the expedition, while the squadron of Admiral Durell steered for the St. Lawrence to intercept the expected ships from France.

In May the whole fleet, except the ten ships with Durell, was united in the harbor of Louisbourg. Twelve thousand troops were to have been employed for the expedition; but several regiments expected from the West Indies were for some reason countermanded, while the accessions from New York and the Nova Scotia garrisons fell far short of the looked-for numbers. Three weeks before leaving Louisbourg, Wolfe writes to his uncle Walter that he has an army of nine thousand men. The actual number seems to have been somewhat less.[1] "Our troops are

[1] See *Grenville Correspondence*, I. 305.

good," he informs Pitt; "and if valor can make amends for the want of numbers, we shall probably succeed."

Three brigadiers, all in the early prime of life, held command under him: Monckton, Townshend, and Murray. They were all his superiors in birth, and one of them, Townshend, never forgot that he was so. "George Townshend," says Walpole, "has thrust himself again into the service; and, as far as wrongheadedness will go, is very proper for a hero."[1] The same caustic writer says further that he was of "a proud, sullen, and contemptuous temper," and that he "saw everything in an ill-natured and ridiculous light."[2] Though his perverse and envious disposition made him a difficult colleague, Townshend had both talents and energy; as also had Monckton, the same officer who commanded at the capture of Beauséjour in 1755. Murray, too, was well matched to the work in hand, in spite of some lingering remains of youthful rashness.

On the sixth of June the last ship of the fleet sailed out of Louisbourg harbor, the troops cheering and the officers drinking to the toast, "British colors on every French fort, port, and garrison in America." The ships that had gone before lay to till the whole fleet was reunited, and then all steered together for the St. Lawrence. From the headland of Cape Egmont, the Micmac hunter, gazing far out over the shimmering sea, saw the horizon flecked with their canvas wings, as they bore northward on their errand of havoc.

[1] Horace Walpole, *Letters* III. 207 (ed. Cunningham, 1857).
[2] Ibid. *George II.*, II. 345.

NOTE.—For the material of the foregoing sketch of Wolfe I am indebted to Wright's excellent Life of him and the numerous letters contained in it. Several autograph letters which have escaped the notice of Mr. Wright are preserved in the Public Record Office. The following is a characteristic passage from one of these, written on board the "Neptune," at sea, on the sixth of June, the day when the fleet sailed from Louisbourg. It is directed to a nobleman of high rank in the army, whose name does not appear, the address being lost (War Office Records: *North America, various, 1756–1763*): "I have had the honour to receive two letters from your Lordship, one of an old date, concerning my stay in this country [*after the capture of Louisbourg*], in answer to which I shall only say that the Marshal told me I was to return at the end of the campaign; and as General Amherst had no other commands than to send me to winter at Halifax under the orders of an officer [*Brigadier Lawrence*] who was but a few months before put over my head, I thought it was much better to get into the way of service and out of the way of being insulted; and as the style of your Lordship's letter is pretty strong, I must take the liberty to inform you that . . . rather than receive orders in the Government [*of Nova Scotia*] from an officer younger than myself (though a very worthy man), I should certainly have desired leave to resign my commission; for as I neither ask nor expect any favour, so I never intend to submit to any ill-usage whatsoever."

Many other papers in the Public Record Office have been consulted in preparing the above chapter, including the secret instructions of the King to Wolfe and to Saunders, and the letters of Amherst to Wolfe and to Pitt. Other correspondence touching the same subjects is printed in *Selections from the Public Documents of Nova Scotia*, 441–450. Knox, Mante, and Entick are the best contemporary printed sources.

A story has gained currency respecting the last interview of Wolfe with Pitt, in which he is said to have flourished his sword and boasted of what he would achieve. This anecdote was told by Lord Temple, who was present at the interview, to Mr. Grenville, who, many years after, told it to Earl Stanhope, by whom it was made public. That the incident underwent essential changes in the course of these transmissions,—which extended over more than half a century, for Earl Stanhope was not born till 1805,—can never be doubted by one who considers the known character of Wolfe, who may have uttered some vehement expression, but who can never be suspected of gasconade.

25

Wolfe at Quebec

1759

In early spring the chiefs of Canada met at Montreal to settle a plan of defence. What at first they most dreaded was an advance of the enemy by way of Lake Champlain. Bourlamaque, with three battalions, was ordered to take post at Ticonderoga, hold it if he could, or, if overborne by numbers, fall back to Isle-aux-Noix, at the outlet of the lake. La Corne was sent with a strong detachment to intrench himself at the head of the rapids of the St. Lawrence, and oppose any hostile movement from Lake Ontario. Every able-bodied man in the colony, and every boy who could fire a gun, was to be called to the field. Vaudreuil sent a circular letter to the militia captains of all the parishes, with orders to read it to the parishioners. It exhorted them to defend their religion, their wives, their children, and their goods

419

from the fury of the heretics; declared that he, the Governor, would never yield up Canada on any terms whatever; and ordered them to join the army at once, leaving none behind but the old, the sick, the women, and the children.[1] The Bishop issued a pastoral mandate: "On every side, dearest brethren, the enemy is making immense preparations. His forces, at least six times more numerous than ours, are already in motion. Never was Canada in a state so critical and full of peril. Never were we so destitute, or threatened with an attack so fierce, so general, and so obstinate. Now, in truth, we may say, more than ever before, that our only resource is in the powerful succor of our Lord. Then, dearest brethren, make every effort to deserve it. 'Seek first the kingdom of God; and all these things shall be added unto you.' " And he reproves their sins, exhorts them to repentance, and ordains processions, masses, and prayers.[2]

Vaudreuil bustled and boasted. In May he wrote to the Minister: "The zeal with which I am animated for the service of the King will always make me surmount the greatest obstacles. I am taking the most proper measures to give the enemy a good reception whenever he may attack us. I keep in view the defence of Quebec. I have given orders in the parishes below to muster the inhabitants who are able to bear arms, and place women, children, cattle, and even hay and grain, in places of safety. Permit me, Monseigneur, to beg you to have the goodness to assure His Majesty that, to whatever hard extremity I may be reduced, my zeal will be equally ardent and indefatigable, and that I shall do the impossible to prevent our enemies from making progress in any direction, or, at least, to make them pay extremely dear for it."[3] Then he writes again to say that Amherst with a great army will, as he learns, attack Ticonderoga; that Bradstreet, with six thousand men, will advance to Lake Ontario; and that six thousand more will march to the Ohio. "Whatever progress they may make," he adds, "I am resolved to yield them nothing, but hold my ground even to annihilation." He promises to do his best to keep on good terms with Montcalm, and ends with a warm eulogy of Bigot.[4]

It was in the midst of all these preparations that Bougainville arrived from France with news that a great fleet was on its way to attack Quebec. The town was filled with consternation mixed with surprise, for the Canadians had believed that the dangerous navigation of the St.

---

[1] *Mémoires sur le Canada, 1749–1760.*
[2] I am indebted for a copy of this mandate to the kindness of Abbé Bois. As printed by Knox, it is somewhat different, though the spirit is the same.
[3] *Vaudreuil au Ministre, 8 Mai, 1759.*
[4] *Vaudreuil au Ministre, 20 [?] Mai, 1759.*

Lawrence would deter their enemies from the attempt. "Everybody," writes one of them, "was stupefied at an enterprise that seemed so bold." In a few days a crowd of sails was seen approaching. They were not enemies, but friends. It was the fleet of the contractor Cadet, commanded by an officer named Kanon, and loaded with supplies for the colony. They anchored in the harbor, eighteen sail in all, and their arrival spread universal joy. Admiral Durell had come too late to intercept them, catching but three stragglers that had lagged behind the rest. Still others succeeded in eluding him, and before the first of June five more ships had come safely into port.

When the news brought by Bougainville reached Montreal, nearly the whole force of the colony, except the detachments of Bourlamaque and La Corne, was ordered to Quebec. Montcalm hastened thither, and Vaudreuil followed. The Governor-General wrote to the Minister in his usual strain, as if all the hope of Canada rested in him. Such, he says, was his activity, that, though very busy, he reached Quebec only a day and a half after Montcalm; and, on arriving, learned from his scouts that English ships-of-war had already appeared at Isle-aux-Coudres. These were the squadron of Durell. "I expect," Vaudreuil goes on, "to be sharply attacked, and that our enemies will make their most powerful efforts to conquer this colony; but there is no ruse, no resource, no means which my zeal does not suggest to lay snares for them, and finally, when the exigency demands it, to fight them with an ardor, and even a fury, which exceeds the range of their ambitious designs. The troops, the Canadians, and the Indians are not ignorant of the resolution I have taken, and from which I shall not recoil under any circumstance whatever. The burghers of this city have already put their goods and furniture in places of safety. The old men, women, and children hold themselves ready to leave town. My firmness is generally applauded. It has penetrated every heart; and each man says aloud: 'Canada, our native land, shall bury us under its ruins before we surrender to the English!' This is decidedly my own determination, and I shall hold to it inviolably." He launches into high praise of the contractor Cadet, whose zeal for the service of the King and the defence of the colony he declares to be triumphant over every difficulty. It is necessary, he adds, that ample supplies of all kinds should be sent out in the autumn, with the distribution of which Cadet offers to charge himself, and to account for them at their first cost; but he does not say what prices his disinterested friend will compel the destitute Canadians to pay for them.[1]

---

[1] *Vaudreuil au Ministre, 28 Mai, 1759.*

Five battalions from France, nearly all the colony troops, and the militia from every part of Canada poured into Quebec, along with a thousand or more Indians, who, at the call of Vaudreuil, came to lend their scalping-knives to the defence. Such was the ardor of the people that boys of fifteen and men of eighty were to be seen in the camp. Isle-aux-Coudres and Isle d'Orléans were ordered to be evacuated, and an excited crowd on the rock of Quebec watched hourly for the approaching fleet. Days passed and weeks passed, yet it did not appear. Meanwhile Vaudreuil held council after council to settle a plan of defence. They were strange scenes: a crowd of officers of every rank, mixed pell-mell in a small room, pushing, shouting, elbowing each other, interrupting each other; till Montcalm, in despair, took each aside after the meeting was over, and made him give his opinion in writing.[1]

He himself had at first proposed to encamp the army on the plains of Abraham and the meadows of the St. Charles, making that river his line of defence;[2] but he changed his plan, and, with the concurrence of Vaudreuil, resolved to post his whole force on the St. Lawrence below the city, with his right resting on the St. Charles, and his left on the Montmorenci. Here, accordingly, the troops and militia were stationed as they arrived. Early in June, standing at the northeastern brink of the rock of Quebec, one could have seen the whole position at a glance. On the curving shore from the St. Charles to the rocky gorge of the Montmorenci, a distance of seven or eight miles, the whitewashed dwellings of the parish of Beauport stretched down the road in a double chain, and the fields on both sides were studded with tents, huts, and Indian wigwams. Along the borders of the St. Lawrence, as far as the eye could distinguish them, gangs of men were throwing up redoubts, batteries, and lines of intrenchment. About midway between the two extremities of the encampment ran the little river of Beauport; and on the rising ground just beyond it stood a large stone house, round which the tents were thickly clustered; for here Montcalm had made his headquarters.

A boom of logs chained together was drawn across the mouth of the St. Charles, which was further guarded by two hulks mounted with cannon. The bridge of boats that crossed the stream nearly a mile above, formed the chief communication between the city and the camp. Its head towards Beauport was protected by a strong and extensive earthwork; and the banks of the stream on the Quebec side were

---

[1] *Journal du Siége de Québec déposé à la Bibliothêque de Hartwell, en Angleterre.* (Printed at Quebec, 1836.)
[2] *Livre d'Ordres, Disposition pour s'opposer à la Descente.*

also intrenched, to form a second line of defence in case the position at Beauport should be forced.

In the city itself every gate, except the Palace Gate, which gave access to the bridge, was closed and barricaded. A hundred and six cannon were mounted on the walls.[1] A floating battery of twelve heavy pieces, a number of gunboats, eight fireships, and several firerafts formed the river defences. The largest merchantmen of Kanon's fleet were sacrificed to make the fireships; and the rest, along with the frigates that came with them, were sent for safety up the St. Lawrence beyond the River Richelieu, whence about a thousand of their sailors returned to man the batteries and gunboats.

In the camps along the Beauport shore were about fourteen thousand men, besides Indians. The regulars held the centre; the militia of Quebec and Three Rivers were on the right, and those of Montreal on the left. In Quebec itself there was a garrison of between one and two thousand men under the Chevalier de Ramesay. Thus the whole number, including Indians, amounted to more than sixteen thousand;[2] and though the Canadians who formed the greater part of it were of little use in the open field, they could be trusted to fight well behind intrenchments. Against this force, posted behind defensive works, on positions almost impregnable by nature, Wolfe brought less than nine thousand men available for operations on land.[3] The steep and lofty heights that lined the river made the cannon of the ships for the most part useless, while the exigencies of the naval service forbade employing the sailors on shore. In two or three instances only, throughout the siege, small squads of them landed to aid in moving and working cannon; and the actual fighting fell to the troops alone.

Vaudreuil and Bigot took up their quarters with the army. The Governor-General had delegated the command of the land-forces to Montcalm, whom, in his own words, he authorized "to give orders everywhere, provisionally." His relations with him were more than ever anomalous and critical; for while Vaudreuil, in virtue of his office, had a right to supreme command, Montcalm, now a lieutenant-general, held a military grade far above him; and the Governor, while always writing himself down in his despatches as the head and front of every movement, had too little self-confidence not to leave the actual command in the hands of his rival.

Days and weeks wore on, and the first excitement gave way to restless

---

[1]This number was found after the siege. Knox, II. 151. Some French writers make it much greater.
[2]See Appendix H.
[3]Ibid.

impatience. Why did not the English come? Many of the Canadians thought that Heaven would interpose and wreck the English fleet, as it had wrecked that of Admiral Walker half a century before. There were processions, prayers, and vows towards this happy consummation. Food was scarce. Bigot and Cadet lived in luxury; fowls by thousands were fattened with wheat for their tables, while the people were put on rations of two ounces of bread a day.[1] Durell and his ships were reported to be still at Isle-aux-Coudres. Vaudreuil sent thither a party of Canadians, and they captured three midshipmen, who, says Montcalm, had gone ashore *pour polissonner*, that is, on a lark. These youths were brought to Quebec, where they increased the general anxiety by grossly exaggerating the English force.

At length it became known that eight English vessels were anchored in the north channel of Orleans, and on the twenty-first of June the masts of three of them could plainly be seen. One of the fireships was consumed in a vain attempt to burn them, and several firerafts and a sort of infernal machine were tried with no better success; the unwelcome visitors still held their posts.

Meanwhile the whole English fleet had slowly advanced, piloted by Denis de Vitré, a Canadian of good birth, captured at sea some time before, and now compelled to serve, under a threat of being hanged if he refused.[2] Nor was he alone; for when Durell reached the place where the river pilots were usually taken on board, he raised a French flag to his mast-head, causing great rejoicings among the Canadians on shore, who thought that a fleet was come to their rescue, and that their country was saved. The pilots launched their canoes and came out to the ships, where they were all made prisoners; then the French flag was lowered, and the red cross displayed in its stead. The spectators on shore turned from joy to despair; and a priest who stood watching the squadron with a telescope is said to have dropped dead with the revulsion of feeling.

Towards the end of June the main fleet was near the mountain of Cape Tourmente. The passage called the Traverse, between the Cape and the lower end of the Island of Orleans, was reputed one of the most dangerous parts of the St. Lawrence; and as the ships successively came up, the captive pilots were put on board to carry them safely through, on pain of death. One of these men was assigned to the transport "Goodwill," in which was Captain Knox, who spoke French,

---

[1] *Mémoires sur le Canada, 1749-1760.*
[2] *Mémorial de Jean-Denis de Vitré au Très-honorable William Pitt.*

and who reports thus in his Diary: "He gasconaded at a most extravagant rate, and gave us to understand that it was much against his will that he was become an English pilot. The poor fellow assumed great latitude in his conversation, and said 'he made no doubt that some of the fleet would return to England, but they should have a dismal tale to carry with them; for Canada should be the grave of the whole army, and he expected in a short time to see the walls of Quebec ornamented with English scalps.' Had it not been in obedience to the Admiral, who gave orders that he should not be ill-used, he would certainly have been thrown overboard." The master of the transport was an old sailor named Killick, who despised the whole Gallic race, and had no mind to see his ship in charge of a Frenchman. "He would not let the pilot speak," continues Knox, "but fixed his mate at the helm, charged him not to take orders from any person but himself, and going forward with his trumpet to the forecastle, gave the necessary instructions. All that could be said by the commanding officer and the other gentlemen on board was to no purpose; the pilot declared we should be lost, for that no French ship ever presumed to pass there without a pilot. 'Ay, ay, my dear,' replied our son of Neptune, 'but, damn me, I'll convince you that an Englishman shall go where a Frenchman dare not show his nose.' The 'Richmond' frigate being close astern of us, the commanding officer called out to the captain and told him our case; he inquired who the master was, and was answered from the forecastle by the man himself, who told him 'he was old Killick, and that was enough.' I went forward with this experienced mariner, who pointed out the channel to me as we passed; showing me by the ripple and color of the water where there was any danger, and distinguishing the places where there were ledges of rocks (to me invisible) from banks of sand, mud, or gravel. He gave his orders with great unconcern, joked with the sounding-boats which lay off on each side with different colored flags for our guidance; and when any of them called to him and pointed to the deepest water, he answered: 'Ay, ay, my dear, chalk it down, a damned dangerous navigation, eh! If you don't make a sputter about it you'll get no credit in England.' After we had cleared this remarkable place, where the channel forms a complete zigzag, the master called to his mate to give the helm to somebody else, saying, 'Damn me if there are not a thousand places in the Thames fifty times more hazardous than this; I am ashamed that Englishmen should make such a rout about it.' The Frenchman asked me if the captain had not been there before. I assured him in the negative;

upon which he viewed him with great attention, lifting at the same time his hands and eyes to heaven with astonishment and fervency."[1]

Vaudreuil was blamed for not planting cannon at a certain plateau on the side of the mountain of Cape Tourmente, where the gunners would have been inaccessible, and whence they could have battered every passing ship with a plunging fire. As it was, the whole fleet sailed safely through. On the twenty-sixth they were all anchored off the south shore of the Island of Orleans, a few miles from Quebec; and, writes Knox, "here we are entertained with a most agreeable prospect of a delightful country on every side; windmills, watermills, churches, chapels, and compact farmhouses, all built with stone, and covered, some with wood, and others with straw. The lands appear to be everywhere well cultivated; and with the help of my glass I can discern that they are sowed with flax, wheat, barley, peas, etc., and the grounds are enclosed with wooden pales. The weather to-day is agreeably warm. A light fog sometimes hangs over the highlands, but in the river we have a fine clear air. In the curve of the river, while we were under sail, we had a transient view of a stupendous natural curiosity called the waterfall of Montmorenci."

That night Lieutenant Meech, with forty New England rangers, landed on the Island of Orleans, and found a body of armed inhabitants, who tried to surround him. He beat them off, and took possession of a neighboring farmhouse, where he remained till daylight; then pursued the enemy, and found that they had crossed to the north shore. The whole army now landed, and were drawn up on the beach. As they were kept there for some time, Knox and several brother officers went to visit the neighboring church of Saint-Laurent, where they found a letter from the parish priest, directed to "The Worthy Officers of the British Army," praying that they would protect the sacred edifice, and also his own adjoining house, and adding, with somewhat needless civility, that he wished they had come sooner, that they might have enjoyed the asparagus and radishes of his garden, now unhappily going to seed. The letter concluded with many compliments and good wishes, in which the Britons to whom they were addressed saw only "the frothy politeness so peculiar to the French." The army marched westward and encamped. Wolfe, with his chief engineer, Major Mackellar, and an escort of light infantry, advanced to the extreme point of the island.

---

[1]Others, as well as the pilot, were astonished. "The enemy passed sixty ships of war where we hardly dared risk a vessel of a hundred tons." "Notwithstanding all our precautions, the English, without any accident, by night, as well as by day, passed through it [*the Traverse*] their ships of seventy and eighty guns, and even many of them together." *Vaudreuil au Ministre, 22 Oct. 1759.*

Here he could see, in part, the desperate nature of the task he had undertaken. Before him, three or four miles away, Quebec sat perched upon her rock, a congregation of stone houses, churches, palaces, convents, and hospitals; the green trees of the Seminary garden and the spires of the Cathedral, the Ursulines, the Recollets, and the Jesuits. Beyond rose the loftier height of Cape Diamond, edged with palisades and capped with redoubt and parapet. Batteries frowned everywhere; the Château battery, the Clergy battery, the Hospital battery, on the rock above, and the Royal, Dauphin's, and Queen's batteries on the strand, where the dwellings and warehouses of the lower town clustered beneath the cliff.

Full in sight lay the far-extended camp of Montcalm, stretching from the St. Charles, beneath the city walls, to the chasm and cataract of the Montmorenci. From the cataract to the river of Beauport, its front was covered by earthworks along the brink of abrupt and lofty heights; and from the river of Beauport to the St. Charles, by broad flats of mud swept by the fire of redoubts, intrenchments, a floating battery, and the city itself. Above the city, Cape Diamond hid the view; but could Wolfe have looked beyond it, he would have beheld a prospect still more disheartening. Here, mile after mile, the St. Lawrence was walled by a range of steeps, often inaccessible, and always so difficult that a few men at the top could hold an army in check; while at Cap-Rouge, about eight miles distant, the high plateau was cleft by the channel of a stream which formed a line of defence as strong as that of the Montmorenci. Quebec was a natural fortress. Bougainville had long before examined the position, and reported that "by the help of intrenchments, easily and quickly made, and defended by three or four thousand men, I think the city would be safe. I do not believe that the English will make any attempt against it; but they may have the madness to do so, and it is well to be prepared against surprise."

Not four thousand men, but four times four thousand, now stood in its defence; and their chiefs wisely resolved not to throw away the advantages of their position. Nothing more was heard of Vaudreuil's bold plan of attacking the invaders at their landing; and Montcalm had declared that he would play the part, not of Hannibal, but of Fabius. His plan was to avoid a general battle, run no risks, and protract the defence till the resources of the enemy were exhausted, or till approaching winter forced them to withdraw. Success was almost certain but for one contingency. Amherst, with a force larger than that of Wolfe, was moving against Ticonderoga. If he should capture it, and advance into the colony, Montcalm would be forced to weaken his army by sending strong detachments to oppose him. Here was Wolfe's best hope. This failing, his only chance was in audacity. The game was desperate; but, intrepid gamester as he was in war, he was a man, in the last resort, to stake everything on the cast of the dice.

The elements declared for France. On the afternoon of the day when Wolfe's army landed, a violent squall swept over the St. Lawrence, dashed the ships together, drove several ashore, and destroyed many of the flat-boats from which the troops had just disembarked. "I never saw so much distress among shipping in my whole life," writes an officer to a friend in Boston. Fortunately the storm subsided as quickly as it rose. Vaudreuil saw that the hoped-for deliverance had failed; and as the tempest had not destroyed the British fleet, he resolved to try the virtue of his fireships. "I am afraid," says Montcalm, "that they have cost us a million, and will be good for nothing after all." This remained to be seen. Vaudreuil gave the chief command of them to a naval officer named Delouche; and on the evening of the twenty-eighth, after long consultation and much debate among their respective captains, they set sail together at ten o'clock. The night was moonless and dark. In less than an hour they were at the entrance of the north channel. Delouche had been all enthusiasm; but as he neared the danger his nerves failed, and he set fire to his ship half an hour too soon, the rest following his example.[1]

There was an English outpost at the Point of Orleans; and, about eleven o'clock, the sentries descried through the gloom the ghostly outlines of the approaching ships. As they gazed, these mysterious strangers began to dart tongues of flame; fire ran like lightning up their masts and sails, and then they burst out like volcanoes. Filled as they were with pitch, tar, and every manner of combustible, mixed with fireworks, bombs, grenades, and old cannon, swivels, and muskets loaded to the throat, the effect was terrific. The troops at the Point, amazed at the sudden eruption, the din of the explosions, and the showers of grapeshot that rattled among the trees, lost their wits and fled. The blazing dragons hissed and roared, spouted sheets of fire, vomited smoke in black, pitchy volumes and vast illumined clouds, and shed their infernal glare on the distant city, the tents of Montcalm, and the long red lines of the British army, drawn up in array of battle, lest the French should cross from their encampments to attack them in the confusion. Knox calls the display "the grandest fireworks that can pos-

---

[1] Foligny,* *Journal mémoratif. Vaudreuil au Ministre, 5 Oct. 1759. Journal du Siége* (Bibliothèque de Hartwell).
* Parkman said in a letter that he would correct this misspelling of Foligné in subsequent editions, but he did not do so.—Ed.

sibly be conceived." Yet the fireships did no other harm than burning alive one of their own captains and six or seven of his sailors who failed to escape in their boats. Some of them ran ashore before reaching the fleet; the others were seized by the intrepid English sailors, who, approaching in their boats, threw grappling-irons upon them and towed them towards land, till they swung round and stranded. Here, after venting their fury for a while, they subsided into quiet conflagration, which lasted till morning. Vaudreuil watched the result of his experiment from the steeple of the church at Beauport; then returned, dejected, to Quebec.

Wolfe longed to fight his enemy; but his sagacious enemy would not gratify him. From the heights of Beauport, the rock of Quebec, or the summit of Cape Diamond, Montcalm could look down on the river and its shores as on a map, and watch each movement of the invaders. He was hopeful, perhaps confident; and for a month or more he wrote almost daily to Bourlamaque at Ticonderoga, in a cheerful, and often a jocose vein, mingling orders and instructions with pleasantries and bits of news. Yet his vigilance was unceasing. "We pass every night in bivouac, or else sleep in our clothes. Perhaps you are doing as much, my dear Bourlamaque."[1]

Of the two commanders, Vaudreuil was the more sanguine, and professed full faith that all would go well. He too corresponded with Bourlamaque, to whom he gave his opinion, founded on the reports of deserters, that Wolfe had no chance of success unless Amherst should come to his aid. This he pronounced impossible; and he expressed a strong desire that the English would attack him, "so that we may rid ourselves of them at once."[2] He was courageous, except in the immediate presence of danger, and failed only when the crisis came.

Wolfe, held in check at every other point, had one movement in his power. He could seize the heights of Point Levi, opposite the city; and this, along with his occupation of the Island of Orleans, would give him command of the Basin of Quebec. Thence also he could fire on the place across the St. Lawrence, which is here less than a mile wide. The movement was begun on the afternoon of the twenty-ninth, when, shivering in a north wind and a sharp frost, a part of Monckton's brigade was ferried over to Beaumont, on the south shore, and the rest followed in the morning. The rangers had a brush with a party of Canadians, whom they drove off, and the regulars then landed unopposed.

[1] *Montcalm à Bourlamaque, 27 Juin, 1759.* All these letters are before me.
[2] *Vaudreuil à Bourlamaque, 8 Juillet, 1759.*

Monckton ordered a proclamation, signed by Wolfe, to be posted on the door of the parish church. It called on the Canadians, in peremptory terms, to stand neutral in the contest, promised them, if they did so, full protection in property and religion, and threatened that, if they presumed to resist the invaders, their houses, goods, and harvests should be destroyed, and their churches despoiled. As soon as the troops were out of sight the inhabitants took down the placard and carried it to Vaudreuil.

The brigade marched along the river road to Point Levi, drove off a body of French and Indians posted in the church, and took possession of the houses and the surrounding heights. In the morning they were intrenching themselves, when they were greeted by a brisk fire from the edge of the woods. It came from a party of Indians, whom the rangers presently put to flight, and, imitating their own ferocity, scalped nine of them. Wolfe came over to the camp on the next day, went with an escort to the heights opposite Quebec, examined it with a spy-glass, and chose a position from which to bombard it. Cannon and mortars were brought ashore, fascines and gabions made, intrenchments thrown up, and batteries planted. Knox came over from the main camp, and says that he had "a most agreeable view of the city of Quebec. It is a very fair object for our artillery, particularly the lower town." But why did Wolfe wish to bombard it? Its fortifications were but little exposed to his fire, and to knock its houses, convents, and churches to pieces would bring him no nearer to his object. His guns at Point Levi could destroy the city, but could not capture it; yet doubtless they would have good moral effect, discourage the French, and cheer his own soldiers with the flattering belief that they were achieving something.

The guns of Quebec showered balls and bombs upon his workmen; but they still toiled on, and the French saw the fatal batteries fast growing to completion. The citizens, alarmed at the threatened destruction, begged the Governor for leave to cross the river and dislodge their assailants. At length he consented. A party of twelve or fifteen hundred was made up of armed burghers, Canadians from the camp, a few Indians, some pupils of the Seminary, and about a hundred volunteers from the regulars. Dumas, an experienced officer, took command of them; and, going up to Sillery, they crossed the river on the night of the twelfth of July. They had hardly climbed the heights of the south shore when they grew exceedingly nervous, though the enemy was still three miles off. The Seminary scholars fired on some of their own party, whom they mistook for English; and the same mishap was repeated a second and a third time. A panic seized the whole body, and Dumas could not control them. They turned and made for their canoes, rolling over each other as they rushed down the heights, and reappeared at Quebec at six in the morning, overwhelmed with despair and shame.[1]

The presentiment of the unhappy burghers proved too true. The English batteries fell to their work, and the families of the town fled to the country for safety. In a single day eighteen houses and the cathedral were burned by exploding shells; and fiercer and fiercer the storm of fire and iron hailed upon Quebec.

Wolfe did not rest content with distressing his enemy. With an ardor and a daring that no difficulties could cool, he sought means to strike an effective blow. It was nothing to lay Quebec in ruins if he could not defeat the army that protected it. To land from boats and attack Montcalm in front, through the mud of the Beauport flats or up the heights along the neighboring shore, was an enterprise too rash even for his temerity. It might, however, be possible to land below the cataract of Montmorenci, cross that stream higher up, and strike the French army in flank or rear; and he had no sooner secured his positions at the points of Levi and Orleans, than he addressed himself to this attempt.

On the eighth several frigates and a bomb-ketch took their stations before the camp of the Chevalier de Lévis, who, with his division of Canadian militia, occupied the heights along the St. Lawrence just above the cataract. Here they shelled and cannonaded him all day; though, from his elevated position, with very little effect. Towards evening the troops on the Point of Orleans broke up their camp. Major Hardy, with a detachment of marines, was left to hold that post, while the rest embarked at night in the boats of the fleet. They were the brigades of Townshend and Murray, consisting of five battalions, with a body of grenadiers, light infantry, and rangers,—in all three thousand men. They landed before daybreak in front of the parish of L'Ange Gardien, a little below the cataract. The only opposition was from a troop of Canadians and Indians, whom they routed, after some loss, climbed the heights, gained the plateau above, and began to intrench themselves. A company of rangers, supported by detachments of regulars, was sent into the neighboring forest to protect the parties who were cutting fascines, and apparently, also, to look for a fording-place.

Lévis, with his Scotch-Jacobite aide-de-camp, Johnstone, had

---

[1] *Événements de la Guerre en Canada* (Hist. Soc. Quebec, 1861). *Mémoires sur le Canada, 1749–1760. Vaudreuil au Ministre, 5 Oct. 1759. L'Abeille,* II. No. 14 (a publication of the Quebec Seminary). *Journal du Siége de Québec* (Bibliothêque de Hartwell). Panet, *Journal du Siége.* Foligny, *Journal mémoratif. Memoirs of the Siege of Quebec,* by John Johnson, Clerk and QuartermasterSergeant to the Fifty-eighth Regiment.

watched the movements of Wolfe from the heights across the cataract. Johnstone says that he asked his commander if he was sure there was no ford higher up on the Montmorenci, by which the English could cross. Lévis averred that there was none, and that he himself had examined the stream to its source; on which a Canadian who stood by whispered to the aide-de-camp: "The General is mistaken; there is a ford." Johnstone told this to Lévis, who would not believe it, and so browbeat the Canadian that he dared not repeat what he had said. Johnstone, taking him aside, told him to go and find somebody who had lately crossed the ford, and bring him at once to the General's quarters; whereupon he soon reappeared with a man who affirmed that he had crossed it the night before with a sack of wheat on his back. A detachment was immediately sent to the place, with orders to intrench itself, and Repentigny, lieutenant of Lévis, was posted not far off with eleven hundred Canadians.

Four hundred Indians passed the ford under the partisan Langlade, discovered Wolfe's detachment, hid themselves, and sent their commander to tell Repentigny that there was a body of English in the forest, who might all be destroyed if he would come over at once with his Canadians. Repentigny sent for orders to Lévis, and Lévis sent for orders to Vaudreuil, whose quarters were three or four miles distant. Vaudreuil answered that no risk should be run, and that he would come and see to the matter himself. It was about two hours before he arrived; and meanwhile the Indians grew impatient, rose from their hiding-place, fired on the rangers, and drove them back with heavy loss upon the regulars, who stood their ground, and at last repulsed the assailants. The Indians recrossed the ford with thirty-six scalps. If Repentigny had advanced, and Lévis had followed with his main body, the consequences to the English might have been serious; for, as Johnstone remarks, "a Canadian in the woods is worth three disciplined soldiers, as a soldier in a plain is worth three Canadians." Vaudreuil called a council of war. The question was whether an effort should be made to dislodge Wolfe's main force. Montcalm and the Governor were this time of one mind, and both thought it inexpedient to attack, with militia, a body of regular troops whose numbers and position were imperfectly known. Bigot gave his voice for the attack. He was overruled, and Wolfe was left to fortify himself in peace.[1]

---

[1] The above is from a comparison of the rather discordant accounts of Johnstone, the *Journal tenu à l'Armée*, the *Journal* of Panet, and that of the Hartwell Library. The last says that Lévis crossed the Montmorenci. If so, he accomplished nothing. This affair should not be confounded with a somewhat similar one which took place on the 26th.

His occupation of the heights of Montmorenci exposed him to great risks. The left wing of his army at Point Levi was six miles from its right wing at the cataract, and Major Hardy's detachment on the Point of Orleans was between them, separated from each by a wide arm of the St. Lawrence. Any one of the three camps might be overpowered before the others could support it; and Hardy with his small force was above all in danger of being cut to pieces. But the French kept persistently on the defensive; and after the failure of Dumas to dislodge the English from Point Levi, Vaudreuil would not hear of another such attempt. Wolfe was soon well intrenched; but it was easier to defend himself than to strike at his enemy. Montcalm, when urged to attack him, is said to have answered: "Let him amuse himself where he is. If we drive him off he may go to some place where he can do us harm." His late movement, however, had a discouraging effect on the Canadians, who now for the first time began to desert. His batteries, too, played across the chasm of Montmorenci upon the left wing of the French army with an effect extremely annoying.

The position of the hostile forces was a remarkable one. They were separated by the vast gorge that opens upon the St. Lawrence; an amphitheatre of lofty precipices, their brows crested with forests, and their steep brown sides scantily feathered with stunted birch and fir. Into this abyss leaps the Montmorenci with one headlong plunge of nearly two hundred and fifty feet, a living column of snowy white, with its spray, its foam, its mists, and its rainbows; then spreads itself in broad thin sheets over a floor of rock and gravel, and creeps tamely to the St. Lawrence. It was but a gunshot across the gulf, and the sentinels on each side watched each other over the roar and turmoil of the cataract. Captain Knox, coming one day from Point Levi to receive orders from Wolfe, improved a spare hour to visit this marvel of nature. "I had very nigh paid dear for my inquisitiveness; for while I stood on the eminence I was hastily called to by one of our sentinels, when, throwing my eyes about, I saw a Frenchman creeping under the eastern extremity of their breastwork to fire at me. This obliged me to retire as fast as I could out of his reach, and, making up to the sentry to thank him for his attention, he told me the fellow had snapped his piece twice, and the second time it flashed in the pan at the instant I turned away from the Fall." Another officer, less fortunate, had a leg broken by a shot from the opposite cliffs.

Day after day went by, and the invaders made no progress. Flags of truce passed often between the hostile camps. "You will demolish the town, no doubt," said the bearer of one of them, "but you shall never get inside of it." To which Wolfe replied: "I will have Quebec if I stay here till the end of November." Sometimes the heat was intense, and sometimes there were floods of summer rain that inundated the tents. Along the river, from the Montmorenci to Point Levi, there were ceaseless artillery fights between gunboats, frigates, and batteries on shore. Bands of Indians infested the outskirts of the camps, killing sentries and patrols. The rangers chased them through the woods; there were brisk skirmishes, and scalps lost and won. Sometimes the regulars took part in these forest battles; and once it was announced, in orders of the day, that "the General has ordered two sheep and some rum to Captain Cosnan's company of grenadiers for the spirit they showed this morning in pushing those scoundrels of Indians." The Indians complained that the British soldiers were learning how to fight, and no longer stood still in a mass to be shot at, as in Braddock's time. The Canadian *coureurs-de-bois* mixed with their red allies and wore their livery. One of them was caught on the eighteenth. He was naked, daubed red and blue, and adorned with a bunch of painted feathers dangling from the top of his head. He and his companions used the scalping-knife as freely as the Indians themselves; nor were the New England rangers much behind them in this respect, till an order came from Wolfe forbidding "the inhuman practice of scalping, except when the enemy are Indians, or Canadians dressed like Indians."

A part of the fleet worked up into the Basin, beyond the Point of Orleans; and here, on the warm summer nights, officers and men watched the cannon flashing and thundering from the heights of Montmorenci on one side, and those of Point Levi on the other, and the bombs sailing through the air in fiery semicircles. Often the gloom was lighted up by the blaze of the burning houses of Quebec, kindled by incendiary shells. Both the lower and the upper town were nearly deserted by the inhabitants, some retreating into the country, and some into the suburb of St. Roch; while the Ursulines and Hospital nuns abandoned their convents to seek harborage beyond the range of shot. The city was a prey to robbers, who pillaged the empty houses, till an order came from headquarters promising the gallows to all who should be caught. News reached the French that Niagara was attacked, and that the army of Amherst was moving against Ticonderoga. The Canadians deserted more and more. They were disheartened by the defensive attitude in which both Vaudreuil and Montcalm steadily persisted; and accustomed as they were to rapid raids, sudden strokes, and a quick return to their homes, they tired of long weeks of inaction. The English patrols caught one of them as he was passing the time in fishing. "He seemed to be a subtle old rogue," says Knox, "of seventy years of age, as he told us. We plied him well with port wine, and then his heart was more open; and seeing that we laughed at the exaggerated accounts he had given us, he said he 'wished the affair was well over, one way or the other; that his countrymen were all discontented, and would either surrender, or disperse and act a neutral part, if it were not for the persuasions of their priests and the fear of being maltreated by the savages, with whom they are threatened on all occasions.' " A deserter reported on the nineteenth of July that nothing but dread of the Indians kept the Canadians in the camp.

Wolfe's proclamation, at first unavailing, was now taking effect. A large number of Canadian prisoners, brought in on the twenty-fifth, declared that their countrymen would gladly accept his offers but for the threats of their commanders that if they did so the Indians should be set upon them. The prisoners said further that "they had been under apprehension for several days past of having a body of four hundred barbarians sent to rifle their parish and habitations."[1] Such threats were not wholly effectual. A French chronicler of the time says: "The Canadians showed their disgust every day, and deserted at every opportunity, in spite of the means taken to prevent them." "The people were intimidated, seeing all our army kept in one body and solely on the defensive; while the English, though far less numerous, divided their forces, and undertook various bold enterprises without meeting resistance."[2]

On the eighteenth the English accomplished a feat which promised important results. The French commanders had thought it impossible for any hostile ship to pass the batteries of Quebec; but about eleven o'clock at night, favored by the wind, and covered by a furious cannonade from Point Levi, the ship "Sutherland," with a frigate and several small vessels, sailed safely by and reached the river above the town. Here they at once attacked and destroyed a fireship and some small craft that they found there. Now, for the first time, it became necessary for Montcalm to weaken his army at Beauport by sending six hundred men, under Dumas, to defend the accessible points in the line of precipices between Quebec and Cap-Rouge. Several hundred more were sent on the next day, when it became known that the English had dragged a fleet of boats over Point Levi, launched them above the town, and despatched troops to embark in them. Thus a new feature

---

[1] Knox, I. 347; compare pp. 339, 341, 346.
[2] *Journal du Siége* (Bibliothêque de Hartwell).

was introduced into the siege operations, and danger had risen on a side where the French thought themselves safe. On the other hand, Wolfe had become more vulnerable than ever. His army was now divided, not into three parts, but into four, each so far from the rest that, in case of sudden attack, it must defend itself alone. That Montcalm did not improve his opportunity was apparently due to want of confidence in his militia.

The force above the town did not lie idle. On the night of the twentieth, Colonel Carleton, with six hundred men, rowed eighteen miles up the river, and landed at Pointe-aux-Trembles, on the north shore. Here some of the families of Quebec had sought asylum; and Wolfe had been told by prisoners that not only were stores in great quantity to be found here, but also letters and papers throwing light on the French plans. Carleton and his men drove off a band of Indians who fired on them, and spent a quiet day around the parish church; but found few papers, and still fewer stores. They withdrew towards evening, carrying with them nearly a hundred women, children, and old men; and they were no sooner gone than the Indians returned to plunder the empty houses of their unfortunate allies. The prisoners were treated with great kindness. The ladies among them were entertained at supper by Wolfe, who jested with them on the caution of the French generals, saying: "I have given good chances to attack me, and am surprised that they have not profited by them."[1] On the next day the prisoners were all sent to Quebec under a flag of truce.

Thus far Wolfe had refrained from executing the threats he had affixed the month before to the church of Beaumont. But now he issued another proclamation. It declared that the Canadians had shown themselves unworthy of the offers he had made them, and that he had therefore ordered his light troops to ravage their country and bring them prisoners to his camp. Such of the Canadian militia as belonged to the parishes near Quebec were now in a sad dilemma; for Montcalm threatened them on one side, and Wolfe on the other. They might desert to their homes, or they might stand by their colors; in the one case their houses were to be burned by French savages, and in the other by British light infantry.

Wolfe at once gave orders in accord with his late proclamation; but he commanded that no church should be profaned, and no woman or child injured. The first effects of his stern policy are thus recorded by Knox: "Major Dalling's light infantry brought in this afternoon to our

[1] *Journal tenu à l'Armée que commandoit feu M. le Marquis de Montcalm.*

camp two hundred and fifty male and female prisoners. Among this number was a very respectable looking priest, and about forty men fit to bear arms. There was almost an equal number of black cattle, with about seventy sheep and lambs, and a few horses. Brigadier Monckton entertained the reverend father and some other fashionable personages in his tent, and most humanely ordered refreshments to all the rest of the captives; which noble example was followed by the soldiery, who generously crowded about those unhappy people, sharing their provisions, rum, and tobacco with them. They were sent in the evening on board of transports in the river." Again, two days later: "Colonel Fraser's detachment returned this morning, and presented us with more scenes of distress and the dismal consequences of war, by a great number of wretched families, whom they brought in prisoners, with some of their effects, and near three hundred black cattle, sheep, hogs, and horses."

On the next night the attention of the excellent journalist was otherwise engaged. Vaudreuil tried again to burn the English fleet. "Late last night," writes Knox, under date of the twenty-eighth, "the enemy sent down a most formidable fireraft, which consisted of a parcel of schooners, shallops, and stages chained together. It could not be less than a hundred fathoms in length, and was covered with grenades, old swivels, gun and pistol barrels loaded up to their muzzles, and various other inventions and combustible matters. This seemed to be their last attempt against our fleet, which happily miscarried, as before; for our gallant seamen, with their usual expertness, grappled them before they got down above a third part of the Basin, towed them safe to shore, and left them at anchor, continually repeating, *All's well*. A remarkable expression from some of these intrepid souls to their comrades on this occasion I must not omit, on account of its singular uncouthness; namely: 'Damme, Jack, didst thee ever take hell in tow before?' "

According to a French account, this aquatic infernal machine consisted of seventy rafts, boats, and schooners. Its failure was due to no shortcoming on the part of its conductors; who, under a brave Canadian named Courval, acted with coolness and resolution. Nothing saved the fleet but the courage of the sailors, swarming out in their boats to fight the approaching conflagration.

It was now the end of July. More than half the summer was gone, and Quebec seemed as far as ever beyond the grasp of Wolfe. Its buildings were in ruins, and the neighboring parishes were burned and ravaged; but its living rampart, the army of Montcalm, still lay in patient defiance along the shores of Beauport, while above the city every point where a wildcat could climb the precipices was watched and guarded, and Dumas with a thousand men held the impregnable heights of Cap-Rouge. Montcalm persisted in doing nothing that his enemy wished him to do. He would not fight on Wolfe's terms, and Wolfe resolved at last to fight him on his own; that is, to attack his camp in front.

The plan was desperate; for, after leaving troops enough to hold Point Levi and the heights of Montmorenci, less than five thousand men would be left to attack a position of commanding strength, where Montcalm at an hour's notice could collect twice as many to oppose them. But Wolfe had a boundless trust in the disciplined valor of his soldiers, and an utter scorn of the militia who made the greater part of his enemy's force.

Towards the Montmorenci the borders of the St. Lawrence are, as we have seen, extremely high and steep. At a mile from the gorge of the cataract there is, at high tide, a strand, about the eighth of a mile wide, between the foot of these heights and the river; and beyond this strand the receding tide lays bare a tract of mud nearly half a mile wide. At the edge of the dry ground the French had built a redoubt mounted with cannon, and there were other similar works on the strand a quarter of a mile nearer the cataract. Wolfe could not see from the river that these redoubts were commanded by the musketry of the intrench-ments along the brink of the heights above. These intrenchments were so constructed that they swept with cross-fires the whole face of the declivity, which was covered with grass, and was very steep. Wolfe hoped that, if he attacked one of the redoubts, the French would come down to defend it, and so bring on a general engagement; or, if they did not, that he should gain an opportunity of reconnoitring the heights to find some point where they could be stormed with a chance of success.

In front of the gorge of the Montmorenci there was a ford during several hours of low tide, so that troops from the adjoining English camp might cross to co-operate with their comrades landing in boats from Point Levi and the Island of Orleans. On the morning of the thirty-first of July, the tide then being at the flood, the French saw the ship "Centurion," of sixty-four guns, anchor near the Montmorenci and open fire on the redoubts. Then two armed transports, each of fourteen guns, stood in as close as possible to the first redoubt and fired upon it, stranding as the tide went out, till in the afternoon they lay bare upon the mud. At the same time a battery of more than forty heavy pieces, planted on the lofty promontory beyond the Montmorenci, began a furious cannonade upon the flank of the French intrenchments. It did no great harm, however, for the works were protected by a great number of traverses, which stopped the shot; and the Canadians, who manned this part of the lines, held their ground with excellent steadiness.

About eleven o'clock a fleet of boats filled with troops, chiefly from Point Levi, appeared in the river and hovered off the shore west of the parish church of Beauport, as if meaning to land there. Montcalm was perplexed, doubting whether the real attack was to be made here, or toward the Montmorenci. Hour after hour the boats moved to and fro, to increase his doubts and hide the real design; but he soon became convinced that the camp of Lévis at the Montmorenci was the true object of his enemy; and about two o'clock he went thither, greeted as he rode along the lines by shouts of *Vive notre Général!* Lévis had already made preparations for defence with his usual skill. His Canadians were reinforced by the battalions of Béarn, Guienne, and Royal Roussillon; and, as the intentions of Wolfe became certain, the right of the camp was nearly abandoned, the main strength of the army being gathered between the river of Beauport and the Montmorenci, where, according to a French writer, there were, towards the end of the afternoon, about twelve thousand men.[1]

At half-past five o'clock the tide was out, and the crisis came. The batteries across the Montmorenci, the distant batteries of Point Levi, the cannon of the "Centurion," and those of the two stranded ships, all opened together with redoubled fury. The French batteries replied; and, amid this deafening roar of artillery, the English boats set their troops ashore at the edge of the broad tract of sedgy mud that the receding river had left bare. At the same time a column of two thousand men was seen, a mile away, moving in perfect order across the Montmorenci ford. The first troops that landed from the boats were thirteen companies of grenadiers and a detachment of Royal Americans. They dashed swiftly forward; while at some distance behind came Monckton's brigade, composed of the fifteenth, or Amherst's regiment, and the seventy-eighth, or Fraser's Highlanders. The day had been fair and warm; but the sky was now thick with clouds, and large rain-drops began to fall, the precursors of a summer storm.

With the utmost precipitation, without orders, and without waiting for Monckton's brigade to come up, the grenadiers in front made a rush for the redoubt near the foot of the hill. The French abandoned it; but the assailants had no sooner gained their prize than the thronged

[1] Panet, *Journal.*

heights above blazed with musketry, and a tempest of bullets fell among them. Nothing daunted, they dashed forward again, reserving their fire, and struggling to climb the steep ascent; while, with yells and shouts of *Vive le Roi!* the troops and Canadians at the top poured upon them a hailstorm of musket-balls and buckshot, and dead and wounded in numbers rolled together down the slope. At that instant the clouds burst, and the rain fell in torrents. "We could not see half way down the hill," says the Chevalier Johnstone, who was at this part of the line. Ammunition was wet on both sides, and the grassy steeps became so slippery that it was impossible to climb them. The English say that the storm saved the French; the French, with as much reason, that it saved the English.

The baffled grenadiers drew back into the redoubt. Wolfe saw the madness of persisting, and ordered a retreat. The rain ceased, and troops of Indians came down the heights to scalp the fallen. Some of them ran towards Lieutenant Peyton, of the Royal Americans, as he lay disabled by a musket-shot. With his double-barrelled gun he brought down two of his assailants, when a Highland sergeant snatched him in his arms, dragged him half a mile over the mud-flats, and placed him in one of the boats. A friend of Peyton, Captain Ochterlony, had received a mortal wound, and an Indian would have scalped him but for the generous intrepidity of a soldier of the battalion of Guienne; who, seizing the enraged savage, held him back till several French officers interposed, and had the dying man carried to a place of safety.

The English retreated in good order, after setting fire to the two stranded vessels. Those of the grenadiers and Royal Americans who were left alive rowed for the Point of Orleans; the fifteenth regiment rowed for Point Levi; and the Highlanders, led by Wolfe himself, joined the column from beyond the Montmorenci, placing themselves in its rear as it slowly retired along the flats and across the ford, the Indians yelling and the French shouting from the heights, while the British waved their hats, daring them to come down and fight.

The grenadiers and the Royal Americans, who had borne the brunt of the fray, bore also nearly all the loss; which, in proportion to their numbers, was enormous. Knox reports it at four hundred and forty-three, killed, wounded, and missing, including one colonel, eight captains, twenty-one lieutenants, and three ensigns.

Vaudreuil, delighted, wrote to Bourlamaque an account of the affair. "I have no more anxiety about Quebec. M. Wolfe, I can assure you, will make no progress. Luckily for him, his prudence saved him from the consequences of his mad enterprise, and he contented himself with losing about five hundred of his best soldiers. Deserters say that he will try us again in a few days. That is what we want; he 'll find somebody to talk to (*il trouvera à qui parler*)."

NOTE.—Among the killed in this affair was Edward Botwood, sergeant in the grenadiers of the forty-seventh, or Lascelles' regiment. "Ned Botwood" was well known among his comrades as a poet; and the following lines of his, written on the eve of the expedition to Quebec, continued to be favorites with the British troops during the War of the Revolution (see *Historical Magazine*, II., First Series, 164). It may be observed here that the war produced a considerable quantity of indifferent verse on both sides. On that of the English it took the shape of occasional ballads, such as "Bold General Wolfe," printed on broadsides, or of patriotic effusions scattered through magazines and newspapers, while the French celebrated all their victories with songs.

HOT STUFF

AIR,—*Lilies of France.*

> Come, each death-doing dog who dares venture his neck,
> Come, follow the hero that goes to Quebec;
> Jump aboard of the transports, and loose every sail,
> Pay your debts at the tavern by giving leg-bail;
> And ye that love fighting shall soon have enough:
> Wolfe commands us, my boys; we shall give them Hot Stuff.
>
> Up the River St. Lawrence our troops shall advance,
> To the Grenadiers' March we will teach them to dance.
> Cape Breton we have taken, and next we will try
> At their capital to give them another black eye.
> Vaudreuil, 't is in vain you pretend to look gruff,—
> Those are coming who know how to give you Hot Stuff.
>
> With powder in his periwig, and snuff in his nose,
> Monsieur will run down our descent to oppose;
> And the Indians will come: but the light infantry
> Will soon oblige *them* to betake to a tree.
> From such rascals as these may we fear a rebuff?
> Advance, grenadiers, and let fly your Hot Stuff!
>
> When the forty-seventh regiment is dashing ashore,
> While bullets are whistling and cannons do roar,
> Says Montcalm: "Those are Shirley's—I know the lappels."
> "You lie," says Ned Botwood, "we belong to Lascelles'!
> Tho' our cloathing is changed, yet we scorn a powder-puff;
> So at you, ye b——s, here 's give you Hot Stuff."

On the repulse at Montmorenci, *Wolfe to Pitt, 2 Sept. 1759. Vaudreuil au Ministre, 5 Oct. 1759.* Panet, *Journal du Siége.* Johnstone, *Dialogue in Hades. Journal tenu à l'Armée,* etc. *Journal of the Siege of Quebec, by a Gentleman in an eminent Station on the Spot. Mémoires sur le Canada, 1749–1760.* Fraser, *Journal of the Siege. Journal du Siége d'après un MS. déposé à la Bibliothêque Hartwell.* Foligny, *Journal mémoratif. Journal of Transactions at the Siege of Quebec,* in *Notes and Queries,* XX. 164. John Johnson, *Memoirs of the Siege of Quebec. Journal of an Expedition on the River St. Lawrence. An Authentic Account of the Expedition against Quebec, by a Volunteer on that Expedition.* J. Gibson to Governor Lawrence, *1 Aug. 1759.* Knox, I. 354. Mante, 244.

26

Amherst–Niagara

1759

AMHERST ON LAKE GEORGE · CAPTURE OF TICONDEROGA AND CROWN POINT · DELAYS OF AMHERST · NIAGARA EXPEDITION · LA CORNE ATTACKS OSWEGO · HIS REPULSE · NIAGARA BESIEGED · AUBRY COMES TO ITS RELIEF · BATTLE · ROUT OF THE FRENCH · THE FORT TAKEN · ISLE-AUX-NOIX · AMHERST ADVANCES TO ATTACK IT · STORM · THE ENTERPRISE ABANDONED · ROGERS ATTACKS ST. FRANCIS · DESTROYS THE TOWN · SUFFERINGS OF THE RANGERS

Pitt had directed that, while Quebec was attacked, an attempt should be made to penetrate into Canada by way of Ticonderoga and Crown Point. Thus the two armies might unite in the heart of the colony, or, at least, a powerful diversion might be effected in behalf of Wolfe. At the same time Oswego was to be reestablished, and the possession of Fort Duquesne, or Pittsburg, secured by reinforcements and supplies; while Amherst, the commander-in-chief, was further directed to pursue any other enterprise which in his opinion would weaken the enemy, without detriment to the main objects of the campaign.[1] He accordingly resolved to attempt the capture of Niagara. Brigadier Prideaux was charged with this stroke; Brigadier Stanwix was sent to conduct the operations for the relief of Pittsburg;

[1] *Pitt to Amherst, 23 Jan., 10 March, 1759.*

and Amherst himself prepared to lead the grand central advance against Ticonderoga, Crown Point, and Montreal.[1]

Towards the end of June he reached that valley by the head of Lake George which for five years past had been the annual mustering-place of armies. Here were now gathered about eleven thousand men, half regulars and half provincials,[2] drilling every day, firing by platoons, firing at marks, practising manœuvres in the woods; going out on scouting parties, bathing parties, fishing parties; gathering wild herbs to serve for greens, cutting brushwood and meadow hay to make hospital beds. The sick were ordered on certain mornings to repair to the surgeon's tent, there, in prompt succession, to swallow such doses as he thought appropriate to their several ailments; and it was further ordered that "every fair day they that can walk be paraded together and marched down to the lake to wash their hands and faces." Courts-martial were numerous; culprits were flogged at the head of each regiment in turn, and occasionally one was shot. A frequent employment was the cutting of spruce tops to make spruce beer. This innocent beverage was reputed sovereign against scurvy; and such was the fame of its virtues that a copious supply of the West Indian molasses used in concocting it was thought indispensable to every army or garrison in the wilderness. Throughout this campaign it is repeatedly mentioned in general orders, and the soldiers are promised that they shall have as much of it as they want at a halfpenny a quart.[3]

The rear of the army was well protected from insult. Fortified posts were built at intervals of three or four miles along the road to Fort Edward, and especially at the station called Half-way Brook; while, for the whole distance, a broad belt of wood on both sides was cut down and burned, to deprive a skulking enemy of cover. Amherst was never long in one place without building a fort there. He now began one, which proved wholly needless, on that flat rocky hill where the English made their intrenched camp during the siege of Fort William Henry. Only one bastion of it was ever finished, and this is still shown to tourists under the name of Fort George.

The army embarked on Saturday, the twenty-first of July. The Reverend Benjamin Pomeroy watched their departure in some concern, and

---

[1]*Amherst to Pitt, 19 June, 1759. Amherst to Stanwix, 6 May, 1759.*
[2]*Mante, 210.*
[3]*Orderly Book of Commissary Wilson in the Expedition against Ticonderoga, 1759. Journal of Samuel Warner, a Massachusetts Soldier, 1759. General and Regimental Orders, Army of Major-General Amherst, 1759. Diary of Sergeant Merriman, of Ruggles's Regiment, 1759.* I owe to William L. Stone, Esq., the use of the last two curious documents.

wrote on Monday to Abigail, his wife: "I could wish for more appearance of dependence on God than was observable among them; yet I hope God will grant deliverance unto Israel by them." There was another military pageant, another long procession of boats and banners, among the mountains and islands of Lake George. Night found them near the outlet; and here they lay till morning, tossed unpleasantly on waves ruffled by a summer gale. At daylight they landed, beat back a French detachment, and marched by the portage road to the saw-mill at the waterfall. There was little resistance. They occupied the heights, and then advanced to the famous line of intrenchment against which the army of Abercromby had hurled itself in vain. These works had been completely reconstructed, partly of earth, and partly of logs. Amherst's followers were less numerous than those of his predecessor, while the French commander, Bourlamaque, had a force nearly equal to that of Montcalm in the summer before; yet he made no attempt to defend the intrenchment, and the English, encamping along its front, found it an excellent shelter from the cannon of the fort beyond.

Amherst brought up his artillery and began approaches in form, when, on the night of the twenty-third, it was found that Bourlamaque had retired down Lake Champlain, leaving four hundred men under Hebecourt to defend the place as long as possible. This was in obedience to an order from Vaudreuil, requiring him on the approach of the English to abandon both Ticonderoga and Crown Point, retreat to the outlet of Lake Champlain, take post at Isle-aux-Noix, and there defend himself to the last extremity;[1] a course unquestionably the best that could have been taken, since obstinacy in holding Ticonderoga might have involved the surrender of Bourlamaque's whole force, while Isle-aux-Noix offered rare advantages for defence.

The fort fired briskly; a cannon-shot killed Colonel Townshend, and a few soldiers were killed and wounded by grape and bursting shells; when, at dusk on the evening of the twenty-sixth, an unusual movement was seen among the garrison, and, about ten o'clock, three deserters came in great excitement to the English camp. They reported that Hebecourt and his soldiers were escaping in their boats, and that a match was burning in the magazine to blow Ticonderoga to atoms. Amherst offered a hundred guineas to any one of them who would point out the match, that it might be cut; but they shrank from the perilous venture. All was silent till eleven o'clock, when a broad, fierce

---

[1] *Vaudreuil au Ministre, 8 Nov. 1759. Instructions pour M. de Bourlamaque, 20 Mai, 1759, signé Vaudreuil. Montcalm à Bourlamaque, 4 Juin, 1759.*

glare burst on the night, and a roaring explosion shook the promontory; then came a few breathless moments, and then the fragments of Fort Ticonderoga fell with clatter and splash on the water and the land. It was but one bastion, however, that had been thus hurled skyward. The rest of the fort was little hurt, though the barracks and other combustible parts were set on fire, and by the light the French flag was seen still waving on the rampart.[1] A sergeant of the light infantry, braving the risk of other explosions, went and brought it off. Thus did this redoubted stronghold of France fall at last into English hands, as in all likelihood it would have done a year sooner, if Amherst had commanded in Abercromby's place; for, with the deliberation that marked all his proceedings, he would have sat down before Montcalm's wooden wall and knocked it to splinters with his cannon.

He now set about repairing the damaged works and making ready to advance on Crown Point; when on the first of August his scouts told him that the enemy had abandoned this place also, and retreated northward down the lake.[2] Well pleased, he took possession of the deserted fort, and, in the animation of success, thought for a moment of keeping the promise he had given to Pitt "to make an irruption into Canada with the utmost vigor and despatch."[3] Wolfe, his brother in arms and his friend, was battling with the impossible under the rocks of Quebec, and every motive, public and private, impelled Amherst to push to his relief, not counting costs, or balancing risks too nicely. He was ready enough to spur on others, for he wrote to Gage: "We must all be alert and active day and night; if we all do our parts the French must fall;"[4] but, far from doing his, he set the army to building a new fort at Crown Point, telling them that it would "give plenty, peace, and quiet to His Majesty's subjects for ages to come."[5] Then he began three small additional forts, as outworks to the first, sent two parties to explore the sources of the Hudson; one party to explore Otter Creek; another to explore South Bay, which was already well known; another to make a road across what is now the State of Vermont, from Crown Point to Charlestown, or "Number Four," on the Connecticut; and another to widen and improve the old French road between Crown

[1] *Journal of Colonel Amherst* (brother of General Amherst). *Vaudreuil au Ministre, 8 Nov. 1759. Amherst to Prideaux, 28 July, 1759. Amherst to Pitt, 27 July, 1759.* Mante, 213. Knox, I., 397–403. *Vaudreuil à Bourlamaque, 19 Juin, 1759.*

[2] *Amherst to Pitt, 5 Aug. 1759.*

[3] *Ibid., 19 June, 1759.*

[4] *Amherst to Gage, 1 Aug. 1759.*

[5] *General Orders, 13 Aug. 1759.*

Point and Ticonderoga. His industry was untiring; a great deal of useful work was done: but the essential task of making a diversion to aid the army of Wolfe was needlessly postponed.

It is true that some delay was inevitable. The French had four armed vessels on the lake, and this made it necessary to provide an equal or superior force to protect the troops on their way to Isle-aux-Noix. Captain Loring, the English naval commander, was therefore ordered to build a brigantine; and, this being thought insufficient, he was directed to add a kind of floating battery, moved by sweeps. Three weeks later, in consequence of farther information concerning the force of the French vessels, Amherst ordered an armed sloop to be put on the stocks; and this involved a long delay. The saw-mill at Ticonderoga was to furnish planks for the intended navy; but, being overtasked in sawing timber for the new works at Crown Point, it was continually breaking down. Hence much time was lost, and autumn was well advanced before Loring could launch his vessels.[1]

Meanwhile news had come from Prideaux and the Niagara expedition. That officer had been ordered to ascend the Mohawk with five thousand regulars and provincials, leave a strong garrison at Fort Stanwix, on the Great Carrying Place, establish posts at both ends of Lake Oneida, descend the Onondaga to Oswego, leave nearly half his force there under Colonel Haldimand, and proceed with the rest to attack Niagara.[2] These orders he accomplished. Haldimand remained to reoccupy the spot that Montcalm had made desolate three years before; and, while preparing to build a fort, he barricaded his camp with pork and flour barrels, lest the enemy should make a dash upon him from their station at the head of the St. Lawrence Rapids. Such an attack was probable; for if the French could seize Oswego, the return of Prideaux from Niagara would be cut off, and when his small stock of provisions had failed, he would be reduced to extremity. Saint-Luc de la Corne left the head of the Rapids early in July with a thousand French and Canadians and a body of Indians, who soon made their appearance among the stumps and bushes that surrounded the camp at Oswego. The priest Piquet was of the party; and five deserters declared that he solemnly blessed them, and told them to give the English no quarter.[3] Some valuable time was lost in bestowing the benediction; yet Haldimand's men were taken by surprise. Many of them were dispersed in

[1] *Amherst to Pitt, 22 Oct. 1759.* This letter, which is in the form of a journal, covers twenty-one folio pages.
[2] *Instructions of Amherst to Prideaux, 17 May, 1759. Prideaux to Haldimand, 30 June, 1759.*
[3] *Journal of Colonel Amherst.*

the woods, cutting timber for the intended fort; and it might have gone hard with them had not some of La Corne's Canadians become alarmed and rushed back to their boats, oversetting Father Piquet on the way.[1] These being rallied, the whole party ensconced itself in a tract of felled trees so far from the English that their fire did little harm. They continued it about two hours, and resumed it the next morning; when, three cannon being brought to bear on them, they took to their boats and disappeared, having lost about thirty killed and wounded, including two officers and La Corne himself, who was shot in the thigh. The English loss was slight.

Prideaux safely reached Niagara, and laid siege to it. It was a strong fort, lately rebuilt in regular form by an excellent officer, Captain Pouchot, of the battalion of Béarn, who commanded it. It stood where the present fort stands, in the angle formed by the junction of the River Niagara with Lake Ontario, and was held by about six hundred men, well supplied with provisions and munitions of war.[2] Higher up the river, a mile and a half above the cataract, there was another fort, called Little Niagara, built of wood, and commanded by the half-breed officer, Joncaire-Chabert, who with his brother, Joncaire-Clauzonne, and a numerous clan of Indian relatives, had so long thwarted the efforts of Johnson to engage the Five Nations in the English cause. But recent English successes had had their effect. Joncaire's influence was waning, and Johnson was now in Prideaux's camp with nine hundred Five Nation warriors pledged to fight the French. Joncaire, finding his fort untenable, burned it, and came with his garrison and his Indian friends to reinforce Niagara.[3]

Pouchot had another resource, on which he confidently relied. In obedience to an order from Vaudreuil, the French population of the Illinois, Detroit, and other distant posts, joined with troops of Western Indians, had come down the Lakes to recover Pittsburg, undo the work of Forbes, and restore French ascendency on the Ohio. Pittsburg had been in imminent danger; nor was it yet safe, though General Stanwix was sparing no effort to succor it.[4] These mixed bands of white men and red, bushrangers and savages, were now gathered, partly at Le Bœuf and Venango, but chiefly at Presquisle, under command of Aubry, Li-

[1] Pouchot, II. 130. Compare Mémoires sur le Canada, 1749–1760; N. Y. Col. Docs., VII. 395; and Letter from Oswego, in Boston Evening Post, No. 1,248.

[2] Pouchot says 515, besides 60 men from Little Niagara; Vaudreuil gives a total of 589.

[3] Pouchot, II. 52, 59. Procès de Bigot, Cadet, et autres, Mémoire pour Daniel de Joncaire-Chabert.

[4] Letters of Colonel Hugh Mercer, commanding at Pittsburg, January–June, 1759. Letters of Stanwix, May–July, 1759. Letter from Pittsburg, in Boston News Letter, No. 3,023. Narrative of John Ormsby.

gneris, Marin, and other partisan chiefs, the best in Canada. No sooner did Pouchot learn that the English were coming to attack him than he sent a messenger to summon them all to his aid.[1]

The siege was begun in form, though the English engineers were so incompetent that the trenches, as first laid out, were scoured by the fire of the place, and had to be made anew.[2] At last the batteries opened fire. A shell from a coehorn burst prematurely, just as it left the mouth of the piece, and a fragment striking Prideaux on the head, killed him instantly. Johnson took command in his place, and made up in energy what he lacked in skill. In two or three weeks the fort was in extremity. The rampart was breached, more than a hundred of the garrison were killed or disabled, and the rest were exhausted with want of sleep. Pouchot watched anxiously for the promised succors; and on the morning of the twenty-fourth of July a distant firing told him that they were at hand.

Aubry and Ligneris, with their motley following, had left Presquisle a few days before, to the number, according to Vaudreuil, of eleven hundred French and two hundred Indians.[3] Among them was a body of colony troops; but the Frenchmen of the party were chiefly traders and bushrangers from the West, connecting links between civilization and savagery; some of them indeed were mere white Indians, imbued with the ideas and morals of the wigwam, wearing hunting-shirts of smoked deer-skin embroidered with quills of the Canada porcupine, painting their faces black and red, tying eagle feathers in their long hair, or plastering it on their temples with a compound of vermilion and glue. They were excellent woodsmen, skilful hunters, and perhaps the best bushfighters in all Canada.

When Pouchot heard the firing, he went with a wounded artillery officer to the bastion next the river; and as the forest had been cut away for a great distance, they could see more than a mile and a half along the shore. There, by glimpses among trees and bushes, they descried bodies of men, now advancing, and now retreating; Indians in rapid movement, and the smoke of guns, the sound of which reached

---

[1] Pouchot, II. 46.

[2] *Rutherford to Haldimand, 14 July, 1759.* Prideaux was extremely disgusted. *Prideaux to Haldimand, 13 July, 1759.* Allan Macleane, of the Highlanders, calls the engineers "fools and blockheads, G—d d—n them." *Macleane to Haldimand, 21 July, 1759.*

[3] "Il n'y avoit que 1,100 François et 200 sauvages." *Vaudreuil au Ministre, 30 Oct. 1759.* Johnson says "1,200 men, with a number of Indians." *Johnson to Amherst, 25 July, 1759.* Portneuf, commanding at Presquisle, wrote to Pouchot that there were 1,600 French and 1,200 Indians. Pouchot, II. 94. A letter from Aubry to Pouchot put the whole at 2,500, half of them Indians. *Historical Magazine,* V., Second Series, 199.

their ears in heavy volleys, or a sharp and angry rattle. Meanwhile the English cannon had ceased their fire, and the silent trenches seemed deserted, as if their occupants were gone to meet the advancing foe. There was a call in the fort for volunteers to sally and destroy the works; but no sooner did they show themselves along the covered way than the seemingly abandoned trenches were thronged with men and bayonets, and the attempt was given up. The distant firing lasted half an hour, then ceased, and Pouchot remained in suspense; till, at two in the afternoon, a friendly Onondaga, who had passed unnoticed through the English lines, came to him with the announcement that the French and their allies had been routed and cut to pieces. Pouchot would not believe him.

Nevertheless his tale was true. Johnson, besides his Indians, had with him about twenty-three hundred men, whom he was forced to divide into three separate bodies,—one to guard the bateaux, one to guard the trenches, and one to fight Aubry and his band. This last body consisted of the provincial light infantry and the pickets, two companies of grenadiers, and a hundred and fifty men of the forty-sixth regiment, all under command of Colonel Massey.[1] They took post behind an abattis at a place called La Belle Famille, and the Five Nation warriors placed themselves on their flanks. These savages had shown signs of disaffection; and when the enemy approached, they opened a parley with the French Indians, which, however, soon ended, and both sides raised the war-whoop. The fight was brisk for a while; but at last Aubry's men broke away in a panic. The French officers seem to have made desperate efforts to retrieve the day, for nearly all of them were killed or captured; while their followers, after heavy loss, fled to their canoes and boats above the cataract, hastened back to Lake Erie, burned Presquisle, Le Bœuf, and Venango, and, joined by the garrisons of those forts, retreated to Detroit, leaving the whole region of the upper Ohio in undisputed possession of the English.

At four o'clock on the day of the battle, after a furious cannonade on both sides, a trumpet sounded from the trenches, and an officer approached the fort with a summons to surrender. He brought also a paper containing the names of the captive French officers, though some of them were spelled in a way that defied recognition. Pouchot, feigning incredulity, sent an officer of his own to the English camp, who soon saw unanswerable proof of the disaster; for here, under a shelter

---

[1] *Johnson to Amherst, 25 July, 1759.* Knox, II. 135. *Captain Delancey to ——, 25 July, 1759.* This writer commanded the light infantry in the fight.

of leaves and boughs near the tent of Johnson, sat Ligneris, severely wounded, with Aubry, Villiers, Montigny, Marin, and their companions in misfortune,—in all, sixteen officers, four cadets, and a surgeon.[1]

Pouchot had now no choice but surrender. By the terms of the capitulation, the garrison were to be sent prisoners to New York, though honors of war were granted them in acknowledgment of their courageous conduct. There was a special stipulation that they should be protected from the Indians, of whom they stood in the greatest terror, lest the massacre of Fort William Henry should be avenged upon them. Johnson restrained his dangerous allies, and, though the fort was pillaged, no blood was shed.

The capture of Niagara was an important stroke. Thenceforth Detroit, Michillimackinac, the Illinois, and all the other French interior posts, were severed from Canada, and left in helpless isolation; but Amherst was not yet satisfied. On hearing of Prideaux's death he sent Brigadier Gage to supersede Johnson and take command on Lake Ontario, directing him to descend the St. Lawrence, attack the French posts at the head of the rapids, and hold them if possible for the winter. The attempt was difficult; for the French force on the St. Lawrence was now greater than that which Gage could bring against it, after providing for the safety of Oswego and Niagara. Nor was he by nature prone to dashing and doubtful enterprise. He reported that the movement was impossible, much to the disappointment of Amherst, who seemed to expect from subordinates an activity greater than his own.[2]

He, meanwhile, was working at his fort at Crown Point, while the season crept away, and Bourlamaque lay ready to receive him at Isle-aux-Noix. "I wait his coming with impatience," writes the French commander, "though I doubt if he will venture to attack a post where we are intrenched to the teeth, and armed with a hundred pieces of cannon."[3] Bourlamaque now had with him thirty-five hundred men, in a position of great strength. Isle-aux-Noix, planted in mid-channel of the Richelieu soon after it issues from Lake Champlain, had been diligently fortified since the spring. On each side of it was an arm of the river, closed against an enemy with *chevaux-de-frise*. To attack it in front

[1]Johnson gives the names in his private *Diary*, printed in Stone, *Life of Johnson*, II. 394. Compare Pouchot, II. 105, 106. *Letter from Niagara*, in Boston Evening Post, No. 1,250. *Vaudreuil au Ministre*, 30 Oct. 1759.

[2]*Amherst to Gage, 28 July, 1 Aug., 14 Aug., 11 Sept. 1759. Diary of Sir William Johnson*, in Stone, *Life of Johnson*, II. 394–429.

[3]*Bourlamaque à (Bernetz?), 22 Sept. 1759.*

in the face of its formidable artillery would be a hazardous attempt, and the task of reducing it was likely to be a long one. The French force in these parts had lately received accessions. After the fall of Niagara the danger seemed so great, both in the direction of Lake Ontario and that of Lake Champlain, that Lévis had been sent up from Quebec with eight hundred men to command the whole department of Montreal.[1] A body of troops and militia was encamped opposite that town, ready to march towards either quarter, as need might be, while the abundant crops of the neighboring parishes were harvested by armed bands, ready at a word to drop the sickle for the gun.

Thus the promised advance of Amherst into Canada would be not without its difficulties, even when his navy, too tardily begun, should be ready to act its part. But if he showed no haste in succoring Wolfe, he at least made some attempts to communicate with him. Early in August he wrote him a letter, which Ensign Hutchins, of the rangers, carried to him in about a month by the long and circuitous route of the Kennebec, and which, after telling the news of the campaign, ended thus: "You may depend on my doing all I can for effectually reducing Canada. Now is the time!"[2] Amherst soon after tried another expedient, and sent Captains Kennedy and Hamilton with a flag of truce and a message of peace to the Abenakis of St. Francis, who, he thought, won over by these advances, might permit the two officers to pass unmolested to Quebec. But the Abenakis seized them and carried them prisoners to Montreal; on which Amherst sent Major Robert Rogers and a band of rangers to destroy their town.[3]

It was the eleventh of October before the miniature navy of Captain Loring—the floating battery, the brig, and the sloop that had been begun three weeks too late—was ready for service. They sailed at once to look for the enemy. The four French vessels made no resistance. One of them succeeded in reaching Isle-aux-Noix; one was run aground; and two were sunk by their crews, who escaped to the shore. Amherst, meanwhile, leaving the provincials to work at the fort, embarked with the regulars in bateaux, and proceeded on his northern way till, on the evening of the twelfth, a head-wind began to blow, and, rising to a storm, drove him for shelter into Ligonier Bay, on the west side of the lake.[4] On the thirteenth, it blew a gale. The lake raged like

[1] *Montcalm à Bourlamaque, 9 Août, 1759. Rigaud à Bourlamaque, 14 Août, 1759. Lévis à Bourlamaque, 25 Août, 1759.*

[2] *Amherst to Wolfe, 7 Aug. 1759.*

[3] *Amherst to Pitt, 22 Oct. 1759. Rogers, Journals,* 144.

[4] *Orderly Book of Commissary Wilson.*

an angry sea, and the frail bateaux, fit only for smooth water, could not have lived a moment. Through all the next night the gale continued, with floods of driving rain. "I hope it will soon change," wrote Amherst on the fifteenth, "for I have no time to lose." He was right. He had waited till the season of autumnal storms, when nature was more dangerous than man. On the sixteenth there was frost, and the wind did not abate. On the next morning it shifted to the south, but soon turned back with violence to the north, and the ruffled lake put on a look of winter, "which determined me," says the General, "not to lose time by striving to get to the Isle-aux-Noix, where I should arrive too late to force the enemy from their post, but to return to Crown Point and complete the works there." This he did, and spent the remnant of the season in the congenial task of finishing the fort, of which the massive remains still bear witness to his industry.

When Lévis heard that the English army had fallen back, he wrote, well pleased, to Bourlamaque: "I don't know how General Amherst will excuse himself to his Court, but I am very glad he let us alone, because the Canadians are so backward that you could count on nobody but the regulars."[1]

Concerning this year's operations on the Lakes, it may be observed that the result was not what the French feared, or what the British colonists had cause to hope. If, at the end of winter, Amherst had begun, as he might have done, the building of armed vessels at the head of the navigable waters of Lake Champlain, where Whitehall now stands, he would have had a navy ready to his hand before August, and would have been able to follow the retreating French without delay, and attack them at Isle-aux-Noix before they had finished their fortifications. And if, at the same time, he had directed Prideaux, instead of attacking Niagara, to co-operate with him by descending the St. Lawrence towards Montreal, the prospect was good that the two armies would have united at that place, and ended the campaign by the reduction of all Canada. In this case Niagara and all the western posts would have fallen without a blow.

Major Robert Rogers, sent in September to punish the Abenakis of St. Francis, had addressed himself to the task with his usual vigor. These Indians had been settled for about three quarters of a century on the River St. Francis, a few miles above its junction with the St. Lawrence. They were nominal Christians, and had been under the control of their missionaries for three generations; but though zealous and

[1] *Lévis à Bourlamaque,* 1 Nov. 1759.

sometimes fanatical in their devotion to the forms of Romanism, they remained thorough savages in dress, habits, and character. They were the scourge of the New England borders, where they surprised and burned farmhouses and small hamlets, killed men, women, and children without distinction, carried others prisoners to their village, subjected them to the torture of "running the gantlet," and compelled them to witness dances of triumph around the scalps of parents, children, and friends.

Amherst's instructions to Rogers contained the following: "Remember the barbarities that have been committed by the enemy's Indian scoundrels. Take your revenge, but don't forget that, though those dastardly villains have promiscuously murdered women and children of all ages, it is my order that no women or children be killed or hurt."

Rogers and his men set out in whaleboats, and, eluding the French armed vessels, then in full activity, came, on the tenth day, to Missisquoi Bay, at the north end of Lake Champlain. Here he hid his boats, leaving two friendly Indians to watch them from a distance, and inform him should the enemy discover them. He then began his march for St. Francis, when, on the evening of the second day, the two Indians overtook him with the startling news that a party of about four hundred French had found the boats, and that half of them were on his tracks in hot pursuit. It was certain that the alarm would soon be given, and other parties sent to cut him off. He took the bold resolution of outmarching his pursuers, pushing straight for St. Francis, striking it before succors could arrive, and then returning by Lake Memphremagog and the Connecticut. Accordingly he despatched Lieutenant McMullen by a circuitous route back to Crown Point, with a request to Amherst that provisions should be sent up the Connecticut to meet him on the way down. Then he set his course for the Indian town, and for nine days more toiled through the forest with desperate energy. Much of the way was through dense spruce swamps, with no dry resting-place at night. At length the party reached the River St. Francis, fifteen miles above the town, and, hooking their arms together for mutual support, forded it with extreme difficulty. Towards evening, Rogers climbed a tree, and descried the town three miles distant. Accidents, fatigue, and illness had reduced his followers to a hundred and forty-two officers and men. He left them to rest for a time, and, taking with him Lieutenant Turner and Ensign Avery, went to reconnoitre the place; left his two companions, entered it disguised in an Indian dress, and saw the unconscious savages yelling and singing in the full enjoyment of a grand dance. At two o'clock in the morning he rejoined his party, and at three led them to the attack, formed them in a semicircle, and burst in upon the town half an hour before sunrise. Many of the warriors were absent, and the rest were asleep. Some were killed in their beds, and some shot down in trying to escape. "About seven o'clock in the morning," he says, "the affair was completely over, in which time we had killed at least two hundred Indians and taken twenty of their women and children prisoners, fifteen of whom I let go their own way, and five I brought with me, namely, two Indian boys and three Indian girls. I likewise retook five English captives."

English scalps in hundreds were dangling from poles over the doors of the houses.[1] The town was pillaged and burned, not excepting the church, where ornaments of some value were found. On the side of the rangers, Captain Ogden and six men were wounded, and a Mohegan Indian from Stockbridge was killed. Rogers was told by his prisoners that a party of three hundred French and Indians was encamped on the river below, and that another party of two hundred and fifteen was not far distant. They had been sent to cut off the retreat of the invaders, but were doubtful as to their designs till after the blow was struck. There was no time to lose. The rangers made all haste southward, up the St. Francis, subsisting on corn from the Indian town; till, near the eastern borders of Lake Memphremagog, the supply failed, and they separated into small parties, the better to sustain life by hunting. The enemy followed close, attacked Ensign Avery's party, and captured five of them; then fell upon a band of about twenty, under Lieutenants Dunbar and Turner, and killed or captured nearly all. The other bands eluded their pursuers, turned southeastward, reached the Connecticut, some here, some there, and, giddy with fatigue and hunger, toiled wearily down the wild and lonely stream to the appointed rendezvous at the mouth of the Amonoosuc.

This was the place to which Rogers had requested that provisions might be sent; and the hope of finding them there had been the breath of life to the famished wayfarers. To their horror, the place was a solitude. There were fires still burning, but those who made them were gone. Amherst had sent Lieutenant Stephen up the river from Charlestown with an abundant supply of food; but finding nobody at the Amonoosuc, he had waited there two days, and then returned, carrying the

---

[1] Rogers says "about six hundred." Other accounts say six or seven hundred. The late Abbé Maurault, missionary of the St. Francis Indians, and their historian, adopts the latter statement, though it is probably exaggerated.

provisions back with him; for which outrageous conduct he was expelled from the service. "It is hardly possible," says Rogers, "to describe our grief and consternation." Some gave themselves up to despair. Few but their indomitable chief had strength to go farther. There was scarcely any game, and the barren wilderness yielded no sustenance but a few lily bulbs and the tubers of the climbing plant called in New England the ground-nut. Leaving his party to these miserable resources, and promising to send them relief within ten days, Rogers made a raft of dry pine logs, and drifted on it down the stream, with Captain Ogden, a ranger, and one of the captive Indian boys. They were stopped on the second day by rapids, and gained the shore with difficulty. At the foot of the rapids, while Ogden and the ranger went in search of squirrels, Rogers set himself to making another raft; and, having no strength to use the axe, he burned down the trees, which he then divided into logs by the same process. Five days after leaving his party he reached the first English settlement, Charlestown, or "Number Four," and immediately sent a canoe with provisions to the relief of the sufferers, following himself with other canoes two days later. Most of the men were saved, though some died miserably of famine and exhaustion. Of the few who had been captured, we are told by a French contemporary that they "became victims of the fury of the Indian women," from whose clutches the Canadians tried in vain to save them.[1]

---

[1] *Événements de la Guerre en Canada, 1759, 1760.* Compare *N. Y. Col. Docs.*, X. 1042.

NOTE.—On the day after he reached "Number Four," Rogers wrote a report of his expedition to Amherst. This letter is printed in his *Journals*, in which he gives also a supplementary account, containing further particulars. The *New Hampshire Gazette, Boston Evening Post*, and other newspapers of the time recount the story in detail. Hoyt (*Indian Wars*, 302) repeats it, with a few additions drawn from the recollections of survivors, long after. There is another account, very short and unsatisfactory, by Thompson Maxwell, who says that he was of the party, which is doubtful. Mante (223) gives horrible details of the sufferings of the rangers. An old chief of the St. Francis Indians, said to be one of those who pursued Rogers after the town was burned, many years ago told Mr. Jesse Pennoyer, a government land surveyor, that Rogers laid an ambush for the pursuers, and defeated them with great loss. This, the story says, took place near the present town of Sherbrooke; and minute details are given, with high praise of the skill and conduct of the famous partisan. If such an incident really took place, it is scarcely possible that Rogers would not have made some mention of it. On the other hand, it is equally incredible that the Indians would have invented the tale of their own defeat. I am indebted for Pennoyer's puzzling narrative to the kindness of R. A. Ramsay, Esq., of Montreal. It was printed, in 1869, in the *History of the Eastern Townships*, by Mrs. C. M. Day. All things considered, it is probably groundless.

Vaudreuil describes the destruction of the village in a letter to the Minister dated October 26, and says that Rogers had a hundred and fifty men; that St. Francis was burned to ashes; that the head chief and others were killed; that he (Vaudreuil), hearing of the march of the rangers, sent the most active of the Canadians to oppose them, and that Longueuil sent all the Canadians and Indians he could muster to pursue them on their retreat; that forty-six rangers were killed, and ten captured; that he thinks all the rest will starve to death; and, finally, that the affair is very unfortunate.

I once, when a college student, followed on foot the route of Rogers from Lake Memphremagog to the Connecticut.

27

The Heights of Abraham

1759

Wolfe was deeply moved by the disaster at the heights of Montmorenci, and in a General Order on the next day he rebuked the grenadiers for their precipitation. "Such impetuous, irregular, and unsoldierlike proceedings destroy all order, make it impossible for the commanders to form any disposition for an attack, and put it out of the general's power to execute his plans. The grenadiers could not suppose that they could beat the French alone."

The French were elated by their success. "Everybody," says the commissary Berniers, "thought that the campaign was as good as ended, gloriously for us." They had been sufficiently confident even before their victory; and the bearer of a flag of truce told the English officers that he had never imagined they were such fools as to attack Quebec with so small a force. Wolfe, on the other hand, had every reason to despond. At the outset, before he had seen Quebec and learned the nature of the ground, he had meant to begin the campaign by taking post on the Plains of Abraham, and thence laying siege to the town; but he soon discovered that the Plains of Abraham were hardly more within his reach than was Quebec itself. Such hope as was left him lay in the composition of Montcalm's army. He respected the French commander, and thought his disciplined soldiers not unworthy of the British steel; but he held his militia in high scorn, and could he but face them in the open field, he never doubted the result. But Montcalm also distrusted them, and persisted in refusing the coveted battle.

Wolfe, therefore, was forced to the conviction that his chances were of the smallest. It is said that, despairing of any decisive stroke, he conceived the idea of fortifying Isle-aux-Coudres, and leaving a part of his troops there when he sailed for home, against another attempt in the spring. The more to weaken the enemy and prepare his future conquest, he began at the same time a course of action which for his credit one would gladly wipe from the record; for, though far from inhuman, he threw himself with extraordinary intensity into whatever work he had in hand, and, to accomplish it, spared others scarcely more than he spared himself. About the middle of August he issued a third proclamation to the Canadians, declaring that as they had refused his offers of protection and "had made such ungrateful returns in practising the most unchristian barbarities against his troops on all occasions, he could no longer refrain in justice to himself and his army from chastising them as they deserved." The barbarities in question consisted in the frequent scalping and mutilating of sentinels and men on outpost duty, perpetrated no less by Canadians than by Indians. Wolfe's object was twofold: first, to cause the militia to desert, and, secondly, to exhaust the colony. Rangers, light infantry, and Highlanders were sent to waste the settlements far and wide. Wherever resistance was offered, farmhouses and villages were laid in ashes, though churches were generally spared. St. Paul, far below Quebec, was sacked and burned, and the settlements of the opposite shore were partially destroyed. The parishes of L'Ange Gardien, Château Richer, and St. Joachim were wasted with fire and sword. Night after night the garrison of Quebec could see the light of burning houses as far down as the mountain of Cape Tourmente. Near St. Joachim there was a severe skirmish, followed by atrocious cruelties. Captain Alexander Montgomery, of the forty-third regiment, who commanded the detachment, and who has been most unjustly confounded with the revolutionary general, Richard Montgomery, ordered the prisoners to be shot in cold blood, to the indignation of his own officers.[1] Robineau de Portneuf, curé of St. Joachim, placed himself at the head of thirty parishioners and took possession of a large stone house in the adjacent parish of Château Richer, where for a time he held the English at bay. At length he and his followers were drawn out into an ambush, where they were surrounded and killed; and, being disguised as Indians, the rangers scalped them all.[2]

Most of the French writers of the time mention these barbarities without much comment, while Vaudreuil loudly denounces them. Yet he himself was answerable for atrocities incomparably worse, and on a far larger scale. He had turned loose his savages, red and white, along a frontier of six hundred miles, to waste, burn, and murder at will. "Women and children," such were the orders of Wolfe, "are to be treated with humanity; if any violence is offered to a woman, the offender shall be punished with death." These orders were generally obeyed. The English, with the single exception of Montgomery, killed none but armed men in the act of resistance or attack; Vaudreuil's war-parties spared neither age nor sex.

Montcalm let the parishes burn, and still lay fast intrenched in his lines of Beauport. He would not imperil all Canada to save a few hundred farmhouses; and Wolfe was as far as ever from the battle that he coveted. Hitherto, his attacks had been made chiefly below the town; but, these having failed, he now changed his plan and renewed on a larger scale the movements begun above it in July. With every fair wind, ships and transports passed the batteries of Quebec, favored by a hot fire from Point Levi, and generally succeeded, with more or less damage, in gaining the upper river. A fleet of flatboats was also sent thither, and twelve hundred troops marched overland to embark in them, under Brigadier Murray. Admiral Holmes took command of the little fleet now gathered above the town, and operations in that quarter were systematically resumed.

To oppose them, Bougainville was sent from the camp at Beauport with fifteen hundred men. His was a most arduous and exhausting duty. He must watch the shores for fifteen or twenty miles, divide his force into detachments, and subject himself and his followers to the strain of

[1] Fraser, *Journal*. Fraser was an officer under Montgomery, of whom he speaks with anger and disgust.
[2] Knox, II. 32. Most of the contemporary journals mention the incident.

incessant vigilance and incessant marching. Murray made a descent at Pointe-aux-Trembles, and was repulsed with loss. He tried a second time at another place, was met before landing by a body of ambushed Canadians, and was again driven back, his foremost boats full of dead and wounded. A third time he succeeded, landed at Deschambault, and burned a large building filled with stores and all the spare baggage of the French regular officers. The blow was so alarming that Montcalm hastened from Beauport to take command in person; but when he arrived the English were gone.

Vaudreuil now saw his mistake in sending the French frigates up the river out of harm's way, and withdrawing their crews to serve the batteries of Quebec. Had these ships been there, they might have overpowered those of the English in detail as they passed the town. An attempt was made to retrieve the blunder. The sailors were sent to man the frigates anew and attack the squadron of Holmes. It was too late. Holmes was already too strong for them, and they were recalled. Yet the difficulties of the English still seemed insurmountable. Dysentery and fever broke out in their camps, the number of their effective men was greatly reduced, and the advancing season told them that their work must be done quickly, or not done at all.

On the other side, the distress of the French grew greater every day. Their army was on short rations. The operations of the English above the town filled the camp of Beauport with dismay, for troops and Canadians alike dreaded the cutting off of their supplies. These were all drawn from the districts of Three Rivers and Montreal; and, at best, they were in great danger, since when brought down in boats at night they were apt to be intercepted, while the difficulty of bringing them by land was extreme, through the scarcity of cattle and horses. Discipline was relaxed, disorder and pillage were rife, and the Canadians deserted so fast, that towards the end of August two hundred of them, it is said, would sometimes go off in one night. Early in the month the disheartening news came of the loss of Ticonderoga and Crown Point, the retreat of Bourlamaque, the fall of Niagara, and the expected advance of Amherst on Montreal. It was then that Lévis was despatched to the scene of danger; and Quebec was deplorably weakened by his absence. About this time the Lower Town was again set on fire by the English batteries, and a hundred and sixty-seven houses were burned in a night. In the front of the Upper Town nearly every building was a ruin. At the General Hospital, which was remote enough to be safe from the bombardment, every barn, shed, and garret, and even the chapel itself, were crowded with sick and wounded, with women and children from the town, and the nuns of the Ursulines and the Hôtel-Dieu, driven thither for refuge. Bishop Pontbriand, though suffering from a mortal disease, came almost daily to visit and console them from his lodging in the house of the curé at Charlesbourg.

Towards the end of August the sky brightened again. It became known that Amherst was not moving on Montreal, and Bourlamaque wrote that his position at Isle-aux-Noix was impregnable. On the twenty-seventh a deserter from Wolfe's army brought the welcome assurance that the invaders despaired of success, and would soon sail for home; while there were movements in the English camps and fleet that seemed to confirm what he said. Vaudreuil breathed more freely, and renewed hope and confidence visited the army of Beauport.

Meanwhile a deep cloud fell on the English. Since the siege began, Wolfe had passed with ceaseless energy from camp to camp, animating the troops, observing everything, and directing everything; but now the pale face and tall lean form were seen no more, and the rumor spread that the General was dangerously ill. He had in fact been seized by an access of the disease that had tortured him for some time past; and fever had followed. His quarters were at a French farmhouse in the camp at Montmorenci; and here, as he lay in an upper chamber, helpless in bed, his singular and most unmilitary features haggard with disease and drawn with pain, no man could less have looked the hero. But as the needle, though quivering, points always to the pole, so, through torment and languor and the heats of fever, the mind of Wolfe dwelt on the capture of Quebec. His illness, which began before the twentieth of August, had so far subsided on the twenty-fifth that Knox wrote in his Diary of that day: "His Excellency General Wolfe is on the recovery, to the inconceivable joy of the whole army." On the twenty-ninth he was able to write or dictate a letter to the three brigadiers, Monckton, Townshend, and Murray: "That the public service may not suffer by the General's indisposition, he begs the brigadiers will meet and consult together for the public utility and advantage, and consider of the best method to attack the enemy." The letter then proposes three plans, all bold to audacity. The first was to send a part of the army to ford the Montmorenci eight or nine miles above its mouth, march through the forest, and fall on the rear of the French at Beauport, while the rest landed and attacked them in front. The second was to cross the ford at the mouth of the Montmorenci and march along the strand, under the French intrenchments, till a place could be found where the troops might climb the heights. The third was to make a general attack from boats at the Beauport flats. Wolfe had before entertained two other plans, one of which was to scale the heights at St. Michel, about a league above Quebec; but this he had abandoned on learning that the French were there in force to receive him. The other was to storm the Lower Town; but this also he had abandoned, because the Upper Town, which commanded it, would still remain inaccessible.

The brigadiers met in consultation, rejected the three plans proposed in the letter, and advised that an attempt should be made to gain a footing on the north shore above the town, place the army between Montcalm and his base of supply, and so force him to fight or surrender. The scheme was similar to that of the heights of St. Michel. It seemed desperate, but so did all the rest; and if by chance it should succeed, the gain was far greater than could follow any success below the town. Wolfe embraced it at once.

Not that he saw much hope in it. He knew that every chance was against him. Disappointment in the past and gloom in the future, the pain and exhaustion of disease, toils, and anxieties "too great," in the words of Burke, "to be supported by a delicate constitution, and a body unequal to the vigorous and enterprising soul that it lodged," threw him at times into deep dejection. By those intimate with him he was heard to say that he would not go back defeated, "to be exposed to the censure and reproach of an ignorant populace." In other moods he felt that he ought not to sacrifice what was left of his diminished army in vain conflict with hopeless obstacles. But his final resolve once taken, he would not swerve from it. His fear was that he might not be able to lead his troops in person. "I know perfectly well you cannot cure me," he said to his physician; "but pray make me up so that I may be without pain for a few days, and able to do my duty: that is all I want."

In a despatch which Wolfe had written to Pitt, Admiral Saunders conceived that he had ascribed to the fleet more than its just share in the disaster at Montmorenci; and he sent him a letter on the subject. Major Barré kept it from the invalid till the fever had abated. Wolfe then wrote a long answer, which reveals his mixed dejection and resolve. He affirms the justice of what Saunders had said, but adds: "I shall leave out that part of my letter to Mr. Pitt which you object to. I am sensible of my own errors in the course of the campaign, see clearly wherein I have been deficient, and think a little more or less blame to a man that must necessarily be ruined, of little or no consequence. I take the blame of that unlucky day entirely upon my own shoulders, and I expect to suffer for it." Then, speaking of the new project of an attack above Quebec, he says despondingly: "My ill state of health prevents me from executing my own plan; it is of too desperate a nature to order others to execute." He proceeds, however, to give directions for it. "It will be necessary to run as many small craft as possible above the town, with provisions for six weeks, for about five thousand, which is all I intend to take. My letters, I hope, will be ready to-morrow, and I hope I shall have strength to lead these men to wherever we can find the enemy."

On the next day, the last of August, he was able for the first time to leave the house. It was on this same day that he wrote his last letter to his mother: "My writing to you will convince you that no personal evils worse than defeats and disappointments have fallen upon me. The enemy puts nothing to risk, and I can't in conscience put the whole army to risk. My antagonist has wisely shut himself up in inaccessible intrenchments, so that I can't get at him without spilling a torrent of blood, and that perhaps to little purpose. The Marquis de Montcalm is at the head of a great number of bad soldiers, and I am at the head of a small number of good ones, that wish for nothing so much as to fight him; but the wary old fellow avoids an action, doubtful of the behavior of his army. People must be of the profession to understand the disadvantages and difficulties we labor under, arising from the uncommon natural strength of the country."

On the second of September a vessel was sent to England with his last despatch to Pitt. It begins thus: "The obstacles we have met with in the operations of the campaign are much greater than we had reason to expect or could foresee; not so much from the number of the enemy (though superior to us) as from the natural strength of the country, which the Marquis of Montcalm seems wisely to depend upon. When I learned that succors of all kinds had been thrown into Quebec; that five battalions of regular troops, completed from the best inhabitants of the country, some of the troops of the colony, and every Canadian that was able to bear arms, besides several nations of savages, had taken the field in a very advantageous situation,—I could not flatter myself that I should be able to reduce the place. I sought, however, an occasion to attack their army, knowing well that with these troops I was able to fight, and hoping that a victory might disperse them." Then, after recounting the events of the campaign with admirable clearness, he continues: "I found myself so ill, and am still so weak, that I begged the general officers to consult together for the general utility. They are all of opinion that, as more ships and provisions are now got above the town, they should try, by conveying up a corps of four or five thousand men (which is nearly the whole strength of the army after the Points of Levi and Orleans are left in a proper state of defence), to draw the enemy from their present situation and bring them to an action. I have acquiesced in the proposal, and we are preparing to put it into execution." The letter ends thus: "By the list of disabled officers, many of whom are of rank, you may perceive that the army is much weakened. By the nature of the river, the most formidable part of this armament is deprived of the power of acting; yet we have almost the whole force of Canada to oppose. In this situation there is such a choice of difficulties that I own myself at a loss how to determine. The affairs of Great Britain, I know, require the most vigorous measures; but the courage of a handful of brave troops should be exerted only when there is some hope of a favorable event; however, you may be assured that the small part of the campaign which remains shall be employed, as far as I am able, for the honor of His Majesty and the interest of the nation, in which I am sure of being well seconded by the Admiral and by the generals; happy if our efforts here can contribute to the success of His Majesty's arms in any other parts of America."

Some days later, he wrote to the Earl of Holdernesse: "The Marquis of Montcalm has a numerous body of armed men (I cannot call it an army), and the strongest country perhaps in the world. Our fleet blocks up the river above and below the town, but can give no manner of aid in an attack upon the Canadian army. We are now here [*off Cap-Rouge*] with about thirty-six hundred men, waiting to attack them when and wherever they can best be got at. I am so far recovered as to do business; but my constitution is entirely ruined, without the consolation of doing any considerable service to the state, and without any prospect of it." He had just learned, through the letter brought from Amherst by Ensign Hutchins, that he could expect no help from that quarter.

Perhaps he was as near despair as his undaunted nature was capable of being. In his present state of body and mind he was a hero without the light and cheer of heroism. He flattered himself with no illusions, but saw the worst and faced it all. He seems to have been entirely without excitement. The languor of disease, the desperation of the chances, and the greatness of the stake may have wrought to tranquillize him. His energy was doubly tasked: to bear up his own sinking frame, and to achieve an almost hopeless feat of arms.

Audacious as it was, his plan cannot be called rash if we may accept the statement of two well-informed writers on the French side. They say that on the tenth of September the English naval commanders held a council on board the flagship, in which it was resolved that the lateness of the season required the fleet to leave Quebec without delay. They say further that Wolfe then went to the Admiral, told him that

EUROPE AT WAR

"The war kindled in the American forest was now raging in full conflagration among the kingdoms of Europe; and in the midst stood Frederick of Prussia (42), a veritable fire-king. He had learned through secret agents that he was to be attacked, and that the wrath of Maria Theresa (43), with her two allies, Pompadour (44) and the Empress of Russia (45), was soon to wreak itself upon him."

CONFLICT IN
NORTH AMERICA

England, dragged into the Continental ~
fared badly until "an event took place
pregnant with glorious consequence." I~
1757 William Pitt (48) was made Secre~
of State with full control of the war and
foreign affairs, and England's course of
Continental victories began. Pitt then tu~
his efforts towards America, sending Co~
Jeffrey Amherst (49) and Admiral Edw~
Boscawen (46) to command an expediti~
against Louisbourg on Cape Breton (47~
Pitt's object was "not to curb the power
France in America, but to annihilate it.~

47

48

49

50

51

A contemporary French map (50) details Amherst's attack on Louisbourg in July of 1758. His troops were put ashore from the ships at left to advance on the French fortress at lower right. In plate 51 Amherst, now a major general, is seen at center with his hat raised, directing the attack and talking to his subordinate, Brigadier General James Wolfe (pointing at left). "The ardent and indomitable" Wolfe was "the life of the siege." On July 22nd he sent a note (52) to Amherst from his post in the trenches. When the victory had been won and Louisbourg, with the two great islands that depended on it, passed to the British Crown, Wolfe remained eager to press on the fight.

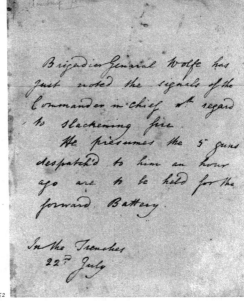

Brigadier General Wolfe has just noted the signals of the Commander in chief with regard to slackening fire.

He presumes the 5 guns despatch'd to him an hour ago are to be held for the forward Battery.

In the Trenches
22.ᵈ July

53

In the same year as the Louisbourg engagement, Pitt also called upon General James Abercromby to lead an expedition against Montcalm at Fort Ticonderoga. Abercromby, "an aged gentleman, infirm in body and mind," was little more than the nominal commander. Brigadier Lord Howe (53), only thirty-four but described by Wolfe as "that great man," led the attack until his death early in the battle. Abercromby, without artillery backup, charged the barricades six times (54), lost the day and nineteen hundred and forty-four officers and men.

54

A year later Amherst reached the head of Lake George, made a camp there (55) and marched on Ticonderoga only to have the French blow up the fort and escape up the lake. This painting, recently found in an English coal shed, is by Thomas Davies, who, while serving in the British army in America, drew and painted many on-the-spot pictures of these events.

55

Admiral Charles Saunders (5
commanded the British fleet c
transported Wolfe to Canada
his ship Neptune. By skilful
manoeuvering he sailed his
whole fleet safely through the
treacherous St. Lawrence to c
few miles from Quebec. On 2
June, 1759, Saunders thwarte
Montcalm's attempt to destro
his fleet by fireships (56),
described by one of his crew a
the "the grandest fireworks th
can possibly be conceived."

Pitt selected thirty-three-
year-old James Wolfe (61) to
command the long-awaited
expedition against Quebec an
permitted him to choose his o
staff. He appointed three
brigadiers, all in the early prir
of life: James Murray (58),
Robert Monckton (59), and
George Townshend (60).
Wolfe, with his narrow
shoulders, long thin limbs, an
receding forehead and chin, u
an incongruous figure.
"Nothing but the clear, bright,
and piercing eye bespoke the
spirit within."

58

59

60

61

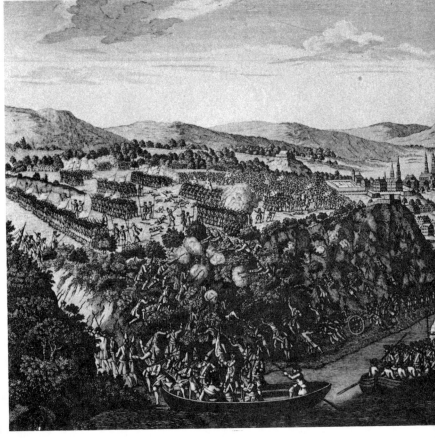

63

Wolfe entrenched himself at Point Levi across the river from Quebec (both seen in the distance in plate 62). From there he bombarded the seemingly impregnable city as he sought ways to attack it. On 31 July, 1759, he made an attempt on the French position at the Falls of Montmorenci (62), where, under cover of his fleet's fire, his men came ashore only to be badly routed.

As summer faded Wolfe settled on a bold plan. With his telescope "he descried a path...up the face of the woody precipice" and determined to try his luck there. In the dawn of September 13th, twenty-four volunteers led the way up the steep hill (63), closely followed by a much larger group. The main body of troops waited in their boats until the signal of success was given and they rushed ashore to meet their enemy on the Plains of Abraham (64).

65

Both Generals Wolfe and Montcalm were killed in the battle for Quebec, and both deaths were commemorated in romantic paintings with no regard for the facts. Benjamin West's heroic "Death of Wolfe" (65) and Louis-Joseph Watteau's "Death of Montcalm" (66) reflected in very different styles their countrymen's deep regard for their heroes. Edward Penny's version of Wolfe's death (67) is closest to the truth—and less satisfactory as art.

67

66

68

...er the battle the victorious
...glish found Quebec in ruins
...? and 69), a devastation accomp-
...ed by their own guns.

69

70

71

72

the fall of Quebec, both Governor Vaudreuil and
~~ral~~ François de Lévis had high hopes of retaking
~~ec~~. Their chance came in April of 1760, when Lévis
~~l~~eft Montreal with over eight thousand men and
~~m~~ed to Ste.-Foy (70), an English outpost not far from
~~ec~~. Here, on his white charger, he engaged the English
~~s~~ under General James Murray and roundly defeated
~~~~. But victory was short lived as English reinforcements
~~l~~ from across the Atlantic. When Montreal (71)
~~dered~~ on 8 September, "Canada and all its dependen-
~~ss~~ed to the British Crown."

~~sinister~~" intendant, François Bigot (73)—together
~~V~~audreuil and others accused of the frauds that had
~~l~~ to ruin Canada—was sent to France for trial. Bigot
~~h~~en banished from France for life.

73

Se here O fair Britania at thy Feet:
The Gallic Genius does her Rage submit:
Her Standards torn of her proud beating hands,
She suppliant brings with her submissive hands;
When the brave Wolfe heroic led the Way,
To Victory, and dying won the Day;
Which brought them under Georges milder sway.

Quebec no more is here, Auspicious Heav'n!
Has that to Britains braver Genius given:
No more Acadian Swains beneath the pow'r
Of Tyrants groan, but bless the happy Hour.

74

PAX EUROPÆ REDDITA
ANNO M.DCC.LXIII.

75

France kneels to Britain, with Quebec in the background, commemorating the British victory in America (74). In plate 75 another allegorical print celebrates peace in Europe after the Treaty of the Peace of Paris was signed in 1763, ending the Seven Years War.

he had found a place where the heights could be scaled, that he would send up a hundred and fifty picked men to feel the way, and that if they gained a lodgment at the top, the other troops should follow; if, on the other hand, the French were there in force to oppose them, he would not sacrifice the army in a hopeless attempt, but embark them for home, consoled by the thought that all had been done that man could do. On this, concludes the story, the Admiral and his officers consented to wait the result.[1]

As Wolfe had informed Pitt, his army was greatly weakened. Since the end of June his loss in killed and wounded was more than eight hundred and fifty, including two colonels, two majors, nineteen captains, and thirty-four subalterns; and to these were to be added a greater number disabled by disease.

The squadron of Admiral Holmes above Quebec had now increased to twenty-two vessels, great and small. One of the last that went up was a diminutive schooner, armed with a few swivels, and jocosely named the "Terror of France." She sailed by the town in broad daylight, the French, incensed at her impudence, blazing at her from all their batteries; but she passed unharmed, anchored by the Admiral's ship, and saluted him triumphantly with her swivels.

Wolfe's first move towards executing his plan was the critical one of evacuating the camp at Montmorenci. This was accomplished on the third of September. Montcalm sent a strong force to fall on the rear of the retiring English. Monckton saw the movement from Point Levi, embarked two battalions in the boats of the fleet, and made a feint of landing at Beauport. Montcalm recalled his troops to repulse the threatened attack; and the English withdrew from Montmorenci unmolested, some to the Point of Orleans, others to Point Levi. On the night of the fourth a fleet of flatboats passed above the town with the baggage and stores. On the fifth, Murray, with four battalions, marched up to the River Etechemin, and forded it under a hot fire from the French batteries at Sillery. Monckton and Townshend followed with three more battalions, and the united force, of about thirty-six hundred men, was embarked on board the ships of Holmes, where Wolfe joined them on the same evening.

These movements of the English filled the French commanders with mingled perplexity, anxiety, and hope. A deserter told them that Ad-

---

[1]This statement is made by the Chevalier Johnstone, and, with some variation, by the author of the valuable *Journal tenu à l'Armée que commandoit feu M. le Marquis de Montcalm*. Bigot says that, after the battle, he was told by British officers that Wolfe meant to risk only an advance party of two hundred men, and to reimbark if they were repulsed.

miral Saunders was impatient to be gone. Vaudreuil grew confident. "The breaking up of the camp at Montmorenci," he says, "and the abandonment of the intrenchments there, the reimbarkation on board the vessels above Quebec of the troops who had encamped on the south bank, the movements of these vessels, the removal of the heaviest pieces of artillery from the batteries of Point Levi,—these and the late-ness of the season all combined to announce the speedy departure of the fleet, several vessels of which had even sailed down the river al-ready. The prisoners and the deserters who daily came in told us that this was the common report in their army."[1] He wrote to Bourlamaque on the first of September: "Everything proves that the grand design of the English has failed."

Yet he was ceaselessly watchful. So was Montcalm; and he, too, on the night of the second, snatched a moment to write to Bourlamaque from his headquarters in the stone house, by the river of Beauport: "The night is dark; it rains; our troops are in their tents, with clothes on, ready for an alarm; I in my boots; my horses saddled. In fact, this is my usual way. I wish you were here; for I cannot be everywhere, though I multiply myself, and have not taken off my clothes since the twenty-third of June." On the eleventh of September he wrote his last letter to Bourlamaque, and probably the last that his pen ever traced. "I am overwhelmed with work, and should often lose temper, like you, if I did not remember that I am paid by Europe for not losing it. Noth-ing new since my last. I give the enemy another month, or something less, to stay here." The more sanguine Vaudreuil would hardly give them a week.

Meanwhile, no precaution was spared. The force under Bougainville above Quebec was raised to three thousand men.[2] He was ordered to watch the shore as far as Jacques-Cartier, and follow with his main body every movement of Holmes's squadron. There was little fear for the heights near the town; they were thought inaccessible.[3] Even Mont-calm believed them safe, and had expressed himself to that effect some time before. "We need not suppose," he wrote to Vaudreuil, "that the enemy have wings;" and again, speaking of the very place where Wolfe afterwards landed, "I swear to you that a hundred men posted there would stop their whole army."[4] He was right. A hundred watchful and

[1] *Vaudreuil au Ministre*, 5 Oct. 1759.

[2] *Journal du Siége* (Bibliothêque de Hartwell). *Journal tenu à l'Armée*, etc. *Vaudreuil au Ministre*, 5 Oct. 1759.

[3] Pontbriand, *Jugement impartial.*

[4] *Montcalm à Vaudreuil*, 27 Juillet. *Ibid.*, 29 Juillet, 1759.

determined men could have held the position long enough for reinforcements to come up.

The hundred men were there. Captain de Vergor, of the colony
troops, commanded them, and reinforcements were within his call; for
the battalion of Guienne had been ordered to encamp close at hand on
the Plains of Abraham.[1] Vergor's post, called Anse du Foulon, was a
mile and a half from Quebec. A little beyond it, by the brink of the
cliffs, was another post, called Samos, held by seventy men with four
cannon; and, beyond this again, the heights of Sillery were guarded by
a hundred and thirty men, also with cannon.[2] These were outposts of
Bougainville, whose headquarters were at Cap-Rouge, six miles above
Sillery, and whose troops were in continual movement along the intervening shore. Thus all was vigilance; for while the French were strong
in the hope of speedy delivery, they felt that there was no safety till
the tents of the invader had vanished from their shores and his ships
from their river. "What we knew," says one of them, "of the character
of M. Wolfe, that impetuous, bold, and intrepid warrior, prepared us
for a last attack before he left us."

Wolfe had been very ill on the evening of the fourth. The troops
knew it, and their spirits sank; but, after a night of torment, he grew
better, and was soon among them again, rekindling their ardor, and
imparting a cheer that he could not share. For himself he had no pity;
but when he heard of the illness of two officers in one of the ships, he
sent them a message of warm sympathy, advised them to return to Point
Levi, and offered them his own barge and an escort. They thanked
him, but replied that, come what might, they would see the enterprise
to an end. Another officer remarked in his hearing that one of the
invalids had a very delicate constitution. "Don't tell me of constitution," said Wolfe; "he has good spirit, and good spirit will carry a man
through everything."[3] An immense moral force bore up his own frail
body and forced it to its work.

Major Robert Stobo, who, five years before, had been given as a
hostage to the French at the capture of Fort Necessity, arrived about
this time in a vessel from Halifax. He had long been a prisoner at
Quebec, not always in close custody, and had used his opportunities to
acquaint himself with the neighborhood. In the spring of this year he
and an officer of rangers named Stevens had made their escape with

---

[1]Foligny, *Journal mémoratif. Journal tenu à l'Armée*, etc.
[2]*Vaudreuil au Ministre, 5 Oct. 1759.*
[3]Knox, II. 61, 65.

extraordinary skill and daring; and he now returned to give his countrymen the benefit of his local knowledge.[1] His biographer says that it was
he who directed Wolfe in the choice of a landing-place.[2] Be this as it
may, Wolfe in person examined the river and the shores as far as
Pointe-aux-Trembles; till at length, landing on the south side a little
above Quebec, and looking across the water with a telescope, he descried a path that ran with a long slope up the face of the woody precipice, and saw at the top a cluster of tents. They were those of Vergor's
guard at the Anse du Foulon, now called Wolfe's Cove. As he could
see but ten or twelve of them, he thought that the guard could not be
numerous, and might be overpowered. His hope would have been
stronger if he had known that Vergor had once been tried for misconduct and cowardice in the surrender of Beauséjour, and saved from mer-
ited disgrace by the friendship of Bigot and the protection of
Vaudreuil.[3]

The morning of the seventh was fair and warm, and the vessels of
Holmes, their crowded decks gay with scarlet uniforms, sailed up the
river to Cap-Rouge. A lively scene awaited them; for here were the
headquarters of Bougainville, and here lay his principal force, while
the rest watched the banks above and below. The cove into which
the little river runs was guarded by floating batteries; the surrounding
shore was defended by breastworks; and a large body of regulars, militia,
and mounted Canadians in blue uniforms moved to and fro, with restless activity, on the hills behind. When the vessels came to anchor,
the horsemen dismounted and formed in line with the infantry; then,
with loud shouts, the whole rushed down the heights to man their
works at the shore. That true Briton, Captain Knox, looked on with a
critical eye from the gangway of his ship, and wrote that night in his
Diary that they had made a ridiculous noise. "How different!" he exclaims, "how nobly awful and expressive of true valor is the customary
silence of the British troops!"

In the afternoon the ships opened fire, while the troops entered the
boats and rowed up and down as if looking for a landing-place. It was
but a feint of Wolfe to deceive Bougainville as to his real design. A
heavy easterly rain set in on the next morning, and lasted two days
without respite. All operations were suspended, and the men suffered
greatly in the crowded transports. Half of them were therefore landed

---

[1]Letters in *Boston Post Boy*, No. 97, and *Boston Evening Post*, No. 1,258.
[2]*Memoirs of Major Robert Stobo*. Curious, but often inexact.
[3]See *supra*, p. 148.

on the south shore, where they made their quarters in the village of St. Nicolas, refreshed themselves, and dried their wet clothing, knapsacks, and blankets.

For several successive days the squadron of Holmes was allowed to drift up the river with the flood tide and down with the ebb, thus passing and repassing incessantly between the neighborhood of Quebec on one hand, and a point high above Cap-Rouge on the other; while Bougainville, perplexed, and always expecting an attack, followed the ships to and fro along the shore, by day and by night, till his men were exhausted with ceaseless forced marches.[1]

At last the time for action came. On Wednesday, the twelfth, the troops at St. Nicolas were embarked again, and all were told to hold themselves in readiness. Wolfe, from the flagship "Sutherland," issued his last general orders. "The enemy's force is now divided, great scarcity of provisions in their camp, and universal discontent among the Canadians. Our troops below are in readiness to join us; all the light artillery and tools are embarked at the Point of Levi; and the troops will land where the French seem least to expect it. The first body that gets on shore is to march directly to the enemy and drive them from any little post they may occupy; the officers must be careful that the succeeding bodies do not by any mistake fire on those who go before them. The battalions must form on the upper ground with expedition, and be ready to charge whatever presents itself. When the artillery and troops are landed, a corps will be left to secure the landing-place, while the rest march on and endeavor to bring the Canadians and French to a battle. The officers and men will remember what their country expects from them, and what a determined body of soldiers inured to war is capable of doing against five weak French battalions mingled with a disorderly peasantry."

The spirit of the army answered to that of its chief. The troops loved and admired their general, trusted their officers, and were ready for any attempt. "Nay, how could it be otherwise," quaintly asks honest Sergeant John Johnson, of the fifty-eighth regiment, "being at the heels of gentlemen whose whole thirst, equal with their general, was for glory? We had seen them tried, and always found them sterling. We knew that they would stand by us to the last extremity."

Wolfe had thirty-six hundred men and officers with him on board the vessels of Holmes; and he now sent orders to Colonel Burton at Point Levi to bring to his aid all who could be spared from that place

[1] Joannès, Major de Québec, *Mémoire sur la Campagne de 1759.*

and the Point of Orleans. They were to march along the south bank, after nightfall, and wait further orders at a designated spot convenient for embarkation. Their number was about twelve hundred, so that the entire force destined for the enterprise was at the utmost forty-eight hundred.[1] With these, Wolfe meant to climb the heights of Abraham in the teeth of an enemy who, though much reduced, were still twice as numerous as their assailants.[2]

Admiral Saunders lay with the main fleet in the Basin of Quebec. This excellent officer, whatever may have been his views as to the necessity of a speedy departure, aided Wolfe to the last with unfailing energy and zeal. It was agreed between them that while the General made the real attack, the Admiral should engage Montcalm's attention by a pretended one. As night approached, the fleet ranged itself along the Beauport shore; the boats were lowered and filled with sailors, marines, and the few troops that had been left behind; while ship signalled to ship, cannon flashed and thundered, and shot ploughed the beach, as if to clear a way for assailants to land. In the gloom of the evening the effect was imposing. Montcalm, who thought that the movements of the English above the town were only a feint, that their main force was still below it, and that their real attack would be made there, was completely deceived, and massed his troops in front of Beauport to repel the expected landing. But while in the fleet of Saunders all was uproar and ostentatious menace, the danger was ten miles away, where the squadron of Holmes lay tranquil and silent at its anchorage off Cap-Rouge.

It was less tranquil than it seemed. All on board knew that a blow would be struck that night, though only a few high officers knew where. Colonel Howe, of the light infantry, called for volunteers to lead the unknown and desperate venture, promising, in the words of one of them, "that if any of us survived we might depend on being recommended to the General."[3] As many as were wanted—twenty-four in all— soon came forward. Thirty large bateaux and some boats belonging to the squadron lay moored alongside the vessels; and late in the evening the troops were ordered into them, the twenty-four vol-

---

[1] See Note, end of chapter.

[2] Including Bougainville's command. An escaped prisoner told Wolfe, a few days before, that Montcalm still had fourteen thousand men. *Journal of an Expedition on the River St. Lawrence.* This meant only those in the town and the camps of Beauport. "I don't believe their whole army amounts to that number," wrote Wolfe to Colonel Burton, on the tenth. He knew, however, that if Montcalm could bring all his troops together, the French would outnumber him more than two to one.

[3] *Journal of the Particular Transactions during the Siege of Quebec.* The writer, a soldier in the light infantry, says he was one of the first eight who came forward. See *Notes and Queries,* XX. 370.

unteers taking their place in the foremost. They held in all about seventeen hundred men. The rest remained on board.

Bougainville could discern the movement, and misjudged it, thinking that he himself was to be attacked. The tide was still flowing; and, the better to deceive him, the vessels and boats were allowed to drift upward with it for a little distance, as if to land above Cap-Rouge.

The day had been fortunate for Wolfe. Two deserters came from the camp of Bougainville with intelligence that, at ebb tide on the next night, he was to send down a convoy of provisions to Montcalm. The necessities of the camp at Beauport, and the difficulties of transportation by land, had before compelled the French to resort to this perilous means of conveying supplies; and their boats, drifting in darkness under the shadows of the northern shore, had commonly passed in safety. Wolfe saw at once that, if his own boats went down in advance of the convoy, he could turn the intelligence of the deserters to good account.

He was still on board the "Sutherland." Every preparation was made, and every order given; it only remained to wait the turning of the tide. Seated with him in the cabin was the commander of the sloop-of-war "Porcupine," his former school-fellow, John Jervis, afterwards Earl St. Vincent. Wolfe told him that he expected to die in the battle of the next day; and taking from his bosom a miniature of Miss Lowther, his betrothed, he gave it to him with a request that he would return it to her if the presentiment should prove true.[1]

Towards two o'clock the tide began to ebb, and a fresh wind blew down the river. Two lanterns were raised into the maintop shrouds of the "Sutherland." It was the appointed signal; the boats cast off and fell down with the current, those of the light infantry leading the way. The vessels with the rest of the troops had orders to follow a little later.

To look for a moment at the chances on which this bold adventure hung. First, the deserters told Wolfe that provision-boats were ordered to go down to Quebec that night; secondly, Bougainville countermanded them; thirdly, the sentries posted along the heights were told of the order, but not of the countermand;[2] fourthly, Vergor at the Anse du Foulon had permitted most of his men, chiefly Canadians from Lorette, to go home for a time and work at their harvesting, on condition, it is said, that they should afterwards work in a neighboring field of his own;[3] fifthly, he kept careless watch, and went quietly to bed; sixthly, the battalion of Guienne, ordered to take post on the Plains of Abra-

[1] Tucker, *Life of Earl St. Vincent*, I. 19. (London, 1844.)
[2] *Journal tenu à l'Armée*, etc.
[3] *Mémoires sur le Canada*, 1749–1760.

ham, had, for reasons unexplained, remained encamped by the St. Charles;[1] and lastly, when Bougainville saw Holmes's vessels drift down the stream, he did not tax his weary troops to follow them, thinking that they would return as usual with the flood tide.[2] But for these conspiring circumstances New France might have lived a little longer, and the fruitless heroism of Wolfe would have passed, with countless other heroisms, into oblivion.

For full two hours the procession of boats, borne on the current, steered silently down the St. Lawrence. The stars were visible, but the night was moonless and sufficiently dark. The General was in one of the foremost boats, and near him was a young midshipman, John Robison, afterwards professor of natural philosophy in the University of Edinburgh. He used to tell in his later life how Wolfe, with a low voice, repeated Gray's *Elegy in a Country Churchyard* to the officers about him. Probably it was to relieve the intense strain of his thoughts. Among the rest was the verse which his own fate was soon to illustrate,—

"The paths of glory lead but to the grave."

"Gentlemen," he said, as his recital ended, "I would rather have written those lines than take Quebec." None were there to tell him that the hero is greater than the poet.

As they neared their destination, the tide bore them in towards the shore, and the mighty wall of rock and forest towered in darkness on their left. The dead stillness was suddenly broken by the sharp *Qui vive!* of a French sentry, invisible in the thick gloom. *France!* answered a Highland officer of Fraser's regiment from one of the boats of the light infantry. He had served in Holland, and spoke French fluently.

À quel régiment?

De la Reine, replied the Highlander. He knew that a part of that corps was with Bougainville. The sentry, expecting the convoy of provisions, was satisfied, and did not ask for the password.

Soon after, the foremost boats were passing the heights of Samos, when another sentry challenged them, and they could see him through the darkness running down to the edge of the water, within range of a pistol-shot. In answer to his questions, the same officer replied, in French: "Provision-boats. Don't make a noise; the English will hear

[1]Foligny, *Journal mémoratif. Journal tenu à l'Armée*, etc.
[2]Johnstone, *Dialogue. Vaudreuil au Ministre, 5 Oct. 1759.*

us."[1] In fact, the sloop-of-war "Hunter" was anchored in the stream not far off. This time, again, the sentry let them pass. In a few moments they rounded the headland above the Anse du Foulon. There was no sentry there. The strong current swept the boats of the light infantry a little below the intended landing-place.[2] They disembarked on a narrow strand at the foot of heights as steep as a hill covered with trees can be. The twenty-four volunteers led the way, climbing with what silence they might, closely followed by a much larger body. When they reached the top they saw in the dim light a cluster of tents at a short distance, and immediately made a dash at them. Vergor leaped from bed and tried to run off, but was shot in the heel and captured. His men, taken by surprise, made little resistance. One or two were caught, and the rest fled.

The main body of troops waited in their boats by the edge of the strand. The heights near by were cleft by a great ravine choked with forest trees; and in its depths ran a little brook called Ruisseau St.-Denis, which, swollen by the late rains, fell plashing in the stillness over a rock. Other than this no sound could reach the strained ear of Wolfe but the gurgle of the tide and the cautious climbing of his advance-parties as they mounted the steeps at some little distance from where he sat listening. At length from the top came a sound of musket-shots, followed by loud huzzas, and he knew that his men were masters of the position. The word was given; the troops leaped from the boats and scaled the heights, some here, some there, clutching at trees and bushes, their muskets slung at their backs. Tradition still points out the place, near the mouth of the ravine, where the foremost reached the top. Wolfe said to an officer near him: "You can try it, but I don't think you'll get up." He himself, however, found strength to drag himself up with the rest. The narrow slanting path on the face of the heights had been made impassable by trenches and abattis; but all obstructions were soon cleared away, and then the ascent was easy. In the gray of the morning the long file of red-coated soldiers moved quickly upward, and formed in order on the plateau above.

Before many of them had reached the top, cannon were heard close on the left. It was the battery at Samos firing on the boats in the rear and the vessels descending from Cap-Rouge. A party was sent to silence it; this was soon effected, and the more distant battery at Sillery was

---

[1]See a note of Smollett, *History of England*, V. 56 (ed. 1805). Sergeant Johnson, Vaudreuil, Foligny, and the *Journal of Particular Transactions* give similar accounts.

[2]*Saunders to Pitt*, 20 Sept. *Journal of Sergeant Johnson*. Compare Knox, II. 67.

next attacked and taken. As fast as the boats were emptied they returned for the troops left on board the vessels and for those waiting on the southern shore under Colonel Burton.

The day broke in clouds and threatening rain. Wolfe's battalions were drawn up along the crest of the heights. No enemy was in sight, though a body of Canadians had sallied from the town and moved along the strand towards the landing-place, whence they were quickly driven back. He had achieved the most critical part of his enterprise; yet the success that he coveted placed him in imminent danger. On one side was the garrison of Quebec and the army of Beauport, and Bougainville was on the other. Wolfe's alternative was victory or ruin; for if he should be overwhelmed by a combined attack, retreat would be hopeless. His feelings no man can know; but it would be safe to say that hesitation or doubt had no part in them.

He went to reconnoitre the ground, and soon came to the Plains of Abraham, so called from Abraham Martin, a pilot known as Maître Abraham, who had owned a piece of land here in the early times of the colony. The Plains were a tract of grass, tolerably level in most parts, patched here and there with cornfields, studded with clumps of bushes, and forming a part of the high plateau at the eastern end of which Quebec stood. On the south it was bounded by the declivities along the St. Lawrence; on the north, by those along the St. Charles, or rather along the meadows through which that lazy stream crawled like a writhing snake. At the place that Wolfe chose for his battle-field the plateau was less than a mile wide.

Thither the troops advanced, marched by files till they reached the ground, and then wheeled to form their line of battle, which stretched across the plateau and faced the city. It consisted of six battalions and the detached grenadiers from Louisbourg, all drawn up in ranks three deep. Its right wing was near the brink of the heights along the St. Lawrence; but the left could not reach those along the St. Charles. On this side a wide space was perforce left open, and there was danger of being outflanked. To prevent this, Brigadier Townshend was stationed here with two battalions, drawn up at right angles with the rest, and fronting the St. Charles. The battalion of Webb's regiment, under Colonel Burton, formed the reserve; the third battalion of Royal Americans was left to guard the landing; and Howe's light infantry occupied a wood far in the rear. Wolfe, with Monckton and Murray, commanded the front line, on which the heavy fighting was to fall, and which, when all the troops had arrived, numbered less than thirty-five hundred men.[1]

[1]See Note, end of chapter.

Quebec was not a mile distant, but they could not see it; for a ridge of broken ground intervened, called Buttes-à-Neveu, about six hundred paces off. The first division of troops had scarcely come up when, about six o'clock, this ridge was suddenly thronged with white uniforms. It was the battalion of Guienne, arrived at the eleventh hour from its camp by the St. Charles. Some time after there was hot firing in the rear. It came from a detachment of Bougainville's command attacking a house where some of the light infantry were posted. The assailants were repulsed, and the firing ceased. Light showers fell at intervals, besprinkling the troops as they stood patiently waiting the event.

Montcalm had passed a troubled night. Through all the evening the cannon bellowed from the ships of Saunders, and the boats of the fleet hovered in the dusk off the Beauport shore, threatening every moment to land. Troops lined the intrenchments till day, while the General walked the field that adjoined his headquarters till one in the morning, accompanied by the Chevalier Johnstone and Colonel Poulariez. Johnstone says that he was in great agitation, and took no rest all night. At daybreak he heard the sound of cannon above the town. It was the battery at Samos firing on the English ships. He had sent an officer to the quarters of Vaudreuil, which were much nearer Quebec, with orders to bring him word at once should anything unusual happen. But no word came, and about six o'clock he mounted and rode thither with Johnstone. As they advanced, the country behind the town opened more and more upon their sight; till at length, when opposite Vaudreuil's house, they saw across the St. Charles, some two miles away, the red ranks of British soldiers on the heights beyond.

"This is a serious business," Montcalm said; and sent off Johnstone at full gallop to bring up the troops from the centre and left of the camp. Those of the right were in motion already, doubtless by the Governor's order. Vaudreuil came out of the house. Montcalm stopped for a few words with him; then set spurs to his horse, and rode over the bridge of the St. Charles to the scene of danger.[1] He rode with a fixed look, uttering not a word.[2]

The army followed in such order as it might, crossed the bridge in hot haste, passed under the northern rampart of Quebec, entered at the Palace Gate, and pressed on in headlong march along the quaint narrow streets of the warlike town: troops of Indians in scalplocks and warpaint, a savage glitter in their deep-set eyes; bands of Canadians whose all was at stake,—faith, country, and home; the colony regulars; the

---

[1]Johnstone, *Dialogue.*
[2]*Malartic à Bourlamaque,* — *Sept. 1759.*

battalions of Old France, a torrent of white uniforms and gleaming bayonets, La Sarre, Languedoc, Roussillon, Béarn,—victors of Oswego,
William Henry, and Ticonderoga. So they swept on, poured out upon
the plain, some by the gate of St. Louis, and some by that of St. John,
and hurried, breathless, to where the banners of Guienne still fluttered
on the ridge.

Montcalm was amazed at what he saw. He had expected a detachment, and he found an army. Full in sight before him stretched the
lines of Wolfe: the close ranks of the English infantry, a silent wall of
red, and the wild array of the Highlanders, with their waving tartans,
and bagpipes screaming defiance. Vaudreuil had not come; but not the
less was felt the evil of a divided authority and the jealousy of the rival
chiefs. Montcalm waited long for the forces he had ordered to join him
from the left wing of the army. He waited in vain. It is said that the
Governor had detained them, lest the English should attack the Beauport shore. Even if they did so, and succeeded, the French might defy
them, could they but put Wolfe to rout on the Plains of Abraham.
Neither did the garrison of Quebec come to the aid of Montcalm. He
sent to Ramesay, its commander, for twenty-five field-pieces which
were on the Palace battery. Ramesay would give him only three, saying
that he wanted them for his own defence. There were orders and
counter-orders; misunderstanding, haste, delay, perplexity.

Montcalm and his chief officers held a council of war. It is said that
he and they alike were for immediate attack. His enemies declare that
he was afraid lest Vaudreuil should arrive and take command; but the
Governor was not a man to assume responsibility at such a crisis. Others say that his impetuosity overcame his better judgment; and of this
charge it is hard to acquit him. Bougainville was but a few miles
distant, and some of his troops were much nearer; a messenger sent
by way of Old Lorette could have reached him in an hour and a half
at most, and a combined attack in front and rear might have been
concerted with him. If, moreover, Montcalm could have come to an
understanding with Vaudreuil, his own force might have been strengthened by two or three thousand additional men from the town and the
camp of Beauport; but he felt that there was no time to lose, for he
imagined that Wolfe would soon be reinforced, which was impossible,
and he believed that the English were fortifying themselves, which was
no less an error. He has been blamed not only for fighting too soon,
but for fighting at all. In this he could not choose. Fight he must, for
Wolfe was now in a position to cut off all his supplies. His men were
full of ardor, and he resolved to attack before their ardor cooled. He
spoke a few words to them in his keen, vehement way. "I remember

very well how he looked," one of the Canadians, then a boy of eighteen, used to say in his old age; "he rode a black or dark bay horse along the front of our lines, brandishing his sword, as if to excite us to do our duty. He wore a coat with wide sleeves, which fell back as he raised his arm, and showed the white linen of the wristband."[1]

The English waited the result with a composure which, if not quite real, was at least well feigned. The three field-pieces sent by Ramesay plied them with canister-shot, and fifteen hundred Canadians and Indians fusilladed them in front and flank. Over all the plain, from behind bushes and knolls and the edge of cornfields, puffs of smoke sprang incessantly from the guns of these hidden marksmen. Skirmishers were thrown out before the lines to hold them in check, and the soldiers were ordered to lie on the grass to avoid the shot. The firing was liveliest on the English left, where bands of sharpshooters got under the edge of the declivity, among thickets, and behind scattered houses, whence they killed and wounded a considerable number of Townshend's men. The light infantry were called up from the rear. The houses were taken and retaken, and one or more of them was burned.

Wolfe was everywhere. How cool he was, and why his followers loved him, is shown by an incident that happened in the course of the morning. One of his captains was shot through the lungs; and on recovering consciousness he saw the General standing at his side. Wolfe pressed his hand, told him not to despair, praised his services, promised him early promotion, and sent an aide-de-camp to Monckton to beg that officer to keep the promise if he himself should fall.[2]

It was towards ten o'clock when, from the high ground on the right of the line, Wolfe saw that the crisis was near. The French on the ridge had formed themselves into three bodies, regulars in the centre, regulars and Canadians on right and left. Two field-pieces, which had been dragged up the heights at Anse du Foulon, fired on them with grapeshot, and the troops, rising from the ground, prepared to receive them. In a few moments more they were in motion. They came on rapidly, uttering loud shouts, and firing as soon as they were within range. Their ranks, ill ordered at the best, were further confused by a number of Canadians who had been mixed among the regulars, and who, after hastily firing, threw themselves on the ground to reload.[3] The British

---

[1] *Recollections of Joseph Trahan*, in *Revue Canadienne*, IV. 856.

[2] Sir Denis Le Marchant, cited by Wright, 579. Le Marchant knew the captain in his old age. Monckton kept Wolfe's promise.

[3] "Les Canadiens, qui étaient mêlés dans les bataillons, se pressèrent de tirer et, dès qu'ils l'eussent fait, de mettre ventre à terre pour charger, ce qui rompit tout l'ordre." *Malartic à Bourlamaque, 25 Sept. 1759.*

advanced a few rods; then halted and stood still. When the French were within forty paces the word of command rang out, and a crash of musketry answered all along the line. The volley was delivered with remarkable precision. In the battalions of the centre, which had suffered least from the enemy's bullets, the simultaneous explosion was afterwards said by French officers to have sounded like a cannon-shot. Another volley followed, and then a furious clattering fire that lasted but a minute or two. When the smoke rose, a miserable sight was revealed: the ground cumbered with dead and wounded, the advancing masses stopped short and turned into a frantic mob, shouting, cursing, gesticulating. The order was given to charge. Then over the field rose the British cheer, mixed with the fierce yell of the Highland slogan. Some of the corps pushed forward with the bayonet; some advanced firing. The clansmen drew their broadswords and dashed on, keen and swift as bloodhounds. At the English right, though the attacking column was broken to pieces, a fire was still kept up, chiefly, it seems, by sharpshooters from the bushes and cornfields, where they had lain for an hour or more. Here Wolfe himself led the charge, at the head of the Louisbourg grenadiers. A shot shattered his wrist. He wrapped his handkerchief about it and kept on. Another shot struck him, and he still advanced, when a third lodged in his breast. He staggered, and sat on the ground. Lieutenant Brown, of the grenadiers, one Henderson, a volunteer in the same company, and a private soldier, aided by an officer of artillery who ran to join them, carried him in their arms to the rear. He begged them to lay him down. They did so, and asked if he would have a surgeon. "There's no need," he answered; "it's all over with me." A moment after, one of them cried out: "They run; see how they run!" "Who run?" Wolfe demanded, like a man roused from sleep. "The enemy, sir. Egad, they give way everywhere!" "Go, one of you, to Colonel Burton," returned the dying man; "tell him to march Webb's regiment down to Charles River, to cut off their retreat from the bridge." Then, turning on his side, he murmured, "Now, God be praised, I will die in peace!" and in a few moments his gallant soul had fled.

Montcalm, still on horseback, was borne with the tide of fugitives towards the town. As he approached the walls a shot passed through his body. He kept his seat; two soldiers supported him, one on each side, and led his horse through the St. Louis Gate. On the open space within, among the excited crowd, were several women, drawn, no doubt, by eagerness to know the result of the fight. One of them recognized him, saw the streaming blood, and shrieked, *"O mon Dieu! mon*

Dieu! le Marquis est tué!" "It's nothing, it's nothing," replied the death-stricken man; "don't be troubled for me, my good friends." (*"Ce n'est rien, ce n'est rien; ne vous affligez pas pour moi, mes bonnes amies."*)

NOTE.—There are several contemporary versions of the dying words of Wolfe. The report of Knox, given above, is by far the best attested. Knox says that he took particular pains at the time to learn them accurately from those who were with Wolfe when they were uttered.

The anecdote of Montcalm is due to the late Hon. Malcolm Fraser, of Quebec. He often heard it in his youth from an old woman, who, when a girl, was one of the group who saw the wounded general led by, and to whom the words were addressed.

Force of the English and French at the Battle of Quebec.—The tabular return given by Knox shows the number of officers and men in each corps engaged. According to this, the battalions as they stood on the Plains of Abraham before the battle varied in strength from 322 (Monckton's) to 683 (Webb's), making a total of 4,828, including officers. But another return, less specific, signed *George Townshend, Brigadier,* makes the entire number only 4,441. Townshend succeeded Wolfe in the command; and this return, which is preserved in the Public Record Office, was sent to London a few days after the battle. Some French writers present put the number lower, perhaps for the reason that Webb's regiment and the third battalion of Royal Americans took no part in the fight, the one being in the rear as a reserve, and the other also invisible, guarding the landing place. Wolfe's front line, which alone met and turned the French attack, was made up as follows, the figures including officers and men:—

Thirty-fifth Regiment	519	Twenty-eighth Regiment	421
Fifty-eighth "	335	Forty-seventh "	360
Seventy-eighth "	662	Forty-third "	327
Louisbourg Grenadiers	241	Light Infantry	400

Making a total of 3,265.

The French force engaged cannot be precisely given. Knox, on information received from "an intelligent Frenchman," states the number, corps by corps, the aggregate being 7,520. This, on examination, plainly appears exaggerated. Fraser puts it at 5,000; Townshend at 4,470, including militia. Bigot says, 3,500, which may perhaps be as many as actually advanced to the attack, since some of the militia held back. Including Bougainville's command, the militia and artillerymen left in the Beauport camp, the sailors at the town batteries, and the garrison of Quebec, at least as many of the French were out of the battle as were in it; and the numbers engaged on each side seem to have been about equal.

For authorities of the foregoing chapter, see Appendix I.

28

Fall of Quebec

1759

AFTER THE BATTLE · CANADIANS RESIST THE PURSUIT · ARRIVAL OF
VAUDREUIL · SCENE IN THE REDOUBT · PANIC · MOVEMENTS OF THE
VICTORS · VAUDREUIL'S COUNCIL OF WAR · PRECIPITATE RETREAT OF
THE FRENCH ARMY · LAST HOURS OF MONTCALM · HIS DEATH AND
BURIAL · QUEBEC ABANDONED TO ITS FATE · DESPAIR OF THE GARRISON ·
LÉVIS JOINS THE ARMY · ATTEMPTS TO RELIEVE THE TOWN · SURRENDER ·
THE BRITISH OCCUPY QUEBEC · SLANDERS OF VAUDREUIL · RECEPTION IN
ENGLAND OF THE NEWS OF WOLFE'S VICTORY AND DEATH · PREDICTION
OF JONATHAN MAYHEW

"Never was rout more complete than that of our
army," says a French official.[1] It was the more so
because Montcalm held no troops in reserve, but launched his whole
force at once against the English. Nevertheless there was some resistance to the pursuit. It came chiefly from the Canadians, many of
whom had not advanced with the regulars to the attack. Those on the
right wing, instead of doing so, threw themselves into an extensive
tract of bushes that lay in front of the English left; and from this cover
they opened a fire, too distant for much effect, till the victors advanced
in their turn, when the shot of the hidden marksmen told severely upon

[1] *Daine au Ministre, 9 Oct. 1759.*

them. Two battalions, therefore, deployed before the bushes, fired volleys into them, and drove their occupants out.

Again, those of the Canadians who, before the main battle began, attacked the English left from the brink of the plateau towards the St. Charles, withdrew when the rout took place, and ran along the edge of the declivity till, at the part of it called Côte Ste.-Geneviève, they came to a place where it was overgrown with thickets. Into these they threw themselves; and were no sooner under cover than they faced about to fire upon the Highlanders, who presently came up. As many of these mountaineers, according to their old custom, threw down their muskets when they charged, and had no weapons but their broadswords, they tried in vain to dislodge the marksmen, and suffered greatly in the attempt. Other troops came to their aid, cleared the thickets, after stout resistance, and drove their occupants across the meadow to the bridge of boats. The conduct of the Canadians at the Côte Ste.-Geneviève went far to atone for the shortcomings of some of them on the battle-field.

A part of the fugitives escaped into the town by the gates of St. Louis and St. John, while the greater number fled along the front of the ramparts, rushed down the declivity to the suburb of St. Roch, and ran over the meadows to the bridge, protected by the cannon of the town and the two armed hulks in the river. The rout had but just begun when Vaudreuil crossed the bridge from the camp of Beauport. It was four hours since he first heard the alarm, and his quarters were not much more than two miles from the battle-field. He does not explain why he did not come sooner; it is certain that his coming was well timed to throw the blame on Montcalm in case of defeat, or to claim some of the honor for himself in case of victory. "Monsieur the Marquis of Montcalm," he says, "unfortunately made his attack before I had joined him."[1] His joining him could have done no good; for though he had at last brought with him the rest of the militia from the Beauport camp, they had come no farther than the bridge over the St. Charles, having, as he alleges, been kept there by an unauthorized order from the chief of staff, Montreuil.[2] He declares that the regulars were in such a fright that he could not stop them; but that the Canadians listened to his voice, and that it was he who rallied them at the Côte Ste.-Geneviève. Of this the evidence is his own word. From other accounts it would appear that the Canadians rallied themselves. Vaudreuil lost

[1] *Vaudreuil au Ministre, 21 Sept. 1759.*
[2] *Ibid., 5 Oct. 1759.*

no time in recrossing the bridge and joining the militia in the redoubt at the farther end, where a crowd of fugitives soon poured in after him.

The aide-de-camp Johnstone, mounted on horseback, had stopped for a moment in what is now the suburb of St. John to encourage some soldiers who were trying to save a cannon that had stuck fast in a marshy hollow; when, on spurring his horse to the higher ground, he saw within musket-shot a long line of British troops, who immediately fired upon him. The bullets whistled about his ears, tore his clothes, and wounded his horse; which, however, carried him along the edge of the declivity to a windmill, near which was a roadway to a bakehouse on the meadow below. He descended, crossed the meadow, reached the bridge, and rode over it to the great redoubt or hornwork that guarded its head.

The place was full of troops and Canadians in a wild panic. "It is impossible," says Johnstone, "to imagine the disorder and confusion I found in the hornwork. Consternation was general. M. de Vaudreuil listened to everybody, and was always of the opinion of him who spoke last. On the appearance of the English troops on the plain by the bakehouse, Montguet and La Motte, two old captains in the regiment of Béarn, cried out with vehemence to M. de Vaudreuil 'that the hornwork would be taken in an instant by assault, sword in hand; that we all should be cut to pieces without quarter; and that nothing would save us but an immediate and general capitulation of Canada, giving it up to the English.' "[1] Yet the river was wide and deep, and the hornwork was protected on the water side by strong palisades, with cannon. Nevertheless there rose a general cry to cut the bridge of boats. By doing so more than half the army, who had not yet crossed, would have been sacrificed. The axemen were already at work, when they were stopped by some officers who had not lost their wits.

"M. de Vaudreuil," pursues Johnstone, "was closeted in a house in the inside of the hornwork with the Intendant and some other persons. I suspected they were busy drafting the articles for a general capitulation, and I entered the house, where I had only time to see the Intendant, with a pen in his hand, writing upon a sheet of paper, when M. de Vaudreuil told me I had no business there. Having answered him that what he had said was true, I retired immediately, in wrath to see them intent on giving up so scandalously a dependency for the preser-

---

[1] Confirmed by *Journal tenu à l'Armée*, etc. "Divers officiers des troupes de terre n'hésitèrent point à dire, tout haut en présence du soldat, qu'il ne nous restoit d'autre ressource que celle de capituler promptement pour toute la colonie," etc.

vation of which so much blood and treasure had been expended." On going out he met Lieutenant-colonels Dalquier and Poulariez, whom he begged to prevent the apprehended disgrace; and, in fact, if Vaudreuil really meant to capitulate for the colony, he was presently dissuaded by firmer spirits than his own.

Johnstone, whose horse could carry him no farther, set out on foot for Beauport, and, in his own words, "continued sorrowfully jogging on, with a very heavy heart for the loss of my dear friend M. de Montcalm, sinking with weariness, and lost in reflection upon the changes which Providence had brought about in the space of three or four hours."

Great indeed were these changes. Montcalm was dying; his second in command, the Brigadier Senezergues, was mortally wounded; the army, routed and demoralized, was virtually without a head; and the colony, yesterday cheered as on the eve of deliverance, was plunged into sudden despair. "Ah, what a cruel day!" cries Bougainville; "how fatal to all that was dearest to us! My heart is torn in its most tender parts. We shall be fortunate if the approach of winter saves the country from total ruin."[1]

The victors were fortifying themselves on the field of battle. Like the French, they had lost two generals; for Monckton, second in rank, was disabled by a musket-shot, and the command had fallen upon Townshend at the moment when the enemy were in full flight. He had recalled the pursuers, and formed them again in line of battle, knowing that another foe was at hand. Bougainville, in fact, appeared at noon from Cap-Rouge with about two thousand men; but withdrew on seeing double that force prepared to receive him. He had not heard till eight o'clock that the English were on the Plains of Abraham; and the delay of his arrival was no doubt due to his endeavors to collect as many as possible of his detachments posted along the St. Lawrence for many miles towards Jacques-Cartier.

Before midnight the English had made good progress in their redoubts and intrenchments, had brought cannon up the heights to defend them, planted a battery on the Côte Ste.-Geneviève, descended into the meadows of the St. Charles, and taken possession of the General Hospital, with its crowds of sick and wounded. Their victory had cost them six hundred and sixty-four of all ranks, killed, wounded, and missing. The French loss is placed by Vaudreuil at about six hundred and forty, and by the English official reports at about fifteen hundred.

---

[1] *Bougainville à Bourlamaque, 18 Sept. 1759.*

Measured by the numbers engaged, the battle of Quebec was but a heavy skirmish; measured by results, it was one of the great battles of the world.

Vaudreuil went from the hornwork to his quarters on the Beauport road and called a council of war. It was a tumultuous scene. A letter was despatched to Quebec to ask advice of Montcalm. The dying General sent a brief message to the effect that there was a threefold choice,—to fight again, retreat to Jacques-Cartier, or give up the colony. There was much in favor of fighting. When Bougainville had gathered all his force from the river above, he would have three thousand men; and these, joined to the garrison of Quebec, the sailors at the batteries, and the militia and artillerymen of the Beauport camp, would form a body of fresh soldiers more than equal to the English then on the Plains of Abraham. Add to these the defeated troops, and the victors would be greatly outnumbered.[1] Bigot gave his voice for fighting. Vaudreuil expressed himself to the same effect; but he says that all the officers were against him. "In vain I remarked to these gentlemen that we were superior to the enemy, and should beat them if we managed well. I could not at all change their opinion, and my love for the service and for the colony made me subscribe to the views of the council. In fact, if I had attacked the English against the advice of all the principal officers, their ill-will would have exposed me to the risk of losing the battle and the colony also."[2]

It was said at the time that the officers voted for retreat because they thought Vaudreuil unfit to command an army, and, still more, to fight a battle.[3] There was no need, however, to fight at once. The object of the English was to take Quebec, and that of Vaudreuil should have been to keep it. By a march of a few miles he could have joined Bougainville; and by then intrenching himself at or near Ste.-Foy he would have placed a greatly superior force in the English rear, where his position might have been made impregnable. Here he might be easily furnished with provisions, and from hence he could readily throw men and supplies into Quebec, which the English were too few to invest.

[1]Bigot, as well as Vaudreuil, sets Bougainville's force at three thousand. "En réunissant le corps de M. de Bougainville, les bataillons de Montréal [laissés au camp de Beauport] et la garnison de la ville, il nous restoit encore près de 5,000 hommes de troupes fraîches." Journal tenu à l'Armée. Vaudreuil says that there were fifteen hundred men in garrison at Quebec who did not take part in the battle. If this is correct, the number of fresh troops after it was not five thousand, but more than six thousand; to whom the defeated force is to be added, making, after deducting killed and wounded, some ten thousand in all.
[2]Vaudreuil au Ministre, 5 Oct. 1759.
[3]Mémoires sur le Canada, 1749–1760.

He could harass the besiegers, or attack them, should opportunity offer, and either raise the siege or so protract it that they would be forced by approaching winter to sail homeward, robbed of the fruit of their victory.

At least he might have taken a night for reflection. He was safe behind the St. Charles. The English, spent by fighting, toil, and want of sleep, were in no condition to disturb him. A part of his own men were in deadly need of rest; the night would have brought refreshment, and the morning might have brought wise counsel. Vaudreuil would not wait, and orders were given at once for retreat.[1] It began at nine o'clock that evening. Quebec was abandoned to its fate. The cannon were left in the lines of Beauport, the tents in the encampments, and provisions enough in the storehouses to supply the army for a week. "The loss of the Marquis de Montcalm," says a French officer then on the spot, "robbed his successors of their senses, and they thought of nothing but flight; such was their fear that the enemy would attack the intrenchments the next day. The army abandoned the camp in such disorder that the like was never known."[2] "It was not a retreat," says Johnstone, who was himself a part of it, "but an abominable flight, with such disorder and confusion that, had the English known it, three hundred men sent after us would have been sufficient to cut all our army to pieces. The soldiers were all mixed, scattered, dispersed, and running as hard as they could, as if the English army were at their heels." They passed Charlesbourg, Lorette, and St. Augustin, till, on the fifteenth, they found rest on the impregnable hill of Jacques-Cartier, by the brink of the St. Lawrence, thirty miles from danger.

In the night of humiliation when Vaudreuil abandoned Quebec, Montcalm was breathing his last within its walls. When he was brought wounded from the field, he was placed in the house of the Surgeon Arnoux, who was then with Bourlamaque at Isle-aux-Noix, but whose younger brother, also a surgeon, examined the wound and pronounced it mortal. "I am glad of it," Montcalm said quietly; and then asked how long he had to live. "Twelve hours, more or less," was the reply. "So much the better," he returned. "I am happy that I shall not live to see the surrender of Quebec." He is reported to have said that since he had lost the battle it consoled him to have been defeated by so brave an enemy; and some of his last words were in praise of his successor, Lévis,

[1] *Livre d'Ordres, Ordre du 13 Sept. 1759.*
[2] Foligny, *Journal mémoratif.*

for whose talents and fitness for command he expressed high esteem. When Vaudreuil sent to ask his opinion, he gave it; but when Ramesay, commandant of the garrison, came to receive his orders, he replied: "I will neither give orders nor interfere any further. I have much business that must be attended to, of greater moment than your ruined garrison and this wretched country. My time is very short; therefore pray leave me. I wish you all comfort, and to be happily extricated from your present perplexities." Nevertheless he thought to the last of those who had been under his command, and sent the following note to Brigadier Townshend: "Monsieur, the humanity of the English sets my mind at peace concerning the fate of the French prisoners and the Canadians. Feel towards them as they have caused me to feel. Do not let them perceive that they have changed masters. Be their protector as I have been their father."[1]

Bishop Pontbriand, himself fast sinking with mortal disease, attended his death-bed and administered the last sacraments. He died peacefully at four o'clock on the morning of the fourteenth. He was in his forty-eighth year.

In the confusion of the time no workman could be found to make a coffin, and an old servant of the Ursulines, known as Bonhomme Michel, gathered a few boards and nailed them together so as to form a rough box. In it was laid the body of the dead soldier; and late in the evening of the same day he was carried to his rest. There was no tolling of bells or firing of cannon. The officers of the garrison followed the bier, and some of the populace, including women and children, joined the procession as it moved in dreary silence along the dusky street, shattered with cannon-ball and bomb, to the chapel of the Ursuline convent. Here a shell, bursting under the floor, had made a cavity which had been hollowed into a grave. Three priests of the Cathedral, several nuns, Ramesay with his officers, and a throng of townspeople were present at the rite. After the service and the chant, the body was lowered into the grave by the light of torches; and then, says the chronicle, "the tears and sobs burst forth. It seemed as if the last hope of the colony were buried with the remains of the General."[2] In truth, the funeral of Montcalm was the funeral of New France.[3]

It was no time for grief. The demands of the hour were too exigent and stern. When, on the morning after the battle, the people of Que-

---

[1] I am indebted to Abbé Bois for a copy of this note. The last words of Montcalm, as above, are reported partly by Johnstone, and partly by Knox.

[2] *Ursulines de Québec*, III. 10.

[3] See Appendix J.

bec saw the tents standing in the camp of Beauport, they thought the army still there to defend them.[1] Ramesay knew that the hope was vain. On the evening before, Vaudreuil had sent two hasty notes to tell him of his flight. "The position of the enemy," wrote the Governor, "becomes stronger every instant; and this, with other reasons, obliges me to retreat." "I have received all your letters. As I set out this moment, I pray you not to write again. You shall hear from me to-morrow. I wish you good evening." With these notes came the following order: "M. de Ramesay is not to wait till the enemy carries the town by assault. As soon as provisions fail, he will raise the white flag." This order was accompanied by a memorandum of terms which Ramesay was to ask of the victors.[2]

"What a blow for me," says the unfortunate commandant, "to find myself abandoned so soon by the army, which alone could defend the town!" His garrison consisted of between one and two hundred troops of the line, some four or five hundred colony troops, a considerable number of sailors, and the local militia.[3] These last were in a state of despair. The inhabitants who, during the siege, had sought refuge in the suburb of St. Roch, had returned after the battle, and there were now twenty-six hundred women and children, with about a thousand invalids and other non-combatants to be supported, though the provisions in the town, even at half rations, would hardly last a week. Ramesay had not been informed that a good supply was left in the camps of Beauport; and when he heard at last that it was there, and sent out parties to get it, they found that the Indians and the famished country people had carried it off.

"Despondency," he says again, "was complete; discouragement extreme and universal. Murmurs and complaints against the army that had abandoned us rose to a general outcry. I could not prevent the merchants, all of whom were officers of the town militia, from meeting at the house of M. Daine, the mayor. There they declared for capitulating, and presented me a petition to that effect, signed by M. Daine and all the principal citizens."

Ramesay called a council of war. One officer alone, Fiedmont, captain of artillery, was for reducing the rations still more, and holding out to the last. All the others gave their voices for capitulation.[4] Ramesay

---

[1] *Mémoire du Sieur de Ramesay.*

[2] *Mémoire pour servir d'Instruction à M. de Ramesay, 13 Sept. 1759.* Appended, with the foregoing notes, to the *Mémoire de Ramesay.*

[3] The English returns give a total of 615 French regulars in the place besides sailors and militia.

[4] *Copie du Conseil de Guerre tenu par M. de Ramesay à Québec, 15 Sept. 1759.*

might have yielded without dishonor; but he still held out till an event fraught with new hope took place at Jacques-Cartier.

This event was the arrival of Lévis. On the afternoon of the battle Vaudreuil took one rational step; he sent a courier to Montreal to summon that able officer to his aid.[1] Lévis set out at once, reached Jacques-Cartier, and found his worst fears realized. "The great number of fugitives that I began to meet at Three Rivers prepared me for the disorder in which I found the army. I never in my life knew the like of it. They left everything behind in the camp at Beauport; tents, baggage, and kettles."

He spoke his mind freely; loudly blamed the retreat, and urged Vaudreuil to march back with all speed to whence he came.[2] The Governor, stiff at ordinary times, but pliant at a crisis, welcomed the firmer mind that decided for him, consented that the troops should return, and wrote afterwards in his despatch to the Minister: "I was much charmed to find M. de Lévis disposed to march with the army towards Quebec."[3]

Lévis, on his part, wrote: "The condition in which I found the army, bereft of everything, did not discourage me, because M. de Vaudreuil told me that Quebec was not taken, and that he had left there a sufficiently numerous garrison; I therefore resolved, in order to repair the fault that had been committed, to engage M. de Vaudreuil to march the army back to the relief of the place. I represented to him that this was the only way to prevent the complete defection of the Canadians and Indians; that our knowledge of the country would enable us to approach very near the enemy, whom we knew to be intrenching themselves on the heights of Quebec and constructing batteries to breach the walls; that if we found their army ill posted, we could attack them, or, at any rate, could prolong the siege by throwing men and supplies into the town; and that if we could not save it, we could evacuate and burn it, so that the enemy could not possibly winter there."[4]

Lévis quickly made his presence felt in the military chaos about him. Bigot bestirred himself with his usual vigor to collect provisions; and before the next morning all was ready.[5] Bougainville had taken no part in the retreat, but sturdily held his ground at Cap-Rouge while the fugitive mob swept by him. A hundred of the mounted Canadians who

---

[1] *Lévis à Bourlamaque, 15 Sept. 1759. Lévis, Guerre du Canada.*

[2] *Bigot au Ministre, 15 Oct. 1759. Malartic à Bourlamaque, 28 Sept. 1759.*

[3] "Je fus bien charmé," etc. *Vaudreuil au Ministre, 5 Oct. 1759.*

[4] *Lévis au Ministre, 10 Nov. 1759.*

[5] *Livre d'Ordres, Ordre du 17–18 Sept. 1759.*

formed part of his command were now sent to Quebec, each with a bag of biscuit across his saddle. They were to circle round to the Beauport side, where there was no enemy, and whence they could cross the St. Charles in canoes to the town. Bougainville followed close with a larger supply. Vaudreuil sent Ramesay a message, revoking his order to surrender if threatened with assault, telling him to hold out to the last, and assuring him that the whole army was coming to his relief. Lévis hastened to be gone; but first he found time to write a few lines to Bourlamaque. "We have had a very great loss, for we have lost M. de Montcalm. I regret him as my general and my friend. I found our army here. It is now on the march to retrieve our fortunes. I can trust you to hold your position; as I have not M. de Montcalm's talents, I look to you to second me and advise me. Put a good face on it. Hide this business as long as you can. I am mounting my horse this moment. Write me all the news."[1]

The army marched that morning, the eighteenth. In the evening it reached St. Augustin; and here it was stopped by the chilling news that Quebec had surrendered.

Utter confusion had reigned in the disheartened garrison. Men deserted hourly, some to the country, and some to the English camp; while Townshend pushed his trenches nearer and nearer to the walls, in spite of the cannonade with which Fiedmont and his artillerymen tried to check them. On the evening of the seventeenth, the English ships of war moved towards the Lower Town, and a column of troops was seen approaching over the meadows of the St. Charles, as if to storm the Palace Gate. The drums beat the alarm; but the militia refused to fight. Their officers came to Ramesay in a body; declared that they had no mind to sustain an assault; that they knew he had orders against it; that they would carry their guns back to the arsenal; that they were no longer soldiers, but citizens; that if the army had not abandoned them they would fight with as much spirit as ever; but that they would not get themselves killed to no purpose. The town-major, Joannès, in a rage, beat two of them with the flat of his sword.

The white flag was raised; Joannès pulled it down, thinking, or pretending to think, that it was raised without authority; but Ramesay presently ordered him to go to the English camp and get what terms he could. He went, through driving rain, to the quarters of Townshend, and, in hope of the promised succor, spun out the negotiation to the utmost, pretended that he had no power to yield certain points de-

---

[1] *Lévis à Bourlamaque, 18 Sept. 1759.*

manded, and was at last sent back to confer with Ramesay, under a promise from the English commander that, if Quebec were not given up before eleven o'clock, he would take it by storm. On this Ramesay signed the articles, and Joannès carried them back within the time prescribed. Scarcely had he left the town, when the Canadian horsemen appeared with their sacks of biscuit and a renewed assurance that help was near; but it was too late. Ramesay had surrendered, and would not break his word. He dreaded an assault, which he knew he could not withstand, and he but half believed in the promised succor. "How could I trust it?" he asks. "The army had not dared to face the enemy before he had fortified himself; and could I hope that it would come to attack him in an intrenched camp, defended by a formidable artillery?" Whatever may be thought of his conduct, it was to Vaudreuil, and not to him, that the loss of Quebec was due.

The conditions granted were favorable, for Townshend knew the danger of his position, and was glad to have Quebec on any terms. The troops and sailors of the garrison were to march out of the place with the honors of war, and to be carried to France. The inhabitants were to have protection in person and property, and free exercise of religion.[1]

In the afternoon a company of artillerymen with a field-piece entered the town, and marched to the place of arms, followed by a body of infantry. Detachments took post at all the gates. The British flag was raised on the heights near the top of Mountain Street, and the capital of New France passed into the hands of its hereditary foes. The question remained, should they keep, or destroy it? It was resolved to keep it at every risk. The marines, the grenadiers from Louisbourg, and some of the rangers were to reimbark in the fleet; while the ten battalions, with the artillery and one company of rangers, were to remain behind, bide the Canadian winter, and defend the ruins of Quebec against the efforts of Lévis. Monckton, the oldest brigadier, was disabled by his wound, and could not stay; while Townshend returned home, to parade his laurels and claim more than his share of the honors of victory.[2] The command, therefore, rested with Murray.

The troops were not idle. Levelling their own field-works, repairing the defences of the town, storing provisions sent ashore from the fleet, making fascines, and cutting firewood, busied them through the autumn

[1] *Articles de Capitulation*, 18 Sept. 1759.
[2] *Letter to an Honourable Brigadier-General* [Townshend], printed in 1760. A *Refutation* soon after appeared, angry, but not conclusive. Other replies will be found in the *Imperial Magazine* for 1760.

days bright with sunshine, or dark and chill with premonition of the bitter months to come. Admiral Saunders put off his departure longer than he had once thought possible; and it was past the middle of October when he fired a parting salute, and sailed down the river with his fleet. In it was the ship "Royal William," carrying the embalmed remains of Wolfe.

Montcalm lay in his soldier's grave before the humble altar of the Ursulines, never more to see the home for which he yearned, the wife, mother, and children whom he loved, the olive-trees and chestnut-groves of his beloved Candiac. He slept in peace among triumphant enemies, who respected his memory, though they hardly knew his resting-place. It was left for a fellow-countryman—a colleague and a brother-in-arms—to belittle his achievements and blacken his name. The jealous spite of Vaudreuil pursued him even in death. Leaving Lévis to command at Jacques-Cartier, whither the army had again withdrawn, the Governor retired to Montreal, whence he wrote a series of despatches to justify himself at the expense of others, and above all of the slain general, against whom his accusations were never so bitter as now, when the lips were cold that could have answered them. First, he threw on Ramesay all the blame of the surrender of Quebec. Then he addressed himself to his chief task, the defamation of his unconscious rival. "The letter that you wrote in cipher, on the tenth of February, to Monsieur the Marquis of Montcalm and me, in common,[1] flattered his self-love to such a degree that, far from seeking conciliation, he did nothing but try to persuade the public that his authority surpassed mine. From the moment of Monsieur de Montcalm's arrival in this colony, down to that of his death, he did not cease to sacrifice everything to his boundless ambition. He sowed dissension among the troops, tolerated the most indecent talk against the government, attached to himself the most disreputable persons, used means to corrupt the most virtuous, and, when he could not succeed, became their cruel enemy. He wanted to be Governor-General. He privately flattered with favors and promises of patronage every officer of the colony troops who adopted his ideas. He spared no pains to gain over the people of whatever calling, and persuade them of his attachment; while, either by himself or by means of the troops of the line, he made them bear the most frightful yoke (*le joug le plus affreux*). He defamed honest people, encouraged insubordination, and closed his eyes to the rapine of his soldiers."

[1] See *ante*, p. 402.

This letter was written to Vaudreuil's official superior and confidant, the Minister of the Marine and Colonies. In another letter, written about the same time to the Minister of War, who held similar relations to his rival, he declares that he "greatly regretted Monsieur de Montcalm."[1]

His charges are strange ones from a man who was by turns the patron, advocate, and tool of the official villains who cheated the King and plundered the people. Bigot, Cadet, and the rest of the harpies that preyed on Canada looked to Vaudreuil for support, and found it. It was but three or four weeks since he had written to the Court in high eulogy of Bigot and effusive praise of Cadet, coupled with the request that a patent of nobility should be given to that notorious public thief.[2] The corruptions which disgraced his government were rife, not only in the civil administration, but also among the officers of the colony troops, over whom he had complete control. They did not, as has been seen already, extend to the officers of the line, who were outside the circle of peculation. It was these who were the habitual associates of Montcalm; and when Vaudreuil charges him with "attaching to himself the most disreputable persons, and using means to corrupt the most virtuous," the true interpretation of his words is that the former were disreputable because they disliked him (the Governor), and the latter virtuous because they were his partisans.

Vaudreuil continues thus: "I am in despair, Monseigneur, to be under the necessity of painting you such a portrait after death of Monsieur the Marquis of Montcalm. Though it contains the exact truth, I would have deferred it if his personal hatred to me were alone to be considered; but I feel too deeply the loss of the colony to hide from you the cause of it. I can assure you that if I had been the sole master, Quebec would still belong to the King, and that nothing is so disadvantageous in a colony as a division of authority and the mingling of troops of the line with marine [*colony*] troops. Thoroughly knowing Monsieur de Montcalm, I did not doubt in the least that unless I condescended to all his wishes, he would succeed in ruining Canada and wrecking all my plans."

He then charges the dead man with losing the battle of Quebec by attacking before he, the Governor, arrived to take command; and this, he says, was due to Montcalm's absolute determination to exercise independent authority, without caring whether the colony was saved or

---

[1] *Vaudreuil au Ministre de la Guerre,* 1 Nov. 1759.
[2] See *ante,* p. 321.

lost. "I cannot hide from you, Monseigneur, that if he had had his way in past years Oswego and Fort George [*William Henry*] would never have been attacked or taken; and he owed the success at Ticonderoga to the orders I had given him."[1] Montcalm, on the other hand, declared at the time that Vaudreuil had ordered him not to risk a battle, and that it was only through his disobedience that Ticonderoga was saved.

Ten days later Vaudreuil wrote again: "I have already had the honor, by my letter written in cipher on the thirtieth of last month, to give you a sketch of the character of Monsieur the Marquis of Montcalm; but I have just been informed of a stroke so black that I think, Monseigneur, that I should fail in my duty to you if I did not tell you of it." He goes on to say that, a little before his death, and "no doubt in fear of the fate that befell him," Montcalm placed in the hands of Father Roubaud, missionary at St. Francis, two packets of papers containing remarks on the administration of the colony, and especially on the manner in which the military posts were furnished with supplies; that these observations were accompanied by certificates; and that they involved charges against him, the Governor, of complicity in peculation. Roubaud, he continues, was to send these papers to France; "but now, Monseigneur, that you are informed about them, I feel no anxiety, and I am sure that the King will receive no impression from them without acquainting himself with their truth or falsity."

Vaudreuil's anxiety was natural; and so was the action of Montcalm in making known to the Court the outrageous abuses that threatened the King's service with ruin. His doing so was necessary, both for his own justification and for the public good; and afterwards, when Vaudreuil and others were brought to trial at Paris, and when one of the counsel for the defence charged the late general with slanderously accusing his clients, the Court ordered the charge to be struck from the record.[2] The papers the existence of which, if they did exist, so terrified Vaudreuil, have thus far escaped research. But the correspondence of the two rivals with the chiefs of the departments on which they severally depended is in large measure preserved; and while that of the Governor is filled with defamation of Montcalm and praise of himself, that of the General is neither egotistic nor abusive. The faults of Montcalm have sufficiently appeared. They were those of an impetuous, excitable, and impatient nature, by no means free from either ambition or vanity;

[1] *Vaudreuil au Ministre de la Marine, 30 Oct. 1759.*
[2] *Procès de Bigot, Cadet, et autres.*

but they were never inconsistent with the character of a man of honor. His impulsive utterances, reported by retainers and sycophants, kept Vaudreuil in a state of chronic rage; and, void as he was of all magnanimity, gnawed with undying jealousy, and mortally in dread of being compromised by the knaveries to which he had lent his countenance, he could not contain himself within the bounds of decency or sense. In another letter he had the baseness to say that Montcalm met his death in trying to escape from the English.

Among the Governor's charges are some which cannot be flatly denied. When he accuses his rival of haste and precipitation in attacking the English army, he touches a fair subject of criticism; but, as a whole, he is as false in his detraction of Montcalm as in his praises of Bigot and Cadet.

The letter which Wolfe sent to Pitt a few days before his death, written in what may be called a spirit of resolute despair, and representing success as almost hopeless, filled England with a dejection that found utterance in loud grumblings against the Ministry. Horace Walpole wrote the bad news to his friend Mann, ambassador at Florence: "Two days ago came letters from Wolfe, despairing as much as heroes can despair. Quebec is well victualled, Amherst is not arrived, and fifteen thousand men are encamped to defend it. We have lost many men by the enemy, and some by our friends; that is, we now call our nine thousand only seven thousand. How this little army will get away from a much larger, and in this season, in that country, I don't guess: yes, I do."

Hardly were these lines written when tidings came that Montcalm was defeated, Quebec taken, and Wolfe killed. A flood of mixed emotion swept over England. Even Walpole grew half serious as he sent a packet of newspapers to his friend the ambassador. "You may now give yourself what airs you please. An ambassador is the only man in the world whom bullying becomes. All precedents are on your side: Persians, Greeks, Romans, always insulted their neighbors when they took Quebec. Think how pert the French would have been on such an occasion! What a scene! An army in the night dragging itself up a precipice by stumps of trees to assault a town and attack an enemy strongly intrenched and double in numbers! The King is overwhelmed with addresses on our victories; he will have enough to paper his palace."[1]

When, in soberer mood, he wrote the annals of his time, and turned, not for the better, from the epistolary style to the historical, he thus

---

[1] *Letters of Horace Walpole,* III. 254, 257 (ed. Cunningham, 1857).

described the impression made on the English public by the touching and inspiring story of Wolfe's heroism and death: "The incidents of dramatic fiction could not be conducted with more address to lead an audience from despondency to sudden exaltation than accident prepared to excite the passions of a whole people. They despaired, they triumphed, and they wept; for Wolfe had fallen in the hour of victory. Joy, curiosity, astonishment, was painted on every countenance. The more they inquired, the more their admiration rose. Not an incident but was heroic and affecting."[1] England blazed with bonfires. In one spot alone all was dark and silent; for here a widowed mother mourned for a loving and devoted son, and the people forbore to profane her grief with the clamor of their rejoicings.

New England had still more cause of joy than Old, and she filled the land with jubilation. The pulpits resounded with sermons of thanksgiving, some of which were worthy of the occasion that called them forth. Among the rest, Jonathan Mayhew, a young but justly celebrated minister of Boston, pictured with enthusiasm the future greatness of the British-American colonies, with the continent thrown open before them, and foretold that, "with the continued blessing of Heaven, they will become, in another century or two, a mighty empire;" adding in cautious parenthesis, "*I do not mean an independent one.*" He read Wolfe's victory aright, and divined its far-reaching consequence.

---

[1]Walpole, *Memoirs of George II.*, II. 384.

NOTE.—The authorities of this chapter are, in the main, the same as those of the preceding, with some additions, the principal of which is the *Mémoire du Sieur de Ramezay, Chevalier de l'Ordre royal et militaire de St.-Louis, cy-devant Lieutenant pour le Roy commandant à Québec, au sujet de la Reddition de cette Ville, qui a été suivie de la Capitulation du 18 7ᵇʳᵉ, 1759* (Archives de la Marine). To this document are appended a number of important "pièces justificatives." These, with the *Mémoire*, have been printed by the Quebec Historical Society. The letters of Vaudreuil cited in this chapter are chiefly from the Archives Nationales.

If Montcalm, as Vaudreuil says, really intrusted papers to the care of the Jesuit missionary Roubaud, he was not fortunate in his choice of a depositary. After the war Roubaud renounced his Order, abjured his faith, and went over to the English. He gave various and contradictory accounts of the documents said to be in his hands. On one occasion he declared that Montcalm's effects left with him at his mission of St. Francis had been burned to prevent their falling into the hands of the enemy (see Verreau, *Report on Canadian Archives, 1874*, p. 183). Again, he says that he had placed in the hands of the King of England certain letters of Montcalm (see Mr. *Roubaud's Deplorable Case, humbly submitted to Lord North's Consideration*, in *Historical Magazine*, Second Series, VIII. 283). Yet again, he speaks of these same letters as "pretended" (Verreau, *as above*). He complains that some of them had been published, without his consent, "by a Lord belonging to His Majesty's household" (Mr. *Roubaud's Deplorable Case*).

The allusion here is evidently to a pamphlet printed in London, in 1777, in French and English, and entitled, *Lettres de Monsieur le Marquis de Montcalm, Gouverneur-Général en Canada, à Messieurs de Berryer et de la Molé, écrites dans les Années 1757, 1758, et 1759, avec une Version Angloise.*

They profess to be observations by Montcalm on the English colonies, their political character, their trade, and their tendency to independence. They bear the strongest marks of being fabricated to suit the times, the colonies being then in revolt. The principal letter is one addressed to Molé, and bearing date Quebec, Aug. 24, 1759. It foretells the loss of her colonies as a consequence to England of her probable conquest of Canada. I laid before the Massachusetts Historical Society my reasons for believing this letter, like the rest, an imposture (see the *Proceedings* of that Society for 1869–1870, pp. 112–128). To these reasons it may be added that at the date assigned to the letter all correspondence was stopped between Canada and France. From the arrival of the English fleet, at the end of spring, till its departure, late in autumn, communication was completely cut off. It was not till towards the end of November, when the river was clear of English ships, that the naval commander Kanon ran by the batteries of Quebec and carried to France the first news from Canada. Some of the letters thus sent were dated a month before, and had waited in Canada till Kanon's departure.

Abbé Verreau—a high authority on questions of Canadian history—tells me a comparison of the handwriting has convinced him that these pretended letters of Montcalm are the work of Roubaud.

On the burial of Montcalm, see Appendix J.

29

Sainte-Foy

1759, 1760

QUEBEC AFTER THE SIEGE · CAPTAIN KNOX AND THE NUNS · ESCAPE OF
FRENCH SHIPS · WINTER AT QUEBEC · THREATS OF LÉVIS · ATTACKS ·
SKIRMISHES · FEAT OF THE RANGERS · STATE OF THE GARRISON · THE
FRENCH PREPARE TO RETAKE QUEBEC · ADVANCE OF LÉVIS · THE ALARM
· SORTIE OF THE ENGLISH · RASH DETERMINATION OF MURRAY · BATTLE
OF STE.-FOY · RETREAT OF THE ENGLISH · LÉVIS BESIEGES QUEBEC ·
SPIRIT OF THE GARRISON · PERIL OF THEIR SITUATION · RELIEF · QUEBEC
SAVED · RETREAT OF LÉVIS · THE NEWS IN ENGLAND

The fleet was gone; the great river was left a solitude; and
the chill days of a fitful November passed over Quebec
in alternations of rain and frost, sunshine and snow. The troops, driven
by cold from their encampment on the Plains, were all gathered within
the walls. Their own artillery had so battered the place that it was not
easy to find shelter. The Lower Town was a wilderness of scorched and
crumbling walls. As you ascended Mountain Street, the Bishop's Palace, on the right, was a skeleton of tottering masonry, and the buildings on the left were a mass of ruin, where ragged boys were playing at
see-saw among the fallen planks and timbers.[1] Even in the Upper Town
few of the churches and public buildings had escaped. The Cathedral

---

[1]Drawings made on the spot by Richard Short. These drawings, twelve in number, were engraved
and published in 1761.

was burned to a shell. The solid front of the College of the Jesuits was pockmarked by numberless cannon-balls, and the adjacent church of the Order was wofully shattered. The church of the Recollets suffered still more. The bombshells that fell through the roof had broken into the pavement, and as they burst had thrown up the bones and skulls of the dead from the graves beneath.[1] Even the more distant Hôtel-Dieu was pierced by fifteen projectiles, some of which had exploded in the halls and chambers.[2]

The Commissary-General, Berniers, thus describes to Bourlamaque the state of the town: "Quebec is nothing but a shapeless mass of ruins. Confusion, disorder, pillage reign even among the inhabitants, for the English make examples of severity every day. Everybody rushes hither and thither, without knowing why. Each searches for his possessions, and, not finding his own, seizes those of other people. English and French, all is chaos alike. The inhabitants, famished and destitute, escape to the country. Never was there seen such a sight."[3]

Quebec swarmed with troops. There were guard-houses at twenty different points; sentinels paced the ramparts, squads of men went the rounds, soldiers off duty strolled the streets, some in mitre caps and some in black three-cornered hats; while a ceaseless rolling of drums and a rigid observance of military forms betrayed the sense of a still imminent danger. While some of the inhabitants left town, others remained, having no refuge elsewhere. They were civil to the victors, but severe towards their late ruler. "The citizens," says Knox, "particularly the females, reproach M. Vaudreuil upon every occasion, and give full scope to bitter invectives." He praises the agreeable manners and cheerful spirit of the Canadian ladies, concerning whom another officer also writes: "It is very surprising with what ease the gayety of their tempers enables them to bear misfortunes which to us would be insupportable. Families whom the calamities of war have reduced from the height of luxury to the want of common necessaries laugh, dance, and sing, comforting themselves with this reflection—*Fortune de guerre*. Their young ladies take the utmost pains to teach our officers French; with what view I know not, if it is not that they may hear themselves praised, flattered, and courted without loss of time."[4]

Knox was quartered in a small stable, with a hayloft above and a

[1] Short's *Views in Quebec, 1759.* Compare Pontbriand, in *N. Y. Col. Docs.*, X. 1,057.

[2] Casgrain, *Hôtel-Dieu de Québec*, 445.

[3] *Berniers à Bourlamaque, 27 Sept. 1759.*

[4] *Alexander Campbell to John Lloyd, 22 Oct. 1759.* Campbell was a lieutenant of the Highlanders; Lloyd was a Connecticut merchant.

rack and manger at one end: a lodging better than fell to the lot of many of his brother officers; and, by means of a stove and some help from a carpenter, he says that he made himself tolerably comfortable. The change, however, was an agreeable one when he was ordered for a week to the General Hospital, a mile out of the town, where he was to command the guard stationed to protect the inmates and watch the enemy. Here were gathered the sick and wounded of both armies, nursed with equal care by the nuns, of whom Knox speaks with gratitude and respect. "When our poor fellows were ill and ordered to be removed from their odious regimental hospital to this general receptacle, they were indeed rendered inexpressibly happy. Each patient has his bed, with curtains, allotted to him, and a nurse to attend him. Every sick or wounded officer has an apartment to himself, and is attended by one of these religious sisters, who in general are young, handsome, courteous, rigidly reserved, and very respectful. Their office of nursing the sick furnishes them with opportunities of taking great latitudes if they are so disposed; but I never heard any of them charged with the least levity." The nuns, on their part, were well pleased with the conduct of their new masters, whom one of them describes as the "most moderate of all conquerors."

"I lived here," Knox continues, "at the French King's table, with an agreeable, polite society of officers, directors, and commissaries. Some of the gentlemen were married, and their ladies honored us with their company. They were generally cheerful, except when we discoursed on the late revolution and the affairs of the campaign; then they seemingly gave way to grief, uttered by profound sighs, followed by an *O mon Dieu!*" He walked in the garden with the French officers, played at cards with them, and passed the time so pleasantly that his short stay at the hospital seemed an oasis in his hard life of camp and garrison.

Mère de Sainte-Claude, the Superior, a sister of Ramesay, late commandant of Quebec, one morning sent him a note of invitation to what she called an English breakfast; and though the repast answered to nothing within his experience, he says that he "fared exceedingly well, and passed near two hours most agreeably in the society of this ancient lady and her virgin sisters."

The excellent nuns of the General Hospital are to-day what their predecessors were, and the scene of their useful labors still answers at many points to that described by the careful pen of their military guest. Throughout the war they and the nuns of the Hôtel-Dieu had been above praise in their assiduous devotion to the sick and wounded.

Brigadier Murray, now in command of Quebec, was a gallant soldier, upright, humane, generous, eager for distinction, and more daring than prudent. He befriended the Canadians, issued strict orders against harming them in person or property, hanged a soldier who had robbed a citizen of Quebec, and severely punished others for slighter offences of the same sort. In general the soldiers themselves showed kindness towards the conquered people; during harvest they were seen helping them to reap their fields, without compensation, and sharing with them their tobacco and rations. The inhabitants were disarmed, and required to take the oath of allegiance. Murray reported in the spring that the whole country, from Cap-Rouge downward, was in subjection to the British Crown.[1]

Late in October it was rumored that some of the French ships in the river above Quebec were preparing to run by the batteries. This was the squadron which had arrived in the spring with supplies, and had lain all summer at Batiscan, in the Richelieu, and at other points beyond reach of the English. After nearly a month of expectancy, they at length appeared, anchored off Sillery on the twenty-first of November, and tried to pass the town on the dark night of the twenty-fourth. Seven or eight of them succeeded; four others ran aground and were set on fire by their crews, excepting one which was stranded on the south shore and abandoned. Captain Miller, with a lieutenant and above forty men, boarded her; when, apparently through their own carelessness, she blew up.[2] Most of the party were killed by the explosion, and the rest, including the two officers, were left in a horrible condition between life and death. Thus they remained till a Canadian, venturing on board in search of plunder, found them, called his neighbors to his aid, carried them to his own house, and after applying, with the utmost kindness, what simple remedies he knew, went over to Quebec and told of the disaster. Fortunately for themselves, the sufferers soon died.

December came, and brought the Canadian winter, with its fierce light and cold, glaring snowfields, and piercing blasts that scorch the cheek like a firebrand. The men were frost-bitten as they dug away the dry, powdery drifts that the wind had piled against the rampart. The sentries were relieved every hour; yet feet and fingers were continually frozen. The clothing of the troops was ill-suited to the climate, and, though stoves had been placed in the guard and barrack rooms, the supply of fuel constantly fell short. The cutting and dragging of wood was the chief task of the garrison for many weeks. Parties of axemen,

---

[1] *Murray to Pitt, 25 May, 1760.* Murray, *Journal, 1759, 1760.*
[2] *Murray to Amherst, 25 Jan. 1760.* Not, as some believed, by a train laid by the French.

strongly guarded, were always at work in the forest of Ste.-Foy, four or five miles from Quebec, and the logs were brought to town on sledges dragged by the soldiers. Eight of them were harnessed in pairs to each sledge; and as there was always danger from Indians and bushrangers, every man carried his musket slung at his back. The labor was prodigious; for frequent snowstorms made it necessary again and again to beat a fresh track through the drifts. The men bore their hardships with admirable good humor; and once a party of them on their return, dragging their load through the street, met a Canadian, also with a load of wood, which was drawn by a team of dogs harnessed much like themselves. They accosted them as yoke-fellows, comrades, and brothers; asked them what allowance of pork and rum they got; and invited them and their owner to mess at the regimental barracks.

The appearance of the troops on duty within the town, as described by Knox, was scarcely less eccentric. "Our guards on the grand parade make a most grotesque appearance in their different dresses; and our inventions to guard us against the extreme rigor of this climate are various beyond imagination. The uniformity as well as nicety of the clean, methodical soldier is buried in the rough, fur-wrought garb of the frozen Laplander; and we rather resemble a masquerade than a body of regular troops, insomuch that I have frequently been accosted by my acquaintances, whom, though their voices were familiar to me, I could not discover, or conceive who they were. Besides, every man seems to be in a continual hurry; for instead of walking soberly through the streets, we are obliged to observe a running or trotting pace."

Early in January there was a storm of sleet, followed by severe frost, which glazed the streets with ice. Knox, being ordered to mount guard in the Lower Town, found the descent of Mountain Street so slippery that it was impossible to walk down with safety, especially as the muskets of the men were loaded; and the whole party, seating themselves on the ground, slid one after another to the foot of the hill. The Highlanders, in spite of their natural hardihood, suffered more from the cold than the other troops, as their national costume was but a sorry defence against the Canadian winter. A detachment of these breechless warriors being on guard at the General Hospital, the nuns spent their scanty leisure in knitting for them long woollen hose, which they gratefully accepted, though at a loss to know whether modesty or charity inspired the gift.

From the time when the English took possession of Quebec, reports had come in through deserters that Lévis meant to attack and recover it. Early in November there was a rumor that he was about to march upon it with fifteen thousand men. In December word came that he was on his way, resolved to storm it on or about the twenty-second, and dine within the walls, under the French flag, on Christmas Day. He failed to appear; but in January a deserter said that he had prepared scaling-ladders, and was training his men to use them by assaults on mock ramparts of snow. There was more tangible evidence that the enemy was astir. Murray had established two fortified outposts, one at Ste.-Foy, and the other farther on, at Old Lorette. War-parties hovered round both, and kept the occupants in alarm. A large body of French grenadiers appeared at the latter place in February, and drove off a herd of cattle; when a detachment of rangers, much inferior in number, set upon them, put them to flight, and recovered the plunder. At the same time a party of regulars, Canadians, and Indians took up a strong position near the church at Point Levi, and sent a message to the English officers that a large company of expert hairdressers were ready to wait upon them whenever they required their services. The allusion was of course to the scalp-lifting practices of the Indians and bushrangers.

The river being now hard frozen, Murray sent over a detachment of light infantry under Major Dalling. A sharp fight ensued on the snow, around the church, and in the neighboring forest, where the English soldiers, taught to use snow-shoes by the rangers, routed the enemy, and killed or captured a considerable number. A third post was then established at the church and the priest's house adjacent. Some days after, the French came back in large numbers, fortified themselves with felled trees, and then attacked the English position. The firing being heard at Quebec, the light infantry went over to the scene of action, and Murray himself followed on the ice, with the Highlanders and other troops. Before he came up, the French drew off and retreated to their breast-work, where they were attacked and put to flight, the nimble Highlanders capturing a few, while the greater part made their escape.

As it became known that the French held a strong post at Le Calvaire, near St. Augustin, two days' march from Quebec, Captain Donald MacDonald was sent with five hundred men to attack it. He found the enemy behind a breastwork of logs protected by an abattis. The light infantry advanced and poured in a brisk fire; on which the French threw down their arms and fled. About eighty of them were captured; but their commander, Herbin, escaped, leaving to the victors his watch, hat and feather, wine, liquor-case, and mistress. The English had six men wounded and nearly a hundred frost-bitten.[1]

---

[1] Knox, II. 275. Murray, *Journal*. Fraser, *Journal*. Vaudreuil, in his usual way, multiplies the English force by three.

Captain Hazen and his rangers soon after had a notable skirmish. They were posted in a house not far from the station at Lorette. A scout came in with news that a large party of the enemy was coming to attack them; on which Hazen left a sergeant and fourteen men in the house, and set out for Lorette with the rest to ask a reinforcement. On the way he met the French, who tried to surround him; and he told his men to fall back to the house. They remonstrated, saying that they "felt spry," and wanted to show the regulars that provincials could fight as well as red-coats. Thereupon they charged the enemy, gave them a close volley of buckshot and bullets, and put them to flight; but scarcely had they reloaded their guns when they were fired upon from behind. Another body of assailants had got into their rear, in order to cut them off. They faced about, attacked them, and drove them back like the first. The two French parties then joined forces, left Hazen to pursue his march, and attacked the fourteen rangers in the house, who met them with a brisk fire. Hazen and his men heard the noise; and, hastening back, fell upon the rear of the French, while those in the house sallied and attacked them in front. They were again routed; and the rangers chased them two miles, killing six of them and capturing seven. Knox, in whose eyes provincials usually find no favor, launches this time into warm commendation of "our simply honest New England men."

Fresh reports came in from time to time that the French were gathering all their strength to recover Quebec; and late in February these stories took a definite shape. A deserter from Montreal brought Murray a letter from an officer of rangers, who was a prisoner at that place, warning him that eleven thousand men were on the point of marching to attack him. Three other deserters soon after confirmed the news, but added that the scheme had met with a check; for as it was intended to carry the town by storm, a grand rehearsal had taken place, with the help of scaling-ladders planted against the wall of a church; whereupon the Canadians rushed with such zeal to the assault that numerous broken legs, arms, and heads ensued, along with ruptures, sprains, bruises, and dislocations; insomuch, said the story, that they became disgusted with the attempt. All remained quiet till after the middle of April, when the garrison was startled by repeated assurances that at the first breaking-up of the ice all Canada would be upon them. Murray accordingly ordered the French inhabitants to leave the town within three days.[1]

In some respects the temper of the troops was excellent. In the petty

[1]*Ordonnance faite à Québec le 21 Avril, 1760, par son Excellence, Jacques Murray.*

warfare of the past winter they had generally been successful, proving themselves a match for the bushrangers and Indians on their own ground; so that, as Sergeant Johnson remarks, in his odd way, "Very often a small number of our men would put to flight a considerable party of those Cannibals." They began to think themselves invincible; yet they had the deepest cause for anxiety. The effective strength of the garrison was reduced to less than half, and of those that remained fit for duty, hardly a man was entirely free from scurvy. The rank and file had no fresh provisions; and, in spite of every precaution, this malignant disease, aided by fever and dysentery, made no less havoc among them than among the crews of Jacques Cartier at this same place two centuries before. Of about seven thousand men left at Quebec in the autumn, scarcely more than three thousand were fit for duty on the twenty-fourth of April.[1] About seven hundred had found temporary burial in the snowdrifts, as the frozen ground was impenetrable as a rock.

Meanwhile Vaudreuil was still at Montreal, where he says that he "arrived just in time to take the most judicious measures and prevent General Amherst from penetrating into the colony."[2] During the winter some of the French regulars were kept in garrison at the outposts, and the rest quartered on the inhabitants; while the Canadians were dismissed to their homes, subject to be mustered again at the call of the Governor. Both he and Lévis were full of the hope of retaking Quebec. He had spies and agents among Murray's soldiers; and though the citizens had sworn allegiance to King George, some of them were exceedingly useful to his enemies. Vaudreuil had constant information of the state of the garrison. He knew that the scurvy was his active and powerful ally, and that the hospitals and houses of Quebec were crowded with the sick. At the end of March he was informed that more than half the British were on the sick-list; and it was presently rumored that Murray had only two thousand men able to bear arms.[3] With every allowance for exaggeration in these reports, it was plain that the French could attack their invaders in overwhelming force.

The difficulty was to find means of transportation. The depth of the snow and the want of draught animals made it necessary to wait till the river should become navigable; but preparation was begun at once. Lévis was the soul of the enterprise. Provisions were gathered from far

[1] *Return of the present State of His Majesty's Forces in Garrison at Quebec, 24 April, 1760* (Public Record Office).
[2] *Vaudreuil au Ministre, 30 Oct. 1759.*
[3] *Vaudreuil au Ministre, 15 Avril, 1760.*

and near; cannon, mortars, and munitions of war were brought from the frontier posts, and butcher-knives were fitted to the muzzles of guns to serve the Canadians in place of bayonets. All the workmen about Montreal were busied in making tools and gun-carriages. Stores were impressed from the merchants; and certain articles, which could not otherwise be had, were smuggled, with extraordinary address, out of Quebec itself.[1] Early in spring the militia received orders to muster for the march. There were doubts and discontent; but, says a contemporary, "sensible people dared not speak, for if they did they were set down as English." Some there were who in secret called the scheme "Lévis' folly;" yet it was perfectly rational, well conceived, and conducted with vigor and skill. Two frigates, two sloops-of-war, and a number of smaller craft still remained in the river, under command of Vauquelin, the brave officer who had distinguished himself at the siege of Louisbourg. The stores and cannon were placed on board these vessels, the army embarked in a fleet of bateaux, and on the twentieth of April the whole set out together for the scene of action. They comprised eight battalions of troops of the line and two of colony troops; with the colonial artillery, three thousand Canadians, and four hundred Indians. When they left Montreal, their effective strength, besides Indians, is said by Lévis to have been six thousand nine hundred and ten, a number which was increased as he advanced by the garrisons of Jacques-Cartier, Déschambault, and Pointe-aux-Trembles, as well as by the Canadians on both sides of the St. Lawrence below Three Rivers; for Vaudreuil had ordered the militia captains to join his standard, with all their followers, armed and equipped, on pain of death.[2] These accessions appear to have raised his force to between eight and nine thousand.

The ice still clung to the river banks, the weather was bad, and the navigation difficult; but on the twenty-sixth the army landed at St. Augustin, crossed the river of Cap-Rouge on bridges of their own making, and moved upon the English outpost at Old Lorette. The English abandoned it and fell back to Ste.-Foy. Lévis followed. Night came on, with a gale from the southeast, a driving rain, and violent thunder, unusual at that season. The road, a bad and broken one, led through the marsh called La Suède. Causeways and bridges broke down under the weight of the marching columns and plunged the men into water,

---

[1] *Vaudreuil au Ministre, 23 Avril, 1760.*
[2] *Vaudreuil aux Capitaines de Milice, 16 Avril, 1760.* I am indebted to Abbé H. R. Casgrain for a copy of this letter.

mud, and half-thawed ice. "It was a frightful night," says Lévis; "so dark that but for the flashes of lightning we should have been forced to stop." The break of day found the vanguard at the edge of the woods bordering the farther side of the marsh. The storm had abated; and they saw before them, a few hundred yards distant, through the misty air, a ridge of rising ground on which stood the parish church of Ste.-Foy, with a row of Canadian houses stretching far to right and left. This ridge was the declivity of the plateau of Quebec; the same which as it approaches the town, some five or six miles towards the left, takes the names of Côte d'Abraham and Côte Ste.-Geneviéve. The church and the houses were occupied by British troops, who, as the French debouched from the woods, opened on them with cannon, and compelled them to fall back. Though the ridge at this point is not steep, the position was a strong one; but had Lévis known how few were as yet there to oppose him, he might have carried it by an assault in front. As it was, he resolved to wait till night, and then flank the enemy by a march to the right along the border of the wood.

It was the morning of Sunday, the twenty-seventh. Till late in the night before, Murray and the garrison of Quebec were unaware of the immediate danger; and they learned it at last through a singular stroke of fortune. Some time after midnight the watch on board the frigate "Racehorse," which had wintered in the dock at the Lower Town, heard a feeble cry of distress from the midst of the darkness that covered the St. Lawrence. Captain Macartney was at once informed of it; and, through an impulse of humanity, he ordered a boat to put out amid the drifting ice that was sweeping up the river with the tide. Guided by the faint cries, the sailors found a man lying on a large cake of ice, drenched, and half dead with cold; and, taking him with difficulty into their boat, they carried him to the ship. It was long before he was able to speak intelligibly; but at last, being revived by cordials and other remedies, he found strength to tell his benefactors that he was a sergeant of artillery in the army that had come to retake Quebec; that in trying to land a little above Cap-Rouge, his boat had been overset, his companions drowned, and he himself saved by climbing upon the cake of ice where they had discovered him; that he had been borne by the ebb tide down to the Island of Orleans, and then brought up to Quebec by the flow; and, finally, that Lévis was marching on the town with twelve thousand men at his back.

He was placed in a hammock and carried up Mountain Street to the quarters of the General, who was roused from sleep at three o'clock in the morning to hear his story. The troops were ordered under arms; and soon after daybreak Murray marched out with ten pieces of cannon and more than half the garrison. His principal object was to withdraw the advanced posts at Ste.-Foy, Cap-Rouge, Sillery, and Anse du Foulon. The storm had turned to a cold, drizzling rain, and the men, as they dragged their cannon through snow and mud, were soon drenched to the skin. On reaching Ste.-Foy, they opened a brisk fire from the heights upon the woods which now covered the whole army of Lévis; and being rejoined by the various outposts, returned to Quebec in the afternoon, after blowing up the church, which contained a store of munitions that they had no means of bringing off. When they entered Quebec a gill of rum was served out to each man; several houses in the suburb of St. Roch were torn down to supply them with firewood for drying their clothes; and they were left to take what rest they could against the morrow. The French, meanwhile, took possession of the abandoned heights; and while some filled the houses, barns, and sheds of Ste.-Foy and its neighborhood, others, chiefly Canadians, crossed the plateau to seek shelter in the village of Sillery.

Three courses were open to Murray. He could defend Quebec, fortify himself outside the walls on the Buttes-à-Neveu, or fight Lévis at all risks. The walls of Quebec could not withstand a cannonade, and he had long intended to intrench his army on the Buttes, as a better position of defence; but the ground, frozen like a rock, had thus far made the plan impracticable. Even now, though the surface was thawed, the soil beneath was still frost-bound, making the task of fortification extremely difficult, if indeed the French would give him time for it. Murray was young in years, and younger still in impulse. He was ardent, fearless, ambitious, and emulous of the fame of Wolfe. "The enemy," he soon after wrote to Pitt, "was greatly superior in number, it is true; but when I considered that our little army was in the habit of beating that enemy, and had a very fine train of field artillery; that shutting ourselves at once within the walls was putting all upon the single chance of holding out for a considerable time a wretched fortification, I resolved to give them battle; and, half an hour after six in the morning, we marched with all the force I could muster, namely, three thousand men."[1] Some of these had left the hospitals of their own accord in their eagerness to take part in the fray.

The rain had ceased; but as the column emerged from St. Louis Gate, the scene before them was a dismal one. As yet there was no sign of spring. Each leafless bush and tree was dark with clammy mois-

---

[1] *Murray to Pitt, 25 May, 1760.*

ture; patches of bare earth lay oozy and black on the southern slopes:
but elsewhere the ground was still covered with snow, in some places
piled in drifts, and everywhere sodden with rain; while each hollow and
depression was full of that half-liquid, lead-colored mixture of snow and
water which New England schoolboys call "slush," for all drainage was
stopped by the frozen subsoil. The troops had with them two howitzers
and twenty field-pieces, which had been captured when Quebec surrendered, and had formed a part of that very battery which Ramesay refused to Montcalm at the battle of the autumn before. As there were
no horses, the cannon were dragged by some of the soldiers, while others carried picks and spades; for as yet Murray seems not to have made
up his mind whether to fortify or fight. Thus they advanced nearly half
a mile; till reaching the Buttes-à-Neveu, they formed in order of battle
along their farther slopes, on the same ground that Montcalm had occupied on the morning of his death.

Murray went forward to reconnoitre. Immediately before him was a
rising ground, and, beyond it, a tract of forest called Sillery Wood, a
mile or more distant. Nearer, on the left, he could see two blockhouses
built by the English in the last autumn, not far from the brink of the
plateau above the Anse du Foulon where Wolfe climbed the heights.
On the right, at the opposite brink of the plateau, was a house and a
fortified windmill belonging to one Dumont. The blockhouses, the
mill, and the rising ground between them were occupied by the vanguard of Lévis' army; while, behind, he could descry the main body
moving along the road from Ste.-Foy, then turning, battalion after battalion, and rapidly marching across the plateau along the edge of Sillery
Wood. The two brigades of the leading column had already reached the
blockhouses by the Anse du Foulon, and formed themselves as the right
wing of the French line of battle; but those behind were not yet in
position.

Murray, kindling at the sight, thought that so favorable a moment
was not to be lost, and ordered an advance. His line consisted of eight
battalions, numbering a little above two thousand. In the intervals between them the cannon were dragged through slush and mud by five
hundred men; and, at a little distance behind, the remaining two battalions followed as a reserve. The right flank was covered by Dalling's
light infantry; the left by Hazen's company of rangers and a hundred
volunteers under Major MacDonald. They all moved forward till they
were on nearly the same ground where Wolfe's army had been drawn
up. Then the cannon unlimbered, and opened on the French with such
effect that Lévis, who was on horseback in the middle of the field, sent

orders to the corps of his left to fall back to the cover of the woods. The movement caused some disorder. Murray mistook it for retreat, and commanded a farther advance. The whole British line, extending itself towards the right, pushed eagerly forward: in doing which it lost the advantage of the favorable position it had occupied; and the battalions of the right soon found themselves on low grounds, wading in half-melted snow, which in some parts was knee deep. Here the cannon could no longer be worked with effect. Just in front, a small brook ran along the hollow, through soft mud and saturated snowdrifts, then gurgled down the slope on the right, to lose itself in the meadows of the St. Charles. A few rods before this brook stood the house and windmill of Dumont, occupied by five companies of French grenadiers. The light infantry at once attacked them. A furious struggle ensued, till at length the French gave way, and the victors dashed forward to follow up their advantage. Their ardor cost them dear. The corps on the French left, which had fallen back into the woods, now advanced again as the cannon ceased to play, rushing on without order but with the utmost impetuosity, led by a gallant old officer, Colonel Dalquier, of the battalion of Béarn. A bullet in the body could not stop him. The light infantry were overwhelmed; and such of them as were left alive were driven back in confusion upon the battalions behind them, along the front of which they remained dispersed for some minutes, preventing the troops from firing on the advancing French, who thus had time to reform their ranks. At length the light infantry got themselves out of the way and retired to the rear, where, having lost nearly all their officers, they remained during the rest of the fight. Another struggle followed for the house and mill of Dumont, of which the French again got possession, to be again driven out; and it remained, as if by mutual consent, unoccupied for some time by either party. For above an hour more the fight was hot and fierce. "We drove them back as long as we had ammunition for our cannon," says Sergeant Johnson; but now it failed, and no more was to be had, because, in the eccentric phrase of the sergeant, the tumbrils were "bogged in deep pits of snow."

While this was passing on the English right, it fared still worse with them on the left. The advance of the line was no less disastrous here than there. It brought the troops close to the woods which circled round to this point from the French rear, and from which the Canadians, covered by the trees, now poured on them a deadly fire. Here, as on the right, Lévis had ordered his troops to fall back for a time; but when the fire of the English cannon ceased, they advanced again, and their artillery, though consisting of only three pieces, played its part with good effect. Hazen's rangers and MacDonald's volunteers attacked and took the two adjacent blockhouses, but could not hold them. Hazen was wounded, MacDonald killed, and their party overpowered. The British battalions held their ground till the French, whose superior numbers enabled them to extend themselves on both sides beyond the English line, made a furious attack on the left wing, in front and flank. The reserves were ordered up, and the troops stood for a time in sullen desperation under the storm of bullets; but they were dropping fast in the blood-stained snow, and the order came at length to fall back. They obeyed with curses: "Damn it, what is falling back but retreating?"[1] The right wing, also outflanked, followed the example of the left. Some of the corps tried to drag off their cannon; but being prevented by the deep mud and snow they spiked the pieces and abandoned them. The French followed close, hoping to cut off the fugitives from the gates of Quebec; till Lévis, seeing that the retreat, though precipitate, was not entirely without order, thought best to stop the pursuit.

The fight lasted about two hours, and did credit to both sides. The Canadians not only showed their usual address and courage when under cover of woods, but they also fought well in the open field; and the conduct of the whole French force proved how completely they had recovered from the panic of the last autumn. From the first they were greatly superior in number, and at the middle and end of the affair, when they had all reached the field, they were more than two against one.[2] The English, on the other hand, besides the opportunity of attacking before their enemies had completely formed, had a vastly superior artillery and a favorable position, both which advantages they lost after their second advance.

Some curious anecdotes are told of the retreat. Colonel Fraser, of the Highlanders, received a bullet which was no doubt half spent, and which, with excellent precision, hit the base of his queue, so deadening the shock that it gave him no other inconvenience than a stiff neck. Captain Hazen, of the rangers, badly wounded, was making his way towards the gate, supported by his servant, when he saw at a great distance a French officer leading a file of men across a rising ground; whereupon he stopped and told the servant to give him his gun. A volunteer named Thompson, who was near by and who tells the story, thought that he was out of his senses; but Hazen persisted, seated himself on the ground, took a long aim, fired, and brought down his man.

[1]Knox, II. 295.
[2]See Appendix K.

Thompson congratulated him. "A chance shot may kill the devil," replied Hazen; and resigning himself again to the arms of his attendant, he reached the town, recovered from his wound, and lived to be a general of the Revolution.[1]

The English lost above a thousand, or more than a third of their whole number, killed, wounded, and missing.[2] They carried off some of their wounded, but left others behind; and the greater part of these were murdered, scalped, and mangled by the Indians, all of whom were converts from the mission villages. English writers put the French loss at two thousand and upwards, which is no doubt a gross exaggeration. Lévis declares that the number did not exceed six or eight hundred; but afterwards gives a list which makes it eight hundred and thirty-three.

Murray had left three or four hundred men to guard Quebec when the rest marched out; and adding them to those who had returned scathless from the fight, he now had about twenty-four hundred rank and file fit for duty. Yet even the troops that were rated as effective were in so bad a condition that the hyperbolical Sergeant Johnson calls them "half-starved, scorbutic skeletons." That worthy soldier, commonly a model of dutiful respect to those above him, this time so far forgets himself as to criticise his general for the "mad, enthusiastic zeal" by which he nearly lost the fruits of Wolfe's victory. In fact, the fate of Quebec trembled in the balance. "We were too few and weak to stand an assault," continues Johnson, "and we were almost in as deep a distress as we could be." At first there was some drunkenness and some plundering of private houses; but Murray stopped the one by staving the rum-barrels of the sutlers, and the other by hanging the chief offender. Within three days order, subordination, hope, and almost confidence were completely restored. Not a man was idle. The troops left their barracks and lay in tents close to their respective alarm posts. On the open space by St. Louis Gate a crowd of convalescents were busy in filling sand-bags to strengthen the defences, while the sick and wounded in the hospitals made wadding for the cannon. The ramparts were faced with fascines, of which a large stock had been provided in the autumn; *chevaux-de-frise* were planted in exposed places; an outwork was built to protect St. Louis Gate; embrasures were cut along the whole length of the walls; and the French cannon captured when the town was taken were planted against their late owners. Every man was

[1] Thompson, deceived by Hazen's baptismal name, Moses, thought that he was a Jew. (*Revue Canadienne*, IV. 865.) He was, however, of an old New England Puritan family. See the Hazen genealogy in *Historic-Genealogical Register*, XXXIII.

[2] *Return of Killed, Wounded, and Missing*, signed J. Murray.

tasked to the utmost of his strength; and the garrison, gaunt, worn, besmirched with mud, looked less like soldiers than like overworked laborers.

The conduct of the officers troubled the spirit of Sergeant Johnson. It shocked his sense of the fitness of things to see them sharing the hard work of the private men, and he thus gives utterance to his feelings: "None but those who were present on the spot can imagine the grief of heart the soldiers felt to see their officers yoked in the harness, dragging up cannon from the Lower Town; to see gentlemen, who were set over them by His Majesty to command and keep them to their duty, working at the batteries with the barrow, pickaxe, and spade." The effect, how-ever, was admirable. The spirit of the men rose to the crisis. Murray, no less than his officers, had all their confidence; for if he had fallen into a fatal error, he atoned for it now by unconquerable resolution and exhaustless fertility of resource. Deserters said that Lévis would assault the town; and the soldiers replied: "Let him come on; he will catch a Tartar."

Lévis and his army were no less busy in digging trenches along the stony back of the Buttes-à-Neveu. Every day the English fire grew hot-ter; till at last nearly a hundred and fifty cannon vomited iron upon them from the walls of Quebec, and May was well advanced before they could plant a single gun to reply. Their vessels had landed artillery at the Anse du Foulon; but their best hope lay in the succors they daily expected from the river below. In the autumn Lévis, with a view to his intended enterprise, had sent a request to Versailles that a ship laden with munitions and heavy siege-guns should be sent from France in time to meet him at Quebec in April; while he looked also for another ship, which had wintered at Gaspé, and which therefore might reach him as soon as navigation opened. The arrival of these vessels would have made the position of the English doubly critical; and, on the other hand, should an English squadron appear first, Lévis would be forced to raise the siege. Thus each side watched the river with an anxiety that grew constantly more intense; and the English presently descried signals along the shore which seemed to say that French ships were moving up the St. Lawrence. Meantime, while doing their best to compass each other's destruction, neither side forgot the courtesies of war. Lévis heard that Murray liked spruce-beer for his table, and sent him a flag of truce with a quantity of spruce-boughs and a message of compliment; Murray responded with a Cheshire cheese, and Lévis rejoined with a present of partridges.

Bad and scanty fare, excessive toil, and broken sleep were telling ominously on the strength of the garrison when, on the ninth of May, Murray, as he sat pondering over the fire at his quarters in St. Louis Street, was interrupted by an officer who came to tell him that there was a ship-of-war in the Basin beating up towards the town. Murray started from his revery, and directed that British colors should be raised immediately on Cape Diamond.[1] The halyards being out of order, a sailor climbed the staff and drew up the flag to its place. The news had spread; men and officers, divided between hope and fear, crowded to the rampart by the Château, where Durham Terrace now overlooks the St. Lawrence, and every eye was strained on the approaching ship, eager to see whether she would show the red flag of England or the white one of France. Slowly her colors rose to the mast-head and unfurled to the wind the red cross of St. George. It was the British frigate "Lowestoffe." She anchored before the Lower Town, and saluted the garrison with twenty-one guns. "The gladness of the troops," says Knox, "is not to be expressed. Both officers and soldiers mounted the parapet in the face of the enemy and huzzaed with their hats in the air for almost an hour. The garrison, the enemy's camp, the bay, and circumjacent country resounded with our shouts and the thunder of our artillery; for the gunners were so elated that they did nothing but load and fire for a considerable time. In short, the general satisfaction is not to be conceived, except by a person who had suffered the extremities of a siege, and been destined, with his brave friends and countrymen, to the scalping-knives of a faithless conqueror and his barbarous allies." The "Lowestoffe" brought news that a British squadron was at the mouth of the St. Lawrence, and would reach Quebec in a few days.

Lévis, in ignorance of this, still clung to the hope that French ships would arrive strong enough to overpower the unwelcome stranger. His guns, being at last in position, presently opened fire upon a wall that was not built to bear the brunt of heavy shot; but an artillery better and more numerous than his own almost silenced them, and his gunners were harassed by repeated sallies. The besiegers had now no real chance of success unless they could carry the place by storm, to which end they had provided abundant scaling-ladders as well as petards to burst in the gates. They made, however, no attempt to use them. A week passed, when, on the evening of the fifteenth, the ship of the line "Vanguard" and the frigate "Diana" sailed into the harbor; and on the next morning the "Diana" and the "Lowestoffe" passed the town to attack the French vessels in the river above. These were six in all,—

---

[1] Thompson in *Revue Canadienne*, IV. 866.

two frigates, two smaller armed ships, and two schooners; the whole under command of the gallant Vauquelin. He did not belie his reputation; fought his ship with persistent bravery till his ammunition was spent, refused even then to strike his flag, and being made prisoner, was treated by his captors with distinguished honor. The other vessels made little or no resistance. One of them threw her guns overboard and escaped; the rest ran ashore and were burned.

The destruction of his vessels was a death-blow to the hopes of Lévis, for they contained his stores of food and ammunition. He had passed the preceding night in great agitation; and when the cannonade on the river ceased, he hastened to raise the siege. In the evening deserters from his camp told Murray that the French were in full retreat; on which all the English batteries opened, firing at random through the darkness, and sending cannon-balls *en ricochet*, bowling by scores together, over the Plains of Abraham on the heels of the retiring enemy. Murray marched out at dawn of day to fall upon their rear; but, with a hundred and fifty cannon bellowing behind them, they had made such speed that, though he pushed over the marsh to Old Lorette, he could not overtake them; they had already crossed the river of Cap-Rouge. Why, with numbers still superior, they went off in such haste, it is hard to say. They left behind them thirty-four cannon and six mortars, with petards, scaling-ladders, tents, ammunition, baggage, intrenching tools, many of their muskets, and all their sick and wounded.

The effort to recover Quebec did great honor to the enterprise of the French; but it availed them nothing, served only to waste resources that seemed already at the lowest ebb, and gave fresh opportunity of plunder to Cadet and his crew, who failed not to make use of it.

After the battle of Ste.-Foy Murray sent the frigate "Racehorse" to Halifax with news of his defeat, and from Halifax it was sent to England. The British public were taken by surprise. "Who the deuce was thinking of Quebec?" says Horace Walpole. "America was like a book one has read and done with; but here we are on a sudden reading our book backwards." Ten days passed, and then came word that the siege was raised and that the French were gone; upon which Walpole wrote to General Conway: "Well, Quebec is come to life again. Last night I went to see the Holdernesses. I met my Lady in a triumphal car, drawn by a Manx horse, thirteen little fingers high, with Lady Emily. Mr. Milbank was walking by himself in ovation after the car, and they were going to see the bonfire at the alehouse at the corner. The whole procession returned with me; and from the Countess's dressing-room we saw a battery fired before the house, the mob crying, 'God bless the good news!' These are all the particulars I know of the siege. My Lord would have showed me the journal; but we amused ourselves much better in going to eat peaches from the new Dutch stoves [*hot-houses*]."

NOTE.—On the battle of Ste.-Foy and the subsequent siege, Lévis, *Guerre du Canada. Relation de la seconde Bataille de Québec et du Siége de cette Ville* (there are several copies of this paper, with different titles and some variation). *Murray to Amherst, 30 April, 1760*. Murray, *Journal kept at Quebec from Sept. 18, 1759, to May 17, 1760* (Public Record Office, *America and West Indies*, XCIX.). *Murray to Pitt, 25 May, 1760. Letter from an Officer of the Royal Americans at Quebec, 24 May, 1760* (in *London Magazine* and several periodical papers of the time). Fraser, *Journal* (Quebec Hist. Soc.); Johnstone, *Campaign of 1760* (Ibid.). *Relation de ce qui s'est passé au Siége de Québec, par une Réligieuse de l'Hôpital Général* (Ibid.). *Memoirs of the Siege of Quebec,* by Sergeant John Johnson. *Mémoires sur le Canada, 1749–1760.* Letters of Lévis, Bourlamaque, and Vaudreuil, May, June, 1760. Several letters from officers at Quebec in provincial newspapers. Knox, II. 292–322. *Plan of the Battle and Situation of the British and French on the Heights of Abraham, the 28th of April, 1760,*—an admirable plan, attached to the great plan of operations at Quebec before mentioned, and necessary to an understanding of the position and movements of the two armies (British Museum, King's Maps).

The narratives of Mante, Entick, Wynne, Smith, and other secondary writers give no additional light. On the force engaged on each side, see Appendix K.

30
Fall of Canada
1760

DESPERATE SITUATION · EFFORTS OF VAUDREUIL AND LÉVIS · PLANS OF
AMHERST · A TRIPLE ATTACK · ADVANCE OF MURRAY · ADVANCE OF
HAVILAND · ADVANCE OF AMHERST · CAPITULATION OF MONTREAL ·
PROTEST OF LÉVIS · INJUSTICE OF LOUIS XV. · JOY IN THE BRITISH
COLONIES · CHARACTER OF THE WAR

The retreat of Lévis left Canada little hope but in a speedy
peace. This hope was strong, for a belief widely prevailed
that, even if the colony should be subdued, it would be restored to
France by treaty. Its available force did not exceed eight or ten thousand men, as most of the Canadians below the district of Three Rivers
had sworn allegiance to King George; and though many of them had
disregarded the oath to join the standard of Lévis, they could venture
to do so no longer. The French had lost the best of their artillery, their
gunpowder was falling short, their provisions would barely carry them
to harvest time, and no more was to be hoped for, since a convoy of
ships which had sailed from France at the end of winter, laden with
supplies of all kinds, had been captured by the English. The blockade
of the St. Lawrence was complete. The Western Indians would not
fight, and even those of the mission villages were wavering and insolent.

Yet Vaudreuil and Lévis exerted themselves for defence with an energy that does honor to them both. "Far from showing the least timid-

ity," says the ever-modest Governor, "I have taken positions such as may hide our weakness from the enemy."[1] He stationed Rochbeaucourt with three hundred men at Pointe-aux-Trembles; Repentigny with two hundred at Jacques-Cartier; and Dumas with twelve hundred at Deschambault to watch the St. Lawrence and, if possible, prevent Murray from moving up the river. Bougainville was stationed at Isle-aux-Noix to bar the approach from Lake Champlain, and a force under La Corne was held ready to defend the rapids above Montreal, should the English attempt that dangerous passage. Prisoners taken by war parties near Crown Point gave exaggerated reports of hostile preparation, and doubled and trebled the forces that were mustering against Canada.

These forces were nevertheless considerable. Amherst had resolved to enter the colony by all its three gates at once, and, advancing from east, west, and south, unite at Montreal and crush it as in the jaws of a vice. Murray was to ascend the St. Lawrence from Quebec, while Brigadier Haviland forced an entrance by way of Lake Champlain, and Amherst himself led the main army down the St. Lawrence from Lake Ontario. This last route was long, circuitous, difficult, and full of danger from the rapids that obstructed the river. His choice of it for his chief line of operation, instead of the shorter and easier way of Lake Champlain, was meant, no doubt, to prevent the French army from escaping up the Lakes to Detroit and the other wilderness posts, where it might have protracted the war for an indefinite time; while the plan adopted, if successful, would make its capture certain. The plan was a critical one. Three armies advancing from three different points, hundreds of miles apart, by routes full of difficulty, and with no possibility of intercommunication, were to meet at the same place at the same time, or, failing to do so, run the risk of being destroyed in detail. If the French troops could be kept together, and if the small army of Murray or of Haviland should reach Montreal a few days before the co-operating forces appeared, it might be separately attacked and overpowered. In this lay the hope of Vaudreuil and Lévis.[2]

After the siege of Quebec was raised, Murray had an effective force of about twenty-five hundred rank and file.[3] As the spring opened the invalids were encamped on the Island of Orleans, where fresh air, fresh provisions, and the change from the pestiferous town hospitals wrought such wonders on the scorbutic patients, that in a few weeks a consid-

[1] *Vaudreuil au Ministre, 22 Juin, 1760.*
[2] *Lévis à Bourlamaque, Juillet, Août, 1760.*
[3] *Return of the Present State of His Majesty's Forces in Garrison at Quebec, 21 May, 1760.*

erable number of them were again fit for garrison duty, if not for the field. Thus it happened that on the second of July twenty-four hundred and fifty men and officers received orders to embark for Montreal; and on the fifteenth they set sail, in thirty-two vessels, with a number of boats and bateaux.[1] They were followed some time after by Lord Rollo, with thirteen hundred additional men just arrived from Louisbourg, the King having ordered that fortress to be abandoned and dismantled. They advanced slowly, landing from time to time, skirmishing with detachments of the enemy who followed them along the shore, or more frequently trading with the farmers who brought them vegetables, poultry, eggs, and fresh meat. They passed the fortified hill of Jacques-Cartier, whence they were saluted with shot and shell, stopped at various parishes, disarmed the inhabitants, administered oaths of neutrality, which were taken without much apparent reluctance, and on the fourth of August came within sight of Three Rivers, then occupied by a body of troops expecting an attack. "But," says Knox, "a delay here would be absurd, as that wretched place must share the fate of Montreal. Our fleet sailed this morning. The French troops, apparently about two thousand, lined their different works, and were in general clothed as regulars, except a very few Canadians and about fifty naked Picts or savages, their bodies being painted of a reddish color and their faces of different colors, which I plainly discerned with my glass. Their light cavalry, who paraded along shore, seemed to be well appointed, clothed in blue, faced with scarlet; but their officers had white uniforms. In fine, their troops, batteries, fair-looking houses; their situation on the banks of a delightful river; our fleet sailing triumphantly before them, with our floating batteries drawn up in line of battle; the country on both sides interspersed with neat settlements, together with the verdure of the fields and trees and the clear, pleasant weather, afforded as agreeable a prospect as the most lively imagination can conceive."

This excellent lover of the picturesque was still more delighted as the fleet sailed among the islands of St. Peter. "I think nothing could equal the beauties of our navigation this morning: the meandering course of the narrow channel; the awfulness and solemnity of the dark forests with which these islands are covered; the fragrancy of the spontaneous fruits, shrubs, and flowers; the verdure of the water by the reflection of the neighboring woods; the wild chirping notes of the feathered inhabitants; the masts and sails of ships appearing as if among the trees, both ahead and astern: formed altogether an enchanting diversity."

[1]Knox, II. 344, 348.

The evening recalled him from dreams to realities; for towards seven o'clock they reached the village of Sorel, where they found a large body of troops and militia intrenched along the strand. Bourlamaque was in command here with two or three thousand men, and Dumas, with another body, was on the northern shore. Both had orders to keep abreast of the fleet as it advanced; and thus French and English alike drew slowly towards Montreal, where lay the main French force under Lévis, ready to unite with Bourlamaque and Dumas, and fall upon Murray at the first opportunity. Montreal was now but a few leagues distant, and the situation was becoming delicate. Murray sent five rangers towards Lake Champlain to get news of Haviland, and took measures at the same time to cause the desertion of the Canadians, who formed the largest part of the opposing force. He sent a proclamation among the parishes, advising the inhabitants to remain peacefully at home, promising that those who did so should be safe in person and property, and threatening to burn every house from which the men of the family were absent. These were not idle words. A detachment sent for the purpose destroyed a settlement near Sorel, the owners of which were in arms under Bourlamaque. "I was under the cruel necessity of burning the greatest part of these poor unhappy people's houses," wrote Murray. "I pray God this example may suffice, for my nature revolts when this becomes a necessary part of my duty."[1] On the other hand, he treated with great kindness all who left the army and returned to their families. The effect was soon felt. The Canadians came in by scores and by hundreds to give up their arms and take the oath of neutrality, till, before the end of August, half Bourlamaque's force had disappeared. Murray encamped on Isle Ste.-Thérèse, just below Montreal, and watched and waited for Haviland and Amherst to appear.[2]

Vaudreuil on his part was not idle. He sent a counter-proclamation through the parishes as an antidote to that of Murray. "I have been compelled," he writes to the Minister, "to decree the pain of death to the Canadians who are so dastardly as to desert or give up their arms to the enemy, and to order that the houses of those who do not join our army shall be burned."[3] Execution was to be summary, without court-martial.[4] Yet desertion increased daily. The Canadians felt themselves doubly ruined, for it became known that the Court had refused to redeem the paper that formed the whole currency of the colony; and,

[1] *Murray to Pitt, 24 Aug. 1760.*
[2] Knox, II. 382, 384. Mante, 340.
[3] *Vaudreuil au Ministre, 29 Août, 1760.*
[4] *Lévis à Bourlamaque, 25 Août, 1760.*

in their desperation, they preferred to trust the tried clemency of the enemy rather than exasperate him by persisting in a vain defence. Vaudreuil writes in his usual strain: "I am taking the most just measures to unite our forces, and, if our situation permits, fight a battle, or several battles. It is to be feared that we shall go down before an enemy so numerous and strong; but, whatever may be the event, we will save the honor of the King's arms. I have the honor to repeat to you, Monseigneur, that if any resource were left me, whatever the progress the English might make, I would maintain myself in some part of the colony with my remaining troops, after having fought with the greatest obstinacy; but I am absolutely without the least remnant of the necessary means. In these unhappy circumstances I shall continue to use every manœuvre and device to keep the enemy in check; but if we succumb in the battles we shall fight, I shall apply myself to obtaining a capitulation which may avert the total ruin of a people who will remain forever French, and who could not survive their misfortunes but for the hope of being restored by the treaty of peace to the rule of His Most Christian Majesty. It is with this view that I shall remain in this town, the Chevalier de Lévis having represented to me that it would be an evil to the colonists past remedy if any accident should happen to me." Lévis was willing to go very far in soothing the susceptibilities of the Governor; but it may be suspected this time that he thought him more useful within four walls than in the open field.

There seemed good hope of stopping the advance of Haviland. To this end Vaudreuil had stationed Bougainville at Isle-aux-Noix with seventeen hundred men, and Roquemaure at St. John, a few miles distant, with twelve or fifteen hundred more, besides all the Indians.[1] Haviland embarked at Crown Point with thirty-four hundred regulars, provincials, and Indians.[2] Four days brought him to Isle-aux-Noix; he landed, planted cannon in the swamp, and opened fire. Major Darby with the light infantry, and Rogers with the rangers, dragged three light pieces through the forest, and planted them on the river-bank in the rear of Bougainville's position, where lay the French naval force, consisting of three armed vessels and several gunboats. The cannon were turned upon the principal ship; a shot cut her cable, and a strong west wind drove her ashore into the hands of her enemies. The other vessels

---

[1] *Vaudreuil au Ministre, 29 Août, 1760.*

[2] *A List of the Forces employed in the Expedition against Canada, 1760.* Compare Mante, 340, Knox, II. 392, and Rogers, 188. Chevalier Johnstone, who was with Bougainville, says "about four thousand," which Vaudreuil multiplies to twelve thousand.

and gunboats made all sail for St. John, but stranded in a bend of the river, where the rangers, swimming out with their tomahawks, boarded and took one of them, and the rest soon surrendered. It was a fatal blow to Bougainville, whose communications with St. John were now cut off. In accordance with instructions from Vaudreuil, he abandoned the island on the night of the twenty-seventh of August, and, making his way with infinite difficulty through the dark forest, joined Roquemaure at St. John, twelve miles below. Haviland followed, the rangers leading the way. Bougainville and Roquemaure fell back, abandoned St. John and Chambly, and joined Bourlamaque on the banks of the St. Lawrence, where the united force at first outnumbered that of Haviland, though fast melted away by discouragement and desertion. Haviland opened communication with Murray, and they both looked daily for the arrival of Amherst, whose approach was rumored by prisoners and deserters.[1]

The army of Amherst had gathered at Oswego in July. On the tenth of August it was all afloat on Lake Ontario, to the number of ten thousand one hundred and forty-two men, besides about seven hundred Indians under Sir William Johnson.[2] Before the fifteenth the whole had reached La Présentation, otherwise called Oswegatchie or La Galette, the seat of Father Piquet's mission. Near by was a French armed brig, the "Ottawa," with ten cannon and a hundred men, threatening destruction to Amherst's bateaux and whaleboats. Five gunboats attacked and captured her. Then the army advanced again, and were presently joined by two armed vessels of their own which had lingered behind, bewildered among the channels of the Thousand Islands.

Near the head of the rapids, a little below La Galette, stood Fort Lévis, built the year before on an islet in mid-channel. Amherst might have passed its batteries with slight loss, continuing his voyage without paying it the honor of a siege; and this was what the French commanders feared that he would do. "We shall be fortunate," Lévis wrote to Bourlamaque, "if the enemy amuse themselves with capturing it. My chief anxiety is lest Amherst should reach Montreal so soon that we may not have time to unite our forces to attack Haviland or Murray." If he had better known the English commander, Lévis would have seen that he was not the man to leave a post of

---

[1] Rogers, *Journals*. *Diary of a Sergeant in the Army of Haviland*. Johnstone, *Campaign of 1760*. *Bigot au Ministre, 29 Août, 1760*.
[2] *A List of the Forces employed in the Expedition against Canada*. Compare Mante, 301, and Knox, II. 403.

the enemy in his rear under any circumstances; and Amherst had also another reason for wishing to get the garrison into his hands, for he expected to find among them the pilots whom he needed to guide his boats down the rapids. He therefore invested the fort, and, on the twenty-third, cannonaded it from his vessels, the mainland, and the neighboring islands. It was commanded by Pouchot, the late commandant of Niagara, made prisoner in the last campaign, and since exchanged. As the rocky islet had but little earth, the defences, though thick and strong, were chiefly of logs, which flew in splinters under the bombardment. The French, however, made a brave resistance. The firing lasted all day, was resumed in the morning, and continued two days more; when Pouchot, whose works were in ruins, surrendered himself and his garrison. On this, Johnson's Indians prepared to kill the prisoners; and, being compelled to desist, three fourths of them went home in a rage. [1]

Now began the critical part of the expedition, the descent of the rapids. The Galops, the Rapide Plat, the Long Saut, the Côteau du Lac were passed in succession, with little loss, till they reached the Cedars, the Buisson, and the Cascades, where the reckless surges dashed and bounded in the sun, beautiful and terrible as young tigers at play. Boat after boat, borne on their foaming crests, rushed madly down the torrent. Forty-six were totally wrecked, eighteen were damaged, and eighty-four men were drowned. [2] La Corne was watching the rapids with a considerable body of Canadians; and it is difficult to see why this bold and enterprising chief allowed the army to descend undisturbed through passes so dangerous. At length the last rapid was left behind; and the flotilla, gliding in peace over the smooth breast of Lake St. Louis, landed at Isle Perrot, a few leagues from Montreal. In the morning, September sixth, the troops embarked again, landed unopposed at La Chine, nine miles from the city, marched on without delay, and encamped before its walls.

The Montreal of that time was a long, narrow assemblage of wooden or stone houses, one or two stories high, above which rose the peaked towers of the Seminary, the spires of three churches, the walls of four convents, with the trees of their adjacent gardens, and, conspicuous at the lower end, a high mound of earth, crowned by a redoubt, where a few cannon were mounted. The whole was surrounded by a shallow

---

[1] On the capture of Fort Lévis, *Amherst to Pitt, 26 Aug. 1760. Amherst to Monckton, same date.* Pouchot, II. 264–282. Knox, II. 405–413. Mante, 303–306. *All Canada in the Hands of the English* (Boston, 1760). *Journal of Colonel Nathaniel Woodhull.*
[2] *Amherst to Pitt, 8 Sept. 1760.*

moat and a bastioned stone wall, made for defence against Indians, and incapable of resisting cannon.[1]

On the morning after Amherst encamped above the place, Murray landed to encamp below it; and Vaudreuil, looking across the St. Lawrence, could see the tents of Haviland's little army on the southern shore. Bourlamaque, Bougainville, and Roquemaure, abandoned by all their militia, had crossed to Montreal with the few regulars that remained with them. The town was crowded with non-combatant refugees. Here, too, was nearly all the remaining force of Canada, consisting of twenty-two hundred troops of the line and some two hundred colony troops; for all the Canadians had by this time gone home. Many of the regulars, especially of the colony troops, had also deserted; and the rest were so broken in discipline that their officers were forced to use entreaties instead of commands. The three armies encamped around the city amounted to seventeen thousand men;[2] Amherst was bringing up his cannon from La Chine, and the town wall would have crumbled before them in an hour.

On the night when Amherst arrived, the Governor called a council of war.[3] It was resolved that since all the militia and many of the regulars had abandoned the army, and the Indian allies of France had gone over to the enemy, further resistance was impossible. Vaudreuil laid before the assembled officers a long paper that he had drawn up, containing fifty-five articles of capitulation to be proposed to the English; and these were unanimously approved.[4] In the morning Bougainville carried them to the tent of Amherst. He granted the greater part, modified some, and flatly refused others. That which the French officers thought more important than all the rest was the provision that the troops should march out with arms, cannon, and the honors of war; to which it was replied: "The whole garrison of Montreal and all other French troops in Canada must lay down their arms, and shall not serve during the present war." This demand was felt to be intolerable. The

---

[1] *An East View of Montreal, drawn on the Spot by Thomas Patten* (King's Maps, British Museum), *Plan of Montreal, 1759. A Description of Montreal*, in several magazines of the time. The recent Canadian publication called *Le Vieux Montréal*, is exceedingly incorrect as to the numbers of the British troops and the position of their camps.

[2] *A List of the Forces employed in the Expedition against Canada.* See Smith, *History of Canada*, I. Appendix xix. Vaudreuil writes to Charles Langlade, on the ninth, that the three armies amount to twenty thousand, and raises the number to thirty-two thousand in a letter to the Minister on the next day. Berniers says twenty thousand; Lévis, for obvious reasons, exaggerates the number to forty thousand.

[3] *Vaudreuil au Ministre, 10 Sept. 1760.*

[4] *Procès-verbal de la Déliberation du Conseil de Guerre tenu à Montréal, 6 Sept. 1760.*

Governor sent Bougainville back to remonstrate; but Amherst was inflexible. Then Lévis tried to shake his resolution, and sent him an officer with the following note: "I send your Excellency M. de la Pause, Assistant Quartermaster-General of the Army, on the subject of the too rigorous article which you dictate to the troops by the capitulation, to which it would not be possible for us to subscribe." Amherst answered the envoy: "I am fully resolved, for the infamous part the troops of France have acted in exciting the savages to perpetrate the most horrid and unheard of barbarities in the whole progress of the war, and for other open treacheries and flagrant breaches of faith, to manifest to all the world by this capitulation my detestation of such practices;" and he dismissed La Pause with a short note, refusing to change the conditions.

On the next morning, September eighth, Vaudreuil yielded, and signed the capitulation. By it Canada and all its dependencies passed to the British Crown. French officers, civil and military, with French troops and sailors, were to be sent to France in British ships. Free exercise of religion was assured to the people of the colony, and the religious communities were to retain their possessions, rights, and privileges. All persons who might wish to retire to France were allowed to do so, and the Canadians were to remain in full enjoyment of feudal and other property, including negro and Indian slaves.[1]

The greatest alarm had prevailed among the inhabitants lest they should suffer violence from the English Indians, and Vaudreuil had endeavored to provide that these dangerous enemies should be sent back at once to their villages. This was refused, with the remark: "There never have been any cruelties committed by the Indians of our army." Strict precautions were taken at the same time, not only against the few savages whom the firm conduct of Johnson at Fort Lévis had not driven away, but also against the late allies of the French, now become a peril to them. In consequence, not a man, woman, or child was hurt. Amherst, in general orders, expressed his confidence "that the troops will not disgrace themselves by the least appearance of inhumanity, or by any unsoldierlike behavior in seeking for plunder; and that as the Canadians are now become British subjects, they will feel the good effects of His Majesty's protection." They were in fact treated with a kindness that seemed to surprise them.

Lévis was so incensed at the demand that the troops should lay down their arms and serve no longer during the war that, before the capitu-

[1] *Articles of Capitulation, 8 Sept. 1760. Amherst to Pitt, same date.*

lation was signed, he made a formal protest[1] in his own name and that of the officers from France, and insisted that the negotiation should be broken off. "If," he added, "the Marquis de Vaudreuil, through political motives, thinks himself obliged to surrender the colony at once, we ask his permission to withdraw with the troops of the line to the Island of St. Helen, in order to uphold there, on our own behalf, the honor of the King's arms." The proposal was of course rejected, as Lévis knew that it would be, and he and his officers were ordered to conform to the capitulation. When Vaudreuil reached France, three months after, he had the mortification to receive from the Colonial Minister a letter containing these words: "Though His Majesty was perfectly aware of the state of Canada, nevertheless, after the assurances you had given to make the utmost efforts to sustain the honor of his arms, he did not expect to hear so soon of the surrender of Montreal and the whole colony. But, granting that capitulation was a necessity, his Majesty was not the less surprised and ill pleased at the conditions, so little honorable, to which you submitted, especially after the representations made you by the Chevalier de Lévis."[2] The brother of Vaudreuil complained to the Minister of the terms of this letter, and the Minister replied: "I see with regret, Monsieur, that you are pained by the letter I wrote your brother; but I could not help telling him what the King did me the honor to say to me; and it would have been unpleasant for him to hear it from anybody else."[3]

It is true that Vaudreuil had in some measure drawn this reproach upon himself by his boastings about the battles he would fight; yet the royal displeasure was undeserved. The Governor had no choice but to give up the colony; for Amherst had him in his power, and knew that he could exact what terms he pleased. Further resistance could only have ended in surrender at the discretion of the victor, and the protest of Lévis was nothing but a device to save his own reputation and that of his brother officers from France. Vaudreuil had served the King and the colony in some respects with ability, always with an unflagging zeal; and he loved the land of his birth with a jealous devotion that goes far towards redeeming his miserable defects. The King himself, and not the

---

[1] *Protêt de M. de Lévis à M. de Vaudreuil contre la Clause dans les Articles de Capitulation qui exige que les Troupes mettront bas les Armes, avec l'Ordre de M. de Vaudreuil au Chevalier de Lévis de se conformer à la Capitulation proposée. Vaudreuil au Ministre de la Marine, 10 Sept. 1760. Lévis au Ministre de la Guerre, 27 Nov. 1760.*

[2] *Le Ministre à Vaudreuil, 5 Déc. 1760.*

[3] *Le Ministre au Vicomte de Vaudreuil, Frère du Gouverneur, 21 Déc. 1760.*

servants whom he abandoned to their fate, was answerable for the loss of New France.

Half the continent had changed hands at the scratch of a pen. Governor Bernard, of Massachusetts, proclaimed a day of thanksgiving for the great event, and the Boston newspapers recount how the occasion was celebrated with a parade of the cadets and other volunteer corps, a grand dinner in Faneuil Hall, music, bonfires, illuminations, firing of cannon, and, above all, by sermons in every church of the province; for the heart of early New England always found voice through her pulpits. Before me lies a bundle of these sermons, rescued from sixscore years of dust, scrawled on their title-pages with names of owners dead long ago, worm-eaten, dingy, stained with the damps of time, and uttering in quaint old letterpress the emotions of a buried and forgotten past. Triumph, gratulation, hope, breathe in every line, but no ill-will against a fallen enemy. Thomas Foxcroft, pastor of the "Old Church in Boston," preaches from the text, "The Lord hath done great things for us, whereof we are glad." "Long," he says, "had it been the common opinion, *Delenda est Carthago*, Canada must be conquered, or we could hope for no lasting quiet in these parts; and now, through the good hand of our God upon us, we see the happy day of its accomplishment. We behold His Majesty's victorious troops treading upon the high places of the enemy, their last fortress delivered up, and their whole country surrendered to the King of Britain in the person of his general, the intrepid, the serene, the successful Amherst."

The loyal John Mellen, pastor of the Second Church in Lancaster, exclaims, boding nothing of the tempest to come: "Let us fear God and honor the King, and be peaceable subjects of an easy and happy government. And may the blessing of Heaven be ever upon those enemies of our country that have now submitted to the English Crown, and according to the oath they have taken lead quiet lives in all godliness and honesty." Then he ventures to predict that America, now thrown open to British colonists, will be peopled in a century and a half with sixty million souls: a prophecy likely to be more than fulfilled.

"God has given us to sing this day the downfall of New France, the North American Babylon, New England's rival," cries Eli Forbes to his congregation of sober farmers and staid matrons at the rustic village of Brookfield. Like many of his flock, he had been to the war, having served two years as chaplain of Ruggles's Massachusetts regiment; and something of a martial spirit breathes through his discourse. He passes in review the events of each campaign down to their triumphant close. "Thus God was our salvation and our strength; yet he who directs the great events of war suffered not our joy to be uninterrupted, for we had to lament the fall of the valiant and good General Wolfe, whose death demands a tear from every British eye, a sigh from every Protestant heart. Is he dead? I recall myself. Such heroes are immortal; he lives on every loyal tongue; he lives in every grateful breast; and charity bids me give him a place among the princes of heaven." Nor does he forget the praises of Amherst, "the renowned general, worthy of that most honorable of all titles, the Christian hero; for he loves his enemies, and while he subdues them he makes them happy. He transplants British liberty to where till now it was unknown. He acts the General, the Briton, the Conqueror, and the Christian. What fair hopes arise from the peaceful and undisturbed enjoyment of this good land, and the blessing of our gracious God with it! Methinks I see towns enlarged, settlements increased, and this howling wilderness become a fruitful field which the Lord hath blessed; and, to complete the scene, I see churches rise and flourish in every Christian grace where has been the seat of Satan and Indian idolatry."

Nathaniel Appleton, of Cambridge, hails the dawning of a new era. "Who can tell what great and glorious things God is about to bring forward in the world, and in this world of America in particular? Oh, may the time come when these deserts, which for ages unknown have been regions of darkness and habitations of cruelty, shall be illuminated with the light of the glorious Gospel, and when this part of the world, which till the later ages was utterly unknown, shall be the glory and joy of the whole earth!"

On the American continent the war was ended, and the British colonists breathed for a space, as they drifted unwittingly towards a deadlier strife. They had learned hard and useful lessons. Their mutual jealousies and disputes, the quarrels of their governors and assemblies, the want of any general military organization, and the absence, in most of them, of military habits, joined to narrow views of their own interest, had unfitted them to the last degree for carrying on offensive war. Nor were the British troops sent for their support remarkable in the beginning for good discipline or efficient command. When hostilities broke out, the army of Great Britain was so small as to be hardly worth the name. A new one had to be created; and thus the inexperienced Shirley and the incompetent Loudon, with the futile Newcastle behind them, had, besides their own incapacity, the disadvantage of raw troops and half-formed officers; while against them stood an enemy who, though weak in numbers, was strong in a centralized military organization, skilful leaders armed with untrammelled and absolute authority, practised soldiers, and a population not only brave, but in good part inured to war.

The nature of the country was another cause that helped to protract the contest. "Geography," says Von Moltke, "is three fourths of military science;" and never was the truth of his words more fully exemplified. Canada was fortified with vast outworks of defence in the savage forests, marshes, and mountains that encompassed her, where the thoroughfares were streams choked with fallen trees and obstructed by cataracts. Never was the problem of moving troops, encumbered with baggage and artillery, a more difficult one. The question was less how to fight the enemy than how to get at him. If a few practicable roads had crossed this broad tract of wilderness, the war would have been shortened and its character changed.

From these and other reasons, the numerical superiority of the English was to some extent made unavailing. This superiority, though exaggerated by French writers, was nevertheless immense if estimated by the number of men called to arms; but only a part of these could be employed in offensive operations. The rest garrisoned forts and blockhouses and guarded the far reach of frontier from Nova Scotia to South Carolina, where a wily enemy, silent and secret as fate, choosing their own time and place of attack, and striking unawares at every unguarded spot, compelled thousands of men, scattered at countless points of defence, to keep unceasing watch against a few hundred savage marauders. Full half the levies of the colonies, and many of the regulars, were used in service of this kind.

In actual encounters the advantage of numbers was often with the French, through the comparative ease with which they could concentrate their forces at a given point. Of the ten considerable sieges or battles of the war, five, besides the great bushfight in which the Indians defeated Braddock, were victories for France; and in four of these— Oswego, Fort William Henry, Montmorenci, and Ste.-Foy—the odds were greatly on her side.

Yet in this the most picturesque and dramatic of American wars, there is nothing more noteworthy than the skill with which the French and Canadian leaders used their advantages; the indomitable spirit with which, slighted and abandoned as they were, they grappled with prodigious difficulties, and the courage with which they were seconded by regulars and militia alike. In spite of occasional lapses, the defence of Canada deserves a tribute of admiration.

31

The Peace of Paris

1758–1763

In accordance with the terms of the capitulation of Mont-real, the French military officers, with such of the soldiers as could be kept together, as well as all the chief civil officers of the colony, sailed for France in vessels provided by the conquerors. They were voluntarily followed by the principal members of the Canadian *noblesse*, and by many of the merchants who had no mind to swear allegiance to King George. The peasants and poorer colonists remained at home to begin a new life under a new flag.

Though this exodus of the natural leaders of Canada was in good part deferred till the next year, and though the number of persons to be immediately embarked was reduced by the desertion of many French soldiers who had married Canadian wives, yet the English authorities were sorely perplexed to find vessels enough for the motley crowd of passengers. When at last they were all on their way, a succession of

furious autumnal storms fell upon them. The ship that carried Lévis
barely escaped wreck, and that which bore Vaudreuil and his wife fared
little better.[1] Worst of all was the fate of the "Auguste," on board of
which was the bold but ruthless partisan, Saint-Luc de la Corne, his
brother, his children, and a party of Canadian officers, together with
ladies, merchants, and soldiers. A worthy ecclesiastical chronicler
paints the unhappy vessel as a floating Babylon, and sees in her fate
the stern judgment of Heaven.[2] It is true that New France ran riot in
the last years of her existence; but before the "Auguste" was well out
of the St. Lawrence she was so tossed and buffeted, so lashed with
waves and pelted with rain, that the most alluring forms of sin must
have lost their charm, and her inmates passed days rather of penance
than transgression. There was a violent storm as the ship entered the
Gulf; then a calm, during which she took fire in the cook's galley. The
crew and passengers subdued the flames after desperate efforts; but their
only food thenceforth was dry biscuit. Off the coast of Cape Breton
another gale rose. They lost their reckoning and lay tossing blindly
amid the tempest. The exhausted sailors took, in despair, to their ham-
mocks, from which neither commands nor blows could rouse them,
while amid shrieks, tears, prayers, and vows to Heaven, the "Auguste"
drove towards the shore, struck, and rolled over on her side. La Corne
with six others gained the beach; and towards night they saw the ship
break asunder, and counted a hundred and fourteen corpses strewn
along the sand. Aided by Indians and by English officers, La Corne
made his way on snow-shoes up the St. John, and by a miracle of
enduring hardihood reached Quebec before the end of winter.[3]

The other ships weathered the November gales, and landed their
passengers on the shores of France, where some of them found a dismal
welcome, being seized and thrown into the Bastille. These were Vaudreuil, Bigot, Cadet, Péan, Bréard, Varin, Le Mercier, Penisseault,
Maurin, Corpron, and others accused of the frauds and peculations that
had helped to ruin Canada. In the next year they were all put on trial,
whether as an act of pure justice or as a device to turn public indignation from the Government. In December, 1761, judges commissioned
for the purpose began their sessions at the Châtelet, and a prodigious
mass of evidence was laid before them. Cadet, with brazen effrontery,
at first declared himself innocent, but ended with full and unblushing

[1]*Lévis à Belleisle,* 27 Nov. 1760.
[2]Faillon, *Vie de Mademoiselle Le Ber,* 363–370.
[3]*Journal du Voyage de M. Saint-Luc de la Corne.* This is his own narrative.

confession. Bigot denied everything till silenced point by point with papers bearing his own signature. The prisoners defended themselves by accusing each other. Bigot and Vaudreuil brought mutual charges, while all agreed in denouncing Cadet. Vaudreuil, as before mentioned, was acquitted. Bigot was banished from France for life, his property was confiscated, and he was condemned to pay fifteen hundred thousand francs by way of restitution. Cadet was banished for nine years from Paris and required to refund six millions; while others were sentenced in sums varying from thirty thousand to eight hundred thousand francs, and were ordered to be held in prison till the money was paid. Of twenty-one persons brought to trial ten were condemned, six were acquitted, three received an admonition, and two were dismissed for want of evidence. Thirty-four failed to appear, of whom seven were sentenced in default, and judgment was reserved in the case of the rest.[1] Even those who escaped from justice profited little by their gains, for unless they had turned them betimes into land or other substantial values, they lost them in a discredited paper currency and dishonored bills of exchange.

While on the American continent the last scenes of the war were drawing to their close, the contest raged in Europe with unabated violence. England was in the full career of success; but her great ally, Frederic of Prussia, seemed tottering to his ruin. In the summer of 1758 his glory was at its height. French, Austrians, and Russians had all fled before him. But the autumn brought reverses; and the Austrian general, Daun, at the head of an overwhelming force, gained over him a partial victory, which his masterly strategy robbed of its fruits. It was but a momentary respite. His kingdom was exhausted by its own triumphs. His best generals were dead, his best soldiers killed or disabled, his resources almost spent, the very chandeliers of his palace melted into coin; and all Europe was in arms against him. The disciplined valor of the Prussian troops and the supreme leadership of their undespairing King had thus far held the invading hosts at bay; but now the end seemed near. Frederic could not be everywhere at once; and while he stopped one leak the torrent poured in at another. The Russians advanced again, defeated General Wedell, whom he sent against them, and made a junction with the Austrians. In August, 1759, he attacked their united force at Kunersdorf, broke their left wing to pieces, took a hundred and eighty cannon, forced their centre to give ground, and

---

[1] *Jugement rendu souverainement et en dernier Ressort dans l'Affaire du Canada.* Papers at the Châtelet of Paris, cited by Dussieux.

after hours of furious fighting was overwhelmed at last. In vain he tried to stop the rout. The bullets killed two horses under him, tore his clothes, and crushed a gold snuff-box in his waistcoat pocket. "Is there no b— of a shot that can hit me, then?" he cried in his bitterness, as his aides-de-camp forced him from the field. For a few days he despaired; then rallied to his forlorn task, and with smiles on his lip and anguish at his heart watched, manœuvred, and fought with cool and stubborn desperation. To his friend D'Argens he wrote soon after his defeat: "Death is sweet in comparison to such a life as mine. Have pity on me and it; believe that I still keep to myself a great many evil things, not wishing to afflict or disgust anybody with them, and that I would not counsel you to fly these unlucky countries if I had any ray of hope. Adieu, mon cher!" It was well for him and for Prussia that he had strong allies in the dissensions and delays of his enemies. But his cup was not yet full. Dresden was taken from him, eight of his remaining generals and twelve thousand men were defeated and captured at Maxen, and "this infernal campaign," as he calls it, closed in thick darkness.

"I wrap myself in my stoicism as best I can," he writes to Voltaire. "If you saw me you would hardly know me: I am old, broken, gray-headed, wrinkled. If this goes on there will be nothing left of me but the mania of making verses and an inviolable attachment to my duties and to the few virtuous men I know. But you will not get a peace signed by my hand except on conditions honorable to my nation. Your people, blown up with conceit and folly, may depend on this."

The same stubborn conflict with overmastering odds, the same intrepid resolution, the same subtle strategy, the same skill in eluding the blow and lightning-like quickness in retorting it, marked Frederic's campaign of 1760. At Liegnitz three armies, each equal to his own, closed round him, and he put them all to flight. While he was fighting in Silesia, the Allies marched upon Berlin, took it, and held it three days, but withdrew on his approach. For him there was no peace. "Why weary you with the details of my labors and my sorrows?" he wrote again to his faithful D'Argens. "My spirits have forsaken me; all gayety is buried with the loved noble ones to whom my heart was bound." He had lost his mother and his devoted sister Wilhelmina. "You as a follower of Epicurus put a value upon life; as for me, I regard death from the Stoic point of view. I have told you, and I repeat it, never shall my hand sign a humiliating peace. Finish this campaign I will, resolved to dare all, to succeed, or find a glorious end." Then came the victory of Torgau, the last and one of the most desperate of his battles: a success dearly bought, and bringing neither rest nor safety. Once more he wrote to D'Argens: "Adieu, dear Marquis; write to me sometimes. Don't forget a poor devil who curses his fatal existence ten times a day." "I live like a military monk. Endless business, and a little consolation from my books. I don't know if I shall outlive this war, but if I do I am firmly resolved to pass the rest of my life in solitude in the bosom of philosophy and friendship. Your nation, you see, is blinder than you thought. These fools will lose their Canada and Pondicherry to please the Queen of Hungary and the Czarina."

The campaign of 1761 was mainly defensive on the part of Frederic. In the exhaustion of his resources he could see no means of continuing the struggle. "It is only Fortune," says the royal sceptic, "that can extricate me from the situation I am in. I escape out of it by looking at the universe on the great scale like an observer from some distant planet. All then seems to be so infinitely small that I could almost pity my enemies for giving themselves so much trouble about so very little. I read a great deal, I devour my books. But for them I think hypochondria would have had me in Bedlam before now. In fine, dear Marquis, we live in troublous times and desperate situations. I have all the properties of a stage hero; always in danger, always on the point of perishing."[1] And in another mood: "I begin to feel that, as the Italians say, revenge is a pleasure for the gods. My philosophy is worn out by suffering. I am no saint, and I will own that I should die content if only I could first inflict a part of the misery that I endure."

While Frederic was fighting for life and crown, an event took place in England that was to have great influence on the war. Walpole recounts it thus, writing to George Montagu on the twenty-fifth of October, 1760: "My man Harry tells me all the amusing news. He first told me of the late Prince of Wales's death, and to-day of the King's; so I must tell you all I know of departed majesty. He went to bed well last night, rose at six this morning as usual, looked, I suppose, if all his money was in his purse, and called for his chocolate. A little after seven he went into the closet; the German *valet-de-chambre* heard a noise, listened, heard something like a groan, ran in, and found the hero of Oudenarde and Dettingen on the floor with a gash on his right temple by falling against the corner of a bureau. He tried to speak, could not, and expired. The great ventricle of the heart had burst. What an enviable death!"

The old King was succeeded by his grandson, George III., a mirror

---

[1] The above extracts are as translated by Carlyle in his *History of Frederick II. of Prussia.*

of domestic virtues, conscientious, obstinate, narrow. His accession produced political changes that had been preparing for some time. His grandfather was German at heart, loved his Continental kingdom of Hanover, and was eager for all measures that looked to its defence and preservation. Pitt, too, had of late vigorously supported the Continental war, saying that he would conquer America in Germany. Thus with different views the King and the Minister had concurred in the same measures. But George III. was English by birth, language, and inclination. His ruling passion was the establishment and increase of his own authority. He disliked Pitt, the representative of the people. He was at heart averse to a war, the continuance of which would make the Great Commoner necessary, and therefore powerful, and he wished for a peace that would give free scope to his schemes for strengthening the prerogative. He was not alone in his pacific inclinations. The enemies of the haughty Minister, who had ridden rough-shod over men far above him in rank, were tired of his ascendency, and saw no hope of ending it but by ending the war. Thus a peace party grew up, and the young King became its real, though not at first its declared, supporter.

The Tory party, long buried, showed signs of resurrection. There were those among its members who, even in a king of the hated line of Hanover, could recognize and admire the same spirit of arbitrary domination that had marked their fallen idols, the Stuarts; and they now joined hands with the discontented Whigs in opposition to Pitt. The horrors of war, the blessings of peace, the weight of taxation, the growth of the national debt, were the rallying cries of the new party; but the mainspring of their zeal was hostility to the great Minister. Even his own colleagues chafed under his spirit of mastery; the chiefs of the Opposition longed to inherit his power; and the King had begun to hate him as a lion in his path. Pitt held to his purpose regardless of the gathering storm. That purpose, as proclaimed by his adherents, was to secure a solid and lasting peace, which meant the reduction of France to so low an estate that she could no more be a danger to her rival. In this he had the sympathy of the great body of the nation.

Early in 1761 the King, a fanatic for prerogative, set his enginery in motion. The elections for the new Parliament were manipulated in his interest. If he disliked Pitt as the representative of the popular will, he also disliked his colleague, the shuffling and uncertain Newcastle, as the representative of a too powerful nobility. Elements hostile to both were introduced into the Cabinet and the great offices. The King's favorite, the Earl of Bute, supplanted Holdernesse as Secretary of State for the Northern Department; Charles Townshend, an opponent of

Pitt, was made Secretary of War; Legge, Chancellor of the Exchequer, was replaced by Viscount Barrington, who was sure for the King; while a place in the Cabinet was also given to the Duke of Bedford, one of the few men who dared face the formidable Minister. It was the policy of the King and his following to abandon Prussia, hitherto supported by British subsidies, make friends with Austria and Russia at her expense, and conclude a separate peace with France.

France was in sore need of peace. The infatuation that had turned her from her own true interest to serve the passions of Maria Theresa and the Czarina Elizabeth had brought military humiliation and financial ruin. Abbé de Bernis, Minister of Foreign Affairs, had lost the favor of Madame de Pompadour, and had been supplanted by the Duc de Choiseul. The new Minister had gained his place by pleasing the favorite; but he kept it through his own ability and the necessities of the time. The Englishman Stanley, whom Pitt sent to negotiate with him, drew this sketch of his character: "Though he may have his superiors, not only in experience of business, but in depth and refinement as a statesman, he is a person of as bold and daring a spirit as any man whatever in our country or in his own. Madame Pompadour has ever been looked upon by all preceding courtiers and ministers as their tutelary deity, under whose auspices only they could exist, and who was as much out of their reach as if she were of a superior class of beings; but this Minister is so far from being in subordination to her influence that he seized the first opportunity of depriving her not of an equality, but of any share of power, reducing her to the necessity of applying to him even for those favors that she wants for herself and her dependents. He has effected this great change, which every other man would have thought impossible, in the interior of the Court, not by plausibility, flattery, and address, but with a high hand, with frequent railleries and sarcasms which would have ruined any other, and, in short, by a clear superiority of spirit and resolution."[1]

Choiseul was vivacious, brilliant, keen, penetrating; believing nothing, fearing nothing; an easy moralist, an uncertain ally, a hater of priests; light-minded, inconstant; yet a kind of patriot, eager to serve France and retrieve her fortunes.

He flattered himself with no illusions. "Since we do not know how to make war," he said, "we must make peace;"[2] and he proposed a congress of all the belligerent Powers at Augsburg. At the same time,

[1] *Stanley to Pitt, 6 Aug. 1761*, in *Grenville Correspondence*, I. 367, note.
[2] Flassan, *Diplomatie Française*, V. 376 (Paris, 1809).

since the war in Germany was distinct from the maritime and colonial war of France and England, he proposed a separate negotiation with the British Court in order to settle the questions between them as a preliminary to the general pacification. Pitt consented, and Stanley went as envoy to Versailles; while M. de Bussy came as envoy to London and, in behalf of Choiseul, offered terms of peace, the first of which was the entire abandonment of Canada to England.[1] But the offers were accompanied by the demand that Spain, which had complaints of its own against England, should be admitted as a party to the negotiation, and even hold in some measure the attitude of a mediator. Pitt spurned the idea with fierce contempt. "Time enough to treat of all that, sir, when the Tower of London is taken sword in hand."[2] He bore his part with the ability that never failed him, and with a supreme arrogance that rose to a climax in his demand that the fortress of Dunkirk should be demolished, not because it was any longer dangerous to England, but because the nation would regard its destruction "as an eternal monument of the yoke imposed on France."[3]

Choiseul replied with counter-propositions less humiliating to his nation. When the question of accepting or rejecting them came before the Ministry, the views of Pitt prevailed by a majority of one, and, to the disappointment of Bute and the King, the conferences were broken off. Choiseul, launched again on the billows of a disastrous war, had seen and provided against the event. Ferdinand VI. of Spain had died, and Carlos III. had succeeded to his throne. Here, as in England, change of kings brought change of policy. While negotiating vainly with Pitt, the French Minister had negotiated secretly and successfully with Carlos; and the result was the treaty known as the Family Compact, having for its object the union of the various members of the House of Bourbon in common resistance to the growing power of England. It provided that in any future war the Kings of France and Spain should act as one towards foreign Powers, insomuch that the enemy of either should be the enemy of both; and the Bourbon princes of Italy were invited to join in the covenant.[4] What was more to the present purpose, a special agreement was concluded on the same day, by which

---

[1]See the proposals in Entick, V. 161.

[2]Beatson, *Military Memoirs*, II. 434. *The Count de Fuentes to the Earl of Egremont, 25 Dec. 1761*, in Entick, V. 264.

[3]On this negotiation, see *Mémoire historique sur la Négociation de la France et de l'Angleterre* (Paris, 1761), a French Government publication containing papers on both sides. The British Ministry also published such documents as they saw fit, under the title of *Papers relating to the Rupture with Spain*. Compare Adolphus, *George III.*, I. 31–39.

[4]Flassan, *Diplomatie Française*, V. 317 (Paris, 1809).

Spain bound herself to declare war against England unless that Power should make peace with France before the first of May, 1762. For the safety of her colonies and her trade Spain felt it her interest to join her sister nation in putting a check on the vast expansion of British maritime power. She could bring a hundred ships of war to aid the dilapidated navy of France, and the wealth of the Indies to aid her ruined treasury.[1]

Pitt divined the secret treaty, and soon found evidence of it. He resolved to demand at once full explanation from Spain; and, failing to receive a satisfactory reply, attack her at home and abroad before she was prepared. On the second of October he laid his plan before a Cabinet Council held at a house in St. James Street. There were present the Earl of Bute, the Duke of Newcastle, Earl Granville, Earl Temple, and others of the Ministry. Pitt urged his views with great warmth. "This," he exclaimed, "is the time for humbling the whole House of Bourbon!"[1] His brother-in-law, Temple, supported him. Newcastle kept silent. Bute denounced the proposal, and the rest were of his mind. "If these views are to be followed," said Pitt, "this is the last time I can sit at this board. I was called to the administration of affairs by the voice of the people; to them I have always considered myself as accountable for my conduct; and therefore cannot remain in a situation which makes me responsible for measures I am no longer allowed to guide." Nothing could be more offensive to George III. and his adherents.

The veteran Carteret, Earl Granville, replied angrily: "I find the gentleman is determined to leave us; nor can I say I am sorry for it, since otherwise he would certainly have compelled us to leave him. But if he is resolved to assume the office of exclusively advising His Majesty and directing the operations of the war, to what purpose are we called to this council? When he talks of being responsible to the people, he talks the language of the House of Commons, and forgets that at this board he is responsible only to the King. However, though he may possibly have convinced himself of his infallibility, still it remains that we should be equally convinced before we can resign our understandings to his direction, or join with him in the measure he proposes."[2]

Pitt resigned, and his colleagues rejoiced.[3] Power fell to Bute and the Tories; and great was the fall. The mass of the nation was with the defeated Minister. On Lord Mayor's Day Bute and Barrington were

[1]Beatson, II. 438.

[2]*Annual Register, 1761*, p. 44. Adolphus, *George III.*, I. 40. Thackeray, *Life of Chatham*, I. 592.

[3]Walpole, *George III.*, I. 80, and note by Sir Denis Le Marchant, 80–82.

passing St. Paul's in a coach, which the crowd mistook for that of Pitt, and cheered lustily; till one man, looking in at the window, shouted to the rest: "This isn't Pitt; it's Bute, and be damned to him!" The cheers turned forthwith to hisses, mixed with cries of "No Bute!" "No New-castle salmon!" "Pitt forever!" Handfuls of mud were showered against the coach, and Barrington's ruffles were besmirched with it.[1]

The fall of Pitt was like the knell of doom to Frederic of Prussia. It meant abandonment by his only ally, and the loss of the subsidy which was his chief resource. The darkness around him grew darker yet, and not a hope seemed left; when as by miracle the clouds broke, and light streamed out of the blackness. The bitterest of his foes, the Czarina Elizabeth, she whom he had called *infâme catin du Nord*, died, and was succeeded by her nephew, Peter III. Here again, as in England and Spain, a new sovereign brought new measures. The young Czar, simple and enthusiastic, admired the King of Prussia, thought him the paragon of heroes, and proclaimed himself his friend. No sooner was he on the throne than Russia changed front. From the foe of Frederic she became his ally; and in the opening campaign of 1762 the army that was to have aided in crushing him was ranged on his side. It was a turn of fortune too sharp and sudden to endure. Ill-balanced and extreme in all things, Peter plunged into headlong reforms, exasperated the clergy and the army, and alienated his wife, Catherine, who had hoped to rule in his name, and who now saw herself supplanted by his mistress. Within six months he was deposed and strangled. Catherine, one of whose lovers had borne part in the murder, reigned in his stead, conspicuous by the unbridled disorders of her life, and by powers of mind that mark her as the ablest of female sovereigns. If she did not share her husband's enthusiasm for Frederic, neither did she share Elizabeth's hatred of him. He, on his part, taught by hard experience, conciliated instead of in-sulting her, and she let him alone.

Peace with Russia brought peace with Sweden, and Austria with the Germanic Empire stood alone against him. France needed all her strength to hold her own against the mixed English and German force under Ferdinand of Brunswick in the Rhine countries. She made spas-modic efforts to seize upon Hanover, but the result was humiliating defeat.

In England George III. pursued his policy of strengthening the pre-rogative, and, jealous of the Whig aristocracy, attacked it in the person of Newcastle. In vain the old politician had played false with Pitt, and

---

[1] *Nuthall to Lady Chatham, 12 Nov. 1761,* in *Chatham Correspondence,* II. 166.

trimmed to please his young master. He was worried into resigning his place in the Cabinet, and Bute, the obsequious agent of the royal will, succeeded him as First Lord of the Treasury. Into his weak and unwilling hands now fell the task of carrying on the war; for the nation, elated with triumphs and full of fight, still called on its rulers for fresh efforts and fresh victories. Pitt had proved a true prophet, and his enemies were put to shame; for the attitude of Spain forced Bute and his colleagues to the open rupture with her which the great Minister had vainly urged upon them; and a new and formidable war was now added to the old.[1] Their counsels were weak and half-hearted; but the armies and navies of England still felt the impulsion that the imperial hand of Pitt had given and the unconquerable spirit that he had roused.

This spirit had borne them from victory to victory. In Asia they had driven the French from Pondicherry and all their Indian possessions; in Africa they had wrested from them Gorée and the Senegal country; in the West Indies they had taken Guadeloupe and Dominica; in the European seas they had captured ship after ship, routed and crippled the great fleet of Admiral Conflans, seized Belleisle, and defeated a bold attempt to invade Ireland. The navy of France was reduced to helplessness. Pitt, before his resignation, had planned a series of new operations, including an attack on Martinique, with other West Indian islands still left to France, and then in turn on the Spanish possessions of Havana, Panama, Manila, and the Philippines. Now, more than ever before, the war appeared in its true character. It was a contest for maritime and colonial ascendency; and England saw herself confronted by both her great rivals at once.

Admiral Rodney sailed for Martinique, and Brigadier Monckton joined him with troops from America. Before the middle of February the whole island was in their hands; and Grenada, St. Lucia, and St. Vincent soon shared its fate. The Earl of Albemarle and Admiral Sir George Pococke sailed in early spring on a more important errand, landed in June near Havana with eleven thousand soldiers, and attacked Moro Castle, the key of the city. The pitiless sun of the tropic midsummer poured its fierce light and heat on the parched rocks where the men toiled at the trenches. Earth was so scarce that hardly enough could be had to keep the fascines in place. The siege works were little else than a mass of dry faggots; and when, after exhausting toil, the grand battery opened on the Spanish defences, it presently took fire, was consumed, and had to be made anew. Fresh water failed, and the

[1] *Declaration of War against the King of Spain*, 4 Jan. 1762.

troops died by scores from thirst; fevers set in, killed many, and disabled nearly half the army. The sea was strewn with floating corpses, and carrion-birds in clouds hovered over the populous graveyards and infected camps. Yet the siege went on: a formidable sally was repulsed; Moro Castle was carried by storm; till at length, two months and eight days after the troops landed, Havana fell into their hands.[1] At the same time Spain was attacked at the antipodes, and the loss of Manila and the Philippines gave her fresh cause to repent her rash compact with France. She was hardly more fortunate near home; for having sent an army to invade Portugal, which was in the interest of England, a small British force, under Brigadier Burgoyne, foiled it, and forced it to retire.

The tide of British success was checked for an instant in Newfoundland, where a French squadron attacked St. John's and took it, with its garrison of sixty men. The news reached Amherst at New York; his brother, Lieutenant-Colonel Amherst, was sent to the scene of the mishap. St. John's was retaken, and its late conquerors were made prisoners of war.

The financial condition of France was desperate. Her people were crushed with taxation; her debt grew apace; and her yearly expenditure was nearly double her revenue. Choiseul felt the need of immediate peace; and George III. and Bute were hardly less eager for it, to avert the danger of Pitt's return to power and give free scope to their schemes for strengthening the prerogative. Therefore, in September, 1762, negotiations were resumed. The Duke of Bedford was sent to Paris to settle the preliminaries, and the Duc de Nivernois came to London on the same errand. The populace were still for war. Bedford was hissed as he passed through the streets of London, and a mob hooted at the puny figure of Nivernois as he landed at Dover.

The great question was, Should Canada be restored? Should France still be permitted to keep a foothold on the North American continent? Ever since the capitulation of Montreal a swarm of pamphlets had discussed the momentous subject. Some maintained that the acquisition of Canada was not an original object of the war; that the colony was of little value and ought to be given back to its old masters; that Guadeloupe should be kept instead, the sugar trade of that island being worth far more than the Canadian fur trade; and, lastly, that the British colonists, if no longer held in check by France, would spread themselves over the continent, learn to supply all their own wants, grow

---

[1] *Journal of the Siege, by the Chief Engineer*, in Beatson, II. 544. Mante, 398–465. Entick, V. 363–383.

independent, and become dangerous. Nor were these views confined to Englishmen. There were foreign observers who clearly saw that the adhesion of her colonies to Great Britain would be jeopardized by the extinction of French power in America. Choiseul warned Stanley that they "would not fail to shake off their dependence the moment Canada should be ceded;" while thirteen years before, the Swedish traveller Kalm declared that the presence of the French in America gave the best assurance to Great Britain that its own colonies would remain in due subjection.[1]

The most noteworthy argument on the other side was that of Franklin, whose words find a strange commentary in the events of the next few years. He affirmed that the colonies were so jealous of each other that they would never unite against England. "If they could not agree to unite against the French and Indians, can it reasonably be supposed that there is any danger of their uniting against their own nation, which it is well known they all love much more than they love one another? I will venture to say union amongst them for such a purpose is not merely improbable, it is impossible;" that is, he prudently adds, without "the most grievous tyranny and oppression," like the bloody rule of "Alva in the Netherlands."[2]

If Pitt had been in office he would have demanded terms that must ruin past redemption the maritime and colonial power of France; but Bute was less exacting. In November the plenipotentiaries of England, France, and Spain agreed on preliminaries of peace, in which the following were the essential points. France ceded to Great Britain Canada and all her possessions on the North American continent east of the River Mississippi, except the city of New Orleans and a small adjacent district. She renounced her claims to Acadia, and gave up to the conqueror the Island of Cape Breton, with all other islands in the Gulf and River of St. Lawrence. Spain received back Havana, and paid for it by the cession of Florida, with all her other possessions east of the Mississippi. France, subject to certain restrictions, was left free to fish in the Gulf of St. Lawrence and off a part of the coast of Newfoundland; and the two little islands of St. Pierre and Miquelon were given her as

[1]Kalm, *Travels in North America*, I. 207.

[2]*Interest of Great Britain in regard to her Colonies* (London, 1760).

Lord Bath argues for retaining Canada in *A Letter addressed to Two Great Men on the Prospect of Peace* (1759). He is answered by another pamphlet called *Remarks on the Letter to Two Great Men* (1760). The *Gentleman's Magazine* for 1759 has an ironical article styled *Reasons for restoring Canada to the French*; and in 1761 a pamphlet against the restitution appeared under the title, *Importance of Canada considered in Two Letters to a Noble Lord*. These are but a part of the writings on the question.

fishing stations on condition that she should not fortify or garrison them. In the West Indies, England restored the captured islands of Guadeloupe, Marigalante, Désirade, and Martinique, and France ceded Grenada and the Grenadines; while it was agreed that of the so-called neutral islands, St. Vincent, Dominica, and Tobago should belong to England, and St. Lucia to France. In Europe, each side promised to give no more help to its allies in the German war. France restored Minorca, and England restored Belleisle; France gave up such parts of Hanoverian territory as she had occupied, and evacuated certain fortresses belonging to Prussia, pledging herself at the same time to demolish, under the inspection of English engineers, her own maritime fortress of Dunkirk. In Africa France ceded Senegal, and received back the small Island of Gorée. In India she lost everything she had gained since the peace of Aix-la-Chapelle; recovered certain trading stations, but renounced the right of building forts or maintaining troops in Bengal.

On the day when the preliminaries were signed, France made a secret agreement with Spain, by which she divested herself of the last shred of her possessions on the North American continent. As compensation for Florida, which her luckless ally had lost in her quarrel, she made over to the Spanish Crown the city of New Orleans, and under the name of Louisiana gave her the vast region spreading westward from the Mississippi towards the Pacific.

On the ninth of December the question of approving the preliminaries came up before both Houses of Parliament. There was a long debate in the Commons. Pitt was not present, confined, it was said, by gout; till late in the day the House was startled by repeated cheers from the outside. The doors opened, and the fallen Minister entered, carried in the arms of his servants, and followed by an applauding crowd. His bearers set him down within the bar, and by the help of a crutch he made his way with difficulty to his seat. "There was a mixture of the very solemn and the theatric in this apparition," says Walpole, who was present. "The moment was so well timed, the importance of the man and his services, the languor of his emaciated countenance, and the study bestowed on his dress were circumstances that struck solemnity into a patriot mind, and did a little furnish ridicule to the hardened and insensible. He was dressed in black velvet, his legs and thighs wrapped in flannel, his feet covered with buskins of black cloth, and his hands with thick gloves." Not for the first time, he was utilizing his maladies for purposes of stage effect. He spoke for about three hours, sometimes standing, and sometimes seated; sometimes with a brief burst of power, more often with the accents of pain and exhaustion. He highly commended the retention of Canada, but denounced the leaving to France a share in the fisheries, as well as other advantages tending to a possible revival of her maritime power. But the Commons listened coldly, and by a great majority approved the preliminaries of peace.

These preliminaries were embodied in the definitive treaty concluded at Paris on the tenth of February, 1763. Peace between France and England brought peace between the warring nations of the Continent. Austria, bereft of her allies, and exhausted by vain efforts to crush Frederic, gave up the attempt in despair, and signed the treaty of Hubertsburg. The Seven Years War was ended.

32

Conclusion

1763–1884

"This," said Earl Granville on his deathbed, "has been the most glorious war and the most triumphant peace that England ever knew." Not all were so well pleased, and many held with Pitt that the House of Bourbon should have been forced to drain the cup of humiliation to the dregs. Yet the fact remains that the Peace of Paris marks an epoch than which none in modern history is more fruitful of grand results. With it began a new chapter in the annals of the world. To borrow the words of a late eminent writer, "It is no exaggeration to say that three of the many victories of the Seven Years War determined for ages to come the destinies of mankind. With that of Rossbach began the re-creation of Germany; with that of Plassey the influence of Europe told for the first time since the days of Alexander on the nations of the East; with the triumph of Wolfe on the Heights of Abraham began the history of the United States."[1]

So far, however, as concerns the war in the Germanic countries, it was to outward seeming but a mad debauch of blood and rapine, ending in nothing but the exhaustion of the combatants. The havoc had been frightful. According to the King of Prussia's reckoning, 853,000 soldiers

[1]Green, *History of the English People*, IV. 193 (London, 1880).

544

of the various nations had lost their lives, besides hundreds of thousands of non-combatants who had perished from famine, exposure, disease, or violence. And with all this waste of life not a boundary line had been changed. The rage of the two empresses and the vanity and spite of the concubine had been completely foiled. Frederic had defied them all, and had come out of the strife intact in his own hereditary dominions and master of all that he had snatched from the Empress-Queen; while Prussia, portioned out by her enemies as their spoil, lay depleted indeed, and faint with deadly striving, but crowned with glory, and with the career before her which, through tribulation and adversity, was to lead her at last to the headship of a united Germany.

Through centuries of strife and vicissitude the French monarchy had triumphed over nobles, parliaments, and people, gathered to itself all the forces of the State, beamed with illusive splendors under Louis the Great, and shone with the phosphorescence of decay under his contemptible successor; till now, robbed of prestige, burdened with debt, and mined with corruption, it was moving swiftly and more swiftly towards the abyss of ruin.

While the war hastened the inevitable downfall of the French monarchy, it produced still more notable effects. France under Colbert had embarked on a grand course of maritime and colonial enterprise, and followed it with an activity and vigor that promised to make her a great and formidable ocean power. It was she who led the way in the East, first trained the natives to fight her battles, and began that system of mixed diplomacy and war which, imitated by her rival, enabled a handful of Europeans to master all India. In North America her vast possessions dwarfed those of every other nation. She had built up a powerful navy and created an extensive foreign trade. All this was now changed. In India she was reduced to helpless inferiority, with total ruin in the future; and of all her boundless territories in North America nothing was left but the two island rocks on the coast of Newfoundland that the victors had given her for drying her codfish. Of her navy scarcely forty ships remained; all the rest were captured or destroyed. She was still great on the continent of Europe, but as a world power her grand opportunities were gone.

In England as in France the several members of the State had battled together since the national life began, and the result had been, not the unchecked domination of the Crown, but a system of balanced and adjusted forces, in which King, Nobility, and Commons all had their recognized places and their share of power. Thus in the war just ended two great conditions of success had been supplied: a people instinct with the energies of ordered freedom, and a masterly leadership to inspire and direct them.

All, and more than all, that France had lost England had won. Now, for the first time, she was beyond dispute the greatest of maritime and colonial Powers. Portugal and Holland, her precursors in ocean enterprise, had long ago fallen hopelessly behind. Two great rivals remained, and she had humbled the one and swept the other from her path. Spain, with vast American possessions, was sinking into the decay which is one of the phenomena of modern history; while France, of late a most formidable competitor, had abandoned the contest in despair. England was mistress of the seas, and the world was thrown open to her merchants, explorers, and colonists. A few years after the Peace the navigator Cook began his memorable series of voyages, and surveyed the strange and barbarous lands which after times were to transform into other Englands, vigorous children of this great mother of nations. It is true that a heavy blow was soon to fall upon her; her own folly was to alienate the eldest and greatest of her offspring. But nothing could rob her of the glory of giving birth to the United States; and, though politically severed, this gigantic progeny were to be not the less a source of growth and prosperity to the parent that bore them, joined with her in a triple kinship of laws, language, and blood. The war or series of wars that ended with the Peace of Paris secured the opportunities and set in action the forces that have planted English homes in every clime, and dotted the earth with English garrisons and posts of trade.

With the Peace of Paris ended the checkered story of New France; a story which would have been a history if faults of constitution and the bigotry and folly of rulers had not dwarfed it to an episode. Yet it is a noteworthy one in both its lights and its shadows: in the disinterested zeal of the founder of Quebec, the self-devotion of the early missionary martyrs, and the daring enterprise of explorers; in the spiritual and temporal vassalage from which the only escape was to the savagery of the wilderness; and in the swarming corruptions which were the natural result of an attempt to rule, by the absolute hand of a master beyond the Atlantic, a people bereft of every vestige of civil liberty. Civil liberty was given them by the British sword; but the conqueror left their religious system untouched, and through it they have imposed upon themselves a weight of ecclesiastical tutelage that finds few equals in the most Catholic countries of Europe. Such guardianship is not without certain advantages. When faithfully exercised it aids to uphold some of the tamer virtues, if that can be called a virtue which needs the constant presence of a sentinel to keep it from escaping: but it is fatal to mental robustness and moral courage; and if French Canada would fulfil its aspirations it must cease to be one of the most priest-ridden communities of the modern world.

Scarcely were they free from the incubus of France when the British provinces showed symptoms of revolt. The measures on the part of the mother-country which roused their resentment, far from being oppressive, were less burdensome than the navigation laws to which they had long submitted; and they resisted taxation by Parliament simply because it was in principle opposed to their rights as freemen. They did not, like the American provinces of Spain at a later day, sunder themselves from a parent fallen into decrepitude; but with astonishing audacity they affronted the wrath of England in the hour of her triumph, forgot their jealousies and quarrels, joined hands in the common cause, fought, endured, and won. The disunited colonies became the United States. The string of discordant communities along the Atlantic coast has grown to a mighty people, joined in a union which the earthquake of civil war served only to compact and consolidate. Those who in the weakness of their dissensions needed help from England against the savage on their borders have become a nation that may defy every foe but that most dangerous of all foes, herself, destined to a majestic future if she will shun the excess and perversion of the principles that made her great, prate less about the enemies of the past and strive more against the enemies of the present, resist the mob and the demagogue as she resisted Parliament and King, rally her powers from the race for gold and the delirium of prosperity to make firm the foundations on which that prosperity rests, and turn some fair proportion of her vast mental forces to other objects than material progress and the game of party politics. She has tamed the savage continent, peopled the solitude, gathered wealth untold, waxed potent, imposing, redoubtable; and now it remains for her to prove, if she can, that the rule of the masses is consistent with the highest growth of the individual; that democracy can give the world a civilization as mature and pregnant, ideas as energetic and vitalizing, and types of manhood as lofty and strong, as any of the systems which it boasts to supplant.

Appendixes
Index

APPENDIXES

Chapter 3. CONFLICT FOR THE WEST

Piquet and his War-Party.—"Ce parti [*de guerre*] pour lequel M. le Général a donné son consentement, sera de plus de 3,800 hommes. . . . 500 hommes de nos domiciliés, 700 des Cinq nations à l'exclusion des Agniers [*Mohawks*] qui ne sont plus regardés que comme des anglais, 600 tant Iroquois que d'autres nations le long de la Belle Rivière d'où ils espèrent chasser les anglais qui y forment des Établissemens contraires au bien des guerriers, 2,000 hommes qu'ils doivent prendre aux têtes plates [*Choctaws*] où ils s'arresteront, c'est la où les deux chefs de guerre doivent proposer à l'armée l'expédition des Miamis au retour de celle contre la Nation du Chien [*Cherokees*]. Un vieux levain, quelques anciennes querelles leur feront tout entreprendre contre les anglais de la Virginie s'ils donnent encore quelques secours à cette derniere nation, ce qui ne manquera pas d'arriver. . . .

"C'est un grand miracle que malgré l'envie, les contradictions, l'opposition presque générale de tous les Villages sauvages, j'aye formé en moins de 3 ans une des plus florissantes missions du Canada. . . . Je me trouve donc, Messieurs, dans l'occasion de pouvoir étendre l'empire de Jésus Christ et du Roy mes bons maitres jusqu'aux extrémités de ce nouveau monde, et de plus faire avec quelques secours que vous me procurerez que la France et l'angleterre ne pourraient faire avec plusieurs millions et toutes leur troupes." *Copie de la Lettre écrite par M. l'Abbé Picquet, dattée à la Présentation du 8 Fév. 1752* (Archives de la Marine).

I saw in the possession of the late Jacques Viger, of Montreal, an illuminated drawing of one of Piquet's banners, said to be still in existence, in which the cross, the emblems of the Virgin and the Saviour, the fleur-de-lis, and the Iroquois totems are all embroidered and linked together by strings of wampum beads wrought into the silk.

Directions of the French Colonial Minister for the Destruction of Oswego.—"La seule voye dont on puisse faire usage en temps de paix pour une pareille opération est celle des Iroquois des cinq nations. Les terres sur lesquelles le poste a été établi leur appartiennent et ce n'est qu'avec leur consentement que les anglois s'y sont placés. Si en faisant regarder à ces sauvages un pareil établissement comme contraire à leur liberté et comme une usurpation dont les anglois prétendent faire usage pour acquérir la propriété de leur terre on pourrait les déterminer à entreprendre de les détruire, une pareille opération ne seroit pas à négliger; mais M. le Marquis de la Jonquière doit sentir avec quelle circonspection une affaire de cette espèce doit être conduite et il faut en effêt qu'il y travaille de façon à ne se point compromettre." *Le Ministre à MM. de la Jonquière et Bigot, 15 Avril, 1750* (Archives de la Marine).

APPENDIX B

Chapter 4. CONFLICT FOR ACADIA

English Treatment of Acadians.—"Les Anglois dans la vue de la Conquête du Canada ont voulu donner aux peuples françois de ces Colonies un exemple frappant de la douceur de leur gouvernement dans leur conduite à l'égard des Accadiens.

"Ils leur ont fourni pendant plus de 35 ans le simple nécessaire, sans élever la fortune d'aucun, ils leur ont fourni ce nécessaire souvent à crédit, avec un excès de confiance, sans fatiguer les débiteurs, sans les presser, sans vouloir les forcer au payement.

"Ils leur ont laissé une apparence de liberté si excessive qu'ils n'ont voulu prendre aucune différence [*sic*] de leur différents, pas même pour les crimes. . . . Ils ont souffert que les accadiens leur refusassent insolemment certains rentes de grains, modiques & très-légitimement dues.

"Ils ont dissimulé le refus méprisant que les accadiens ont fait de prendre d'eux des concessions pour les nouveaux terreins qu'ils voulaient occuper.

"Les fruits que cette conduite a produit dans la dernière guerre nous le savons [*sic*] et les anglois n'en ignorent rien. Qu'on juge là-dessus de leur ressentiment et des vues de vengeance de cette nation cruelle. . . . Je prévois notamment la dispersion des jeunes accadiens sur les vaisseaux de guerre anglois, où la seule règle pour la ration du pain suffit pour les detruire jusqu'au dernier." *Roma, Officier à l'Isle Royale à —— , 1750.*

Indians, directed by Missionaries, to attack the English in Time of Peace.—"La lettre de M. l'Abbé Le Loutre me paroit si intéressante que j'ay l'honneur de vous en envoyer Copie. . . . Les trois sauvages qui m'ont porté ces dépêches m'ont parlé relativement à ce que M. l'Abbé Le Loutre marque dans sa lettre; je n'ay eu garde de leur donner aucun Conseil là-dessus et je me suis borné à leur promettre que je ne les abandonnerai point, aussy ai-je pourvu à tout, soit pour les armes, munitions de guerre et de bouche, soit pour les autres choses nécessaires.

"Il seroit à souhaiter que ces Sauvages rassemblés pussent parvenir à traverser les anglois dans leurs entreprises, même dans celle de Chibouctou [*Halifax*], ils sont dans cette résolution et s'ils peuvent mettre à execution ce qu'ils ont projetté il est assuré qu'ils seront fort incommodes aux Anglois et que les vexations qu'ils exerceront sur eux leur seront un très grand obstacle.

"Ces sauvages doivent agir seuls, il n'y aura ny soldat ny habitant, tout se fera de leur pur mouvement, et sans qu'il paraisse que j'en eusse connoissance.

"Cela est très essentiel, aussy ai-je écrit au Sr de Boishébert d'observer beaucoup de prudence dans ses démarches et de les faire très secrètement pour que les Anglois ne puissent pas s'apercevoir que nous pourvoyons aux besoins des dits sauvages.

"Ce seront les missionnaires qui feront toutes les négociations et qui dirigeront les pas des dits sauvages, ils sont en très bonnes mains, le R. P. Germain et M. l'Abbé Le Loutre étant fort au fait d'en tirer tout le party possible et le plus avantageux pour nos interêts, ils ménageront leur intrigue de façon à n'y pas paroitre. . . .

"Je sens, Monseigneur, toute la delicatesse de cette negociation, soyez persuadé que je la conduirai avec tant de précautions que les anglois ne pourront pas dire que mes ordres y ont eu part." *La Jonquière au Ministre, 9 Oct. 1749.*

Missionaries to be encouraged in their Efforts to make the Indians attack the English.—"Les sauvages . . . se distinguent, depuis la paix, dans les mouvements qu'il y a du côté de l'Acadie, et sur lesquels Sa Majesté juge à propos d'entrer dans quelques details avec le Sieur de Raymond. . . .

"Sa Majesté luy a déjà observé que les sauvages ont été jusqu'à présent dans les dispositions les plus favorables. Il est de la plus grande importance, et pour le présent et pour l'avenir, de ne rien négliger pour les y maintenir. Les missionnaires qui sont auprès d'eux sont plus à portés d'y contribuer que personne, et Sa Majesté a lieu d'être satisfaite des soins qu'ils y donnent. Le Sr de Raymond doit exciter ces missionnaires à ne point se relacher sur cela; mais en même temps il doit les avertir de contenir leur zèle de manière qu'ils ne se compromettent pas mal à propos avec les anglois et qu'ils ne donnent point de justes sujets de plaintes." *Mémoire du Roy pour servir d'Instruction au Comte de Raymond, 24 Avril, 1751.*

Acadians to join the Indians in attacking the English.—"Pour que ces Sauvages agissent avec beaucoup de Courage, quelques accadiens habillés et matachés comme les Sauvages pourront se joindre à eux pour faire coup sur les Anglois. Je ne puis éviter de consentir à ce que ces Sauvages feront puisque nous avons les bras liés et que nous ne pouvons rien faire par nous-mêmes, au surplus je ne crois pas qu'il y ait de l'inconvenient de laisser mêler les accadiens parmi les Sauvages, parceque s'ils sont pris, nous dirons qu'ils ont agi de leur propre mouvement." *La Jonquière au Ministre, 1 Mai, 1751.*

Cost of Le Loutre's Intrigues.—"J'ay déjà fait payer a M. Le Loutre depuis l'année dernière la somme de 11183*l.* 18*s.* pour acquitter les dépenses qu'il fait journellement et je ne cesse de luy recommander de s'en tenir aux indispensables en evitant toujours de rien compromettre avec le gouvernement anglois." *Prévost au Ministre, 22 Juillet, 1750.*

Payment for English Scalps in Time of Peace.—"Les Sauvages ont pris, il y a un mois, 18 chevelures angloises [*English scalps*], et M. Le Loutre a été obligé de les payer 1800*l.*, argent de l'Acadie, dont je luy ay fait le remboursement." *Ibid., 16 Août, 1753.*

Many pages might be filled with extracts like the above. These, with most of the other French documents used in Chapter IV., are taken from the Archives de la Marine et des Colonies.

APPENDIX C
Chapter 5. WASHINGTON

Washington and the Capitulation at Fort Necessity.—Villiers, in his Journal, boasts that he made Washington sign a virtual admission that he had assassinated Jumonville. In regard to this point, a letter, of which the following is an extract, is printed in the provincial papers of the time. It is from Captain Adam Stephen, an officer in the action, writing to a friend five weeks after.

"When Mr. Vanbraam returned with the French proposals, we were obliged to take the sense of them from his mouth; it rained so heavy that he could not give us a written translation of them; we could scarcely keep the candle lighted to read them by; they were written in a bad hand, on wet and blotted paper, so that no person could read them but Vanbraam, who had heard them from the mouth of the French officer. Every officer there is ready to declare that there was no such word as *assassination* mentioned. The terms expressed were, *the death of Jumonville.* If it had been mentioned we would by all means have had it altered, as the French, during the course of the interview, seemed very condescending, and desirous to bring things to an issue." He then gives several other points in which Vanbraam had misled them.

Dinwiddie, recounting the affair to Lord Albemarle, says that Washington, being ignorant of French, was deceived by the interpreter, who, through poltroonery, suppressed the word assassination.

Captain Mackay, writing to Washington in September, after a visit to Philadelphia, says: "I had several disputes about our capitulation; but I satisfied every person that mentioned the subject as to the articles in question, that they were owing to a bad interpreter, and contrary to the translation made to us when we signed them."

At the next meeting of the burgesses they passed a vote of thanks for gallant conduct to Washington and all his officers by name, except Vanbraam and the major of the regiment, the latter being charged with cowardice, and the former with treacherous misinterpretation of the articles.

Sometime after, Washington wrote to a correspondent who had questioned him on the subject: "That we were wilfully or ignorantly deceived by our interpreter in regard to the word *assassination* I do aver, and will to my dying moment; so will every officer that was present. The interpreter was a Dutchman little acquainted with the English tongue, therefore might not advert to the tone and meaning of the word in English; but, whatever his motives for so doing, certain it is that he called it the *death* or the *loss* of the Sieur Jumonville. So we received and so we understood it, until, to our great surprise and mortification, we found it otherwise in a literal translation." Sparks, *Writings of Washington*, II. 464, 465.

APPENDIX D
Chapter 7. BRADDOCK

It has been said that Beaujeu, and not Contrecœur, commanded at Fort Duquesne at the time of Braddock's expedition. Some contemporaries, and notably the chaplain of the fort, do, in fact, speak of him as in this position; but their evidence is overborne by more numerous and conclusive authorities, among them Vaudreuil, governor of Canada, and Contrecœur himself, in an official report. Vaudreuil says of him: "Ce commandant s'occupa le 8 [*Juillet*] à former un parti pour aller au devant des Anglois;" and adds that this party was commanded by Beaujeu and consisted of 250 French and 650 Indians (*Vaudreuil au Ministre, 5 Août, 1755*). In the autumn of 1756 Vaudreuil asked the Colonial Minister to procure a pension for Contrecœur and Ligneris. He says: "Le premier de ces Messieurs a commandé longtemps au fort Duquesne; c'est luy qui a ordonné et dirigé tous les mouvements qui se sont faits dans cette partie, soit pour faire abandonner le premier établissement des Anglois, soit pour les forcer à se retirer du fort Nécessité, et soit enfin pour aller au devant de l'armée du Général Braddock qui a été entièrement défaite" (*Vaudreuil au Ministre, 8 Nov. 1756*). Beaujeu, who had lately arrived with a reinforcement, had been named to relieve Contrecœur (*Dumas au Ministre, 24 Juillet, 1756*), but had not yet done so.

As the report of Contrecœur has never been printed, I give an extract from it (*Contrecœur à Vaudreuil, 14 Juillet, 1755*, in Archives de la Marine):—

"Le même jour [8 *Juillet*] je formai un party de tout ce que je pouvois mettre hors du fort pour aller à leur rencontre. Il étoit composé de 250 François et de 650 sauvages, ce qui faisoit 900 hommes. M. de Beaujeu, capitaine, le commandoit. Il y avoit deux capitaines qui estoient M.ʳˢ Dumas et Ligneris et plusieurs autres officiers subalternes. Ce parti se mit en marche le 9 à 8 heures du matin, et se trouva à midi et demie en présence des Anglois à environ 3 lieues du fort. On commença à faire feu de part et d'autre. Le feu de l'artillerie ennemie fit reculer un peu par deux fois notre parti. M. de Beaujeu fut tué à la troisième décharge. M. Dumas prit le commandement et s'en acquitta au mieux. Nos François, pleins de courage, soutenus par les sauvages, quoiqu'ils n'eussent point d'artillerie, firent à leur tour plier les Anglois qui se battirent en ordre de bataille et en bonne contenance. Et ces derniers voyant l'ardeur de nos gens qui fonçoient avec une vigueur infinie furent enfin obligés de plier tout à fait après 4 heures d'un grand feu. Mrs Dumas et Ligneris qui n'avoient plus avec eux q'une vingtaine de François ne s'engagerent point dans la poursuite. Ils rentrerent dans le fort, parceq'une grande partie des Canadiens qui n'estoient malheureusement que des enfants s'estoient retirés à la première décharge."

The letter of Dumas cited in the text has been equally unknown. It was written a year after the battle in order to draw the attention of the minister to services which the writer thought had not been duly recognized. The following is an extract (*Dumas au Ministre, 24 Juillet, 1756*, in Archives de la Marine):—

"M. de Beaujeu marcha donc, et sous ses ordres M. de Ligneris et moi. Il attaqua avec beaucoup d'audace mais sans nulle disposition; notre première décharge fut faite hors de portée; l'ennemi fit la sienne de plus près, et dans le premier instant du combat, cent miliciens, qui fasaient la moitié de nos Français lâcherent honteusement le pied en criant 'Sauve qui peut.' Deux cadets qui depuis ont été faits officiers autorisait cette fuite par leur exemple. Ce mouvement en arrière ayant encouragé l'ennemi, il fit retentir ses cris de Vive le Roi et avança sur nous à grand pas. Son artillerie s'étant preparée pendant ce temps là commença à faire feu ce qui épouvanta tellement les Sauvages que tout prit la fuite; l'ennemi faisait sa troisième décharge de mousqueterie quand M. de Beaujeu fut tué.

"Notre déroute se présenta a mes yeux sous le plus désagréable point de vue, et pour n'être point chargé de la mauvaise manœuvre d'autrui, je ne songeai plus qu'à me faire tuer. Ce fut alors, Monseigneur, qu'excitant de la voix et du geste le peu de soldats qui restait, je m'avançai avec la contenance qui donne le désespoir. Mon peloton fit un feu si vif que l'ennemi en parut étonné; il grossit insensiblement et les Sauvages voyant que mon attaque faisait cesser les cris de l'ennemi revinrent à moi. Dans ce moment j'envoyai M. le Chev.^{r} Le Borgne et M. de Rocheblave dire aux officiers qui étaient à la tête des Sauvages de prendre l'ennemi en flanc. Le canon qui battit en tête donna faveur à mes ordres. L'ennemi, pris de tous cotés, combattit avec la fermeté la plus opiniâtre. Des rangs entiers tombaient à la fois; presque tous les officiers périrent; et le désordre s'etant mis par là dans cette colonne, tout prit la fuite."

Whatever may have been the conduct of the Canadian militia, the French officers behaved with the utmost courage, and shared with the Indians the honors of the victory. The partisan chief Charles Langlade seems also to have been especially prominent. His grandson, the aged Pierre Grignon, declared that it was he who led the attack (Draper, *Recollections of Grignon*, in the *Collections of the Wisconsin Historical Society*, III.). Such evidence, taken alone, is of the least possible weight; but both the traveller Anbury and General John Burgoyne, writing many years after the event, speak of Langlade, who was then alive, as the author of Braddock's defeat. Hence there can be little doubt that he took an important part in it, though the contemporary writers do not mention his name. Compare Tassé, *Notice sur Charles Langlade*. The honors fell to Contrecœur, Dumas, and Ligneris, all of whom received the cross of the Order of St. Louis (*Ordres du Roy et Dépêches des Ministres*, *1755*).

APPENDIX E

Chapter 14. MONTCALM AND VAUDREUIL

To show the style of Montcalm's familiar letters, I give a few examples. Literal translation is often impossible.

À MADAME DE MONTCALM, *à Montréal,*
16 Avril, 1757.
(*Extrait.*)

"Ma santé assez bonne, malgré beaucoup de travail, surtout d'ecriture. Estève, mon secretaire, se marie. Beau caractère. Bon autographe, écrivant vite. Je lui procure un emploi et le moyen de faire fortune s'il veut. Il fait un meilleur mariage que ne lui appartient; malgré cela je crains qu'il ne la fasse pas comme un autre; fat, frivole, joueur, glorieux, petit-maître, dépensier. J'ai toujours Marcel, des soldats copistes dans le besoin. . . . Tous les soldats de Montpellier se portants bien, hors le fils de Pierre mort chez moi. Tout est hors de prix. Il faut vivre honorablement et je le fais, tous les jours seize personnes. Une fois tous les quinze jours chez M. le Gouverneur général et M.ʳ le Chev. de Lévis qui vit aussi très bien. Il a donné trois beaux grands bals. Pour moi jusqu'au carême, outre les diners, de grands soupers de dames trois fois la semaine. Le jour des devotes prudes, des concerts. Les jours des jeûnes des violons d'hazard, parcequ'on me les demandait, cela ne menait que jusqu'à deux heures du matin et il se joignait l'après-souper compagnie dansante sans être priée, mais sure d'être bien reçue à celle qui avait soupé. Fort cher, peu amusant, et souvent ennuyeux. . . . Vous connaissiez ma maison, je l'ai augmentée d'un cocher, d'un frotteur, un garçon de cuisine, et j'ai marié mon aide de cuisine; car je travaille à peupler la colonie: 80 mariages de soldats cet hiver et deux d'officiers. Germain a perdu sa fille. Il a epousé mieux que lui; bonne femme mais sans bien, comme toutes. . . ."

À Madame de Montcalm, *à Montréal*,
6 Juin, 1757.
(*Extrait.*)

"J'addresse la première de cette lettre à ma mère. Il n'y a pas une heure dans la journée que je ne songe à vous, à elle, et à mes enfants. J'embrasse ma fille; je vous adore, ma très chère, ainsi que ma mère. Mille choses à mes sœurs. Je n'ai pas le temps de leur écrire, ni à Naujac, ni aux abbesses. . . . Des compliments au château d'Arbois, aux Du Cayla, et aux Givard. P. S. N'oubliez pas d'envoyer une douzaine de bouteilles d'Angleterre de pinte d'eau de lavande; vous en mettrez quatre pour chaque envoi."

À Bourlamaque, *à Montréal*,
20 Février, 1757.
(*Extrait.*)

"Dimanche j'avais rassemblé les dames de France hors Mad. de Parfouru qui m'a fait l'honneur de me venir voir il y a trois jours et en la voyant je me suis apperçu que l'amour avait des traits de puissance dont on ne pouvait pas rendre raison, non pas par l'impression qu'elle a faite sur mon cœur, mais bien par celle qu'elle a faite sur celui de son époux. Mercredi une assemblée chez Mad. Varin. Jeudi un bal chez le Chev. de Lévis qui avait prié 65 Dames ou demoiselles; Il n'y en avait que trente—autant d'hommes qu'à la guerre. Sa salle bien éclairée, aussi grand que celle de l'Intendance, beaucoup d'ordre, beaucoup d'attention, des rafraichissements en abondance toute la nuit de tout genre et de toute espèce et on ne se retira qu'à sept heures du matin. Pour moi qui ay quitté le séjour de Québec, Je me couchai de bonne heure. J'avais eu ce jour-là huit dames à souper et ce souper était dedié à Mad. Varin. Demain j'en aurai une demi douzaine. Je ne scai encore a qui il est dedié, Je suis tenté de croire que c'est à La Roche Beaucourt Le galant Chev. nous donne encore un bal."

APPENDIX F
Chapter 15. FORT WILLIAM HENRY

Webb to Loudon, *Fort Edward,* 11 *Aug. 1757.*
Public Record Office. (*Extract.*)

"On leaving the Camp Yesterday Morning they [*the English soldiers*] were stript by the Indians of everything they had both Officers and Men the Women and Children drag'd from among them and most inhumanly butchered before their faces, the party of about three hundred Men which were given them as

an escort were during this time quietly looking on, from this and other circumstances we are too well convinced these barbarities must have been connived
at by the French, After having destroyed the women and children they fell
upon the rear of our Men who running in upon the Front soon put the whole
to a most precipitate flight in which confusion part of them came into this
Camp about two o'Clock yesterday morning in a most distressing situation,
and have continued dropping in ever since, a great many men and we are
afraid several Officers were massacred."

The above is independent of the testimony of Frye, who did not reach Fort
Edward till the day after Webb's letter was written.

FRYE TO THOMAS HUBBARD, Speaker of the House of
Representatives of Massachusetts, Albany, 16 Aug. 1757.
Public Record Office. (Extract.)

"We did not march till ye 10th at which time the Savages were let loose
upon us, Strips, Kills, & Scalps our people drove them into Disorder Rendered
it impossible to Rally, the French Gaurds we were promised shou'd Escort us
to Fort Edward Could or would not protect us so that there Opened the most
horrid Scene of Barbarity immaginable, I was strip'd myself of my Arms &
Cloathing that I had nothing left but Briches Stockings Shoes & Shirt, the
Indians round me with their Tomehawks Spears &c threatening Death I flew
to the Officers of the French Gaurds for Protection but they would afford me
none, therefore was Oblig'd to fly and was in the woods till the 12th in the
Morning of which I arriv'd at Fort Edward almost Famished . . . with what of
Fatigue Starving &c I am obliged to break off but as soon as I can Recollect
myself shall write to you more fully."

FRYE, Journal of the Attack of Fort William Henry.
Public Record Office. (Extract.)

"*Wednesday, August 10th.*—Early this morning we were ordered to prepare
for our march, but found the Indians in a worse temper (if possible) than last
night, every one having a tomahawk, hatchett or some other instrument of
death, and Constantly plundering from the officers their arms &ca this Col?
Monro Complained of, as a breach of the Articles of Capitulation but to no
effect, the french officers however told us that if we would give up the baggage
of the officers and men, to the Indians, they thought it would make them
easy, which at last Col° Monro Consented to but this was no sooner done,
then they began to take the Officers Hatts, Swords, guns & Cloaths, stripping
them all to their Shirts, and on some officers, left no shirt at all, while this
was doing they killed and scalp'd all the sick and wounded before our faces
and then took out from our troops, all the Indians and negroes, and Carried
them off, one of the former they burnt alive afterwards.

"At last with great difficulty the troops gott from the Retrenchment, but they were no sooner out, then the savages fell upon the rear, killing & scalping, which Occasioned an order for a halt, which at last was done in great Confusion but as soon as those in the front knew what was doing in the rear they again pressed forward, and thus the Confusion continued & encreased till we came to the Advane'd guard of the French, the savages still carrying away Officers, privates, Women and Children, some of which latter they kill'd & scalpt in the road. This horrid scene of blood and slaughter obliged our officers to apply to the Officers of the French Guard for protection, which they refus'd & told them they must take to the woods and shift for themselves which many did, and in all probability many perish't in the woods, many got into Fort Edward that day and others daily Continued coming in, but vastly fatigued with their former hardships added to this last, which threw several of them into Deliriums."

Affidavit of MILES WHITWORTH, *Surgeon of the Massachusetts Regiment, taken before Governor Pownall 17 Oct. 1757. Public Record Office. (Extract.)*

"Being duly sworn on the Holy Evangelists doth declare . . . that there were also seventeen Men of the Massachusetts Regiment wounded unable to March under his immediate Care in the Intrenched Camp, that according to the Capitulation he did deliver them over to the French Surgeon on the ninth of August at two in the Afternoon . . . that the French Surgeon received them into his Custody and placed Centinals of the French Troops upon the said seventeen wounded. That the French Surgeon going away to the French Camp, the said Miles Whitworth continued with the said wounded Men till five o'Clock on the Morn of the tenth of August, That the Centinals were taken off and that he the said Whitworth saw the French Indians about 5 O'Clock in the Morn of the 10th of August dragg the said seventeen wounded men out of their Hutts, Murder them with their Tomohawks and scalp them, That the French Troops posted round the lines were not further than forty feet from the Hutts where the said wounded Men lay, that several Canadian Officers particularly one Lacorne were present and that none, either Officer or Soldier, protected the said wounded Men.

"MILES WHITWORTH.

"*Sworn before me* T. POWNALL."

APPENDIX G
Chapter 20. TICONDEROGA

The French accounts of the battle at Ticonderoga are very numerous, and consist of letters and despatches of Montcalm, Lévis, Bougainville, Doreil, and other officers, besides several anonymous narratives, one of which was printed in pamphlet form at the time. Translations of many of them may be found in *N. Y. Colonial Documents*, X. There are, however, various others preserved in the archives of the War and Marine Departments at Paris which have not seen the light. I have carefully examined and collated them all. The English accounts are by no means so numerous or so minute. Among those not already cited, may be mentioned a letter of Colonel Woolsey of the New York provincials, and two letters from British officers written just after the battle and enclosed in a letter from Alexander Colden to Major Halkett, 17 July. (*Bouquet and Haldimand Papers*.)

The French greatly exaggerated the force of the English and their losses in the battle. They place the former at from twenty thousand to thirty-one thousand, and the latter at from four thousand to six thousand. Prisoners taken at the end of the battle told them that the English had lost four thousand,—a statement which they readily accepted, though the prisoners could have known little more about the matter than they themselves. And these figures were easily magnified. The number of dead lying before the lines is variously given at from eight hundred to three thousand. Montcalm himself, who was somewhat elated by his victory, gives this last number in one of his letters, though he elsewhere says two thousand; while Lévis, in his *Journal de la Guerre*, says "about eight hundred." The truth is that no pains were taken to ascertain the exact number, which, by the English returns, was a little above five hundred, the total of killed, wounded, and missing being nineteen hundred and forty-four. A friend of Knox, writing to him from Fort Edward three weeks after the battle, gives a tabular statement which shows nineteen hundred and fifty in all, or six more than the official report. As the name of every officer killed or wounded, with the corps to which he belonged, was published at the time (*London Magazine*, 1758), it is extremely unlikely that the official return was falsified. Abercromby's letter to Pitt, on July 12, says that he retreated "with the loss of four hundred and sixty-four regulars killed, twenty-nine missing eleven hundred and seventeen wounded; and eighty-seven provincials killed, eight missing, and two hundred and thirty-nine wounded, officers of both included." In a letter to Viscount Barrington, of the same date (Public Record Office), Abercromby encloses a full detail of losses, regiment by regiment and company by company, being a total of nineteen hundred and forty-five. Several of the French writers state correctly that about fourteen thousand men (including reserves) were engaged in the attack; but they add erroneously that there were thirteen thousand more at the Falls. In fact there was only a small provincial regiment left there, and a battalion of the New York regiment, under Colonel Woolsey, at the landing.

A LEGEND OF TICONDEROGA.—Mention has been made of the death of Major Duncan Campbell of Inverawe. The following family tradition relating to it was told me in 1878 by the late Dean Stanley, to whom I am also indebted for various papers on the subject, including a letter from James Campbell, Esq., the present laird of Inverawe, and great-nephew of the hero of the tale. The same story is told, in an amplified form and with some variations, in the *Legendary Tales of the Highlands* of Sir Thomas Dick Lauder. As related by Dean Stanley and approved by Mr. Campbell, it is this:—

The ancient castle of Inverawe stands by the banks of the Awe, in the midst of the wild and picturesque scenery of the western Highlands. Late one evening, before the middle of the last century, as the laird, Duncan Campbell, sat alone in the old hall, there was a loud knocking at the gate; and, opening it, he saw a stranger, with torn clothing and kilt besmeared with blood, who in a breathless voice begged for asylum. He went on to say that he had killed a man in a fray, and that the pursuers were at his heels. Campbell promised to shelter him. "Swear on your dirk!" said the stranger; and Campbell swore. He then led him to a secret recess in the depths of the castle. Scarcely was he hidden when again there was a loud knocking at the gate, and two armed men appeared. "Your cousin Donald has been murdered, and we are looking for the murderer!" Campbell, remembering his oath, professed to have no knowledge of the fugitive; and the men went on their way. The laird, in great agitation, lay down to rest in a large dark room, where at length he fell asleep. Waking suddenly in bewilderment and terror, he saw the ghost of the murdered Donald standing by his bedside, and heard a hollow voice pronounce the words: *"Inverawe! Inverawe! blood has been shed. Shield not the murderer!"* In the morning Campbell went to the hiding-place of the guilty man and told him that he could harbor him no longer. "You have sworn on your dirk!" he replied; and the laird of Inverawe, greatly perplexed and troubled, made a compromise between conflicting duties, promised not to betray his guest, led him to the neighboring mountain, and hid him in a cave.

In the next night, as he lay tossing in feverish slumbers, the same stern voice awoke him, the ghost of his cousin Donald stood again at his bedside, and again he heard the same appalling words: *"Inverawe! Inverawe! blood has been shed. Shield not the murderer!"* At break of day he hastened, in strange agitation, to the cave; but it was empty, the stranger was gone. At night, as he strove in vain to sleep, the vision appeared once more, ghastly pale, but less stern of aspect than before. *"Farewell, Inverawe!"* it said; *"Farewell, till we meet at TICONDEROGA!"*

The strange name dwelt in Campbell's memory. He had joined the Black Watch, or Forty-second Regiment, then employed in keeping order in the turbulent Highlands. In time he became its major; and, a year or two after the war broke out, he went with it to America. Here, to his horror, he learned that it was ordered to the attack of Ticonderoga. His story was well known among his brother officers. They combined among themselves to disarm his fears; and when they reached the fatal spot they told him on the eve of the battle, "This is not Ticonderoga; we are not there yet; this is Fort George." But in the morning he came to them with haggard looks. "I have seen him!

You have deceived me! He came to my tent last night! This is Ticonderoga! I shall die to-day!" and his prediction was fulfilled.

Such is the tradition. The indisputable facts are that Major Duncan Campbell of Inverawe, his arm shattered by a bullet, was carried to Fort Edward, where, after amputation, he died and was buried. (*Abercromby to Pitt, 19 August, 1758.*) The stone that marks his grave may still be seen, with this inscription: "*Here lyes the Body of Duncan Campbell of Inverawe, Esqre, Major to the old Highland Regiment, aged 55 Years, who died the 17th July, 1758, of the Wounds he received in the Attack of the Retrenchment of Ticonderoga or Carrillon, on the 8th July, 1758.*"

His son, Lieutenant Alexander Campbell, was severely wounded at the same time, but reached Scotland alive, and died in Glasgow.

Mr. Campbell, the present Inverawe, in the letter mentioned above, says that forty-five years ago he knew an old man whose grandfather was foster-brother to the slain major of the forty-second, and who told him the following story while carrying a salmon for him to an inn near Inverawe. The old man's grandfather was sleeping with his son, then a lad, in the same room, but in another bed. This son, father of the narrator, "was awakened," to borrow the words of Mr. Campbell, "by some unaccustomed sound, and behold there was a bright light in the room, and he saw a figure, in full Highland regimentals, cross over the room and stoop down over his father's bed and give him a kiss. He was too frightened to speak, but put his head under his coverlet and went to sleep. Once more he was roused in like manner, and saw the same sight. In the morning he spoke to his father about it, who told him that it was Macdonno-chie [*the Gaelic patronymic of the laird of Inverawe*] whom he had seen, and who came to tell him that he had been killed in a great battle in America. Sure enough, said my informant, it was on the very day that the battle of Ticon-deroga was fought and the laird was killed."

It is also said that two ladies of the family of Inverawe saw a battle in the clouds, in which the shadowy forms of Highland warriors were plainly to be descried; and that when the fatal news came from America, it was found that the time of the vision answered exactly to that of the battle in which the head of the family fell.

The legend of Inverawe has within a few years found its way into an English magazine, and it has also been excellently told in the *Atlantic Monthly* of September of this year, 1884, by Miss C. F. Gordon Cumming. Her version differs a little from that given above from the recital of Dean Stanley and the present laird of Inverawe, but the essential points are the same. Miss Gordon Cumming, however, is in error when she says that Duncan Campbell was wounded in the breast, and that he was first buried at Ticonderoga. His burial-place was near Fort Edward, where he died, and where his remains still lie, though not at the same spot, as they were long after removed by a family named Gilchrist, who claimed kinship with the Campbells of Inverawe.

APPENDIX H

Chapter 25. WOLFE AT QUEBEC

Force of the French and English at the Siege of Quebec.

"Les retranchemens que j'avois fait tracer depuis la rivière St. Charles jusqu'au saut Montmorency furent occupés par plus de 14,000 hommes, 200 cavaliers dont je formai un corps aux ordres de M. de la Rochebeaucour, environ 1,000 sauvages Abenakis et des différentes nations du nord des pays d'en haut. M. de Boishébert arriva ensuite avec les Acadiens et sauvages qu'il avoit rassemblés. Je réglai la garnison de Québec à 2,000 hommes." *Vaudreuil au Ministre,* 5 Oct. 1759.

The commissary Berniers says that the whole force was about fifteen thousand men, besides Indians, which is less than the number given by Vaudreuil.

Bigot says: "Nous avions 13,000 hommes et mille à 1,200 sauvages, sans compter 2,000 hommes de garnison dans la ville." *Bigot au Ministre,* 25 Oct. 1759.

The Hartwell *Journal du Siége* says: "Il fut décidé qu'on ne laisseroit dans la place que 1,200 hommes, et que tout le reste marcheroit au camp, où l'on comptoit se trouver plus de 15,000 hommes, y compris les sauvages."

Rigaud, Vaudreuil's brother, writing from Montreal to Bourlamaque on the 23d of June, says: "Je compte que l'armée campée sous Québec sera de 17,000 hommes bien effectifs, sans les sauvages." He then gives a list of Indians who have joined the army, or are on the way, amounting to thirteen hundred.

At the end of June Wolfe had about eight thousand six hundred effective soldiers. Of these the ten battalions, commonly mentioned as regiments, supplied six thousand four hundred; detached grenadiers from Louisbourg, three hundred; artillery, three hundred; rangers, four hundred; light infantry, two hundred; marines, one thousand. The complement of the battalions was in some cases seven hundred and in others one thousand (Knox, II. 25); but their actual strength varied from five hundred to eight hundred, except the Highlanders, who mustered eleven hundred, their ranks being more than full. Fraser, in his *Journal of the Siege*, gives a tabular view of the whole. At the end of the campaign Lévis reckons the remaining English troops at about six thousand (*Lévis au Ministre,* 10 Nov. 1759), which answers to the report of General Murray: "The troops will amount to six thousand" (*Murray to Pitt,* 12 Oct. 1759). The precise number is given in the *Return of the State of His Majesty's Forces left in Garrison at Quebec,* dated 12 Oct. 1759, and signed, Robert Monckton (Public Record Office, *America and West Indies,* XCIX.). This shows the total of rank and file to have been 6,214, which the addition of officers, sergeants, and drummers raises to about seven thousand, besides 171 artillerymen.

APPENDIX I
Chapter 27. THE HEIGHTS OF ABRAHAM

One of the most important unpublished documents on Wolfe's operations against Quebec is the long and elaborate *Journal mémoratif de ce qui s'est passé de plus remarquable pendant qu'a duré le Siége de la Ville de Québec* (Archives de la Marine). The writer, M. de Foligny, was a naval officer who during the siege commanded one of the principal batteries of the town. The official correspondence of Vaudreuil for 1759 (Archives Nationales) gives the events of the time from his point of view; and various manuscript letters of Bigot, Lévis, Montreuil, and others (Archives de la Marine, Archives de la Guerre) give additional particulars. The letters, generally private and confidential, written to Bourlamaque by Montcalm, Lévis, Vaudreuil, Malartic, Berniers, and others during the siege contain much that is curious and interesting.

Siége de Québec en 1759, d'après un Manuscrit déposé à la Bibliothêque de Hartwell en Angleterre. A very valuable diary, by a citizen of Quebec; it was brought from England in 1834 by the Hon. D. B. Viger, and a few copies were printed at Quebec in 1836. *Journal tenu à l'Armée que commandoit feu M. le Marquis de Montcalm.* A minute diary of an officer under Montcalm (printed by the Quebec Historical Society). *Mémoire sur la Campagne de 1759, par M. de Joannès, Major de Québec* (Archives de la Guerre). *Lettres et Dépêches de Montcalm* (Ibid.). These touch chiefly the antecedents of the siege. *Mémoires sur le Canada depuis 1749 jusqu'à 1760* (Quebec Historical Society). *Journal du Siége de Québec en 1759, par M. Jean Claude Panet, notaire* (Ibid.). The writer of this diary was in Quebec at the time. Several other journals and letters of persons present at the siege have been printed by the Quebec Historical Society, under the title *Événements de la Guerre en Canada durant les Années 1759 et 1760. Relation de ce qui s'est passé au Siége de Québec, par une Réligieuse de l'Hôpital Général de Québec* (Quebec Historical Society). *Jugement impartial sur les Opérations militaires de la Campagne, par M.ᵍʳ de Pontbriand, Évêque de Québec* (Ibid.). *Memoirs of the Siege of Quebec, from the Journal of a French Officer on board the Chezine Frigate, taken by His Majesty's Ship Rippon, by Richard Gardiner, Esq., Captain of Marines in the Rippon,* London, 1761.

General Wolfe's Instructions to Young Officers, Philadelphia, 1778. This title is misleading, the book being a collection of military orders. *General Orders in Wolfe's Army* (Quebec Historical Society). This collection is much more full than the foregoing, so far as concerns the campaign of 1759. *Letters of Wolfe* (in Wright's *Wolfe*), *Despatches of Wolfe, Saunders, Monckton, and Townshend* (in contemporary magazines). *A Short Authentic Account of the Expedition against Quebec, by a Volunteer upon that Expedition,* Quebec, 1872. This valuable diary is ascribed to James Thompson, a volunteer under Wolfe, who died at Quebec in 1830 at the age of ninety-eight, after holding for many years the position of overseer of works in the Engineer Department. Another manuscript, for the most part identical with this, was found a few years ago among old papers in the office of the Royal Engineers at Quebec. *Journal of the Expedition on the River St. Lawrence.* Two entirely distinct diaries bear this name. One is printed in the *New York Mercury* for December, 1759; the other was found among the papers of George Alsopp, secretary to Sir Guy Carleton, who served under Wolfe (Quebec Historical Society). Johnstone, *A Dialogue in Hades* (Ibid.). The Scotch Jacobite, Chevalier Johnstone, as aide-de-camp to Lévis, and afterwards to Montcalm, had great opportunities of acquiring information during the campaign; and the results, though produced in the fanciful form of a dialogue between the ghosts of Wolfe and Montcalm, are of substantial historical value. The *Dialogue* is followed by a plain personal narrative. Fraser, *Journal of the Siege of Quebec* (Ibid.). Fraser was an officer in the Seventy-eighth Highlanders. *Journal of the Siege of Quebec, by a Gentleman in an Eminent Station on the Spot,* Dublin, 1759. *Journal of the Particular Transactions during the Siege of Quebec* (*Notes and Queries,* XX.). The writer was a soldier or non-commissioned officer serving in the light infantry.

Memoirs of the Siege of Quebec and Total Reduction of Canada, by John Johnson, Clerk and Quarter-master Sergeant to the Fifty-eighth Regiment. A manuscript of 176 pages, written when Johnson was a pensioner at Chelsea (England). The handwriting is exceedingly neat and clear; and the style, though often grandiloquent, is creditable to a writer in his station. This curious production was found among the papers of Thomas McDonough, Esq., formerly British Consul at Boston, and is in possession of his grandson, my relative, George Francis Parkman, Esq., who, by inquiries at the Chelsea Hospital, learned that Johnson was still living in 1802.

I have read and collated with extreme care all the above authorities, with others which need not be mentioned.

Among several manuscript maps and plans showing the operations of the siege may be mentioned one entitled, *Plan of the Town and Basin of Quebec and Part of the Adjacent Country, shewing the principal Encampments and Works of the British Army commanded by Major Gen! Wolfe, and those of the French Army by Lieut. Gen! the Marquis of Montcalm.* It is the work of three engineers of Wolfe's army, and is on a scale of eight hundred feet to an inch. A facsimile from the original in possession of the Royal Engineers is before me.

Among the "King's Maps," British Museum (CXIX. 27), is a very large colored plan of operations at Quebec in 1759, 1760, superbly executed in minute detail.

APPENDIX J
Chapter 28. FALL OF QUEBEC

Death and Burial of Montcalm.—Johnstone, who had every means of knowing the facts, says that Montcalm was carried after his wound to the house of the surgeon Arnoux. Yet it is not quite certain that he died there. According to

Knox, his death took place at the General Hospital; according to the modern author of the *Ursulines de Québec*, at the Château St.-Louis. But the General Hospital was a mile out of the town, and in momentary danger of capture by the English; while the Château had been made untenable by the batteries of Point Levi, being immediately exposed to their fire. Neither of these places was one to which the dying general was likely to be removed, and it is probable that he was suffered to die in peace at the house of the surgeon.

It has been said that the story of the burial of Montcalm in a grave partially formed by the explosion of a bomb, rests only on the assertion in his epitaph, composed in 1761 by the Academy of Inscriptions at the instance of Bougainville. There is, however, other evidence of the fact. The naval captain Foligny, writing on the spot at the time of the burial, says in his Diary, under date of September 14: "A huit heures du soir, dans l'église des Ursulines, fut enterré dans une fosse faite sous la chaire *par le travail de la Bombe*, M. le Marquis de Montcalm, décédé du matin à 4 heures après avoir reçu tous les Sacrements. Jamais Général n'avoit été plus aimé de sa troupe et plus universellement regretté. Il étoit d'un esprit supérieur, doux, gracieux, affable, familier à tout le monde, ce qui lui avoit fait gagner la confiance de toute la Colonie: *requiescat in pace*."

The author of *Les Ursulines de Québec* says : "Un des projectiles ayant fait une large ouverture dans le plancher de bas, on en profita pour creuser la fosse du général."

The *Boston Post Boy and Advertiser*, in its issue of Dec. 3, 1759, contains a letter from "an officer of distinction" at Quebec to Messrs. Green and Russell, proprietors of the newspaper. This letter contains the following words: "He [Montcalm] died the next day; and, with a little Improvement, one of our 13-inch Shell-Holes served him for a Grave."

The particulars of his burial are from the *Acte Mortuaire du Marquis de Montcalm* in the registers of the Church of Notre Dame de Québec, and from that valuable chronicle, *Les Ursulines de Québec*, composed by the Superior of the convent. A nun of the sisterhood, Mère Aimable Dubé de Saint-Ignace, was, when a child, a witness of the scene, and preserved a vivid memory of it to the age of eighty-one.

APPENDIX K
Chapter 29. SAINTE-FOY

Strength of the French and English at the Battle of Ste.-Foy.

In the Public Record Office (*America and West Indies*, XCIX.) are preserved the tabular returns of the garrison of Quebec for 1759, 1760, sent by Murray to the War Office. They show the exact condition of each regiment, in all ranks, for every month of the autumn, winter, and spring. The return made out on the 24th of April, four days before the battle, shows that the total number of rank and file, exclusive of non-commissioned officers and drummers, was 6,808, of whom 2,612 were fit for duty in Quebec, and 654 at other places in Canada; that is, at Ste.-Foy, Old Lorette, and the other outposts. This gives a total of 3,266 rank and file fit for duty at or near Quebec; besides which there were between one hundred and two hundred artillerymen, and a company of rangers. This was Murray's whole available force at the time. Of the rest of the 6,808 who appear in the return, 2,299 were invalids at Quebec, and 669 in New York; 538 were on service in Halifax and New York, and 36 were absent on furlough. These figures nearly answer to the condensed statement of Fraser, and confirm the various English statements of the numbers that took part in the battle; namely, 3,140 (Knox), 3,000 (John Johnson), 3,111, and elsewhere, in round numbers, 3,000 (Murray). Lévis, with natural exaggeration, says 4,000. Three or four hundred were left in Quebec to guard the walls when the rest marched out.

I have been thus particular because a Canadian writer, Garneau, says: "Murray sortit de la ville le 28 au matin à la tête de toute la garnison, dont les seules troupes de la ligne comptaient encore 7,714 combattants, non compris les officiers." To prove this, he cites the pay-roll of the garrison; which, in fact, corresponds to the returns of the same date, if non-commissioned officers, drummers, and artillerymen are counted with the rank and file. But Garneau falls into a double error. He assumes, first, that there were no men on the sick list; and secondly, that there were none absent from Quebec; when in reality, as the returns show, considerably more than half were in one or the other of these categories. The pay-rolls were made out at the headquarters of each corps, and always included the entire number of men enlisted in it, whether sick or well, present or absent. On the same fallacious premises Garneau affirms that Wolfe, at the battle on the Plains of Abraham, had eight thousand soldiers, or a little less than double his actual force.

Having stated, as above, that Murray marched out of Quebec with at least 7,714 effective troops, Garneau, not very consistently, goes on to say that he advanced against Lévis with six thousand or seven thousand men; and he adds that the two armies were about equal, because Lévis had left some detachments behind to guard his boats and artillery. The number of the French, after they had all reached the field, was, in truth, about seven thousand; at the beginning of the fight it seems not to have exceeded five thousand. The *Relation de la seconde Bataille de Québec* says: "Notre petite armée consistoit *au moment de l'action* en 3,000 hommes de troupes reglées et 2,000 Canadiens ou sauvages." A large number of Canadians came up from Sillery while the affair went on; and as the whole French army, except the detachments mentioned by Garneau, had passed the night at no greater distance from the field than Ste.-Foy and Sillery, the last man must have reached it before the firing was half over.

INDEX

Other titles of interest

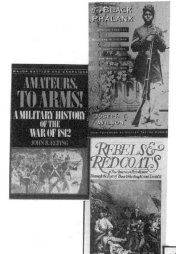

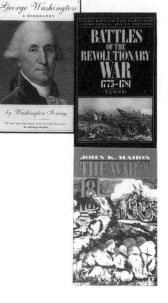

DECISIVE BATTLES OF THE U.S.A.
J.F.C. Fuller
428 pp., 29 maps and plans
80532-4 $14.95

**THE ENCYCLOPEDIA OF COLONIAL
AND REVOLUTIONARY AMERICA**
Edited by John Mack Faragher
494 pp., 126 illus. & maps
80687-8 $24.50

**GEORGE WASHINGTON
A Biography**
Washington Irving
Edited and abridged with an
introduction by Charles Neider
790 pp., 3 illus, 5 maps
80593-6 $18.95

**GEORGE WASHINGTON'S
GENERALS AND OPPONENTS
Their Exploits and Leadership**
Edited by George Athan Billias
766 pp., 23 photos, 9 maps
80560-X $19.95

**AMATEURS, TO ARMS!
A Military History of the War of
1812**
John R. Elting
318 pp., 19 photos, 16 maps
80653-3 $14.95

**BATTLES OF THE
REVOLUTIONARY WAR 1775–1781**
W. J. Wood
Introd. by John S. D. Eisenhower
363 pp., 40 illus., 30 maps and dia-
grams
80617-7 $14.95

**BENJAMIN FRANKLIN
A Biography**
Ronald W. Clark
544 pp., 30 illus.
80368-2 $15.95

**THE BLACK PHALANX
African American Soldiers
in the War of Independence,
the War of 1812, and the
Civil War**
Joseph T. Wilson
New introduction by
Dudley Taylor Cornish
534 pp., 64 illus.
80550-2 $16.95

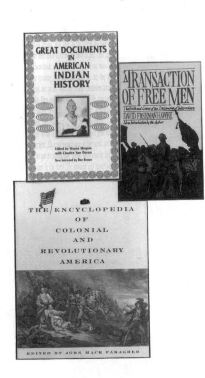
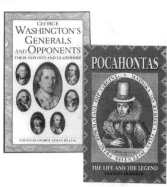